LEARNING

6

EDITION

This book is dedicated to my wife Marie and my children—Dora, David, Jason, Katherine, and William—for the joy that they have brought to my life.

LEARNING

Principles and Applications

6
EDITION

STEPHEN B. KLEIN

MISSISSIPPI STATE UNIVERSITY

Los Angeles | London | New Delhi
Singapore | Washington DC

SP

Los Angeles | London | New Delhi
Singapore | Washington DC

FOR INFORMATION:

SAGE Publications, Inc.
2455 Teller Road
Thousand Oaks, California 91320
E-mail: order@sagepub.com

SAGE Publications Ltd.
1 Oliver's Yard
55 City Road
London EC1Y 1SP
United Kingdom

SAGE Publications India Pvt. Ltd.
B 1/I 1 Mohan Cooperative Industrial Area
Mathura Road, New Delhi 110 044
India

SAGE Publications Asia-Pacific Pte. Ltd.
33 Pekin Street #02-01
Far East Square
Singapore 048763

Acquisitions Editor: Christine Cardone
Editorial Assistant: Sarita Sarak
Production Editor: Eric Garner
Copy Editor: Gretchen Treadwell
Typesetter: C&M Digitals (P) Ltd.
Proofreader: Wendy Jo Dymond
Cover Designer: Janet Kiesel
Marketing Manager: Liz Thornton
Permissions Editor: Karen Ehrmann

Printed in the United States of America

Library of Congress Cataloging-in-Publication Data

Klein, Stephen B.

Learning : principles and applications/Stephen B.
Klein. — 6th ed.

p. cm.
Includes bibliographical references and index.

ISBN 978-1-4129-8734-9 (pbk.)

1. Learning. 2. Conditioned response. I. Title.

LB1060.K59 2012
370.15'23—dc22
2011008082

This book is printed on acid-free paper.

11 12 13 14 15 10 9 8 7 6 5 4 3 2 1

12/19/11

Brief Contents

Detailed Contents

Preface

Learning: Principles and Applications seeks to provide students with an up-to-date understanding of learning. Basic principles are described and supplemented by research studies, including classic experiments and important contemporary studies. The sixth edition continues to uphold the same uncompromising scholarship of earlier editions. Psychologists who study the nature of the learning process have uncovered many important principles about the way in which we acquire information about the structure of our environment and how we use this understanding to interact effectively with our environment. As in earlier editions, the sixth edition provides thorough, current coverage of such principles and applications.

Much exciting new research in learning has occurred in the last few years. Key new discoveries include the identification of behavioral economic principles in operant conditioning, a determination of the conditions that lead to a reinforcer being devalued, the recognition of the processes that provide the reinforcing power of psychoactive drugs, the study of the influence of expectancies in classical and operant conditioning, the determination of whether language learning occurs in primates, and the study of the relevance of memory reconstruction to understanding the validity of repressed memories.

As in previous editions, the text presents the important contributions of both animal and human research, as both are crucial to our understanding of the learning process. In many instances, animal studies and human research have yielded identical results, indicating the generality of the processes governing learning. While there are many general laws of learning, there are also instances in which species differ in their ability to learn a particular behavior. The study of learning in different animal species has shown that biological character affects learning. Furthermore, in some situations, only animal research can be ethically conducted, while in other cases, only human research can identify the learning process that is unique to people.

ORGANIZATION

Based on feedback from users of the previous edition of the book, the discussion of theories of learning has been moved to follow the presentation of a historical perspective of how behavior changes as a result of experience. Further, there are separate chapters for the principles and applications, along with theories, of classical conditioning, appetitive conditioning, and aversive conditioning. Brief descriptions of chapter coverage follow.

Chapter 1 gives a brief introduction to learning as well as a discussion of the origins of behavior theory. Basic learning principles are first introduced through a description of the research findings and theories of Thorndike, Pavlov, and Watson. The importance of their work is subsequently evident throughout the text. A brief presentation of the ethics of conducting research is also included in this chapter.

Chapter 2 describes traditional learning theory. The theories of Hull, Spence, Guthrie, Tolman, and Skinner are explored in this chapter. The chapter illustrates the changes that have taken place in the understanding of the nature of the learning process during the first half of the twentieth century.

Chapter 3 describes how instinctive processes govern behavior. This chapter also describes two learning processes, habituation and sensitization, by which experience can alter instinctive behaviors. Opponent process theory, which describes the affective responses both during and following an event, also is introduced in this chapter.

Chapter 4 details the principles and applications of classical conditioning, a process that involves learning when and where events will or will not occur. This discussion first explores the factors that govern the acquisition or elimination of conditioned responses. Several procedures (higher-order conditioning, sensory preconditioning, and vicarious conditioning) in which a conditioned response can be learned without direct conditioned stimulus–unconditioned stimulus (CS-UCS) pairings are found in this chapter. Several of the Pavlovian conditioning principles that have been used to establish effective conditioned responses and to eliminate impairment of conditioned responses are also presented.

Chapter 5 describes theories of classical conditioning. This chapter discusses theoretical perspectives about the nature of the classical conditioning process and the nature of the conditioned response.

Chapter 6 discusses principles and applications of appetitive conditioning, a process that involves learning how to behave in order to obtain the positive aspects (reinforcers) that exist in the environment. The variables influencing the development or extinction of appetitive or reinforcer-seeking behavior are described in this chapter. The use of reinforcement to establish appropriate and to eliminate inappropriate behavior also is described in this chapter.

Chapter 7 discusses principles and applications of aversive conditioning, a process that involves learning how to react to the negative aspects (punishers) that exist in our environment. The determinants of escape and avoidance behavior as well as the influence of punishment on behavior are described. Several negative consequences that result from using punishment are also explored in this chapter. The use of several punishment techniques (positive punishment, response cost, time-out from reinforcement) to suppress inappropriate behavior also is described in this chapter.

Chapter 8 describes theories of appetitive and aversive conditioning. Theories about the nature of reinforcement and behavioral economics are discussed. Theories about the nature of avoidance learning and punishment also are discussed.

Chapter 9 discusses the biological processes that influence learning. In some instances, learning is enhanced by instinctive systems, whereas in others, learning is impaired by our biological character. This chapter also describes the biological processes that provide the pleasurable aspects of reinforcement.

Chapter 10 discusses the environmental control of behavior and how the stimulus environment can exert a powerful influence on how we act. A discussion of stimulus generalization and discrimination learning is the major focus of the chapter. Special attention is given to understanding the difference between the eliciting and occasion-setting functions of environmental events.

Chapter 11 describes the cognitive processes that affect how and when we behave. This chapter examines the relative contributions of expectations and habits to determining one's actions. The relevance of cognitive learning for understanding the causes of depression and phobias also is discussed in this chapter.

Chapter 12 describes three complex learning processes. This chapter explores how we identify concepts, solve problems, and learn to use language. A discussion of animal cognition is an important focus of this chapter, and the issue of whether language is unique to humans is one of the key areas of this discussion.

Chapters 13 and 14 discuss memory, the process that allows us to retain the influence of a learning experience into the future. The nature of memory storage and the encoding or organization of our experiences is described in Chapter 13.

Chapter 14 discusses the processes that allow us to retrieve some experiences or forget others. Further, the biological basis of memory storage is presented in Chapter 13 and retrieval is presented in Chapter 14.

PEDAGOGICAL FEATURES

Pedagogy remains a central feature of this new edition, but approaches have been reworked to enhance their impact. In addition, all-new pedagogical features have been added to promote students' understanding of the learning process and to better enable them to see its relevance to their everyday lives.

Vignettes. A vignette opens each chapter, and some chapters include vignettes within the chapter as well. This pedagogical feature serves three purposes. First, it lets students know what type of material will be presented in the chapter and provides a frame of reference. Second, the vignette arouses the student's curiosity and enhances the impact of the text material. Third, references to the vignette have been incorporated into the text to give it a seamless quality. I have found that students like the chapter-opening vignettes, and I believe that their use solidifies the link between the text material and the students' lives.

"Before You Go On" Sections. I have included two critical thinking questions in each of these sections, which appear throughout each chapter. These questions ensure that students understand the material and allow them to apply this knowledge in original, creative ways. My students report that the use of this pedagogy is quite helpful in understanding what can be difficult concepts.

"Application" Sections. Although applications of the text material are presented throughout, most chapters have at least one stand-alone application section. Many of the discoveries made by psychologists have been applied to solving real-world problems. The application sections enhance the relevance of the abstract ideas presented in the text, showing students that the behaviors described are not just laboratory phenomena.

Photographs and Biographies of Noted Researchers. Each chapter presents the photographs and biographies of individuals who have made significant contributions to an understanding of learning. This new pedagogy allows students to gain a better understanding of the principles and applications presented in the text by learning about the background of the individuals whose work contributed to that understanding.

Section Reviews. I have provided a review of key concepts at significant points in each chapter, as another tool for students to check their understanding of the material that has just been covered. Once the students have read the chapter, they can easily use the review sections as a study guide to prepare for examinations.

Critical Thinking Questions. Critical thinking questions in the form of scenarios are presented at the end of each chapter. Answering these questions requires creative application of one or more of the major concepts presented in the chapter, further assisting students in relating the principles presented in the text to situations that they may encounter in the real world.

SUPPLEMENTS

The password-protected **Instructor Teaching Site** includes a test bank with multiple-choice, true/false, and fill-in-the-blank questions for each chapter; PowerPoint® slides; chapter overviews and lecture outlines; suggested classroom activities; artwork from the book; and tips for teaching a "Psychology of Learning" course. To obtain a password, please contact SAGE Customer Service at 800-818-7243.

The open-access **Student Study Site** includes eFlashcards, web quizzes, chapter-specific internet resources and activities, and SAGE journal articles with discussion questions. These materials are available at **www.sagepub.com/klein6e**.

ACKNOWLEDGMENTS

The textbook has had input from many people. I thank the students in my learning classes who read drafts of the chapters and pointed out which sections they liked, which they disliked, and which were unclear. The staff at SAGE played an important role in the creation of this edition. Christine Cardone and Sarita Sarak have guided the development of the text from its inception to this final product.

I also thank my colleagues who reviewed chapters of the sixth edition. I am especially grateful to the following reviewers for their detailed and constructive comments:

Steven E. Meier, University of Idaho

Charles A. Gramlich, Xavier University of Louisiana

Rob Mowrer, Angelo State University

Michael A. Burman, University of New England

Nancy J. Karlin, University of Northern Colorado

Melissa D. Blank, Virginia Commonwealth University

I wish to thank Donna Barnes and Sheridan Hatcher for their technical support. Their help allowed the project to progress quite smoothly.

My family has been very supportive of my work on this edition, and I am grateful for their help and understanding.

—Stephen B. Klein
Mississippi State University

An Introduction to Learning

THE GIFT OF KNOWLEDGE

Marcus entered college three years ago with the intention to study chemistry. However, over the past year, he has found several of his psychology courses more exciting and challenging than his chemistry classes, and he now wants to obtain a degree in clinical psychology. Marcus's concern over his younger sister Yolanda's drug problems has stimulated this interest in psychology. Yolanda, an excellent student before she began to experiment with drugs several years ago, is now addicted, has quit school, and has left home. Marcus wants to understand the factors that can lead to drug addiction, and he hopes to contribute someday to the development of an effective drug addiction therapy. Dr. Martinez, Marcus's advisor, suggested that Marcus enroll in a course on learning in order to fulfill the Psychology Department's degree requirements. However, spending endless hours watching rats run through mazes and analyzing pages and pages of data did not appeal to Marcus. Interested in the human aspect of psychology, Marcus wondered how this course would benefit him. In spite of this, he trusted Dr. Martinez's advice, so he enrolled in the class. Marcus soon discovered that his preconceived ideas about the learning course were incorrect. The course covered research with both human and nonhuman subjects, and the various types of experimentation complemented each other in revealing the nature of the learning processes that govern behavior. The experiments, far from boring, made the learning principles described in class seem real. Marcus soon discovered that learning involves the acquisition of behaviors that are needed to obtain reward or avoid punishment. It also involves an understanding of when and where these behaviors are appropriate. Marcus became interested in discovering how basic research has stimulated the development of behavior modification techniques and how understanding the application of learning principles benefits the student of clinical psychology.

Psychology relies heavily on theory to guide its research; theory is especially important in investigations of the learning process. As Marcus discovered, many generations of psychologists have speculated about the nature of learning, and they have shown that the learning process is governed by complex, yet lawful, principles. He learned psychologists initially thought that learning involved the acquisition of associations between environmental events and behavior, whereas contemporary psychologists now recognize that learning involves both cognitive and associative processes.

Marcus now thinks that the knowledge gained from the learning class will undoubtedly help in his search for an effective treatment of addictive behavior. You will learn from this book what Marcus discovered about learning in his course. I hope your experience will be as positive as his. We begin our exploration by defining **learning**.

A DEFINITION OF LEARNING

What do we mean by the term *learning?* Learning can be defined as *a relatively permanent change in behavior potential that results from experience.* This definition of learning has two important components. First, learning reflects a change in the potential for a behavior to occur; it does not automatically lead to a change in behavior. We must be sufficiently motivated to translate learning into behavior. For example, although you may know the location of the campus cafeteria, you will not be motivated to go there until you are hungry. Also, we are sometimes unable to exhibit a particular behavior even though we have learned it and are sufficiently motivated to exhibit it. For example, you may learn from friends that a good movie is playing but not go because you cannot afford it.

Second, the behavior changes that learning causes are not always permanent. As a result of new experiences, previously learned behavior may no longer be exhibited. For example, you may learn a new and faster route to work and no longer take the old route. Also, we sometimes forget a previously learned behavior, and therefore are no longer able to exhibit that behavior. Forgetting the story line of a movie is one instance of the transient aspect of learning.

It is important to note that changes in behavior can be due to performance processes (e.g., maturation, motivation) rather than learning. Our behavior can change as the result of a motivational change rather than because of learning. For example, we eat when we are hungry or study when we are worried about an upcoming exam. However, eating or studying may not necessarily be due to learning. Motivational changes, rather than learning, could trigger eating or studying. You have already learned to eat, and your hunger motivates your eating behavior. Likewise, you have learned to study to prevent failure, and your fear motivates studying behavior. These behavioral changes are temporary; when the motivational state changes again, the behavior will also change. Therefore, you will stop eating when you are no longer hungry and quit studying when you no longer fear failing the examination. Becoming full or unafraid and ceasing to eat or study is another instance when a temporary state, rather than learning, leads to a change in behavior.

Many behavioral changes are the result of maturation. For example, a young child may fear darkness, while an adult may not show an emotional reaction to the dark. The change in emotionality could reflect a maturational process and may not be dependent on experiences with darkness. Another example of the impact of maturation is a child who cannot open a door at age 1, but can do so at age 2. The child may have learned that turning the doorknob opens the door, but physical growth of the child is necessary for the child to reach the doorknob.

Not all psychologists agree on the causes of behavior. Some even argue that instinct, rather than experience, determines behavior. We begin our discussion by examining the view that instinctive processes govern human actions. Later in the chapter, we explore the origins of behavior theory—the view that emphasizes the central role of experience in determining behavior. Throughout the rest of the text, we discuss what we now know about the nature of learning.

FUNCTIONALISM

Functionalism was an early school of psychology that emphasized the instinctive origins and adaptive function of behavior. According to this theory, the function of behavior is to promote survival through adaptive behavior. The functionalists expressed various ideas concerning the mechanisms controlling human behavior. The father of functionalism, John Dewey (1886), suggested that, in humans, the mind replaced the reflexive behaviors of lower animals, and the mind has evolved as the primary mechanism for human survival. The mind enables the individual to adapt to the environment. The main idea in Dewey's functionalism was that the manner of human survival differs from that of lower animals.

In contrast to Dewey, William James, also a nineteenth-century psychologist, argued that the major difference between humans and lower animals lies in the character of their respective inborn or instinctual motives. According to James (1890), human beings possess a greater range of **instincts** that guide behavior (e.g., rivalry, sympathy, fear, sociability, cleanliness, modesty, and love) than do lower animals. These social instincts directly enhance (or reduce) our successful interaction with our environment and, thus, our survival. James also proposed that all instincts, both human and nonhuman, have a mentalist quality, possessing both purpose and direction. Unlike Dewey, James believed that instincts motivated the behavior of both humans and lower animals.

Some psychologists (see Troland, 1928) who opposed a mentalist concept of instinct argued that internal biochemical forces motivate behavior in all species. Concepts developed in physics and chemistry during the second half of the nineteenth century provided a framework for this mechanistic approach. Ernst Brucke stated, in his *Lectures on Physiology* (1874), that "the living organism is a dynamic system to which the laws of chemistry and physics apply"—a view that led to great advances in physiology. This group of functionalists used a physiochemical approach to explain the causes of human and animal behavior.

A number of scientists strongly criticized the instinct concept that the functionalists proposed. First, anthropologists pointed to a variety of values, beliefs, and behaviors among different cultures, an observation inconsistent with the idea of universal human instincts. Second, some argued that the widespread and uncritical use of the instinct concept did not advance our understanding of the nature of human behavior. L. L. Bernard's (1924) analysis illustrates the weaknesses of the instinct theories of the 1920s. Bernard identified several thousand often-conflicting instincts the functionalists had proposed. For example, Bernard described one instinct as "with a glance of the eye we can estimate instinctively the age of a passerby" (p. 132). With this type of proposed "instinct," it is not surprising that many psychologists reacted so negatively to the instinct concept.

In the 1920s, American psychology moved away from the instinct explanation of human behavior and began to emphasize the learning process. The psychologists who viewed experience as the major determinant of human actions were called behaviorists. Contemporary views suggest that behavior is traceable to both instinctive and experiential processes. In Chapter 3, we look at instinctive processes and how experience alters instinctive reactions. In this chapter, we briefly examine the behaviorists' ideas concerning the nature of the learning process. We discuss theories about the nature of the learning process throughout the text.

BEHAVIORISM

Behaviorism is a school of thought that emphasizes the role of experience in governing behavior. According to behaviorists, the important processes governing our behavior are learned. We learn both the motives that initiate behavior and specific behaviors that occur in response to these motivates through our interaction with the environment. A major goal of the behaviorists is to determine the laws governing learning. A number of ideas contributed to the behavioral view. The Greek philosopher Aristotle's concept of the association of ideas is one important origin of behaviorism.

Associationism

Suppose a friend approaches you after class and remarks that your party last week was terrific. This remark causes you to recall meeting a very attractive person at your party, which in turn reminds you to ask this person for a date. This whole thought process reflects the concept of the association of ideas: Two events become associated with each other; thus, when you think of one event, you automatically recall the other. Aristotle proposed that in order for an **association** to develop, the two events must be contiguous (temporally paired) and either similar to or opposite each other.

During the seventeenth and eighteenth centuries, British empiricists described the association process in greater detail. John Locke (1690/1964) suggested that there are no innate ideas, but instead we form ideas as a result of experience. Locke distinguished simple from complex ideas. **Simple ideas** are passive impressions received by the senses, or the mind's representation of that sensory impression. In contrast, **complex ideas** represent the combination of simple ideas, or the association of ideas. The following example illustrates the difference between simple and complex ideas. You approach a rose in a garden. Your senses detect the color, odor, and texture of the rose. Each of these sensory impressions represents a simple idea. Your mind also infers that the smell is pleasant, which also is a simple idea. The combination or association of these simple ideas creates the perception of a rose, which is a complex idea.

David Hume (1748/1955) hypothesized that three principles connect simple ideas into a complex idea. One of these principles is **resemblance**, the second is **contiguity** in time or place, and the third is **cause and effect**. Hume's own words best illustrate these three principles, which, he proposed, are responsible for the association of ideas:

> A picture naturally leads our thoughts to the original [resemblance]. The mention of the apartment in a building naturally introduces an inquiry . . . concerning the others [contiguity]; and if we think of a wound, we can scarcely forebear reflecting on the pain which follows it [cause and effect]. (Hume, 1748/1955, p. 32)

Locke and Hume were philosophers, and it was left to later scientists to evaluate the validity of the principle of the association of ideas. One of these scientists was Edward Thorndike, whose work we discuss next.

Thorndike

The work of Edward Thorndike had important influence on the development of behaviorism. Thorndike's 1898 publication of his studies established that animal behavior could change as a consequence of experience. Thorndike's ideas on learning and motivation developed from his research with his famous puzzle box (see Figures 1.1a and 1.1b). He tested 13 kittens and young cats in 15 different puzzle boxes. In his studies, he placed a hungry cat in a locked box and put food just beyond its reach, outside the box. The cat could escape to obtain food by exhibiting one of a number of possible behaviors. A different response or sequence of responses was required to activate a release mechanism and escape from each box. For example, two effective behaviors were pulling on a string and pressing a pedal.

Edward Lee Thorndike (1874–1949)

Thorndike studied under William James at Harvard University. His research on associative learning in animals began in James's basement when he was unable to secure research space at Harvard. He continued his animal learning studies at Columbia University, where he obtained his doctorate under the direction of James McKeen Cattell, who is considered one of the founding fathers of psychometrics. He then taught for 36 years at Teachers College, Columbia University. Considered a pioneer in the field of educational psychology, he applied the psychological principles to the teaching of reading, language acquisition, and intelligence testing. He served as president of the American Psychological Association in 1912.

Figure 1.1   Thorndike's famous puzzle box: The hungry cat can escape and obtain access to food by exhibiting the appropriate response (top). Photograph of Thorndike's puzzle box C (bottom).

Thorndike (1898) observed that when a cat was initially placed into the puzzle box, the cat would engage in a number of behaviors, such as clawing, biting, meowing, and rubbing. Eventually, the cat would respond in a way that activated the release mechanism and opened the door to the puzzle box. The cat would then escape from the puzzle box and consume the food outside. On subsequent trials, the cat would engage in the other behaviors, but eventually would respond in the manner needed to activate the release mechanism and escape from the puzzle box. Thorndike found that not only did the cats escape but that with each successive trial, the time needed to activate the release also decreased (see Figure 1.2). Further, Thorndike observed that the time the cat spent engaging in the other behaviors declined until the only behavior seen in the puzzle box was the one that activated the release mechanism.

Figure 1.2   The escape time of one cat declined over 24 trials in one of Thorndike's puzzle boxes.

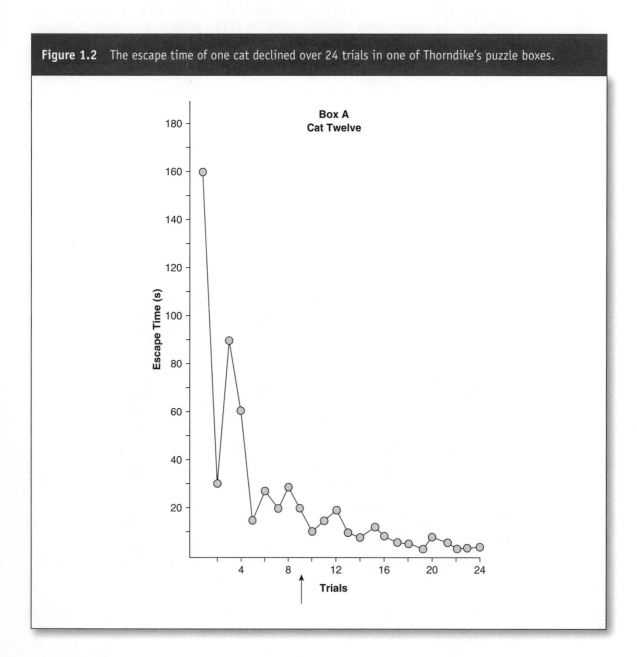

Thorndike (1898) proposed that the cat formed an association between the stimulus (the box) and the effective response. Learning, according to Thorndike, reflects the development of a stimulus-response (S-R) association. As the result of learning, the presence of the stimulus elicits the appropriate response. Thorndike asserted that the animal is not conscious of this association but is instead exhibiting a mechanistic **habit** in response to a particular stimulus. The S-R connection developed because the cat received a **reward**: The effective response resulted in the cat obtaining reward (food), which produced a satisfying state and strengthened the S-R bond. Thorndike labeled this strengthening of an S-R association by reward or a satisfying state the **law of effect**. Thus, the law of effect selects the appropriate response and connects it to the environment, thereby changing a chance act into a learned behavior.

Thorndike did not think that the law of effect applied only to animal behavior; he argued that it also describes the human learning process. Thorndike (1932) presented his human subjects with a concept to learn. Telling his subjects that they had responded correctly enabled the subjects to learn the appropriate response.

Although Thorndike's views concerning the nature of the learning process were quite specific, his ideas on the motivational processes that determine behavior were vague. According to Thorndike (1898), learning occurs, or previously learned behavior is exhibited, only if the animal or human is "ready." Thorndike's **law of readiness** proposes that the animal or human must be motivated to develop an association or to exhibit a previously established habit. Thorndike did not hypothesize about the nature of the motivation mechanism, leaving such endeavors to future psychologists. Indeed, the motivational basis of behavior became a critical concern of the behaviorists.

Thorndike (1913) suggested a second means by which learning can occur. According to Thorndike, associating the stimulus that elicited a response with another stimulus could result in the association of that response with the other stimulus. Thorndike referred to this learning process as **associative shifting**. To illustrate the associative shifting process, consider Thorndike's example of teaching a cat to stand up on command. At first, a piece of fish is placed in front of a cat; when the cat stands to reach the fish, the trainer says, "Stand up." After a number of trials, the trainer omits the fish stimulus, and the verbal stimulus alone can elicit the standing response, even though this S-R association has not been rewarded. Although Thorndike believed that conditioning, or the development of a new S-R association, could occur through associative shifting, he proposed that the law of effect, rather than associative shifting, explains the learning of most S-R associations. In the next section, we will discover that Thorndike's associative shifting process bears a striking resemblance to classical conditioning.

BEFORE YOU GO ON

- What could Marcus learn about drug addiction from our discussion of behaviorism?

- How could Marcus use Thorndike's law of effect to explain a possible cause of drug addiction?

SECTION REVIEW

- Learning is a relatively permanent change in behavioral potential that results from experience.

- The functionalists emphasized the instinctive character of human behavior, but could not agree on the nature of instinctive processes or the number of instincts.

- The behaviorists' view is that most human behavior is due to experience.

- Thorndike repeatedly placed individual cats in a puzzle box and found that the cats increasingly used the behavior that enabled them to escape from the box.

- Thorndike believed that the effect of the food reward was to strengthen the association between the stimulus of the puzzle box and the effective response.

- Thorndike's law of readiness proposed that motivation was necessary for learning to occur.

- Thorndike believed that association of a stimulus that elicited a response with another stimulus results in the other stimulus also eliciting the response through the associative shifting process.

Pavlov

How did the cat select the correct response in Thorndike's puzzle box studies? Thorndike explained the process as one of trial and error; the cat simply performed various behaviors until it discovered a correct one. Reward then functioned to strengthen the association of the stimulus environment with that response. However, the research of Ivan Pavlov (1927) suggests that the learning process is anything but trial and error. According to Pavlov, definite rules determine which behavior occurs in the learning situation.

Pavlov was a physiologist, not a psychologist; his initial plan was to uncover the laws governing digestion. He observed that animals exhibit numerous reflexive responses when food is placed in their mouths (e.g., salivation, gastric secretion). The function of these responses is to aid in the digestion process.

Ivan Petrovich Pavlov (1849–1936)

Pavlov received a doctorate in physiology from the University of Saint Petersburg and for 45 years directed the Department of Physiology at the Institute of Experimental Medicine, which became a leading center of physiological research. His early research was on the physiology of pancreatic nerves. He received the Nobel Prize in Physiology or Medicine in 1904 for his work on the physiology of digestion. He is most noted for his studies on the conditioning of digestive reflexes. Toward the end of his career, he turned his attention to the use of conditioning to induce experimental neurosis in animals by overstraining the excitatory or the inhibitory process, or by quickly alternating excitation and inhibition. He continued to work in his lab until the age of 87. His lectures are in the public domain and can be read at www .ivanpavlov.com.

Pavlov observed during the course of his research that his dogs began to secrete stomach juices when they saw food or when it was placed in their food dishes. He concluded that the dogs had learned a new behavior because he had not observed this response during their first exposure to the food. To explain his observation, he suggested that both humans and nonhuman animals possess innate or **unconditioned reflexes**. An unconditioned reflex consists of two components—an **unconditioned stimulus** (UCS; e.g., food), which involuntarily elicits the second component, the **unconditioned response** (UCR; e.g., release of saliva). A new or **conditioned reflex** develops when a neutral environmental event occurs along with the unconditioned stimulus. As conditioning progresses, the neutral stimulus becomes the **conditioned stimulus** (CS; e.g., the sight of food) and is able to elicit the learned or **conditioned response** (CR; e.g., the release of saliva).

The demonstration of a learned reflex in animals was an important discovery, illustrating not only an animal's ability to learn but the mechanism responsible for the learned behavior. According to Pavlov, any neutral stimulus paired with an unconditioned stimulus could, through conditioning, develop the capacity to elicit a CR. In his classic demonstration of the **classical conditioning** process, he first implanted a tube, called a fistula, in a dog's salivary glands to collect saliva (see Figures 1.3a and 1.3b). He then presented the conditioned stimulus (the sound of a metronome) and, shortly thereafter, placed the unconditioned stimulus (meat powder) in the dog's mouth. On the first presentation, only the meat powder produced saliva (UCR). However, with repeated pairings of the metronome with food, the metronome sound (CS) began to elicit saliva (CR), and the strength of the conditioned response increased with increased pairings of the conditioned and unconditioned stimuli.

Figure 1.3 Pavlov's salivary-conditioning apparatus. The experimenter can measure saliva output when either a conditioned stimulus (e.g., the tick of a metronome) or an unconditioned stimulus (e.g., meat powder) is presented to the dog. The dog is placed in a harness to minimize movement, thus ensuring an accurate measure of the salivary response (top). Photograph of Pavlov and one of his dogs (bottom).

Pavlov conducted an extensive investigation of the conditioning process, identifying many procedures that influence an animal's learned behaviors. Many of his ideas are still accepted today. He observed that stimuli similar to the CS can also elicit the CR through a process he called **generalization**; further, the more similar the stimulus is to the CS, the greater the generalization of the CR. Pavlov also showed that if, after conditioning, the conditioned stimulus is presented without the unconditioned stimulus, the strength of the conditioned response diminishes. Pavlov named this process of eliminating a conditioned response **extinction**.

Pavlov's observations had a profound influence on psychology. The conditioning process he described, often called Pavlovian conditioning, has been demonstrated in various animals, including humans. Many different responses can become conditioned responses and most environmental stimuli can become conditioned stimuli.

Watson

The learning processes Thorndike and Pavlov described became the foundation of behaviorism. However, it was John B. Watson who was responsible for the emergence of behaviorism as the dominant point of view in American psychology. Watson's *Psychology from the Standpoint of a Behaviorist* was first published in 1919. His introductory psychology text presented a coherent stimulus-response view of human behavior, which was extremely successful and provided the structure for later behavioral theories.

Although Pavlov's research excited Watson, the work of another Russian, Vladimir Bechterev, was an even greater influence. Whereas Pavlov used positive or pleasant UCSs, Bechterev employed aversive or unpleasant stimuli (e.g., shock) to study the conditioning process. Bechterev found that a conditioned leg withdrawal response could be established in dogs by pairing a neutral stimulus with the shock. In his duplication of Bechterev's studies, Watson (1916) showed that after several pairings with electric shock, a previously neutral stimulus elicited a leg withdrawal response in dogs. Watson also was able to condition a toe or a finger withdrawal in human subjects. Further, Watson conditioned not only a toe or a finger withdrawal response but also an emotional arousal (revealed by increased breathing).

Watson believed that abnormal, as well as normal, behavior is learned. He was particularly concerned with demonstrating that human **fears** are acquired through classical conditioning. To illustrate this point, Watson and his assistant Rosalie Rayner (1920) showed a white rat to Albert, a healthy 9-month-old infant attending a day-care center at Johns Hopkins University. As the child reached for the rat, he heard a loud sound (UCS) produced as Watson hit a heavy iron rail with a hammer (see Figures 1.4a and 1.4b). After three CS–UCS pairings, Watson and Rayner observed that the presentation of the rat (CS) alone produced a fear response in the child. The rat elicited strong emotional arousal, as the child's attempts to escape from it demonstrated, after six CS–UCS pairings. The authors observed a strong generalized response to similar objects: The child also showed fear of a white rabbit and a white fur coat.

John Broadus Watson (1878–1958)

Watson studied under Jacques Loeb and John Dewey and received his doctorate from the University of Chicago. Considered the founder of the field of behaviorism, he taught at Johns Hopkins University for 13 years. At Johns Hopkins, he and his assistant Rosalie Rayner conducted his famous "little Albert" study. He served as president of the American Psychological Association in 1915. In 1920, he was dismissed from Johns Hopkins due to his affair with Rosalie Rayner, whom he subsequently married. After leaving John Hopkins, he served as a vice president of the J. Walter Thompson Advertising Agency, where he applied behavioral principles to advertising, most notably with popularizing the "coffee break" during an ad campaign for Maxwell House coffee.

Figure 1.4 While "little Albert" was playing with a white rat, Watson struck a suspended bar with a hammer. The loud sound disturbed the child, causing him to develop a conditioned fear of the white rat. Rosalie Rayner, Watson's assistant, distracted little Albert as Watson approached the bar (top). Photograph of Watson, Rayner, Albert, and white rat (bottom).

Although Watson had intended to extinguish Albert's fear, Albert's mother withdrew him from the daycare center before Watson could eliminate the infant's fear. There has been much speculation about what happened to "little Albert." Watson and Rayner (1920) suggested that fears like Albert's were "likely to persist indefinitely, unless an accidental method for removing them is hit upon" (p.12). Contemporary behaviorists have suggested that not only did Albert develop a phobia of white rats and indeed all furry animals (Eysenck, 1960), but that the "little Albert study" also indicates "that it is quite possible for one experience to induce a phobia" (Wolpe & Rachman, 1960, p. 146). It would, however, be a mistake to base the idea that a phobia can develop after a single experience on the little Albert study (B. Harris, 1979). Watson and Rayner used a single subject in their study, their accounts of little Albert's fears were very subjective, and they provided no reliable assessment of Albert's emotional response (Sherman, 1930). Further, attempts to condition fears in infants using loud noises have consistently been unsuccessful (Bregman, 1934; Valentine, 1930). Thus, it seems highly unlikely that the methodology Watson and Rayner employed was sufficient for little Albert to develop a phobia of white rats. As we will discover in Chapter 4, there is substantial evidence that phobias in humans can be acquired through experience, but probably not the experience described in the Watson and Rayner study.

In 1924, Mary Cover Jones, a student working with Watson, developed an effective technique to eliminate fears. Jones observed that Peter, a 3-year-old boy, was quite frightened of white rabbits. When Peter was at ease, she brought the rabbit into the same room while Peter was eating, keeping enough distance between the rabbit and Peter that the child was not alarmed. She then moved the rabbit closer and closer to Peter, allowing him to grow accustomed to it in gradual steps. Eventually, the child was able to touch and hold the formerly fear-inducing animal. According to Jones, this procedure had eliminated fear by conditioning a positive emotional response to the rabbit, produced by eating. The elimination of fear by the acquisition of a fear-inhibiting emotional response occurs through the conditioning of an opponent or antagonistic response, a process called **counterconditioning**. Approximately 30 years later, Jones's study played an important role in the development of an effective treatment of human phobic behavior. We discuss this treatment, systematic desensitization, in Chapter 4.

Mary Cover Jones (1896–1987)

Cover Jones studied with John B. Watson and received her doctorate from Columbia University. Considered a pioneer in the field of behavior therapy, her counterconditioning of a fear of rabbits in 3-year old Peter played a central role in the development of systematic desensitization. When her husband, Harold Jones, accepted a position as director of research at the Institute for Child Welfare at the University of California, she took a position as research associate at the institute, where she remained for 20 years conducting longitudinal studies of child development. She later served on the faculty at the University of California, Berkeley for 8 years prior to her retirement. She received the G. Stanley Hall Award for Distinguished Contribution to Developmental Psychology by the American Psychological Association in 1968.

BEFORE YOU GO ON

- How might classical conditioning lead to addictive behavior?
- What could Marcus learn from the Mary Cover Jones study about a potential way to eliminate addictive behavior?

SECTION REVIEW

- Pavlov demonstrated that pairing a novel stimulus (the conditioned stimulus) with a biologically significant event (the unconditioned stimulus) results in the conditioning of a new reflex.

- Prior to conditioning, only the unconditioned stimulus elicited the unconditioned response, while after the pairing of the conditioned and unconditioned stimuli, the conditioned stimulus elicited the conditioned response.

- Watson suggested that emotional responses develop as a result of classical conditioning experiences in humans.

- Watson and Rayner observed that a young child would become frightened of a rat if the rat was paired with a loud noise.

- Watson and Rayner suggested that little Albert's fear could also generalize the fear to other white animals and objects.

- Jones discovered that pairing a feared rabbit with food could eliminate a child's fear of the rabbit through counterconditioning.

Many different views of human nature developed during the early part of the twentieth century. Some of these views stressed the mentalist aspect of our behavior; others presented human beings as automatically responding to events in our environment. The role of instincts was central to some theories of behavior; learning as the determinant of human action was the core of others. However, psychology was just in its infancy, and all these views remained essentially untested. Our understanding of the learning process has increased during the past 75 years, as you will discover from the remainder of the text.

THE ETHICS OF CONDUCTING RESEARCH

In this text, we discuss many studies that used both nonhuman animals and humans as subjects. There are limits to both types of research. Research must never violate principles of ethical conduct. This chapter ends by examining the research that is permissible.

Conducting Research With Human Subjects

Psychological research with human subjects must be conducted in accordance with the principles published by the American Psychological Association (APA) in the book titled *Ethical Principles in the Conduct of Research With Human Participants* (APA, 2002). Let's briefly discuss the ethical principles a psychologist must follow when conducting research with humans.

When a psychologist plans to conduct research using human subjects, an ethics committee decides whether that research is permissible under the guidelines. The main principle that determines whether the ethics committee approves the research project is the demonstration that the planned study maximizes potential gain in knowledge and minimizes the costs and potential risks to human subjects. In conducting human research, the psychologist typically enters into an agreement with the subject. The subject learns the general purpose of the study and the potential risks of participating. It also is essential that no subject be coerced into participation in the study. For example, at many schools, students are required to participate in psychological experiments as a course requirement in general psychology. This requirement is permissible only if an alternative activity is available to the student. Students at other universities can volunteer to participate, but failing to volunteer cannot be counted against the student. The subject must also be free to withdraw from the study at any time.

As part of the agreement between the researcher and subject, the subject is informed that he or she will receive some tangible rewards (such as money), personal help (such as counseling), or information regarding the study (primarily results of the study). The researcher must live up to this agreement because it is a contract between the researcher and participant. After the study is completed, the experimenter **debriefs** the subject, by providing information about the nature of the study. Further, the anonymity of the subject and confidentiality regarding the subject's behavior in the study must be maintained. All of this information must be explained in a written agreement, and the subject must sign an **informed consent** agreement indicating that he or she is willing to participate in the study.

The Use of Nonhuman Animals in Research

Many of the studies described in this text used nonhuman animals as subjects, including mice, rats, birds, cats, dogs, and monkeys. Why do psychologists use nonhuman animals in their research? There are several reasons. One is the problem of documenting causal relationships. People differ greatly in terms of their behavior, which makes it difficult to obtain a representative sample. Because the behavior of animals is less variable, it is easier to show causal relationships in lower animals than in humans.

Another reason for using nonhuman animals is that some types of research cannot be ethically conducted with humans. For example, suppose that a psychologist suspects that damage to a certain area of the brain impairs memory storage. This idea may come from case histories of individuals with memory disorders who have tumors in this brain area. But these case histories cannot be used to infer causality. The only way to demonstrate causality is to damage this area of the brain and see whether memory storage problems result. Obviously, we cannot do this type of research with humans; it would be unethical to expose a person to any treatment that would lead to behavior pathology. The use of animals provides a way to show that this brain area controls memory storage and that damage to this area leads to memory disorders.

Some people object to the use of animals for demonstrating that a certain area of the brain controls memory storage, or for any other reason. Several arguments have been offered in defense of the use of animals for psychological research. Humans suffer from many different behavior disorders, and animal research can provide us with knowledge concerning the causes of these disorders as well as treatments that can prevent or cure behavioral problems. As the noted psychologist Neal Miller (1985) pointed out, animal research has led to a variety of programs, including rehabilitation treatments for neuromuscular disorders and the development of drug and behavioral treatments for phobias, depression, schizophrenia, and other behavior pathologies.

Certainly, animals should not be harmed needlessly, and their discomfort should be minimized. Yet, when a great deal of human suffering may be prevented, the use of animals in studies seems appropriate (Feeney, 1987). Animal research also has led to significant advances in veterinary medicine, and far more animals are sacrificed for food, hunting, or fur coats than for research and education (Nichols & Russell, 1990). Currently, animal research is conducted only when approved by a committee, such as an Institutional Animal Use and Care Committee (IACUC), that acts to ensure that animals are used humanely and in strict accordance with local, state, and federal guidelines.

BEFORE YOU GO ON

- What would Marcus need to do to conduct a study using human subjects?
- How would Marcus justify the use of animals to study addictive behavior?

SECTION REVIEW

- Ethical principles established by the American Psychological Association govern the kind of research that is permissible with human subjects.

- A researcher must demonstrate to an ethics committee that the planned study maximizes the potential gain in psychological knowledge and minimizes the costs and potential risks to human subjects.

- Many psychologists use nonhuman animals as subjects in their research.

- One reason for using animal subjects is that causal relationships can be demonstrated with animals in certain types of studies that cannot be ethically conducted with humans.

- The discomfort experienced by the animals should be minimized; however, a great deal of human suffering can be prevented by conducting research with animals.

- Animal research must be approved by a committee, such as the IACUC, which acts to ensure that animals are used in accordance with local, state, and federal guidelines.

CRITICAL THINKING QUESTIONS

1. Functionalism and behaviorism present quite different explanations for the causes of behavior. Explain the differences between functionalism and behaviorism. Then, select a behavior and explain that behavior using both the functionalist and behaviorist perspectives.

2. Pavlov and Thorndike had a significant impact on our understanding of the learning process. Describe their work and indicate why it is important for learning theory.

3. Many individuals object to the use of animals in psychological research. Discuss the basis of their objections. Explain why some psychologists use animals in their studies. Is there any way to reconcile these opposing perspectives?

KEY TERMS

association	associative shifting
behaviorism	cause and effect
classical conditioning	complex ideas
conditioned reflex	conditioned response (CR)
conditioned stimulus (CS)	contiguity
counterconditioning	debrief
extinction	fear
functionalism	generalization
habit	informed consent
instinct	law of effect
law of readiness	learning
resemblance	reward
simple ideas	unconditioned reflex
unconditioned response (UCR)	unconditioned stimulus (UCS)

Traditional Learning Theories

THE OLDIES BUT GOODIES

Justin goes to the movies every Friday night. The Cinema Theatre shows classic movies like On the Waterfront *and* To Kill a Mockingbird. *Although he has not missed a show in almost a year, Justin was not always a fan of the classics. Before going to college, his favorite movies were science fiction and adventure films. Justin especially enjoyed the* Star Wars *movies; he probably saw each one at least three times. Some of his friends are not as avid about movies, but Justin enjoys them so much that he often goes by himself. His latest preference developed in his first semester at school. He met with his advisor during enrollment to discuss the courses he should take. Four courses were required, but he could enroll in one course of his choosing. His advisor gave him a list of courses that would fulfill the university's General Education Program. As he looked over the list, he spotted a course titled "Introduction to Motion Pictures" offered by the Theatre Department. Since he liked movies so much, Justin decided to take the course. At the first class, he received a list of 15 movies the class would see that semester. Justin had not seen most of the movies on the list, and several of the films were not familiar to him. His instructor informed the class that they would discuss each film's strengths and weaknesses after seeing it. The first movie the class saw was* High Noon. *Justin had seen many Western movies, but none compared with this one. It was not only action packed; it also revealed well-defined characters. The next week, he saw* Grapes of Wrath. *He could not believe he would like a black-and-white movie, but it was wonderful. Every week, he saw a new and exciting movie. Around the middle of the semester, Justin started going to the theatre in town every Friday night. The theatre showed a Humphrey Bogart film festival, and several students in the class asked Justin to go. The Bogart movies were great, and he had a super time. He is now hooked on classic movies. Justin also discovered the Cinema Theatre has the best buttered popcorn in town, which made going to the theatre even more enjoyable.*

Why does Justin go to the movies every Friday night? It seems his past enjoyable experiences are responsible for his present behavior. Yet how have Justin's experiences been translated into actions? Many psychologists have speculated on the nature of the learning process. Some theories attempt to explain the basis of all human actions, while others focus on specific aspects of the learning process. Some theories would attempt to describe both why Justin likes movies and why he goes to the theatre every Friday. In contrast, other theories would tell us either why Justin enjoyed movies or why he went on Friday nights.

In this chapter, we examine several different global theories of learning, that is, several views that attempt to explain all aspects of behavior. Global theories emerged in the 1930s and were especially popular into the late 1960s. These global views have provided us with considerable knowledge concerning the nature of learning. Over the past 40 years, psychologists have focused on more specific aspects of the learning process. We discuss what these psychologists discovered about the nature of specific learning processes throughout the remainder of the text.

TRADITIONAL LEARNING THEORIES

Clark Leonard Hull (1884–1952)

Hull received his doctorate from the University of Wisconsin-Madison under the direction of Joseph Jastrow. He then taught at Wisconsin for 10 years where he conducted research on the effects of tobacco on performance. In addition, he developed a course on aptitude testing, and even built a machine that automatically prepared the correlations for his test-construction work. He later taught at Yale University for 23 years, where along with his colleague Kenneth Spence, developed a drive theory of learning. While at Yale, he conducted the first systematic evaluation of the effects of hypnosis on behavior. Judson Brown, John Dollard, Neal E. Miller, and O. H. Mowrer were some of the eminent American psychologists who were his students at Yale. He served as president of the American Psychology Association in 1936.

Two major theoretical approaches have been proposed to explain the nature of the learning process. The stimulus-response (S-R) associative theorists advocate a mechanistic view of the learning process. Learning, according to the S-R approach, occurs when an originally neutral environmental stimulus develops the ability to elicit a specific response. In contrast, the cognitive theory approach assumes that learning involves recognizing when important events are likely to occur and developing an understanding of how to obtain those events. Cognitive theorists propose a flexible view of behavior, which contrasts with the inflexible approach of the S-R theorists.

The S-R approach assumes that the stimulus environment controls behavior, while the cognitive approach proposes that mental processes control behavior. We begin by describing the S-R theories and then discuss the cognitive approach. In Chapter 10, we further examine the stimulus environment's control of behavior. A detailed discussion of the cognitive control of behavior follows in Chapter 11.

Two very different **S-R associative theories** exist: One proposes that **reward** is necessary in order to learn an S-R association, while the other proposes that the only necessity is for the response to occur in the stimulus context. We begin by looking at the view that reward is necessary to learn an S-R association, followed by a discussion of the theory that contiguity is sufficient for S-R learning.

HULL'S DRIVE THEORY

Clark Hull (1943, 1952) proposed that primary drives such as hunger and thirst are produced by states of deprivation and, when aroused, elicit internal arousal. This internal arousal, which Hull called **drive**, motivates behavior that will reduce the drive and, thereby, restore bodily balance. This tendency to maintain a steady internal state is called **homeostasis**. Hull also suggested that intense environmental events can produce the drive state, that animals can learn behaviors to reduce internal tension and that drives, which Hull called acquired drives, can be learned through experience.

In 1918, Robert S. Woodworth defined drive as an intense internal force that motivates behavior. Hull incorporated Woodworth's concept of drive into an S-R associative theory. According to Hull, drive motivates behavior and drive reduction is responsible for the S-R associative learning that was described in Chapter 1.

Hull thought that several factors determine the intensity of behavior. In addition to drive (D), Hull suggested that the **incentive motivation** for reward (K); the **habit strength**, or strength of the S-R association (H); and the level of **inhibition** (I) control **excitatory potential**. The excitatory potential reflects the likelihood that a specific event (S) will cause the occurrence of a specific behavior (R).

Hull assumed that the excitatory potential level is increased by drive (D), incentive motivation (K), and habit strength (H) and is reduced by inhibition (I). Drive is an internal arousal state produced by deprivation, the presence of intense environmental events, or stimuli associated with deprivation or intense environmental events. Incentive motivation is an internal arousal produced by reward or the stimuli associated with reward. Habit strength is the strength of the connection between the stimulus and response produced when the response reduces drive. Inhibition is the suppression of a response produced when that response fails to produce reward.

Hull also developed a mathematical equation to express how these variables jointly determine the intensity of a response. According to Hull, *Excitatory potential ($_sE_R$) = drive (D) × incentive motivation (K) × habit strength (H)—inhibition (I)*. The factors influencing each aspect of the theory are presented in Figure 2.1. In Hull's view, the accurate prediction of behavior is possible only if each factor in the mathematical relationship is known.

Figure 2.1 Diagram of Hull's theory. The terms in the circles show the major variables influencing the likelihood of behavior. Drive (D), habit strength (H), and incentive (K) increase the excitatory potential ($_sE_R$), enhancing the likelihood that the stimulus will elicit a particular response. By contrast, inhibition (I) decreases excitatory potential. The terms in the rectangles represent the secondary processes that influence each major process.

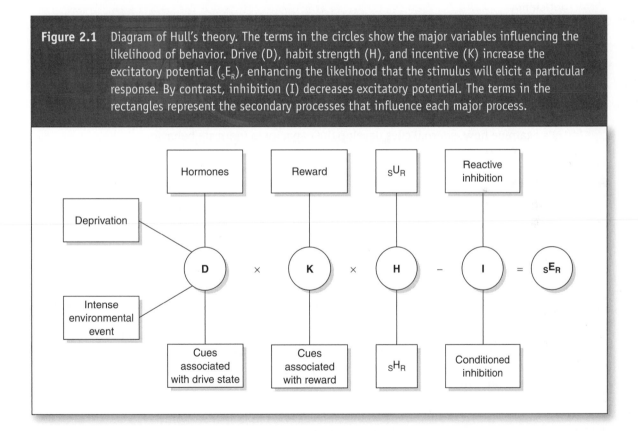

Consider the following example to illustrate Hull's theory. Imagine the butterflies that you experience before taking a test. The scheduled exam creates this arousal, or nervousness; the prior scheduling of the exam is an antecedent condition producing the internal drive state. Your nervousness motivates behavior that in the past reduced this drive; ideally, this behavior includes studying. We begin by examining the antecedent conditions inducing drive and motivating behavior.

Unconditioned Sources of Drive

Hull (1943) proposed that events that threaten survival (for example, failure to obtain food) activate the internal drive state. Survival requires that internal biological systems operate effectively. A deficit in these internal systems threatens survival and thus represents, according to Hull, an antecedent condition that will motivate behavior designed to restore biological systems to normal. In some cases, an internal adjustment may restore normal functioning. For instance, in the absence of food, an individual will use stored energy to maintain normal functioning. However, if the deficiency persists, behavior will be initiated to resolve the deficiency. Thus, using too much stored energy motivates the animal to obtain food.

In 1952, Hull acknowledged that events that do not threaten survival can also motivate behavior. Several types of studies forced Hull to acknowledge that an internal drive state can appear even in the absence of deprivation. First, animals show a strong preference for saccharin, consuming large quantities even when they are not hungry. Although saccharin has no caloric value, deprived animals will eat it rather than a more nutritionally valuable food. In addition, hungry rats can learn an instrumental behavior to obtain saccharin (Sheffield & Roby, 1950). These observations suggest that behavior can occur in the absence of a biologically induced deficiency.

Several classes of nondeprivation events can induce drive and motivate behavior. Hull assumed that intense environmental events motivate behavior by activating the internal drive state. Electrical shock is one external stimulus that can induce internal arousal and motivate defensive behavior. The shock may be aversive, but it does not necessarily threaten survival.

A number of circumstances, including deprivation and intense environmental events, can produce the internal drive state that motivates behavior. These events instinctively produce drive. However, many stimuli in our environment acquire the capacity to induce the internal drive state. Let's examine how external cues develop the capacity to motivate behavior.

Acquired Drives

Hull (1943) suggested that, through classical conditioning, environmental stimuli can acquire the ability to produce an internal drive state. According to this view, the association of environmental cues with the antecedent conditions that produce an unconditioned drive state cause the development of a conditioned drive state. Once this conditioned drive state has developed, these cues can induce internal arousal and motivate behavior on subsequent occasions, even in the absence of the stimuli that induce the unconditioned drive state.

Consider the following example to illustrate Hull's **acquired drive** concept. A person goes to the ball park on a very hot day. Thirst, produced by the heat, motivates this person to go to the concession stand and consume several beers. The beers reduce the thirst, and because of this experience, the person will feel thirst even on cool days when walking past the concession stand and may well purchase a beer. This person has acquired a conditioned drive associated with the stimulus of the concession stand.

The Reinforcing Function of Drive Reduction

From the Hullian view, drive motivates behavior, but each specific behavior depends on the environment; that is, environmental events direct behavior. Which behavior does a specific stimulus elicit? Hull thought that when an animal is motivated (drive exists), the environmental cue present automatically elicits a specific response—the response with the strongest habit strength. The strength of the habit can be innate ($_sU_R$) or can be acquired through experience ($_sH_R$).

How does habit strength develop? If a response reduces the drive state, the bond between the stimulus and response is strengthened; thus, habit strength can increase as the result of drive reduction. Habit strength increases each time the behavior produces drive reduction.

Let's examine how the Hullian view of reinforcement would explain a person eating a hot dog at the ballpark. This person's primary drive initially motivated behavior to reduce hunger. After a trip to the concession stand and the purchase and consumption of a hot dog, hunger was eliminated. Hull would assert that the drive reduction strengthened the bond between the concession stand and eating a hot dog. Each subsequent experience strengthens the bond until the behavior becomes habitual.

The Elimination of Unsuccessful Behavior

According to Hull, unsuccessful behavior causes drive to persist. If drive persists, all behavior is temporarily inhibited—a process referred to as **reactive inhibition**. When the reactive inhibition declines, the habitual behavior will occur again. The continued failure of the response to reduce drive leads to a permanent **conditioned inhibition**.

Conditioned inhibition is specific to a particular response, and it acts to reduce the excitatory strength of the habit. The continued failure of one response may lead the drive state to elicit the second strongest response in the **habit hierarchy**. If this behavior successfully reduces drive, the habit strength of this response increases. This effective habit will become the dominant habit and will again be elicited when the animal is motivated. If the second habit in the hierarchy is ineffective, the animal will continue down the habit hierarchy until a successful response occurs.

Incentive Motivation

To suggest that a person would continue to visit the concession stand if it no longer sold quality hot dogs is probably inaccurate; the likelihood of the behavior is determined, to some degree, by the quality of a hot dog served at the concession stand. Yet, Hull's 1943 theory assumed that drive reduction or reward only influences the strength of the S-R bond; a more valuable reward produces greater drive reduction and, therefore, establishes a stronger habit. Once the habit is established, motivation depends on the drive level but not the reward value.

However, numerous studies have shown that the value of the reward has an important influence on motivational level. For example, Crespi (1942) found that shifts in reward magnitude produced a rapid change in rats' runway performance for food. When he increased the reward magnitude from 1 to 16 pellets on the twentieth trial, the rats' performance after just two or three trials equaled that of animals that had always received the higher reward. If reward magnitude influenced only the learning level, as Hull suggested, the change in runway speed should have been gradual. The rapid shift in the rats' behavior indicates that reward magnitude influenced their motivation; the use of a larger reward increased the rats' motivational level. A similar rapid change in behavior occurred when the reward was decreased from 256 to 16 pellets. These rats quickly decreased their running speed to a level equal to that of rats receiving the lower reward on each trial. Figure 2.2 presents the results of Crespi's study.

The results of these experiments convinced Hull (1952) that reward magnitude affects the intensity of the motivation producing instrumental behavior. According to Hull, a large reward produces a greater arousal level, and thereby more motivation to act, than does a small reward. Furthermore, he theorized that the environmental stimuli associated with reward acquire incentive motivation properties and that the cues present with a large reward will produce a greater conditioned incentive motivation than stimuli associated with a small reward. The importance of these acquired incentive cues is most evident when the reward cannot be seen; the cues associated with large reward elicit a greater approach to reward than do cues associated with a small reward.

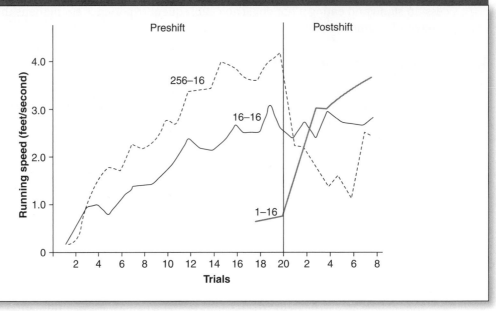

Figure 2.2   Speed in the runway as a function of the magnitude of reinforcement. The rats received 1, 16, and 256 pellets of food. (The acquisition data for the 1-pellet group are not represented.) Sixteen pellets were given to each rat after trial 20. A shift from 1 to 16 pellets produced a rapid increase in performance, while a rapid decline in speed occurred when reward magnitude was lowered from 256 to 16 pellets.

How would Hull's view explain the fact that Justin goes to the Cinema Theatre every Friday night to watch classic movies? Recall that the Cinema Theatre has the best buttered popcorn in town. As a result of his eating buttered popcorn, Justin associates the Friday night (stimulus) with going to the Cinema Theatre (response). This habit develops because buttered popcorn is very arousing, perhaps because it tastes so good. And since buttered popcorn is very arousing, it is a large reward that motivates Justin to go to the Cinema Theatre every Friday night.

An Evaluation of Drive Theory

Hull's drive theory represented the dominant behavioral theory from the 1930s to the 1960s. Many of Hull's ideas do accurately reflect important aspects of human behavior: (1) intense arousal can motivate behavior; (2) environmental stimuli can develop the ability to produce arousal, thereby motivating behavior; and (3) the value of reward influences the intensity of responding. Evidence of the validity of these aspects of Hull's drive theory appears throughout the text. Although Hull's drive theory developed from research with animals, psychologists have used it to explain the basis of many human behaviors.

However, Hull's drive theory has encountered some difficulties. His concept of reward has proved to be inaccurate; that is, reward and drive reduction are not synonymous. Two types of evidence challenge the drive-reduction view of reward. First, numerous experiments—the initial study by Olds and Milner in 1954 is classic—demonstrate that direct stimulation of the brain is reinforcing. Olds and Milner placed a small wire, an electrode, into a rat's brain and passed an electrical current through the electrode. They noted that their rats learned to bar press to obtain brain stimulation. Other studies have reported that rats will learn the correct path in a maze for this reward (Mendelson & Chorover, 1965). The rewarding property of brain stimulation argues against a drive-reduction interpretation.

Sheffield (1966) argued that drive induction rather than reduction strengthens responding. In addition, according to Sheffield, the presentation of a reward is arousing, which subsequently acts to motivate behavior. For example, the excitement produced by the presentation of food motivates approach behavior; the food itself subsequently motivates eating. This interpretation of reward explains how secondary rewards acquire the ability to elicit behavior through association with primary rewards; this characteristic of secondary, or learned, rewards was an enigma in the Hullian view. A secondary reward (e.g., money) not only rewards behavior but also motivates future behavior.

Hull's drive theory focused on the acquisition of habitual reactions. Although he did indicate that environmental stimuli associated with reward could acquire the ability to motivate behavior through the classical conditioning process, Hull did not specify the mechanism responsible for the motivational influence of these environmental stimuli. Following Hull's death in 1952, Kenneth Spence (1956) described the process responsible for the acquisition of incentive motivation.

Other psychologists subsequently used the system Spence detailed to describe the conditioning of other motives. We briefly examine this approach next; their contribution is evident throughout the text.

Kenneth Wartinbee Spence (1907–1967)

Spence received his doctorate from Yale University under the direction of Robert Mearns Yerkes. While at Yale, he began a two-decade long collaboration with Clark Hull, developing a drive theory of learning. After graduating, he spent 4 years at the Yale Laboratories of Primate Biology in Orange Park, Florida, studying discrimination learning in chimpanzees. Spence also taught for 1 year at the University of Virginia before spending the next 26 years teaching at the University of Iowa. While at Iowa, he served as chair of the Department of Psychology and a number of eminent American Psychologists, including Abram Amsel, Janet Taylor Spence, and Allan Wagner, were his students. He was awarded the first Distinguished Scientific Contribution Award from the American Psychological Association in 1956. He taught at the University of Texas-Austin for 3 years until to his death from cancer in 1967.

SPENCE'S ACQUIRED MOTIVE APPROACH

The Anticipation of Reward

To explain the influence of reward value on behavior, Hull (1952) introduced the concept of incentive motivation, or K. Although Hull indicated that an animal or human would be more motivated after receiving a large reward than a small one, Kenneth Spence (1956), Hull's colleague, detailed the transformation of K into behavior. Let's use the behavior of the person who orders a hot dog at the ballpark to describe Spence's view.

Spence suggested that when a reward (the hot dog) is obtained in a goal environment (concession stand), this reward elicits an unconditioned goal response (R_G). For example, when the hungry person smells and tastes the hot dog, the hot dog initiates an internal response. This internal response (e.g., salivation, gastric secretion) produces an internal stimulus state (S_G) that motivates the person to eat the hot dog. The characteristics of S_G resemble those of Hull's drive state (D): They represent an internal arousal that motivates behavior. The internal response intensifies as the person eats. Until eating is inhibited, the hot dog continues to elicit the internal goal response. The reward value determines the intensity of the goal response; the greater the reward magnitude, the stronger the goal response.

Spence thought that during the first few experiences, the environmental cues present during reward (e.g., the concession stand) become associated with reward and subsequently produce a conditioned or **anticipatory goal response** (r_G). This anticipatory goal response then causes internal stimulus changes (s_G) that motivate approach behavior. Thus, the person becomes aroused when he or she sees the ballpark concession stand. The arousal motivates the person to go to the concession stand and buy a hot dog.

The reward magnitude used during conditioning determines the maximum level of response. Since a large reward creates a more intense R_G than does a smaller reward, Spence (1956) reasoned that the environmental cues associated with the large reward produce a stronger r_G than those paired with a small reward. This idea conforms to basic classical conditioning principles: The strength of a CR depends on UCS intensity; the stronger the UCS, the greater the CR. Observations that performance level improves with greater reward (e.g., Crespi, 1942) lend support to Spence's incentive motivation concept. As noted earlier, Crespi found that rats ran down a runway faster for a larger reward than for a smaller one.

Let's see how Spence's view would explain the fact that Justin goes to the Cinema Theatre every Friday night. Recall that the Cinema Theatre serves the best buttered popcorn in town. According to Spence's view, eating popcorn (S_G) elicits an intense goal response (R_G). Justin associates the stimulus environment (Friday night) with the popcorn, which results in Friday night eliciting an anticipatory goal response. The anticipatory goal response, elicited by Friday night, motivates Justin to go to the Cinema Theatre.

Spence's (1956) theory suggests that classical conditioning is responsible for motivating the behaviors that approach reward. Other psychologists have adopted this acquired motive view to explain the motivation to avoid frustrating or painful circumstances. We look briefly at how this approach explained the avoidance of nonreward. The application of this approach to explain the avoidance of painful events is discussed in Chapter 8.

Avoidance of Frustrating Events

According to Hull (1943), the absence of reward acts to inhibit behavior. Hull suggested that by inhibiting habitual behavior, nonreward allows the strengthening of other behaviors. However, this view does not completely describe the influence of nonreward on behavior. Abram Amsel's (1958) frustration theory proposes that frustration both motivates avoidance behavior and suppresses approach behavior.

Amsel (1958) proposed that the frustration state differs from the goal response. Nonreward presented in a situation that was previously rewarded produces an unconditioned frustration response (R_F). This frustration response has motivational properties: The stimulus aftereffects (S_F) energize escape behavior. The cues present during the frustration (R_F) become conditioned to produce an **anticipatory frustration response** (r_F). The anticipatory frustration response also produces distinctive internal stimuli (s_F); these stimuli (s_F) motivate the animal to avoid a potentially frustrating situation.

The following example illustrates the central aspects of Amsel's (1958) frustration model. Suppose that Justin has 10 minutes to reach the theatre before a movie begins. Justin gets into his car, but it will not start. The failure of Justin's car to start is a nonreward, which in turn produces frustration (R_F). The stimulus aftereffects of frustration (S_F) motivate escape behavior; that is, Justin leaves the car and returns home. According to Amsel's view, the car becomes associated with nonreward and, therefore, produces an anticipatory frustration response (r_F). If Justin's car continues to fail to start, he probably will sell it to avoid future frustration.

Nature of Anticipatory Behavior

Robert Rescorla and Richard Solomon (1967) pointed to a serious problem with the r_G-s_G mechanism that Kenneth Spence (1956) proposed. Spence envisioned the r_G to be a peripheral physiological response, such as salivation. Although incentive value does influence motivation level, there are no peripheral physiological changes that are always related to instrumental behavior. Psychologists who have attempted to observe r_G directly and evaluate its influence on behavior have found that salivation might precede or follow instrumental behavior; other times, an animal might salivate without responding, or respond without salivating (Kintsch & Witte, 1962; Lewis, 1959).

Rescorla and Solomon (1967) suggested that r_G is a central, rather than peripheral, nervous system response. According to Rescorla and Solomon, this central nervous system response is classically conditioned, with its strength determined by reward magnitude. Conditioned activity in the central nervous system motivates behavior. Rescorla and Solomon also suggested that frustration reflects activity in the central rather than the peripheral nervous system.

BEFORE YOU GO ON

- What S-R association did Justin learn as a result of going to the movies?

- How would changes in the level of drive, and the incentive value of the movie, influence Justin's behavior?

SECTION REVIEW

- Hull theorized that a nonspecific intense internal arousal—drive—motivates behavior.

- Several classes of stimuli (deprivation and intense environmental events) are inherently capable of initiating drive, and any stimuli associated with these innate drive stimuli develop the capacity to produce drive through the classical conditioning process.

- Reward, and stimuli associated with reward, is also able to produce arousal and motivate behavior.

- According to Hull, specific stimuli are capable of eliciting several behaviors, and the behavior with the strongest bond (or habit strength) will be repeated; the bond strengthens if the behavior produces drive reduction.

- Spence suggested that the association of environmental events with reward causes the development of a conditioned anticipatory goal response (r_G), and the stimuli (s_G) produced by this conditioned response motivate the approach to reward.

- Amsel proposed that an anticipatory frustration response (r_F) is conditioned as a result of the association of environmental events with nonreward, and the stimuli (s_F) produced by this conditioned response motivate avoidance of nonreward.

GUTHRIE'S CONTIGUITY VIEW

Hull's drive theory proposed that reward was responsible for the establishment of S-R associations. Although most psychologists during the 1930s and 1940s accepted this S-R approach, Edwin Guthrie (1935, 1942, 1959) rejected the view that reward strengthened the bond between a stimulus and a response. Instead, Guthrie proposed that **contiguity** was sufficient to establish an S-R association. According to Guthrie, if a response occurs when a particular stimulus is present, the stimulus and response will automatically become associated.

Guthrie believed that learning is a simple process governed entirely by the contiguity principle: Whenever a particular stimulus and response occur simultaneously, a person reencountering

Edwin Ray Guthrie (1886-1959)

Guthrie received his doctorate in philosophy from the University of Pennsylvania. He taught high school mathematics for five years before joining the philosophy department at the University of Washington in 1914. Guthrie spent 42 years at the University of Washington, switching from the philosophy department to the psychology department after 5 years. Guthrie's contiguity theory emphasized the role of attention in learning. He is best known for applying his learning principles to everyday life with his methods of breaking old habits being an integral part of behavior therapy. Guthrie served as president of the American Psychological Association in 1945.

that stimulus will exhibit that response. Guthrie provided many real-life examples of how a behavior could change, based on his theory. Consider the following illustration of Guthrie's view of learning:

> The mother of a ten-year-old girl complained to a psychologist that for two years her daughter had annoyed her by habitually tossing her coat and hat on the floor as she entered the house. On a hundred occasions the mother had insisted that the girl pick up the clothing and hang it in its place. These wild ways were changed only after the mother, on advice, began to insist not only that the girl pick up the fallen garments from the floor, but that she also put them on, return to the street, and reenter the house, this time removing the coat and hat and hanging them properly. (Guthrie, 1935, p. 21)

Why was this technique effective? According to Guthrie (1935), the desired response is for the child to hang up her clothes upon entering the house, that is, to associate hanging up her clothes with entering the house. Having the child hang up the clothes after being in the house will not establish the correct association; learning, in Guthrie's view, will occur only when stimulus (entering the house) and response (hanging up the coat and hat) occur together.

The Impact of Reward

Guthrie (1935) proposed that reward has an important effect on the response to a specific environmental circumstance; however, he did not believe that reward strengthens the S-R association. According to Guthrie, many responses can become conditioned to a stimulus, and the response exhibited just prior to reward will be associated with the stimulus and occur when the stimulus is experienced again. For example, a child may draw, put together a puzzle, and study at the same desk. If her parents reward the child by allowing her to play outside after she studies but not after she draws or works on the puzzle, the next time the child sits down at the desk, she will study rather than draw or play with a puzzle. In Guthrie's view, a person must respond in a particular way (to study) in the presence of a specific stimulus (the desk) in order to obtain reward (playing outside).

Once the person exhibits the appropriate response, a reward acts to change the stimulus context (internal and/or external) that was present prior to reward. For example, suppose the child is rewarded by going outside to ride her bike. Any new actions will be conditioned to this new stimulus circumstance—being outside—and therefore, they will allow the appropriate response—studying—to be produced by the original stimulus context—the desk—when it is experienced again. Thus, the reward functions to prevent further conditioning and not to strengthen an S-R association. In the example of the studying child, the reward of going outside prevents her from doing anything else at the desk; the reward does not per se strengthen the child's association between studying and the desk.

Guthrie (1935) believed that a reward must be presented immediately after the appropriate response if that response is to occur on the next stimulus exposure. If the reward is delayed, the actions occurring between the appropriate response and the reward will be exhibited when the stimulus is encountered again. For example, if the child did not go outside immediately after studying but instead watched television at the desk and then went outside, the child would watch television at the desk rather than study.

The Impact of Punishment

What if a child is punished for hitting a younger sibling? Will the punishment cause the child to stop hitting his younger sibling? Guthrie suggested that **punishment** may not always eliminate the undesired, punished behavior. Punishment will work only if the response elicited by punishment, and conditioned to the punishment situation, is incompatible with the inappropriate response. Punishment often acts to elicit aggression. Because the punished response—hitting a younger sibling—is not incompatible with the response elicited by punishment—aggression—punishing the child may not suppress the inappropriate behavior.

How did Guthrie explain the influence of punishment on behavior? Guthrie (1935) suggested that punishment is an unconditioned stimulus capable of eliciting a number of responses, such as crying, pouting, or fleeing. If the response terminates the punishment, the response will become conditioned to the stimulus context in which the punishment occurred. When the person encounters this stimulus circumstance again, the conditioned response will be elicited. If this conditioned response is effective, punishment will not occur. However, if the response that terminates punishment does not prevent punishment, punishment cannot be avoided, only escaped.

The Importance of Practice

According to Guthrie (1935), learning occurs in a single trial; that is, the strength of an S-R association reaches its maximum value following a single pairing of the stimulus and a response. You might wonder why Guthrie believed that learning occurred on a single trial when it is obvious that the efficiency and strength of behavior improves with experience. Guthrie did not deny that behavior improves with experience; however, he rejected the Hullian view that the strength of the S-R bond slowly increases with experience.

According to Guthrie (1935), performance gradually improves for three reasons. First, although many potential stimuli are present during initial conditioning, the subject will attend to only some of these stimuli. The stimuli present when an animal or person responds vary from trial to trial. For a stimulus attended to during the particular trial to produce a response, this stimulus must have also been attended to during a previous response. For example, suppose that in an instrumental conditioning situation, a rat is rewarded in the black compartment of a T-maze but is not attending to the color of the goal box. On a future trial, the rat does not go to the black side, even though it was rewarded in that environment on the previous trial. Although the rat's behavior may change from trial to trial, this change reflects an attentional process rather than a learning process.

A second reason for improvement in performance is that many different stimuli can become conditioned to produce a particular response. As more stimuli begin to elicit a response, the strength of the response will increase. However, a stronger S-R association does not cause this increased intensity, but rather the increased number of stimuli able to produce the response. Third, a complex behavior consists of many separate responses. For the behavior to be efficient, each response element must be conditioned to the stimulus. As each element is conditioned to the stimulus, the efficiency of the behavior will improve. Guthrie (1935) suggested that the more varied the stimuli and/or the responses that must be associated to produce effective performance, the more practice is needed to make behavior efficient.

Let's see how Guthrie's view would explain Justin going to the Cinema Theatre every Friday night. According Guthrie's view, Justin developed a stimulus (Friday night)-response (going to the

Cinema Theatre) merely as a result of going to the Cinema Theatre as part of the requirements of his Introduction to Motion Pictures class. And he will continue to go as long as no other response occurs on Friday night.

Breaking a Habit

What if Justin's girlfriend wanted to go dancing rather than watch an old movie on a Friday night? You would think that it would be easy to break his old habit by just going dancing. As Guthrie (1952) unfortunately recognized, doing something else does not always work:

> I once had a caller to whom I was explaining that an apple I had just finished was a splendid for avoiding a smoke. The caller pointed out that I was smoking at that moment. The habit of lighting a cigarette was so attached to the finish of eating that smoking had been started automatically. (p. 116)

Guthrie did not believe that an old undesired habit would be forgotten, but that it could only be replaced by a new habit. He proposed three methods to break a habit, or replacing an old undesired habit with a new habit. The three methods are (1) fatigue method, (2) threshold method, and (3) incompatible stimuli method. With the fatigue method, the stimulus eliciting the response is presented so often that the person is too fatigued to perform the old habit. At this point, a new response occurs and a new S-R association is learned, or no response occurs. For example, to break the old habit of a student staring out of the window, the student could be required to spend a lot of time staring out of the window. Justin's girlfriend could use the fatigue method to break Justin of going to the movies every Friday night by having him repeatedly view movies until he grows tired of them, which would allow him to go dancing. With the threshold method, a below-threshold level of the stimulus is initially presented so that the old habit is not elicited. The intensity of the stimulus is slowly increased until it reaches the full intensity, but the old habit is not elicited. For example, a person who cannot read in a noisy environment could slowly increase the background noise level until reading can occur with the television blaring. In the incompatible method, the person is placed in a situation where the old habit cannot occur. For example, a habitual smoker could break this old habit by chewing gum (one cannot chew gum and smoke at the same time).

An Evaluation of Contiguity Theory

The S-R contiguity view that Guthrie proposed during the 1930s and 1940s was not accepted by many psychologists. During his career as a professor at the University of Washington, Guthrie conducted few studies to validate his approach. The lack of empirical evaluation meant that Guthrie's theory remained unrevised from its original proposal in 1935 until his final writings in 1959. More recent experiments to test Guthrie's theory have found some ideas accurate and others inaccurate.

Some parts of Guthrie's theory accurately describe aspects of the learning process. First, punishment can intensify an inappropriate behavior when punishment elicits a behavior that is compatible with the punished response; however, an intense punishment suppresses the punished response even if the responses the punishment elicits are compatible with the punished response. Second, contiguity between a response and reward is critical to prevent the acquisition of competing associations. (The child must go outside immediately after studying; if she watches television first, she will associate her desk with watching television rather than with studying.) Third, only a portion of the environmental stimuli are active at a particular moment; therefore, only some of the potential conditioned stimuli become associated with the response. Later chapters examine the evidence that supports these aspects of Guthrie's view. Fourth, Guthrie's methods of breaking habits have been widely adopted, usually without recognizing the source.

Some aspects of Guthrie's theory, however, do not accurately describe the learning process. First, Guthrie rejected the law of effect, suggesting instead that reward changes the stimulus situation. However, numerous experiments have disproved his concept of a reward (Bower & Hilgard, 1981). An experimenter can arrange for many changes to occur after a response, but if these actions do not serve as rewards, then the response will not be conditioned, even though substantial stimulus change followed the response.

Second, Guthrie believed that recency and frequency determined which response a particular stimulus would produce. However, C. E. Noble's (1966) extensive research indicated that reward predicted response significantly better than did either frequency or recency.

Third, Guthrie assumed that learning occurs on a single trial; that is, a single, simultaneous pairing of a stimulus and response results in the development of the maximum S-R associative strength. Many studies have evaluated Guthrie's view that learning occurs after a single S-R pairing. To test this view, the conditioning situation must be simple, and the trial-to-trial behavior of each subject must be assessed. In an eyeblink conditioning study using humans, Voeks (1954) conducted a well-controlled evaluation of Guthrie's view. Voeks observed that most subjects showed all-or-none learning; that is, they showed no CR on one trial and an intense CR on the next trial (see Figure 2.3). However, other studies have not reported single-trial learning for individual subjects. Instead, they have found a gradual increase in the strength of a response (Bower & Hilgard, 1981).

Spence (1956), accepting that rapid response changes do occur in some circumstances, suggested that an incremental learning approach could explain these results. (An incremental view holds that the strength of learned behavior increases slowly over trials.) According to Spence, although S-R habit strength increases slowly over trials, the response will not be elicited until its strength exceeds the threshold of response evocation. Spence suggested that if the threshold is near maximum strength, the learning process will appear to be of the all-or-none type. Spence's

Figure 2.3   The performance of six subjects on a conditioned eyeblink study. The rapid change in performance of each subject from one trial to the next supports one-trial learning. Note the mean performance of all subjects slowly increases across trials, which could erroneously suggest an incremental increase in learning over trials.

analysis allowed an incremental theory to explain the apparent single-trial learning, but more-recent theories suggest that some aspects of learning can develop on a single trial, while others develop slowly. For example, we learn in Chapter 10 that it is likely that the emotional components of discrimination are learned slowly, while the attentional aspects of discrimination learning develop on a single trial.

BEFORE YOU GO ON

- What competing associations could cause Justin to stop going to the movies on Friday night?

- How would punishment affect Justin's habit of going to the movies?

SECTION REVIEW

- Guthrie suggested that when a stimulus and response occur together, they automatically become associated, and when the stimulus is encountered again, it will produce the response.

- According to Guthrie, reward alters the stimulus environment, thereby precluding the acquisition of any new competing S-R associations.

- In Guthrie's view, punishment suppresses an inappropriate behavior only if the response the punishment produces is incompatible with the behavior.

- Punishment can actually increase a behavior if the response the punishment elicits is compatible with the undesired behavior.

- Practice increases the number of stimuli associated with a response and thereby increases the intensity of that response.

- Guthrie proposed three methods (fatigue, threshold, and incompatible stimuli) of breaking a habit or for replacing an old undesired habit with a new habit.

The S-R theories propose that a mechanistic process governs our behavior. In contrast, the cognitive approach suggests that actions are guided by purpose rather than by internal and external forces. Furthermore, the cognitive approach argues that behavior is a flexible reaction rather than a habitual response. We briefly examine the cognitive view of learning next; Chapter 11 discusses this view in greater detail.

TOLMAN'S PURPOSIVE BEHAVIORISM

Edward Tolman (1932, 1959) proposed a cognitive view of learning during the 1930s and 1940s that most psychologists did not accept. Instead, Hull's mechanistic drive theory was the accepted view of learning during that period. During the 1950s, the cognitive view gained ground, and other psychologists expanded Tolman's original approach. Over the last three decades, **cognitive theories** have made many important contributions to our understanding of learning. We briefly discuss Tolman's theory in this chapter. In Chapter 11, we examine Tolman's work more closely as well as describe several contemporary cognitive approaches to learning.

**Edward Chace Tolman
(1886–1959)**

Tolman received his doctorate from Harvard University where he studied under Robert Mearns Yerkes. His study with Kurt Koffa, one of the founders of Gestalt psychology, greatly influenced his purposive behaviorism. He taught for 36 years at the University of California, Berkeley, and was suspended in 1950 when he refused to sign a loyalty oath because he felt it infringed upon his academic freedom. When the courts upheld his position, he was reinstated to the faculty. His work contributed greatly to the emergence of cognitive psychology, and the psychology building, Tolman Hall, at the University of California, Berkeley was named in his honor when it opened in 1963. He served as president of the American Psychological Association in 1937.

Flexibility of Behavior

Tolman's (1932, 1959) view conflicted in several ways with Hull's drive theory. Tolman did not believe that behavior was an automatic response to an environmental event. Instead, he proposed that our behavior has both direction and purpose. Tolman argued that behavior is goal oriented; that is, we are motivated either to achieve a desired condition or to avoid an aversive situation. According to Tolman, certain paths lead to our goals and certain tools can help us attain these goals. In Tolman's view, we can understand the structure of our environment through experience. This knowledge allows us to reach desired goals.

According to Tolman (1932, 1959), our behavior is not only goal oriented, but we also expect specific outcomes to follow specific behavior. For example, you may expect to receive an A for working hard in this class. If you do not receive an A, you will continue to work hard for the reward and will not be satisfied with a less-valued goal. Thus, if you received a B on your first test, you would not be satisfied with the B and would work even harder for an A on the next test.

Tolman (1932, 1959) also believed that certain events in the environment convey information about where our goals are located. We can reach our goals only after we have learned to read the signs leading to reward or punishment in our environment. For example, you must learn the signs leading to the cafeteria to obtain food. Although Tolman believed that behavior is purposeful, he did not mean that we are always aware of either the purpose or the direction of our behavior. Tolman proposed only that we act *as if* we expect a particular behavior to lead to a specific goal.

Motivation Processes

According to Tolman (1932, 1959), there are two types of motivations. Deprivation is one source of motivation. In Tolman's view, deprivation produces an internal drive state that increases demand for the goal object. Tolman (1959) also suggested that environmental events can acquire motivational properties through association with either a primary drive or a reward. The following example illustrates Tolman's view. A thirsty child sees a soda. According to Tolman, the ability of thirst to motivate behavior transfers to the soda. Tolman called this transference process **cathexis**, a term he borrowed from psychoanalytic theory. As a result of cathexis, the soda is now a preferred goal object, and in the future, this child—even when not thirsty—will be motivated to obtain a soda. The preference for the soda is a positive cathexis. In contrast, avoiding a certain place could reflect a negative cathexis. In Tolman's opinion, if we associate a certain place with an unpleasant experience, we will think of the place itself as an aversive object.

You might remember that Hull (1943) suggested that drives could be conditioned. Tolman's (1932, 1959) cathexis concept is very similar to Hull's view of acquired drive. And Tolman's **equivalence belief principle** is comparable to Spence's (1956) anticipatory goal concept. Animals or people react to a secondary reward (or subgoal) as they do to the original goal object; for instance, our motivation to obtain money reflects our identification of money with desired goal objects such as shelter and food.

Is Reward Necessary for Learning?

We learned in Chapter 1 that Thorndike (1898) argued that S-R associations form when the response leads to a satisfying state of affairs. Hull (1943) adopted Thorndike's law of effect concept and suggested that habit strength increases when a particular response decreases the drive state. In contrast to these views, Tolman (1932) proposed that reward is not necessary for learning to occur and that the simultaneous experience of two events is sufficient for learning. Thus, according to Tolman, an understanding of when events will occur can develop without reward. What is the influence of reward, in Tolman's view? He proposed that reward affects performance but not learning. The presence of a reward will motivate an animal or person to exhibit a previously learned behavior. For example, a child may have learned how to mow the yard, but he needs to be rewarded to actually do the job.

Recall that Justin went to the Cinema Theatre every Friday night to watch classic movies. In Tolman's view, Justin expects classic movies to be enjoyable and has learned to follow the signs to the Cinema Theatre every Friday night. As long as Justin continues to find classic movies enjoyable (rewarding), he will continue to go to the Cinema Theatre every Friday night.

An Evaluation of Purposive Behaviorism

Tolman (1932) proposed that the expectation of future reward or punishment motivates behavior. Further, knowledge of the paths and/or the tools that enable us to obtain reward or avoid punishment guides our behavior. Although the research Tolman and his students designed did not provide conclusive evidence for his cognitive approach, his work caused Hull to make major changes in his theory to accommodate Tolman's observations. For example, the idea that a conditioned anticipation of reward (r_G) motivates us to approach reward is clearly similar to Tolman's view that the expectation of reward motivates behavior intended to produce reward. Furthermore, the view that frustration can motivate both the avoidance of a less preferred reward and the continued search for the desired reward parallels the cognitive explanation that not just any reward will be acceptable. However, once Tolman's observations were incorporated into drive theory, most psychologists ignored Tolman's cognitive view and continued to accept the drive view of learning. When problems developed with the drive approach during the 1960s and 1970s, the cognitive view gained wider approval. Psychologists began to use a cognitive approach to explain how behavior is learned. We explore further evidence of the important role cognitive processes play in determining our behavior in Chapter 11.

SKINNER'S BEHAVIORISTIC METHODOLOGY

The work of B. F. Skinner, a noted American behaviorist, spans more than half a century and has contributed greatly to our understanding of the learning process. Skinner's concept of behaviorism differs from theories advocated by the other behaviorists discussed in this chapter. In his 1938 text *The Behavior of Organisms,* Skinner argued that the goal of behaviorism should be to identify and isolate the environmental factors that govern behavior. Skinner stated that we understand a particular behavior only when we learn how to predict and control the behavior. Also, Skinner suggested that the ability to predict and control a behavior depends on understanding the circumstances governing the occurrence of the behavior.

The Importance of the Environment

Skinner designed many studies to examine the factors that govern behavior. He first studied the conditions responsible for a rat's behavior—pressing a lever for food—in an operant chamber (see Figure 2.4). Much of his research focused on reinforcement's influence on behavior. Skinner defined a **reinforcer** as an event whose occurrence increases the frequency of behavior that preceded the event. According to Skinner, the environment identifies the behavior necessary to produce reinforcement, called the **operant response**. Skinner referred to the specified relationship between the operant response and the reinforcement as a **contingency**. Skinner found that contingencies had an important impact on the rat's behavior. The rats were sensitive to contingencies and performed the behavior the contingency specified as needed to produce reinforcement.

Skinner then expanded his analysis of behavior to include other animals, both human and nonhuman animals, and situations and behaviors that differ greatly from operant chambers and bar pressing. For example, in his 1957 text *Verbal Behavior,* Skinner argued that people do not have an instinctive capacity for expressing ideas. Instead, he believed, verbal behavior, like any

Figure 2.4   Photograph of B. F. Skinner and one of his laboratory animals in an operant chamber.

Burrhus Frederick Skinner (1904–1990)

Skinner received his doctorate from Harvard University under physiologist William Crozier. He then taught at the University of Minnesota and Indiana University for 9 years before returning to a faculty position at Harvard University. During his 42-year tenure at Harvard, some of the leading American psychologists—including Nathan H. Azrin, A. Charles Catania, Richard J. Herrnstein, and Herbert S. Terrace—studied with him. His research led to the emergence of applied behavior analysis, which is the application of reinforcement principles to modify behavior in a variety of applied settings. In *Walden II,* he describes a utopialike commune run on operant conditioning principles that is still both controversial and thought provoking. The American Psychological Association honored him with the Distinguished Scientific Contribution Award in 1950 and the Lifetime Achievement Award in 1990.

other operant behavior, is controlled by differential reinforcement and punishment administered by significant others, such as parents and friends. Skinner's methodology led to the development of **behavior modification**, an approach effective in treating behavior pathology. Chapter 6 presents evidence of Skinner's contribution to our understanding of how to establish desired behaviors and eliminate undesired behaviors.

The Role of Theory?

How does Skinner's view differ from those of the other behaviorists described in this chapter? Skinner (1938) argued that the use of "hypothetical constructs," such as drives and expectancies, does not contribute to our understanding of behavior. In Skinner's view, the search for evidence to validate a particular hypothetical construct interferes with the functional analysis of the variables controlling the behavior and thereby limits our understanding of the circumstances that govern behavior.

Consider the following example to illustrate Skinner's approach. Many psychologists have speculated that stimulus-response associations strengthen as the result of reinforcement, and years of research have been devoted to validating this view. According to Skinner, understanding the "theoretical construct" that underlies the effect that reinforcement has on stimulus-response associations is useful in only one respect: It points out that reinforcement is one environmental variable that can control how frequently a specific behavior occurs in a particular context.

How might Skinner's view explain Justin going to the Cinema Theatre every Friday night? His view would not explain Justin's behavior by relying on concepts such as an S-R association or an expectation. Instead, Skinner's view would merely suggest that eating popcorn or watching a great classic movie serves as an effective reinforcement for Justin to go the Cinema Theatre on Friday night.

Many psychologists do not agree with Skinner's view. These psychologists argue that theory guides research, which in turn identifies the variables that control behavior as well as explains similar results from various experiments. The work of psychologists who use theory to guide their research has contributed greatly to our understanding of learning and has increased our ability to predict and control behavior. For example, Hull's drive theory, discussed earlier, greatly influenced the development of systematic desensitization, a behavior therapy that can effectively modify phobic behavior. (We describe systematic desensitization in Chapter 4.) The contribution of Hull and other theorists is also evident throughout the text.

BEFORE YOU GO ON

- What expectancies led Justin to go to the movies every Friday night?

- How would Skinner explain Justin's going to the movies?

SECTION REVIEW

- Tolman proposed that behavior is goal oriented; an animal is motivated to reach specific goals and will continue to search until the goal is reached.

- According to Tolman, expectations determine the specific behavior we perform to obtain reward or avoid punishment.

- According to Skinner, an animal's level of operant responding increases when a contingency between the operant behavior and reinforcement is established.

- Skinner argued that attempts to explain the theoretical basis of behavior interfere with the discovery of the causes of behavior.

- Skinner believed that psychologists should seek to identify the environmental factors governing behavior.

- Once these environmental factors have been discovered, the accurate prediction and the control of behavior are possible.

- The theoretical emphasis that Skinner criticized has also contributed to our understanding of the common elements of various situations and behaviors, and that has produced effective procedures for controlling behaviors.

CRITICAL THINKING QUESTIONS

1. Alan drinks a couple of beers while watching sports on television. Cynthia has a glass of wine with dinner. Using what you have learned from Hull's theory of learning, explain Alan and Cynthia's behavior.

2. Tim believes that studying leads to good grades. Gerald assumes that good grades depend on whether or not an instructor grades on the curve. Explain the differences in Tim's and Gerald's beliefs using Tolman's theory. How would Tolman's theory predict Tim's and Gerald's preparation for an examination?

3. Some psychologists argue that environmental contingencies govern behavior. Others believe that cognitive processes determine how we act. Select a behavior and show how stimulus-response and cognitive processes could control that behavior. Use the ideas presented in the text to substantiate your statements.

KEY TERMS

acquired drive
anticipatory goal response (r_G)
cathexis
conditioned inhibition
contingency
equivalence belief principle
habit hierarchy
homeostasis
inhibition
punishment
reinforcer
S-R (stimulus-response) associative theories

anticipatory frustration response (r_F)
behavior modification
cognitive theories
contiguity
drive
excitatory potential
habit strength
incentive motivation
operant response
reactive inhibition
reward

The Modification of Instinctive Behavior

DO YOU HAVE A LIGHT?

For two days, Greg has resisted his urge to smoke. Having attempted to quit on more occasions than he can count, he's determined not to let his extreme nervousness and irritability keep him from succeeding this time. His family tries to distract his thoughts from cigarettes, but these attempts work only temporarily. Anticipating tonight's televised championship boxing match helped him for a while, but even this cannot prevent his recurrent, intense impulses to smoke. Greg began smoking cigarettes when he was 15. All his friends smoked, so it seemed like the natural thing to do. At first, he did not like to smoke; it made him cough and sometimes feel slightly nauseated. Greg smoked only with his friends to feel part of the group, and he pretended to inhale. However, as the unpleasant effects began to disappear, he learned to inhale and began to smoke more. By the age of 18, Greg smoked two to three packs of cigarettes each day. He never thought about stopping until he met Paula. A nonsmoker, she tried to convince him to quit. Finding himself unable to completely break his habit, he simply did not smoke while with Paula. After they married, Paula continued to plead with Greg to stop smoking. He has tried every now and then over the past 10 years to resist cigarettes, usually avoiding his habit for a day or two. This time has to be different. At age 35, Greg felt himself in perfect health, but a routine checkup with the family physician two days ago proved him wrong. Greg learned that his extremely high blood pressure makes him a prime candidate for a heart attack. The doctor told Greg that he must lower his blood pressure through special diet, medication, and not smoking. Continued smoking would undoubtedly interfere with the other treatments. The threat of a heart attack frightened Greg; he saw his father suffer the consequences of an attack several years ago. Determined now to quit, he only hopes he can endure his withdrawal symptoms.

Millions of people share Greg's intense desire to smoke, as well as his record of repeated attempts to stop. Their addiction, stemming from dependence on the effects of cigarettes, motivates their behavior. Evidence of this dependence includes the aversive withdrawal symptoms that many people experience when they attempt to stop smoking. When the symptoms are strong enough, the withdrawal state motivates them to resume smoking.

Cigarette smoking is just one example of addictive behavior. People become addicted to many drugs that exert quite different effects. For example, the painkilling effects of heroin contrast sharply with the arousing effects of cocaine. Although the effects of drugs may differ, the cycle of drug effects, withdrawal symptoms, and the resumption of addictive behavior characterizes all addictive behaviors.

Addictive behavior is thought to reflect the combined influence of instinctive and experiential processes. In this chapter, we focus on the influence of instinct on addictive behavior, as well as on other behaviors. The role that experience plays in addictive behavior, as well as in other behaviors, is also addressed in this chapter and throughout the rest of the text.

This chapter discusses how experience alters instinctive behaviors. But first, the Lorenz-Tinbergen theory of instinctive behavior provides the background necessary to appreciate the way in which experience modifies instinctive behavior.

Konrad Zacharias Lorenz (1903–1989)

Lorenz (right) received a doctorate in medicine and a doctorate in zoological studies from the University of Vienna in Austria. He taught at the University of Vienna Institute of Anatomy for 5 years and the Department of Psychology at the University of Königsberg for 1 year before World War II. He also conducted research at the Max Planck Institute for Behavioral Physiology for 25 years after the war. His text, *Behind the Mirror, a Search for a Natural History of Human Knowledge,* was written while he was a prisoner of war in the Soviet Union. He was awarded the Nobel Prize in Medicine or Physiology in 1973 for his research on the instinctive basis of social behavior.

Nikolass "Niko" Tinbergen (1907–1988)

Tinbergen (left) received a doctorate in biology from the University of Leiden in the Netherlands. He taught at the University of Leiden where he began his classic research on the nature of instinctive behavior of stickleback fish. During World War II, he was imprisoned for 2 years in a Nazi camp for supporting Jewish faculty colleagues. After the war, he taught at the University of Leiden for 2 years before moving to the University of Oxford in England for 39 years. Richard Dawkins and Desmond Morris, two prominent biologists, were students of his at Oxford University. He was awarded the Nobel Prize in Medicine or Physiology in 1973 for his research on the instinctive basis of social behavior.

THE INSTINCTIVE BASIS OF BEHAVIOR

Greg smokes a cigarette when he wakes up in the morning. After about 30 minutes, he goes outside to smoke another cigarette because Paula does not allow him to smoke in the house. He does the same at work; after about 30 minutes or so, he goes outside to smoke. If he sees a coworker smoking, Greg often goes outside to smoke, even if less than 30 minutes has passed since his last cigarette. What causes Greg to smoke a cigarette about every 30 minutes? Why will seeing a coworker smoke a cigarette cause Greg to smoke even if less than 30 minutes has passed since his last cigarette? The instinctive theory of behavior proposed by Konrad Lorenz and Niko Tinbergen provides a reasonable explanation of Greg's behavior.

The Interaction of Energy and Environment

Lorenz and Tinbergen developed their instinctive theory from years observing animal behavior. To illustrate their theory, we present one of Lorenz and Tinbergen's classic observations, followed by their analysis of the systems controlling this observed behavior.

In 1938, Lorenz and Tinbergen reported their observations of the egg-rolling behavior of the greylag goose. This species builds a shallow nest on the ground to incubate its eggs. When an egg rolls to the side of the nest, the goose reacts by stretching toward the egg and bending its neck, bringing its bill toward its breast. This action causes the bill to nudge the egg to the center of the nest. If, during transit, the egg begins to veer to one side, the goose adjusts the position of its bill to reverse the direction of the egg. What causes the goose to react to the rolling egg? Lorenz's energy model addresses this question.

Energy Model

According to Lorenz (1950), **action-specific energy** constantly accumulates (see Figure 3.1). This accumulation of energy resembles

Figure 3.1 Diagram of Lorenz's energy system. The energy flows constantly from the tap T into the reservoir R. The cone valve V represents the releasing mechanism, which is open when the sign stimulus exerts pressure on the scale pan SP. The weight on the pan corresponds to the intensity of stimulation. The spring S represents inhibition from higher centers. Energy released from the reservoir R flows in the reservoirs of internal pressure that occur from the accumulation of action-specific energy and the external stimulation of the sign stimulus; both act to release the stored energy.

filling a reservoir with water; the more liquid in the reservoir, the greater the internal pressure for its release. In behavioral terms, the greater the pressure, the more motivated the animal is to behave in a specific way. The internal pressure (action-specific energy) motivates **appetitive behavior**, which enables the animal to approach and contact a specific and distinctive event called a **sign stimulus**. The presence of the sign stimulus releases the accumulated energy. In our goose example, the stretching movement and adjustment reaction are appetitive behaviors directed toward the rolling egg, which is the sign stimulus.

The goose does not exhibit the retrieving behavior until it has reached the egg. The retrieving behavior is an example of a **fixed action pattern**, an instinctive behavior that the presence of a specific environmental cue, the sign stimulus, triggers. An internal block exists for each fixed action pattern, preventing the behavior from occurring until the appropriate time. The animal's appetitive behavior, motivated by the buildup of action-specific energy, allows the animal to come into contact with the appropriate releasing stimulus. According to Lorenz and Tinbergen (1938), the sign stimulus acts to remove the block by stimulating an internal **innate releasing mechanism (IRM)**. The IRM removes the block, thereby releasing the fixed action pattern. The sight of the egg stimulates the appropriate IRM, which triggers the retrieving response in the goose. After the goose has retrieved one egg and its energy reserve dissipates, the bird will allow another egg to remain at the side of the nest until sufficient action-specific energy has accumulated to motivate the bird to return the second egg to the middle of the nest.

In some situations, a chain of fixed action patterns occurs. In these cases, a block exists for each specific fixed action pattern in the sequence, and the appropriate releasing mechanism must be activated for each behavior. For example, a male Siamese fighting fish exhibits a ritualistic aggressive display when he sees another male or even when he sees a reflection of himself in a mirror. However, no actual aggressive behavior occurs until one male intrudes on the other's territory. The second fixed action pattern is blocked until the two males come into close proximity. If neither fish retreats after the ritualistic display, the fish approach each other (an appetitive act), and fighting behavior is released.

Environmental Release

In some cases, the sign stimulus for a particular fixed action pattern is a simple environmental stimulus. For example, Tinbergen (1951) observed that the red belly of the male stickleback is the sign stimulus that releases fighting behavior between two male sticklebacks. An experimental dummy stickleback, which resembles the stickleback only in color, releases aggressive behavior in a real male stickleback, supporting this conclusion.

The releasing sign stimulus can be quite complex for other fixed action patterns; for example, consider the sexual pursuit of the male grayling butterfly (Tinbergen, 1951). Tinbergen found that a male grayling would pursue a female flying past. Although the color and shape of a model grayling did not influence the male's flight behavior, the darkness of the female, the distance from the male, and the pattern of movement that simulated the male's forward and backward flight all influenced pursuit. Tinbergen noticed that an increased value in another component could compensate for the absence of one female characteristic. For instance, one model passing by at a certain distance from the male did not elicit a flight reaction. However, a darker model at the same distance did elicit pursuit.

The likelihood of eliciting a fixed action pattern depends upon both the accumulated level of action-specific energy and the intensity of the sign stimulus. Research (Lorenz, 1950; Tinbergen, 1951) indicates that the greater the level of accumulated energy, the weaker the sign stimulus that can release a particular fixed action pattern. For example, Baerends, Brouwer, and Waterbolk (1955) examined the relationship between a male guppy's readiness to respond and the size of the female. They found that a large female model released courtship behavior even in a male that was typically unresponsive.

Lorenz (1950) envisioned an IRM as a gate blocking the release of stored energy. The gate opens either by pulling from external stimulation or by pushing from within. As the internal pressure increases, the amount of external pull needed to open the gate and release the behavior decreases. And because the amount of accumulated energy increases during the time since the last fixed action pattern, the reliance on a sign stimulus to activate the IRM and release the fixed action pattern decreases.

Another view, proposed by Tinbergen (1951), suggested that sensitivity to the sign stimulus changes as a function of time passed since the occurrence of the specific behavior. According to Tinbergen, the sensitivity of the innate releasing mechanism to the sign stimulus increases when no recent fixed action pattern occurs.

How would the Lorenz-Tinbergen model explain Greg's addiction to cigarettes? According to the Lorenz-Tinbergen model, after Greg smokes a cigarette, action-specific energy builds up until Greg encounters an effective sign stimulus (cigarette). The appetitive behavior of going outside puts Greg into contact with a cigarette, which releases the stored action-specific energy and elicits the instinctive smoking behavior. In Greg's case, after about 30 minutes, enough action-specific energy accumulates for the cigarette to motivate the appetitive behavior of going outside to smoke.

Hierarchical System

Lorenz proposed that action-specific energy exists for each fixed action pattern. It is now clear, however, that the internal motivation for functionally equivalent behaviors depends on a common source. Tinbergen (1951) suggested that a central instinctive system (e.g., the reproductive instinct of stickleback fish) controls the occurrence of a number of potential behaviors (see Figure 3.2).

Energy accumulates in a specific brain center for each major instinct, and numerous systems can contribute energy for each instinct. Internal impulses can develop from the release of energy from a higher center following the occurrence of a fixed action pattern, from energy buildup at the level on which the animal is presently operating, or from both. Hormones or other internal stimuli as well as external forces can also generate energy. All of these factors influence the level of accumulated energy and the likelihood of additional behavior.

Once an effective sign stimulus releases energy, this energy flows to lower centers. The next fixed action pattern (or patterns) occurring in the chain depends on prevailing environmental

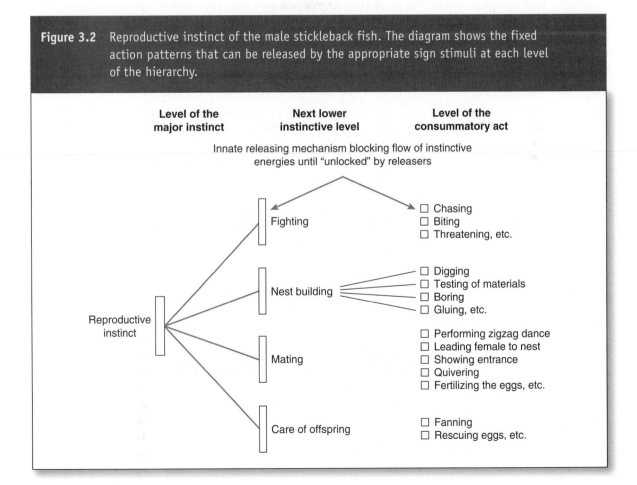

Figure 3.2   Reproductive instinct of the male stickleback fish. The diagram shows the fixed action patterns that can be released by the appropriate sign stimuli at each level of the hierarchy.

conditions. Several fixed action patterns might be released, but the sign stimulus determines the specific fixed action pattern that occurs.

Let's consider the reproductive instinct of the male stickleback fish to illustrate Tinbergen's (1951) hierarchical system (refer again to Figure 3.2). The reproductive instinct will be activated when a mature male is placed in an aquarium, if sufficient space exists. The stimulation of the reproductive instinct causes the male to establish a territory and releases energy to lower brain systems that control specific instinctive behaviors. The presence of specific environmental events determines which of the lower center's IRMs will be activated and, therefore, which specific fixed action pattern (or patterns) will occur. Thus, the male stickleback will defend his territory and use threadlike weeds to build a nest, but the nest-building instinct is not activated if there are no weeds in the territory. Similarly, the mating and care-of-offspring instincts also depend on the presence of appropriate releasing stimuli. If a female swollen with eggs approaches the male's territory, the male displays a ritualistic courtship pattern, first exhibiting a zigzag dance, then leading the female to his nest. The male's quivering behavior causes the female to lay her eggs in his nest, and the male fertilizes them. The presence of the eggs then activates the care-of-offspring instinct and motivates the male to fan the eggs, enabling them to hatch. Thus, the presence of appropriate sign stimuli determines which of the behaviors that the reproductive instinct controls will actually occur.

Von Holst and Von St. Paul in 1962 found support for Tinbergen's hierarchical theory in their study of the manner in which chickens go to sleep. A chicken exhibits a ritualistic behavior pattern before sleeping, standing on one leg and putting its head under one wing. Von Holst and Von St. Paul discovered that electrical stimulation of one brain site elicited the whole behavioral sequence; however, stimulation of other locations elicited only specific behavioral components, such as the presleeping ritual. These results suggest that different brain systems mediate the central instinctive motive and the specific fixed action patterns that this motive controls.

Conflicting Motives

An often-observed phenomenon occurs when two incompatible sign stimuli are experienced. The response is different from the fixed action patterns typically released by either sign stimuli acting alone. According to Tinbergen (1951), when a human or nonhuman animal experiences conflict due to the presence of two antagonistic sign stimuli, energy overflows into another motivational instinct system and releases a behavior from this other system. The process of activating a third instinct system, different from the two involved in the conflict, is called **displacement**.

Naturalistic settings are ideal for observing displacement behaviors. Tinbergen and Van Iersel (1947) reported that the stickleback, when between its own territory and the territory of another stickleback, often displays nest-building behavior. This out-of-context nest building is presumably due to the fish's conflict between attacking the neighbor's territory and escaping into its own. A person who whistles nervously before a date may be exhibiting displaced activity resulting from the conflict between anticipation of the date and fear of acting inappropriately.

The Importance of Experience

You might have the impression that an instinctive response is inflexible or that the releasing sign stimulus cannot be altered. Although this view is often accurate, in some circumstances, experience can modify instinctive systems. Lorenz (1950) suggested that the instinctive processes of many animals are programmed to change as the result of experience.

According to Lorenz (1950), a conditioning experience can alter instinctive behavior, the releasing mechanism for instinctive behavior, or both. Only the consummatory response at the end of the behavior chain, according to Lorenz, is resistant to modification. Conditioning can alter the effectiveness of existing appetitive behavior or change the sensitivity of the releasing mechanism to the sign stimulus. Depending on the nature of the conditioning experience, this change can be either increased or decreased sensitivity. In addition, conditioning can establish new behaviors or new releasing stimuli. All of these modifications increase the organism's ability to adapt to the environment.

Lorenz's (1950) observations of the jackdaw's nest building illustrate his view of the importance of learning in adaptation. He discovered that the jackdaw does not instinctively know the best type of twigs to use as nesting material. This bird displays an instinctive nest-building response—stuffing twigs into a foundation—but must try different twigs until it finds one that lodges firmly and does not break. Once it has discovered a suitable type of twig, the bird selects only that type. According to Lorenz, the twig gained the ability to release instinctive behavior as the result of the bird's success.

Returning again to Greg's addiction to cigarettes, according to the Lorenz-Tinbergen model, a number of stimuli (e.g., end of a meal, party) released cigarette smoking behavior and a number of behaviors (e.g., buying a pack of cigarettes, asking a friend for a cigarette) became appetitive behaviors as a result of Greg's experiences.

Evaluation of Lorenz-Tinbergen Model

It is important to distinguish the general aspects of the Lorenz-Tinbergen instinctive approach from the specific aspects of their hypothetical energy system. Our understanding of the factors that govern a wide range of behaviors has benefited from the instinctive approach. Further, the hypothetical energy system is an excellent way to conceptualize the processes motivating instinctive behavior. Environmental stimuli do release instinctive behaviors, and the likelihood of environmental release depends upon both the time since the last occurrence of the behavior and the intensity of the releaser. Animals do approach environmental releasers, and the animal's motivation level influences the approach's intensity. However, recent physiological research has raised questions concerning certain aspects of Lorenz and Tinbergen's theory. Although scientists (Friesen, 1989; Willows & Hoyle, 1969) have identified brain systems responsible for the release of both appetitive behavior and fixed action patterns, no physiological system operates according to the structure of the energy model. Energy does not appear to accumulate in any identified brain systems, nor does it appear to flow from one system to another. Brain structures do communicate and interact, but not in accordance with Lorenz and Tinbergen's energy model. Let's examine one study that illustrates this interaction.

Willows and Hoyle (1969) examined the brain structures controlling the innate escape response of the sea slug, elicited by contact with a predatory starfish. Contact with the starfish releases a chemical from the starfish's tentacles that receptors on the sea slug's body detect. The sea slug's chemical sensory receptors then send a message through the sea slug's nervous system that elicits alternating contractions of the muscles on the sea slug's back and underside.

Willows and Hoyle (1969) traced the neural circuit from the sensory receptors to the muscles (see Figure 3.3). The neural message is first sent to Area 1 in the slug's brain. Activity in Area 1 causes the muscles in the sea slug's back to contract and inhibits brain Area 2, which controls the muscles on the slug's underside. Willows and Hoyle found that activity in brain Area 1 lasted for a set time. When activity in brain Area 1 stopped, the inhibition of brain Area 2 was removed, thereby allowing activity in brain Area 3 to stimulate brain Area 2. (Activity in brain Area 3 began when the message reached the brain, but Area 3 could not stimulate brain Area 2 until the inhibition from brain Area 1 ended.) Activity in brain Area 2 causes the sea slug's underside to contract and inhibits brain Area 1. The neural activity in brain Area 2 continues for a set time and then stops, removing the inhibition on brain Area 1. The removal of this inhibition allows brain

Figure 3.3   A schematic representation of the neural network controlling the sea slug's escape behavior.

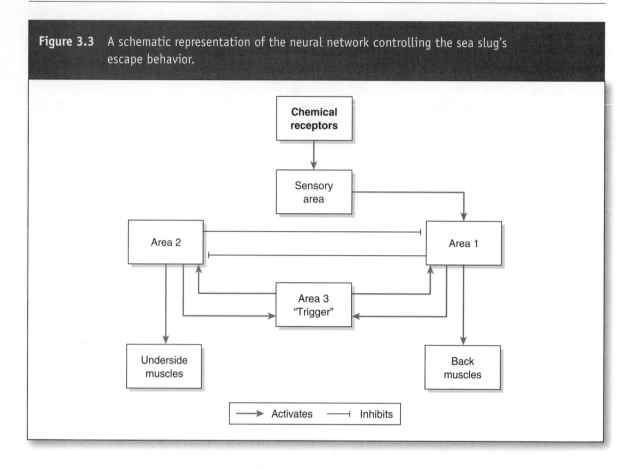

Area 3 to stimulate brain Area 1. Activity in brain Areas 1 and 2 will continue to cycle, resulting in alternating contractions of the sea slug's back and underside muscles. What is the function of the alternating contractions? This innate sequence of muscle responses can propel the slug to safety away from the predatory starfish.

Lorenz (1950) believed that conditioning enhanced a species' adaptation to its environment and that the ability to learn is programmed into each species' genetic structure. However, Lorenz did not detail the mechanism responsible for translating learning into behavior. In addition, neither Lorenz nor Tinbergen investigated the factors determining the effectiveness of conditioning.

BEFORE YOU GO ON

- Are any aspects of Greg's smoking explainable as instinctive?

- How might experience interact with these instinctive aspects of Greg's smoking?

SECTION REVIEW

- Lorenz and Tinbergen proposed that a specific internal tension (or action-specific energy) exists for each major instinct.

- The accumulation of internal action-specific energy motivates appetitive behavior, which continues until a specific environmental cue, called a sign stimulus, is encountered.

- This sign stimulus can activate an innate releasing mechanism (IRM), which releases the stored energy and activates the appropriate fixed action pattern.

- According to Lorenz and Tinbergen, the instinctive system is not inflexible; experience can sometimes alter the releasing stimuli, the instinctive behavior, or both.

- In some cases, the modification involves altering the effectiveness of the existing instinctive actions, while at other times, new releasing stimuli, new behaviors, or both enable the organism to adapt.

We next examine the changes in instinctive behavior that occur with experience. In later chapters, we discuss how new releasing stimuli or new behaviors are acquired as a result of experience.

HABITUATION AND SENSITIZATION

Students who have to give speeches in a class show different reactions to this experience. Some students become less nervous with experience; for others, the anxiety increases rather than declines with experience. Why do some students experience less distress after several speeches, while others find the experience more distressing? The phenomena of habituation and sensitization provide one reason.

With **habituation**, responsiveness to a specific stimulus declines with repeated experiences with that stimulus (R. F. Thompson, 2009). In our example, the lessened anxiety some students feel after several experiences giving a speech may be due to habituation. **Sensitization** refers to an increased reaction to environmental events. The greater nervousness other students feel after several instances of giving a speech may be due to sensitization. It is also possible that classical conditioning leads to the increased or decreased reactions to giving a speech; for example, a change in nervousness may be the result of negative or positive aspects of giving the speech. We look at classical conditioning in Chapter 4. There are many real-world examples of habituation and sensitization; we examine these phenomena next.

Suppose an animal is given a new food. Most animals would only eat a little of this novel food, an avoidance referred to as **ingestional neophobia**. This neophobic response has considerable adaptive significance. Many foods in the natural environment contain poisons. If the animal eats too much of a poisoned food, it will die. To determine whether the food can be safely consumed, the animal eats only a small quantity of the food on the first exposure. After repeated experiences with a food, the neophobic response habituates and the animal consumes greater amounts.

Michael Domjan's 1976 study documents the habituation of ingestional neophobia. Rats received either a 2% saccharin and water solution or just water. Figure 3.4 shows that the rats drank very little saccharin solution when first exposed to this novel flavor. However, intake of saccharin increased with each subsequent experience. Eventually, the animals drank as much as rats given only plain water. These results indicate that the habituation of the neophobic response led to the increasing consumption of saccharin.

Animals also can show an increased neophobic response. Suppose that an animal is sick. Under this illness condition, the animal will exhibit an increased ingestional neophobia (Domjan, 1977). The sensitization process causes the greater neophobic response.

The properties of a reward also have been found to change with experience. It has generally been assumed that this decreased effectiveness of a reward is due to satiation; that is, the animal is no longer motivated to obtain the reward. Or, increased deprivation can cause a reward to be more effective; that is, the animal is more motivated to obtain the reward. Thus, homeostasis (satiation or deprivation) has been assumed to be the mechanism responsible for either the

Figure 3.4   Animals show a reluctance to consume novel foods, but repeated exposure to a food will lead to habituation of neophobia. Animals in group S were given access each day to a 2% saccharin solution for 30 minutes, followed by 30 minutes of tap water. Over a 20-day period, the intake of saccharin in group S increased, while their consumption of tap water declined. The animals in group W received only 30 minutes of tap water each day, and their intake of water remained steady.

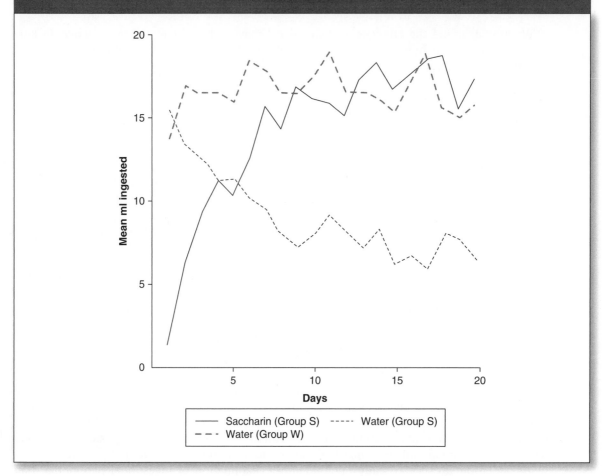

decreased or increased effectiveness of a reward. However, considerable evidence suggests that habituation can lead a reward to lose its effectiveness (McSweeney & Murphy, 2009). Similarly, sensitization can cause an increase in reward effectiveness. According to McSweeney and Murphy, habituation and sensitization explains many observations about changes in reward effectiveness that cannot be explained by homeostasis. For example, Blass and Hall (1976) observed that animals often drink before there is a physiological need and stop drinking before any physiological needs are met. McSweeney and Murphy suggest that sensitization can cause a reward to be effective in the absence of a physiological need and habituation can cause a reward to lose its effectives before the need is met. Additional evidence that habituation and sensitization can modify the effectiveness of a reward is presented in the next section.

Characteristics of Habituation and Sensitization

Habituation or sensitization doe not always occur with repeated experience (see R. F. Thompson, 2009; R. F. Thompson & Spencer, 1966). A number of variables affect the occurrence of habituation or sensitization.

First, stimulus intensity determines the rate of habituation and sensitization. With habituation, the weaker the stimulus, the more rapid habituation occurs to that stimulus. In fact, habituation to very intense stimuli may not occur. The opposite is true with sensitization; that is, a more intense stimulus produces stronger sensitization than does a weaker one.

Second, habituation increases with more frequent stimulus presentations, although the amount of habituation becomes progressively smaller over the course of habituation. Similarly, greater sensitization occurs when a strong stimulus is experienced more frequently.

Third, habituation to a stimulus appears to depend upon the specific characteristics of the stimulus. A change in any characteristic of the stimulus results in an absence of habituation. For example, many birds become alarmed when seeing a hawklike object flying overhead (Tinbergen, 1951). Any novel object flying overhead can elicit this alarm reaction and will habituate when the stimulus is repeatedly experienced. However, the reaction will return if any quality of the object is altered. For example, in one study, Schleidt (1961) reported habituation of the alarm reaction in young turkeys when either a circular or rectangular silhouette flew overhead. However, if the shape of stimulus changed, habituation ceased, and the alarm reaction returned.

What is the significance of these observations? There appears to be no specific sign stimulus eliciting alarm in young turkeys. In the natural environment, the birds habituate their alarm reaction to members of their species. When a hawk approaches (or the shape changes), the turkeys experience a new shape, and their alarm reaction is elicited.

By contrast, a change in the properties of the stimulus typically does not affect sensitization. For example, illness elicits enhanced neophobia even if the characteristics of the sensitizing stimulus (illness) change.

Finally, both habituation and sensitization can be relatively transient phenomena. When a delay intervenes between stimulus presentations, habituation weakens. In some instances, habituation is lost if several seconds or minutes intervene between stimuli. Yet, at other times, delay does not lead to a loss of habituation. This long-term habituation does not appear to reflect a change in an innate response to a stimulus. Instead, it seems to represent a more complex type of learning. We look at the long-term habituation of responding to a stimulus in Chapter 5.

Time also affects sensitization. Sensitization is lost shortly after the sensitizing event ends. For example, M. Davis (1974) noted that sensitization of the startle response to a tone was absent 10 to 15 minutes after a loud noise terminated. Unlike the long-term habituation effect, sensitization is always a temporary effect. This observation suggests that sensitization is due to a nonspecific increased responsiveness produced by the sensitizing stimulus.

We learned in the last section that habituation may lead to a decreased reward effectiveness and sensitization may lead to an increased reward effectiveness. Support for this view comes from research showing that the characteristics of habituation and sensitization described previously also affect the influence of a rewarding stimulus on behavior (Raynor & Epstein, 2001; McSweeney & Murphy, 2009). For example, the intensity of responding does not decline when a variety of rewards are used (Ernst & Epstein, 2002). In the Ernst and Epstein study, human subjects participated in a computer game for food reward (either three pieces of turkey sandwiches or three different sandwiches that were the same caloric value as the three turkey sandwiches). Ernst and Epstein reported that decreases in responding within a session were steeper for those subjects given the same food than the different food. According to McSweeney & Murphy, satiation should still occur when different rewards are used, whereas habituation of reward effectiveness should be reduced when a variety of rewards are used. The fact that variety of rewards results in the continued effectiveness of reward supports the view that habituation plays an important role in the reduced effectiveness of reward over time on motivated behavior. It also has been observed that once an animal stops eating food, giving the animal a nibble of the food restores eating, presumably due to that nibble producing sensitization of reward effectiveness.

I have frequently observed people overeat at a restaurant with a buffet or view the desert tray and order a desert after having eaten a large meal. Decreased habituation likely causes the first example, due to the presence of a variety of reward, and sensitization provided by the desert tray likely causes the second example.

The Nature of Habituation and Sensitization

Dual Process Theory

Why do animals show a decreased (habituated) or increased (sensitized) reaction to environmental events? Groves and Thompson (1970) suggested that habituation reflects a decreased responsiveness of innate reflexes; that is, a stimulus becomes less able to elicit a response resulting from repeated exposure to that stimulus. By contrast, sensitization reflects an increased readiness to react to all stimuli. This increased reactivity operates on the animal's central nervous system. According to Groves and Thompson, drugs that stimulate the central nervous system increase an animal's overall readiness to respond, while depressive drugs suppress reactivity. Emotional distress can also affect responsiveness: Anxiety increases reactivity; depression decreases responsiveness.

Research on the startle response (M. Davis, 1974) supports Groves and Thompson's (1970) view. When animals are exposed to an unexpected stimulus, they show a sudden jump reaction due to tensing muscles. A variety of stimuli, such as a brief tone or light, elicits the startle response. As an example, imagine your reaction when you are working on a project and someone talks to you unexpectedly. In all likelihood, you would exhibit the startle reaction to the unexpected sound.

Repeated presentations of unexpected stimuli can lead to either a decreased or increased intensity of the startle reaction. M. Davis (1974) investigated habituation and sensitization of the startle reaction in rats. A brief 90-millisecond, 110-decibel (db) tone was presented to two groups of rats. For one group of rats, the unexpected tone was presented against a relatively quiet 60-db noise background. Davis noted that repeated presentation of the tone under this condition produced a decreased startle response (see Figure 3.5). The other group of rats experienced the unexpected tone against a louder 80-db noise background. In contrast to the habituation observed with the quiet background, repeated experiences with the tone against the louder background intensified the startle reaction (refer also to Figure 3.5).

Why does the startle response habituate with a quiet background but sensitize with a loud background? A loud background is arousing and should lead to enhanced reactivity. This greater reactivity should lead to a greater startle reaction (sensitization). In contrast, in a quiet background, arousal of the central nervous system would be minimal. This should reduce the ability of the unexpected stimulus to elicit the startle reaction (habituation).

John Garcia and his associates (Garcia, 1989; Garcia, Brett, & Rusiniak, 1989) suggested that changes in animals' innate reactions to environmental events have considerable adaptiveness. For example, the reduced neophobia to safe foods allows the animal to consume nutritionally valuable foods. We discuss the modification of innate feeding responses further when we look at biological influences on learning in Chapter 9.

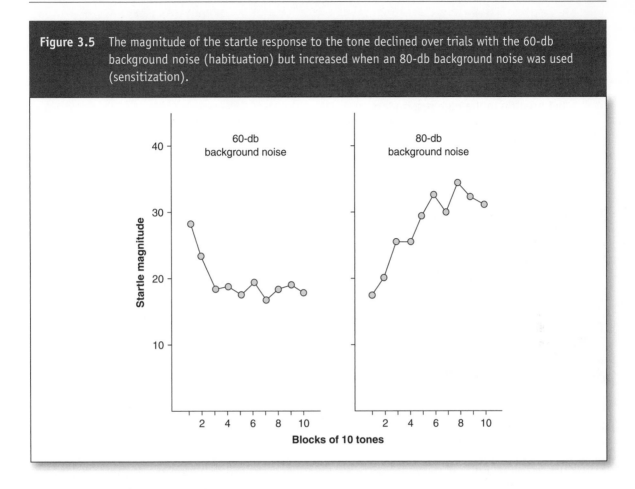

Figure 3.5   The magnitude of the startle response to the tone declined over trials with the 60-db background noise (habituation) but increased when an 80-db background noise was used (sensitization).

Evolutionary Theory

Edward Eisenstein and his associates (Eisenstein & Eisenstein, 2006; Eisenstein, Eisenstein, & Smith, 2001) suggested that the survival of an animal depends upon its ability to recognize biologically significant stimuli. According to these researchers, an animal needs to set sensory thresholds to maximize its probability of detecting potentially significant external events. If sensory thresholds are too sensitive, the animal will be flooded by irrelevant events and not notice the important ones. By contrast, if sensory thresholds are too insensitive, the animal also will not detect important external events. Obviously, the challenge for the animal is to set sensory thresholds at a level to maximize the detection of environmental events.

Eisenstein and Eisenstein (2006) proposed that the habituation and sensitization processes evolved as nonassociative forms of learning in order to modify sensory thresholds so that only significant external events will be detected. They interpret habituation as a process that filters out external stimuli of little relevance by raising the sensory threshold to those stimuli. By contrast, sensitization decreases sensory thresholds to potentially relevant external events. In Eisenstein and Eisenstein's view, habituation and sensitization are homeostatic processes that optimize an animal's likelihood of detecting significant external events.

Support for their evolutionary view comes from research showing that the same stimulus can produce both habituation and sensitization depending upon an animal's initial level of response to that stimulus. Eisenstein and colleagues (2001) reported that some human subjects (high responders) react (galvanic skin response, GSR) intensely to a particular stimulus (shock), while other humans (low responders) will respond very little to the same stimulus. They report that the GSR response decreased over trials to a shock stimulus in high responders. By contrast, low responders show an increased GSR response to the shock stimulus over trials. In other words, they found that low responders' sensitization occurred to the same shock stimulus that produced habituation in the high responders.

Eisenstein and Eisenstein (2006) suggested that the initial responsiveness to a new stimulus is a function of an animal's sensory threshold just prior to that event's occurrence. According to Eisenstein and Eisenstein, high responders initially receive more sensory input than do low responders. As a result, high responders progressively decrease their responsiveness to a nonthreatening stimulus (habituation). Low responders initially receive less sensory input than do high responders. As a result, low responders steadily increase their sensory threshold and show an increased response to the next stimulus occurrence (sensitization). Eisenstein and Eisenstein assumed that the level of responsiveness achieved in both low responders and high responders balances between being too sensitive to an unimportant stimulus (and possibly missing other significant stimuli) and being too insensitive and missing a change in the relevance of the present stimulus. In other words, Eisenstein and Eisenstein posited that habituation and sensitization represents an animal's way to achieve an appropriate threshold level to events in its environment.

Eric Richard Kandel (1929–   )

Kandel received his doctorate in medicine from New York University. In 1939, at age 10, he and his brother Ludwig, age 14, fled Austria and the Nazi invasion to join their uncle in the United States. After receiving his MD degree, he taught at Harvard University and the New York University Medical School for 11 years before going to the Columbia University College of Physicians and Surgeons to become the founding director of the Center for Neurobiology and Behavior, where he has been for the last 36 years. After completing his residency in psychiatry in 1962, he went to Paris to learn, from Ladislav Tauc, about the marine mollusc *Aplysia californica*. He has spent almost a half a century studying the physiological basis of learning and memory in *Aplysia* and received the Nobel Prize in Physiology or Medicine in 2000 for that research.

Learning in the *Aplysia Californica*

Many scientists (Bailey, Kandel, & Si, 2004; M. A. Lynch, 2004) have proposed that permanent memory represents changes in neural responsiveness. This view, referred to as **cellular modification theory**, suggests that learning permanently alters the functioning of specific neural systems. This change can reflect either the enhanced functioning of existing neural circuits or the establishment of new neural connections. We briefly examine evidence in this chapter that neural circuits are modified as a result of habituation and sensitization. The view that conditioning reflects modification of neural circuitry is explored in Chapter 13.

Nobel Prize winner Eric Kandel and his associates (Antonov, Antonova, Kandel, & Hawkins, 2001; Bailey, Giustetto, Zhu, Chen, & Kandel, 2000; Kandel, 2000) have investigated changes in synaptic responsivity following learning in the sea snail *Aplysia californica* (see Figure 3.6). This simple, shell-less marine mollusk has three external organs—the gill, the mantle, and the siphon—that retract when either the mantle or the siphon is touched. This defensive withdrawal response either increases or decreases as a result of experience and is analogous to the withdrawal responses found in almost all higher animals.

Repeatedly presenting a weak tactile stimulus to *Aplysia* decreases the strength of its withdrawal reaction (see Figure 3.7 on page 52), which satisfies our definition of habituation. Further, habituation of *Aplysia*'s defensive reaction is stimulus specific; that

Figure 3.6   In this shell-less marine mollusk, touching either the siphon or the mantle elicits a defensive retraction of the three external organs—the gill, the mantle, and the siphon. (a) The external organs are relaxed and (b) withdrawn.

is, the decreased withdrawal response occurs only in response to a weak touch on a particular part of the animal's body. If the tail of *Aplysia* is electrically shocked before its siphon is touched, the result is an exaggerated defensive response because of sensitization—an increase in the innate reactivity to a stimulus following exposure to an intense stimulus. Unlike habituation, which occurs in response to a specific stimulus, the sensitizing effect is nonspecific. After exposure to an electric shock, any stimulus, even a weak one, will elicit a strong defensive response in *Aplysia*.

Habituation of the defensive response of *Aplysia* lowers the responsivity of the synapses between the sensory and motor neurons involved in the withdrawal response (see Figure 3.7; R. D. Hawkins, Kandel, & Siegelbaum, 1993). This decreased synaptic responsiveness reflects a decreased neurotransmitter release from the sensory neuron and decreased activity of the motor

Figure 3.7   (a) Repeated exposure to a weak tactile stimulus leads to a reduced withdrawal reaction (habituation), whereas either a rest period or another tactile stimulus reinstates the withdrawal reaction (dishabituation). (b) The neural circuit that mediates the habituation of the gill withdrawal response includes the sensory neuron, an inhibitory interneuron, and the motor neuron.

neuron. In other words, habituation results from a decrease in neurotransmitter release in the neural circuit that produces the withdrawal response in *Aplysia*.

By contrast, sensitization results from an increased responsiveness of the synapses between the sensory and motor neurons controlling the withdrawal reflex. The increased responsiveness reflects a greater neurotransmitter release from the sensory neuron and increased activity in the motor neuron.

Dishabituation

You are driving to school and thinking about going to the movies after class when suddenly a car turns into your lane. Startled by the car, you notice that you are going too fast and put your foot on the brake to slow down. Why did you notice your speed after, but not before, the car turned into your lane? The phenomenon of **dishabituation** is one likely reason.

The Dishabituation Process

Dishabituation refers to the recovery of a habituated response as a result of the presentation of a sensitizing stimulus (G. Hall & Channell, 1985; Wagner, 1981). G. Hall and Channell (1985) provided one study demonstrating dishabituation. In this study, rats habituated to a light stimulus in one context. A reduced orienting response (turning toward the light and rearing in front of it) demonstrated habituation. Hall and Channell then presented the light stimulus to the rats in a context where they had never experienced the light. The second context was either another familiar context or a novel environment. An orienting response to the light stimulus was observed in the novel context. In contrast, the orienting response was not observed in the familiar environment.

Why did exposure to the novel, but not the familiar, context lead to dishabituation? According to the Groves and Thompson dual-process theory (Groves & Thompson, 1970), the arousing effect of the sensitizing stimulus causes the habituated response to return. In the absence of a sensitizing stimulus, habituation remains. Exposure to a novel context is arousing, and this arousal caused the rats' orienting response to the light to return in the Hall and Channell (1985) study. In contrast, the orienting response did not return when the rats were exposed to a nonarousing, familiar environment. In our automobile example, the car turning into your lane aroused your central nervous system, which caused you to again notice the setting on the speedometer.

R. D. Hawkins, Cohen, and Kandel (2006) also have observed dishabituation of the withdrawal response in *Aplysia*. Hawkins, Cohen, and Kandel first touched the *Aplysia*'s siphon, which produced withdrawal of the *Aplysia*'s external organs. Repeated touch stimulations with a 5-minute intertrial interval produced reduced withdrawal response (habituation). After five touch stimulations, the *Aplysia*'s mantle shelf was shocked. Hawkins, Cohen, and Kandel reported that this shock produced an increased withdrawal response, or dishabituation (see Figure 3.7).

Dishabituation can also restore the effectiveness of a reward produced by habituation (McSweeney & Murphy, 2009). For example, Aoyama & McSweeney (2001) observed rats' wheel-running rates decrease over the course of a 30-minute training session. These researchers found that when a flashing light was introduced 20 minutes into a 30-minute session, the rate of running increased.

What process is responsible for dishabituation? We examine this question next.

The Nature of Dishabituation

Pavlov (1927) suggested that a reversal of habituation caused dishabituation. In Pavlov's view, the cause of dishabituation of the withdrawal response in *Aplysia* would be a return to the prehabituation level of neurotransmitter released from the sensory neuron to the motor neuron that controls the withdrawal response. By contrast, Grether (1938) proposed that dishabituation results from a process similar to sensitization that was superimposed on habituation. In terms of *Aplysia,* this "dual process" view would suggest that the cause of dishabituation is due to two processes: (1) a decreased neurotransmitter release as a result of habituation and (2) an increased neurotransmitter release produced as a result of a sensitization experience.

Which of the two views is correct? One way to test whether dishabituation is due to a process similar to sensitization that counteracts habituation is to determine whether the specific factors influence both dishabituation and sensitization in the same way. Most of the evidence suggests that sensitization and dishabituation are due to similar processes.

Marcus, Nolen, Rankin, and Carew (1988) found that weak tail stimulation produced maximal dishabituation of a siphon withdrawal response, whereas strong tail stimulation produced maximum sensitization. Further, they observed that a short delay (1.5 minutes) after the tail stimulation produced maximum dishabituation, whereas a longer delay (20 minutes) produced maximum sensitization. By contrast, T. E. Cohen, Kaplan, Kandel, and Hawkins (1997) did not find any differences in the gill withdrawal response produced by either a sensitizing or dishabituating stimulus;

that is, the same noxious stimulus could produce either sensitization or dishabituation with similar time courses.

R. D. Hawkins, Cohen, and Kandel (2006) analyzed the sensitization and dishabituation of the *Aplysia's* gill withdrawal response. They reported that sensitization and dishabituation can be dissociated, but only under very limited conditions. These researchers found that varying the intensity of a sensitizing shock stimulus or a dishabituation shock stimulus had different effects only when presented 2.5 minutes before a nontouch (water) stimulus to the *Aplysia's* gill. There was no effect of shock intensity when the sensitizing stimulus or dishabituation stimulus was presented 12.5 minutes before the nontouch stimulus or when either the sensitizing or the dishabituation stimulus were presented either 2.5 or 12.5 minutes before the gill was touched (touch stimulus). These results suggest that dishabituation generally is due to a process similar to sensitization. Only under very limited circumstances—a very short interval that is not conducive to sensitization—does dishabituation reflect a reversal of habituation. What process, then, could lead to a reversal of habituation? At this time, that mechanism remains unclear.

Our discussion suggests that habituation and sensitization represent independent, but also interdependent, processes. Habituation results in a stimulus that is no longer able to elicit a response, while an arousing stimulus can cause either a return to normal response in the case of dishabituation or a heightened response in the case of sensitization. This interdependence of habituation and sensitization has adaptive value. Habituation allows us to ignore unimportant or irrelevant stimuli, while sensitization reinstates the response in case those stimuli now have become important. While it is not essential that you know exactly how fast you are going while you are just driving down the road, a car turning in front of you makes noticing your speed important again. It might just prevent you from having an accident (or getting a speeding ticket).

BEFORE YOU GO ON

- Would habituation cause Greg to smoke less?

- Would sensitization cause Greg to smoke more?

SECTION REVIEW

- Habituation is a decreased response to a stimulus following repeated experiences with that stimulus; sensitization reflects an increased reaction to a stimulus.

- Groves and Thompson suggest that habituation results from the decreased ability of the stimulus to elicit the response (innate reflexes) that occurs by filtering out external stimuli of little present relevance through increased sensory threshold to those irrelevant stimuli.

- Sensitization represents an increased reactivity to all stimuli (central nervous system) that occurs by decreasing the sensory threshold to significant external events.

- Dishabituation is the recovery of a habituated response resulting from the presentation of a sensitizing stimulus, which is a process similar to sensitization that is superimposed on habituation triggers.

- Animals exposed to a novel food show ingestional neophobia, or avoidance of the food.

- With repeated experience, ingestional neophobia habituates and more food is consumed; when an animal is ill, it becomes sensitized and shows enhanced ingestional neophobia.

- Habituation can lead to decrease in reward effectiveness, while sensitization and dishabituation can increase reward effectiveness.

- Studies on *Aplysia* have demonstrated that habituation decreases neurotransmitter release from the sensory neuron to the motor neuron controlling the withdrawal response, whereas sensitization increases neurotransmitter release.

Experience can lead to either a more intense (sensitization) or less intense (habituation) reaction to environmental events. Our discussion has focused on the response produced during exposure to a situation. However, responses also occur following an experience. Solomon and Corbit (1974) examined this aspect of the innate reaction to events. We now turn our attention to their opponent-process theory.

OPPONENT-PROCESS THEORY

Recall Greg's addiction to cigarettes, described in the chapter-opening vignette. Why does Greg crave cigarettes and find it so difficult to stop smoking? Opponent-process theory provides us with one answer to this question.

The Initial Reaction

Richard Solomon and John Corbit (1974) observed that all experiences (both biological and psychological) produce an initial affective reaction, the **A state** (see Figure 3.8), which can either be

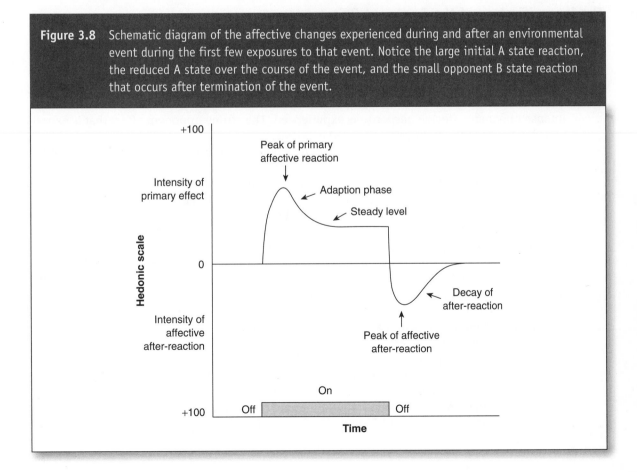

Figure 3.8   Schematic diagram of the affective changes experienced during and after an environmental event during the first few exposures to that event. Notice the large initial A state reaction, the reduced A state over the course of the event, and the small opponent B state reaction that occurs after termination of the event.

pleasant or unpleasant. For example, drinking alcohol usually produces a pleasurable A state, while taking an exam often produces an unpleasant A state. According to **opponent-process theory**, the intensity of an experience influences the strength of the A state; that is, the more intense the event, the stronger the A state.

The A state arouses a second affective reaction, the **B state**. The B state is the opposite of the A state; if A state is positive, then the B state will be negative, and vice versa. Thus, the pleasurable A state aroused by drinking initiates an opposing, or opponent, aversive affective state. Similarly, the pain produced during the examination creates a pleasurable relief response. In Solomon and Corbit's (1974) view, our biological systems automatically initiate an opposite, or opponent, response to counter the initial effect of all events.

Several important aspects of the opponent process must be described in order to understand the system Figure 3.8 depicts. First, the B state is initially less intense than the A state. Second, the B state intensifies more slowly than the A state. Finally, after an event has terminated, the strength of the B state diminishes more slowly than the A state. As a result of the slower decline of the B state than the A state, the opponent affective response will only be experienced when the event ends.

Consider Greg's addiction to smoking to illustrate how these rules operate. Smoking a cigarette activates a positive A state—pleasure. Automatic arousal of the opponent B state—pain or withdrawal—causes his initial A state (pleasure) to diminish as he continues smoking the cigarette. When Greg stops smoking, the A state declines quickly, and he experiences the B state (pain or withdrawal).

The Intensification of the Opponent B State

Solomon and Corbit (1974) discovered that repeated experience with a certain event often increases the strength of the opponent B state (see Figure 3.9), which in turn reduces the magnitude of the affective reaction experienced during the event. Thus, the strengthening of the opponent B state may well be responsible for the development of **tolerance**. Tolerance represents a decreased reactivity to an event with repeated experience. Furthermore, when the event ends, an intense opponent affective response is experienced. The strong opponent affect that is experienced in the absence of the event is called **withdrawal**.

Let's return to our example of Greg's cigarette smoking to illustrate this intensification of the B state process. Greg has smoked for many years, causing him to experience only mild pleasure from smoking. Yet, he feels intense prolonged pain or withdrawal when he stops smoking. Thus, the increased intensity of the B state not only produces reduced pleasure in smoking a cigarette, but it also increases withdrawal when the effects of smoking end.

Katcher, Solomon, Turner, LoLordo, Overmeir, and Rescorla's (1969) study demonstrates this process. These experimenters observed physiological reactions in dogs during and after electric shock. After the termination of shock, physiological responses (e.g., heart rate) declined below preshock levels for several minutes before returning to baseline. After many presentations, the decline was greater and lasted longer. These observations show (1) a strong A state and a weak opponent B state during the first presentations of shock and (2) a diminished A state (tolerance) and an intensified B state (withdrawal) after many experiences.

The opponent process operates in many different situations (see Solomon & Corbit, 1974). Epstein's (1967) description of the emotional reactions of military parachutists is one real-world example of the opponent process. Epstein reported that during the first free fall, all the parachutists showed an intense aversive A state (terror). This A state diminished after they had landed, and they looked stunned for several minutes. Then, the parachutists began to talk enthusiastically with friends. This opponent B state (relief) lasted for about 10 minutes.

Figure 3.9 Schematic diagram of the affective changes experienced during and after an environmental event after many presentations of that event. As a result of experiencing an event many times, there is a small A state response (tolerance) and a large and long B state reaction (withdrawal).

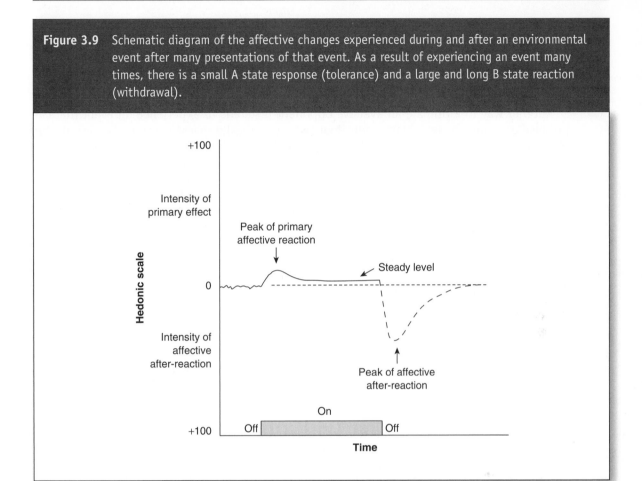

The affective response of experienced parachutists is quite different. During the free fall, experienced parachutists seemed tense, eager, or excited, reporting only a mildly aversive A state. Their opponent B state was exhilaration. Having landed safely, experienced parachutists showed (1) a high level of activity, (2) euphoria, and (3) intense social interaction. This opponent B state (exhilaration) decreased slowly, lasting for several hours.

People who consume cocaine report that the drug produces an initial and profound euphoria that is followed by an affective state described as anxiety, fatigue, agitation, and depression (Anthony, Tien, & Petronis, 1989; Resnick & Resnick, 1984). Ettenberg (2004) has reported a similar two-stage response to cocaine in rats. In his study, rats were placed in a distinctive environment either immediately after a cocaine injection, 5 minutes after a cocaine injection, or 15 minutes after a cocaine injection. Ettenberg reported that rats came to prefer the distinctive environment when placed there either immediately after or 5 minutes after the cocaine injection, presumably because the distinctive environment was associated with the positive effects (A state) of cocaine. By contrast, the rats avoided the distinctive environment when placed there 15 minutes after the cocaine injection, presumably because the distinctive environment became associated with the negative effects (B state) from cocaine use.

The Addictive Process

Opponent-process theory (Solomon, 1977, 1980) offers an explanation for the development of addiction. In Solomon's view, addictive behavior is a coping response to an aversive opponent B state. Addictive behavior is an example of behavior motivated to terminate (or prevent) the unpleasant withdrawal state.

Another way to terminate an aversive opponent B state is to experience an event that can produce a positive A state. Many individuals who chronically ingest cocaine also use alcohol (Anthony, Warner, & Kessler, 1994; Magura & Rosenblum, 2000). Cocaine users who also ingest alcohol report that the positive effects of cocaine are prolonged and the negative effects of cocaine withdrawal reduced (McCance-Katz et al., 1993; Perez-Reyes & Jeffcoat, 1992). Knackst-edt, Samimi, and Ettenberg (2002) reported that rats placed in a distinctive environment 15 minutes after being administered cocaine and alcohol showed no avoidance of the distinctive environment, presumably because the positive effects of alcohol, which has a longer half-life than does cocaine, negated the negative effects of cocaine withdrawal. Rats placed in the distinctive environment 30 minutes after drug use show a weak avoidance of the distinctive place. Ettenberg suggested that the negative effects of alcohol produced the avoidance of the distinctive environment, but the avoidance was weak because the withdrawal (B state) from alcohol is weaker than that from cocaine.

Most people who drink alcohol do not become alcoholics. Similarly, people who consume other drugs do not always become drug addicts. Solomon (1980) suggests that for addiction to develop, people must recognize that abstinence causes withdrawal symptoms and that the resumption of the addictive behavior after abstinence eliminates or prevents aversive feelings. People who think that the discomfort they experience is caused by factors other than the absence of the drug are not motivated to resume taking the drug. Under these circumstances, addiction does not develop.

There is another reason why addiction may not occur following repeated exposure. The number of exposures to a substance or event alone does not determine the intensification of the B state. If sufficient time intervenes between experiences, the opponent state does not intensify. And without the aversive withdrawal B state, the motivation for addiction does not exist. In support of Solomon's view, Starr (1978) discovered that young ducklings showed no distress in the absence of their mother when a 5-minute interval lapsed between separations. In contrast, with a 1- or 2-minute interval, strong withdrawal symptoms occurred. The importance of the interval between experiences in strengthening the opponent state might explain why some people can take a drug infrequently and never experience intense withdrawal symptoms after its effect has ended.

Once an addiction is established, an addict is motivated to prevent or terminate withdrawal symptoms. One consequence of addiction is the sacrifice of potential reinforcers (e.g., friends or a job). Most addicts recognize the serious consequences of their addiction and try to stop their self-destructive behavior.

Why is it so difficult for addicts to change their behavior? The aversive withdrawal reaction is a nonspecific unpleasant affective state. Therefore, any event that arouses the aversive state will motivate the addictive behavior. Usually, alcoholics who attempt to stop drinking face multiple problems. The suppression of drinking while experiencing the B state is only part of the problem for the alcoholic. Many daily stressors, such as problems at work or home, can activate the aversive motivational state, which can motivate the habitual addictive behavior.

For example, suppose that an alcoholic's mother-in-law arrives and that her presence is a very aversive event. Under these conditions, the mother-in-law's presence will activate the aversive state, thus intensifying the pressure to drink. Solomon (1980) believes that all potential aversive events must be prevented for addicts to break their habits. Other reasons for why it is so difficult to eliminate addictive behavior are described in Chapter 4.

The Search for Pleasure

Most of us equate addictive behavior with situations in which people are motivated to terminate the aversive withdrawal state and reinstate a pleasant initial state. However, some people deliberately expose themselves to an aversive A state in order to experience the pleasant opponent B state (Solomon, 1977, 1980). The behavior of experienced parachutists is one example. Most people who anticipate parachuting from an aircraft never jump at all or quit after one jump. However, those who do jump and experience a strong reinforcing B state are often motivated to jump again. Epstein (1967) reported that some experienced jumpers become extremely depressed when bad weather cancels a jump. The reaction of these parachutists when denied the opportunity to jump resembles that of drug addicts who cannot obtain the desired drug. Other behaviors in which the positive opponent state may lead to addiction include running in marathons (Milvy, 1977) and jogging (Booth, as cited in Solomon, 1980).

R. L. Craig and Siegel (1980) discovered that introductory psychology students taking a test felt apprehensive and experienced a euphoric feeling when the test ended. However, it is unlikely that students' level of positive affect after taking a test is as strong as that of an experienced parachutist after jumping. Perhaps students are not tested often enough to develop a strong opponent reinforcing B state. You might suggest that your instructor test you more frequently to decrease your initial aversive apprehension and to intensify your positive affective relief when the test ends.

BEFORE YOU GO ON

- How would opponent-process theory explain Greg's addiction to smoking cigarettes?

- Does opponent-process theory make a prediction regarding how Greg might best quit smoking cigarettes?

SECTION REVIEW

- Solomon and Corbit suggested that all experiences produce an initial affective reaction (A state) that can either be pleasant or unpleasant.

- The A state arouses a second affective reaction, called the B state, which is the opposite of the A state; if the A state is positive, then the B state will be negative, and vice versa.

- The B state is initially less intense, develops more slowly, and declines more slowly than the A state.

- When an event is experienced often, the strength of the B state increases, which reduces the affective reaction (A state) experienced during the event.

- After the event ends, the increased B state leads to a strong opponent B state.

- The reduced A response to the event is called tolerance, and the intensified opponent B reaction in the absence of the event is called withdrawal.

- According to opponent-process theory, one form of addiction develops when people learn that withdrawal occurs after the event ends and that resuming the addictive behavior terminates the aversive opponent withdrawal state.

- A second form of addiction occurs when a person learns that an intense, pleasurable opponent state can be produced following exposure to an initial aversive state.

- Although early experience with the event was unpleasant, "the pleasure addict" now finds the initial affective response only mildly aversive and the opponent state very pleasurable. The anticipated pleasure motivates the addict to experience the aversive event.

CRITICAL THINKING QUESTIONS

1. Ming can usually pass a bakery without buying a donut, but sometimes she cannot resist the temptation. Using Lorenz and Tinbergen's energy model, explain Ming's behaviors.

2. Jamaal no longer notices the high pitch of his friend's voice. LaToya finds the friend's voice piercing. Explain how habituation and sensitization might be responsible for the different reactions of Jamaal and LaToya to their friend's voice.

3. Neal enjoys a few beers after work. He claims that it calms him after a hard day at the office. Using what you have learned about opponent-process theory, explain as much as you can about Neal's behavior. Focus on the conditions that cause Neal to drink, how we feel while drinking, and how he might feel in the morning.

KEY TERMS

action-specific energy	withdrawal
A state	appetitive behavior
cellular modification theory	B state
displacement	dishabituation
fixed action pattern (FAP)	habituation
ingestional neophobia	innate releasing mechanism (IRM)
opponent-process theory	sensitization
sign stimulus	tolerance

Principles and Applications of Classical Conditioning

A LINGERING FEAR

Juliette is a teacher at the local high school. Although her coworkers often ask her to socialize after work, Juliette always rejects their requests; instead, after driving home, she proceeds hurriedly from her car to her apartment. Once inside, Juliette locks the door and refuses to leave until the next morning. On weekends, Juliette shops with her sister, who lives with their parents several blocks away. However, once darkness approaches, Juliette compulsively returns to her apartment. Although her sister, her parents, or close friends sometimes visit during the evening, Juliette refuses any of their invitations to go out after dark. Several men—all seemingly pleasant, sociable, and handsome—have asked Juliette for dates during the past year. Juliette has desperately wanted to socialize with them, yet she has been unable to accept any of their invitations. Juliette's fear of going out at night and her inability to accept dates began 13 months ago. She had dined with her parents at their home and had left about 9:30 p.m. Because it was a pleasant fall evening, she decided to walk the several blocks to her apartment. Within a block of her apartment, a man grabbed her and dragged her to a nearby alley. The man kicked her intensely several times before running away upon hearing another person approach. Since Juliette did not see her assailant, the police doubted they could apprehend him. The few friends and relatives whom Juliette told about the attack tried to support her, yet she found no solace. Juliette still has nightmares about the attack and often wakes up terrified. On the few occasions after the attack that Juliette did go out after dark, she felt very uncomfortable and had to return home. She has become fearful even thinking about having to go out at night and arranges her schedule so she is home before dark. Juliette wants to overcome her fears, but she does not know how to do it.

Juliette's fear of darkness is a classically conditioned emotional response that she acquired as a result of the attack. This fear motivates Juliette to avoid going out at night. In this chapter, we describe the classical conditioning process responsible for Juliette's intense fear reaction. The learning mechanism that causes Juliette to avoid darkness is discussed in Chapter 8.

Juliette does not have to remain afraid of going out into the darkness. There are two effective behavior therapies, systematic desensitization and flooding, that use the classical conditioning process to eliminate intense, conditioned fear reactions like Juliette's. We discuss systematic desensitization later in this chapter and response prevention or flooding in Chapter 7.

Juliette's fear of darkness is one example of emotional reactions becoming attached to environmental events. In this chapter, we discuss the process by which environmental conditions become able to elicit emotional responses, as well as how those associations can be eliminated if they are harmful.

PRINCIPLES OF CLASSICAL CONDITIONING

The Conditioning Process

Basic Components

As you learned in Chapter 1, there are four basic components of classical conditioning: (1) the **unconditioned stimulus** (UCS), (2) the **unconditioned response** (UCR), (3) the **conditioned stimulus** (CS), and (4) the **conditioned response** (CR). Prior to conditioning, the biologically significant event—or UCS—elicits the UCR, but the neutral environmental stimulus—or CS—cannot elicit the CR. During conditioning, the CS is experienced with the UCS. Following conditioning, the CS is able to elicit the CR, and the strength of the CR increases steadily during acquisition until a maximum or **asymptotic level** is reached (see Figure 4.1). The UCS-UCR complex is the **unconditioned reflex**; the CS-CR complex is the **conditioned reflex**.

Although the pairing of the CS and UCS is essential to the development of the CR, other factors determine both whether conditioning occurs as well as the final strength of the CR. We detail the conditions that influence the ability of the CS to elicit the CR later in the chapter. Let's use two examples to illustrate the basic components of conditioning.

Figure 4.1 Acquisition and extinction of a conditioned response. The strength of the conditioned response increases during acquisition, when the CS and UCS are paired, while presentation of the CS without the UCS during extinction lowers the strength of the conditioned response. The strength of the conditioned response will spontaneously recover when a short interval follows extinction, but it will decline again with additional presentations of the CS alone.

The Conditioning of Hunger

Suppose you often arrive home late in the day, and you go into the kitchen and see the refrigerator. Opening the refrigerator, you notice the milk and pie. Why does the sight of the refrigerator and the food increase your hunger and your motivation to obtain food? The answer lies in the association of the kitchen, the refrigerator, and the sight of food (CSs) with the taste and the smell of the food (UCSs).

When animals or people are exposed to food, they exhibit a set of unconditioned responses that prepare them to digest, metabolize, and store ingested food. These unconditioned feeding responses include the secretion of saliva, gastric juices, pancreatic enzymes, and insulin. One important action of insulin is to lower blood glucose, which in turn stimulates hunger and motivates eating (Campfield & Smith, 2003). Thus, we become hungry when we taste or smell food. The intensity of these unconditioned feeding responses directly relates to the palatability of food. The more attractive the food, the greater the unconditioned feeding responses and the more we eat.

These unconditioned feeding responses to food can be conditioned (Weingarten & Martin, 1989). The conditioning of these feeding responses to environmental cues can lead to a desire to eat when encountering specific stimuli, such as your kitchen. Since cues such as the cupboard and the refrigerator have been associated with food, they are capable of eliciting these feeding responses. As a result of this conditioning experience, when you go to the kitchen and see the cupboard or refrigerator, your body reflexively releases insulin, which lowers your blood glucose level and makes you hungry. As we discover shortly, the strength of the conditioned response (CR) depends upon the intensity of the unconditioned stimulus (UCS). If you have associated the environment of the kitchen with highly palatable foods capable of eliciting an intense unconditioned feeding reaction, the stimuli in the kitchen will elicit an intense conditioned feeding response, and your hunger will be acute.

Environmental events associated with food can develop sufficient motivational properties to override satiety and elicit eating even in nondeprived or satiated animals (Holland & Petrovich, 2005; Holland, Petrovich, & Gallagher, 2002; Petrovich & Gallagher, 2007; Petrovich, Ross, Gallagher, & Holland, 2007). Food consumption in satiated rats has been conditioned to a discrete stimulus, such as a tone (Holland & Petrovich, 2005) or to a distinctive contextual environment (Petrovich et al., 2007). In these studies, either the discrete or contextual stimulus was initially paired with food delivery in food-deprived (hungry) rats. The cues were then presented prior to food availability in satiated rats. The presence of these environmental events elicited eating even though the rats were not hungry. Not only can these environmental events motivate the consumption of the food experienced during conditioning, but they can also motivate the consumption of either novel food (Petrovich et al., 2007) or other familiar foods (Petrovich, Ross, Holland, & Gallagher, 2007).

The elicitation of eating behavior by environmental events also has been reported in humans (Petrovich & Gallagher, 2007). For example, L. L. Birch, McPhee, Sullivan, and Johnson (1989) presented visual and auditory stimuli with snacks on some days and other visual and auditory stimuli without snacks on other days. On test days, the children were satiated and the cues associated with food or those stimuli not previously paired with food were presented. The researchers reported that the stimuli associated with food led to greater snack consumption in satiated children than did the stimuli that had not been previously associated with food.

Petrovich and Gallagher (2007) suggested that the elicitation of eating by conditioned stimuli helps us understand the causes of overeating and obesity in humans. The settings of fast-food and other chain restaurants—with a relatively uniform, recognizable appearance and relatively limited menu items—are ideal for specific food contexts to become conditioned stimuli, capable of overriding satiety cues, and, thereby, leading to overeating and obesity.

The basolateral region of the amygdala appears to be responsible for the elicitation of feeding behavior by conditioned stimuli (Petrovich & Gallagher, 2007). Research with human subjects shows that the amygdala becomes active in satiated subjects while viewing the names of preferred foods, but not neutral foods (Arana et al., 2003) and while thinking about liked or craved foods (Pelchat, Johnson, Chan, Valdez, & Ragland, 2004).

Damage to the basolateral region of the amygdala has been found to prevent the conditioning of feeding in satiated rats when the damage occurs prior to conditioning and to abolish it when it occurs following training (Holland & Petrovich, 2005; Petrovich & Gallagher, 2007). The basolateral region of the amygdala has projections to areas of the hypothalamus that control hunger and satiety and to nucleus accumbens (S. B. Klein & Thorne, 2007). As we will discover in Chapter 9, activity in the nucleus accumbens motivates reward seeking behavior.

The Conditioning of Fear

For most people, experiencing turbulence in an airplane is an unpleasant event. When the plane drops suddenly and sharply (the UCS), an unconditioned aversive reaction is elicited (the UCR). The psychological distress you experience when the airplane drops is one aspect of your aversive reaction; the increased physiological arousal is another aspect. Although the unpleasantness may lessen as the airplane continues to shake, you will most likely not experience relief until the turbulence ends.

Experiences with turbulence differ considerably in their degree of aversiveness. You respond intensely to some experiences; others elicit only a mild aversive reaction. Many factors determine the level of aversiveness. The severity of the turbulence is one factor influencing how intensely you respond; a lot of air movement elicits a stronger aversive reaction than a little air movement. This is one example of the influence of the strength of the UCS on the intensity of the UCR. Another factor that often affects the aversiveness of experiencing turbulence is the number of times you have experienced it before. You may experience less distress if you have never before encountered turbulence than if you have often experienced the unsettling motion of a plane (sensitization).

As a result of past experiences, the cues that predict turbulence can elicit an anticipatory aversive reaction (the CR). We typically call this anticipatory aversive reaction fear. One stimulus associated with turbulence is the fasten seatbelt light. Thus, you may become frightened (CR) when the pilot puts on the fasten seatbelt light (CS). Another cue may be storm clouds or a darkening sky. Each of these CSs may have been associated with sudden and sharp movement of the airplane; if so, each can become able to elicit fear. Even a forecast of bad weather might become a conditioned stimulus that elicits fear.

Recall Juliette's fear of darkness described in the chapter-opening vignette. Classical conditioning provides an explanation of Juliette's fear. Being attacked was an unconditioned stimulus that elicited pain as the unconditioned response. As the result of pairing nighttime with the attack, the darkness of nighttime has become a conditioned stimulus that elicits fear as the conditioned response.

Psychologists have consistently observed that fear is conditioned when a novel stimulus (the CS) is associated with an aversive event. The Russian physiologist Bechterev's (1913) observation that a conditioned response (e.g., withdrawal of the leg) can occur by pairing a neutral stimulus with shock was the first experimental demonstration of fear conditioning. In 1916, John Watson showed that emotional arousal can be conditioned during the pairing of a novel stimulus with shock. Other researchers have consistently reported the development of fear through classical conditioning in animals (N. E. Miller, 1948) and humans (Staats & Staats, 1957).

Fear also motivates an escape response to an aversive event. Neal Miller's classic 1948 study demonstrates the motivational properties of fear. Miller first conditioned fear in rats by administering electric shock in the white compartment of a shuttle box apparatus (see Figure 4.2).

Figure 4.2   Apparatus similar to the one Neal Miller (1948) employed to investigate acquisition of a fear response. The rat's emotional response to the white chamber, previously paired with shock, motivates the rat to learn to turn the wheel, which raises the gate and allows escape.

After administering the shock, Miller allowed the rats to escape into the black compartment. After the initial pairings of the white compartment with shock, he confined the animals in the white compartment without presenting any additional shock. However, each rat could escape the white chamber by turning a wheel to open the door to the black compartment. Miller found that about half the rats learned to turn the wheel to escape the aversive white chamber; the other half "froze" and did not learn the required response. The results show that the association of an environment (the white chamber) with an unconditioned aversive event (shock) can cause the environment to acquire motivational properties.

We learned earlier that the degree of hunger that various environmental cues induce depends upon the UCS intensity: the stronger the UCS, the more intense our conditioned hunger reaction. The strength of the aversive unconditioned event also influences our conditioned fear reaction. We are more fearful of flying when the weather is bad than when the sun is shining and there are no storm clouds in the sky.

Juliette's fear of the darkness of nighttime (CS) developed motivational properties as a result of pairing with the attack (UCS). As being attacked is a very intense event, it is not surprising that Juliette developed a strong fear of the darkness of nighttime. The darkness of nighttime now motivates Juliette to stay at home at night.

Not all people are frightened by flying in turbulent conditions, and some do not learn that driving is a way to avoid an unpleasant airplane ride. This chapter describes the conditions that influence the development of a conditioned fear response. Chapter 7 details the factors that govern avoidance acquisition.

Other Examples of Conditioned Responses

Hunger and fear are not the only examples of conditioned responses. Other examples include feeling nauseous when seeing a type of food that has previously made you ill, becoming thirsty at a ball game as a result of previously consuming drinks in that setting, and experiencing sexual arousal during a candlelight dinner because of previous sexual activity. These examples not only demonstrate three additional conditioned responses—nausea, thirst, and sexual arousal—but also show that stimuli other than food or shock can be involved in the conditioning process. The three unconditioned stimuli in the previous examples are poison, fluid, and sexual activity. Of course, people encounter many more conditioned responses and unconditioned stimuli in the real world. Other examples are presented throughout the chapter.

Most of the experiments on classical conditioning have investigated the conditioning of only a single conditioned response. In most cases, several responses are conditioned during CS-UCS pairings. The conditioning of several responses has an obvious adaptive value. For example, when a CS is experienced along with food, several different digestive responses occur: The conditioned salivary reflex aids in swallowing, the conditioned gastric secretion response facilitates digestion, and the conditioned insulin release enhances food storage.

Conditioning Techniques

Psychologists now use several techniques to investigate the conditioning process. Pavlov's surgical technique to measure the visceral reactions (saliva, gastric juices, insulin) to stimuli associated with food is the most familiar measure of conditioning. Other techniques that reveal the strength of conditioning include eyeblink conditioning, fear conditioning, and flavor aversion learning. Brief descriptions of these conditioning measures will familiarize you with the techniques; their widespread use is evident in our discussion of classical conditioning principles and applications in this chapter.

Eyeblink Conditioning

A puff of air is presented to a rabbit's eye. The rabbit reflexively blinks its eye. If a tone is paired with the puff of air, the rabbit will come to blink in response to the tone as well as to the puff of air. The pairing of a tone (CS) with the puff of air (UCS) leads to the establishment of an eyeblink response (CR). The process that leads to the rabbit's response is called **eyeblink conditioning** (see Figure 4.3).

Eyeblink conditioning is possible because the rabbit not only has an outer eyelid similar to that found in humans, but also has an inner eyelid called a nictitating membrane. The nictitating membrane reacts by closing whenever it detects any air movement near the eye. The closure of the nictitating membrane then causes the rabbit's eye to blink. Researchers have widely used eyeblink conditioning to investigate the nature of classical conditioning (Domjan, 2005). They have also used it to study the brain mechanisms that underlie conditioning (Robleto, Poulos, & Thompson, 2004). While most eyeblink conditioning studies have used rabbits as subjects, eyeblink conditioning also occurs in humans.

We need to make several important points about eyeblink conditioning. A puff of air or a mild irritation of the skin below the eye with a brief electrical shock (UCSs) will elicit a rapid, unconditioned eyeblink response. By contrast, a tone, light, or tactile stimulus (CSs) will produce a slow, gradual closure of the eye. Further, eyeblink conditioning is quite slow, taking as many as 100 CS-UCS pairings before the rabbit responds to the CS on 50% of the trials.

Figure 4.3   Illustration of an apparatus used to condition an eyeblink response. The potentiometer records the closure of the eye following its exposure to a puff of air (UCS) or a tone (CS).

Fear Conditioning

We discussed several examples of **fear conditioning** earlier in the chapter. Fear can be measured in several ways. One measure is escape or avoidance behavior in response to a stimulus associated with a painful UCS. However, while avoidance behavior is highly correlated with fear, avoidance performance does not automatically provide a measure of fear. As we discover in Chapter 8, animals show no overt evidence of fear with a well-learned avoidance behavior (Kamin, Brimer, & Black, 1963). Further, animals can fail to avoid despite being afraid (Monti & Smith, 1976).

Another measure of fear is the **conditioned emotional response** (CER). Animals may freeze in an open environment when exposed to a feared stimulus. They will suppress operant behavior reinforced by food or water when a feared stimulus is present. Estes and Skinner (1941) developed a CER procedure for detecting the level of fear, and their methodology has been used often to provide a measure of conditioned fear (H. Davis, 1968). Fear conditioning develops rapidly, and significant suppression can be found within 10 trials.

To obtain a measure of conditioned fear, researchers first have animals learn to bar press or key peck to obtain food or water reinforcement. Following operant training, a neutral stimulus (usually a light or tone) is paired with an aversive event (usually electric shock or a loud noise). The animals are then returned to the operant chamber, and the tone or light CS is presented during the training session. The presentation of the CS follows an equal period when the CS is not present. Fear conditioned to the tone or light will lead to suppression of operant behavior.

If fear is conditioned only to the CS, the animal will exhibit the operant behavior when the CS is not present.

Calculating a **suppression ratio** determines the level of fear conditioned to the CS. This suppression ratio compares the response level during the interval when the CS is absent to the response level when the CS is present. To obtain the ratio, the number of responses during the CS is divided by the total number of responses (responses without the CS and with the CS).

$$\text{Suppression ratio} = \frac{\text{Responses with CS}}{\text{Responses with CS } + \text{ Responses without CS}}$$

How can we interpret a particular suppression ratio? A suppression ratio of 0.5 indicates that fear has not been conditioned to the CS because the animal responds equally when the CS is on and off. For example, if the animal responds 15 times when the CS is on and 15 times when it is off, the suppression ratio will be 0.5. A suppression ratio of 0 indicates that the animal responds only when the CS is off; for example, an animal might respond 0 times when the CS is on and 15 times when the CS is off. Only on rare occasions will the suppression ratio be as low as 0 or as high as 0.5. In most instances, the suppression ratio will fall between 0 and 0.5.

Flavor Aversion Learning

I have a friend who refuses to walk down a supermarket aisle where tomato sauce is displayed; he says that even the sight of cans of tomatoes makes him ill. My oldest son once got sick after eating string beans, and now he refuses to touch them. I once became nauseous several hours after eating at a local restaurant, and I have not returned there since. Almost all of us have some food we will not eat or a restaurant we avoid. Often, the reason for this behavior is that at some time, we experienced illness after eating a particular food or dining at a particular place, and we associated the food or the place with the illness, through classical conditioning. Such an experience creates a conditioned **flavor aversion** to the taste (or smell or sight) of the food or the place itself. Subsequently, we avoid it.

The classic research of John Garcia and his associates (Garcia, Kimeldorf, & Hunt, 1957; Garcia, Kimeldorf, & Koelling, 1955) demonstrated that animals learn to avoid a flavor associated with illness. Although rats have a strong preference for saccharin and will consume large quantities even when nondeprived, Garcia and colleagues discovered that the animals will not drink saccharin if illness follows its consumption. In their studies, after consuming saccharin, rats were made ill by agents such as X-ray irradiation or lithium chloride; the rats subsequently avoided the saccharin. The measure of conditioning is the amount of the fluid or food consumed. Flavor aversion learning is quite rapid, with significant avoidance observed after a single trial.

Does a person's dislike for a particular food reflect the establishment of a flavor aversion? It seems reasonable that people's aversion to a specific food often develops after they eat it and become ill. Informally questioning the students in my learning class last year, I found that many of them indeed had had an experience in which illness followed eating a certain food and that these students no longer could eat that food. If you have had a similar experience, perhaps you, too, can identify the cause of your aversion to some food. In a more formal investigation, Garb and Stunkard (1974) questioned 696 subjects about their food aversions, reporting that 38% of the subjects had at least one strong food aversion. The researchers found that 89% of the people reporting a strong food aversion could identify a specific instance associated with illness after eating the food. Even though most often the illness did not begin until several hours after consumption of the food, the subjects still avoided the food subsequently. Also, Garb and Stunkard's survey indicated that the subjects were more likely to develop aversions between the ages of 6 and 12 than at any other age.

More recent surveys suggest that the number of persons with flavor aversions is even higher than Garb and Stunkard (1974) reported. For example, Logue, Ophir, and Strauss (1981) found that over half the college students they surveyed reported at least one food aversion. Further, many people have an aversion to a flavor even when they know that the flavor did not cause the illness. This observation suggests that mechanistic rather than cognitive processes control aversions; we have more to say about the nature of flavor aversion learning in Chapter 9.

Temporal Relationships Between the CS and the UCS

Five different temporal relationships have been used in conditioning studies (see Figure 4.4). These temporal relationships represent the varied ways to pair a CS with a UCS. As we will discover, they are not equally effective.

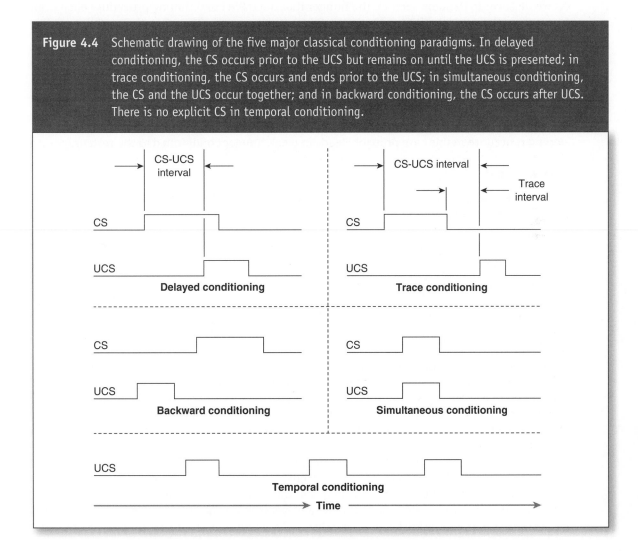

Figure 4.4 Schematic drawing of the five major classical conditioning paradigms. In delayed conditioning, the CS occurs prior to the UCS but remains on until the UCS is presented; in trace conditioning, the CS occurs and ends prior to the UCS; in simultaneous conditioning, the CS and the UCS occur together; and in backward conditioning, the CS occurs after UCS. There is no explicit CS in temporal conditioning.

Delayed Conditioning

In **delayed conditioning**, the CS onset precedes UCS onset. The termination of the CS occurs either with UCS onset or during UCS presentation. In other words, there is no time delay between the CS and onset of the UCS. If, for instance, a darkening sky precedes a severe storm, delayed conditioning may occur. The darkening sky is the CS; its occurrence precedes the storm, and it remains present until the storm occurs. A person who has experienced this type of conditioning may be frightened whenever seeing a darkened sky.

Juliette's fear of nighttime darkness was conditioned using the delayed conditioned procedure. Nighttime darkness (CS) preceded the attack (UCS) and continued during the course of the attack.

Trace Conditioning

With this conditioning procedure, the CS is presented and terminated prior to UCS onset. In other words, there are delays of varying lengths between the termination of the CS and the onset of the UCS. A parent who calls a child to dinner is using a **trace conditioning** procedure. In this example, the announcement of dinner (CS) terminates prior to the presentation of food (UCS). As we discover in the next section, the hunger that the trace conditioning procedure elicits can be quite weak unless the interval between CS termination and UCS onset (the trace interval) is very short.

Simultaneous Conditioning

The CS and UCS are presented together when the **simultaneous conditioning** procedure is used. An example of simultaneous conditioning is walking into a fast food restaurant. In this setting, the restaurant (CS) and the smell of food (UCS) occur at the same time. The simultaneous conditioning procedure in this case probably leads to weak hunger conditioned to the restaurant.

Backward Conditioning

In the **backward conditioning** procedure, the UCS is presented and terminated prior to the CS. Suppose that a candlelight dinner (CS) follows sexual activity (UCS). With this example of backward conditioning, sexual arousal to the candlelight dinner may not develop. In fact, contemporary research (Tait & Saladin, 1986) demonstrates that the backward conditioning procedure is also a conditioned inhibition procedure; that is, the CS is actually paired with the absence of the UCS. In some instances, a person experiences a conditioned inhibition rather than conditioned excitation when exposed to the CS. In Chapter 5, we look at the factors that determine whether a backward conditioning paradigm conditions excitation or **inhibition**.

Temporal Conditioning

There is no distinctive CS in **temporal conditioning**. Instead, the UCS is presented at regular intervals, and over time, the CR occurs just prior to the onset of the UCS. To show that conditioning has occurred, the UCS is omitted and the strength of the CR assessed. What mechanism allows for temporal conditioning? In temporal conditioning, a specific biological state often provides the CS. When the same internal state precedes each UCS exposure, that state will be conditioned to elicit the CR.

Consider the following example to illustrate the temporal conditioning procedure. You set your alarm to awaken you at 7:00 a.m. for an 8:00 a.m. class. After several months, you awaken just prior to the alarm's sounding. The reason lies in the temporal conditioning process. The alarm (UCS) produces an arousal reaction (UCR), which awakens you. Your internal state every day just before the alarm rings (the CS) becomes conditioned to produce arousal; this arousal (CR) awakens you prior to the alarm's sounding.

The five different procedures for presenting the CS and UCS are not equally effective (Keith-Lucas & Guttman, 1975). The delayed conditioning paradigm usually is the most effective; the backward conditioning is usually the least. The other three procedures typically have an intermediate level of effectiveness.

BEFORE YOU GO ON

- How might a clinical psychologist measure Juliette's fear of darkness?

- What conditioning paradigm was responsible for the conditioning of Juliette's fear?

SECTION REVIEW

- The ability of environmental events to produce emotional reactions that in turn motivate instrumental behavior develops through the classical conditioning process.

- Conditioning involves the pairing of a neutral environmental cue with a biologically important event. Prior to conditioning, only the biologically important stimulus, called an unconditioned stimulus (UCS), can elicit a response.

- As the result of conditioning, the neutral environmental stimulus, now a conditioned stimulus (CS), can also elicit a response, called the conditioned response (CR).

- With delayed conditioning, the CS remains present until the UCS begins, while with trace conditioning the CS ends prior to the onset of the UCS.

- With simultaneous conditioning, the CS and UCS occur at the same time, while backward conditioning presents the CS following the presentation of the UCS.

- Temporal conditioning takes place when the UCS is presented at regular intervals of time.

- Delayed conditioning is usually the most efficient and backward conditioning the least.

Conditions Affecting the Acquisition of a Conditioned Response

In the previous section, we learned that a conditioned response develops when a novel stimulus is paired with an unconditioned stimulus. However, the pairing of a CS and a UCS does not automatically ensure that the subject will acquire a conditioned response. A number of factors determine whether a CR will develop following CS-UCS pairings. Let us now look at the factors that play an important role in classical conditioning.

Contiguity

Consider the following example to illustrate the importance of contiguity to the development of a conditioned response. An 8-year-old girl hits her 6-year-old brother. The mother informs her aggressive daughter that her father will punish her when he gets home from work. Even though this father frequently punishes his daughter for aggression toward her younger brother, the mother's threat instills no fear. The failure of her threat to elicit fear renders the mother unable to curb her daughter's inappropriate behavior.

Why doesn't the girl fear her mother's threat, even though it has been consistently paired with her father's punishment? The answer to this question relates to the importance of the close temporal pairing, or **contiguity**, of the CS and UCS in classical conditioning. A threat (the CS) provides information concerning future punishment and elicits the emotional state that motivates avoidance behavior. Although the mother's threat does predict future punishment, the child's fright at the time of the threat is not adaptive because the punishment will not occur for several hours. Instead of being frightened from the time that the threat is made until the father's arrival, the girl becomes afraid only when her father arrives. This girl's fear now motivates her to avoid punishment, perhaps by crying and promising not to hit her little brother again. Similarly, the contiguity between nighttime darkness and the attack contributed to Juliette's intense fear and her avoidance of going out at night.

The Optimal CS-UCS. Many studies document the importance of contiguity to the acquisition of a conditioned response. Experiments designed to evaluate the influence of contiguity on classical conditioning have varied the interval between the CS and UCS and then evaluated the strength of the CR. The results of these studies show that the optimal **CS-UCS interval**, or interstimulus interval (ISI), is very short. Intervals even shorter than the optimal ISI produce weaker conditioning, with the strength of the CR increasing as the ISI becomes longer, until the optimal CS-UCS interval is reached. An ISI longer than the optimal CS-UCS interval also leads to weaker conditioning, with the intensity of the CR decreasing as the ISI increases beyond the optimal.

   The optimal CS-UCS interval is different for different responses. For example, the optimal conditioning interval is 450 milliseconds for eyeblink conditioning. This 450-millisecond ISI for the conditioning of the eyelid closure reflex has been observed in both animals (M. C. Smith, Coleman, & Gormezano, 1969) and humans (Kimble & Reynolds, 1967). Figure 4.5 presents the

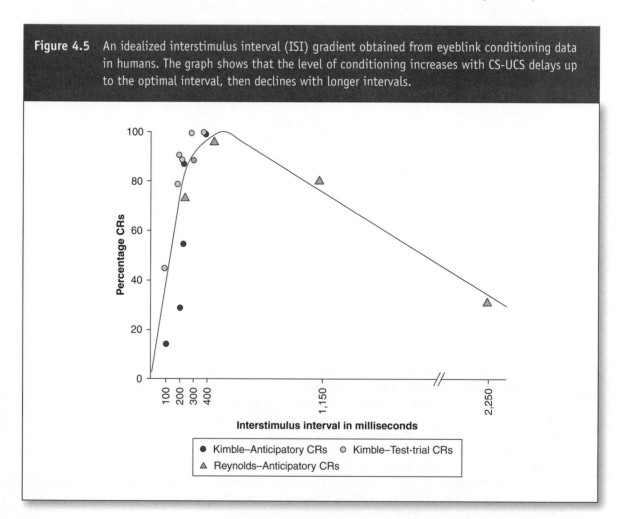

Figure 4.5   An idealized interstimulus interval (ISI) gradient obtained from eyeblink conditioning data in humans. The graph shows that the level of conditioning increases with CS-UCS delays up to the optimal interval, then declines with longer intervals.

CS-UCS interval gradient for eyeblink conditioning in humans. Some other optimal ISIs include 2.0 seconds for skeletal movements (M. Noble & Harding, 1963), 4.0 seconds for salivary reflexes (Gormezano, 1972), and 20 seconds for heart rate responses (Church & Black, 1958).

Why does the optimal CS-UCS interval vary among responses? The optimal ISI is thought to reflect the latency to respond in a particular reflex system (Hilgard & Marquis, 1940). Hilgard and Marquis suggested that the different optimal CS-UCS intervals occur because the response latency of the autonomic nervous system is longer than that of the eyeblink closure reflex. Wagner and Brandon's theory (1989) addresses the question of how response latency affects the optimal ISI; we look at their view in Chapter 5.

Long-Delay Learning. There is one noteworthy exception to the contiguity principle. Animals and humans are capable of associating a flavor stimulus (CS) with an illness experience (UCS) that occurs several hours later. The association of taste with illness, called flavor aversion learning, contrasts sharply with the other forms of classical conditioning, in which no conditioning occurs if the CS-UCS interval is longer than several minutes. While flavor aversion learning can occur even with long delays, a CS-UCS interval gradient does exist for it, with the strongest conditioning occurring when the flavor and illness are separated only by 30 minutes (Garcia, Clark, & Hankins, 1973). We take a more detailed look at flavor aversion learning in Chapter 9.

The Influence of Intensity

CS Intensity. Suppose that you were bitten by a dog. Would you be more afraid if it was a large dog or if it was a small dog? If we assume that the pain induced by bites (the UCS) from each are equivalent, research on the intensity of the CS and the strength of intensity conditioning indicates your fear would be equivalent only if one dog bites you. However, you would be more afraid of the more intense CS, the large dog, even if its bite was no more painful. Let's now look at research examining the influence of CS intensity on CR strength if you were bitten by both sizes of dogs (not necessarily at the same time).

Initial research indicated that the intensity of the CS does not affect CR strength. For example, D. A. Grant and Schneider (1948, 1949) reported that CS intensity did not influence the classical conditioning of the eyeblink response in humans. Carter (1941) and Wilcott (1953) showed similar results. However, more-recent research clearly demonstrates that CS intensity can affect the strength of the conditioned response. A greater CR strength produced by a more intense CS has been shown in dogs (G. W. Barnes, 1956), rabbits (Frey, 1969), rats (Kamin & Schaub, 1963), and humans (Grice & Hunter, 1964).

Why does a more intense CS only sometimes elicit a stronger CR? An intense CS does not produce an appreciably greater CR than does a weak CS when an animal or person experiences only a single stimulus (either weak or intense). However, if the animal experiences both the intense and the weak CS, the intense CS will produce a greater CR.

A study by Grice and Hunter (1964) shows the important influence of the type of training procedure on the magnitude of CS intensity effect. In Grice and Hunter's study, one group of human subjects received 100 eyelid conditioning trials of a loud (100-db) tone CS paired with an air puff UCS. A second group of subjects had a soft (50-db) tone CS paired with the air puff for 100 trials, and a third group was given 50 trials with the loud tone and 50 with the soft tone. Grice and Hunter's results show that CS intensity (loudness of tone) had a much greater effect on conditioning when a subject experienced both stimuli than when a subject was exposed to only the soft or the loud tone.

UCS Intensity. Recall Juliette's intense fear of darkness and men described in the chapter-opening vignette. The intensity of the attack was a critical factor in causing Juliette's extreme fear of darkness and men. Yet, not all experiences are as aversive as Juliette's attack. Suppose that you have the misfortune of being in an automobile accident. How much fear will arise the next time you get into a car? Research on UCS intensity and CR strength indicates that your level of fear will depend upon the intensity of the accident; the more severe the accident, the greater your fear of automobiles. Thus, if the accident was a minor one causing only slight discomfort, your subsequent fear will be minimal. A more severe accident will cause an intense fear.

The literature provides conclusive documentation that the strength of the CR increases with higher UCS intensity. To show the influence of UCS intensity on eyelid response conditioning, Prokasy, Grant, and Myers (1958) gave their human subjects either a 50-, 120-, 190-, or 260-mm intensity air puff UCS paired with a light CS. They found that the strength of the CR was directly related to the UCS intensity, that is, the more intense the air puff, the stronger the eyeblink CR (see Figure 4.6).

The Salience of the CS

Martin Seligman (1970) suggested that animals or humans have an evolutionary predisposition or **preparedness** to associate some particular stimulus with some specific unconditioned stimulus, but that other CS-UCS associations cannot be learned. The concept of **contrapreparedness** suggests that some stimuli, despite repeated CS-UCS pairings, cannot become associated with a particular UCS. The likelihood that a particular neutral stimulus will become able to elicit a conditioned response after pairing with an unconditioned stimulus reflects the salience of the

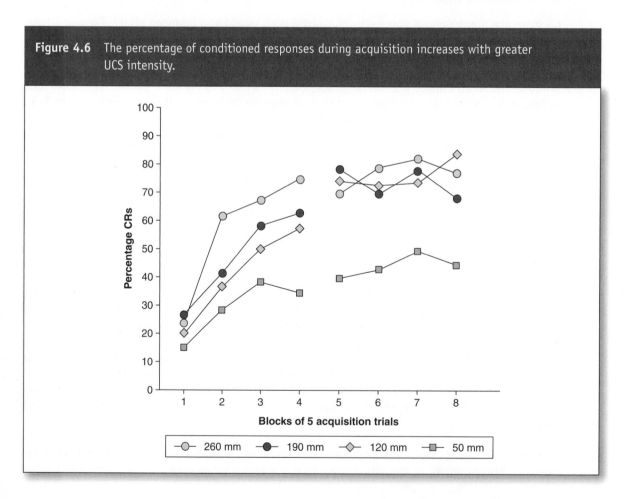

Figure 4.6   The percentage of conditioned responses during acquisition increases with greater UCS intensity.

neutral stimulus. Seligman proposed that preparedness makes a stimulus more salient. Thus, salient stimuli rapidly become associated with a particular unconditioned stimulus, while non-salient stimuli do not, despite repeated CS-UCS pairings.

Many, perhaps most, stimuli are not particularly salient or nonsalient; instead, most stimuli will gradually develop the ability to elicit a conditioned response as the result of conditioning experiences. In addition, **salience** is species dependent; that is, a stimulus may be salient to one species but not to another. Chapter 9 discusses the biological significance of stimulus salience in classical conditioning; we examine the influence of species-specific stimulus salience on the acquisition of a conditioned response in that chapter.

The Predictiveness of the CS

Robert Bolles (1972, 1979) proposed that contiguity alone is not sufficient for the development of a conditioned response. In Bolles's view, events must consistently occur together before we can acquire a conditioned response. A neutral stimulus may be paired with a UCS, but unless the neutral stimulus reliably predicts the occurrence of the UCS, it will not elicit the CR. Additionally, when two or more stimuli are presented with the UCS, only the most reliable predictor of the UCS becomes able to elicit the CR.

The following example illustrates the importance of **cue predictiveness** to the development of a conditioned response. Many parents threaten their children prior to punishment, yet their threats instill no fear, despite repeated threat (CS)–punishment (UCS) pairings. Why is parental threat ineffective? One likely reason is that these parents often threaten their children without punishing them. Under these circumstances, the threat is not a reliable predictor of punishment. Thus, its presentation will elicit little or no fear, even though the threat and punishment have frequently been experienced together. We next examine evidence showing that CR acquisition is impaired if the UCS is often presented without the CS. Then we review research that shows how presentations of the CS alone decrease the development of the CR.

Robert A. Rescorla (1940–   )

Rescorla received his doctorate from the University of Pennsylvania under the direction of Richard Solomon. He then taught at Yale University for 15 years before spending the last 29 years at the University of Pennsylvania. While at Penn, he served as chair of the Department of Psychology and dean of the College of Arts and Sciences. His research has contributed significantly to an understanding of the classical conditioning process. He received the Distinguished Scientist Contribution Award from the American Psychological Association in 1986.

UCS-Alone Presentations. Robert Rescorla's (1968) research demonstrates the influence of cue predictiveness in classical conditioning. After his rats learned to bar press for food, Rescorla divided the 2-hour training sessions into 2-minute segments. One of three events occurred in each segment: (1) a distinctive cue (CS; tone) was paired with a shock (UCS); (2) a shock was presented without the distinctive cue; or (3) neither tone nor shock occurred. Rescorla varied the likelihood that the shock would occur with (or without) the tone in each 2-minute segment. He found that the tone suppressed the bar-press response for food when the tone reliably predicted shock, indicating that the rats had formed an association between the tone and shock. However, the influence of the tone on the rats' behavior diminished as the frequency of the shock occurring without the tone increased. The tone had no effect on behavior when the shock occurred as frequently with no tone as it did when the tone was present. Figure 4.7 presents the results for the subjects that received a .4 CS-UCS probability (or CS paired with the UCS on 40% of the 2-minute segments).

Figure 4.7   Suppression of bar-pressing behavior during six test sessions (a low value indicates that the CS elicits fear and thereby suppresses bar pressing for food). The probability of the UCS occurring with the CS is 0.4 for all groups, and the values shown in the graph represent the probability that the UCS will occur alone in a 2-minute segment. When the two probabilities are equal, the CS does not elicit fear and, therefore, does not suppress the response. Only when the UCS occurs more frequently with than without the CS will the CS elicit fear and suppress bar pressing.

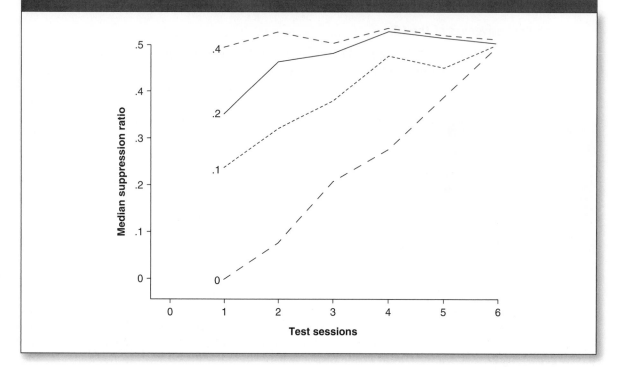

One important finding from Rescorla's data is that even with only a few pairings, the presentation of the tone produced intense fear and suppressed bar pressing if the shock was administered only with the tone. However, when the shock occurred without the tone as frequently as it did with it, no conditioning appeared to occur, even with a large number of tone-shock pairings. These results indicate that the predictability of a stimulus, not the number of CS-UCS pairings, determines an environmental event's ability to elicit a CR.

CS-Alone Presentations. The acquisition of a CR is also impaired or prevented when the CS is presented alone during conditioning. Many studies (see J. F. Hall, 1976) have documented the attenuation of conditioning when the CS is presented without, as well as with, the UCS. The level of conditioning depends upon the percentage of trials pairing the CS with the UCS: the greater the percentage, the greater the conditioning.

Hartman and Grant's (1960) study provides one example of the influence of the percentage of paired CS-UCS presentations on CR strength. All of Hartman and Grant's human subjects received 40 light (CS) and air puff (UCS) pairings. For subjects in the 25% group, the UCS occurred following 40 of the 160 CS presentations; for subjects in the 50% group, the air puff followed the tone on 40 of 80 CS presentations; for subjects in the 75% group, the UCS followed the CS on 40 of 54 trials; and for subjects in the 100% group, the air puff was presented after the light on 40 of 40 trials. Hartman and Grant's results showed that conditioning was strengthened as the percentage of trials that paired the CS with the UCS increased.

The Redundancy of the CS

Recall from the previous section the example of parental threats that fail to instill fear. In addition to a lack of predictiveness, another possible explanation for this lack of fear is that the child is already afraid when the threat is presented. Perhaps she is afraid of her parents; if so, parental presence (the CS) will interfere with the acquisition of fear to the threat, despite repeated threat-punishment pairings. For a cue to elicit a CR, and thereby influence behavior, Bolles (1978) suggested that the cue must not only predict the occurrence of the UCS but must also provide information not signaled by the other cues in the environment.

The research of Leon Kamin (1968) suggests that the presence of a predictive cue (CS_1) will prevent the development of an association between a second cue (CS_2) also paired with the UCS. To demonstrate the importance of relative cue predictability, Kamin presented to all of his subjects a distinctive cue (CS_1, a light) paired with a shock (UCS) eight times during the first phase of the study (see Figure 4.8). In the second phase of the study, the experimental group subjects received eight pairings of the light (CS_1), a new cue (CS_2, a tone), and shock (UCS). Kamin observed that while presentation of the light (CS_1) suppressed bar pressing, the tone cue (CS_2) alone had no influence on it. The light had become associated with the shock, while tone had apparently not. Kamin's results do not indicate that a tone cannot be associated with shock. Control group animals that received only tone (CS_2)–shock pairings during the second phase of the study showed strong suppression in response to the tone (CS_2). The prevention of conditioning to CS_2 by the CS_1 is called **blocking**.

Figure 4.8   The design of Kamin's blocking study. In Phase 1, the CS_1 (light) is paired with the UCS (shock); in the second phase, both the CS_1 and CS_2 (tone) are paired with the UCS (shock). The ability of the CS_2 (tone) to elicit fear is assessed during Phase 3.

Phase 1 CS_1 (Light)
          UCS (Shock)

Phase 2 CS_1 (Light)
          CS_2 (Tone)
          UCS (Shock)

Phase 3 CS_2 (Tone)   Test

- How did the intensity of the attack contribute to the conditioning of Juliette's fear of darkness?

- Was salience a factor in the conditioning of Juliette's fear? Predictiveness? Redundancy?

SECTION REVIEW

- Temporal contiguity affects the strength of conditioning; the longer the interval between the CS and UCS, the weaker the conditioning.

- An aversion to a flavor cue paired with illness is an exception; it can develop despite a lack of contiguity.

- An intense stimulus typically leads to a stronger CR, while some stimuli are more salient than others and therefore are more likely to elicit a CR following pairing with a UCS.

- The stimulus must also be a reliable predictor of the UCS; the more often the CS occurs without the UCS, or the UCS without the CS, the weaker the CR.

- The presence of a conditioned stimulus can prevent or block the development of a conditioned response to a new stimulus when both stimuli are paired with the UCS.

Extinction of the Conditioned Response

Earlier in the chapter, you learned that environmental stimuli, through their association with deprivation, food, or both, can acquire the ability to elicit hunger. Our conditioned responses typically have an adaptive function; the development of a conditioned hunger enables us to eat at regularly scheduled times. However, the conditioning of hunger can also be harmful. For example, people can eat too much and become obese.

Clinical research (Masters, Burish, Hollon, & Rimm, 1987) has revealed that overweight people eat in many situations (e.g., while watching television, driving, or at the movies). In order to lose weight, overweight people must restrict their food intake to the dining room (or the room where they usually eat), a process called **stimulus narrowing**. Yet, how can those who are overweight control their intake in varied environmental circumstances? One answer is through extinction, a method of eliminating a conditioned response. As the person's hunger response to varied environmental circumstances has developed through the classical conditioning process, so the conditioned hunger reaction can be extinguished through this process.

Extinction can also be effective for people who are extremely fearful of flying. Because fear of flying may be acquired through the classical conditioning process, extinction again represents a potentially effective method for eliminating the conditioned reaction. Extinction also represents a way that Juliette could eliminate her fear of nighttime darkness; that is, if she were to experience nighttime darkness (CS) in the absence of being attacked (UCR), her fear of nighttime darkness would be extinguished.

In the next section, we describe the extinction process and explain how extinction might eliminate a person's hunger reaction to an environmental event like watching television or reduce someone's fear reaction to flying in an airplane. We also explore the reason that extinction is not always an effective method of eliminating a conditioned response. Let's begin by looking at the extinction procedure.

Extinction Procedure

The **extinction of a conditioned response** will occur when the conditioned stimulus is presented without the unconditioned stimulus. The strength of the CR decreases as the number of CS-alone experiences increases, until eventually the CS elicits no CR (refer again to Figure 4.1).

Pavlov reported in his classic 1927 book that a classically conditioned salivation response in dogs could rapidly be extinguished by presenting the CS (tone) without the UCS (meat powder). Since Pavlov's initial observations, many psychologists have documented the extinction of a CR by using CS-alone presentations; the extinction process is definitely one of the most reliable conditioning phenomena.

Extinction is one way to eliminate a person's hunger reaction to environmental stimuli such as watching television. In this case, the person can eliminate the hunger response by repeatedly watching television without eating food (the UCS). However, people experiencing hunger-inducing circumstances are not always able to refrain from eating. Other behavioral techniques (e.g., aversive counterconditioning or reinforcement therapy) are often necessary to inhibit eating and, thereby, to extinguish the conditioned hunger response. The use of reinforcement is examined in Chapter 6; the use of punishment is discussed in Chapter 7.

Extinction can also eliminate fear of flying. Fear is diminished if a person flies and does not experience extreme plane movements. However, fear is not only an aversive emotion; it can also be an intense motivator of avoidance behavior. Thus, people who are afraid of flying may not be able to withstand the fear and inhibit their avoidance of flying. Similarly, Juliette probably would not be able to experience the nighttime darkness sufficiently to extinguish her fear. Other techniques (e.g., desensitization, response prevention, and modeling) also are available to eliminate fears. Desensitization is discussed later in this chapter, response prevention in Chapter 7, and modeling in Chapter 11.

How Rapidly Does a Conditioned Response Extinguish?

We have learned that many factors can facilitate or hinder the acquisition of the CR; we next discuss the variables that determine its rate of extinction.

The Strength of the CR. Hull (1943) envisioned the extinction process as a mirror image of acquisition; that is, the stronger the CS-CR bond, the more difficult it is to extinguish the CR. Thus, Hull assumed that the stronger the CR, the slower the extinction of that response. Although many studies have found that acquisition level does influence resistance to extinction, other research shows the relationship between the strength of the CR during acquisition and the rate of the extinction of that response is not a perfect correspondence. As J. F. Hall (1976) stated, one reason for this discrepancy is that the omission of the UCS during extinction changes the subject's motivational level from that which existed during acquisition. This altered motivation level makes extinction differ from acquisition, and thereby decreases the correlation between the CR acquisition level and the resistance to extinction.

The Influence of Predictiveness. In 1939, Humphreys examined how the percentage of trials in which the UCS followed the CS during acquisition influenced resistance to extinction. To study this effect, he conditioned an eyelid response in humans. During acquisition, subjects in Group 1 received 96 CS-UCS pairings and no CS-alone presentations; subjects in Group 2 received 48 CS-UCS pairings and 48 CS-alone presentations; and subjects in Group 3 were given 48 CS-UCS pairings and no CS-alone presentations. Humphreys discovered that in the subjects who received CS-UCS pairings on 50% of the trials (Group 2), the conditioned eyeblink response extinguished significantly more slowly than in those subjects given CS-UCS pairings on 100% of the trials (Groups 1 and 3). Humphrey's results, presented in Figure 4.9, show that the number of CS-UCS

Figure 4.9   The extinction of the CR as a function of the percentage of trials in which the UCS followed the CS during acquisition. Subjects in Groups 1 and 3 received CS-UCS pairings on 100% of the acquisition trials, and those in Group 2 on 50% of the acquisition trials. Resistance to extinction was greater with only partial pairings of CS and UCS during acquisition.

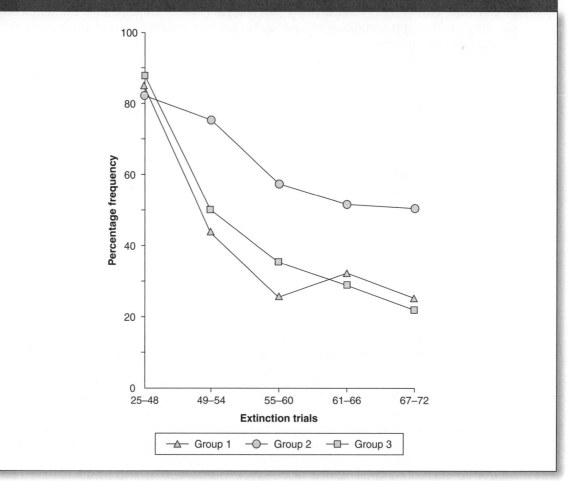

pairings during acquisition does not determine resistance to extinction; the rates of extinction were equal in animals given only 48 or 96 CS-UCS pairings. Instead, extinction was more rapid when the CS was more predictive of the UCS during acquisition.

Duration of CS Exposure. We have discovered that the strength of the conditioned response declines as the CS-alone experience increases. You might think that the number of CS-alone presentations would determine the level of extinction; that is, as the number of extinction trials increases, the strength of the CR declines. However, research clearly shows that the total duration of CS-alone exposure, not the number of extinction trials, determines the rate of extinction. These studies demonstrate that as the duration of CS-alone exposure increases, the strength of the CR weakens.

Let's briefly look at Shipley's study to see the influence of CS-alone duration on the extinction of a CR. Shipley (1974) initially trained water-deprived rats to lick a water tube to obtain liquid reinforcement. Following lick training, the animals received 20 exposures to a tone paired with electric shock. Extinction occurred following fear conditioning. Half the animals were given 25-second CS-alone exposures during extinction; the other half received 100-second CS-alone experiences during extinction. One-third of the animals in both the 25-second and the 100-second CS duration groups were given sufficient extinction experience that they received a total of 200 seconds of CS exposure; another third received 400 seconds, and the last third 800 seconds of exposure. For example, to have 200 total seconds of CS exposure, the animals given 25 seconds on each trial received 8 trials, compared to 2 trials for subjects receiving 100 seconds on each. Shipley reported that neither the number of CS-alone exposures nor the duration of each exposure affected the suppression of licking by the CS. Only the total duration of CS exposure during extinction determined the rate of extinction for the CR: The greater the length of the total CS exposure during extinction, the less suppression the tone produced (see Figure 4.10).

We have examined the variables that affect extinction rate; let's next look at the spontaneous recovery of responding following the extinction of a CR.

Spontaneous Recovery

Pavlov (1927) proposed that the extinction of a CR is caused by the inhibition of the CR. This **inhibition** develops because of the activation of a central inhibitory state that occurs when the CS is presented without the UCS. The continued presentation of the CS without the UCS strengthens this inhibitory state and acts to prevent the occurrence of the CR.

The initial inhibition of the CR during extinction is only temporary. According to Pavlov (1927), the arousal of the inhibitory state declines following the initial extinction. As the strength of the inhibitory state diminishes, the ability of the CS to elicit the CR returns (see Figure 4.1). The return

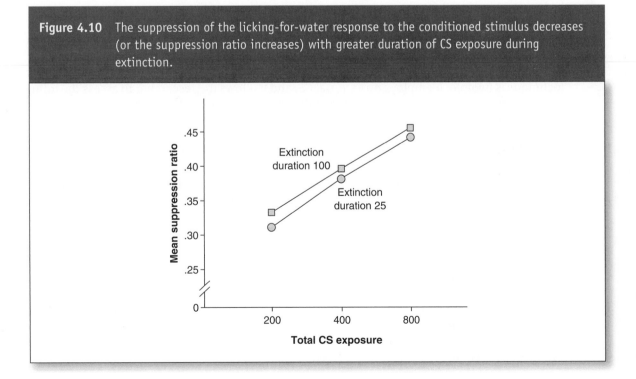

Figure 4.10 The suppression of the licking-for-water response to the conditioned stimulus decreases (or the suppression ratio increases) with greater duration of CS exposure during extinction.

of the CR following extinction is called **spontaneous recovery**. The continued presentation of the CS without the UCS eventually leads to the long-term suppression of the CR. The inhibition of a CR can become permanent as the result of conditioned inhibition; we discuss the conditioned inhibition process next.

Other Inhibitory Processes

We have learned that a temporary inhibition is involved in the extinction of a conditioned response. The inhibition of the CR can also become permanent, a process Pavlov (1927) called conditioned inhibition. There are also several other types of inhibition: external inhibition, latent inhibition, and inhibition of delay. Inhibition can be disrupted through a process called disinhibition.

Conditioned Inhibition

The temporary inhibition of a CR can become permanent. If a new stimulus (CS–) similar to the conditioned stimulus (CS+) is presented in the absence of the unconditioned stimulus, the CS– will act to inhibit a CR to the CS+. The process of developing a permanent inhibitor is called **conditioned inhibition**. Conditioned inhibition is believed to reflect the ability of the CS– to activate the inhibitory state, which can suppress the CR.

Consider the following example to illustrate the conditioned inhibition phenomenon. Recall our discussion of conditioned hunger: Because of past experiences, you became hungry when arriving home after your classes. Suppose that when you open the food pantry, you find it empty. It is likely that the empty food pantry would act to inhibit your hunger. This inhibitory property of the empty food pantry developed as a result of past pairings of the empty food pantry with an absence of food. Many studies have shown that associating new stimuli with the absence of the UCS causes these stimuli to develop permanent inhibitory properties. Let's examine one of these studies.

Rescorla and LoLordo (1965) initially trained dogs to avoid electric shock using a Sidman avoidance schedule. With this procedure, the dogs received a shock every 10 seconds unless they jumped over a hurdle dividing the two compartments of a shuttle box (see Chapter 7). If a dog avoided a shock, the next shock was postponed for 30 seconds. The advantage of this technique is twofold: It employs no external CS, and it allows the researcher to assess the influence of fear-inducing cues (CS+) and fear-inhibiting cues (CS–). After three days of avoidance conditioning, the dogs were locked in one compartment of the shuttle box and exposed on some trials to a 1200-hertz tone (CS+) and shock (UCS) and on other trials to a 400-hertz tone (CS–) without shock. Following conditioned inhibition training, the CS+ aroused fear and increased avoidance responses. In contrast, the CS– inhibited fear, causing the dogs to stop responding. These results indicate that the CS+ elicited fear and the CS– inhibited fear and that conditioned stimuli have an important influence on avoidance behavior. We examine that influence in Chapter 10.

External Inhibition

Pavlov (1927) suggested that inhibition could occur in situations other than extinction. In support of his theory, he observed that the presentation of a novel stimulus during conditioning reduces the strength of the conditioned response. Pavlov labeled this temporary activation of the inhibitory state **external inhibition**. The inhibition of the CR will not occur on a subsequent trial unless the novel stimulus is presented again; if the novel stimulus is not presented during the next trial, the strength of the conditioned response will return to its previous level.

Latent Inhibition

Preexposure to the CS impairs conditioning of the CR when the CS and UCS are later presented together. Lubow and Moore (1959) attributed the effect of CS preexposure to **latent inhibition**; that is, they argued that exposure to the CS prior to conditioning caused the CS to acquire inhibitory properties that subsequently interfered with excitatory conditioning when the CS and the UCS were paired. Mackintosh (1983) believes that CS preexposure leads to **learned irrelevance**—the subject learns that a stimulus does not predict any significant event. The subject therefore has difficulty recognizing the correlation between the stimulus and the UCS.

A number of studies (Baker & Mackintosh, 1977; Rescorla, 1971) have examined the effect of CS preexposure on the acquisition of conditioned inhibition. If the impact of CS preexposure resulted from inhibition, then CS preexposure should enhance conditioned inhibition training. However, these studies show that preexposure to a stimulus not only retards excitatory conditioning, it interferes with inhibitory conditioning. Thus, it appears that CS preexposure does not lead to the development of latent inhibition. We look more closely at the influence of CS preexposure on classical conditioning in Chapter 5.

You might be wondering why preexposure to nighttime darkness did not prevent Juliette from associating nighttime darkness with her attack. Lots of people have accidents at night and do not become afraid of nighttime darkness. In all likelihood, the severe intensity of the attack attenuated the CS preexposure effect, which resulted in Juliette associating the nighttime darkness and the attack. In support of this statement, De la Casa, Diaz, and Lubow (2005) reported that the CS preexposure effect was attenuated when an intense UCS was used during CS-UCS pairings.

Inhibition of Delay

There are many occasions when a short delay separates the CS and the UCS. For example, several minutes elapse from the time we enter a restaurant until we receive our food. Under these conditions, we inhibit our responses until just before we receive the food. (If we did begin to salivate as soon as we entered the restaurant, our mouths would be dry when we were served our food and our digestion impaired.) Further, the ability to inhibit the response until the end of the CS-UCS interval improves with experience. At first, we respond immediately when a CS is presented; our ability to withhold the CR improves with increased exposure to CS-UCS pairings.

Pavlov's (1927) classic research demonstrated that the dogs developed the ability to suppress the CR until the end of the CS-UCS interval, a phenomenon he labeled **inhibition of delay**. Other experimenters (Kimmel, 1965; Sheffield, 1965) have also shown that animals and humans can inhibit the CR until just before the UCS presentation. For example, Kimmel (1965) gave human subjects 50 trials of a red light (CS) paired with shock (UCS). The red light was presented 7.5 seconds prior to shock, and both terminated simultaneously. Kimmel reported that the latency of the galvanic skin response (GSR) increased with increased training trials (see Figure 4.11).

Disinhibition

Pavlov (1927) reported that the presentation of a novel stimulus during extinction leads to an increased strength of the conditioned response. The extinction process will proceed normally on the next trial if the novel stimulus is not presented. Pavlov labeled the process of increasing the strength of the CR as a result of presenting a novel stimulus during extinction **disinhibition**.

Kimmel's (1965) study shows the disinhibition phenomenon in an inhibition-of-delay paradigm. Kimmel observed that a novel tone presented with the CS disrupted the ability of the subjects to withhold the CR during the 7.5-second CS-UCS interval. Whereas the subjects exhibited the CR approximately 4.0 seconds after the CS was presented following 50 acquisition trials, the latency dropped to 2.3 seconds when the novel stimulus was presented along with the CS. These results

Figure 4.11   The average latency of GSR response to a conditioned stimulus, which preceded the unconditioned stimulus by 7.5 seconds, increases as the number of CS-UCS pairings increases.

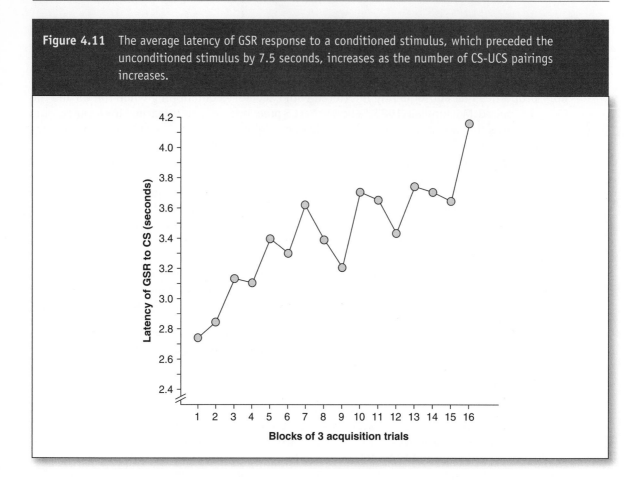

indicate that a novel stimulus can disrupt the inhibition of a CR. They also show that inhibition is responsible for the suppression of the CR observed in the inhibition-of-delay phenomenon.

BEFORE YOU GO ON

- How might Juliette's fear of nighttime darkness be extinguished?
- What problems might a clinical psychologist encounter trying to extinguish Juliette's fear?

SECTION REVIEW

- Extinction, or the presentation of the CS without the UCS, will cause a reduction in CR strength; with continued CS-alone presentations, the conditioned stimulus will eventually fail to elicit the CR.
- Spontaneous recovery is the return of a CR following an interval between extinction and testing without additional CS-UCS pairings.
- Conditioned inhibition develops when the CS+ is paired with the UCS and the CS– with the absence of the UCS.
- External inhibition occurs when a novel stimulus is experienced prior to the CS during acquisition. Inhibition of delay reflects the suppression of the CR until presentation of the UCS.

- These inhibitory processes can be disrupted during extinction by the presentation of a novel stimulus, causing a disinhibition effect and resulting in an increased CR strength.

A CR Without CS-UCS Pairings

Although many conditioned responses are acquired through direct experience, many stimuli develop the ability to elicit a conditioned response indirectly; that is, a stimulus that is never directly paired with the UCS nevertheless elicits a CR. For example, although many people with test anxiety have developed their fear because of the direct pairing of a test and failure, many others who have never failed an examination also fear tests. We will next discuss three ways—higher-order conditioning, sensory preconditioning, and vicarious conditioning—that a CR can develop without CS-UCS pairings. A fourth way—stimulus generalization—is explored further in Chapter 10.

Higher-Order Conditioning

You did poorly last semester in Professor Jones's class. Not only do you dislike Professor Jones, but you also dislike Professor Rice, who is Professor Jones's friend. Why do you dislike Professor Rice, with whom you have never had a class? **Higher-order conditioning** provides one likely reason for your dislike.

The Higher-Order Conditioning Process. Pavlov (1927) observed that following several CS_1-UCS pairings, presenting the CS_1 with another neutral stimulus (CS_2) enabled the CS_2 to elicit the CR. In one of Pavlov's studies using dogs, a tone (the beat of a metronome) was paired with meat powder. After this first-order conditioning, the tone was presented with a black square, but the meat powder was omitted. Following the black square CS_2-tone CS_1 pairings, the black square (CS_2) alone was able to elicit salivation. Pavlov called this conditioning process higher-order conditioning. (In this particular study, the higher-order conditioning was of the second order.) Figure 4.12 presents a diagram of the higher-order conditioning process.

Figure 4.12 The higher-order conditioning process. In Phase 1, the CS_1 (light) is paired with the UCS; in Phase 2, the CS_1 (light) and the CS_2 (buzzer) are presented together. The ability of the CS_2 to elicit the CR is evaluated in Phase 3.

Research on Higher-Order Conditioning. The strength of a CR acquired through higher-order conditioning is weaker than that developed through first-order conditioning. Pavlov (1927) discovered that a second-order CR is approximately 50% as strong as a first-order CR, and a third-order CR is very weak. He found it impossible to develop a fourth-order CR.

Psychologists since the time of Pavlov's original studies have not always been successful in producing a CR through higher-order conditioning. Rescorla's (Holland & Rescorla, 1975; Rescorla, 1973, 1978; Rizley & Rescorla, 1972) elegant analysis of the higher-order conditioning process demonstrates the reason for these failures. According to Rescorla, the problem with higher-order conditioning is that the pairing of CS_2-CS_1 without the UCS during the second phase of conditioning also represents a conditioned inhibition paradigm. Thus, not only are the CS_2-CS_1 pairings conditioning the excitation of the CR to the CS_2, but they are also conditioning the inhibition of the CR by pairing the compound stimulus (CS_2 & CS_1) in the absence of the UCS.

When will higher-order conditioning occur? Rescorla and his associates (Holland & Rescorla, 1975; Rescorla, 1973, 1978; Rizley & Rescorla, 1972) have discovered that conditioned excitation develops more rapidly than conditioned inhibition. Thus, with only a few pairings, a CS_2 will elicit the CR. However, as conditioned inhibition develops, CR strength declines until the CS_2 can no longer elicit the CR. At this time, the conditioned inhibition equals the conditioned excitation produced by the CS_2, and the presentation of the CS_2 will not elicit the CR.

Rizley and Rescorla's (1972) study illustrates the influence of the number of CS_2-CS_1 pairings on the strength of a higher-order conditioned fear. Rizley and Rescorla presented eight pairings of a 10-second flashing light (CS_1) paired with a 1 mA (one milliamp or one thousandth of an ampere) 0.5-second electric shock (UCS). Following first-order conditioning, the light (CS_1) was paired with a 1800-Hz tone (CS_2). Rizley and Rescorla discovered that the strength of the fear conditioned to the CS_2 increased with initial CS_2-CS_1 pairings, reaching a maximum strength after four pairings (see Figure 4.13). However, the intensity of fear elicited by the CS_2 declined with each additional pairing until the CS_2 produced no fear after 15 CS_2-CS_1 presentations. Holland and Rescorla (1975)

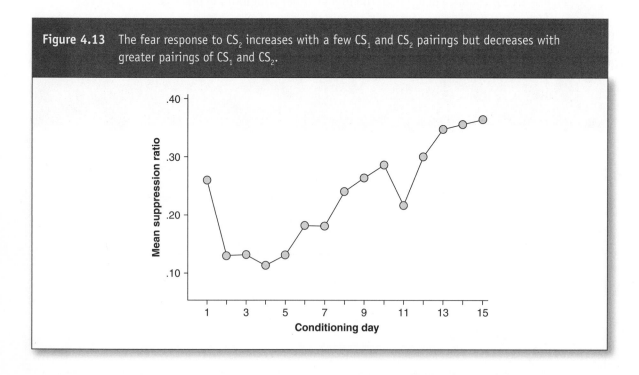

Figure 4.13   The fear response to CS_2 increases with a few CS_1 and CS_2 pairings but decreases with greater pairings of CS_1 and CS_2.

obtained similar results in measuring the effects of higher-order conditioning on the development of a conditioned appetitive response.

The observation that the strength of a second-order CR diminishes after the presentation of more than a few CS_2-CS_1 pairings does not indicate that higher-order conditioning has no role in real-world settings. For example, once a CR, such as fear, is conditioned to a CS_2, such as high places, the fear the CS_2 produces will motivate avoidance behavior, resulting in only a brief exposure to the CS_2. This rapid avoidance response will result in slow development of conditioned inhibition. The slow acquisition of conditioned inhibition permits the CS_2 to elicit fear for a very long, possibly indefinite, time.

Sensory Preconditioning

Consider the following example to illustrate the **sensory preconditioning** process. Your neighbor owns a large German shepherd; you associate the neighbor with his dog. As you are walking down the street, the dog bites you, causing you to become afraid of the dog. You may also develop a dislike for your neighbor as the result of your previous association of the neighbor with the dog.

The Sensory Preconditioning Process. In sensory preconditioning, two neutral stimuli, CS_1 and CS_2, are paired (see Figure 4.14). Following the association of CS_1 and CS_2 (dog and neighbor), CS_1 is presented with an unconditioned stimulus (bite). The CS_1-UCS pairing results in the ability of the CS_2, as well as the CS_1, to elicit the CR (fear). Thus, as a result of the initial CS_2-CS_1 association, the CS_2 is able to produce the CR even though it was never directly paired with the UCS.

Research on Sensory Preconditioning. Brogden's (1939) classic research represents an early successful sensory preconditioning study. In the first phase of Brogden's experiment, dogs in the experimental condition received 200 simultaneous pairings of a light and a buzzer. Control animals did not receive light-buzzer pairings. Following this initial conditioning, one of the cues (either the light or the buzzer) was presented with an electric shock to the dog's foot. Brogden reported that

Figure 4.14   The sensory preconditioning process. In Phase 1, the CS_1 (light) and CS_2 (bzzer) are paired; in Phase 2, the CS_1 (light) is presented with the UCS. The ability of the CS_2 (buzzer) to elicit the CR is evaluated in Phase 3.

presentation of the cue not paired with shock elicited the CR (leg flexion) in experimental animals but not in control animals. Although Brogden's results showed that a cue can develop the ability to elicit a CR through the sensory preconditioning process, the leg flexion CR to the CS_2 was weaker than the CR to the CS_1. Other researchers (see Kimble, 1961) during the 1940s and 1950s also observed that the magnitude of the sensory preconditioning effect was small.

Subsequent studies (Rizley & Rescorla, 1972; Tait, Marquis, Williams, Weinstein, & Suboski, 1969) indicate that the earlier studies did not employ the best procedures to produce a strong, reliable sensory preconditioning effect. These later studies found that the CS_2 will elicit a strong CR if, during the initial conditioning, (1) the CS_2 precedes the CS_1 by several seconds and (2) only a few CS_2-CS_1 pairings are used in order to prevent the development of learned irrelevance. Recall that when the CS is presented without the UCS prior to conditioning, it diminishes the conditioning of a CR when the CS and UCS are later paired during training.

Vicarious Conditioning

A person can develop an emotional response to a specific stimulus through direct experience; a person can also learn to respond to a particular stimulus after observing the experiences of others. For example, a person can become afraid of dogs after being bitten or after seeing another person being bitten. The development of a CS's ability to elicit a CR following such an observation is called **vicarious conditioning**. Although many emotional responses are clearly developed through direct conditioning experience, the research (see Bandura, 1971) also demonstrates that CS-CR associations can be acquired through vicarious conditioning experiences. Let's examine several studies which show the vicarious conditioning of a CR.

Research on Vicarious Conditioning. Berger's study (1962) demonstrates the vicarious conditioning of a conditioned fear reaction to a neutral stimulus. Berger's subjects listened to a neutral tone and then saw another person receiving an electric shock and exhibiting pain reactions (this other person, a confederate, pretended to be shocked and hurt). Berger found that subjects who repeatedly heard the tone and then witnessed the scene developed an emotional response to the tone. Bandura and Rosenthal (1966) also observed that vicarious conditioning of fear occurred when a subject observed another person being shocked.

One can also develop an emotional reaction by observing people fail at a task (Bandura, Blanchard, & Ritter, 1969; K. D. Craig & Weinstein, 1965). In the Craig and Weinstein study, subjects watched another person either succeed or fail at a motor task. The subjects who witnessed the other person failing showed a stronger conditioned stress reaction to the task than subjects who saw the other person succeed. This indicates we can learn to fear a task merely by watching others fail at it.

Vicarious conditioning is not unique to humans. Crooks (1967) reported that monkeys can develop a fear of certain objects after viewing the experience of another monkey with these objects. In Crooks's study, the monkeys heard a tape-recorded distress sound when a model monkey touched some particular objects; they did not hear the emotional reaction when the model touched other objects. Crooks discovered that the monkeys subsequently played with the objects not associated with distress but would not touch the objects that appeared to have hurt the other monkey. In a more recent study, Mineka, Davidson, Cook, and Keir (1984) found that monkeys learned to fear snakes after seeing another monkey react fearfully to a snake. In the absence of this experience, the monkeys showed no evidence of a fear of snakes.

The Importance of Arousal. We do not always develop a CR after watching the experiences of others. For vicarious conditioning to occur, we must respond emotionally to the scene we witness. Bandura and Rosenthal (1966) evaluated the level of vicarious CR conditioning as a function of the subject's arousal level during conditioning. They found that observers moderately aroused by seeing another person being shocked subsequently showed a strong autonomic reaction to the tone that was paired with the scene; subjects either minimally distressed or intensely upset by viewing the shock displayed only weak vicarious conditioning. The highly aroused subjects stopped attending to the person receiving the shock; Bandura and Rosenthal suggested that the subjects' altered attention reduced the association of the tone with shock. These results indicate that we must be aroused—but not too aroused—if we are to develop conditioned responses from observing the experiences of others.

We have learned that the strength of higher-order conditioning, sensory preconditioning, and vicarious conditioning is weaker than conditioning developed through the direct pairing of the CS and the UCS. Does this weaker conditioning mean that an intense CR cannot develop indirectly? The answer to this question is no. Several sources may contribute to the intensity of the conditioned response. For example, the combined influence of vicarious conditioning and sensory preconditioning may cause an intense conditioned reaction to the CS.

BEFORE YOU GO ON

- How might Juliette have developed a fear of darkness through higher-order conditioning? Sensory preconditioning? Vicarious conditioning?

- Would the intensity of Juliette's fear be equivalent to first-order and higher-order conditioning, sensory preconditioning, or vicarious conditioning?

SECTION REVIEW

- A conditioned stimulus can develop the ability to elicit the conditioned response indirectly, that is, without being directly paired with the UCS.

- Higher-order conditioning occurs when, after CS_1 and UCS pairings, a new stimulus (CS_2) is presented with the CS_1; the CS_1 and CS_2 occur together prior to CS_1 and UCS pairings with sensory preconditioning.

- In both higher-order conditioning and sensory preconditioning, the CS_2 elicits the CR even though it has never been directly paired with the UCS.

- A CR can be established through vicarious conditioning when one person observes another person experiencing the pairing of CS and UCS.

APPLICATIONS OF CLASSICAL CONDITIONING

We discuss two applications of classical conditioning in this chapter. The first involves the use of classical conditioning principles to eliminate phobias or irrational fears. This procedure, called systematic desensitization, has been used for over 40 years to eliminate the fears of people with phobias. The second application, which involves extinction of a person's craving for a drug, has only recently been used to treat drug addiction.

Systematic Desensitization

Recall that Juliette is extremely frightened of nighttime darkness. This fear causes Juliette to refuse invitations to go out at night. What can be done to allow Juliette to go out at night with minimal or no fear? **Systematic desensitization**, a therapy developed by Joseph Wolpe, would allow Juliette to no longer be afraid of darkness.

Systematic desensitization acts to inhibit fear and suppress phobic behavior (a **phobia** is an unrealistic fear of an object or situation). Wolpe's therapy can help people with extreme anxiety. His treatment is based on classical conditioning principles and represents an important application of classical conditioning. Let's examine this technique to discover how classical conditioning can alleviate extreme fear.

Original Animal Studies

Wolpe's therapy developed from his animal research. In an initial study (Wolpe, 1958), he shocked one group of cats in their home cages after they heard a buzzer. For the other cats, he paired the buzzer with food in the home cages and then shocked them. Both groups of cats later showed extreme fear of the buzzer; one indication of their fear was their refusal to eat when hearing the buzzer. Since fear inhibited eating, Wolpe reasoned that eating could—if sufficiently intense—suppress fear. As we learned in Chapter 1, counterconditioning is the process of establishing a response that competes with a previously acquired response.

Wolpe suggested that counterconditioning is a potentially effective way of treating human phobic behavior. He based this idea on three lines of evidence: (1) Sherrington's (1906) statement that an animal can only experience one emotional state at a time—a phenomenon Wolpe termed **reciprocal inhibition**; (2) M. C. Jones's (1924) report that she had successfully eliminated a young boy's conditioned fear of rabbits by presenting the feared stimulus (a rabbit) while the boy was eating (see Chapter 1); and (3) Wolpe's own research using cats.

Wolpe (1958) initially placed the cats—which had developed a conditioned fear of the buzzer and the environment in which the buzzer was experienced—in a cage with food; this cage was quite dissimilar to their home cage. He used the dissimilar cage, which produced only a low fear level due to little generalization (see Chapter 1), because the home cage would produce too intense a fear and therefore inhibit eating. Wolpe observed that the cats ate in the dissimilar cage and did not appear afraid either during or after eating. Wolpe concluded that in the dissimilar environment, the eating response had replaced the fear response. Once the fear in the dissimilar cage was eliminated, the cats were less fearful in another cage more closely resembling the home cage. The reason for this reduced fear was that the inhibition of fear conditioned to the dissimilar cage generalized to the second cage. Using the counterconditioning process with this second cage, Wolpe found that presentation of food in this cage quickly reversed the cats' fear.

Wolpe continued the gradual counterconditioning treatment by slowly changing the characteristics of the test cage until the cats were able to eat in their home cages without any evidence of fear. Wolpe also found that a gradual exposure of the buzzer paired with food modified the cats' fear response to the buzzer.

Clinical Treatment

Wolpe (1958) believed that human phobias could be eliminated in a manner similar to the one he used with his cats. He chose not to use eating to inhibit human fears, but instead used three classes of inhibitors: relaxation, assertion, and sexual responses. We limit our discussion in this chapter to the use of relaxation.

Wolpe's (1958) therapy using relaxation to counter human phobic behavior is called systematic desensitization. Basically, desensitization involves relaxing while imagining anxiety-inducing scenes. To promote relaxation, Wolpe used a series of muscle exercises Jacobson developed in 1938. These exercises involve tensing a particular muscle and then releasing this tension. Presumably, tension is related to anxiety, and tension reduction is relaxing. The patient tenses and relaxes each major muscle group in a specific sequence.

Relaxation is most effective when the tension phase lasts approximately 10 seconds and is followed by 10 to 15 seconds of relaxation for each muscle group. The typical procedure requires about 30 to 40 minutes to complete; however, later in therapy, patients need less time as they become more readily able to experience relaxation. Once relaxed, patients are required to think of a specific word (for example, *calm*). This procedure, which Russell and Sipich (1973) labeled **cue-controlled relaxation**, promotes the development of a conditioned relaxation response that enables a word cue to elicit relaxation promptly; the patient then uses the cue to inhibit any anxiety occurring during therapy.

The desensitization treatment consists of four separate stages: (1) the construction of the anxiety hierarchy; (2) relaxation training; (3) counterconditioning, or the pairing of relaxation with the feared stimulus; and (4) an assessment of whether the patient can successfully interact with the phobic object. In the first stage, patients are instructed to construct a graded series of anxiety-inducing scenes related to their phobia. A 10- to 15-item list of low-, moderate-, and high-anxiety scenes is typically employed. The patient writes descriptions of the scenes on index cards and then ranks them from those that produce low anxiety to those that produce high anxiety.

Paul (1969) identified two major types of hierarchies: thematic and spatial-temporal. In a **thematic hierarchy**, the scenes are related to a basic theme. Table 4.1 presents a hierarchy detailing the anxiety an insurance salesman experienced when anticipating interactions with coworkers or clients. Each scene in the hierarchy is somewhat different, but all are related to his fear of possible failure in professional situations.

Table 4.1   Thematic Hierarchy

Level	Scene
1	In your office with an agent, R.C., discussing a prospective interview. The client in question is stalling on his payment, and you must tell R.C. what to do.
2	Monday morning working in your office. In a few minutes you will attend the regularly scheduled sales meeting. You are prepared for the meeting.
3	Conducting an exploratory interview with a prospective client.
4	Sitting at home. The telephone rings.
5	Anticipating returning a call from the district director.
6	Anticipating returning a call from a stranger.
7	Entering the Monday sales meeting unprepared.
8	Anticipating a visit from the regional director.
9	Listening as a fellow agent requests a joint visit with a client.
10	Conducting a joint visit with a fellow agent.
11	Attempting to close a sale.
12	Thinking about attending an agents and managers' meeting.
13	Thinking of contacting a client who should have been contacted earlier.
14	Thinking about calling a prospective client.
15	Thinking about the regional director's request for names of prospective agents.
16	Alone, driving to prospective client's home.
17	Calling a prospective client.

Note: In the fear hierarchy, a higher level represents greater fear.

A **spatial-temporal hierarchy** is based on phobic behavior in which the intensity of fear is determined by distance (either physical or temporal) to the phobic object. The test anxiety hierarchy shown in Table 4.2 indicates that the level of anxiety is related to the proximity to exam time.

Table 4.2	Spatial-Temporal Hierarchy
Level	**Scene**
1	Four days before an examination.
2	Three days before an examination.
3	Two days before an examination.
4	One day before an examination.
5	The night before an examination.
6	The examination paper lies face down before the student.
7	Awaiting the distribution of examination papers.
8	Standing before the unopened doors of the examination room.
9	In the process of answering an examination paper.
10	On the way to the university on the day of the examination.

Note: In the fear hierarchy, a higher level represents greater fear.

We need to point out one important aspect of the hierarchy presented in Table 4.2. Perhaps contrary to your intuition, this student experienced more anxiety en route to the exam than when in the test area. Others may have a different hierarchy; when taking the exam, they experience the most fear. As each individual's phobic response is highly idiosyncratic and dependent on that person's unique learning experience, a hierarchy must be specially constructed for each person. Some phobias require a combination of thematic and spatial-temporal hierarchies. For example, a person with a height phobia can experience varying levels of anxiety at different places and at different distances from the edges of these places.

After the hierarchy is constructed, the patient learns to relax. Relaxation training follows the establishment of the hierarchy to prevent the generalization of relaxation to the hierarchical stimuli and thereby preclude an accurate assessment of the level of fear to each stimulus. The counterconditioning phase of treatment begins following relaxation training. The patient is instructed to relax and imagine as clearly as possible the lowest scene on the hierarchy. Since even this scene elicits some anxiety, Masters, Burish, Hollon, and Rimm (1987) suggested that the first exposure be quite brief (5 seconds). The duration of the imagined scene can then be slowly increased as the counterconditioning progresses.

It is important that the patient not become anxious while picturing the scene; otherwise, additional anxiety, rather than relaxation, will be conditioned. The therapist instructs the patient to signal when experiencing anxiety, and the therapist terminates the scene. After a scene has ended, the patient is instructed to relax. The scene can again be visualized when relaxation has been reinstated. If the individual can imagine the first scene without any discomfort, the next scene in the hierarchy is imagined. Counterconditioning at each level of the hierarchy continues until the patient can imagine the most aversive scene without becoming anxious.

Clinical Effectiveness

The last phase of desensitization evaluates the therapy's success. To test the effectiveness of desensitization, the individual must encounter the feared object. The success of desensitization as a treatment for phobic behavior is quite impressive. Wolpe (1958) reported that 90% of 210 patients showed significant improvement with desensitization, compared to a 60% success rate when psychoanalysis was used. The comparison is more striking when one considers that desensitization produced a rapid extinction of phobic behavior—according to Wolpe (1976), a range of 12 to 29 sessions was effective—compared to the longer length of treatment (3 to 5 years) necessary for psychoanalysis to cure phobic behavior. Although Lazarus (1971) reported that some patients showed a relapse 1 to 3 years after therapy, the renewed anxiety could be readily reversed with additional desensitization.

The range of phobias successfully extinguished by desensitization is impressive: fears of heights, driving, snakes, dogs, insects, tests, water, flying, rejection by others, crowds, enclosed places, and injections are a few in a long list. In addition, desensitization apparently can be used with any behavior disorder initiated by anxiety. For instance, desensitization should help treat an alcoholic whose drinking occurs in response to anxiety. In general, research has demonstrated that systematic desensitization is a very effective way to successfully treat phobic behavior (Hersen & Rosqvist, 2005).

However, systematic desensitization therapy requires that patients be able to vividly imagine the fearful scene. Approximately 10% of patients cannot imagine the phobic object sufficiently to experience anxiety (Masters et al., 1987); for these patients, another form of therapy is needed. Further, Rachman (1990) observed that therapy is more effective when a patient confronts a real, rather than imagined, phobic object. Imagined scenes are used in the initial phase of systematic desensitization in order to control the duration of exposure and prevent the association of the phobic objects with anxiety. You might be wondering whether a patient can confront a phobic object but be able to control the duration of exposure to that object. Fortunately, modern technology appears to have made this possible. What is that technology? Perhaps you guessed: the use of a virtual reality environment.

Rothbaum, Hodges, Kooper, and Opdyke (1995) evaluated whether graded exposure to height-related stimuli in a virtual reality environment could effectively treat acrophobia. The researchers constructed a number of height-related stimuli, such as standing on a bridge, standing on a balcony, or riding in a glass elevator. The height of the stimuli varied: The bridge could be up to 80 meters above water, while the balcony or elevator could be as high as 49 floors.

Rothbaum et al. (1995) reported that a graded virtual reality exposure to height-related stimuli was an effective treatment for acrophobia. Following treatment, patients were able to stand on a real bridge or balcony or ride in a glass elevator. Similarly, Rothbaum, Hodges, Anderson, Price, and Smith (2002) reported that a virtual reality environment was as effective as a standard exposure treatment for fear of flying, while Garcia-Palacious, Hoffman, Carlin, Furness, and Botella (2002) found that a virtual reality environment can be used to treat a spider phobia. Virtual reality is a relatively new technology. As the technology improves, it seems highly likely that its use in systematic desensitization treatment will become more widespread.

Our discussion indicates that systematic desensitization is a very effective treatment for fears. It seems highly likely that should Juliette seek systematic desensitization treatment, her fear of nighttime darkness would be eliminated and she could then go out at night.

Explorations for the Future

Desensitization is a well-established application of classical conditioning. Researchers are developing new applications based on current research; we look at one of these new applications in this section.

In Chapter 3, we discovered that animals and people experience withdrawal following a drug exposure. The withdrawal from the drug can be intense and can act to motivate continued use of the drug. An opponent withdrawal state can be conditioned to the environmental cues surrounding drug administration, and exposure to these cues can produce withdrawal as a conditioned response. The **conditioned withdrawal response** produces a drug craving, which then motivates use of the drug; the greater the intensity of the withdrawal response, the greater the craving and the higher the likelihood of continued drug use.

Can an environmental stimulus produce withdrawal symptoms? Wikler and Pescor (1967) demonstrated that the conditioned withdrawal reaction can be elicited even after months of abstinence. They repeatedly injected dogs with morphine when the animals were in a distinctive cage. The addicted dogs were then allowed to overcome their unconditioned withdrawal reaction in their home cages and were not injected for several months. When placed in the distinctive cages again, these dogs showed a strong withdrawal reaction, including excessive shaking, hypothermia, loss of appetite, and increased emotionality.

Why is it so difficult for an addict to quit using drugs? Whenever an addict encounters the cues associated with a drug (e.g., the end of a meal for a smoker), a conditioned withdrawal will be elicited. The experience of this withdrawal may motivate the person to resume taking the drug. According to Solomon (1980), conditioned withdrawal reactions are what make eliminating addictions so difficult.

Any substance abuse treatment needs to pay attention to conditioned withdrawal reactions. To ensure a permanent cure, an addict must not only stop "cold turkey" and withstand the pain of withdrawal, he or she must also extinguish the conditioned withdrawal reactions that all of the cues associated with the addictive behavior produce. Ignoring these conditioned withdrawal reactions increases the likelihood that addicts will eventually return to their addictive behavior. Consider the alcoholic who goes to a bar just to socialize. Even though this alcoholic may have abstained for weeks, the environment of the bar can produce a conditioned withdrawal reaction and motivate this person to resume drinking.

Can exposure to drug-related stimuli enhance an addict's ability to avoid relapse? Charles O'Brien and his colleagues (Childress, Ehrman, McLellan, & O'Brien, 1986; Ehrman, Robbins, Childress, & O'Brien, 1992) have addressed this issue. Childress et al. (1986) repeatedly exposed cocaine addicts to the stimuli they associated with drug taking. Extinction experiences for these cocaine abusers involved watching videotapes of their "cook-up" procedure, listening to audiotapes of cocaine talk, and handling their drug paraphernalia. Childress et al. reported that their patients' withdrawal responses and craving for drugs decreased as a result of exposure to drug-related cues. Further, the extinction treatment significantly reduced the resumption of drug use.

Other researchers (S. T. Higgins, Budney, & Bickel, 1994; Kasvikis, Bradley, Powell, Marks, & Gray, 1991) also have reported that exposure to drug-related stimuli reduced drug craving and consumption. However, the therapeutic success seems to be relatively short-lived; that is, drug craving returned with a subsequent reinstatement of drug use (O'Brien, Childress, Ehrman, & Robbins, 1998).

Why does drug craving and drug use return? Di Ciano and Everitt (2002) suggested that spontaneous recovery of drug craving occurs following extinction and results in the relapse of drug taking seen in treatment studies. To support this view, they trained rats to self-administer cocaine and then extinguished the cues present during cocaine consumption. After a 7-day extinction period, rats were tested after either 1 or 28 days. While the level of response to cocaine was significantly reduced 1 day after extinction, responding significantly increased on the 28-day test. Di Ciano and Everitt assumed that spontaneous recovery of drug craving (CR) was responsible for the resumption of drug use on the 28-day test. They also suggest that for an extinction procedure to be more effective, the spontaneous recovery of drug craving needs to be eliminated, perhaps by repeated extinction trials over a longer time.

BEFORE YOU GO ON

- How might systematic desensitization be used to overcome Juliette's fear of nighttime darkness?

- What might prevent systematic desensitization from eliminating Juliette's fear of nighttime darkness?

SECTION REVIEW

- Systematic desensitization is a graduated counterconditioning procedure to eliminate phobias.

- The patient first constructs a hierarchy of feared stimuli; relaxation is then paired with the feared stimuli.

- The patient then imagines the least feared stimulus for a brief time, with the time increased until the feared stimulus can be imagined without any discomfort, and continues until the patient can imagine the most aversive stimulus without becoming anxious.

- The success of desensitization is considerable; the elimination of fear of heights, driving, tests, flying, and enclosed places are a few examples of its successful application.

- As part of a treatment program for addiction, exposure to the stimuli associated with drug use can extinguish the conditioned craving and reduce the likelihood of continued use.

CRITICAL THINKING QUESTIONS

1. Classical conditioning has a significant influence on human emotions. Identify your emotional response to several environmental events. Describe the experiences that led to the establishment of these emotional responses. Indicate the CS, CR, UCS, and UCR in these examples. How have these conditioned emotional responses affected your life?

2. Tamiko becomes extremely anxious prior to giving a speech. Mia feels only slightly tense when speaking in public. Using the principles presented in the text, suggest possible explanations for the differences in fear Tamiko and Mia show.

3. Greg has an intense desire to smoke cigarettes. His nicotine craving occurs after a meal, a class, or a movie, as well as at other times. Describe the process responsible for Greg's craving. How might Greg eliminate his craving? What problems might Greg encounter? How can he avoid these problems?

KEY TERMS

asymptotic level

blocking

conditioned inhibition

conditioned reflex

conditioned withdrawal response

contrapreparedness

cue-controlled relaxation

delayed conditioning

external inhibition

eyeblink conditioning

flavor aversion

inhibition

latent inhibition

phobia

reciprocal inhibition

sensory preconditioning

spatial-temporal hierarchy

stimulus narrowing

systematic desensitization

thematic hierarchy

unconditioned reflex

unconditioned stimulus

vicarious conditioning

backward conditioning

conditioned emotional response

conditioned response (CR)

conditioned stimulus (CS)

contiguity

CS-UCS interval

cue predictiveness

disinhibition

extinction of a conditioned response

fear conditioning

higher-order conditioning

inhibition of delay

learned irrelevance

preparedness

salience

simultaneous conditioning

spontaneous recovery

suppression ratio

temporal conditioning

trace conditioning

unconditioned response (UCR)

CHAPTER 5

Theories of Classical Conditioning

HE NEVER SAW IT COMING

Clarence started dating Felicia several months ago. Their very different personalities—Clarence is quiet and shy, and Felicia is outgoing and social—did not keep them from becoming close. Felicia introduced Clarence to a social life he had never before experienced; they enjoyed romantic dinners and exciting parties. Felicia was an excellent dancer, which made dancing fun. However, Clarence was not used to partying late. He had to get up early for work and felt drained the entire day after a late night out. The late nights did not seem to bother Felicia, and she was wide-awake the next day, even with only a few hours of sleep. Last month, Felicia started to drink a lot of alcohol. Clarence rarely drinks more than a beer or two, and he was quite concerned about Felicia's drinking. She called him a "lightweight" for only having one or two drinks. Clarence did not mind the teasing, but he really did not want to drink much. He thought he was in love with Felicia; however, he was troubled by some of her actions toward him. The last several times they were out, Felicia became angry and verbally abusive to him for no apparent reason. The verbal comments were very harsh, and Clarence was hurt. The next day, Felicia apologized for her behavior and promised not to be nasty again. Yet the next time that they went out, Felicia again became angry and abusive. Clarence could not figure out why she became hostile, and he considered breaking off their relationship. He mentioned his concerns to his friend Jared. To Clarence's surprise, Jared said he knew why Felicia became hostile: The alcohol was to blame. Jared also said he felt frightened when Felicia started to drink. Clarence was not sure that Jared was right, but he decided he would pay close attention to the amount Felicia drank and whether she became hostile afterward. He was hopeful that this was the reason for her hostility, but he was not sure what he would do if it was.

Why did Clarence fail to see the relationship between Felicia's drinking and her hostility? The answer may lie in a phenomenon called the CS preexposure effect. When a stimulus is first presented without a UCS, subsequent conditioning is impaired when that stimulus is presented with the UCS. Clarence had seen people drinking without becoming aggressive, and this experience may have caused him to fail to recognize the relationship between Felicia's drinking and her hostility. We examine the CS preexposure effect later in the chapter; our discussion may tell us what caused Clarence to fail to associate the sight of Felicia's drinking (CS) with her hostility toward him (UCS).

Clarence's friend Jared recognized the relationship between Felicia's drinking and her hostility. As a result of this recognition, Jared became frightened when he saw Felicia drinking. One of the main questions we address in this chapter is why Jared was able to associate Felicia's drinking and her hostility. We answer this question by examining the nature of classical conditioning.

Pavlov (1927) conducted an extensive investigation of the principles governing the acquisition and extinction of a conditioned response. During the past 30 years, many studies have examined both how conditioned responses are acquired and whether the CR is similar or different from the UCR. This research has challenged Pavlov's assumptions regarding both the nature of conditioning and the conditioned response. New theories have subsequently emerged to explain these recent research findings.

THE NATURE OF THE CONDITIONED RESPONSE

One important question in classical conditioning concerns the nature of the conditioned response. As we learned in the last chapter, when the UCS is food, both the CR and UCR is salivation. This observation seems to indicate that the CR is just the UCR elicited by the CS rather than the UCS. Yet, when electric shock is used as the UCS, the CR is fear and the UCR pain, an observation that seems to suggest that the CR is a behavior distinctively different from the UCR. In this section, we address the issue whether the CR is the same or a different response than the UCR.

Stimulus-Substitution Theory

Pavlov (1927) suggested that conditioning enables the conditioned stimulus to elicit the same response as the unconditioned stimulus. Why would Pavlov assume that the CR and UCR were the same response? Pavlov was observing the same digestive responses (e.g., saliva, gastric juices, insulin release) as both the CR and UCR. The fact that both the CS and UCS elicit similar responses logically leads to the conclusion that the CR and UCR are the same.

How does the CS become able to elicit the same response as the UCS? According to Pavlov (1927), the presentation of the UCS activates one area of the brain. Stimulation of the neural area responsible for processing the UCS leads to the activation of a brain center responsible for generating the UCR. In Pavlov's view, an innate, direct connection exists between the UCS brain center and the brain center controlling the UCR; this neural connection allows the UCS to elicit the UCR.

How might the connection between the CS and CR develop? When the conditioned stimulus is presented, it excites a distinct brain area. When the UCS follows the CS, the brain centers responsible for processing the CS and UCS are active at the same time. According to Pavlov (1927), the simultaneous activity in two neural centers leads to a new functional neural pathway between the active centers. The establishment of this neural connection causes the CS to activate the neural center processing the CS, which then arouses the UCS neural center. Activity in the UCS center leads to activation in the response center for the UCR, which then allows the CS to elicit the CR. In other words, Pavlov is suggesting that the CS becomes a substitute for the UCS and elicits the same response as the UCS; that is, the CR is the UCR, only elicited by the CS instead of the UCS. Figure 5.1 provides an illustration of Pavlov's **stimulus-substitution theory** of conditioning.

Pavlov's stimulus-substitution theory proposes that the CS elicits the CR by way of the UCS. Holland and Rescorla's (1975) study provides strong support for this view. In their study, two groups of food-deprived rats received tone CS and food UCS pairings. After conditioning, one group of rats was fed until satiated, while the other group remained food deprived. The animals then received a series of CS-alone extinction trials. Holland and Rescorla reported that the CS

Figure 5.1   Pavlov's stimulus-substitution theory of classical conditioning. (a) The UCS activates the UCS brain center, which elicits the UCR; (b) the CS arouses the area of the brain responsible for processing it; (c) a connection develops between the CS and UCS brain centers with contiguous presentation of CS and UCS; and (d) the CS elicits the CR as a result of its ability to activate the UCS brain center.

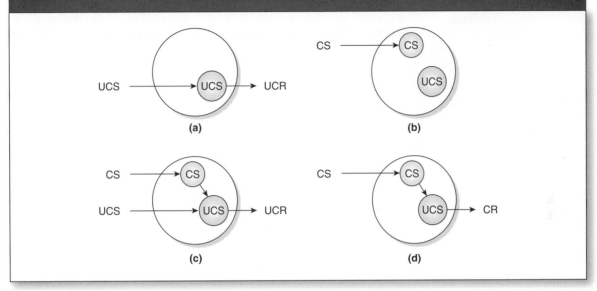

elicited a weaker CR in the satiated than in the hungry rats. Why did the removal of food deprivation reduce the strength of the CR? According to Holland and Rescorla, food satiation reduces the value of food and thereby reduces the ability of the UCS to elicit the UCR. The reduced value of the UCS causes the CS to elicit a weaker CR.

The Conditioning of an Opponent Response

While the conditioned and unconditioned responses are often similar, in many cases, they seem dissimilar. For example, the conditioned response of fear differs in many ways from the unconditioned response of pain. While both involve internal arousal, the sensory aspects of the two responses are not the same. Warner's 1932 statement that "whatever response is grafted onto the sound (CS), it is not snipped from the shock (UCS) (p. 108) indicates a recognition of CR and UCR differences.

The research of Shepard Siegel and his colleagues represents the most impressive accumulation of evidence suggesting that the conditioned and unconditioned responses are different (McDonald & Siegel, 2004; Siegel, 1978, 1991, 2001, 2005; Siegel, Baptista, Kim, McDonald, & Weiss-Kelly, 2000; Siegel, Hinson, & Krank, 1978; Siegel & Ramos, 2002). In several of their studies, Siegel and his associates used morphine as the unconditioned stimulus (Siegel, 1978; Siegel et al., 1978). **Analgesia**, or reduced sensitivity to pain, is one unconditioned response to morphine. Siegel reported that the conditioned response to stimuli, such as lights or tones, that have been paired with morphine is **hyperalgesia**, or an increased sensitivity to pain.

How did Siegel know that a conditioned stimulus associated with morphine makes an event more unpleasant? To illustrate both the analgesic effect of morphine and the hyperalgesic effect of a

Shepard Siegel (1940–   )

Siegel received his doctorate from Yale University under the direction of Allan Wagner. He has subsequently taught at McMaster University in Canada for the last 35 years. His research has contributed significantly to understanding the role of classical conditioning in the development of drug tolerance, drug withdrawal, and drug addiction. He was awarded the D. O. Hebb Distinguished Scientific Contribution Award by the American Psychological Association in 2002 and the Donald O. Hebb Distinguished Contribution Award by the Canadian Society for Brain, Behaviour and Cognitive Sciences in 2006.

stimulus paired with morphine, Siegel placed a rat's paw on a hot plate and measured how long it took the rat to remove its paw. He observed that rats injected with morphine (the UCS) took longer to remove their paws from the heated plate than did animals that had not received the morphine injection. The light or tone paired with morphine, by contrast, caused the rats to remove their paws more quickly than did animals that had been presented with a stimulus not paired with the morphine (UCS).

Siegel (1975) also found that while the UCR to insulin is hypoglycemia, the CR to a stimulus paired with insulin is hyperglycemia. Additional studies reported that the UCR to alcohol is hypothermia, while the CR to a stimulus associated with alcohol is hyperthermia (Crowell, Hinson, & Siegel, 1981; Le, Poulos, & Cappell, 1979).

Recall from the chapter-opening vignette that Felicia became hostile when drinking alcohol. Classical conditioning might explain why alcohol consumption made Felicia hostile. Alcohol consumption has an analgesic effect (UCR) (Chester, Price, & Froehlich, 2002). Conditioned hyperalgesia would increase Felicia's sensitivity to painful events and as we will discover in Chapter 7, cause her hostility.

This research suggests not only that the CR can be the opposite of the UCR, but also that conditioning is responsible, at least in part, for the phenomenon of **drug tolerance** (Siegel, 2001; Siegel et al., 2000). Tolerance to a drug develops when, with repeated use of a drug, the effectiveness of the drug declines and larger doses are necessary to achieve the same pharmacological effect (see Chapter 3). According to Siegel, tolerance represents the conditioning of a response that is opposite to the unconditioned drug effects. Thus, the environmental cues present during drug administration antagonize the drug's action and result in a lower pharmacological reaction to the drug.

The interoceptive cues that occur early in the morphine drug experience also can become able to elicit a conditioned hyperalgesia response (Sokolowska, Siegel, & Kim, 2002). An **interoceptive cue** is a stimulus originating within the body that is related to the functioning of an internal organ or the receptors that internal organ activates. According to Sokolowska et al., the association of these interoceptive early-onset cues plays an important role in the development of tolerance to morphine.

Two lines of evidence support the idea that conditioning plays a role in tolerance to morphine. First, Siegel (1977) found that exposure to the CS (environment) without the UCS (drug), once the association has been conditioned, results in the extinction of the opponent CR; the elimination of the response to the CS results in a stronger reaction to the drug itself (see Figure 5.2). Second, Siegel et al. (1978) reported that changing the stimulus context in which the drug is administered can also induce an increased response to the drug. The novel environment does not elicit a CR opposite to the drug's unconditioned effect; in turn, the absence of the opposing CR results in a stronger unconditioned drug effect. A change in context also has been reported to lead to a reduced tolerance to alcohol (Larson & Siegel, 1998) and caffeine (Siegel, Kim, & Sokolowska, 2003). And a reduced tolerance can lead to a heightened drug response. Siegel (1984) reported that 7 out of 10 victims of a drug overdose recalled that a change in environment was associated with the drug overdose, while Siegel, Hinson, Krank, and McCully (1982) observed that a drug overdose typically occurs when an addict takes his or her usual drug dose, but in an unfamiliar environment. Without the

Figure 5.2   Tolerance develops to morphine injection (as indicated by lowered pain threshold) during first 6 injection sessions. The presentation of 12 placebo sessions (injections without morphine) in M-P-M (morphine-placebo-morphine) group animals extinguished the conditioned opponent response and reduced tolerance (as indicated by an increased pain threshold). Animals given a 12-day rest period between morphine injections (M-Rest-M group) showed no change in pain threshold from the sixth to the seventh session.

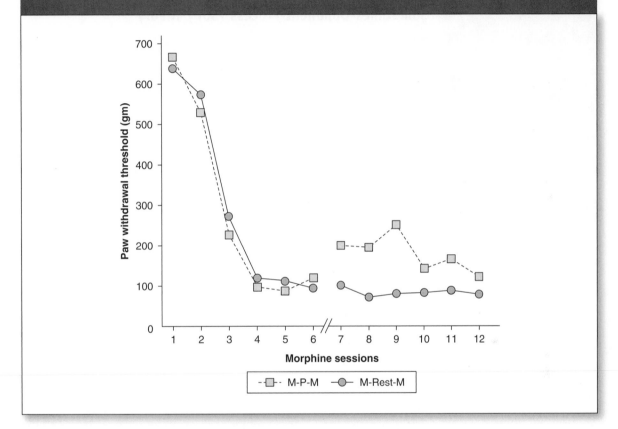

protective conditioned opposing response, the effect of the drug is increased, resulting in the overdose (Siegel & Ramos, 2002).

The conditioned opponent response not only contributes to the development of drug tolerance, but also to the withdrawal symptoms that lead to drug addiction (McDonald & Siegel, 2004; Siegel, 2005). Contextual cues associated with drug exposure have been shown to produce the withdrawal symptoms when the contextual cues are experienced without the drug (Siegel 2005). McDonald and Siegel (2004) reported that drug-onset cues, or pharmacological cues that signal the drug's effect, can produce a **conditioned withdrawal response**. They found that after rats had been injected on a number of occasions with 50 mg/kg of morphine, a 5 mg/kg morphine injection produced the same withdrawal symptoms that the larger dose previously produced. According to Siegel, the reason why exposure to small drug doses have frequently been associated with relapse to drug use is that even a small exposure to the drug will produce the same symptoms as a larger dose and thereby, motivate a resumption of drug use. In support of this view, Zironi, Burattini, Aicardi, and Janak (2006) found that exposure to the contextual cues associated with alcohol

Allan R. Wagner (1934–   )

Wagner received his doctorate from the University of Iowa under the direction of Kenneth Spence. He has taught at Yale University for the last 51 years. While at Yale, he has served as chair of the Department of Philosophy and the Department of Psychology and as the director of the Division of Social Sciences. His research has contributed significantly to an understanding of the nature of the classical conditioning process. He was awarded the Distinguished Scientific Contribution Award by the American Psychological Association in 1998.

consumption produced increased lever-press responding in rats that had self-administered alcohol when alcohol was not available.

While the conditioned response is sometimes dissimilar to the UCR, it is also sometimes similar to the UCR. Why is this? Allan Wagner's **sometimes-opponent-process (SOP) theory** provides one answer to this question; we look at his view next.

Sometimes-Opponent-Process (SOP) Theory

Recall our discussion of Solomon and Corbit's (1974) opponent-process theory in Chapter 3. We learned that an event elicits not only a primary affective response, but also a secondary opponent affective reaction. Wagner's SOP theory (Brandon, Vogel, & Wagner, 2002; Brandon & Wagner, 1991; Wagner & Brandon, 1989, 2001) is an extension of opponent-process theory that can explain why the CR sometimes seems the same as and sometimes different from the UCR. According to Wagner, the UCS elicits two unconditioned responses—a primary A1 component and a secondary A2 component. The primary A1 component is elicited rapidly by the UCS and decays quickly after the UCS ends. In contrast, both the onset and decay of the secondary A2 component are very gradual.

The Importance of the Nature of the A2 Response

The secondary A2 component of the UCR can be the same as the A1 component, or the A1 and A2 components can differ. Whether A1 and A2 are the same or different is important. A key aspect of Wagner's view is that conditioning only occurs to the secondary A2 component; that is, the CR is always the secondary A2 reaction (see Figure 5.3). The CR and UCR will appear to be the same when the A1 and A2 components are the same.

Different A1 and A2 components will yield a CR and UCR that look different; however, the CR and UCR are really the same in this case. This is true because the A1 component is the response we associate with the

Figure 5.3   Wagner's SOP theory. (a) The UCS elicits the A1 and A2 components of the UCR. (b) The pairing of the CS and UCS leads to the CS being able to elicit the A2 component of the UCR.

UCR. When the A2 reaction is opponent to the A1, it looks as if the CR (A2) and UCR (A1 and A2) are different. Yet, the CR is merely the secondary A2 component of the UCR. Several examples help clarify this aspect of SOP theory.

Suppose an animal receives a brief electric shock. The initial reaction to shock is agitated hyperactivity. This initial increased reactivity is followed by a long-lasting hypoactivity or "freezing" response (Blanchard & Blanchard, 1969; Bolles & Riley, 1973). The freezing response, or **conditioned emotional reaction**, is the response conditioned to a stimulus paired with electric shock.

Paletta and Wagner (1986) demonstrated the two-phase reaction of an animal to a morphine injection. The initial A1 reaction to morphine is sedation or hypoactivity. Figure 5.4 shows that the initial activity level is lower in rats given morphine rather than saline. However, two hours after the injection, the morphine-receiving rats are significantly more active than the control rats who received saline.

What is the conditioned reaction to an environmental stimulus paired with morphine? As Figure 5.4 shows, the morphine-receiving animals were hyperactive when tested in the environment where they received morphine. Testing the morphine animals in their home cages produced a level of activity comparable to that of control animals not receiving morphine injections. These observations indicate that the conditioned reaction morphine produces is hyperactivity, which is the A2 secondary component of the UCR.

We have looked at two examples in which the A1 and A2 components of the UCR were opposite. In other cases, A1 and A2 are the same. Grau (1987) observed that the unconditioned response to radiant heat consisted of an initial short-duration **hypoalgesia**, or decreased sensitivity to pain,

Figure 5.4 Illustration of activity levels following injections of morphine or saline. Activity first decreases, then increases above normal after morphine injections. Animals given morphine in a distinctive environment show increased activity, or a conditioned A2 response, when placed in that environment without morphine (shown in bar graph).

followed by a more persistent hypoalgesia. How do we know that both A1 and A2 reactions to a painful stimulus such as radiant heat are hypoalgesia? The use of the opiate antagonist naloxone can demonstrate this similarity of A1 and A2 response. Naloxone blocks the long-term, persistent hypoalgesia (A2) but has no effect on the short-term, immediate hypoalgesia (A1). This differential effect means that the A1 hypoalgesic response is nonopioid, while the A2 hypoalgesia involves the opioid system. Furthermore, Fanselow and his colleagues (Fanselow & Baackes, 1982; Fanselow & Bolles, 1979) showed that it is the A2 opioid hypoalgesia reaction that is conditioned to environmental stimuli paired with a painful unconditioned stimulus such as radiant heat. These researchers observed that administration of naloxone prior to conditioning prevented the conditioning of the hypoalgesic response to environmental cues that were paired with a painful event.

A study by R. F. Thompson et al. (1984) provides perhaps the most impressive support for SOP theory. These researchers investigated the conditioning of an eyeblink response to a tone paired with a corneal air puff to a rabbit's eye. They found that two neural circuits mediate the rabbits' unconditioned eyeblink response (see Figure 5.5). A fast-acting A1 response is controlled by a

Figure 5.5 The two neural circuits that mediate the influence of tone (CS) and corneal air puff (UCS) on the nictitating membrane response. The UCS activates a direct route between sensory (trigeminal nucleus) and motor (accessory abducens nucleus) neurons and an indirect route through the inferior olive nucleus, cerebellum (interpositus and dendrites of Purkinje cell), and red nucleus before reaching the motor nuclei controlling the nictitating membrane response. The pairing of CS and UCS produces simultaneous activity in the pontine nucleus and the inferior olive nucleus and allows the CS to activate the longer neural circuit, eliciting the nictitating membrane response.

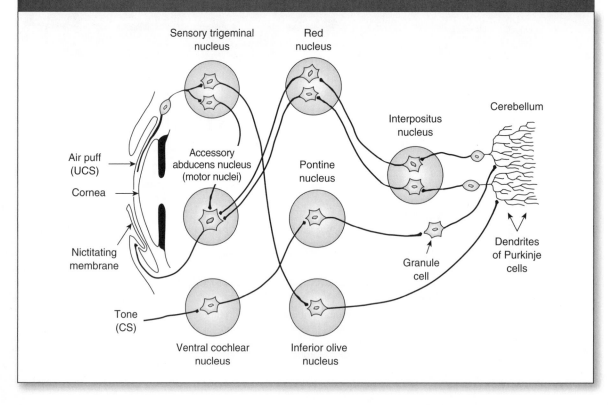

direct path from the brain area (sensory trigeminal area in the medulla) activated by the UCS to the cranial motor neurons controlling the eyeblink response. Stimulation of this neural circuit produces a fast-acting and rapid-decay eyeblink response. A secondary A2 circuit begins at the trigeminal nucleus and goes through the inferior olive nucleus, several cerebellar structures, and red nucleus before reaching the cranial motor neurons. Activation of this A2 circuit produces a slow-acting eyeblink response. Thompson and his colleagues also found that destruction of the indirect pathway eliminated a previously conditioned eyeblink response but did not affect the short-latency, unconditioned eyeblink response. Destruction of the indirect A2 pathways also precluded any reconditioning of the eyeblink response.

Recall from the chapter-opening vignette that Clarence's friend Jared became frightened when Felicia started to drink. According to SOP theory, Jared associated Felicia's drinking (CS) with her hostility (UCS) and became afraid (CR) when Felicia drank. As hostility elicits fear as the UCR, SOP theory would assume that both the A1 and A2 unconditioned responses when Felicia became hostile were a fear response (UCR).

Backward Conditioning of an Excitatory CR

We learned in Chapter 4 that a forward conditioning procedure produces a more reliable acquisition of the CR than does a backward conditioning procedure. While this statement is generally correct, Wagner's SOP theory indicates that backward conditioning can yield an excitatory CR if the CS is presented just prior to the peak of the A2 unconditioned response.

Larew (1986) provided support for this aspect of Wagner's SOP theory. In Larew's study, rats received a 2-second footshock UCS followed by a 30-second tone. The tone occurred 1 second, 31 seconds, or 60 seconds after the UCS. Control rats received no UCS-CS pairings. Larew observed an excitatory conditioned response with the 31-second UCS-CS backward conditioning procedure, but no excitatory conditioning with either a 1-second UCS-CS interval or a 60-second UCS-CS interval. These results suggest that excitatory conditioning occurs with a backward procedure when the CS immediately precedes the A2 response.

Problems With SOP Theory

Wagner and Brandon (Brandon & Wagner, 1991; Brandon et al., 2002; Wagner & Brandon, 1989, 2001) commented that despite the strong support for SOP theory, some research seems to be inconsistent with this view. One significant problem concerns divergent results obtained from different measures of conditioning. SOP theory suggests that all response measures should yield a comparable indication of conditioning and that variations in the training conditions should have a similar effect on all response measures. Suppose that heart rate and eyeblink response are recorded during conditioning. Since both responses are assumed to reflect A2 neural activity, the optimal CS-UCS interval should be equal for both response measures. Yet, Vandercar and Schneiderman (1967) found maximum heart rate conditioning with a 2.25-second CS-UCS interval, while the strongest eyeblink response occurred with a 7.5-second CS-UCS interval.

Recall our earlier discussion of the R. F. Thompson et al. (1984) study. We learned that destruction of the indirect inferior olive-cerebellar-red nucleus pathway eliminated the conditioned eyeblink response. However, the authors reported that this same surgical procedure had no effect on a conditioned heart rate response. To address these inconsistent findings, Wagner and Brandon modified SOP theory; we look at this revision next.

Affective Extension of SOP, or AESOP

Wagner and Brandon (Brandon & Wagner, 1991; Brandon, Vogel, & Wagner, 2003; Wagner & Brandon, 1989, 2001) suggested there are two distinct unconditioned response sequences—a sensory sequence and an emotive one. The sensory and emotive attributes of an unconditioned stimulus activate separate sequences of A1 and A2 activity. Further, the latency of the sensory and emotive activity sequences (A1 & A2) can differ; that is, A2 may take longer to develop for one component than the other. This difference leads to different optimal CS-UCS intervals for the emotive and sensory components. For example, a shorter-latency A2 activity for the sensory than emotive component of a UCS causes a shorter optimal CS-UCS interval for the sensory than the emotive CR. The differences in latencies between sensory and emotive A2 responses can result in one CS eliciting an emotive CR and another CS eliciting a sensory CR.

Wagner and Brandon's **affective extension of SOP theory (AESOP)** has several additional aspects. A conditioned stimulus may activate a strong sensory conditioned response but only a weak emotive CR, or vice versa. This difference would explain the lack of correspondence between response measures of conditioning. Further, while the sensory A2 neural activity elicits a discrete response, the emotive A2 neural activity produces a diffuse reaction. For example, the sensory CR might be an eyeblink response, while the emotive CR could be a startle response. Finally, two unconditioned stimuli might activate the same emotive A2 activity but different sensory A2 activities. This would lead to both similarities and differences in the responses that separate UCSs condition.

Consider two studies that support AESOP theory. Tait and Saladin (1986) trained rabbits to respond to a 1,000-millisecond (msec) tone CS by presenting the tone 5,000-msec after a 100-msec shock UCS to the rabbits' eyes. Two conditioned response measures were taken in this study: The tendency of the CS to (1) suppress ongoing drinking behavior (emotive CR) and (2) elicit the eyeblink response (sensory CR). Tait and Saladin found a strong emotive CR; that is, the CS suppressed drinking. In contrast, the CS did not elicit the eyeblink response. In fact, the CS inhibited an eyeblink response to another CS, a common result with backward conditioning. Why did the rabbits acquire an emotive CR, but not a sensory CR? AESOP theory proposes that the CS occurred prior to the emotive A2 response but after the sensory A2 response.

A study by Betts, Brandon, and Wagner (1996) provides additional support for AESOP theory. These researchers paired a vibratory stimulus with a shock UCS in the first phase of an eyeblink conditioning study in rabbits. In the second phase, the researchers presented a tone, the vibratory stimulus used in the first stage, and a shock UCS. (Recall from Chapter 4 that this is using a blocking paradigm and that the presence of the vibratory stimulus should block conditioning to the tone.) The key variable in this study was whether the UCS in the second phase was presented to the same or to a different eye than was used in the first phase. Betts, Brandon, and Wagner reported that both a reduced startle reaction and a reduced eyeblink response were conditioned to the tone when the UCS was presented to the same eye in both phases of the study. In contrast, when the UCS was presented to different eyes in each phase, the startle response to the tone was reduced, but the eyeblink response was equal to that elicited by the vibratory stimulus.

Why did blocking occur to the startle response even when the location of the UCS changed, while changing the UCS location eliminated the blocking of the eyeblink response? According to Betts, Brandon, and Wagner, the startle response reflects the association of a stimulus and its emotional aspects, while the eyeblink response reflects an association between a stimulus and its sensory aspects. Changing the location of the UCS eliminated blocking of the eyeblink response because the sensory aspects of the UCS change with a change in UCS location, but this change had no effect on the startle response because the emotive aspects of the UCS do not change with a change in location.

BEFORE YOU GO ON

- Was Jared's response to Felicia's drinking different from or similar to his response to her hostility?

- Would Clarence become fearful of Felicia's drinking if it followed her hostility?

- Pavlov suggested that the simultaneous activity of CS and UCS brain areas creates a neural pathway between the CS and UCS brain centers, which allows the CS to elicit the UCR because of its ability to arouse the UCS and UCR brain areas.

- Siegel found that the UCR to morphine is analgesia, or reduced sensitivity to pain, and the CR is hyperalgesia, or an increased sensitivity to pain; the UCR to insulin is hypoglycemia, and the CR is hyperglycemia; the UCR to alcohol is hypothermia, and the CR is hyperthermia.

- Siegel suggested that the conditioning of the opponent CR contributes to drug tolerance.

- Sometimes-opponent-process (SOP) theory suggests that the UCS elicits two unconditioned responses—a primary A1 component and a secondary A2 component.

- The primary A1 component is elicited rapidly by the UCS and decays quickly after the UCS ends. In contrast, the onset and decay of the secondary A2 component is gradual.

- SOP theory assumes that the secondary A2 component becomes the CR.

- The CR will seem different from the UCR when the A1 and A2 components differ, while the CR will appear to be similar to the UCR when the A1 and A2 components are similar.

- AESOP proposes that the UCS elicits separate emotive and sensory unconditioned responses.

- According to AESOP, the emotive and sensory UCRs can have different time courses, which can lead to divergent conditioning outcomes for sensory and emotive CRs.

THE NATURE OF THE CLASSICAL CONDITIONING PROCESS

In Chapter 4, we learned that the predictiveness of the conditioned stimulus influences how readily an animal acquires a conditioned response. We also discovered that the predictive value of other stimuli also affects conditioning to the CS. How does an animal judge the relative predictiveness of a stimulus? Psychologists have developed several different views to explain the mechanism by which predictiveness affects classical conditioning process. The Rescorla-Wagner associative view suggests that the availability of associative strength determines whether a CR develops to a CS paired with the UCS; comparator theory argues that performance of a conditioned response involves a comparison of the response strength to the CS and to competing stimuli; Mackintosh's attentional theory proposes that the relevance of and attention to a stimulus determine whether that stimulus will become associated with the UCS; and Baker's retrospective processing approach suggests that conditioning involves the continuous monitoring of contingencies between a CS and UCS, with the recognition of a lack of predictiveness diminishing the value of the CS.

The Rescorla-Wagner theory was developed to explain the influence of predictiveness on conditioning. We begin our discussion of the nature of classical conditioning with a description of this theory. We then examine several classical conditioning phenomena used to test the validity of the **Rescorla-Wagner associative model**. Some of this research has supported this theory, while other studies have pointed to its weaknesses. We then look at alternatives to the Rescorla-Wagner associative model of conditioning.

Rescorla-Wagner Associative Model

The associative model of classical conditioning that Robert Rescorla and Allan Wagner (1972) developed expresses four main ideas. First, there is a maximum associative strength that can develop between a CS and UCS. The UCS determines the limit of associative strength; different UCSs support different maximum levels of conditioning, and therefore have different asymptotic values.

Second, while the associative strength increases with each training trial, the amount of associative strength gained on a particular training trial depends on the level of prior training. Since the typical learning curve in classical conditioning negatively accelerates (see Figure 5.6), more associative strength will accrue on early training trials than on later trials. In fact, as Figure 5.6 indicates, the increment on each conditioning trial declines with each CS-UCS pairing.

Third, the rate of conditioning varies depending on the CS and the UCS used. Associative strength accrues quickly to some stimuli, but slowly to others. As seen in Figure 5.6, one stimulus readily gains associative strength, while conditioning to the other stimulus occurs slowly. Further, some UCSs produce more rapid learning than other UCSs.

Fourth, the level of conditioning on a particular trial is influenced not only by the amount of prior conditioning to the stimulus, but also by the level of previous conditioning to other stimuli also paired with the UCS. A particular UCS can only support a certain amount of conditioning, even when more than one stimulus is paired with the UCS. When two (or more) stimuli are presented, these stimuli must share the associative strength the UCS can support. Thus, associative strength that accrues to one stimulus is not available to be conditioned to the other stimuli. For example, suppose two stimuli are paired with a UCS, and the maximum associative strength that the UCS can support is 10 units. If 7 units are conditioned to one cue paired with the UCS, only 3 units can develop to the other cue.

Rescorla and Wagner (1972) developed a mathematical equation based on the four ideas just outlined. Their mathematical model of classical conditioning is $\Delta V_A = K (\lambda - V_{AX})$. In this formula,

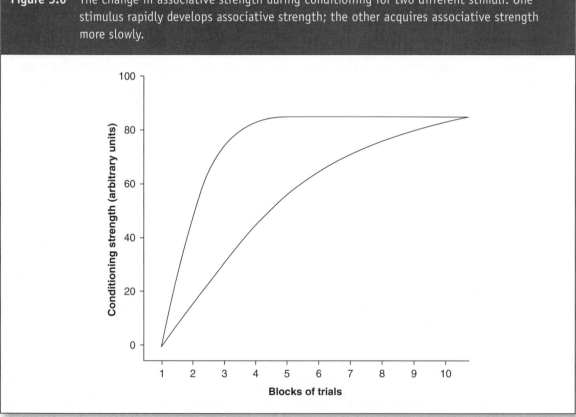

Figure 5.6   The change in associative strength during conditioning for two different stimuli. One stimulus rapidly develops associative strength; the other acquires associative strength more slowly.

V_A is the associative strength between the conditioned stimulus A and the UCS, and the ΔV_A is the change in associative strength that develops on a specific trial when the CS_A and the UCS are paired. The symbol K refers to the rate of conditioning determined by the nature of the CS_A and the intensity of the UCS. (The K value can be separated into α, or alpha, which refers to the power of CS_A, and β, or beta, which reflects the intensity of the UCS.) The symbol λ defines the maximum level of conditioning the UCS supports. The term V_{AX} indicates the level of conditioning that has already accrued to the conditioned stimulus (A) as well as to other stimuli (X) present during conditioning. Thus, $V_{AX} = V_A + V_X$.

To see how this mathematical model works, suppose a light stimulus is paired with shock on five trials. Prior to training, the value of K is .5, λ is 90 and $V_A = 0$. When we apply these values to the Rescorla-Wagner model, we get the following:

Trial 1: ΔV_A = .5 (90 − 0) = 45
Trial 2: ΔV_A = .5 (90 − 45) = 22.5
Trial 3: ΔV_A = .5 (90 − 67.5) = 11.25
Trial 4: ΔV_A = .5 (90 − 78.8) = 5.6
Trial 5: ΔV_A = .5 (90 − 84.4) = 2.8
Total associative strength after 5 trials = 87.2

The data in this example show that conditioning to CS_A occurs rapidly; associative strength grows 45 units on Trial 1, 22.5 units on Trial 2, 11.25 units on Trial 3, 5.6 units on Trial 4, and 2.8 units on Trial 5. Thus, 87.2 units of associative strength accrued to the CS_A after just five trials of conditioning. The rapid development of associative strength indicates that CS_A is an intense and/ or a salient stimulus or that the UCS is a strong stimulus, or both.

The Rescorla-Wagner model has been used to explain a number of conditioning phenomena. Let's see how it explains blocking (see Chapter 4). Suppose that we pair a light with a shock for five trials. The K value for the light is .5 and the maximum level of conditioning, or λ, is 90 units of associative strength. As we learned earlier, 87.2 units of associative strength would accrue to the light after five pairings with the shock. Next we pair the light, tone, and shock for five more trials. The K value for the tone is .5, and we would expect that five pairings of the tone and shock would yield strong conditioning. However, only 2.8 units of associative strength are still available to be conditioned, according to the Rescorla-Wagner model. And the tone must share this associative strength with the light cue. Because strong conditioning has already occurred to the light, the Rescorla-Wagner equation predicts little conditioning to the tone. The weak conditioning to the tone due to the prior accrued associative strength to light is illustrated in the calculations as follows:

Trial 6: ΔV_{light} = .5 (90 − 87.2) = 1.4	ΔV_{tone} = .5 (90 − 87.2) = 1.4
Trial 7: ΔV_{light} = .5 (90 − 90) = 0	ΔV_{tone} = .5 (90 − 90) = 0
Trial 8: ΔV_{light} = .5 (90 − 90) = 0	ΔV_{tone} = .5 (90 − 90) = 0
Trial 9: ΔV_{light} = .5 (90 − 90) = 0	ΔV_{tone} = .5 (90 − 90) = 0
Trial 10: ΔV_{light} = .5 (90 − 90) = 0	ΔV_{tone} = .5 (90 − 90) = 0
Total associative strength of light = 88.6	Total associative strength of tone = 1.4

We learned earlier that blocking occurs when a stimulus previously paired with a UCS is presented with a new stimulus and the UCS. The Rescorla-Wagner model suggests that blocking occurs because the initial CS has already accrued most or all of the associative strength, and little is left to condition to the other stimulus. As the previous equations show, little conditioning occurred to the tone because most of the associative strength had been conditioned to the light prior to the compound pairing of light, tone, and shock. Based on this explanation, the equation the Rescorla-Wagner model generates predicts cue blocking.

Recall our discussion of Clarence's failure to associate Felicia's drinking (CS) with her hostility (UCS) in the chapter-opening vignette. The Rescorla-Wagner model could explain Clarence's failure to associate drinking and hostility as caused by blocking. Perhaps Clarence previously associated another stimulus (CS_1; e.g., work-related stress) with hostility. The presence of work-related stress (CS_1) while Felicia was drinking blocked the association of Felicia's drinking (CS_2) and hostility (UCS).

An Evaluation of the Rescorla-Wagner Model

Many studies have evaluated the validity of the Rescorla-Wagner model of classical conditioning. While many of these studies have supported this view, other observations have not been consistent with the Rescorla-Wagner model. We first discuss one area of research—the UCS preexposure effect—that supports the Rescorla-Wagner view. Next, we describe three areas of research—potentiation, CS preexposure, and cue deflation—that provide findings the Rescorla-Wagner model does not predict. Finally, we discuss several alternative views of classical conditioning.

Suppose you have had several bouts of the flu recently and again become sick after eating a distinctive food. Would you develop an aversion to this food? Your previous experiences with sickness, independent of the particular food, would likely prevent the conditioning of an association between eating this food and being sick.

This example illustrates the effect of preexposure to the UCS (illness) without the CS (food) on the acquisition of a CR (aversion) when the CS is later presented with the UCS. Psychologists refer to this phenomenon as the **UCS preexposure effect**. Many studies have consistently observed that preexposure to the UCS impairs subsequent conditioning; for example, several researchers (Ford & Riley, 1984; Mikulka, Leard, & Klein, 1977) have demonstrated that the presentation of a drug that induces illness (UCS) prior to conditioning impairs the subsequent association of a distinctive food (CS) with illness. Similar preexposure interference has been reported with other UCSs (shock: Baker, Mercier, Gabel, & Baker, 1981; and food: Balsam & Schwartz, 1981).

Why does preexposure to the UCS impair subsequent conditioning? The Rescorla-Wagner model provides an explanation: The presentation of the UCS without the CS occurs in a specific environment or context, which results in the development of associative strength to the context.

Since the UCS can only support a limited amount of associative strength, conditioning of associative strength to the stimulus context reduces the level of possible conditioning to the CS. Thus, the presence of the stimulus context will block the acquisition of a CR to the CS when the CS is presented with the UCS in the stimulus context. (Referring back to blocking described in Chapter 4, it is helpful to think of the context as CS_1 and the new stimulus as CS_2.)

How can one validate the **context blocking** explanation of the UCS preexposure effect? One method is to change the context when the CS is paired with the UCS. Randich and Ross (1985) found that the UCS preexposure effect was attenuated when the preexposure context (noise from a fan, but no light, painted walls, and the odor of Pine-Sol) was different from the conditioning context (light, black-and-white-striped walls, and Pine-Sol odor, but no fan) presented prior to noise CS and shock pairings (see Figure 5.7). As a result of the change in

Figure 5.7   The inflfluence of context change on the UCS preexposure effect. Animals in the +C1/C1 experimental group, which received both preexposure and conditioning in Context 1, showed significantly slower acquisition of a conditioned emotional response than did animals in the +C1/C2 experimental group (given preexposure in Context 1 and conditioning in Context 2). Control animals in the –C1/C1 and –C1/C2 groups who did not receive UCS preexposure readily conditioned fear to either Context 1 or 2.

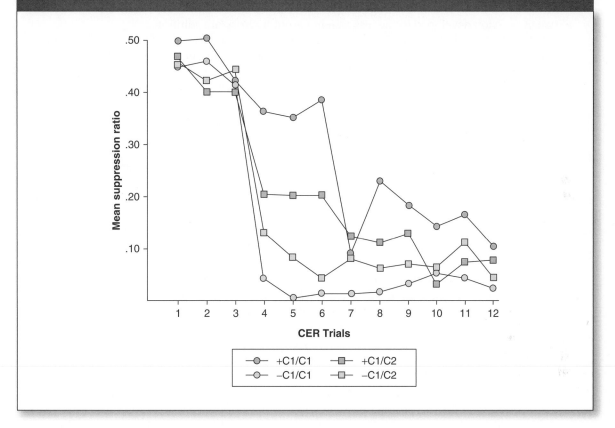

context, no stimuli were present during conditioning that could compete with the association of the CS and the UCS. Thus, the CR was readily conditioned to the CS when paired with the UCS in the new context.

Other researchers also have reported that context change attenuates the UCS preexposure effect. Hinson (1982) found that the effect of UCS preexposure on eyelid conditioning in the rabbit was attenuated by a change in contextual stimuli between preexposure and eyelid conditioning, while de Brugada, Hall, and Symonds (2004) reported the UCS preexposure effect was reduced when lithium chloride was injected during preexposure and orally consumed during flavor aversion conditioning. These results strongly suggest that contextual associations formed during UCS preexposure are responsible for the decrease in the conditioning to a CS paired with a UCS.

In the next three sections, we discuss several findings that the Rescorla-Wagner model does not predict. The first problem area is the potentiation effect.

The Potentiation of a Conditioned Response

The Rescorla-Wagner model predicts that when a salient and a nonsalient cue are presented together with the UCS, the salient cue will accrue more associative strength than the nonsalient cue. This phenomenon, called **overshadowing**, was originally observed by Pavlov (1927). Pavlov found that a more intense tone overshadowed the development of an association between a less intense tone and the UCS. Overshadowing is readily observed in other situations. For example, Lindsey and Best (1973) presented two novel fluids (saccharin and casein hydrosylate) prior to illness. They found that a strong aversion developed to the salient saccharin flavor, but only a weak aversion developed to the less salient casein hydrosylate solution.

Overshadowing does not always occur when two cues of different salience are paired with a UCS; in fact, in some circumstances, the presence of a salient cue produces a stronger CR than would have occurred had the less salient cue been presented alone with the UCS. The increased CR to a less salient stimulus because of the simultaneous pairing of a more salient cue during conditioning was first described by John Garcia and his associates (Garcia & Rusiniak, 1980; Rusiniak, Palmerino, & Garcia, 1982). They observed that the presence of a salient flavor cue potentiated rather than overshadowed the establishment of an aversion to a less salient odor cue paired with illness.

Batsell (2000) suggested that there are occasions when overshadowing is adaptive and potentiation harmful. Consider the following example provided by Batsell to illustrate when overshadowing would be adaptive and potentiation not. An animal consumes some toxic cheese and becomes ill. During a second feeding, the animal consumes less cheese, eats some safe cereal, and becomes ill. If the developing aversion to the toxic cheese potentiated an aversion to the safe cereal, the animal would also develop an aversion to the safe cereal. By contrast, overshadowing would prevent an aversion from developing to the safe cereal, leaving the animal with something to eat.

Batsell also assumed that there are occasions when potentiation is adaptive and overshadowing not. The following example illustrates when potentiation would be adaptive and overshadowing not: The animal consumes some toxic cheese and becomes ill. On its second encounter with the cheese, a smelly odor emanates from the cheese. Potentiation would allow the animal to develop an aversion to the odor and not even have to encounter the cheese, while overshadowing would prevent the animal from developing an aversion to the odor. In this example, potentiation is adaptive and overshadowing not.

Why does the presence of a salient taste cue potentiate rather than overshadow the acquisition of an odor aversion? According to Garcia and Rusiniak (1980), the taste stimulus "indexes" the odor as a food cue, and thereby mediates the establishment of a strong odor aversion. This indexing has considerable adaptive value. The taste cue's **potentiation** of the odor aversion enables an animal to recognize a potentially poisonous food early in the ingestive sequence. Thus, an odor aversion causes animals to avoid dangerous foods before even tasting them.

Rescorla (1981) presented a different view of the potentiation effect, a view consistent with the Rescorla-Wagner model. According to Rescorla, potentiation occurs because an animal perceives the compound stimuli (taste and odor) as a single unitary event and then mistakes each individual element for the compound. If Rescorla's view is accurate, the potentiation effect should depend upon the strength of the taste-illness association. Weakening of the taste-illness association should result in an elimination of the potentiation effect. Rescorla (1981) presented evidence to support his view; that is, he found that extinction of the taste aversion also attenuated the animal's aversion to an odor cue. However, Lett (1982) observed that taste-alone exposure eliminated the taste aversion but not the odor aversion.

Why did extinction of the taste aversion reduce the animal's odor aversion in the Rescorla study, but not the Lett study? We address this question alongside Rescorla's within-compound view later in the chapter.

The CS Preexposure Effect

Recall our discussion of Clarence's failure to associate Felicia's drinking and hostility in the chapter-opening vignette. The **CS preexposure effect** provides one explanation for his failure to develop apprehension about Felicia's drinking. When Clarence first met Felicia, she did not become hostile when consuming alcohol, perhaps because she limited her alcohol consumption. Only after they dated for a while did she consume enough alcohol to become hostile. Unfortunately, Clarence's preexposure to Felicia drinking without become hostile prevented the association of drinking and hostility from being conditioned.

Many studies (Bonardi & Yann Ong, 2003) have reported that preexposure to a specific stimulus subsequently retarded the development of a CR to that stimulus when paired with a UCS. The CS preexposure effect has been reported in a variety of classical conditioning situations, including conditioned water licking in rats (Baker & Mackintosh, 1979), conditioned fear in rats (Pearce, Kaye, & Hall, 1982) and humans (Booth, Siddle, & Bond, 1989), eyelid conditioning in rabbits (Rudy, 1994), leg-flexion conditioning in sheep and goats (Lubow & Moore, 1959), and flavor aversion learning in rats (Fenwick, Mikulka, & Klein, 1975).

Why is the CS preexposure effect a problem for the Rescorla-Wagner model? According to Rescorla and Wagner (1972), exposure to the CS prior to conditioning should have no effect on the subsequent association of the CS with the UCS. This prediction is based on the assumption that the readiness of a stimulus to be associated with a UCS depends only on the intensity and salience of the CS; the parameter K represents these values in the Rescorla-Wagner model. While neither the intensity nor the salience of the CS changes as the result of CS preexposure in the Rescorla-Wagner model, the subsequent interference with conditioning indicates that the associability of the CS changes when the CS is experienced without the UCS prior to conditioning.

How can we explain the influence of CS preexposure on subsequent conditioning? One explanation involves modifying the Rescorla-Wagner model to allow for a change in the value of K as the result of experience. Yet, the effect of CS preexposure on the acquisition of a CR appears to involve more than just a reduction in the value of K. Instead, Mackintosh (1983) argued that animals learn that a particular stimulus is irrelevant when it predicts no significant event; stimulus irrelevance causes the animal to ignore that stimulus in the future. This failure to attend to the CS and the events that follow it may well be responsible for the interference with conditioning that CS preexposure produces. We look more closely at this view of CS preexposure when we describe Mackintosh's attentional model of conditioning.

The Cue Deflation Effect

The Rescorla-Wagner model suggests that the overshadowing phenomenon involves greater conditioning to a more salient rather than a less salient stimulus; that is, greater associative strength accrues to the more salient rather than less salient cue. What do you suppose would happen to an animal's response to the less salient stimulus if the conditioned response to the more salient stimulus were extinguished? The Rescorla-Wagner model does not suggest any change in the reaction to the less salient cue. However, a number of studies (Kaufman & Bolles, 1981; Matzel, Schachtman, & Miller, 1985) reported that extinction of the more salient (or overshadowing) stimulus increased the response to the less salient (or overshadowed) stimulus. Not all studies find a **cue deflation effect**, or increased responding to the less salient stimulus, following extinction to a more salient cue; instead, some studies report a decreased response to both the overshadowing and overshadowed stimuli (Durlach, 1989).

An increased response to a CS without additional experience also occurs with the extinction of context associations acquired with UCS preexposure. Recall that exposure to the UCS prior to CS-UCS pairings produces a weaker response to the CS than when no UCS preexposure is given.

We learned earlier that context-UCS associations acquired during UCS preexposure block strong conditioning to the CS. Several studies (Matzel, Brown, & Miller, 1987; Timberlake, 1986) show that postconditioning extinction of the response to the training context results in an enhanced response to the CS. Again, not all studies that extinguish the response to the training context have noted an increased responding to the CS (refer to Durlach, 1989). What process is responsible for the change in response to one stimulus following the extinction of a response to another stimulus? Why do some studies report that diminished response to one stimulus increased the reaction to the CS, while other studies find that this same procedure decreased the reaction to the CS? The next two sections address both of these questions.

The Importance of Within-Compound Associations

Suppose that a tone and light are paired together with food. According to the Rescorla-Wagner model, the light and tone will compete for associative strength. More recently, Rescorla and Durlach (1981) suggested that rather than two stimuli competing for associative strength, a **within-compound association** can develop between the light and tone during conditioning. This within-compound association will result in a single level of conditioning to both stimuli. One procedure, the simultaneous pairing of both stimuli, facilitates a within-compound association. As a result of developing a within-compound association, any change in the value of one stimulus will have a similar impact on the other stimulus.

We described earlier the observation that a salient taste cue potentiated the aversion to a nonsalient odor cue. Garcia and Rusiniak (1980) suggested that the taste stimulus indexes the odor stimulus as a food cue and thereby mediates the establishment of a strong odor aversion. If this view were accurate, then a taste could potentiate an aversion to an odor, but an odor would not potentiate an aversion to a taste cue. However, Batsell, Trost, Cochran, Blankenship, and Batson (2003) observed that an odor can potentiate the aversion to a taste, a result suggesting that the taste and odor association is symmetrical. We also learned earlier that Rescorla explains the potentiation phenomenon by suggesting that the within-compound association of a salient taste cue and a nonsalient odor cue leads to a strong aversion (potentiation) when both cues were paired with illness. Batsell et al.'s (2003) observation that a taste and odor association is symmetrical provides support for Rescorla's within-compound explanation of potentiation.

The within-compound conditioning view suggests that potentiation is dependent upon the establishment of an association between the odor and taste cues. According to this view, the failure to form a within-compound association between odor and flavor should eliminate potentiation. One procedure used to prevent within-compound associations is pairing the odor and taste cues sequentially rather than simultaneously. This procedure eliminates the flavor stimulus's potentiation of the odor cue (S. F. Davis, Best, & Grover, 1988; Holder & Garcia, 1987).

Ralph Miller and his colleagues (Wheeler & Miller, 2007; Urcelay & Miller, 2009) provided additional support for the within-compound explanation of potentiation. Their research also demonstrates that observations of overshadowing and potentiation are not limited to odor and flavor aversions. In their studies, two auditory stimuli of different salience were paired with an aversive electric shock using either a delayed or trace conditioning procedure. According to Miller and his colleagues, when contiguity is not good (trace conditioning), animals encode each stimulus as a compound (configural encoding), while if contiguity is good (delayed conditioning), animals encode each stimulus separately (elemental encoding). Because elemental encoding leads each stimulus to be separately associated with the aversive event, overshadowing should occur. In contrast, because configural encoding leads both stimuli to be associated with the aversive event as a compound stimulus, potentiation should occur. In support of this view, Miller and his colleagues found that overshadowing of the less salient auditory stimulus by the more salient auditory stimulus occurred with a delay conditioning procedure and potentiation with a trace conditioning procedure.

Miller and his colleagues also found that procedures that lead to elemental encoding of a compound stimulus attenuated potentiation. For example, Urcelay and Miller (2009) gave animals a treatment that would lead two auditory stimuli to be separately encoded. One auditory stimulus signaled the presence of a flashing light, the other, the lights absence. Two different auditory stimuli were then paired with an aversive conditioning using a trace conditioning procedure. Urcelay and Miller reported attenuated potentiation, presumably because the animals' prior experience led the auditory stimuli to be separately associated with the aversive stimulus even though the trace conditioning procedure normally leads to configural encoding and potentiation.

Recall that Rescorla (1981) found that extinction of the taste aversion also attenuated the animal's aversion to an odor cue. A similar result was recently reported with an appetitive classical conditioning procedure using food as the unconditioned stimuli (Esber, Pearce, & Haselgrove, 2009). These researchers reported that the presence of a salient auditory stimulus potentiated an appetitive conditioned response to a less salient auditory stimulus. Extinction of the appetitive conditioned response to the salient auditory stimulus reduced the level of responding to the less salient auditory stimulus. It would appear that the establishment of a within-compound association leads to potentiation in both appetitive and aversive classical conditioning situations.

While within-compound associations definitely contribute to the potentiation phenomenon, it is not the entire story. A number of studies (Bouton, Jones, McPhillips, & Swartzentruber, 1986; Mikulka, Pitts, & Philput, 1982; Schneider & Pinnow, 1994; Symonds & Hall, 1999) have found that a taste cue overshadows rather than potentiates an odor aversion. In these studies, overshadowing occurred under conditions that were favorable to within-compound associations. Processes other than within-compound associations that contribute to the potentiation phenomenon remain to be determined.

BEFORE YOU GO ON

- How would the Rescorla-Wagner model explain Clarence's failure to develop an association between Felicia's drinking and her hostility?
- How would the Rescorla-Wagner model explain Jared's association between Felicia's drinking and her hostility?

SECTION REVIEW

- The Rescorla-Wagner model proposes that (1) the UCS supports a maximum level of conditioning; (2) the associative strength increases readily early in training, but more slowly later in conditioning; (3) the rate of conditioning is more rapid with some CSs or UCSs than with others; and (4) the level of conditioning on a particular trial depends upon the level of prior conditioning to the CS and to the other stimuli present during conditioning.
- According to the Rescorla-Wagner theory, blocking occurs as a result of conditioning associative strength to one stimulus, thereby preventing conditioning to a second stimulus due to a lack of available associative strength.
- Preexposure to the UCS impairs subsequent conditioning due to contextual blocking; a change in context eliminates the UCS preexposure effect.

- In a compound conditioning situation, overshadowing occurs when the presence of a salient stimulus prevents conditioning to a less salient stimulus, while potentiation occurs when the presence of a salient stimulus enhances the conditioning to the less salient stimulus.

- Rescorla suggests that under some conditions, two stimuli paired with a UCS develop a within-compound association (potentiation) instead of competing for associative strength (overshadowing).

Recall our discussion of the cue deflation effect, presented in the previous section. We learned that several studies showed that the extinction of a response to one component of a compound stimulus enhanced the response to the other component. Yet, other experiments reported that extinction to one component also reduced response to the other component. The latter result is consistent with the within-compound analysis; that is, a within-compound association is established to both components. Consequently, reducing the response to one has a comparable effect on the other. However, the former studies are not consistent with the within-compound analysis. Comparator theory offers an explanation why the extinction of a response to one component would increase the response to the other.

A Comparator Theory of Classical Conditioning

Ralph Miller and his associates (Denniston, Savastano, Blaisdell, & Miller, 2003; Denniston, Savastano, & Miller, 2001; Miller & Matzel, 1989; Urcelay & Miller, 2006) have proposed that animals learn about all CS-UCS relationships. However, a particular association may not be evident in the animal's behavior. A strong CS-UCS association may exist but not be expressed in behavior, when compared with another CS even more strongly associated with the UCS. Thus, the ability of a particular stimulus to elicit a CR depends upon its level of conditioning compared to other stimuli. Only when the level of conditioning to that stimulus exceeds that of other stimuli will that CS elicit the CR.

Consider the blocking phenomenon to illustrate **comparator theory**. The comparator approach proposes that an association may exist between CS_2 and the UCS but not be evident in terms of response because of the stronger CS_1-UCS association. (Recall that the Rescorla-Wagner model assumes that the presence of the CS_1 blocks or prevents the establishment of the CS_2-UCS association.) The comparator theory suggests that there is one condition in which the CS_2 can elicit the CR in a blocking paradigm. The extinction of the conditioned response to the CS_1 can allow the CS_2 to now elicit the CR. The reason that extinction of the response to the CS_1 results in response to the CS_2 is that the comparison now favors the CS_2-UCS association. Prior to extinction, the CS_1-UCS association was stronger than the CS_2-UCS association. After extinction, the CS_2-UCS association is stronger than CS_1-UCS association.

We learned in an earlier section that extinction of response to the training context eliminated the UCS preexposure effect. These studies (Matzel et al., 1987; Timberlake, 1986) show that deflation of response to the training context leads to an increased response to the CS. This greater response occurred even though no additional CS-UCS pairings were given. Additional support for the comparator theory comes from experiments in which devaluation of the overshadowing stimulus caused an increased response to the overshadowed stimulus (Kaufman & Bolles, 1981; Matzel et al., 1985). This observation suggests that an association between the overshadowed stimulus and the UCS did form, but it was not evident because of its unfavorable comparison with an overshadowing stimulus.

While these observations provided support for the comparator theory, not all studies have found that the deflation of one stimulus increases the response to another stimulus. In fact, many studies have reported that extinguishing the response to one stimulus produces a comparable reduction in the other stimulus, a result that favors the within-compound associative view presented in the previous section.

What is responsible for this discrepancy in results? Durlach (1989) suggested that the presence of strong within-compound associations might overwhelm the comparator effect. In her view, the comparator effect would only be evident when within-compound associations are weak.

However, Blaisdell, Gunther, and Miller (1999) reported that the amount of posttraining extinction (deflation) is the critical variable that determines whether the CS elicits the CR. These researchers found that extensive extinction trials are needed to eliminate the conditioning to the comparator stimulus and increase the response to the CS.

So what causes the cue deflation effect? Van Hamme and Wasserman (1994) modified the Rescorla-Wagner theory to account for the cue deflation effect. In their view, extinguishing the response to one conditioned stimulus (the deflated stimulus) changes the value of K to a second conditioned stimulus, which serves to increase the associative strength of the second conditioned stimulus (see Van Hamme & Wasserman, 1994, for the mathematical revision of the Rescorla-Wagner associative model that explains the cue deflation effect). Denniston, Savastano, and Miller (2001) have presented several research findings that this modified associative theory cannot explain but that the comparator theory can. For example, these researchers reported that extinction of a second-order comparator stimulus (or a comparator stimulus for the comparator stimulus) increases the response to the first-order comparator stimulus, which then serves to decrease the response to the CS. Future research is needed to clarify the processes responsible for the cue deflation effect, as well as evaluate the validity of the associative and comparator theories of classical conditioning.

Mackintosh's Attentional View

Nicholas Mackintosh (1975) suggested that animals seek information from the environment that predicts the occurrence of biologically significant events (UCSs). Once an animal has identified a cue that reliably predicts a specific event, it ignores other stimuli that also provide information about the event. According to Mackintosh, animals attend to stimuli that are predictive and ignore those that are not essential. Thus, conditioning depends not only on the physical characteristics of stimuli, but also on the animal's recognition of the correlation (or lack of correlation) between events (CS and UCS).

Mackintosh's attentional view of classical conditioning can explain the CS preexposure effect that poses a problem for the Rescorla-Wagner model. We discovered earlier in the chapter that CS preexposure impairs the acquisition of the CR when the CS and UCS are later paired. According to Mackintosh, an animal learns that the CS is irrelevant as a result of preexposure to the CS. Once the animal discovers that a stimulus is irrelevant, it stops attending to that stimulus and will have difficulty learning that the CS correlates with the UCS.

Support for this **learned irrelevance** view of CS preexposure comes from studies in which uncorrelated presentations of the CS and UCS prior to conditioning led to substantial interference with the acquisition of the CR. In fact, Baker and Mackintosh (1977) found that uncorrelated presentations of the CS and the UCS produced significantly greater interference than did CS preexposure or UCS preexposure alone. In their study, the response of water licking to a tone was significantly less evident in animals receiving prior unpaired presentations of the tone (CS) and water (UCS) than either tone alone, water alone, or no preexposure (see Figure 5.8). This greater impairment of subsequent conditioning when the CS and UCS are unpaired has also been demonstrated in studies of conditioning fear in rats (Baker, 1976) and the eyeblink response in rabbits (Siegel & Domjan, 1971).

Figure 5.8 The amount of licking to a tone (CS) paired with water (UCS) is significantly less in animals preexposed to both the tone and water than for those to only the water or only the tone, or with no preexposure.

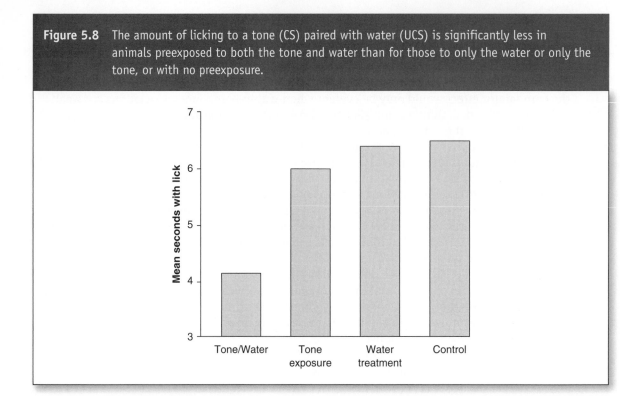

Uncorrelated CS and UCS preexposure not only impairs subsequent excitatory conditioning; it also impairs inhibitory conditioning (Bennett, Wills, Oakeshott, & Mackintosh, 2000). The fact that uncorrelated CS and UCS exposures impaired inhibitory as well as excitatory conditioning provides additional evidence for the learned irrelevance explanation of the CS preexposure effect.

Several studies by Geoffrey Hall and his associates (Hall & Channell, 1985; Hall & Honey, 1989) provided additional evidence for an attentional view of the CS preexposure effect. Animals exposed to a novel stimulus exhibit an orienting response to the novel stimulus. G. Hall and Channell (1985) showed that repeated exposure to light (CS) leads to habituation of the orienting response to that stimulus (see Chapter 3). They also found that later pairings of the light (CS) with milk (UCS) yield a reduced CR compared with control animals who did not experience preexposure to the light CS. These results suggest that habituation of an orienting response to a stimulus is associated with the later failure of conditioning to that stimulus.

What if the orienting response could be reinstated to the conditioned stimulus? Would this procedure restore conditionability to the stimulus? G. Hall and Channell (1985) reported that the presentation of the conditioned stimulus in a novel context reinstated the orienting response. They also found that pairing the CS and UCS in the new context led to a strong CR. These results indicate that a reinstatement of the orienting response eliminated the CS preexposure effect; that is, the CS now elicited a strong CR.

Why would reinstatement of the orienting response cause CS conditionability to return? An orienting response indicates that an animal is attending to the stimulus, and attention allows the stimulus to be associated with the UCS. These observations provide further support for an attentional view of the CS preexposure effect.

We learned earlier that uncorrelated CS and UCS exposures impaired both excitatory and inhibitory conditioning. Bonardi, Hall, and Ong (2005) reported that while uncorrelated CS and UCS exposures impaired excitatory conditioning, inhibitory conditioning was facilitated by uncorrelated CS and UCS presentations, a result that they attributed to latent learning (see Chapter 4) rather than to learned irrelevance. The reasons for these different results remain to be investigated.

The Retrospective Processing View

Theories of classical conditioning have traditionally held that learning occurs at the time of training and that response is based upon the level of training. Baker and Mercier (1989) referred to these models of classical conditioning as input-based theories. The Rescorla-Wagner associative theory, Rescorla's within-compound association view, and Mackintosh's attentional perspective are input-based theories of classical conditioning. In contrast, Miller's comparative theory is an output-based model because it suggests that performance is determined by comparing the level of prior conditioning to each stimulus at the time of testing. However, all of these theories assume that unless further conditioning is provided, the level of learning remains constant after training.

Baker and Mercier (1989) presented a very different view of classical conditioning. They contend that the level of conditioning to a CS can change even with no additional CS-UCS pairings. According to Baker and Mercier, animals constantly assess the contingencies between events in their environment. Rather than viewing learning as a static representation of the degree of correlation between events, these researchers suggest that learning changes over time as an animal encounters new information about the degree of contingency between a CS and UCS. For example, what may seem to be two highly correlated events may later be viewed as having little correlation. This change in learning would occur if initial CS-UCS pairings were followed by many UCS-alone experiences. Baker and Mercier referred to the constant assessment of contingencies as **retrospective processing**. New data may cause an animal to reassess past experiences and to form a new representation of the relationship between the CS and UCS.

Retrospective processing requires the ability to remember past experiences. It also assumes that an animal has a representation of past encounters that it can modify. In this section, we look at several studies that support retrospective processing.

Suppose that after a tone and light were paired with a shock, only the tone was presented prior to the shock. How would the animal respond to the light? Baker and Baker (1985) performed such a study and found that fear of the light was reduced compared to a control group that did not receive tone-shock pairings. This study is similar to the blocking paradigm described in Chapter 4. In fact, the only difference between the procedures is the order of tone-light-shock and tone-shock pairings. Baker and Mercier (1989) referred to a procedure in which the tone-shock follows rather than precedes tone-light-shock pairing as **backward blocking**.

What causes backward blocking? Baker and Mercier (1989) argued that when animals receive tone-shock after tone-light-shock pairings, they discover that the tone is a better predictor of shock than the light. Through retrospective processing, the animals learn that the light is not an adequate predictor of shock. This recognition causes the animal to no longer fear the light.

Recall our discussion of the UCS preexposure effect. We learned that exposure to the UCS impaired later conditioning of the CS and UCS. A similar impairment of conditioning occurs when UCS-alone experiences occur after CS-UCS pairings (Jenkins, Barnes, & Barrera, 1981). According to Baker and Mercier (1989), the animal revises its view of the contingency between the CS and UCS as a result of UCS-alone experience. In other words, the animal retrospectively recognizes that the CS no longer correlates well with the UCS.

Miller and his colleagues (Denniston et al., 2001; Savastano, Escobar, & Miller, as cited in Denniston et al.) have reported that backward blocking does not always occur. These researchers found that if a CS has developed a "robust responding" ability—the CS consistently produces an intense CR—the CS appears to become "immune" to backward blocking, and additional training to a competing stimulus will not reduce the response to the CS. For example, if a CS is "inherently biologically significant" or acquires biological significance through conditioning, attempts to reduce response to the CS by pairing a competing (comparator) cue with the UCS will have little effect on response to the CS. You might wonder what the term *biological significance* means. We leave you in suspense until Chapter 9.

We have described four very different theories about the nature of the classical conditioning process. Our discussion suggests that classical conditioning is a very complex process. In all likelihood, each theory accounts for some aspects of what happens when a conditioned stimulus and an unconditioned occur together. Table 5.1 shows how these four theories explain overshadowing, blocking, and potentiation.

Table 5.1 Explanation of Three Conditioning Phenomena by Four Models of Classical Conditioning			
Model or Theory	**Overshadowing**	**Blocking**	**Predictiveness**
Rescorla-Wagner Model	Salient stimulus acquires associative strength more readily than nonsalient stimulus.	Associative strength to blocking stimulus prevents conditioning to blocked stimulus.	Context associations prevent conditioning to conditioned stimulus.
Comparator Theory	Conditioning to salient stimulus is stronger than to nonsalient stimulus.	Conditioning is stronger for blocking stimulus than for blocked stimulus.	Context associations are stronger than conditioning to conditioned stimulus.
Attentional Theory	Salient stimulus is more associable than nonsalient stimulus.	Absence of surprise prevents conditioning to blocked stimulus.	Animals learn that conditioned stimulus does not reliably predict unconditioned stimulus.
Retrospective Processing Theory	Animals recognize the salience of different stimuli.	Animals recognize greater contingency between blocking and unconditioned stimuli.	Animals recognize the lack of contingency between conditioned stimulus and unconditioned stimulus.

BEFORE YOU GO ON

- How would Mackintosh's attentional view explain the difference in Jared's and Clarence's responses to Felicia's drinking?

- What prediction would Baker's retrospective processing model make for the development of a drinking–hostility association following Clarence's conversation with his friend Jared?

SECTION REVIEW

- Comparator theory argues that animals learn about all CS-UCS relationships and blocking occurs when the animal does not respond to the CS_2 because the CS_2-UCS association is weaker than the CS_1-UCS association.

- Deflation of the value of the CS_1 by extinction results in an increased response to the CS_2 due to the favorable comparison of the CS_2-UCS association to the CS_1-UCS association.

- Mackintosh's attentional view suggests that animals seek information to predict the occurrence of biologically significant events (UCSs).

- As the result of preexposure to the CS, an animal learns that the CS is irrelevant, which makes it difficult to later learn that the CS correlates with the UCS.

- Baker's retrospective processing theory proposes that animals are continuously monitoring the contingency between CS and UCS and that experience with a CS or UCS alone after conditioning can lead the animal to reevaluate the predictive value of the CS.

- The backward blocking phenomenon occurs when there is a reduced response to the CS_2 when CS_1-UCS pairings follow CS_1-CS_2-UCS pairings.

CRITICAL THINKING QUESTIONS

1. Yancy initially experienced intense euphoria after injecting heroin. His response to heroin is now much less intense. Using Siegel's research, provide an explanation for Yancy's current reaction to heroin. What would happen if Yancy injected heroin while he was in a new place?

2. Diane becomes ill after drinking several beers, yet she does not develop an aversion to beer. Describe the process(es) responsible for these preexposure effects.

3. Susan really likes chocolate. Suggest how several theories of classical conditioning would explain Susan's emotional response to chocolate. What experiences might change Susan's liking of chocolate? Explain the conditioning processes responsible for that change.

KEY TERMS

affective extension of SOP theory (AESOP)	analgesia
backward blocking	comparator theory
conditioned emotional reaction	conditioned withdrawal response
context blocking	CS preexposure effect
cue deflation effect	drug tolerance
hyperalgesia	hypoalgesia
interoceptive cue	learned irrelevance
Mackintosh's attentional view	overshadowing
potentiation	Rescorla-Wagner associative model
retrospective processing	sometimes-opponent-process (SOP) theory
stimulus-substitution theory	UCS preexposure effect
within-compound association	

CHAPTER 6

Principles and Applications of Appetitive Conditioning

A LOSS OF CONTROL

Traci and her husband Andre moved to Las Vegas last month. His accounting firm had asked him to move. They discussed the move for several weeks before he agreed to the transfer; the new position paid more and was more challenging than his old position. At first, Traci was upset by the move. She was a sophomore in college and would have to transfer to a new school. Andre assured her that there were good schools in Nevada. Traci was also concerned about being so far from home, but Andre promised that they would visit her family several times each year. The company took care of all the moving details, and they found a great apartment near Andre's office. As the move approached, Traci became excited. She had never been to Las Vegas and was especially looking forward to visiting the casinos. Her friends asked her whether she was going to do any gambling. Traci did enjoy playing the state lottery and thought that gambling in a casino would be fun. She and Andre arrived in Las Vegas several days early and decided to stay at one of the large hotels. Arriving at the hotel, Traci was struck by the glitter of the casino. She could hardly wait to unpack and go to the casino. Andre, on the other hand, did not seem interested in gambling. He told her to go down to the casino because he was tired, and he would nap. When he awoke, he told her, he would get her for dinner. Traci decided to play the $10 blackjack table. To her surprise, she got a blackjack on her first hand and won $15. The thrill of winning was fantastic, and she bet another $10 on the next hand. She lost that hand and was disappointed. She continued to play for the next two hours, until Andre came for dinner. Traci did not want to leave. She was down $40 but felt her luck was changing. Reluctantly, she agreed to go to dinner but thought of nothing else but getting back to the blackjack table. After dinner, they returned to the casino. Andre had wanted to tour the town, but Traci insisted on returning to the casino. Had she not been self-conscious, she would have run back to the table. She decided to try her luck at the $25 table and grew quite excited when the first card she received was an ace.

Why was Traci so anxious to return to the blackjack table? Winning a hand of blackjack can be a very powerful reinforcer, and Traci's excitement reflects the reinforcing power of winning. However, gambling can become an addictive behavior. Unless Traci can limit her gambling activities, she might be headed for serious trouble. Other examples of reinforcers include getting an A on an examination, going to the movies, or dining out at a favorite restaurant. However, reinforcers also have the potential to cause problems. For example, students who do little else but watch television are unlikely to do well in school. This chapter describes the use of reinforcement and nonreinforcement to alter undesired behavior.

PRINCIPLES OF APPETITIVE CONDITIONING

Skinner's Contribution

B. F. Skinner (1938) conducted an extensive investigation into the influence of reinforcement on behavior. His work showed that reinforcement has a significant impact on our actions. The concept of **contingency** is a central aspect of Skinner's theory. As we learned in Chapter 2, a contingency is a specified relationship between behavior and reinforcement. According to Skinner, the environment determines contingencies, and people must perform the appropriate behavior to obtain a reinforcer.

What is a **reinforcer**? We learned in Chapter 1 that Thorndike (1898) thought of a reward as a satisfying state. Skinner (1938) rejected such internal explanations of reinforcement; instead, he proposed that an event is reinforcing if it increases the frequency of the behavior that precedes the event. Thus, Skinner defined reinforcement merely by its influence on future behavior. In Skinner's view, any event that increases the probability of a behavior occurring is a reinforcer.

You might wonder why Skinner defined reinforcement this way. One reason is that the same event may be reinforcing to one person but not to another. Rather than using one's own perspective on what is satisfying, a psychologist can select a reinforcer based on its observed effect on behavior. This definition forces the psychologist to ignore preconceptions about what might be an effective reinforcer and to select one that actually works. We will have more to say about the use of reinforcement to modify behavior later.

The Distinction Between Instrumental and Operant Conditioning

Psychologists have used many different procedures to study the impact of reinforcement on behavior. Some psychologists have examined learning in a setting where the opportunity to respond is constrained; that is, the animal has limited opportunity to behave. For example, suppose a psychologist rewards an animal for running down an alley or turning left in a T-maze (see Figure 6.1). In both of these situations, the animal has a limited opportunity to gain reward. The rat can run down the alley or turn left in the maze and be rewarded, but whether the researcher puts the rat back in the alley or maze determines future opportunities. The rat has no control over how often it has the opportunity to obtain the reward.

When the environment constrains the opportunity for reward, the researcher is investigating **instrumental conditioning**. Evidence of the acquisition of an instrumental response could be the speed at which the rat runs down the alley or the number of errors the rat makes in the maze.

Consider the following example to illustrate the instrumental conditioning process. A parent is concerned about a child's failure to do required homework. The parent could reward the child each evening following the completion of assigned homework. The child can obtain the reward by doing homework; however, the child only has a single opportunity to gain the reward each evening.

In **operant conditioning,** there is no constraint on the amount of reinforcement the subject can obtain. In an operant conditioning situation, an animal controls the frequency of response and thereby determines the amount of reinforcement obtained. The lack of response constraint allows the animal to repeat the behavior, and evidence of learning is the frequency and consistency of

Figure 6.1   (a) A simple T-maze. In this maze, the rat must learn whether to turn left or right to obtain reward. (b) A runway or alley. In this apparatus, the rat receives a reward when it reaches the goal box; latency to run down the alley is the index of performance.

(a)

(b)

responding. (There often is some limit on the length of time that reinforcement is available, but within that time, the animal or person controls the amount of reinforcement received.)

B. F. Skinner needed a simple structured environment to study operant behavior, so he invented his own. This apparatus, which Skinner called an **operant chamber**, is an enclosed environment with a small bar on the inside wall. There is a dispenser for presenting either food or liquid reinforcement when the bar is pressed. A more elaborate version of an operant chamber has the capacity to present tones or lights, in order to study generalization and discrimination. The operant chamber also has been modified to accommodate many different animal species. Figure 6.2 presents a basic operant chamber for use with rats, in which a bar-press response causes the pellet dispenser to release food reinforcement.

Skinner also developed his own methodology to study behavior. More interested in observing the rate of a behavior than the intensity of a specific response, he developed the cumulative recorder. A pen attached to the recorder moves at a specific rate across the page; at the same time, each bar-press response produces an upward movement on the pen, enabling the experimenter to determine the rate of behavior. Modern technology has replaced the cumulative recorder with a computer that generates sophisticated graphics showing the animal's behavior.

There are many real-world examples of operant conditioning. Traci, in the chapter-opening vignette, was being reinforced in an operant conditioning situation. There were no constraints on the number of reinforcers she could earn, and the amount of reinforcement she received was

Figure 6.2   Operant chamber designed for rats. When the rat presses the bar, reinforcement (a food pellet) is delivered.

partly determined by the number of times she played blackjack. Other instances of operant conditioning include fishing—where a person can freely cast—or dating—where an individual can ask out one or many different people.

Skinner believed that operant behavior is not elicited by a stimulus. Instead, he believed that an animal voluntarily emits a specific behavior in order to gain reinforcement. Yet, environmental stimuli do affect operant responding. According to Skinner, environmental events set the occasion for operant behavior; that is, they inform the animal or person when reinforcement is available. We examine the occasion-setting function of environmental stimuli in Chapter 10.

Environmental circumstance also influences instrumental behavior. Thorndike (1898) proposed that stimulus-response connections develop as a result of reward (see Chapter 1). Conditioned stimuli have a powerful influence over instrumental activity; we will see how this influence works in Chapter 10.

One further point deserves mention. Reward and reinforcer are two concepts frequently referred to in psychology. The concept of reward is typically used in instrumental conditioning situations, while a reinforcer usually refers to operant conditioning. We will maintain this distinction between reward and reinforcer to help distinguish instrumental and operant conditioning.

Types of Reinforcers

Skinner (1938) identified several different categories of reinforcers. A **primary reinforcer** has innate reinforcing properties; a **secondary reinforcer** has developed its reinforcing properties through its association with primary reinforcers. For example, food is a primary reinforcer, while money is a secondary reinforcer. The three $5 chips that Traci received for getting a 21 playing blackjack were secondary reinforcers. The beer that she was served while playing blackjack was a primary reinforcer.

A number of variables affect the strength of a secondary reinforcer. First, the magnitude of the primary reinforcer paired with the secondary reinforcing stimulus influences the reinforcing power of the secondary reinforcer. Butter and Thomas (1958) presented a click prior to either an 8% sucrose solution or a 24% solution. These investigators found that rats made significantly more responses to the cue associated with the larger reinforcer. This indicates that a stimulus paired with a larger reinforcer acquires more reinforcing properties than a cue associated with a smaller reinforcer. Similar results were reported by D'Amato (1955) in a runway environment.

Second, the greater the number of pairings between the secondary reinforcing stimulus and the primary reinforcer, the stronger the reinforcing power of the secondary reinforcer. Bersh (1951) presented a 3-second light cue prior to either 10, 20, 40, 80, or 120 reinforcements (food pellets) for bar pressing. After training, primary reinforcement was discontinued and the bar-press response extinguished; this procedure equated the bar-press response strength for all subjects. The testing phase consisted of the presentation of the light following a bar press response. As Figure 6.3 shows, the number of responses emitted to produce the light increased as a function of light–food pairings. These results show that the reinforcing power of a secondary reinforcer increases with a greater number of pairings of the secondary reinforcer and the primary reinforcer. Jacobs (1968) also reported that the number of pairings of the primary and secondary reinforcer influenced the power of a secondary reinforcer.

Third, the elapsed time between the presentation of a secondary reinforcer and the primary reinforcer affects the strength of the secondary reinforcer. Bersh (1951) varied the interval

Figure 6.3   The strength of a secondary reinforcer increases as a function of the number of secondary and primary reinforcer pairings during acquisition. The measure of the power of the secondary reinforcer is the number of responses emitted during the first 10 minutes of testing.

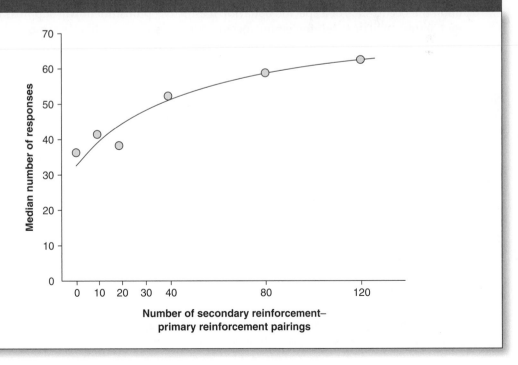

between light and food reinforcement in an operant chamber; the food followed the light stimulus by either .5, 1.0, 2.0, 4.0, or 10.0 seconds. Bersh observed that the number of responses emitted to obtain the light cue decreased as the interval between the secondary and the primary reinforcer increased. Bersh's results indicate that the power of a secondary reinforcer decreases as the interval between the secondary reinforcer and the primary reinforcer increases. Silverstein and Lipsitt (1974) also found that contiguity between the secondary reinforcer (tone) and the primary reinforcer (milk) was necessary to establish the tone as a secondary reinforcer in 10-month-old human infants.

We have learned that the value of the primary reinforcer, the number of pairings, and the temporal delay affect the reinforcing strength of a secondary reinforcer. The influence of these variables is not surprising: Secondary reinforcers acquire their reinforcing ability through the classical conditioning process. As we learned in Chapter 4, these variables influence the association of a conditioned stimulus and an unconditioned stimulus.

Skinner also distinguished between positive and negative reinforcers. A **positive reinforcer** is an event added to the environment that increases the frequency of the behavior that produces it. Examples of positive reinforcers are food and money. Taking away an unpleasant event can also be reinforcing. When the reinforcer is the removal of an unpleasant event, the reinforcer is referred to as a **negative reinforcer**.

In an experimental demonstration of a negative reinforcer, Skinner (1938) observed that rats learned to bar press to turn off electric shock. Animals also will learn to jump over a hurdle to terminate electric shock (Appel, 1964). For a real-world example, suppose that a teacher stands over a child doing schoolwork, encouraging the child to complete the assignment. As a result of the teacher's presence, the child rapidly finishes the assignment. When the child completes the homework, the teacher no longer stands over the child. In our example, the child considers the teacher's presence unpleasant, and the child's completion of the homework is reinforced by the teacher's departure.

It is important to point out that negative reinforcement and punishment is not the same thing. As we discover in Chapter 7, punishment is the application of an unpleasant event contingent upon the occurrence of a specific behavior. If effective, punishment will suppress that behavior. By contrast, **negative reinforcement** occurs when a specific behavior removes an unpleasant event. If the negative reinforcer is effective, the behavior will occur whenever the unpleasant event is encountered.

Shaping

The environment usually specifies the behavior necessary to obtain reinforcement. However, many operant behaviors occur infrequently or not at all, making it unlikely that the behavior-reinforcement contingency will be experienced. Under such conditions, the result is either no change or a slow change in the frequency of the behavior. Skinner (1938) developed a procedure called **shaping**, also known as the **successive approximation procedure**, to increase the rate at which an operant behavior is learned. During shaping, a behavior with a higher baseline rate of response than the desired behavior is selected and reinforced. When this behavior increases in frequency, the contingency is then changed and a closer approximation to the desired final behavior is reinforced. The contingency is slowly changed until the only way that the animal can obtain reinforcement is by performing the appropriate behavior.

Training a Rat to Bar Press

Many scientists have demonstrated that the successive approximation technique effectively and quickly modifies behavior. This technique has been used, for example, to train a rat to bar press to obtain reinforcement. A rat's initial rate of bar pressing is not necessarily zero because an animal exploring a small operant chamber may occasionally hit the bar. Therefore, the rat might learn that pressing the bar obtains food on its own. However, this self-training procedure is often slow, and the rate of learning varies considerably among animals. Shaping of bar pressing helps to ensure a rapid acquisition of desired behavior.

The first stage of the shaping procedure involves reinforcing the rat for eating out of the food dispenser (see Figure 6.4). When this feeding response occurs consistently (which occurs only a short time after training begins), the contingency must be changed to a closer approximation of the final bar-press response. The second stage of shaping consists of reinforcing the rat when it is moving away from the food dispenser. The moving-away response continues to be reinforced until this behavior occurs consistently; then the contingency is changed again.

In the third phase of shaping, the rat is reinforced only for moving away from the dispenser in the direction of the bar. The change in contingency at first causes the rat to move in a number of directions. The experimenter must wait, reinforcing only movement toward the bar. The shaping procedure is continued, with closer and closer approximations reinforced until the rat presses the bar. At this point, shaping is complete. The use of shaping to develop a bar-press response is a reliable technique that can be used to train most rats to bar press in approximately an hour. Let's next consider a real-world application of the shaping technique.

Figure 6.4   Shaping a bar-press response in rats. In the initial phase, the rat is reinforced for eating out of the pellet dispenser (Scene 1). During the second phase of shaping (Scenes 2, 3, 4, and 5), the rat must move away from the dispenser to receive reinforcement. Later in the shaping process (Scenes 6 and 7), the rat must move toward the bar to receive the food reinforcer.

Shaping Social Discourse

Many parents struggle to teach their children social skills. Even simple social skills like talking with company can be difficult for many children. Many parents undoubtedly use reinforcement (probably praise) as well as punishment (probably scolding) to try to teach their children social skills. Yet, parents typically reinforce only the final response. Since children need considerable practice to learn effective social skills, children may experience much frustration and give up.

Parents can employ the shaping technique to teach social skills to their children. Beginning by reinforcing a behavior that their children can readily perform (e.g., opening the door for company), parents should then gradually change the contingencies to train more complex behaviors. Now the child must say "hello" to company in order to be reinforced. Next, a question such as "How are you today?" or "Would you like something to drink?" would yield reinforcement. By successively reinforcing behaviors that more and more closely resemble the final desired behavior, parents can teach their children to converse with others.

BEFORE YOU GO ON

- What does Traci find so reinforcing about playing blackjack?

- How might the shaping process explain why Traci plays blackjack and Andre does not?

SECTION REVIEW

- In instrumental conditioning, constraints are placed on the opportunity to gain reward; operant conditioning has no constraints, and the animal or person can freely respond to obtain reinforcement.

- Primary reinforcers possess innate reinforcing ability; secondary reinforcers develop the capacity to reinforce operant or instrumental behavior.

- The reinforcing property of a secondary reinforcer is determined by (1) the strength of the primary reinforcer it is associated with, (2) the number of pairings of the primary and secondary reinforcers, and (3) the delay between primary and secondary reinforcement.

- A positive reinforcer is an event that has reinforcing properties; a negative reinforcer is the removal of an unpleasant event.

- Shaping involves reinforcing a response that occurs at a high rate and then changing the contingency so that closer and closer approximations to the final behavior are required to produce reinforcement.

We must not only learn how to act to be reinforced but also how often and/or when to act. Skinner called this aspect of the contingency the **schedule of reinforcement**, and the schedule specifies how often or when we must act to receive reinforcement.

Schedules of Reinforcement

Reinforcement can be programmed using two basic methods. First, behavior can be reinforced based on the number of responses emitted. Skinner (1938) labeled a situation in which the contingency requires a certain number of responses to produce reinforcement a **ratio schedule of reinforcement**.

Reinforcement also can be scheduled on a time basis; Skinner (1938) called the timed programming of reinforcement an **interval schedule of reinforcement**. With an interval schedule, reinforcement becomes available at a certain period of time after the last reinforcement. Any behavior occurring during the interval receives no reinforcement, while the first response occurring at the end of the interval is reinforced. In an interval schedule, reinforcement must be obtained before another interval begins.

There are two classes of both ratio and interval schedules: fixed and variable reinforcement schedules. With a **fixed-ratio (FR) schedule**, a constant number of responses is necessary to produce reinforcement. In contrast, with a **variable-ratio (VR) schedule**, an average number of responses produces reinforcement; that is, the number of responses needed to obtain reinforcement varies from one reinforcer to the next. Similarly, reinforcement can be programmed on a **fixed-interval (FI) schedule** of reinforcement, in which the same interval always separates available reinforcements, or it can become available after a varying interval of time. With a **variable-interval (VI) schedule**, there is an average interval between available reinforcements, but the exact interval differs.

We have discussed four types of reinforcement schedules that have an important influence on our behavior. The pattern and rate of behavior is very different depending on the type of reinforcement schedule. Let's now briefly examine the behavioral characteristics of these reinforcement schedules. The interested reader should refer to Ferster and Skinner (1957) for a detailed discussion of schedules of reinforcement.

Fixed-Ratio Schedules

On a **fixed-ratio (FR) schedule**, a specific number of responses is necessary to produce reinforcement. With an FR-1 (or continuous) schedule, reinforcement is given after a single response. Likewise, 10 responses must occur to receive reinforcement on an FR-10 schedule. As an example of a fixed-ratio schedule, a rat may be reinforced after every 10 bar presses. This would be an FR-10 schedule. Two real-world examples of a fixed-ratio schedule are an adult earning a free round-trip ticket for travel after getting 25,000 frequent-flyer miles or a child receiving a toy from a company for sending in five cereal box tops.

Fixed-ratio schedules produce a consistent response rate; that is, an animal or person responds at a steady rate during the entire time that reinforcement is possible, until habituation occurs to the reinforcer (see Chapter 3) or until the animal is satiated (refer to Figure 6.5). Furthermore, the rate of response increases with higher FR schedules. For example, Collier, Hirsch, and Hamlin (1972) noted that rats bar press at a higher rate on an FR-20 than an FR-10 schedule and higher still on an FR-60 than an FR-40 (see Figure 6.6). Similar results were obtained with pigeons (Felton & Lyon, 1966), cats (Kanarek, 1974), prairie dogs (Todd & Cogan, 1978), possum (Hudson, Foster, & Temple, 1999), and children (Stephens, Pear, Wray, & Jackson, 1975).

Fixed-ratio schedules have another distinctive characteristic. Following reinforcement, responding will temporarily stop. The pause after reinforcement is called a **postreinforcement pause**. After the pause, responding resumes at the rate present before reinforcement. Therefore, the animal or person on a fixed-ratio schedule either responds at the intensity characteristic of that ratio or does not respond at all.

A postreinforcement pause is not observed with all fixed-ratio schedules. The higher the number of responses needed to obtain reinforcement, the more likely a pause will follow reinforcement. Further, the length of the pause also varies; the higher the ratio schedule, the longer the pause in prairie dogs (Todd & Cogan, 1978) and humans (Wallace & Mulder, 1973). Collier et al. (1972) noted that the greater the effort necessary to obtain reinforcement, the longer the pause after receiving reinforcement. The length of the pause also depends upon satiation; the greater

Figure 6.5 Samples of cumulative records of bar-press responding under the simple schedules of reinforcement. The slash marks on the response records indicate presentations of reinforcement: The steeper the cumulative response gradient, the higher the animal's rate of response.

Figure 6.6 Cumulative response records on various fixed-ratio schedules. Behavior is affected by the fixed ratio used during conditioning. The rate of response increases with higher fixed ratios, and the postreinforcement pause occurs only at the highest FR schedules.

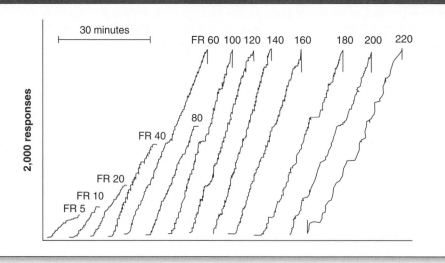

the satiation, the longer the pause following reinforcement in rats (Sidman & Stebbins, 1954) and pigeons (Wald & Cheney, 1975).

Variable-Ratio Schedules

On a **variable-ratio (VR) schedule**, an average number of responses produces reinforcement, but the actual number of responses required to produce reinforcement varies over the course of training. Suppose that a rat is reinforced for bar pressing on a VR-20 schedule. While the rat must bar press 20 times on average to receive reinforcement, the rat may press the bar 10 times to get the reinforcer one time, but have to respond 30 times to obtain the next reinforcer. Two real-world examples of a variable-ratio schedule are a door-to-door salesperson who makes two consecutive sales and then has to knock on 50 doors before making another sale, or a child who receives a star card in the first baseball pack opened, but then has to open five more packs before getting another star card.

Like the FR schedules, VR schedules produce a consistent response rate (see Figure 6.5). Furthermore, the greater the average number of responses necessary to produce reinforcement are, the higher the response rate. For example, Felton and Lyon (1966) found that rats bar press at a higher rate on a VR-200 than a VR-50. Similarly, Ferster and Skinner (1957) observed that the rate at which pigeons key peck is higher on a VR-100 than a VR-50 and still higher on a VR-200 schedule of reinforcement. Recall Traci playing blackjack in the chapter-opening vignette. Traci is being reinforced on a variable-ratio schedule, which explains the fact that she continues to respond at a high rate for long periods as some hands of blackjack are reinforced while others are not, but it is impossible to know from one hand to the next whether playing will be reinforced.

In contrast to the pause after reinforcement on a fixed-ratio schedule, postreinforcement pauses occur only occasionally on variable-ratio schedules (Felton & Lyon, 1966). The relative absence of pause behavior after reinforcement on VR schedules results in a higher response rate on a VR than a comparable FR schedule. Thus, rats bar press more times during an hour-long session with a VR-50 than an FR-50 schedule (see Figure 6.5).

The high response rate that occurs with VR schedules can explain the persistent and vigorous behavior characteristic of gambling. For example, a slot machine is programmed to pay off after an average number of operations. However, the exact number of operations necessary to obtain reinforcement is unpredictable. Individuals who play a slot machine for hours, constantly putting money into it, do so because of the variable-ratio programming of the slot machines.

Fixed-Interval Schedules

With a **fixed-interval (FI) schedule**, reinforcement depends upon both the passage of time and the exhibition of the appropriate behavior. Reinforcement is available only after a specified period of time, and the first response emitted after the interval has elapsed is reinforced. Therefore, a rat on an FI 1-minute schedule is reinforced for the first bar press after the minute interval has elapsed; in contrast, a rat on an FI 2-minute schedule must wait 2 minutes before its first response is reinforced.

One example of a fixed-interval schedule is having the mail delivered at about the same time every day. Making gelatin is another real-world example of a fixed-interval schedule. After it is mixed and dissolved, gelatin is placed in the refrigerator to set. After a few hours, the gelatin is ready to be eaten. However, while the cook may eat the gelatin as soon as it is ready, a few hours or even a few days may elapse before the cook actually goes to the refrigerator and obtains the gelatin reinforcement.

Have you ever seen the behavior of a child waiting for gelatin to set? The child will go to the refrigerator, shake the dish, recognize the gelatin is not ready, and place it back in the refrigerator.

The child will repeat this action every once in awhile. A similar behavior occurs when someone is waiting for an important piece of mail. With each check, the gelatin is closer to being ready or the mail nearer to being delivered. These behaviors illustrate one aspect of a fixed-interval schedule. After receiving reinforcement on a fixed-interval schedule, an animal or person stops responding; then the rate of response slowly increases as the time approaches when reinforcement once more becomes available (see Figure 6.5). This characteristic response pattern produced by an FI schedule was referred to as the **scallop effect** by Ferster and Skinner (1957). The scallop effect has been observed with a number of species, including pigeons (Catania & Reynolds, 1968), rats (Innis, 1979), and humans (Shimoff, Catania, & Matthews, 1981).

Two variables affect the length of the pause on FI schedules. First, the ability to withhold responding until close to the end of the interval increases with experience (Cruser & Klein, 1984). Second, the pause is longer with longer FI schedules (Gentry, Weiss, & Laties, 1983).

Variable-Interval Schedules

On a **variable-interval (VI) schedule**, an average interval of time elapses between available reinforcements; however, the length of time varies from one interval to the next. For example, the average interval is 2 minutes on a VI 2-minute schedule; yet, one time, the rat may wait only 1 minute between reinforcements and the next time, 5 minutes. Consider the following illustration of a variable-interval schedule. Suppose you go fishing. How successful will your fishing trip be? The number of times you cast is not important. Instead, when the fish swims by the bait is critical. You may have to wait only a few minutes between catches on one occasion, but wait many minutes on another.

VI schedules are characterized by a steady rate of response (see Figure 6.5). Furthermore, VI length affects the rate of response; the longer the average interval between reinforcements, the lower the response rate. For example, Catania and Reynolds (1968) discovered that pigeons responded 60 to 100 times per minute on a VI .2-minute schedule, but only 20 to 70 times per minute on a VI 7.1-minute schedule. Nevin (1973) obtained similar results with rats, as did Todd and Cogan (1978) with prairie dogs.

The scallop effect characteristic of FI schedules does not occur on VI schedules: There is no pause following reinforcement on a VI schedule. However, Catania and Reynolds (1968) reported that the maximum rate of response on VI schedules occurred just prior to reinforcement.

Differential Reinforcement Schedules

In many situations, a specific number of behaviors must occur or not occur within a specified amount of time to produce reinforcement. When reinforcement depends on both time and the number of responses, the contingency is a **differential reinforcement schedule**. For example, students required to complete an assignment during a semester are reinforced on a differential reinforcement schedule. Why isn't this an example of a fixed-interval schedule? A fixed-interval schedule imposes no time limit on the occurrence of the appropriate behavior; with a differential reinforcement schedule, if the behavior does not occur within the time limit, no reinforcement is provided. We now discuss three important types of differential reinforcement schedules.

Differential Reinforcement of High Responding (DRH) Schedules. Reinforcement can be made contingent on a high rate of response; such a schedule is called a **differential reinforcement of high responding (DRH) schedule**. Consider the following example of a DRH schedule. Your instructor assigns a paper due in two weeks. It must be at least 10 typed pages. In this situation, a substantial amount of effort must be exerted in a short time to complete the assignment.

Although you may not enjoy it, you are likely to work hard to complete the assignment if your behavior is controlled by the DRH schedule of reinforcement.

DRH schedules are extremely effective. Animals exhibit a consistently high rate of response when reinforcement is provided on a DRH schedule (Catania, 1979). For example, a pigeon on such a schedule can learn to peck a key more than 10 times per second. However, DRH schedules contain an inherent danger. If the high level of response needed to produce reinforcement cannot be maintained, the animal will receive less reinforcement. This lowered reinforcement further decreases the response rate. In a vicious cycle, the response rate and the obtained reinforcement decline until no responses are performed. Therefore, to ensure consistent response, the response rate of the DRH schedule must be high, but not too high.

People can also learn to respond at a high rate on a DRH schedule (P. Reed, 2003). Reed reported that response rate was higher in human subjects on a DRH than a VI schedule that was matched for reinforcement rate. Interestingly, people often respond to a DRH schedule as if it were an FI schedule. For example, a series of exams scheduled during a semester is a DRH schedule; that is, a high rate of response (studying) is necessary to obtain a good grade. However, most students treat exams as they would an FI: They stop responding after an exam and slowly increase their response rate until they are "cramming" for the next test. By limiting studying to the times just prior to examinations, students are not likely to respond enough to do well. The more effective strategy would be to respond consistently throughout the interval, which is the response pattern characteristic of DRH schedules.

Differential Reinforcement of Low Responding (DRL) Schedules. Reinforcement can also be scheduled contingent upon a low rate of response; this schedule is a **differential reinforcement of low responding (DRL) schedule**. With this schedule, a certain interval of time must elapse without a response, and the first response at the end of the interval is reinforced. If an animal responds during the interval, the interval is reset and the response withheld for the length of time specified in the contingency. The following example illustrates the DRL schedule. As you attempt to start your car, you flood the engine. If you try to start it before waiting several minutes, it will flood again, and you will have to wait a few more minutes before it will start. Thus, to start your engine after flooding it, you must withhold your starting behavior for several minutes.

DRH schedules produce high rates of response. By contrast, DRL schedules limit the response rate. DRL schedules, like DRH schedules, effectively control behavior; that is, individuals learn to respond according to the schedule of reinforcement. However, DRL schedules, unlike DRH schedules, require time to become effective (G. S. Reynolds, 1968). The effect of reinforcement is an increase in the response rate, which subsequently acts to prevent reinforcement. The absence of reinforcement lowers the response rate. Eventually, the influence of the schedule appears, and the individual is able to withhold responding until the end of the interval (see Figure 6.7).

Differential Reinforcement of Other Behaviors (DRO) Schedule. Providing reinforcement only in the absence of a particular response in a specified period of time is called a **differential reinforcement of other behaviors (DRO) schedule**. The DRO schedule is unique because it reinforces the failure to exhibit a specific behavior during a particular time period. Suppose that a parent informs a child that hitting a younger sibling again before dinner will result in no television viewing that evening. In this situation, the parent is using a DRO schedule; that is, in order for the child to watch television (obtain reinforcement), no aggressive responses can occur prior to dinner.

A differential reinforcement of other behaviors schedule has been widely used in behavior modification (Poling & Ryan, 1982). We look at the use of DRO schedules further in the discussion of the application of appetitive conditioning later in this chapter.

Figure 6.7 Relative frequency distribution of interresponse times(IRTs) in rats receiving reinforcement on a 10-second DRL schedule.

Compound Schedules

The contingency between behavior and reinforcement sometimes involves more than one schedule. With a **compound schedule**, two or more schedules are combined. As an example of a compound schedule, consider the rat that must bar press 10 times (FR-10) and wait 1 minute after the last bar press (FI 1 minute) until another bar press will produce reinforcement. The rat must complete both schedules in the appropriate sequence in order to obtain reinforcement. The rat learns to respond appropriately, supporting animals and humans' sensitivity to the complexities of schedules. While an extensive discussion of compound schedules of reinforcement is beyond the scope of this text, interested readers should consult Commons, Mazur, Nevin, and Rachlin (1987) for a detailed discussion of the varied compound schedules of reinforcement.

BEFORE YOU GO ON

- What schedule of reinforcement was responsible for Traci's high level of playing blackjack?

- What might the casino do to cause Traci to wager more on each hand of blackjack?

SECTION REVIEW

- A fixed number of responses are necessary to produce reinforcement on fixed-ratio (FR) schedules; an average number of responses lead to reinforcement on variable-ratio (VR) schedules.

- On an FR schedule, responding stops following reinforcement, called a postreinforcement pause. After the pause, responding resumes at the rate present before reinforcement.

- On a VR schedule, response rate is high, with only an occasional postreinforcement pause.

- The first response occurring after a specified interval of time produces reinforcement on a fixed-interval (FI) schedule; an average interval of time elapses between available reinforcements on a variable-interval (VI) schedule; the length of time varies from one interval to the next.

- On a FI schedule, responding stops after reinforcement, with the rate of response increasing slowly as the time approaches when reinforcement will once more become available; the behavior characteristic of a FI schedule is called the scallop effect.

- The scallop effect does not occur on VI schedules, and there is no pause following reinforcement on a VI schedule.

- The response requirement is high within a specified amount of time with a differential reinforcement of high responding (DRH) schedule and low with a differential reinforcement of low responding (DRL) schedule.

- A differential reinforcement of other behaviors (DRO) schedule requires an absence of response during the specified time.

How Readily Is an Instrumental or an Operant Response Learned?

Although many variables affect the development of instrumental or operant behavior, we look at two factors that play a significant role in determining the strength of conditioning.

The Importance of Contiguity

You help a friend change a tire on his car; you're thanked for your assistance. The effect of the social reward is to increase your likelihood of future helping behavior. However, if your friend waits several days before thanking you, the impact of the reward is reduced. This observation points to the importance of contiguity in instrumental or operant conditioning: Reward can lead to the acquisition of an instrumental or operant response if it immediately follows the behavior, while learning is impaired if reward is delayed. Many studies have documented the effect of delay on the acquisition of an instrumental or operant behavior; we discuss several of them next.

The Effect of Delay. In a classic study, Grice (1948) investigated the role of reward delay on the rat's learning to go into a black chamber instead of a white one. Grice varied the delay between the correct response and reward. In his study, the delay interval was either 0, .5, 1.2, 2, 5, or 10 seconds. As Figure 6.8 shows, there is a very steep delay gradient: Little conditioning occurred with delay intervals as short as 1.2 seconds.

However, not all experiments (Logan, 1952; Perin, 1943) have reported a delay gradient comparable to Grice's data. For example, Perin (1943) found moderate levels of conditioning of bar-press responses even with a 10-second delay, while with a delay of 30 seconds or more, rats were unable to learn to bar press to obtain reinforcement.

Why do the delay gradients differ in Grice's (1948) and Perin's (1943) experiments? The presence or absence of secondary reward cues is important. The presence of a secondary reward during the interval can lessen the influence of delay. In contrast, when cues associated with reward are not present during the interval, even a very short delay produces little conditioning. In support

Figure 6.8   The level of learning decreases with an increased delay between the instrumental response and reward. The measure of learning is the reciprocal × 1,000 of the number of trials to reach 75% correct choices: Thus, the higher the value, the greater the level of learning.

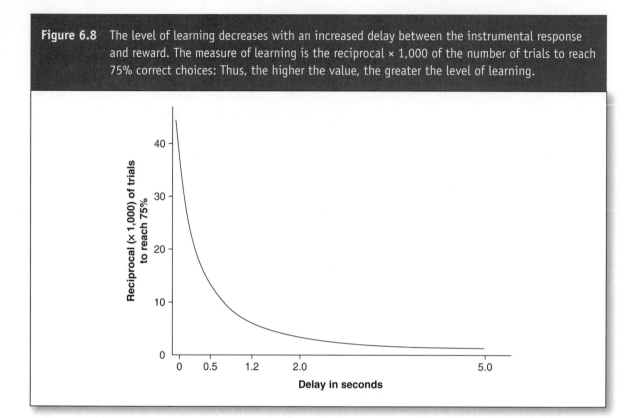

of this view, animals in Grice's study spent the delay interval in an environment not associated with reward. In contrast, the rats in Perin's experiment remained in the conditioning environment associated with reinforcement during the interval between responding and primary reinforcement. If this analysis is correct, the presence of a secondary reward should reduce the effects of a delay of reward. As expected, B. A. Williams (1991b) found that the presence of a secondary reward could "bridge" the interval and reduce the effect of a delayed primary reward.

Delay of Reward and Conditioning in Humans. When Traci wins a hand of blackjack, she receives immediate reinforcement. The immediacy of reinforcement contributes to the effectiveness of reinforcement that motivates gambling behavior.

The importance of reward delay has also been demonstrated by studies using children as subjects. These studies (see J. F. Hall, 1976) consistently show that the longer the delay between the instrumental behavior and reward, the poorer the conditioning of the instrumental response. Let's examine one of these studies more closely.

Terrell and Ware (1961) gave kindergarten and first-grade children two choice problems to solve. The children received immediate reward for responding correctly to the correct stimulus; a 7-second delay of reward followed the correct response for the other choice problem. Terrell and Ware reported that the children required approximately 7 trials with immediate reward to learn to respond correctly compared with an average of 17 trials when reward was delayed. These observations indicate that a delay between the correct response and the reward interferes with the acquisition of choice behavior.

The Impact of Reward Magnitude

The Acquisition of an Instrumental or Operant Response. Suppose that parents decide to reward their children for learning vocabulary words. The rate of acquisition of the vocabulary words depends upon the magnitude of the reward provided; the larger the reward magnitude, the faster the vocabulary words will be acquired. Many studies have shown that the magnitude of reward affects the rate of acquisition of an instrumental or operant response; let's look at several of these studies.

Crespi's 1942 study demonstrates the influence of reward magnitude on the acquisition of an instrumental running response in an alley. Upon reaching the goal box, Crespi's rats received either 1, 4, 16, 64, or 256 units of food. Crespi observed that the greater the reward magnitude, the faster the animals learned to run down the alley.

Researchers have also shown that reinforcer magnitude affects the acquisition of a bar-press response in an operant chamber. For example, N. Guttman (1953) varied the amount of reinforcement rats received for bar pressing; animals were given either a 4%, 8%, 16%, or 32% sucrose solution following the operant response. Guttman discovered that the greater the reinforcer magnitude, the faster the animals learned to bar press to obtain reinforcement (see Figure 6.9).

The Performance of an Instrumental or Operant Response. A while back, my middle son informed me that $20 was no longer enough money for mowing the yard; he now wants $30 to do the job. His behavior indicates the critical influence that the magnitude of reward has on the performance of an instrumental behavior. The likelihood and intensity of an instrumental or operant response depends upon the magnitude of reward provided following a particular response. In many instances, the magnitude of reward must be of a sufficient level to cause the behavior to occur;

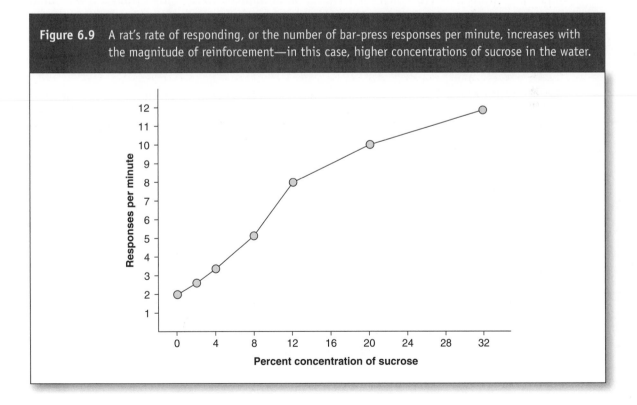

Figure 6.9   A rat's rate of responding, or the number of bar-press responses per minute, increases with the magnitude of reinforcement—in this case, higher concentrations of sucrose in the water.

thus, my son's mowing response would occur only if the payment was sufficiently high. At other times, the instrumental or operant behavior may occur, and the intensity of the response will depend upon the reward magnitude. The literature consistently shows that reward magnitude affects performance. This section examines several studies documenting this influence.

Crespi's 1942 study also evaluated the level of instrumental performance as a function of reward magnitude. Crespi discovered that the greater the magnitude, the faster the rats ran down the alley to obtain the reward, an observation that indicates that the magnitude of reward influences the level of instrumental behavior. Other studies also show that reward magnitude determines the level of performance in the runway situation (Mellgren, 1972) and in the operant chamber (A. Gutman, Sutterer, & Brush, 1975).

Why does reward magnitude affect instrumental or operant behavior? Recall from Chapter 2 that Clark Hull (1943) first thought that reward magnitude influences the level of conditioning. Hull (1952) later came to think that the differences in performance reflect motivational differences. How did Hull come to the conclusion that a greater reward magnitude motivates behavior more than does a lesser reward value? Suppose that after a behavior is rewarded and an asymptotic performance reached, the reward value is shifted to a higher (or lower) level. If the reward magnitude shift causes a gradual alteration in behavior, the change in response would reflect a learning influence because learning changes are thought to occur slowly; however, if the alteration in behavior following the shift is rapid, the inference would be that motivational processes are causing the behavior change.

Many studies (Crespi, 1942; Zeaman, 1949) reported a rapid change in behavior when reward magnitude is shifted, which suggests that motivational differences are responsible for the performance differences associated with differences in reward magnitude (see Figure 6.10). For example, Crespi (1942) shifted some animals from a high reward magnitude (256 units) to a moderate reward level (16 units) on Trial 20; other animals were shifted from a low (1 unit) reward magnitude to the moderate reward magnitude. The animals showed a rapid change in behavior on the trial following the shift in reward magnitude: The high-to-moderate-shift animals exhibited a significantly lowered response time on Trial 21, while the low-to-moderate-shift subjects ran significantly faster on Trial 21 than on the preceding trial.

The Importance of Past Experience. Suppose that your boss's marginal profits cause a cut in your salary. Under these conditions, your behavior will be less efficient as a result of the lowered magnitude of reward. How much will your output decline? Research (Crespi, 1942) indicates that you will exhibit less output now than if your salary had always been low (see Figure 6.10). The lower than predicted level of performance due to a shift from a high to a low reward magnitude is called the **depression effect**.

Perhaps your boss's profits increase and you receive a raise. Under these conditions, your behavior will become more efficient as a result of the higher magnitude of reward. A shift from low to high reward magnitude produces a level of performance greater than it would be if the higher reward level had always been used. The heightened performance produced by a shift from low to high reward is called an **elation effect**.

Zeaman (1949) suggested replacing the terms *elation* and *depression effects* with *positive* and *negative contrast effects* to indicate that the specific context in which a stimulus is experienced can produce exaggerated or reduced effects. Thus, experience with low reward heightens the influence of a high reward, called a **positive contrast effect**; that is, a large reward is more effective than it normally would be because of previous experience with a smaller reward. In contrast, experience exaggerates the impact of a low reward magnitude, called a **negative contrast effect**; that is, a small reward is less effective than it would normally be because of experience with a larger reward.

Figure 6.10   A higher level of performance occurs with a larger reward magnitude during the preshift phase. Not only does the level of response decline following a shift from high to low reward magnitude, but it is even lower than it would be if the level of reward had always been low (a depression or negative contrast effect). By contrast, a shift from low to high reward magnitude not only leads to a higher level of response, but it also produces a response level that is greater than it would be if the level of reward had always been high (an elation or positive contrast effect). The contrast effects last for only a few trials; then responding returns to the level appropriate for that reward magnitude.

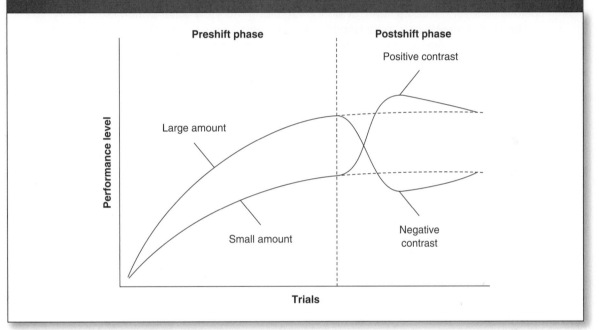

Investigations (Flaherty, 1996) since Crespi's original study have consistently produced a negative contrast effect, yet research conducted during the 1960s seemed to indicate that the positive contrast effect could not be induced (Black, 1968). However, Bower (1981) suggested that a ceiling effect was responsible for the inability to produce a positive contrast effect; that is, high reward magnitude alone was causing maximum responding, and therefore, the shift from low to high could not raise performance. More recent studies (A. Gutman & Fenner, 1982; Shanab, Molayem, Gordon, & Steinhauer, 1981) demonstrated that a positive contrast effect can be induced if animals are initially responding at a level below the upper limit.

We should note that the contrast effects last for only short periods. Thus, animals shifted from high to low (or low to high) reward respond at a lower (or higher) level than animals always experiencing the low (or high) reward magnitude for only a few trials. Further, animals exposed to a series of reward shifts eventually show neither negative not positive contrast effects (Goomas, 1981). Goomas observed both the negative and positive contrast effects early in training (after only one or two reward magnitude shifts), while later in training (after six or seven reward magnitude shifts) neither contrast effect was observed. It would seem that the processes producing the reward magnitude contrast effects are eliminated when subjects have multiple shift experiences.

Why do the contrast effects occur? The emotion of frustration seems to play an important role in the negative contrast effect. According to Flaherty (1996), an animal establishes an expected level of reward during initial acquisition training. The presentation of a lower-than-expected level of reward in the second phase causes frustration, which interferes with instrumental activity and thereby produces a response level lower than it would have been for the expected reward. The observation that drugs that reduce anxiety in humans eliminate the negative contrast effect supports this view; this result has been found in rats with the tranquilizer Librium (Becker & Flaherty, 1983), with alcohol (Becker & Flaherty, 1982), with barbiturates (Flaherty & Driscoll, 1980), and with antipsychotics (Genn, Barr, & Phillips, 2002). Flaherty suggested that the emotional response of elation produced by receiving a reward greater than the expected magnitude may explain the positive contrast effect; however, evidence validating this view is not available.

The medial amygdala plays a significant role in producing the emotion of frustration when a goal is blocked (Amaral, Price, Pitkanen, & Carmichael, 1992). Lesions in the medial amygdala have been found to eliminate the frustration experienced by rats following the omission of reward in a goal box and to produce a decreased speed running to that goal box (Henke & Maxwell, 1973). Not surprisingly, Becker, Jarvis, Wagner, and Flaherty (1984) reported that localized lesions of the medial amygdala eliminated the negative contrast effect.

The Influence of Reward Magnitude in Humans. Recall our example of Traci playing blackjack in the chapter-opening vignette. For Traci, winning $15 with a hand of 21 was a large reward enough to keep her playing well into the night.

Although most of the research on reward magnitude has used animals as subjects, some research with people has indicated that reward value affects the performance of an instrumental or operant response. Research with young children (see Hall, 1976) has shown that the magnitude of reward does affect the development of an instrumental or operant response. For example, Siegel and Andrews (1962) found that 4- and 5-year-old children responded correctly more often on a task when given a large reward (e.g., a small prize) rather than a small reward (e.g., a button). Studies have also shown that reward magnitude influences instrumental or operant behavior in adults. For example, J. W. Atkinson's research (1958) found that the amount of money paid for successful performance influences the level of achievement behavior.

BEFORE YOU GO ON

- How does knowing right away whether a hand of blackjack is a winner or loser contribute to Traci's gambling behavior?

- What would happen if Traci increased the amount of a wager and then won a hand of blackjack? What if she lost?

SECTION REVIEW

- An instrumental or operant response is learned rapidly if reward immediately follows the response.

- The performance of the instrumental or operant response is higher with a larger rather than smaller reward, which is due to the greater motivational impact of a large reward.

- A shift from large to small reward leads to a rapid decrease in response; a shift from small to large reward causes a significant increase in response.

- The negative contrast (or depression) effect is a lower level of performance when the reward magnitude is shifted from high to low than when the reward magnitude is always low.

- The positive contrast (or elation) effect is a higher level of performance when the reward magnitude is shifted from low to high than when the reward magnitude is always high.

Extinction of an Appetitive Response

An operant or instrumental response, acquired when reinforcement follows the occurrence of a specific behavior, can be extinguished when the reinforcer no longer follows the response. Continued failure of behavior to produce reinforcement causes the strength of the response to diminish until the operant or instrumental response is no longer performed.

Consider the following example to illustrate the **extinction of an operant or instrumental response.** A child shopping with her mother sees a favorite candy bar and discovers that a temper tantrum persuades her mother to buy the candy. The contingency between the temper tantrum and candy teaches the child to have a tantrum every time she wants a candy bar. The child's mother, tired of being manipulated, decides to no longer submit to her child's unruly behavior. The mother no longer reinforces the child's tantrums with candy, and the incidence of tantrums declines slowly until the child learns to enter a store and behave when candy is refused.

The Discontinuance of Reinforcement

In 1938, Skinner observed that the failure to reinforce a previously acquired bar-press response in rats caused the **extinction** of that response. When reinforcement is first discontinued, the rate of response remains high (see Figure 6.11) or, under some conditions, actually increases. Consider the child whose temper tantrums are no longer reinforced by a parent. Anyone who has spent some time with a young child has certainly observed the increased intensity of temper

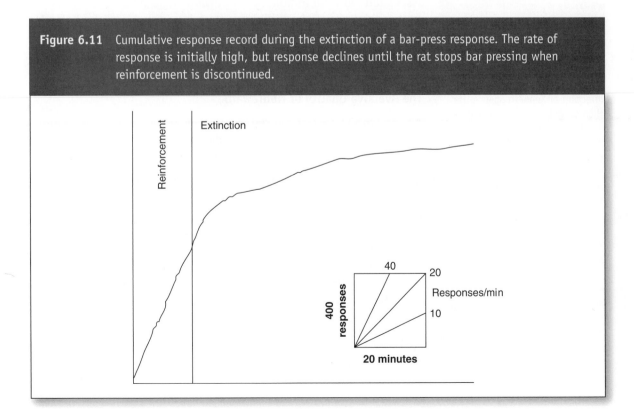

Figure 6.11   Cumulative response record during the extinction of a bar-press response. The rate of response is initially high, but response declines until the rat stops bar pressing when reinforcement is discontinued.

tantrums once they are no longer reinforced. The continued failure to produce reinforcement causes the rate of response to then decline, until the behavior stops; that is, the child eventually stops having temper tantrums.

Extinction of a previously reinforced behavior has also been documented in humans. For example, Lewis and Duncan (1958) reinforced college students for pulling the lever of a slot machine. When reinforcement (a disk exchangeable for 5 cents) was discontinued, the students eventually stopped pulling the lever. Lewis (1952) noted a similar extinction pattern in 6- and 7-year-old children who were no longer reinforced with toys for pressing a button.

Spontaneous Recovery

Abram Amsel (1922–2006)

Amsel received his doctorate from the University of Iowa under the direction of Kenneth Spence. He then taught at Tulane University and the University of Toronto for 21 years. In 1969, he was invited to join the faculty at the University of Texas, Austin, to replace Spence, who had moved to Texas from Iowa a few years earlier but died unexpectedly of cancer. He taught at Texas for the next 20 years before retiring in 1999. His research has contributed significantly to understanding the role of classical conditioning in the development of frustration and its influence on behavior. He kept an old Jaguar two-seater in his garage because the smell of the leather reminded him of his courtship with his wife Tess many years earlier.

In Chapter 4, we learned that when a conditioned response (CS) is presented without the unconditioned response (UCS), a temporary inhibition develops that suppresses all responding. When this temporary inhibition dissipates, the CR reappears. This increase in response shortly after extinction is called **spontaneous recovery**. A similar recovery occurs when an interval of time follows the extinction of an instrumental or operant behavior.

We also learned that if the CS continues in the absence of the UCS, conditioned inhibition develops specifically to the CS. The conditioning of inhibition to the CS leads to a loss of spontaneous recovery. The loss of spontaneous recovery is also seen in instrumental or operant conditioning if the response continues to be unrewarded. According to Hull (1943), conditioned inhibition develops because the environmental events that are present during the nonrewarded behavior become associated with the inhibitory nonreward state. When these cues are experienced again, the inhibitory state is aroused and the behavior suppressed, leading to a loss of spontaneous recovery. Inhibition is not the only cause of the suppression of undesired behavior; the influence of the aversive quality of nonreward is examined next.

The Aversive Quality of Nonreward

Abram Amsel (1958) suggested that nonreward elicits an aversive internal frustration state. Stimuli associated with nonreward become able to elicit frustration as a conditioned response, and escape from this aversive situation is rewarded. Exploring this effect of nonreward further, Adelman and Maatsch (1956) provided evidence of the aversiveness of frustration and the rewarding quality of escaping from a frustrating situation. They found that animals would jump out of a box previously associated with reward and onto a ledge within 5 seconds if they were not rewarded. In contrast, animals that had been rewarded with food for jumping onto the ledge took 20 seconds to jump. Further, while the rewarded animals stopped jumping after about 60 extinction trials, the frustrated animals did not quit responding after 100 trials, even though their only reward was escape from a frustrating situation.

Other researchers (Brooks, 1980; Daly, 1974) have shown that the cues associated with nonreward develop aversive qualities. Let's briefly examine Daly's study to demonstrate the aversive quality of cues associated with nonreward. Daly presented a cue (either a distinctive box or a light) during nonrewarded trials in the first phase of her study; during the second part of the experiment, the rats learned a response—jumping a hurdle—that enabled them to turn off the light or to escape from the box. Apparently, the cues (distinctive box or light) had acquired aversive qualities during nonrewarded trials; the presence of these cues subsequently motivated the escape response. Termination of these cues rewarded the acquisition of the hurdle jump response.

Activation of an Instrumental or Operant Behavior

One additional point about the influence of nonreward on instrumental or operant behavior deserves our attention. Nonreward sometimes increases, rather than decreases, the intensity of the behavior. Nonreward motivates appetitive responding when frustration cues have been conditioned to elicit appetitive instead of avoidance behavior. An animal's behavior on a single alternation task illustrates that nonreward can become conditioned to motivate an appetitive response (Flaherty & Davenport, 1972). In the single alternation situation, reward and nonreward trials alternate. Studies using the single alternation task report that the latency of response shortens following a nonrewarded trial, but lengthens after a rewarded trial.

Why does response latency become shorter after nonreward but longer after reward in the single alternation task? E. J. Capaldi's sequential theory (1971, 1994) explains this conditioning process. According to Capaldi, at the beginning of each trial, a subject remembers whether reward or nonreward occurred on the last trial; Capaldi labels the memory of reward S^R and the memory of nonreward S^N. When reward follows a nonrewarded trial, the memory of the nonreward (S^N) becomes associated with the appetitive response. The conditioning of the memory of nonreward (S^N) to the appetitive response leads to a faster response following nonreward. Furthermore, since nonreward always follows a rewarded trial, the memory of reward (S^R) is associated with nonreward, which results in the conditioning of an avoidance response to S^R. Thus, the memory of reward elicits avoidance behavior. The longer latency of the appetitive response after rewarded trials provides support for Capaldi's approach.

Resistance to Extinction

The magnitude of reward and the consistency of reward experienced during acquisition influence the resistance to extinction of an instrumental or operant response. We examine this influence next.

The Influence of Reward Magnitude. D'Amato (1970) suggested that the influence of reward magnitude on resistance to extinction depends upon the amount of acquisition training. As Figure 6.12 demonstrates, when the level of acquisition training is low, a large reward produces a greater resistance to extinction than does a small reward. However, the opposite effect is observed with extended acquisition: A small reward in acquisition produces more resistance to extinction of the instrumental behavior than a larger reward magnitude.

The literature provides support for D'Amato's (1970) suggestion. Hill and Spear (1963), who gave their subjects only a few acquisition trials in the runway and provided either a small or large reward in the goal box, found that the large reward was associated with more resistance to extinction than was the small reward. Armus (1959) and Hulse (1958) used a large number of acquisition trials in the runway and presented either a small or large reward magnitude in the goal box. Both studies observed that resistance to extinction was greater for the animals given the small rather than large reward during extended acquisition. Furthermore, several other studies (Senkowski, 1978; Traupmann, 1972) varied both the acquisition reward magnitude and the number of acquisition trials; the results of the studies support the relationship Figure 6.12 depicts.

Figure 6.12   Hypothesized resistance to extinction of an instrumental response as a function of level of acquisition training and magnitude of reward.

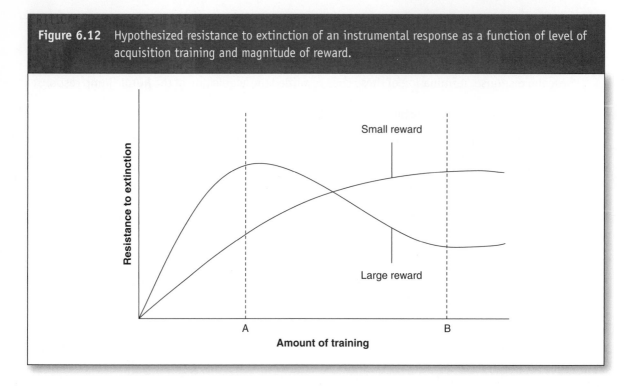

Why does the influence of reward magnitude on resistance to extinction depend on the amount of acquisition training? According to D'Amato (1970), when a small reward magnitude is provided during acquisition, an anticipatory goal response (a conditioned anticipation of impending reward) develops very slowly. (A detailed discussion of the anticipatory goal concept, originally proposed by Kenneth Spence, was presented in Chapter 2.) During extinction, substantial differences in the level of the anticipatory goal response will not occur, and therefore, the frustration produced during extinction will be small. This conclusion is based on the view that frustration is not produced until a reward is anticipated and that the amount of frustration produced is dependent upon the strength of the anticipatory goal response. Since frustration is minimal, resistance to extinction should depend only on the amount of acquisition training. The results of studies using a small reward magnitude support this prediction; the greater the level of acquisition training with a small reward magnitude, the more resistant the appetitive behavior is to extinction.

In contrast, the anticipatory goal response is conditioned rapidly when a large reward is provided during acquisition. Once the anticipatory goal response is strong enough to produce frustration, increases in the strength of the anticipatory goal response should lead to higher levels of frustration during extinction. These increases in frustration, produced as a result of extended training with a large reward, lead to a more rapid extinction of the appetitive response. Researchers employing a large reward magnitude have observed that increased acquisition training first leads to an increase and then to a decrease in resistance to extinction.

The Importance of Consistency of Reward. Earlier in the chapter, we described an example of a mother extinguishing her child's temper tantrums in a grocery store. Suppose that after several nonrewarded trips to the store, and a reduction in the duration and intensity of the temper tantrums, the mother, on the next trip to the store, has a headache when the child starts to cry.

The headache intensifies the unpleasantness of the tantrum; thus, she decides to buy her child candy to stop the crying. If the mother has headaches infrequently but rewards a tantrum whenever she does have a headache, this mother is now intermittently rather than continuously rewarding her child's temper tantrums. This intermittent reward causes the intensity of the temper tantrum to return to its original strength. Further, the intensity of the child's behavior will soon exceed the intensity produced when the response was continuously rewarded. Despite how she feels, in all likelihood, the mother will eventually become so annoyed that she decides to no longer tolerate her child's temper tantrums; unfortunately, extinguishing this behavior will be extremely difficult because she has intermittently rewarded the child's temper tantrums.

The previous example illustrates consistency of reinforcement's influence on the extinction of an instrumental or operant behavior: Extinction is slower following partial rather than continuous reinforcement. The greater resistance to extinction that occurs with intermittent rather than continuous reinforcement is referred to as the **partial reinforcement effect (PRE)**. Humphreys (1939) and Skinner (1938) were the first to describe this greater resistance to extinction with partial rather than continuous reinforcement. Many subsequent studies have demonstrated a partial reinforcement effect; this effect is one of the most reliable phenomena in psychology.

Many studies have documented the effect of consistency of reinforcement of a bar-press response during acquisition on resistance to extinction. For example, W. O. Jenkins, McFann, and Clayton (1950) trained rats to bar press for food reinforcement. Half of the rats were reinforced on an intermittent schedule of reinforcement, the other half of the subjects on a continuous schedule. As Figure 6.13 shows, rats receiving intermittent reinforcement emitted five times as many responses during extinction as rats given continuous reinforcement.

Much research on the partial reinforcement effect has used the runway apparatus; the results of these studies have consistently demonstrated the PRE effect. Consider Weinstock's 1958 study.

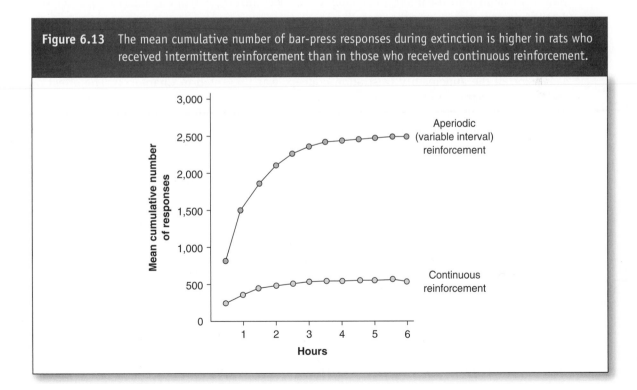

Figure 6.13   The mean cumulative number of bar-press responses during extinction is higher in rats who received intermittent reinforcement than in those who received continuous reinforcement.

Weinstock's rats received 108 acquisition trials with reward occurring on either 16.7%, 33.5%, 50.0%, 66.7%, 83.3%, or 100% of the trials; each rat was then given 60 extinction trials. Weinstock found an inverse relationship between resistance to extinction and the percentage of rewarded trials. These results indicate that as the likelihood that an instrumental response will produce reward during acquisition decreases, resistance to extinction increases. Lehr (1970) observed greater resistance to extinction following partial rather than continuous reward in a T-maze. In a more recent study, Prados, Sansa, and Artigas (2008) observed the partial reinforcement effect in a water maze.

The partial reinforcement effect has also been demonstrated with human adults (Lewis & Duncan, 1958) and children (Lewis, 1952). To illustrate the impact of partial reinforcement on humans, let's again examine the Lewis and Duncan (1958) study. College students were given reinforcement (a disk exchangeable for 5 cents) for pulling the arm of a slot machine. The percentage of reinforced lever-pull responses varied: Subjects received reinforcement after either 33%, 67%, or 100% of the responses. Lewis and Duncan allowed subjects to play the slot machine as long as they liked during extinction, reporting that the lower the percentage of responses reinforced during acquisition, the greater the resistance to extinction. In a more recent study, Pittenger and Pavlik (1988) found that college students receiving partial reinforcement for moving a joystick in one of four directions showed greater resistance to extinction than subjects given continuous reinforcement.

The Nature of the Partial Reinforcement Effect. Psychologists have proposed many explanations of the partial reinforcement effect since Humphreys's and Skinner's initial observations. Abram Amsel's frustration theory (Amsel, 1967, 1994) and E. J. Capaldi's sequential theory (Capaldi, 1971, 1994) seem best able to describe the processes responsible for increased resistance to extinction following intermittent rather than continuous reinforcement. A brief summary of each view is provided here; the interested reader should see Amsel (1994) or Capaldi (1994) for a more detailed description of these theories.

Amsel (1967, 1994) proposed a frustration-based theory for the partial reinforcement effect. According to Amsel, in animals that received continuous rewards, the elicitation of an anticipatory frustration response during extinction led to a rapid suppression of response (a detailed discussion of the anticipatory frustration concept was presented in Chapter 2). The effect of anticipatory frustration in animals that received intermittent reward is quite different. Early in acquisition, the anticipation of nonreward does not produce sufficient frustration to suppress behavior, due to the low associative strength of the instrumental or operant response, which causes continued responding on subsequent trials. When reward then follows nonreward during acquisition, the anticipatory frustration response becomes associated with responding. The conditioning of the anticipatory frustration response to the operant or instrumental behavior causes the nonreward experienced during extinction to elicit, rather than suppress, responding. In other words, animals receiving intermittent reward learn to persist when they experience frustration. As a result of this conditioned persistence, the anticipation of nonreward elicits responding, rather than inhibiting it, during the early stages of extinction. Eventually, continued nonreward leads to a suppression of responding, but the intermittently rewarded animal responds for longer periods during extinction than does the continuously reinforced animal.

Evidence for Amsel's frustration theory can be found in studies varying the amount of reward experienced prior to nonreward during acquisition. For example, Hulse (1958) provided rats with either a large (1.0 gram) or small (0.08 gram) reward during acquisition in the runway. Half of the animals in each reward magnitude condition received either continuous (100%) or intermittent (46%) reward. Hulse found greater resistance to extinction in the intermittent than in the continuous reward groups (see Figure 6.14). He also observed significantly greater resistance to

Figure 6.14 This figure presents the latency of running (1/response time × 100) during extinction as a function of the percentage of reward (46% or 100%) and the magnitude of reward (0.08 or 1.0 gram). The reference point contains the latency from the last training trial and the first extinction trial.

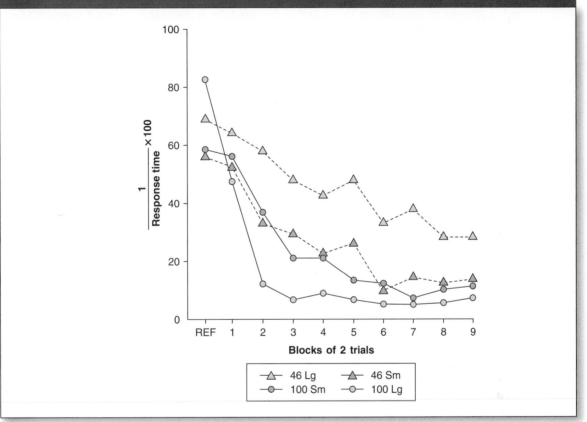

extinction in intermittently rewarded animals given a large rather than a small reward, but no difference as a function of reward magnitude in animals given continuous reward.

Why did reward magnitude affect resistance to extinction in intermittently but not continuously rewarded animals? A large reward followed by nonreward elicits greater frustration than a small reward followed by nonreward. The greater anticipatory frustration response produced by the removal of the large reward leads to a stronger association of the anticipatory frustration response to the instrumental response. This greater conditioning produces more persistence and slower extinction in animals receiving a large rather than a small reward. However, the conditioning of the anticipatory frustration response only occurs in intermittently rewarded animals because continuously rewarded animals never experience reward following nonreward.

Capaldi (1971, 1994) presents a quite different view of the partial reinforcement effect. According to Capaldi, if reward follows a nonrewarded trial, the animal will then associate the memory of the nonrewarded experience (S^N) with the operant or instrumental response. Capaldi suggests that the conditioning of the S^N to the operant, or instrumental behavior, causes the increased resistance to extinction with partial reward. During extinction, the only memory present after the first nonrewarded experience is S^N. Animals receiving continuous reward do not experience S^N during acquisition; therefore, they do not associate S^N with the operant or instrumental response.

The presence of S^N in continuously rewarded animals during extinction changes the stimulus context from that present during acquisition. This change produces a reduction in response strength because of a generalization decrement, a reduced intensity of a response when the stimulus present is dissimilar to the stimulus conditioned to the response (see Chapter 10 for a discussion of generalization). The loss of response strength because of generalization decrement, combined with the inhibition developed during extinction, produces a rapid extinction of the operant or instrumental response in animals receiving continuous reward in acquisition.

However, a different process occurs in animals receiving partial reward in acquisition: These animals associate S^N with the operant or instrumental response during acquisition and, therefore, no generalization decrement occurs during extinction. The absence of the generalization decrement causes the strength of the operant or instrumental response at the beginning of extinction to remain at the level conditioned during acquisition. Thus, the inhibition developed during extinction only slowly suppresses the operant or instrumental response, and extinction is slower with partial than with continuous reward.

Capaldi and his associates (Capaldi, Hart, & Stanley, 1963; Capaldi & Spivey, 1964) conducted several studies to demonstrate the influence of S^N experienced during a rewarded trial on resistance to extinction. In these studies, during the interval between the nonrewarded and the rewarded trials, reward was given in an environment other than the runway. The effect of this intertrial reward procedure is the replacement of the memory of nonreward (S^N) with a memory of reward (S^R) and thus a reduced resistance to extinction. Rats given intertrial reward showed a faster extinction of the instrumental response than control animals receiving only partial reward.

We have presented two views of the partial reinforcement effect. While these two views seem opposite, it is possible that both are valid. The partial reinforcement effect could result from both conditioned persistence and the conditioning of the memory of nonreward to the instrumental or operant response.

What is the significance of the partial reinforcement effect? According to Flaherty (1985), observations of animals in their natural environments indicate that an animal's attempts to attain a desired goal are sometimes successful and at other times, not. Flaherty asserts that the PRE effect is adaptive because it motivates animals not to give up too easily and thus lose the opportunity to succeed. Yet, animals receiving partial reward do not continue to respond indefinitely without reward; this observation indicates that animals will not persist forever in the face of continued frustration.

BEFORE YOU GO ON

- What might cause Traci to stop playing blackjack?

- Does the partial reinforcement effect have anything to say about the likelihood that Traci will stop gambling?

SECTION REVIEW

- The frequency and intensity of an instrumental or operant behavior declines during extinction when that behavior no longer produces reward.

- Nonreward can increase the intensity of instrumental or operant behavior when the memory of nonreward has been conditioned to elicit the behavior.

- Nonreward eventually leads to an inhibition of an instrumental or operant behavior response, as well as elicitation of an escape response from the frustration the nonreward state induces.

- The environmental cues present during nonreward can develop aversive properties, which motivates escape from situations associated with nonreward.

- A large reward produces greater resistance to extinction than does a small reward when the amount of acquisition training is low, but the opposite is true with extended acquisition training.

- Partial rather than continuous reinforcement leads to a slower extinction of the instrumental or operant behavior.

- Conditioned persistence and/or the memory of nonreward associated with the appetitive behavior cause the partial reinforcement effect.

APPLICATION OF APPETITIVE CONDITIONING

Contingency Management

In 1953, B. F. Skinner suggested that poorly arranged reinforcer contingencies are sometimes responsible for people's behavior problems. In many instances, effective instrumental or operant responding does not occur because reinforcement is unavailable. At other times, reinforcing people's behavior problems sustains their occurrence. Skinner believed that rearranging reinforcement contingencies could eliminate behavior pathology and increase the occurrence of more effective ways of responding. Many psychologists (e.g., Ullman & Krasner, 1965) accepted Skinner's view, and the restructuring of reinforcement contingencies emerged as an effective way to alter human behavior. The use of reinforcement and nonreinforcement to control people's behavior was initially labeled **behavior modification**. However, behavior modification refers to all types of behavioral treatments; thus, psychologists now use the term **contingency management** to indicate that contingent reinforcement is being used to increase the frequency of appropriate behaviors and to eliminate or reduce inappropriate responses.

There are three main stages in the effective implementation of a contingency management program (see Cooper, Heron, & Heward, 2007, for a more detailed discussion of these procedures). The first stage (assessment stage) calculates the frequency of appropriate and inappropriate behaviors and determines the situations in which these behaviors occur. In addition, the reinforcers maintaining the inappropriate response, as well as potential reinforcers for the appropriate behavior, are determined in the assessment phase.

The second stage (contingency contracting stage) specifies the relationship between responding and reinforcement. Also, the method of administering the reinforcement contingent upon the appropriate behaviors is determined in this stage.

The contingencies are implemented in the last stage. The changes in response during and following treatment are evaluated in the implementation stage of contingency management; this ensures that (1) the contingency management program produces behavioral changes and (2) these changes continue after the termination of formal treatment. As we will discover shortly, contingency management is an effective way to alter behavior; if the treatment fails to change behavior, it often means that the program was not developed and/or implemented correctly, and modifications are needed to ensure behavioral change.

The Assessment Stage

In the assessment stage, the behavioral problem must be defined and the situations in which it does or does not occur must be determined. Discussions with the individual, others who are familiar with the individual, or both, are the initial source of information concerning the problem behavior. However, subjective reporting cannot be the sole basis for assessing the behavioral problem; it merely provides an impression of the behavioral problem. Direct observations are necessary to establish the precise baseline level of the target behavior. These observations may be made by anyone around the individual. Regardless of who observes the target behavior, accurate observations are essential, and training is needed to ensure reliable data recording.

Consider the following example to illustrate the observational training process. Parents complain to a behavior therapist that their child frequently has temper tantrums, which they have tried but failed to eliminate. The therapist instructs the parents to fill in a chart (see Table 6.1) indicating both the number and duration of tantrums occurring each day for a week, as well as their response to each tantrum. The parents' observations provide a relatively accurate recording of the frequency and intensity of the problem behavior.

The parents' observations also indicate the reinforcement of the problem behavior. As Table 6.1 shows, a parental response to the tantrum increased the frequency of the behavior; when parents ignored the behavior, the temper tantrums decreased in frequency. It is essential in the assessment phase to record the events following the target behavior; this information identifies the reinforcer of the problem behavior.

The assessment must also indicate when and where the target behavior occurs. For example, the child may be having tantrums at home every day after school but not at school. This information about the target behavior shows the extent of the behavioral problem, as well as the stimulus conditions that precipitate the response.

The therapist can determine, based on information obtained in the assessment phase, the reinforcement to be used during therapy. In some cases, the behavioral recording indicates an effective

Table 6.1 Instances of Tantrum Behavior and Parental Reaction to Tantrums During 7-Day Baseline Assessment Period

Day	Tantrums	Duration (minutes)	Response
1	1	4	Parent comforted child when he slipped and banged head during crying.
2	1	5	Parent told child to be quiet but finally gave cookie to quiet him down.
	2	6	Parent ignored crying until couldn't stand it, then gave cookie.
3	1	5	Parent ignored.
	2	6	Parent ignored.
	3	8	Parent ignored until child took cookie himself, and then spanked child.
4	1	4	Parent ignored; child stopped spontaneously.
5	1	4	With company present, parent gave child cookie to quiet him.
	2	5	Parent ignored, and then finally gave in with cookie.
6	1	8	Parent ignored; went into bathroom, had cigarette, and read magazine until child quieted himself.
	2	4	Parent ignored; just as parent was about to give in, child stopped.
7	1	3	Parent ignored; child stopped, and then began to play.

reinforcement for appropriate behavior; in other instances, the therapist must discover what works. There are a number of reinforcement assessment techniques. For example, the Mediation-Reinforcer Incomplete Blank (MRB), a modified incomplete-sentence test developed by Tharp and Wetzel (1969), reveals the client's view of a reinforcement. A client's response to the question, "I will do almost anything to get _____" shows what the client considers a reinforcement.

The Contingency Contracting Stage

In the contingency contracting stage, the desired response is determined and the precise relationship between that response and reinforcement is specified. This involves deciding the schedule of reinforcement necessary to establish the desired response. In addition, if a shaping procedure is needed, the contract will detail the changes in contingency to occur at various stages of treatment. Furthermore, because an inappropriate instrumental or operant response has often elicited reinforcement in the past, the contingency will indicate that this inappropriate response will no longer be reinforced.

Who will administer the reinforcement? In the traditional application of contingency management, people other than the individual (e.g., a nurse in a mental hospital, a teacher in a school setting, or a parent in the home) provide reinforcement contingent upon the appropriate behavior. During the contracting stage, the individuals administering reinforcement are trained to identify and reinforce appropriate behavior.

Enlisting people around the client to provide reinforcement is ideally suited to many types of situations. However, in some circumstances, this technique is not feasible. This is especially true for adults seeking to change their behavior by using outpatient therapy; instead, the use of the self-reinforcement procedure has often proven effective in these situations. Although psychologists (see Skinner, 1953) were initially skeptical of the efficacy of self-reinforcement in behavioral management, Bandura and Perloff (1967) demonstrated that the self-reinforcement technique is as effective in changing behavior as the typical reinforcement procedure. In their study, 7- to 10-year-old children received reinforcement for exerting effort on a wheel-turning task. At the beginning of the experiment, some children were given a supply of tokens they could exchange for prizes. They then used the tokens to provide their own reinforcement for attaining a high level of performance. Other children attaining a high level of performance received tokens from the experimenter. Bandura and Perloff reported that both the self-imposed reinforcement groups and the externally imposed reinforcement groups showed an equivalent level of performance, responding at a higher level than children receiving reinforcement prior to the task or no reinforcement.

Self-reinforcement procedures have effectively modified a number of undesired behaviors, including impulsive overspending (Paulsen, Rimm, Woodburn, & Rimm, 1977), inadequate study habits (Greiner & Karoly, 1976), and smoking (Glasgow, Kleisges, Mizes & Pechacek, 1985). Self-reinforcement also has been found to promote healthy behaviors including weight control (Castro & Rachlin, 1980) and breast examinations (Grady, Goodenow, & Borkin, 1988).

Contingency management has yielded impressive results for changing a wide variety of behaviors. A brief discussion of the effectiveness of such programs completes our examination of contingency management.

The Implementation of the Contingency Management Program

In the early 1960s, Teodoro Ayllon and Nathan Azrin at Anna State Hospital in Illinois tested Skinner's idea that systematically employing reinforcement could modify behavior (see Ayllon & Azrin, 1965, 1968). Ayllon and Azrin established a contingency management program for institutionalized adult female psychotic clients. These clients received tokens, which they could later exchange for desired primary reinforcers, when they engaged in instrumental or operant responses they would need for effective adjustment outside the hospital. Two classes of instrumental or operant behaviors were reinforced: (1) self-care activities such as grooming and bathing and (2) job activities such as washing dishes and serving food. Ayllon and Azrin reported that the frequency of appropriate responses significantly increased as the result of the contingency management program (see Figure 6.15). Their approach is often called a **token economy** program because of the use of tokens as secondary reinforcers.

Ayllon and Azrin's treatment shows that psychiatric patients often develop the behaviors necessary for successful adjustment when they are reinforced for those behaviors. In fact, many

Figure 6.15 The presentation of reinforcement contingent upon target behaviors increases the frequency of appropriate response. The frequency of the target behaviors declined when reinforcement was discontinued but increased when contingent reinforcement was restored.

studies (Hikita, 1986; Lippman & Motta, 1993) have found that psychotic patients receiving a contingency management treatment exhibit a significantly better adjustment to daily living than patients given standard hospital treatment programs. The efficacy of operant conditioning in altering the behavior of hospitalized psychotic clients appears to be well established.

Contingency management programs have been successfully used to alter behavior in a wide variety of settings. A sample of these programs is shown in Table 6.2. Contingency management

Table 6.2   Sample of Behaviors Influenced by a Contingency Management Program

Target Behavior/Competency	Population	Outcome
Social		
Prosocial behavior	Adolescents	Increased
Sharing, praising	Children	Increased
Sharing	Adults	Increased
Social disruption	Adults	Decreased
Social greeting	Children with mental retardation	Increased
Social speech	Children with mental retardation	Increased
Self-control		
Classroom disruption	Preschool children	Decreased
Classroom disruption	Children	Decreased
Classroom attention	Children	Increased
Drug abstinence	Adolescents	Eliminated
Enuresis	Adolescents	Eliminated
Hyperactivity/attention span	Children with mental retardation	Decreased/increased
Hyperactivity	Children	Decreased
Self-injurious behavior	Children with mental retardation	Decreased
Self-stimulation	Children with mental retardation	Decreased
Cognitive-emotional		
Arithmetic competence	Children	Improved
Complex language	Children with autism	Acquired
Creativity	Children	Increased
Reading	Adolescents with delinquent behavior	Improved
School phobia	Children	Eliminated
Stuttering	Adults	Reduced
Vocabulary	Children with hyperactive behavior	Increased

appears to be an effective treatment for a number of behavior pathologies. Depression is one behavior problem that has been modified by contingent reinforcement (Antonuccio, Ward, & Tearnan, 1989). Contingency management has also been employed in the treatment of anxiety (Marshall, Boutilier, & Minnes, 1974) and pain (Ramsden, Friedman, & Williamson, 1983). In these studies, reinforcement occurred when the clients showed decreases in anxiety, depression, or pain and increases in responses incompatible with the behavioral problem.

Token economy systems have been established at a number of residential treatment centers for delinquent and predelinquent children and adolescents. The aim of these contingency management programs is to establish adaptive behaviors. For example, children with mental retardation have received contingent reinforcement to learn toilet training (Azrin, Sneed, & Foxx, 1973), personal grooming (Horner & Keilitz, 1975), and mealtime behavior (Plummer, Baer, & LeBlanc, 1977). Furthermore, contingency management can suppress several maladaptive behaviors characteristic of some children with mental retardation; for example, the incidence of self-injurious behavior (Lockwood & Bourland, 1982), agitated and disruptive behavior (Reese, Sherman, Sheldon, 1998), and self-stimulation (Aurand, Sisson, Aach, & Van Hasselt, 1989) will decrease when reinforcement is made contingent upon the suppression of these behaviors.

The contingent use of reinforcement has been used to increase academic performance in individuals with mental retardation. Henderson, Jenson, and Erken (1986) found that providing token reinforcement on a variable interval schedule significantly improved on-task behavior and academic performance in sixth graders with mental retardation, while J. R. Jenkins and Gorrafa (1974) found that a token economy system increased both reading and math performance in 6- to 11-year-old children with mental retardation.

The academic performance of normal children and adults is also responsive to contingency management treatment. For example, Lovitt, Guppy, and Blattner (1969) found that contingent free time and permission to listen to the radio increased spelling accuracy in fourth-grade children. Other studies (V. W. Harris & Sherman, 1973; Rapport & Bostow, 1976) have also found that contingency management procedures can increase academic competency in children. Also, contingent reinforcement has been shown to increase the studying behavior of college students; however, this procedure appears to be effective only with students of below-average ability (Bristol & Sloane, 1974) or students with low or medium grade averages (DuNann & Weber, 1976). Most likely, the other students are already exhibiting effective studying behavior.

Disruptive behavior can be a real problem for promoting learning in the classroom. Not surprisingly, contingency management has proved to be a successful approach to reducing disruptive behavior in a variety of classroom settings. For example, Filcheck, McNeil, Greco, and Bernard (2004) reported that a token economy reduced disruptive classroom behavior in preschool children. Mottram, Bray, Kehle, Broudy, and Jenson (2002) found that oppositional and defiant behavior in elementary school boys was significantly reduced by the implementation of a token economy system, while De Martini-Scully, Bray, and Kehle (2000) reported similar results with elementary school girls. Further, J. W. Higgins, Williams, and McLaughlin (2001) reported that a token economy using a DRO 1-minute schedule with free time as a reinforcement decreased such disruptive behaviors as out-of-seat behavior, talking out, and poor seating posture in a third-grade student with learning disabilities. Two follow-up observations indicated that the decreased disruptive behaviors were maintained over time (see Figure 6.16).

The use of a token economy system to reduce disruptive behavior in the classroom also improves academic performance. S. J. Simon, Ayllon, and Milan (1982) found that a token economy system to reduce disruptive behavior in low-math-achieving middle school–aged boys not only reduced disruptive behaviors but also increased academic math performance. In fact, these researchers observed a reciprocal relationship between increases in academic performance and decreases in disruptive behaviors in the classroom. More recently, Ward-Maguire (2008) reported that a token economy decreased classroom disruptions (off-task behavior) and increased on-task

Figure 6.16 The number of disruptive classroom behaviors (talk-outs, out-of-seat behavior, and poor posture) decreases on a DRO schedule with free time as a reinforcement for an absence of each disruptive behavior for 1 minute in a third-grade student with learning disabilities.

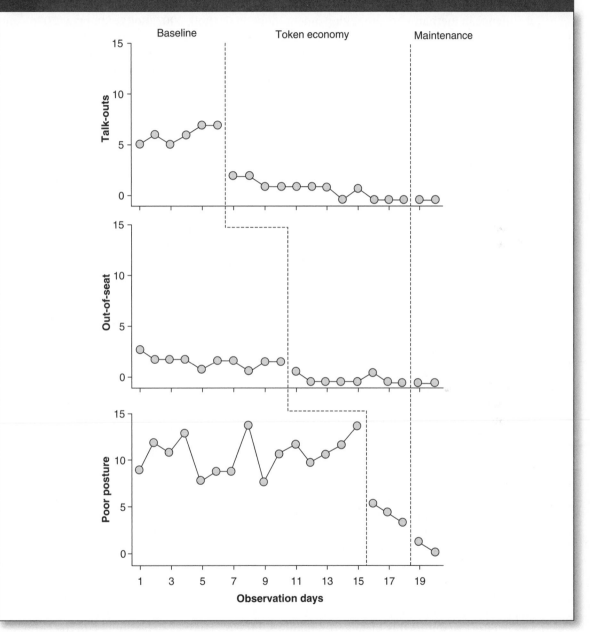

behavior and work completion in high school students with emotional/behavioral disorders. Further, Young Welch (2009) implemented a token economy system in 400 fifth- to eighth-grade students in an inner-city school. She found that the token economy system significantly decreased discipline referrals and student suspensions and improved literacy proficiency and performance on writing assignments.

Contingency management programs have been successfully employed to produce drug absti-nence (Prendergast, Podus, Finney, Greenwell, & Roll, 2006). In these programs, reinforcement is provided when an individual abstains from drug use and is withheld when drug use is detected. The reinforcement provided is typically a voucher with some monetary value that can be exchanged for goods or services. The contingent use of reinforcement has successfully produced abstinence in methamphetamine-dependent individuals (Roll, 2007; Roll & Shoptaw, 2006), and cocaine- or heroin-dependent individuals (Olmstead & Petry, 2009). Contingency management not only produced abstinence in cocaine-abusing methadone patients, but also significantly reduced HIV risk behaviors, especially risky drug injection practices (T. Hanson, Alessi, & Petry, 2008). Further, contingency management has been found to produce abstinence in nicotine-dependent adolescents (Krishnan-Sarin et al., 2006) and college students (Correia & Benson, 2006).

Several studies have reported that an Internet-based voucher program can promote abstinence from cigarette smoking (Dallery, Glenn, & Raiff, 2007; Dunn, Sigmon, Thomas, Heil, & Higgins, 2008; Heil et al., 2008; B. Reynolds, Dallery, Shroff, Patak, & Leraas, 2008). Adolescent smokers in the Reynolds et al. study (2008) took three daily recordings of themselves taking carbon mon-oxide (CO) samples, which provided an objective measure of whether or not the participants were smoking. The samples were then sent electronically to the researchers for analysis. Par-ticipants received a monetary reinforcement for smoking abstinence. Reynolds and his colleagues reported that the adolescent participants in their study took 97.2% of all possible samples and maintained prolonged abstinence from smoking for the 30-day program. Similar results were found with adult woman participants (Dallery et al., 2007), with pregnant women participants (Heil et al., 2008), and with adult male and female methadone-maintained partici-pants (Dunn et al., 2008).

Before a substance-dependent individual can be reinforced for drug abstinence, the individual must enter treatment and remain in treatment. Sorensen, Masson, and Copeland (1999) reported that the use of a coupon-based reinforcement program increased treatment-seeking behavior and entry into a treatment program for opiate-dependent individuals.

Contingency management programs can also increase the use of medications that make absti-nence more likely. For example, Silverman, Preston, Stitzer, and Schuster (1999) found that a voucher-reinforcement program maintained naltrexone (an opiate antagonist that eases drug craving) use in opiate-dependent individuals. In a similar study, Mooney, Babb, Jensen, and Hatsukami (2005) reported that a voucher-based reinforcement program increased nicotine gum use in a smoking cessation program.

Token economy programs also have been used to increase exercise behavior and improve health. Wiggam, French, and Henderson (1986) reported that the use of reinforcement significantly increased walking distance in women aged 70 to 92 living in a retirement home, while Croce (1990) found that contingent reinforcement with obese adults with mental retardation increased aerobic exercise and substantially improved cardiovascular fitness. A similar positive effect of a token economy program was found with children with attention-deficit/hyperactivity disorder (Trocki-Ables, French, & O'Connor, 2001) and children with cystic fibrosis (Bernard, 2005).

Businesses have used contingency management programs to reduce tardiness, decrease employee theft, improve worker safety, and enhance employee productivity (G. Martin & Pear, 1999). Effective reinforcers include pay bonuses, time off, and being mentioned in the company newsletter. Raj, Nelson, and Rao (2006) evaluated the effects of different reinforcers on the per-formance of employees in the business information technology department of a major retail company. These researchers found that performance was improved by either providing money or paid leave as the reinforcers or allowing the employees to select their reinforcers (casual dress code and flexible working hours). Businesses also have used contingency management to influence the behavior of their customers: Young children want to eat at the fast-food restaurant offering the best kid's meal toy, and adults try to fly on one particular airline to accumulate frequent-flyer miles. You can probably think of several purchases you have made based on the reinforcement that a particular company offers.

Contingency management can also be used to change the behavior of large groups of people. For example, S. C. Hayes and Cone (1977) found that direct payments to efficient energy users produced large reductions in energy consumption, while Seaver and Patterson (1976) discovered that informational feedback and a decal for efficient energy use resulted in a significant decrease in home fuel consumption. Also, McCalden and Davis (1972) discovered that reserving a special lane of the Oakland–San Francisco Bay Bridge for cars with several passengers increased car pooling and improved traffic flow.

Scott Geller and his colleagues (Fournier, Ehrhart, Glindemann, & Geller, 2004; Geller & Hahn, 1984; Ludwig, Biggs, Wagner, & Geller, 2001; Needleman & Geller, 1992) have found that contingency management programs can change human behavior when applied in social settings. For example, Geller and Hahn (1984) reported that seat belt use increased at a large industrial plant when the opportunity to obtain reinforcement was made contingent upon the use of seatbelts. Reinforcement applied in social settings also has been found to increase safe driving behaviors in pizza drivers (Ludwig, Biggs, Wagner, & Geller, 2001), to increase use of work-site collection of home-generated recyclable materials (Needleman & Geller, 1992), and to decrease excessive alcohol consumption at fraternity parties (Fournier et al., 2004).

We have learned that contingency management programs are quite effective in establishing appropriate behaviors and eliminating inappropriate behaviors, which would lead you to expect that it would be widely used. Kazdin (2000) reported that contingency management is widely applied in classrooms and in psychiatric hospitals. Yet, every school does not have a store, nor does every major highway have a carpool lane. The success of contingency management programs does not always lead to its use. The failure to adopt contingency management programs is nowhere more evident than in the treatment of psychiatric patients at Veterans Administration (VA) medical centers (G. C. Davidson & Neale, 1994). Boudewyns, Fry, and Nightingale (1986) reported that in 1983, only 20 of 152 VA medical centers used token economy programs in their treatment of psychiatric patients. Some reasons the centers gave for the lack of more widespread implementation of this effective treatment were that they were under pressure to reduce the time patients were hospitalized and that poorly paid staff resisted taking on additional responsibilities. Paul and Menditto (1992) surveyed VA medical centers almost a decade later and found that the use of token economies had not significantly changed.

BEFORE YOU GO ON

- Could a contingency management program help Traci control her gambling behavior?

- If so, how would you design such a program?

SECTION REVIEW

- Contingent reinforcers have been useful in many real-world situations to increase appropriate behaviors and decrease inappropriate behaviors.

- There are three stage of contingency management: assessment, contracting, and implementation.

- In the assessment stage, the baseline levels of appropriate and inappropriate behaviors, the situations in which these behaviors occur, and potential reinforces are determined.

- In the contracting stage, the precise relationship between the operant response and the reinforcement is decided.

- Implementation of the contingency contract involves providing reinforcement contingent upon the appropriate response or upon the absence of the inappropriate behavior, or both.

- Contingency management has successfully modified many different behaviors, including inadequate living skills, drug use, poor study habits, antisocial responses, and energy consumption.

CRITICAL THINKING QUESTIONS

1. Tyrone's roommate never does his share of the household chores, such as washing the dishes, vacuuming the carpet, or taking out the garbage. Tyrone finds his roommate's lack of cooperation unpleasant. Using what you know about reinforcement, suggest several reasons for the roommate's lack of cooperation. How might Tyrone shape his roommate to change his behavior and help out with the household chores?

2. Ebony stayed out past her curfew and her parents have grounded her for the next week. She must come home right after school and cannot leave the house until she goes to school the next morning. The weekend will be spent helping out around the house. Ebony is really angry at her parents and is thinking about running away. Using the principles described in the text, explain why Ebony is so mad at her parents and considering running away.

3. Elizabeth has made the mistake of intermittently reinforcing her son's temper tantrums. Why is her use of intermittent reinforcement a mistake? How might she now extinguish the boy's temper tantrums? What problems might Elizabeth encounter, and how might she overcome these problems?

KEY TERMS

Behavior modification

Compound schedule

Contingency

Contingency management

Depression effect

Differential reinforcement of high (DRH)
  responding schedule

Differential reinforcement of low
  (DRL) responding schedule

Differential reinforcement of other
  behaviors (DRO) schedule

Elation effect

Extinction

Extinction of an operant or instrumental
  response

Fixed-interval (FI) schedule

Fixed-ratio (FR) schedule

Instrumental conditioning

Interval schedule of reinforcement

Negative contrast effect

Negative reinforcement

Negative reinforcer

Operant chamber

Operant conditioning

Partial reinforcement effect (PRE)

Positive contrast effect

Positive reinforcer

Postreinforcement pause

Primary reinforcer

Ratio schedule of reinforcement

Reinforcer

Scallop effect

Schedule of reinforcement

Secondary reinforcer

Shaping

Spontaneous recovery

Successive approximation procedure

Token economy

Variable-interval (VI) schedule

Variable-ratio (VR) schedule

Principles and Applications of Aversive Conditioning

A GOOD WHIPPING

Noah moved last summer. His father got a promotion and a big raise when he transferred to Nashville, Tennessee. Noah liked their big new house, especially since he no longer had to share a bedroom with his brother, Ethan. Ethan was a pest, always bothering Noah's toys. Noah complained to his parents, but nothing seemed to deter Ethan. His mother would yell at Ethan for bothering Noah, but Ethan paid no attention to his mother. Ethan was afraid of his father. Sometimes his Dad would talk to Ethan, and at other times, Ethan would get a spanking. After a spanking, Ethan would leave Noah's stuff alone for a while. Yet, several days later, Ethan would be bothering him and his stuff again. Noah asked his parents if he could lock his door, but they did not think that would be a good idea. As badly as Ethan bothered him at home, Noah was tormented even more at his new school. Noah is small for his age and several of the boys in his class are much bigger than he is. Especially troubling is Billy. Right from Noah's first day at school, Billy took a disliking to Noah. He would walk past in the hall and knock Noah's books onto the floor. At recess, Billy would push Noah to the ground and take his lunch money. Noah told his parents about what Billy and the other boys were doing to him in class, and Noah's parents went to school to talk with Ms. Evans, Noah's teacher. Ms. Evans told Noah's parents that she had observed Billy and the other boys picking on Noah. She had talked to the boys, had sent them to the principal's office, and had talked to their parents. The boys' parents seemed to understand the problem and promised to punish their sons. Billy's father had been especially punitive with Billy and had given him a good whipping. Unfortunately, the whipping had only worked for a few days, and Billy was again tormenting Noah. Ms. Evans was afraid that Billy was headed for suspension and wondered what kind of whipping Billy would get for being suspended.

Why didn't Noah's parents' punishment cause Ethan to stop pestering Noah? Why didn't Billy's father's spanking cause Billy to stop tormenting Noah? In this chapter, we discuss punishment and examine when punishment can suppress undesired behaviors. Chapter 8 examines why punishment works.

PRINCIPLES OF AVERSIVE CONDITIONING

Throughout life, we encounter many unpleasant events. No one is immune from experiencing them; each of us experiences an unpleasant circumstance from time to time. Unless we learn how to cope with aversive events, our lives can be quite miserable.

Some aversive events can be escaped but not avoided. We cannot anticipate these circumstances, but we must be prepared to respond to terminate them. For example, while walking to the store, you are attacked by a thief who wants your money. You might be able to end the mugging by counterattacking. You will escape if your aggressive response is effective; however, if it is not, your counterattack probably will lead to even more aversive events.

Other aversive events are avoidable. To prevent aversive events, you must learn when the aversive event will occur and how you can act to prevent it. For example, many elderly people know they may be mugged if they go out at night; therefore, they do not leave their homes after dark. This chapter describes the factors that affect whether a person learns to avoid an aversive event.

Suppose a parent punishes a child after receiving a teacher's note about the child's poor behavior. The punishment is intended to inhibit future misbehavior in the classroom. If punishment is effective, the child will no longer misbehave in school. The factors that determine whether punishment suppresses inappropriate behavior are detailed later in the chapter.

You might think that a parent punishing a child for misbehaving has no relationship to an elderly person remaining inside at night to avoid being mugged. Yet, punishment and avoidance conditioning typically deal with two aspects of the same process: The child can avoid punishment by not misbehaving in school, and the elderly person can avoid being mugged by not going out at night. Thus, for punishment to be effective, it must motivate the inhibition of an inappropriate response. However, in some circumstances, a person or an animal learns to prevent punishment with a response other than inhibition of the inappropriate behavior. For example, a child may be able to prevent punishment by crying after misbehavior, rather than by not misbehaving. Although we describe punishment and avoidance behavior separately in this chapter, it is important to realize that punishment will only be successful if inhibition of the inappropriate behavior is the only response that will prevent punishment.

Some aversive events cannot be escaped or avoided. For example, a child who is abused by a parent cannot escape or prevent the abuse. In Chapter 11, we will discover that helplessness can develop when a person or animal learns that aversive events can neither be escaped nor avoided. We begin this chapter by examining escape conditioning; then we discuss avoidance learning and punishment.

Escape Conditioning

Many people close their eyes during a scary scene in a horror movie, opening them when they believe the unpleasant scene has ended. This behavior is one example of an **escape response**, which is a behavior motivated by an aversive event (e.g., the scary scene) and reinforced by the termination of the aversive event. Similarly, Noah, described in the chapter-opening vignette, can escape his classmate tormentors by running into a classroom whenever Billy or his friends start abusing him.

Many studies show that people and animals will try to escape aversive events. Let's examine two of these experiments. N. E. Miller's classic 1948 study (see Chapter 4) showed that rats could learn to escape painful electric shock. Miller placed rats in the white compartment of a shuttle box and exposed them to electric shock. The rats could escape the shock by turning a wheel that opened a door and then running into the black compartment; Miller reported that the rats rapidly learned to use this escape route. In a similar study using human subjects, Hiroto (1974) exposed college students to an unpleasant noise; they could terminate it by moving their finger from one side of a shuttle box to the other. Hiroto found that his subjects quickly learned how to escape the noise.

The Escape From Aversive Events

Several factors play important roles in determining whether a person or animal learns to escape aversive events, as well as determining the efficiency of the escape response. We look at these factors next.

The Intensity of the Aversive Event. Walking to class, you see a student stumble and fall. Will you stop to help? A number of variables affect helping behavior. One critical factor is the aversiveness of the emergency. According to Jane Piliavin and her associates (J. A. Piliavin, Dovidio, Gaertner, & Clark, 1981), the more unpleasant the situation, the higher the cost of helping, and, therefore, the greater the motive to escape from the emergency. Thus, the more serious the injury, the less likely you are to help.

Many studies have supported this cost analysis of helping. For example, I. M. Piliavin, Piliavin, and Rodin (1975) simulated an emergency on subway cars in New York City. A confederate acting as a victim would moan and then "faint." The experimenters increased the discomfort of some bystanders by having the victim expose an ugly birthmark just before fainting. The victim did not expose the unpleasant birthmark to other bystanders. Piliavin et al.'s results indicate that the bystanders who saw the ugly birthmark helped the victim less often than those who did not. As the cost of helping increases—in this case, the cost included enduring the sight of an ugly birthmark—the likelihood of helping behavior decreases.

The escape response when anticipating failure on a task further illustrates the intensity of the aversive event's influence: the more unpleasant the task, the greater the expectation of failure, the higher the motivation to escape, and, therefore, the less persistence the subjects exhibit (J. W. Atkinson, 1964; Feather, 1967).

Research with animals has also documented the effect of the intensity of the aversive event on escape behavior. Most studies have used electric shock as the aversive event. For example, Trapold and Fowler (1960) trained rats to escape electric shock in the start box of an alley by running to an uncharged goal box. The rats received either 120, 160, 240, 300, or 400 volts of electric shock in the start box. Trapold and Fowler reported that the greater the shock intensity, the shorter the latency (or time) to escape from the start box (see Figure 7.1). Other research has shown that the intensity of a loud noise (Masterson, 1969) or of light (Kaplan, Jackson, & Sparer, 1965) influences escape latency.

The Absence of Reinforcement. Many people experience unsatisfying social relationships but remain in those relationships. Why do these people fail to escape from their unpleasant social relationships? One likely reason is that past escape reactions from other unpleasant social relationships did not lead to positive relationships, but instead continued negative reactions (e.g., other negative relationships). In these situations, individuals do not learn to escape from aversive social situations. Many studies have shown that the strength of escape behavior depends on the amount of negative reinforcement (or the degree of decrease in the severity of an aversive event). The findings of these experiments show that the greater the negative reinforcement, the higher the asymptotic level of escape performance. Let's now examine one of these studies.

Campbell and Kraeling (1953) exposed rats to a 400-volt electric shock in the start box of an alley. Upon reaching the goal box, the shock was reduced to either 0, 100, 200, or 300 volts. Campbell and Kraeling reported that the greater the reduction in shock intensity, the faster the rats escaped from the 400-volt electric shock. Other experiments (Bower, Fowler, & Trapold, 1959) have found that

---

Figure 7.1   The mean escape performance for both starting and running speed increases over the last eight training trials with a higher shock intensity.

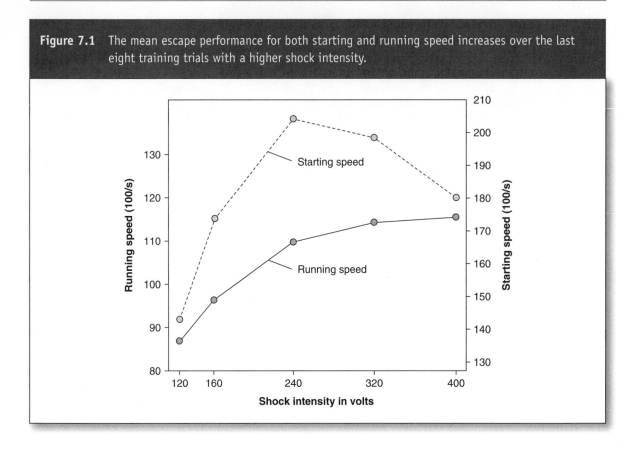

the level of escape behavior directly relates to the level of shock reduction the escape response induces. The magnitude of the negative reinforcement's influence on the asymptotic level of escape performance also is evident with cold water as the aversive stimulus (Woods, Davidson, & Peters, 1964).

The Impact of Delayed Reinforcement. Research has indicated that escape behavior also depends on the delay of reinforcement. The longer reinforcement is delayed after an escape response, the slower the acquisition of the escape behavior and the lower the final level of escape performance.

Fowler and Trapold's (1962) study illustrates the impact of reinforcement delay on escape conditioning. In their study, the termination of electric shock was delayed either 0, 1, 2, 4, 8, or 16 seconds after the rats entered the goal box of the alley. Fowler and Trapold reported that the time it took the rats to reach the goal box was a direct function of reward delay: the longer the delay, the slower the speed of the escape response (see Figure 7.2). Furthermore, the maximum escape speed depended on the delay of reinforcement: the longer the delay, the lower the final level of escape performance. Other studies using animals (Leeming & Robinson, 1973) and humans (Penney, 1967) have also found that a delay of negative reinforcement impairs escape conditioning.

However, some researchers report that a delay of even three seconds eliminates escape conditioning. According to Tarpy and Sawabini (1974), differences in delay gradients reflect the presence or absence of cues associated with negative reinforcement (termination of an aversive event). The experiments showing very short delay gradients have used the operant chamber, with bar pressing as the escape response to terminate shock. Since no cues are typically associated

Figure 7.2   The mean escape performance declines with a longer delay in shock termination.

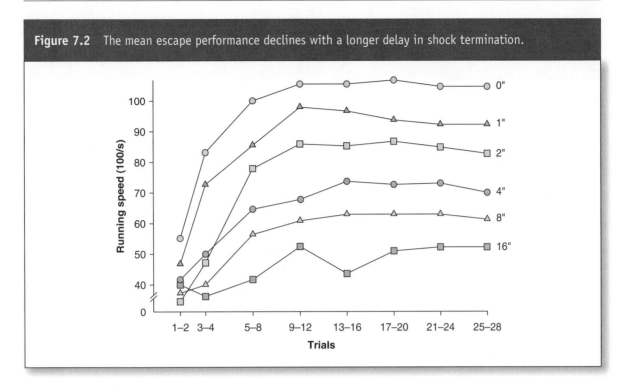

with shock termination in the bar-press situation, no secondary reinforcement cues can enhance performance when reinforcement is delayed. If cues are presented following a bar-press response, these stimuli will be associated with shock termination, and some escape conditioning will occur despite a short delay in reinforcement.

Returning to the chapter-opening vignette, Noah's tormentors have been especially cruel. As a result of their cruelty, Noah is highly motivated to escape their presence. When Billy and his friends start teasing or hitting Noah, Noah is highly motivated to turn and walk into a classroom. Noah experiences significant negative reinforcement when he is no longer abused by his tormentors.

The Elimination of an Escape Response

A rat shocked in the start box of an alley learns to escape by running into the goal box. A researcher can train the rat to no longer escape the start box. No longer presenting the aversive event, or no longer terminating the aversive event following the escape response, can eliminate the escape response.

The Removal of Negative Reinforcement. An escape response is eliminated when the aversive event continues despite the escape response. However, an animal will continue to respond for some time; the aversive event continues to motivate the escape response until an animal learns that the escape response no longer terminates the aversive event.

The strength of the escape response during acquisition affects resistance to extinction: The greater the acquisition training, the slower the extinction of the escape behavior. To illustrate the influence of the acquisition level on resistance to extinction, Fazzaro and D'Amato (1969) trained rats to bar press to terminate electric shock. Rats received either 200, 400, 800, or 1,600 training trials prior to extinction. Fazzaro and D'Amato found that the number of bar-press responses emitted during extinction increased with greater numbers of acquisition trials (see Figure 7.3).

Figure 7.3 The mean number of escape responses during extinction increases with the number of acquisition trials.

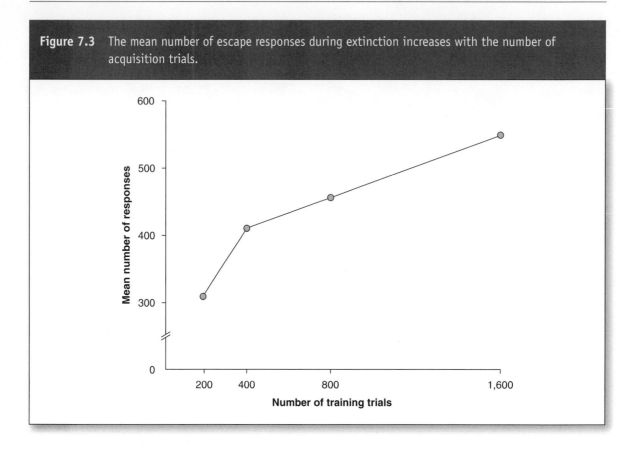

The Absence of Aversive Events. Elimination of an escape response also occurs when the aversive event is no longer experienced; yet an animal exhibits a number of escape responses even when the aversive event no longer occurs. Why do escape responses occur when the aversive event is not present?

D'Amato (1970) suggested an explanation. According to D'Amato, the cues present when the aversive event occurred become able to elicit an anticipatory pain response (a conditioned anticipation of an impending aversive event). The physiological aftereffects of the anticipatory pain response motivate the escape response even though the aversive event is no longer presented. Escape responses will continue until the anticipatory pain response is extinguished.

Vicious Circle Behavior

Judson Brown and his associates observed that punishment does not always eliminate escape behavior. In the J. S. Brown, Martin, and Morrow (1964) study, three groups of rats were initially placed in a 6-foot alley that was electrified except for the goal box. All of these animals learned to run to the goal box to escape the shock. For some animals, shock was eliminated in the second phase of study. As Figure 7.4 shows, the speed of their escape response declined quickly when shock was stopped. The animals in the long-shock group continued to receive shock in the alley but not in the start box; the rats in the short-shock group received shock only in the final 2-foot segment before the goal box. Brown et al. observed that the escape response continued despite punishment of the escape response in both the long-shock and short-shock

Judson S. Brown (1910-2005)

Brown received his doctorate from Yale University under the direction of Clark Hull. His first academic appointment at Harvard was interrupted by World War II. After the war, Brown joined the faculty at the University of Iowa, where he taught for 21 years. While at the University of Iowa, Brown served as chair of the Department of Psychology. Brown also taught at the Oregon Health Science University for 33 years. His research has contributed significantly to understanding the role of drive as a motivational variable and the origins of self-punitive behavior. Brown also was a gifted photographer, whose work was shown in numerous art galleries.

groups (see Figure 7.4). Brown et al. referred to these animals' actions as self-punitive or **vicious circle behavior**.

Vicious circle behavior has also been observed in human subjects. Renner and Tinsley (1976) trained human subjects to key press to escape shock in reaction to a warning light. These subjects stopped responding when the shock was discontinued. Other subjects only received shock on their first key press on each trial. These subjects failed to stop key pressing.

Why do animals engage in vicious circle behavior? Dean, Denny, and Blakemore (1985) suggested that fear motivates running, and the conditioning of fear to the start box maintained the escape response. In contrast, Renner and Tinsley (1976) argued that vicious circle behavior occurs because the animals or people fail to recognize that punishment will not occur if they do not respond. Renner and Tinsley observed that human subjects in a vicious circle condition stop responding when they are told that key pressing will be shocked. This indicates that the subjects' behavior is affected by their perception of behavior-outcome contingencies. R. B. Martin (1984) presents evidence that both fear conditioned to the start box and the failure to recognize that not responding does not lead to punishment contributes to the occurrence of vicious circle behavior. In this chapter we learned that fear is an important factor in motivating escape behavior; we look at the importance of contingency learning in Chapter 11.

BEFORE YOU GO ON

- What might Noah do to stop Billy from bullying him?

- Why might Noah not learn to escape Billy's bullying?

SECTION REVIEW

- Animals and people can learn to escape from an aversive event.

- The more intense the aversive event, the faster an escape response is acquired.

- The greater the decrease in the severity of the aversive event following the escape behavior, the faster the escape response is learned.

- The shorter the delay of reinforcement following the escape behavior, the faster the escape response is acquired.

- Extinction typically occurs if the escape response is punished.

- An animal or person may stop responding if the aversive event is no longer presented. However, fear conditioned during escape learning may impair the extinction of the escape response.

- In vicious circle behavior, the escape response continues despite the fact that the failure to escape is not punished.

Figure 7.4 The mean escape latency during extinction for animals receiving either no shock in the alley, shock in the entire 6-foot alley (long-shock condition), or shock only in the last 2 feet of alley before the goal box (short-shock condition). The resistance to extinction is higher in the long- and short-shock conditions than in the no-shock condition.

Our discussion indicates that we can learn how to escape from aversive situations. However, it is more desirable, when possible, to avoid rather than escape an aversive event. In the next section, we examine the development of responses that allow us to prevent aversive events.

The Avoidance of Aversive Events

A teenage girl is invited to a party by a boy she does not like. Not wanting to hurt his feelings, she says that she would like to go, but she can't because she must study for a test. This girl exhibits an **avoidance response**: Her "little white lie" allows her to prevent an unpleasant evening.

Types of Avoidance Behavior

There are two classes of avoidance behavior: active and passive avoidance responses. Under some circumstances, an overt response, or an **active avoidance response**, is necessary to avoid the aversive event. The teenage girl exhibited an active avoidance response: She formulated an excuse in order to prevent an aversive event. In other circumstances, simply not responding, or a **passive avoidance response**, will prevent an aversive event. Suppose you receive a note from your dentist indicating it is time for your 6-month checkup. Since you do not like going to the dentist, you ignore the note. This is an example of passive avoidance behavior: You avoid the dentist by not responding to the note.

Active Avoidance Learning. O. H. Mowrer's (1938, 1939) classic research showed that rats could learn to exhibit an overt response to avoid electric shock. In these studies, a cue (e.g., a light) was paired with painful electric shock in one chamber of a shuttle box (see Figure 7.5). The rats could avoid shock by jumping across a barrier between the two compartments when the cue (CS) was presented but before the shock (UCS) onset. The animals in Mowrer's studies learned to exhibit the active avoidance hurdle-jumping response when exposed to the CS, and therefore, they avoided the electric shock. Many other psychologists since Mowrer have observed that rats can learn to cross a barrier to avoid electric shock in the shuttle box apparatus (Bower, Starr, &

Figure 7.5   A shuttle box used to study avoidance learning. When the conditioned stimulus (a light) is presented in one side of the box, the animal must jump to the other compartment to avoid the electric shock.

Neal Elgar Miller (1909–2002)

Miller received his doctorate from Yale University under the direction of Clark Hull. After receiving his doctorate, he spent a year at the Institute of Psychoanalysis in Vienna studying with Heinz Hartman, who was a student of Freud. He then taught at Yale University for 30 years before moving to Rockefeller University, where he taught for another 15 years. His text, with John Dollard, *Personality and Psychotherapy: An Analysis in Terms of Learning, Thinking, and Culture* applied the concepts in Hull's drive theory to Freud's psychoanalytic theory. He served as president of the American Psychological Association in 1961 and received its Distinguished Scientific Contribution Award in 1959.

Lazarovitz, 1965; Theios, Lynch, & Lowe, 1966). The shuttle box apparatus has also been used to train other animal species to avoid an aversive event. This research indicates that to avoid shock, dogs (A. Moscovitch & LoLordo, 1968), cats (Steinbrecher & Lockhart, 1966), and rabbits (Flakus & Steinbrecher, 1964) can learn to jump over the hurdle in a shuttle box.

The hurdle-jumping response is one of many behaviors animals can learn in order to avoid aversive events. Neal Miller (1941, 1948) discovered that rats could learn to turn a wheel to avoid electric shock. Other psychologists have reported that rats can learn to press a bar in an operant chamber (Biederman, D'Amato, & Keller, 1964) or even rear up on their hind legs (Bolles & Tuttle, 1967) to prevent shock.

People learn many different responses that enable them to avoid aversive events. A person opening an umbrella in order to stay dry, a child doing homework to avoid failing, or an adult paying the mortgage to avoid foreclosure are three examples of humans responding to avoid unpleasant events. Recall Noah being tormented by Billy and his friends described in the chapter-opening vignette. Noah running the other way when he sees Billy and his friends is an example of an active avoidance response.

Many, perhaps most, of our avoidance responses are acquired during childhood. Research conducted with children shows that they are very adept in learning to avoid aversive events. Several studies (Penney & Kirwin, 1965; N. M. Robinson & Robinson, 1961) using loud tones as the unpleasant event reported that preschool-aged children can learn to press a bar to prevent the noise.

Passive Avoidance Learning. Psychologists have also shown that animals can learn to avoid aversive events passively. In one setting, an animal placed on top of a ledge above a grid floor receives an electric shock upon stepping down. Noah in our chapter-opening vignette could passively avoid Billy and his friends' abuse by not going out to the playground during recess.

Some studies show that rats refuse to leave the platform after a single training trial (Hines & Paolino, 1970; McGaugh & Landfield, 1970). Other studies demonstrate that animals readily learn to avoid shock by not entering an environment where they received shock the previous day (Baron, 1965) or by failing to bar press after being shocked for bar pressing (Camp, Raymond, & Church, 1967).

How Readily Is Avoidance Behavior Learned?

Two variables appear to have an important influence on avoidance learning: the severity of the aversive event and the length of the delay between the CS and the UCS.

The Severity of the Aversive Event. You might suspect that the more aversive an event, the more likely it is the situation will be avoided. This relationship is true in most avoidance situations; that is, the greater the severity of the aversive event, the more readily the subject will learn the avoidance response and the higher the final level of avoidance performance will be. However, the opposite relationship is true in a two-way active avoidance task. In this type of task, the greater the severity of aversive event, the more slowly the subject will acquire the avoidance response and the lower the final level of avoidance performance will be. We first examine evidence of the influence of the severity of the aversive event on avoidance learning, and then we will discuss why severity influences two-way avoidance behavior differently than it does other avoidance responses.

Investigators (Camp et al., 1967; Seligman & Campbell, 1965) have evaluated the effect of shock severity on the acquisition of a passive avoidance response. In these studies, rats were initially trained to bar press for food. After learning to bar press, the animals were shocked following a bar-press response; each rat could avoid shock by not pressing the bar. The severity of shock was either low, moderate, or high. The results showed that the higher the shock severity, the faster the acquisition of the passive avoidance response and the higher the final performance level of the passive avoidance behavior.

Shock severity also has an important influence on the acquisition and performance of a one-way active avoidance response. In this situation, the animal is shocked in one chamber of a shuttle box and can avoid shock by running to the other chamber. The shocked chamber is painted one color (e.g., white), while the goal box is another color (e.g., black). Many studies have found that increasing the severity of the shock leads to faster acquisition of the one-way active avoidance response, as well as a higher level of asymptotic avoidance performance. Let's examine the Moyer and Korn (1966) study to document the role of shock intensity on a one-way active avoidance response.

Moyer and Korn (1966) placed rats on one side of a shuttle box, shocking them if they did not run to the other compartment within 5 seconds. Each rat remained in the "safe" chamber for 15 seconds and was then placed in the "dangerous" chamber to begin another trial. Animals received either .5, 1.5, 2.5, or 3.5 mA of shock during acquisition training, and each subject was given 50 acquisition trials on a single day. Moyer and Korn reported that the greater the severity of shock, the faster the animals learned to avoid the shock (see Figure 7.6). Furthermore, the higher the intensity of shock, the more rapidly the animals ran from the dangerous to the safe compartment of the shuttle box.

In a two-way active avoidance situation, the animal is placed in one chamber (Side A) of the shuttle box and exposed to a specific stimulus (e.g., a light) prior to the presentation of shock. To avoid the shock, the animal must run to the other chamber (Side B) before the electric shock is presented. After this trial, the animal remains in Side B for a short time (e.g., 60 seconds). At the end of this intertrial interval (ITI), the stimulus is again presented, and the animal must run from Side B to Side A to avoid being shocked; thus, the animal avoids the aversive event only by returning to the place where it was previously shocked. Learning a two-way active avoidance response requires an animal to ignore situational cues (the place where the shock was presented) and to attend to a specific cue (e.g., the light). The two-way active avoidance training continues until the animal responds consistently to the specific cue (CS) and avoids the aversive electric shock.

We learned earlier that increases in the aversiveness of an event facilitate the acquisition of a passive avoidance response and a one-way active avoidance behavior. In contrast, the literature clearly shows that a severe aversive event impairs rather than enhances the acquisition and the asymptotic performance level of a two-way active avoidance response. Let's examine one study to illustrate the influence of aversive event severity on two-way active avoidance learning.

Moyer and Korn (1964) gave rats two-way active avoidance response training in periods of 30 trials a day for 4 days. In their study, after the CS (a tone) was presented in one chamber, the rats had 5 seconds to run to the other chamber to avoid being shocked. Rats failing to respond within the 5-second interval received either a .5-, 1.0-, 1.5-, or 2.5-mA shock. Moyer and Korn found that as shock intensity increased, the percentage of avoidance responses made during acquisition declined (see Figure 7.6). These results show that high levels of electric shock impair an animal's ability to avoid shock in a two-way active avoidance task.

Figure 7.6 The influence of shock intensity on the acquisition of a one-way and a two-way active avoidance response. Increases in shock intensity facilitate one-way avoidance learning but impair two-way avoidance acquisition.

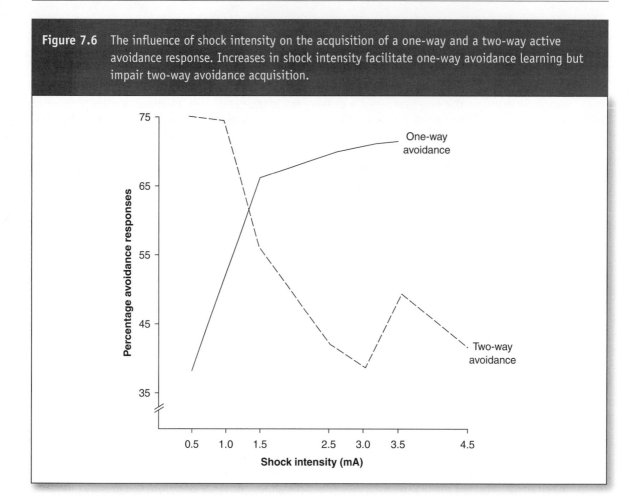

Why do increases in shock severity impair two-way active avoidance learning, yet facilitate other forms of avoidance learning? Theios et al. (1966) suggested that in a two-way active avoidance, the animal experiences conflict between running away from the feared stimulus and running into an environment where the aversive event previously occurred. According to Theios et al., the more severe the aversive event, the greater the animal's reluctance to enter the environment associated with the aversive event and, therefore, the poorer the acquisition of an avoidance response. Many studies (Tarpy & Mayer, 1978) support Theios et al.'s view; let's examine one of them.

P. E. Freedman, Hennessy, and Groner (1974) compared the efficiency of avoidance behavior when animals ran from a compartment associated with a high level of aversiveness into a compartment associated with less aversiveness to avoidance performance when both compartments were associated with equal shock severity. Freedman et al. theorized that the reluctance to avoid shock would decrease if animals were required to run to a less aversive compartment rather than an equally aversive compartment. In support of this view, they found that avoidance performance was enhanced if an animal was required to run into a chamber associated with a lower shock intensity.

The Delay Interval Between the CS and the UCS. We learned in Chapter 4 that the level of fear conditioning depends upon the CS-UCS interval: the longer the interval, the weaker the conditioning of the fear response. The interval between the CS and the UCS also affects the acquisition of an avoidance response. The literature (G. Hall, 1979) shows that the longer the CS-UCS interval, the slower the acquisition of the avoidance behavior. It seems reasonable to assume that the influence of the CS-UCS interval on fear conditioning is also responsible for its effect on avoidance learning; as the level of fear diminishes with longer CS-UCS intervals, motivation to escape the feared stimulus weakens and, therefore, the opportunity to learn to avoid it lessens. Let's next consider one study that examined the influence of the CS-UCS interval on avoidance behavior.

Kamin (1954) trained dogs to avoid shock by jumping over a barrier in a two-way active avoidance situation. The CS, a 2-second buzzer, preceded the shock UCS. The interval between the CS-UCS varied: Subjects received either a 5-, 10-, 20-, or 40-second CS-UCS interval. Kamin reported that the shorter the interval between the CS and UCS, the quicker the acquisition of the avoidance response.

Recall our example of Noah learning to avoid Billy and his friends by running the other way when he sees them (active avoidance response) or by not going out on the playground during recess (passive avoidance response). Noah will quickly learn to avoid Billy and his friends because their abuse is severe and immediate.

BEFORE YOU GO ON

- Why did Ethan fail to avoid his father's spankings?
- How could Ethan prevent future spankings?

SECTION REVIEW

- In active avoidance learning, a specific overt behavior can be used to avoid an aversive event.
- In passive avoidance learning, the suppression of response will prevent the aversive event.
- In passive avoidance learning and one-way active avoidance learning, increases in the severity of the aversive event lead to faster avoidance learning.
- In two-way active avoidance learning, an increase in the intensity of the aversive event produces slower acquisition.
- The longer the interval between the CS and UCS, the slower the acquisition of the avoidance response.

Punishment

A parent takes away a child's television privileges for hitting a younger sibling. A teacher sends a disruptive student to the principal to be suspended for 3 days from school. A soldier absent without leave (AWOL) is ordered to the stockade by the military police. An employee who is late for work faces a reprimand from the boss. Each of these situations is an example of **punishment**. Punishment is defined as the use of an aversive event contingent upon the occurrence of an inappropriate behavior. The intent of punishment is to suppress an undesired behavior; if punishment is effective, the frequency and intensity, or both, of the punished behavior will decline. For example, the parent who takes away a child's television privileges for hitting a younger sibling is using punishment to decrease the occurrence of the child's aggressive behavior. The loss of television is an effective punishment if, after being punished, the youngster hits the sibling less frequently.

Billy receiving a spanking from his father described in the chapter-opening vignette is another example of the use of punishment to suppress his tormenting Noah. Unfortunately, the effects of the spanking only lasted for a few days and Billy went back to his abusive ways. The reasons why the spanking only temporarily stopped Billy's abuse are discussed shortly.

Types of Punishment

We have defined punishment as the response-contingent presentation of an aversive event. If effective, the punishment decreases the likelihood that a response will occur. While peanut butter is reinforcing for many children, it will act as a punishment to a child with a peanut butter allergy. In other words, for most children, peanut butter is reinforcing, but for a child with a food allergy, it is aversive.

There are two types of punishment: positive and negative. **Positive punishment** refers to the use of a physically or psychologically aversive event as the punishment. A spanking is one example of a positive punisher; verbal criticism is another. In **negative punishment**, reinforcement is lost or unavailable as the consequence of an inappropriate behavior. The term **omission training** often is used in place of negative punishment. In omission training, reinforcement is provided when the undesired response does not occur, while the inappropriate behavior leads to no reinforcement.

Recall that Billy received a spanking from his father for bullying Noah in the chapter-opening vignette. The spanking that Billy received is an example of positive punishment. Should Billy be suspended for continuing to torment Noah, the suspension would be an example of negative punishment.

There are two categories of negative punishment. One of these is **response cost**, in which an undesired response results in either the withdrawal of or failure to obtain reinforcement. In laboratory settings, a response cost contingency means that an undesired response will cause an animal or person to lose or not obtain either a primary reinforcer (e.g., candy or food) or a secondary reinforcer (e.g., chips, tokens, or points). Real-world examples of response cost punishment include the withdrawal or failure to obtain material reinforcers (e.g., money) or social reinforcers (e.g., approval). Losing television privileges for hitting a sibling is one example of response cost; being fined by an employer for being late for work is another.

The other kind of negative punishment is called **time-out from reinforcement** (or time-out). Time-out from reinforcement is a period during which reinforcement is unavailable. A child who is sent to his room after misbehaving is enduring time-out; so is the soldier going to the stockade for being AWOL. Billy being suspended for tormenting Noah, described in the chapter-opening vignette, is an example of time-out from reinforcement.

Is punishment effective? Its extensive use in our society suggests that we believe punishment is an effective technique to suppress inappropriate behavior. However, psychology's view of the effectiveness of punishment has changed dramatically during the past 50 years. In the next section, we examine how psychologists have viewed the effectiveness of punishment as a method of suppressing behavior.

The Effectiveness of Punishment

Skinner (1953) believed that punishment could only temporarily suppress behavior. The classic Skinner study (1938) supports this view. In his experiment, two rats were trained to bar press for food reinforcement. The rats' bar-press response was then extinguished by discontinuing reinforcement. One rat was also punished for bar pressing by having its paw slapped when it touched the bar during the first few responses of extinction. The other rat did not receive punishment. Skinner observed that the initial effect of punishment was that the punished rat showed a lower response rate than the unpunished rat (see Figure 7.7). However, the suppressive

Figure 7.7 The effect of punishment on the extinction of the bar-press response. Punishment produced a temporary reduction in bar pressing, but by the end of the second day, punishment no longer had any effect.

effect of punishment was short-lived; bar pressing was equivalent in the punished and the non-punished rats within 30 minutes after punishment. Skinner also noted that the punished rat continued to respond at a high rate even after the nonpunished rat had slowed down. When both rats had finally stopped responding, both had made the same total number of responses. Skinner's observations show that punishment may temporarily suppress responding, but it does not eliminate it. Skinner suggested that extinction instead of punishment should be used to permanently suppress an inappropriate response. His conclusion certainly conflicts with our society's belief that punishment is an effective method of suppressing inappropriate behavior.

Research evaluating the influence of punishment on behavior during the 1950s and 1960s shows that under some conditions, punishment does permanently suppress inappropriate behavior (Campbell & Church, 1969). However, in other circumstances, punishment either has no effect on behavior or only temporarily suppresses behavior.

A number of variables determine whether punishment will suppress behavior. We next discuss the conditions necessary for effective punishment and the circumstances in which punishment does not suppress inappropriate behavior.

When Is Punishment Effective?

Three factors influence the effectiveness of punishment: severity, consistency, and immediacy. We will examine them next.

The Severity of Punishment. Most people in our society recognize the dangers of driving under the influence of alcohol. Local newspapers routinely report traffic fatalities caused by drunk drivers. In

2006, 42,642 persons were killed in all traffic accidents in the United States. Of these 42,642 people, 15,121 died in alcohol-related crashes in which at least one driver had a blood alcohol content (BAC) over .08 (National Highway Traffic Safety Administration, 2007). And every 30 minutes, a person is killed in an alcohol-related motor vehicle accident. Yet people continue to drive while intoxicated, and thousands of drunk drivers are ticketed each year. These drivers, though punished when apprehended, are likely to drink and drive again. About one-third of all drivers who are arrested or convicted of driving under the influence of alcohol have a previous driving-while-intoxicated (DWI) conviction (National Highway Traffic Safety Administration, 2004).

Why haven't previous DWI convictions been effective? One reason may be that the punishments have, in the past, been too mild to suppress drunk driving behavior. First offenses were generally punished with participation in an alcohol treatment program rather than a jail sentence. In addition, repeat offenders rarely spent more than one year in prison. In recent years, laws have been passed that punish repeat offenders more severely (National Highway Traffic Safety Administration, 2004). These more punitive measures include suspending or revoking the license of repeat offenders, impounding or immobilizing the repeat offender's vehicle, installing an interlock system that will not allow the vehicle to start if the driver's blood alcohol level is above a certain threshold, and a mandatory minimum imprisonment and/or a community service requirement for repeat DWI offenders.

These more severe penalties for repeat offenders appear to be successful. The National Highway Traffic Safety Administration (2004) reports that license revocation for a DWI significantly reduced alcohol-related fatalities. These studies also show that while many repeat DWI offenders continue to drive with a suspended license, they drive less and more carefully. Further, the use of a breath-analyzed ignition interlock device significantly reduced recidivism for repeat DWI offenders (Fulkerson, 2003; Marques, Tippetts, & Voas, 2003). Our discussion suggests that mild punishment has little effect on drinking and driving behavior, while a more severe penalty has greater effect. We next look at a large body of evidence that indicates that the more severe the punishment, the more effective it will be.

Research has consistently shown that mild punishment produces little, if any, suppression of the punished response. Moreover, if any suppression does occur, it will be short-lived. The effectiveness of punishment has been found to increase as its severity increases (Campbell & Church, 1969). Thus, a moderately severe punishment produces more suppression of an inappropriate behavior than a mild punishment, while a strong punishment is more likely to produce complete suppression of the punished behavior. Also, the more severe the punishment, the longer the punished behavior is inhibited. In fact, a severe punishment may lead to a permanent suppression of the punished response.

Numerous studies using animal subjects have reported that the greater the intensity of punishment, the more complete the suppression of the punished behavior (Church, 1969). Camp et al.'s 1967 study provides an excellent example of the influence of the intensity of punishment on the degree of suppression of an operant behavior. In their study, 48 rats initially were given eight training sessions to bar press for food reinforcement on a variable-interval (VI) 1-minute schedule. Following initial training, the rats were divided into six groups and given either 0-, 0.1-, 0.2-, 0.3-, 0.5-, or 2.0-mA shock punishments lasting for 2.0 seconds. Punishment was administered when the rat's response rate did not decline. As illustrated in Figure 7.8, the higher the intensity of shock, the greater the suppression of the operant response. These results indicate that the more severe the punisher, the more effective the shock will be in suppressing the punished response. The effect of shock intensity on the suppression of an operant response has been shown in a number of animal species, including monkeys (Hake, Azrin, & Oxford, 1967), pigeons (Azrin & Holz, 1966), and rats (Storms, Boroczi, & Broen, 1962).

Figure 7.8   The mean suppression ratio decreases, or the level of suppression increases, with higher intensities of electric shock during punishment training.

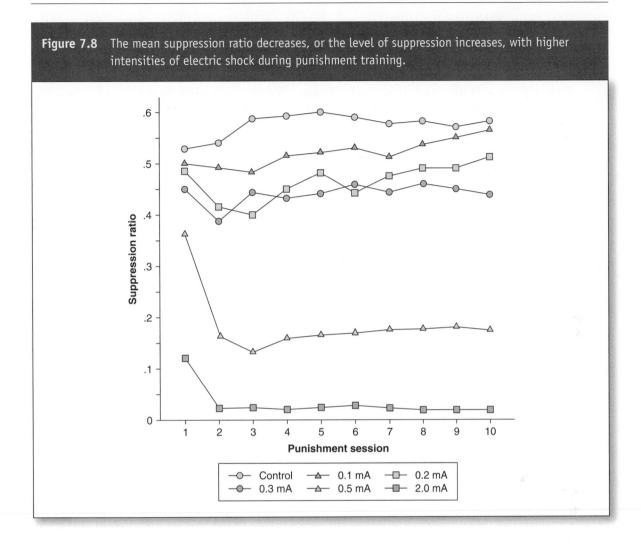

Research conducted with human subjects has also demonstrated that the severity of punishment affects its effectiveness. A number of studies (Cheyne, Goyeche, & Walters, 1969; Parke & Walters, 1967) have evaluated the effect of the intensity of punishment on the suppression of playing with a forbidden toy. In these studies, children were punished with a loud noise for selecting one of a pair of toys. The noises ranged from 52 to 96 decibels, with 60 decibels being the loudness of normal conversation. After punishment, each child was isolated with toys that were either identical or similar to the toys presented at the beginning of the experiment. The studies recorded the latency for each child to touch the "wrong" toy as well as the length of time the child played with this toy. The results of these experiments show that the more intense the punishment, the greater the suppression of the child's play with the toy associated with punishment.

The severity of punishment also affects the level of response suppression in adults. Powell and Azrin (1968) punished their subjects for smoking cigarettes by using a specially designed cigarette case that delivered an electric shock when opened. Powell and Azrin reported that the smoking rate decreased as the intensity of shock increased. Similarly, R. S. Davidson (1972) found that as electric shock intensity increased, the rate of an alcoholic client's pressing a bar to obtain alcohol declined.

Addiction to smoking cigarettes generally begins in adolescence. The cigarette companies have been criticized for targeting advertising campaigns to children, and laws have been passed to prevent the sale of cigarettes to minors. Do these laws work? The answer depends upon whether the punishment for selling to minors is severe. Leonard Jason and his colleagues (Jason, Ji, Anes, & Birkhead, 1991; Jason, Ji, Anes, & Xaverious, 1992) have evaluated the influence of the severity of punishment on a store's compliance with laws prohibiting the sale of cigarettes to minors. Jason et al. (1991) measured the percentage of stores selling cigarettes to minors both before and after the Woodbridge, Illinois, town council passed a local ordinance banning the sale of cigarettes to minors. Minors were sent into stores that sold cigarettes and the sale of (or refusal to sell) cigarettes to these minors was recorded. Prior to the ordinance, 70% of the stores sold cigarettes to minors. The ordinance provided a warning for the first offense. A $400 fine and a 1-day suspension of the ability to sell cigarettes was the punishment for the second offense. Jason et al. (1991) reported that the percentage of stores selling to minors dropped to 33% after the ordinance was instituted. Many of the merchants who received a warning continued to sell to minors, but after the merchants received a $400 fine and 1-day suspension, the percentage selling to minors dropped to 0% and remained at that level for the remainder of the 2-year study.

Recall that the spanking that Billy received from his father for abusing Noah, described in the chapter opening, only temporarily suppressed Billy's bullying behavior. As a "good whipping" would seem to be an intense punishment, why did it not suppress Billy's abuse behavior toward Noah? We address this question in the next two sections.

The Consistency of Punishment. In the last section, we learned that punishment must be severe to eliminate an undesired behavior, such as drunk driving. However, a severe punishment may not always be an effective method of suppressing this behavior. The literature shows that punishment must be consistently administered if it is to successfully eliminate inappropriate behavior. Thus, punishment should be given every time a person drives while intoxicated. Unfortunately, the odds of a drunk driver being caught are 1 in 2,000 (National Transportation Safety Board, 2003).

Rigorous observation of drivers is essential to detecting drunk drivers because a higher probability of being caught leads to a greater deterrence (Ross, 1981). In New South Wales, Australia, the likelihood of detection is high and the incidence of drunk driving low (Homel, McKay, & Henstridge, 1995). Further, once a person is caught drinking and driving, he or she should be punished. Unfortunately, effective penalties for drinking and driving are not always imposed. For example, even though California law mandates the use of ignition interlocking devices for DWI-suspended drivers arrested for driving under the influence, very few judges actually order vehicle ignition interlocks for convicted drivers (DeYoung, 2002).

Numerous studies (Walters & Grusec, 1977) have demonstrated the importance of administering punishment consistently. In one of these studies, Azrin, Holz, and Hake (1963) trained rats to bar press for food reinforcement on a 3-minute VI schedule. A 240-volt shock was delivered following the response on fixed-ratio (FR) punishment schedules ranging from FR-1 to FR-1,000. As Figure 7.9 indicates, the level of suppression decreases as the punishment schedule increases. These results indicate that the less consistently the punishment is administered, the less effective the punishment is.

Consistency also influences the effectiveness of punishment in humans. Parke and Deur (1972) reinforced 6- to 9-year-old boys with marbles for hitting a life-size doll. Then, without informing the subjects, Parke and Deur began punishing half of them with a loud buzzer every time they hit the doll; the other half were punished only 50% of the time they hit the doll and were reinforced the other 50% of the time. Parke and Deur found that the boys who received

Figure 7.9   This graph shows that the rate of bar-press responding for food reinforcement delivered on a 3-minute variable-interval schedule increases with higher fixed-ratio schedules of punishment. The short, oblique lines indicate when punishment was delivered.

consistent punishment stopped hitting the doll sooner than those boys who were punished intermittently. In another experiment, Leff (1969) demonstrated that continuous punishment, compared with intermittent punishment, more effectively caused children to stop choosing an attractive toy and to select an unattractive toy instead.

Several correlational studies have evaluated the relationship between delinquency and the consistency of parental punishment. This research (Glueck & Glueck, 1950; McCord, McCord, & Zola, 1959) reported that delinquent boys were more likely to have received inconsistent parental discipline than were nondelinquent boys. These findings suggest that parents who want to suppress their children's socially inappropriate behavior should be consistent in punishing that behavior.

Returning to our example of Billy's being spanked for tormenting Noah in the chapter-opening vignette, it is likely that Billy is not spanked every time he torments Noah. The lack of consistency between the Billy's bullying behavior and his father's spanking undoubtedly contributed to the fact that the spanking was only temporarily effective.

Delay of Punishment. We have learned that in order for punishment to suppress undesired behavior such as drunk driving, the punishment must be both severe and consistently administered. In this section, we will discover that punishment must also be immediate. The literature shows that the longer the delay between the inappropriate response and punishment, the less effective the punishment will be in suppressing the punished behavior. In our society, there is usually a long delay between a person's apprehension for drunk driving and the administration of a fine or jail sentence. Research on the delay of punishment shows this method is ineffective, suggesting that a shorter interval between the time of the offense and the time of sentencing should be implemented in order to maximize the effects of punishment.

The literature using animal subjects consistently demonstrates that immediate punishment is more effective than delayed punishment. The Camp et al. (1967) study provides an excellent example of this observation. After being trained to bar press for food reinforcement, rats in this experiment received a .25-mA 1-second shock punishment either immediately, 2.0, 7.5, or 30 seconds after a bar-press response. Camp et al. reported greatest suppression of the bar-press response when shock occurred immediately after responding (see Figure 7.10).

Banks and Vogel-Sprott (1965) investigated the influence of delay of punishment (electric shock) on the level of suppression of their human subjects' reaction to a tone. These authors reported that although an immediate punishment inhibited responding, delayed punishment (for either 30, 60, or 120 seconds) did not affect response levels. Trenholme and Baron (1975) found a similar lack of effectiveness of delayed punishment in college students, and Abramowitz and O'Leary (1990) found the same in children. In the A. J. Abramowitz and O'Leary study, children were scolded in a classroom setting. A teacher's scolding was most effective when the punishment immediately followed the misbehavior. In terms of our chapter-opening vignette, Billy did not receive an immediate spanking for his abusive behavior, which very likely contributed to the fact that the suppressive effects of the spanking were only temporary.

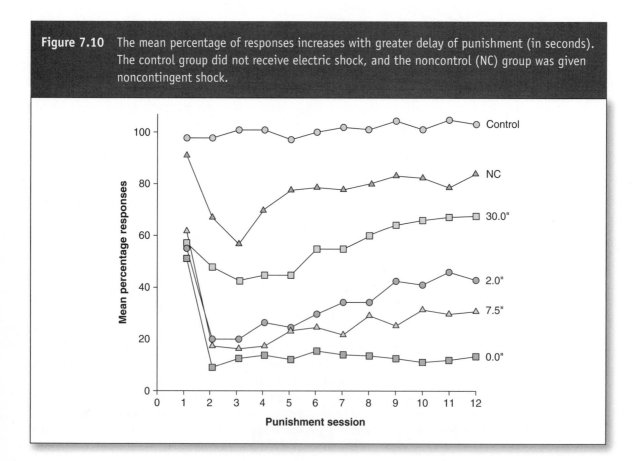

Figure 7.10   The mean percentage of responses increases with greater delay of punishment (in seconds). The control group did not receive electric shock, and the noncontrol (NC) group was given noncontingent shock.

The Negative Consequences of Punishment

The use of punishment has a number of negative consequences. We examine some of these undesirable effects next.

Pain-Induced Aggression. A high school basketball coach was suspended for several months for whipping his players with a weight belt for performance deemed inadequate, even though the use of corporate punishment was prohibited by his school district. Upon his reinstatement, the basketball coach benched the top scorer on the team, who was one of the team's players whose parents complained about the coach's use of corporal punishment (*Clarion Ledger,* December, 25, 2010). In this section, we explore one reason why the coach benched his star player.

Nathan H. Azrin (1927–)

Azrin received his doctorate from the Harvard University under the direction of B. F. Skinner. He then taught at Southern Illinois University for 14 years before moving to Nova Southeastern University for the last 30 years. His research has contributed significantly to the application of operant conditioning principles to the modification of negative patterns of behavior for which he was awarded the Lifetime Achievement Award by the Society for the Advancement of Behavior Analysis. He was president of the Society of the Experimental Analysis of Behavior from 1963 to 1970.

When animals or people are punished, they experience pain. Nathan Azrin's research (Azrin, 1970) clearly shows that this pain response may elicit the emotion of anger, which, in turn, may arouse aggressive behavior. Our discussion begins by looking at evidence of **pain-induced aggression**, followed by a review of studies that show why punishment can lead to aggression.

Azrin, Hutchinson, and Sallery (1964) observed that when primates are shocked, they attack other monkeys, rats, or mice. In addition, monkeys who are shocked will attack a toy tiger (Plotnick, Mir, & Delgado, 1971) or a ball (Azrin, 1964). Shock-induced aggressive attack has also been reported in cats (Ulrich, Wolff, & Azrin, 1964).

Leon Berkowitz (1971, 1978) has provided considerable support for the theory that anger induced by exposure to painful events can lead to aggression in humans. In one study (Berkowitz & LePage, 1967), subjects were to list, within a period of 5 minutes, ideas a publicity agent could use to increase sales of a product. A confederate then rated some subjects' performance as poor by giving these subjects seven electric shocks; this confederate shocked other subjects only once, to indicate a positive evaluation. According to Berkowitz and LePage, the seven-shock evaluation angered subjects, but the one-shock evaluation did not. Next, all the subjects evaluated the confederate's performance by giving the confederate from one to seven shocks. Subjects who had received seven shocks retaliated by giving the confederate significantly more shocks than did the other subjects. These results indicate that painful events can motivate aggressive behavior.

We have seen that anger can result in aggressive behavior. However, this aggressive reaction is not motivated by the expectation of avoiding punishment; rather, it reflects an impulsive act energized by the emotional arousal characteristic of anger. Furthermore, the expression of aggressive behavior in angry animals or people appears to be highly reinforcing. Many studies show that annoyed animals will learn a behavior that gives them the opportunity to be aggressive. For example, Azrin, Hutchinson, and McLaughlin (1965) found that squirrel monkeys bit inanimate objects (e.g., balls) after being shocked. However, if no object was present, they learned to pull a chain that provided them with a ball to bite.

Unfortunately, punishment-induced anger and aggression is not a rare occurrence. Eric Harris and Dylan Klebold entered Columbine High School in Columbine, Colorado on Tuesday, April 20, 1999, armed with two 9 mm firearms and two 12-gauge shotguns and began shooting. When the shooting ended, Harris and Klebold had killed 12 students and 1 teacher. They also injured 21 other students directly, and 3 people were injured while attempting to escape. The two boys then committed suicide. Both Harris and Klebold were two angry young men who had often been tormented by other students. Unfortunately, the Columbine massacre is not an isolated incident.

Will the abuse that Noah received, described in the chapter-opening vignette, cause him to become violent? We address this question next.

Punishment does not always elicit aggressive behavior. Hokanson (1970) reported that people's previous experiences influence their reaction to painful events. If individuals have been reinforced for nonaggressive reactions to aversive events, punished for aggressive responses to painful events, or both, the likelihood that punishment will elicit aggression diminishes. Furthermore, the level of anger that pain produces differs among individuals (S. B. Klein & Thorne, 2007). Some people react intensely to an aversive event that only elicits mild anger in others. Since the probability that painful events will motivate aggression depends upon the level of anger the aversive circumstance induces, individuals who respond strongly to aversive events are much more likely to become aggressive than are people who are not very angered by aversive events.

The Modeling of Aggression. Spanking a child for misbehaving may suppress the inappropriate behavior, may cause the child to become aggressive, or may prompt the child to imitate the parent's aggressive behavior. The behavior we learn not by receiving explicit reinforcement but by observing another person's actions is called **modeling** (Bandura, 1971).

Bandura, Ross, and Ross's (1963) classic experiment illustrates the influence of a model on aggressive behavior. In this study, children saw an adult act aggressively toward a life-sized plastic doll called a Bobo doll. The model sat on this doll, punched it, hit it with a mallet, kicked it, and tossed it up and down. Other children in the study did not watch a model behave in this manner. After the initial phase of the study, all children were allowed to play with attractive toys and then were frustrated by being required to leave these attractive toys for less attractive ones, including a Bobo doll. Bandura et al. recorded the level of imitative aggression (attacking the Bobo doll) and nonimitative aggression (aggressive behaviors the model had not performed). They found that while all the children exhibited nonimitative forms of aggression when they were frustrated, only the children who had watched the model showed the imitative patterns of aggression. These findings indicate that we can learn how to perform a particular behavior merely by watching others.

Other studies have also reported that children will imitate a model's aggressive behavior. For example, Steur, Applefield, and Smith (1971) discovered that children who had viewed cartoons depicting aggressive behavior became more aggressive toward other children than children who had not seen the cartoons. The imitated aggression included hitting, pushing, kicking, squeezing, choking, or throwing objects at the other children. Furthermore, Hanratty, Liebert, Morris, and Fernandez (1969) reported that as the result of a modeling experience, children may even act aggressively toward an adult. In their study, young boys, after watching an aggressive model, attacked an adult dressed as a clown.

Do children who are physically punished, in turn, model this aggressive behavior? Two types of evidence support the view that they do. First, experimental research shows that children punished during a study use the same method of punishment when attempting to control the actions of other children. In one study, Mischel and Grusec (1966) verbally punished preschool-aged children for certain actions during a game; the children, in turn, employed verbal abuse toward other children playing the game. Similarly, Gelfand, Hartmann, Lamb, Smith, Mahan, and Paul (1974) found that children who had been penalized for incorrect responses during a game used this form of punishment when teaching another child to play.

Second, correlational studies report a strong relationship between parental use of punishment and the level of aggressive behavior in their children. Many parents use aggression in the form of a spanking or paddling to punish their children's behavior. Numerous studies show that the use of aggression in the form of punishment leads to aggressive behavior in children, both at school and at home (Larzelere, Schneider, Larson, & Pike, 1996; B. Weiss, Dodge, Bates, & Pettit, 1992). And not surprisingly, the more physical punishment parents use, the more aggressively their children act. Furthermore, many studies have found that parents who abuse their children were themselves likely to have been abused by their parents (Rohner, 1986; Straus & Kantor, 1994). This observation suggests that children will imitate the abusive behavior of their parents and, in turn, may abuse their own children.

The Aversive Quality of a Punisher. We learned in Chapter 4 that environmental events present during an aversive event will become classically conditioned to elicit fear. In addition, we saw earlier in this chapter that fear motivates escape behavior. On the basis of these two observations, we should expect that because punishment is a painful event, the person providing the punishment, or the punisher, will become a conditioned stimulus capable of eliciting fear, which, in turn, should motivate the individual to escape from the punisher.

Recall our example Billy and his friends bullying Noah in the chapter-opening vignette. Noah became afraid of Billy and his fiends as a result of their abuse, and this fear motivated his escape behavior when Noah was confronted by his tormentors.

Azrin, Hake, Holz, and Hutchinson's study (1965) provides evidence that escape behavior occurs as the result of punishment. These psychologists first trained pigeons to key peck for food reinforcement on a fixed-ratio schedule and then punished each key-peck response with electric shock. A distinctive stimulus was present during the punishment period, and the pigeons could peck at another key to terminate the cue that signaled punishment. The escape response also produced another stimulus that indicated that the original reinforcement-punishment key could be pecked safely. After the pigeons pecked the original key and received reinforcement, the safe cue was terminated and the dangerous stimulus reintroduced. Azrin et al. reported that although the pigeons emitted few escape responses if the punishment was mild, the frequency of the escape response increased as the intensity of punishment increased until the pigeons spent the entire punishment period escaping from the cues associated with punishment.

A study by Redd, Morris, and Martin (1975) illustrates the aversive quality of a punisher in humans. In their study, 5-year-old children performed a task in the presence of an adult who made either positive comments ("You're doing well") or negative comments ("Stop throwing the tokens around" or "Don't play with the chair"). Redd et al. reported that although the punitive person was more effective in keeping the children on task, the children preferred working with the complimentary person.

However, little evidence supports the idea that clients escape punitive behavior therapists (Walters & Grusec, 1977). For example, Risley (1968) discovered that punishing autistic children's undesirable behavior with electric shock did not alter the children's eye contact with the therapist, who also reinforced the children's desirable responses. Other studies (Lovaas & Simmons, 1969) have also reported the absence of fear of and escape behavior from a punitive therapist. Walters and Grusec (1977) suggested that the therapist's use of reinforcement as well as punishment prevented the therapist and the therapy situation from becoming aversive and motivating escape behavior.

Additional Negative Effects of Punishment. There are two additional negative effects of punishment. First, the suppressive effects of punishment may generalize to similar behaviors, and the inhibition of these responses may be undesirable. For example, if a parent punishes a child for fighting with other children in the neighborhood, the punishment may generalize, causing the child to stop playing with these children. However, the effects of punishment do not always generalize to similar behaviors. Chapter 10 discusses the circumstances under which punishment does or does not generalize to other responses.

A second negative effect of punishment is that the subject may not recognize the contingency between punishment and the undesired behavior; the aversive events may be perceived as being independent of behavior. In Chapter 11, we will discover that experiencing noncontingent aversive events can lead to helplessness and depression. Punishment is most likely to be perceived as being noncontingent when a delay occurs between the undesired behavior and the punishment. The interval between a response and punishment makes it difficult for an animal or person to recognize that the behavior is responsible for the punishment. People thus must be informed of the relationship between their actions and punishment so that helplessness does not result from seemingly noncontingent aversive events.

We have learned that there are several potential negative consequences of punishment. Given these negative consequences, one might then wonder why the use of punishment is still so prevalent in our society. The most likely answer is that punishment is used because it can be an effective means of behavioral control. Differential reinforcement also is an effective means of behavioral control. Why not just use differential reinforcement to suppress undesired behaviors? There are a number of possible reasons why punishment continues to be used as a means of behavioral control. One likely reason is that we observe punishment being modeled as a means of behavioral control. While modeling can be a negative consequence of using punishment, it also can demonstrate that punishment is an effective means of behavioral control. For example, suppose a child sees an older sibling being grounded for staying out past curfew, and the older sibling no longer misses curfew. Modeling not only will lead the younger child to be home on time, but she is likely to use this means of punishment when she becomes a parent. Another likely reason why punishment is so prevalent in our society is that there are situations where differential reinforcement contingencies cannot be easily applied but punishment can be readily employed as an agent of behavioral change. For example, it may be quite difficult to reinforce a person with a DWI for not drinking and driving, but taking away a repeat offender's driver's license or installing a ignition interlock system in the repeat offender's automobile can be implemented to suppress drinking and driving behavior.

In this chapter, we have described the factors that determine whether or not punishment will effectively suppress behavior. The negative consequences of punishment also were discussed in this chapter. We next explore evidence that punishment has been successfully employed to modify undesired behavior and when it should be used instead of other means of changing behavior. The ethics of using punishment as a means of behavioral control are also discussed in this chapter.

BEFORE YOU GO ON

- What were the negative consequences of Billy's father's whipping?

- How could these negative consequences be prevented?

SECTION REVIEW

- Punishment is the presentation of an aversive event contingent on the occurrence of an undesired response.

- Positive punishment represents the presentation of a painful event after the occurrence of an undesired response.

- Negative punishment is the loss of reinforcement (response cost) or the inability to obtain reinforcement for a specified time (time-out), which is contingent on the occurrence of an inappropriate behavior.

- Punishment usually only temporarily suppresses the punished response, but in some circumstances it can permanently suppress undesired behavior.

- The more severe the punishment, the more consistent the administration of punishment, and the shorter the delay between punishment and the undesired behavior, the more effective the punishment.

- Punishment can elicit aggressive behavior and/or serve as a model of the use of punishment as a means of behavioral control.

- An environment associated with punishment may become aversive, thereby motivating escape behavior.

- The effects of punishment may generalize to other nonpunished behavior and the contingency between behavior and punishment may go unrecognized, leading to learned helplessness.

APPLICATIONS OF AVERSIVE CONDITIONING

Response Prevention or Flooding

Some psychologists, beginning with Watson (1916), have hypothesized that phobias are learned avoidance behaviors. On the basis of this belief, techniques that are effective in eliminating avoidance behaviors in animals should be effective in eliminating phobic behaviors in humans. The problem with trying to extinguish phobic behavior is that because fear motivates avoidance of the phobic stimulus, the person will not experience the CS long enough to learn to associate the CS with the absence of the UCS. Two treatments of phobic behavior, **flooding** and systematic desensitization, have been used to overcome this problem. We learned in Chapter 4 that systematic desensitization works by conditioning a relaxation response antagonistic to fear of the phobic object. Flooding forces the person to experience the feared stimulus and associate the CS with the absence of the UCS, thereby eliminating the avoidance behavior.

Flooding differs from the typical extinction procedure because the feared stimulus cannot be escaped. Otherwise, the two procedures are identical: An animal is exposed to the conditioned fear stimulus without an aversive consequence. Research investigating flooding, also known as **response prevention**, has demonstrated it to be an effective technique for eliminating avoidance behavior in animals (Baum, 1970). Baum found that the effectiveness of flooding increased with longer exposure to the fear stimulus. In addition, Coulter, Riccio, and Page (1969) found that flooding suppressed an avoidance response faster than a typical extinction procedure did.

Can flooding successfully eliminate avoidance behavior in humans? Malleson (1959) first reported the successful use of flooding to treat avoidance behavior in humans. Since Malleson's experiment, a large number of studies have demonstrated the effectiveness of flooding in treating a wide variety of behavior disorders, including obsessive-compulsive behavior in children (Bolton & Perrin, 2008; Freeman & Marrs Garcia, 2009), adolescents

(Bolton & Perrin, 2008; Whiteside & Brown, 2008), and adults (Albert & Brunatto, 2009; Rowa, Antony, & Swinson, 2007); panic disorder (Clum, Clum, & Surls, 1993); posttraumatic stress disorder in children and adolescents (Saigh, Yasik, Oberfield, & Inamder, 1999), and adults (Moulds & Nixon, 2006; Turek, Grubaugh, Hamner, & Foa, 2009); simple phobias (Kneebone & Al-Daftary, 2006; Narayana, Chakrabarti, & Grover, 2004); and social phobias (Javidi, Battersby, & Forbes, 2007; Omdal & Galloway, 2008).

Flooding appears to eliminate fear quite readily (Levis, 2008; Zoellner, Abramowitz, Moore, & Slagle, 2008). For example, Marks (1987) reported that an agoraphobic's fear of a specific situation (e.g., going to a crowded shopping mall) can be eliminated in as few as three sessions. Further, the elimination of fear seems to be long lasting. Emmelkamp, van der Helm, van Zanten, and Plochg (1980) used flooding to treat a compulsive behavior. The level of the client's anxiety was measured before exposure to the feared stimulus, immediately afterward, and 1 and 6 months later. Emmelkamp et al. reported that the level of anxiety decreased significantly following exposure to the feared stimulus (see Figure 7.11). Most important, the client's decreased anxiety level persisted for at least 6 months following treatment.

While flooding has been shown to produce a faster decrease in anxiety than systematic desensitization (see Chapter 4), many patients have difficulty tolerating flooding (Gelder, 1991). In fact, many individuals will not participate in flooding because the initial anxiety is so great. For those individuals, other treatments are used. One such treatment is systematic desensitization, which we discussed in Chapter 4. Cognitive-based treatments also can be used to treat anxiety disorders. We discuss a modeling treatment in Chapter 11.

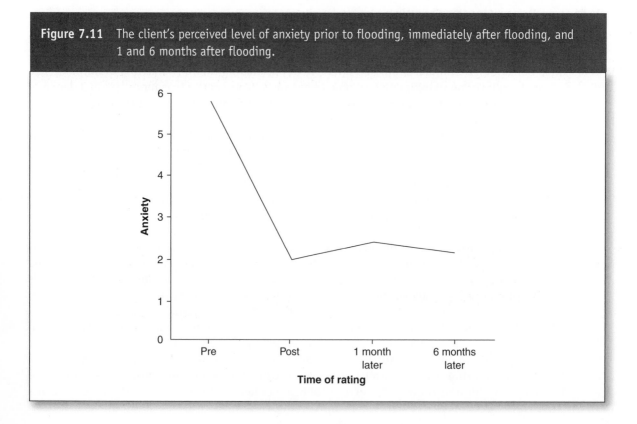

Figure 7.11 The client's perceived level of anxiety prior to flooding, immediately after flooding, and 1 and 6 months after flooding.

Punishment

The use of punishment to control human behavior is widespread in our society. A parent spanks a toddler for throwing a temper tantrum at the grocery store, a middle school child receives an afterschool reflection (ASR) for being late to school, a teenager is grounded for a week for failing a class, a police officer gives a ticket to a woman texting while driving, the IRS puts a tax evader in jail for failing to pay taxes, the army court-martials an AWOL soldier, and an employer fires an employee who does poor work are but a few examples of the use of punishment. The following sections examine several punishment procedures that psychologists report are successful in modifying undesired human activity.

Positive Punishment

We learned earlier in the chapter that positive punishment is the presentation of an aversive event contingent upon the occurrence of an undesired behavior. We also learned that punishment will be effective when it is severe, occurs immediately after the undesired response, and is consistently presented. But how effective is positive punishment in altering problem behaviors in humans? The literature (Cooper et al., 2007) shows that punishment can be quite successful in suppressing human behavior. Let's examine the evidence.

Lang and Melamed (1969) described the use of punishment to suppress the persistent vomiting of a 12-pound, 9-month-old child (see Figure 7.12). The child vomited most of his food within 10 minutes after eating, despite the use of various treatments (e.g., dietary changes, use of antinauseants, and frequent small feedings). Lang and Melamed detected the beginning of

Figure 7.12   The photo on the left shows a 12-pound, 9-month-old child whose persistent vomiting left him seriously ill. The use of punishment suppressed vomiting within six sessions (one per day) and, as the photo on the right shows, enabled the child to regain normal health.

vomiting with an electromyogram (EMG), which measures muscle activity. When the EMG indicated vomiting had begun, the child received an electric shock to the leg; the shock stopped when the child ceased vomiting. After the child had received six punishment sessions (one per day), he no longer vomited after eating. Six months following treatment, the child showed no further vomiting and was of normal weight. Sajwaj, Libet, and Agras (1989) also found punishment an effective way to suppress life-threatening vomiting in a very young child. Furthermore, Galbraith, Byrick, and Rutledge (1970) successfully used punishment to curtail the vomiting of a 13-year-old boy with mental retardation, while Kohlenberg (1970) reported that punishment suppressed the vomiting of a 21-year-old adult with mental retardation.

Chronic head banging can be life threatening in children and adults with mental retardation. This self-injurious behavior has proved difficult to manage. Thomas Linscheid and his associates (Linscheid, Iwata, Ricketts, Williams, & Griffin, 1990; Linscheid & Reichenbach, 2002; Salvy, Mulick, Butter, Bartlett, & Linscheid, 2004) have successfully used an electric shock punishment to suppress head banging. In their treatment, an electric shock (84V, 3.5 mA) is presented for 0.08 seconds to the individual's arm contingent upon blows to his or her head or face. These researchers described the intensity of this shock as similar to having a rubber band snapped on the individual's arm. They reported a very rapid, complete suppression of head banging as the result of the contingent electric shock (see Figure 7.13). Other researchers also have found that contingent electric shock

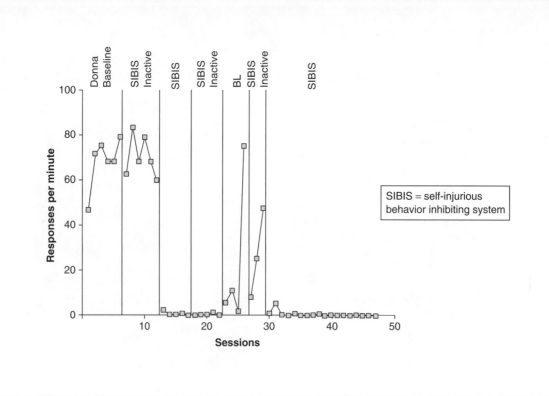

Figure 7.13   This graph shows the number of head bangings per minute by a 17-year-old girl (Donna) with profound mental retardation during baseline (BL), during the application of contingent electric shocks, and during the removal of the contingent shocks for head banging.

suppresses self-injurious head-banging behavior (Duker & Seys, 2000; D. E. Williams, Kirkpatrick-Sanchez, & Crocker, 1994).

Many other behaviors have also been successfully modified through response-contingent punishment. Behaviors reported to have been suppressed by punishment include obsessive ideation (Kenny, Solyom, & Solyom, 1973), chronic cough (Creer, Chai, & Hoffman, 1977), and gagging (Glasscock, Friman, O'Brien, & Christopherson, 1986).

Although positive punishment has been effectively used to suppress a wide variety of undesired behaviors, one problem that sometimes arises with punishment therapy is the patient's difficulty generalizing suppression from the therapy situation to the real world. The Risley (1968) study provides evidence that the suppression of a punished behavior can be generalized. Risley used electric shock punishment to treat the continual climbing behavior of a 6-year-old girl with hyperactivity disorder. Although Risley's treatment suppressed the climbing during the therapy situation, no change occurred in the frequency of this behavior at home. Risley then visited the home and showed the mother how to use the electric shock device. When the mother punished her daughter's climbing, the frequency of this behavior declined from 29 to 2 instances a day within 4 days and disappeared completely within a few weeks. While you might initially feel this procedure is barbaric, the mother had attempted to control the climbing by spanking the child, and she believed the spanking was more unpleasant and "brutalizing" for both herself and her daughter, as well as less effective, than was the shock. It would certainly seem that a minimal number of mild shocks are more humane than the continual but ineffective spanking or shaming of a child.

A spanking is assuredly the most widely used form of positive punishment. The literature shows that most parents use corporal punishment to influence the actions of their children. For example, Regalado, Sareen, Inkelas, Wissow, and Halfron (2008) reported that 63% of the parents of 1- and 2- year old children used spanking as a form of punishment. Further, Gershoff and Bitensky (2007) found that by the time children reached the fifth grade, 80% had been corporally punished by their parents. And Bender, Allen, McElhaney, Antonishak, Moore, Kelly, and Davis (2007) reported that 85% of adolescents had been slapped or spanked by their parents and 51% had been hit with a belt or similar object.

Teachers and administrators in schools also use corporal punishment. While 28 states and the District of Columbia have banned the use of corporal punishment in public schools, it is still allowed in 22 states (Bitensky, 2006). In places where corporal punishment is still permitted, over 250,000 school children received corporal punishment during the 2004–2005 school year (Office of Civil Rights, 2007).

Concerns over the negative effects of corporal punishment led many professionals in the 1970s and 1980s to discourage the use of spanking as a means of behavioral control (Rosellini, 1998). Yet, many of my students report having been spanked by a parent for some misconduct. Has any irreparable harm been done to my students? Some psychologists (Baumrind, Larzelere, & Cowan, 2002) argue that under certain conditions, a spanking can be an effective means of behavioral control but not lead to the negative effects of punishment described earlier the chapter.

Robert Larzelere (2000, 2008) reviewed 38 studies that assessed the outcomes of spanking with preadolescent children and concluded that an occasional spanking, as long as it is combined with other forms of discipline and the use of positive reinforcement for desired behavior, has not been found to be detrimental to a child's development. Larzelere reported detrimental outcomes only with overly frequent use of physical punishment. Further, Larzelere (2000) noted that detrimental outcomes also were found for every alternative disciplinary tactic. Similarly, Diana Baumrind (1996, 1997, 2001) stated that a blanket injunction against the use of a spanking is not warranted and that an occasional spanking, as long as it is not harsh, can be an effective form of discipline. In Baumrind's view, harsh punishment will lead to aggressive behavior and should be avoided.

Other psychologists (Gershoff & Bitensky, 2007) advocate a ban on any use of corporal punishment. Elizabeth Gershoff (2002) analyzed 88 studies that examined the effects of corporal punishment and concluded that the use of spanking as means of behavioral control can have several undesirable outcomes (aggression in childhood and adulthood, childhood delinquent and antisocial behavior, adult criminal or antisocial behavior, anxiety and depression in childhood and adulthood) and only one beneficial outcome (compliance). Gershoff and Bitensky (2007) advocate a ban on the use of corporal punishment by parents and schools, like the ban that has been instituted in 23 countries. Murray Straus (2001) suggests that the believed-to-be "minor" form of physical violence (a spanking) is a precursor to much of the violence that plagues our world. Like Gershoff, Straus advocates a ban of the use of corporal punishment.

How can these totally opposing views (an occasional spanking can be beneficial versus corporal punishment always have negative consequences) be reconciled? Kazdin and Benjet (2003) compared the methodology used by Baumrind, Larzelere, and Cowan (2002) and Gershoff (2002) that lead to very different conclusions about whether corporal punishment should be banned. Kazdin and Benjet found that while there was some overlap in studies analyzed by Baumrind, Larzelere, and Cowan and by Gershoff, most of the studies reviewed used different inclusion criterion. For example, Larzelere did not include studies where a child was frequently punched or hit with a belt, stick, or similar object. While Larzelere and Gershoff agree that overly frequent spanking is detrimental, they disagree on whether an occasional spanking can be beneficial. Kazdin and Benjet (2003) argue that more research is needed to determine whether the use of a spanking in children is ever warranted.

Response Cost

A colleague recently told me of a problem with his daughter, who was having trouble seeing the blackboard at school. When he suggested that she move to the front row of her classes, she informed him that she was already sitting there. An optometrist examined her and discovered that her eyesight was extremely poor; she was to wear glasses all of the time. Despite choosing a pair of glasses she liked, she indicated an extreme dislike for wearing them. After waiting for a reasonable adjustment period and discovering that encouragement and praise were ineffective in persuading his daughter to wear the glasses, the father informed her that she would lose 50 cents of her weekly allowance every time he saw her without them. Although she was not pleased with this arrangement, she did not lose much of her allowance and no longer expresses unhappiness about wearing her glasses.

My colleague was able to modify his daughter's behavior by using a response cost procedure, which is a form of negative punishment. As we discovered earlier in the chapter, response cost refers to a penalty or fine contingent upon the occurrence of an undesired behavior. Thus, my colleague's daughter was to be fined when she did not wear her glasses. Psychologists (Kalish, 1981) have consistently observed that response cost is an effective technique for suppressing inappropriate behavior. Let's look at one study that has examined the use of response cost to alter behavior.

R. F. Peterson and L. R. Peterson's (1968) study illustrates the effectiveness of response cost in suppressing self-injurious behavior. The subject was a 6-year-old boy who had been severely mutilating himself; the experimenters reinforced him with a small amount of food when he refrained from self-injurious behavior during a 3- to 5-second period. However, if the boy exhibited self-injurious behavior, the reinforcer did not occur. Peterson and Peterson reported that they completely eliminated the boy's self-injurious behavior with the response cost procedure.

A wide range of other undesired behaviors has been successfully eliminated by using a response cost procedure. In an extensive investigation of the application of response cost, Kazdin (1972) discovered that response cost has been used to inhibit smoking, overeating, stuttering, psychotic speech, aggressiveness, and tardiness. In addition, response cost significantly reduced or eliminated sleep problems in a 2-year-old child (Ashbaugh & Peck, 1998), inappropriate sucking in a 7-year-old girl (Bradley & Houghton, 1992), and thumb-sucking in two 7-year-old girls (Lloyd, Kauffman, & Weygant, 1982). Response cost also suppressed aggressive behavior in preschool children (L. K. Reynolds & Kelley, 1997) and adolescents (D. S. Stein, 1999), led to less disruptive classroom behavior in preschool children (Conyers et al., 2004) and in school-aged children (Musser, Bray, Kehle, & Jenson, 2001), and reduced self-destructive behavior in a woman with mental retardation (Keeney, Fisher, Adelinis, & Wilder, 2000). Further, tobacco use in minors in 24 Illinois towns was significantly reduced when they were given a fine for violating possession-use-purchase laws (Jason, Pokorny, Adams, Hunt, Gadiraju, & Schoeny, 2007).

Response cost for the occurrence of undesired behaviors also has been found to increase desired behaviors. For example, response cost has been found to lead to increased accuracy on mathematics problems in school-aged children with attention-deficit/hyperactivity disorder (Carlson, Mann, & Alexander, 2000) and to improved handwriting legibility in junior high school students (McLaughlin, Mabee, Byram, & Reiter, 1987).

Time-Out From Reinforcement

Time-out from reinforcement, another form of negative punishment introduced earlier in the chapter, refers to a program in which the occurrence of an inappropriate behavior results in a loss of access to reinforcement for a specified period of time. In time-out, the individual can either be removed from a reinforcing environment or from the reinforcement itself. For example, a parent sends a child to her room for half an hour because she hit a sibling while watching television, and an overweight person decides he cannot dine out for a week because he violated his diet.

If a time-out area is employed, it must not be reinforcing. Thus, sending a disruptive child to his room as a time-out may not stop the disruptive behavior if the room contains attractive toys and the child finds it pleasurable to be there. In fact, the frequency of disruptive behavior may actually increase if the time-out area is reinforcing. Solnick, Rincover, and Peterson's (1977) study illustrates this. They established a time-out contingent upon tantrum behavior in the treatment of a 6-year-old child with autism. Exposure to a sterile time-out environment was contingent upon the occurrence of self-stimulating behavior, and presentation of this environment increased rather than decreased the occurrence of tantrum behavior. When the investigators made physical restraint contingent upon tantrum behavior, the frequency of tantrums rapidly declined.

A wide variety of behaviors have been suppressed using time-out from reinforcement. For example, Drabman and Spitalnik (1973) reported that time-out suppressed disruptive behavior of male adolescents in a psychiatric hospital. Initial recordings showed that the adolescents exhibited very high rates of several disruptive behaviors, including physical aggression, verbal abuse, and disregard of rules. The researchers implemented a time-out procedure that placed the boys in a small room for 10 minutes if they had been physically aggressive or had left their seats without permission. The verbal abuse was not a target of intervention, and therefore, its occurrence did not result in time-out. Drabman and Spitalnik found that the level of physical aggression and disregard of rules decreased significantly after the time-out procedure had been established. In contrast, the unpunished verbal abuse did not decline. These observations demonstrate that time-out from reinforcement produces a specific reduction of behaviors contingent upon it but does not affect unpunished activity.

Elementary school children often exhibit disruptive behavior during school. A. G. White and Bailey (1990) punished disruptive behavior in a gym class by having the misbehaving child go sit on the side of the room, where the child remained until all the sand had flowed through a large hourglass (which took about 3 minutes). Following the implementation of this time-out procedure, the level of misbehavior during gym class dropped by 95%. MacPherson, Candee, and Hohman (1974) found that time-out could inhibit disruptive lunchroom activity in elementary school children, while Barton, Guess, Garcia, and Baer (1970) observed that the use of a time-out reinforcement procedure could suppress mealtime disruptive behavior in children with mental retardation. Other behaviors that time-out has suppressed include thumb-sucking (Baer, 1962), tantrum behavior in children with autism (Wolf, Risley, & Mees, 1964) and in normal children (Wahler, Winkel, Peterson, & Morrison, 1965), and noncompliance at home in an 8-year-old boy (D. Reitman & Drabman, 1999).

We have discussed several behavioral approaches to suppressing undesired behaviors. Differential reinforcement procedures are one behavioral suppression method. Nonreinforcement (extinction) is another means of suppressing undesired behavior. Punishment (positive punishment, response cost, time-out from reinforcement) are other ways to suppress problem behavior. Which approach, then, should be used to suppress a specific behavior? Alberto and Troutman (2006) describe a hierarchy of procedures that have been used in educational systems to decide which behavioral approach should be employed to suppress undesired behavior. The hierarchy begins with the most socially acceptable and least intrusive approach and ends with the least socially acceptable and most intrusive approach. In this hierarchy, differential reinforcement procedures are Level I (most socially acceptable and least intrusive) procedures, nonreinforcement procedures are Level II procedures, response cost and time-out are Level III procedures, and unconditioned aversive stimuli such as a paddling or electric shock or conditioned aversive stimuli (verbal warnings or yelling) are Level IV (least socially acceptable and most intrusive) procedures. According to Alberto and Troutman, the guiding principle should be to use the least intrusive but most effective intervention for a student displaying a specific problem behavior. In some cases, Level I procedures would be the approach used, while in other instances, only a Level IV procedure will work. In our discussion of punishment, we described several behaviors (e.g., persistent vomiting, chronic head banging) for which only positive punishment was an effective means of behavioral control. Under these and similar circumstances, a Level IV procedure would be the best intervention to use.

Are there any aversive treatments that are just not permissible to modify behavior? We address this question next.

The Ethical Use of Punishment

When should the use of punishment be permissible? The Eighth Amendment of the Constitution of the United States mandates as follows: "Excessive bail shall not be required, nor excessive fines imposed, nor cruel and unusual punishments inflicted." What constitutes cruel and unusual punishment? When can a teacher use punishment to discipline a disruptive student, or a psychologist use punishment in therapy? The federal courts have indicated that some use of aversive remedial treatment is permissible. However, the treatment may be considered unconstitutional if it "violates minimal standards of decency, is wholly disproportionate to the alleged offense, or goes beyond what is necessary" (Schwitzgebel & Schwitzgebel, 1980, p. 84).

Many unjustified uses of punishment have occurred in our society. For example, the courts ruled in *Wright v. McMann* (1972) that punishing an inmate in a "psychiatric observation cell" by forcing him to sleep nude on a concrete floor in cold temperatures without soap, towels, or toilet paper constituted cruel and unusual punishment. Similarly, the courts found that it is cruel and unusual punishment to administer apormorphine (to induce vomiting) to nonconsenting mental patients (*Knecht v. Gillman*, 1973) or to forcefully administer an intramuscular injection of a tranquilizer to a juvenile inmate for a rules infraction (*Nelson v. Heyne*, 1974).

Do these abuses mean that aversive punishment procedures may never be employed? Punishment can be used to eliminate undesired behavior; however, the rights of the individual must be safeguarded. The preamble to the American Psychological Association's *Ethical Principles of*

Psychologists and Code of Conduct (2002) clearly states that psychologists respect the dignity and worth of the individual and strive for the presentation and protection of fundamental human rights. They are committed to increasing knowledge of human behavior and of people's understanding of themselves and others and to using such knowledge for the promotion of human welfare. While pursuing these objectives, they make every effort to protect the welfare of those who seek their skills.

The welfare of the individual has been safeguarded in a number of ways (see Schwitzgebel & Schwitzgebel, 1980). For example, the doctrine of "the least restrictive alternative" dictates that less severe methods of punishment must be tried before severe treatments are used. For example, Ohio law (Ohio Rev. Code Ann., 1977) allows "aversive stimuli" to be used for seriously disruptive behavior only after other forms of therapy have been attempted. Further, an institutional review board or human rights committee must evaluate whether the use of punishment is justified. According to Stapleton (1975), justification should be based on "the guiding principle that the procedure should entail a relatively small amount of pain and discomfort relative to a large amount of pain and discomfort if left untreated" (p. 35).

Concern for the individual should not be limited to the institutional use of punishment. The ethical concerns the American Psychological Association outlines should apply to all instances in which punishment is used. Certainly, abuse by parents, family, and peers is of as great or greater concern than is punishment administered by psychologists in the treatment of behavior disorders. A child has as much right to protection from cruel and unusual punishment at the hands of a parent as a patient does with a therapist. Adherence to ethical standards in administering punishment ensures an effective yet humane method of altering inappropriate behavior.

BEFORE YOU GO ON

- What type of punishment is Noah's Dad using?

- Would another type of punishment be more effective? Why or why not?

SECTION REVIEW

- Flooding is one option for treating human phobias and obsessive-compulsive behaviors.

- The flooding technique prevents a person from exhibiting the avoidance response.

- The success of flooding depends upon providing sufficient exposure to the feared stimulus to extinguish the avoidance response.

- Positive punishment presents a painful event contingent upon the occurrence of an undesired behavior.

- Response cost refers to a penalty or fine contingent upon the occurrence of an undesired behavior.

- Time-out from reinforcement refers to a program in which the occurrence of an inappropriate behavior results in a loss of access to reinforcement for a specified period of time.

- Safeguards have been established to protect individuals from cruel and unusual punishment.

- Adherence to ethical standards of conduct should allow the use of punishment as a method of influencing behavior while ensuring that those punished will experience less discomfort than they would if the treatment had not been employed.

CRITICAL THINKING QUESTIONS

1. Raul immediately drops a class as soon as he earns a poor grade. Suggest several reasons for Raul's behavior. How might Raul's friends persuade him not to withdraw from classes?

2. Several state legislatures recently have enacted "three strikes and you're out" laws to punish serious offenders. Based on your knowledge of punishment, are these laws likely to act as a deterrent to criminal activity? Incorporate into your answer the key principles of punishment described in this chapter.

3. Jane constantly bites her nails, and her parents have decided to punish her nail-biting. Describe a psychologically sound punishment procedure that Jane's parents can use to suppress her nail biting. Why did you use the procedure that you selected? Discuss any problems that might be expected and how you would prevent these problems.

KEY TERMS

active avoidance response

escape response

modeling

omission training

passive avoidance response

punishment

response prevention

vicious circle behavior

avoidance response

flooding

negative punishment

pain-induced aggression

positive punishment

response cost

time-out from reinforcement

Theories of Appetitive and Aversive Conditioning

A LACK OF CONTROL

Professor Simpkins, Julia's teacher for her introductory psychology course, has just finished lecturing to the class about instrumental conditioning. Impressed by the powerful influence of reinforcement on behavior, Julia asks whether conditioning could be used to teach her 6-year-old son Evan to make his bed and clean his room. All other attempts to instill a sense of responsibility have been futile. Professor Simpkins tells Julia that reinforcement could, indeed, alter Evan's behavior, and he gives her a brief outline to follow to obtain the desired results. First, Julia must decide exactly what she wants Evan to do to receive reinforcement. Julia decides that her Evan should return his toys to the toy box before going to bed, put his clothes in the hamper, and make his bed. Second, a reinforcer must be chosen. Because watching television and playing computer games are Evan's favorite pastimes, Julia chooses watching television and playing computer games as reinforces. Professor Simpkins suggests writing a contract specifying exactly what the boy must do to obtain his reinforcement. Professor Simpkins also tells Julia that initially, people sometimes have difficulty performing the required behavior and maintaining consistency. To ensure that Julia's son learns to behave effectively and consistently, Professor Simpkins suggests using shaping—selecting a level of behavior that can be easily performed and then slowly changing the response requirement until only the final desired behavior will produce reinforcement. Julia decides that to obtain reinforcement, Evan initially has to make his bed and clean his room only on weekends. Over several weeks, Julia's son will be required to perform the tasks every other day. Furthermore, during the early phases of shaping, the boy needs only to provide a path to his bed and to place his clothes in the hamper. Also, he only has to spread the cover over his bed until required to clean his room every day; then, the efficiency of bed making must improve until the bed is made neatly. To ensure accurate recording of the boy's behavior, Professor Simpkins suggests keeping a chart on his door and marking it for appropriate behavior. He also emphasizes that this shaping procedure works only if record keeping is accurate and if reinforcement is provided for appropriate behavior.

In this chapter, we discuss why a reinforcement procedure similar to that outlined by Professor Simpkins has successfully altered behavior. We do so by examining the nature of appetitive conditioning.

THEORIES OF APPETITIVE CONDITIONING

The Nature of Reinforcement

Skinner (1938) defined a reinforcer as an event whose occurrence will increase the frequency of any behavior that produces it. While Skinner was not concerned about when an event would be reinforcing, other psychologists have been interested in specifying the conditions that determine whether an event is reinforcing. David Premack's probability-differential theory addresses this issue; we start our discussion of the nature of reinforcement with his view.

Premack's Probability-Differential Theory

David Premack (1925–   )

Premack received his doctorate from the University of Minnesota. He taught at the University of Missouri at Columbia for 9 years and the University of California at Santa Barbara for 10 years before going to the University of Pennsylvania, where he taught for 15 years. His first 2 chimpanzee subjects, Sarah and Gussie, started at the University of Missouri and stayed with him through his tenure at the University of Pennsylvania. His research contributed to an understanding of the nature of reinforcement, comparative cognition, and symbol use in chimpanzees. He was awarded the William James Fellow Award by the Association for Psychological Science in 2005.

We typically assume that reinforcers are things like food or water. However, activities can also be reinforcers. Recall our discussion of Julia's son Evan in the chapter-opening vignette. Julia can use watching television or playing computer games as reinforcers for other behavior, such as picking up his clothes and making his bed. Although watching television and playing computer games appear to be very different types of reinforcers, Premack's (1959, 1965) **probability-differential theory** suggests that all reinforcers share a common attribute. According to Premack, a reinforcer is any activity whose probability of occurring is greater than that of the reinforced activity. Therefore, watching television can be a reinforcer for making one's bed if the likelihood of watching television is greater than the probability of making one's bed. In Premack's view, watching television is the reinforcer for Evan. In the same vein, it is the eating response to food, not food, that is the reinforcer for a rat. Since eating is a more probable behavior than bar pressing, eating can reinforce a rat's bar pressing.

Premack's (1959) study of children illustrates the reinforcing character of high- probability activities. He placed a pinball machine next to a candy dispenser. In the first phase of the study, Premack observed the children's relative rate of responding to each activity. Some children played pinball more frequently than they ate candy and were labeled "manipulators"; other children ate candy more often than they played pinball and were labeled "eaters." During the second phase of the study, manipulators had to eat in order to play the pinball machine, while eaters were required to play the pinball machine in order to get candy. Premack reported that the contingency increased the number of times the "eaters" played the pinball machine and the number of pieces of candy the "manipulators" ate.

Application: The Use of Activity Reinforcers

The use of activities as reinforcers to establish desired modes of behavior has been widespread and quite successful (Iwata & Michael, 1994). We will examine several studies that are representative of the application of Premack's probability-differential theory to establish desired behaviors. These studies demonstrate that techniques that alter the behavior-reinforcement contingencies of an individual can be used to establish desired, and eliminate undesired, behaviors.

Preschool-aged children have short attention spans and a tendency to become unruly. Homme, de Baca, Devine, Steinhorst, and Rickert (1963) provided an early application of Premack's probability-differential theory to encourage desired behavior in young children. High-probability behaviors, such as running around the room and pushing chairs, were used as reinforcers for low-probability behaviors like sitting quietly and looking at the blackboard. These researchers reported that in a few days, this procedure produced relatively quiet and attentive children. In a more recent application of the Premack principle to increase attentive behavior, Azrin, Vinas, and Ehle (2007) found that physical activity (high-probability activity) increased attentive calmness (low-probability activity) in children with attention-deficit/hyperactivity disorder.

Konarski and his associates (Konarski, 1985; Konarski, Johnson, Crowell, & Whitman, 1980) found that activities could be used as reinforcers to increase academic performance in educable students with mental retardation. The academic behaviors involved were reading, coloring, cursive writing, and arithmetic. These researchers found that making the more preferred activity contingent upon performance of the less preferred activity increases the level of the less preferred activity. For example, if reading was a low-frequency behavior, its incidence increased if it was necessary in order to color, a higher-frequency behavior. Similarly, McEvoy and Brady (1988) reported that the accuracy and completion rate of mathematics worksheets increased in three special education students when access to playing with toys (high-frequency behavior) was contingent upon meeting a criterion for completing math problems (low-frequency behavior; see Figure 8.1).

The applications of Premack's ideas have not been limited to educational settings. The business environment has also proven to be an ideal arena in which to modify behavior using activities as reinforcers. For example, Luthans, Paul, and Baker (1981) reported that total sales increased among department store salespersons when a contingency was established between low-probability sales activity and high-probability time off with pay. K. O'Hara, Johnson, and Beehr (1985) noted a similar increase in the sales telephone solicitors made when this contingency was set in place.

In another demonstration of the application of Premack's probability-differential theory, Welsh, Bernstein, and Luthans (1992) instituted a contingency whereby employees in a fast-food restaurant earned access to work time at their favorite station if the quality of their performance exceeded baseline at a targeted workstation. These researchers found that this contingency improved the quality of the employees' performance. Makin and Hoyle (1993) observed a similar effect on the performance of professional engineers, while Raj, Nelson, and Rao (2006) observed that a causal dress code and flexible working hours led to improved performance in the information technology department of a major retail industry.

Using activities as reinforcers, psychologists have made an important discovery. Not only can the use of an activity as a reinforcer increase performance of the target behavior, but it can also decrease the level of the activity used as the reinforcer (Allison, 1993). If the activity used as a reinforcer is undesirable, an effective method exists to suppress the inappropriate behavior. To illustrate this application, suppose that a child occasionally screams. Even though screaming may not occur frequently, it can be annoying. A parent could decrease screaming by allowing a child to scream contingent upon the occurrence of the target behavior (e.g., reading). This contingency would act to increase a desired activity such as reading and decrease an undesired behavior like screaming.

Recall our discussion of Julia's son Evan in the chapter-opening vignette. Not only would Julia like for her son to put his clothes in the hamper and make his bed but also to watch less television and play computer games less often. By establishing a contingency so that watching television and playing computer games were contingent upon putting his clothes in the hamper and making his

Figure 8.1 The number of mathematics problems solved correctly in each minute period increases when solving math problems correctly leads to contingent access to toys for three in special education students.

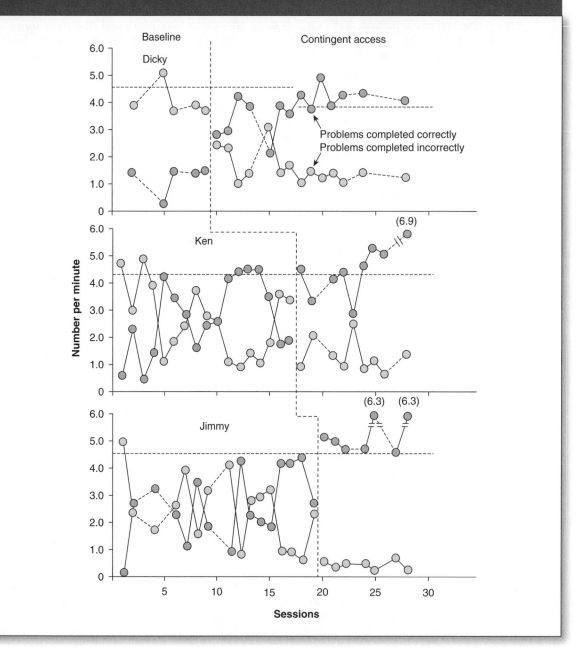

bed, Julia will have killed two birds with one stone; that is, Evan will pick up his clothes and make his bed more and watch television and play computer games less.

Premack's probability-differential theory assumes that a high-probability activity will reinforce a less probable activity. Timberlake and Allison's (1974) response deprivation theory presents a different view of the nature of reinforcers.

Response Deprivation Theory

William Timberlake and James Allison proposed that response deprivation created by the establishment of a behavior-reinforcer contingency causes an activity to become a reinforcer (Timberlake & Allison, 1974). According to Timberlake and Allison, animals respond at a specific level when given free access to objects important to their survival. For example, a rat given free access to food will consume approximately the same amount of food each day; the animal responds to food at the same level each day because its behavior is adaptive and enhances the rat's chance of survival. When an animal's access to an object is restricted and, therefore, its level of response is lowered, the animal will be motivated to return to its previous level of response. Thus, food deprivation will cause a rat to engage in behaviors that will allow it to gain access to food and restore its response to the predeprivation level. Further, Timberlake and Allison assert that a certain activity becomes a reinforcer because the establishment of a behavior-reinforcer contingency restricts the opportunity to participate in that activity. When a contingency is established, the level of operant behavior increases in order to return the performance of the restricted activity to its baseline level.

Timberlake and Allison (1974) conducted a number of studies that support their **response deprivation theory**. Let's briefly examine one of these studies. Rats were deprived access to a running wheel, and a contingency was established so that the rats were required to drink to gain access to the wheel. Even though the rats' baseline level of response was higher for drinking than for running, Timberlake and Allison found that the contingency between drinking and running led to an increase in the rats' level of drinking. These results indicate that restricting access to an activity results in that activity becoming a reinforcer. These results also show that the relative level of response does not determine whether or not an activity acts as a reinforcer. Instead, restricting access to a low-frequency activity, such as running, can increase the response level of another, high-frequency activity, such as drinking, if performing the first activity will provide access to the restricted activity.

The validity of the response deprivation theory has also been demonstrated in an applied setting with human clients (Timberlake & Farmer-Dougan, 1991). The research of Konarski and his colleagues (Konarski et al., 1980; Konarski, Crowell, & Duggan, 1985) especially supports the view that restricting access to an activity makes that activity a potential reinforcer. In a group of grade-school children, Konarski et al. (1980) measured the baseline level of coloring and working simple arithmetic problems. Not surprisingly, these young children had a much higher baseline level of coloring than of doing arithmetic problems. The researchers established a contingency so that having access to the lower-probability arithmetic problems was contingent upon doing the higher-probability coloring. Perhaps surprisingly, Konarski et al. found the children increased their coloring in order to gain the opportunity to complete math problems.

In a later study, using a special education population, Konarski et al. (1985) assessed the baseline levels of working arithmetic problems and writing. Regardless of which activity was the higher-probability behavior, restricting assess to the lower-probability behavior increased the level of the higher-probability behavior.

Returning to Evan in the chapter-opening vignette, the contingency that Julia established would restrict Evan's access to watching television and playing computer games. This restriction would motivate Evan to put his clothes in the hamper and make his bed in order to have access to the television and the computer.

Principles of Behavioral Economics

We have learned that a contingency can restrict an animal's access to an activity. Consider an animal, such as a rat, that cannot eat freely but instead must bar press to have access to food. How many times will the rat bar press? Intuitively, one might say that the rat would bar press until it was no longer motivated to eat. However, in many circumstances, the contingency requires more responses than the animal is willing to emit to satisfy its need for the food. Under these conditions, the rat will not bar press enough to reach its predeprivation level of food consumption. A number of psychologists (Allison, 1993; Staddon, 1988) have examined the question of how many times a rat will bar press to obtain reinforcement.

Behavioral Allocation

Suppose that an animal could freely engage in two activities. It might not respond equally; instead, its level of response might be higher for one behavior than the other. As an example, the animal might show 50 responses of one type, the Response A, and 150 instances of another, Response B. Allison (1993) referred to the free operant level of two responses as the paired basepoint, or **blisspoint**. The blisspoint is the unrestricted level of performance of both behaviors.

When a contingency is established, free access to one behavior is restricted, and the animal must emit a second behavior to access the first. Returning to our example, the contingency could be that one Response A allows the animal to engage in one Response B. This contingency means that the animal cannot attain blisspoint; that is, it cannot emit Response B three times as often as Response A.

What does an animal do when it cannot attain blisspoint? According to Allison (1993), the animal will respond in a manner that allows it to be as close to the blisspoint as possible. Figure 8.2 shows how this process works: Blisspoint is 3 Response Bs to 1 Response A, but the contingency specifies 1 Response B to 1 Response A. Does the animal emit 50, 100, 150, or 200 Response As? The closest point on the contingency line to the blisspoint is Point 1 (see again Figure 8.2). At this point, the animal would emit 100 Response As to receive 100 Response Bs (reinforcer). This level of Response As would bring the animal closest to blisspoint.

Figure 8.2   This graph shows the blisspoint (open circle) for Responses A and B. The contingency states that one Response A is necessary for access to one Response B. The equilibrium point, or minimum distance to blisspoint, on the contingency line is Point 1. Responding at other points takes the animal farther away from blisspoint.

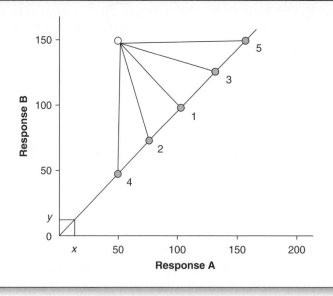

The concept of blisspoint assumes that an animal does not randomly emit contingent responses. Instead, the animal allocates the number of responses that bring it closest to blisspoint. The concept of blisspoint comes from economic theory and assumes that a person acts to minimize cost and maximize gain. If we think of a contingent activity as a cost and reinforcing activity as a gain, the **behavioral allocation view** predicts that the animal emits the minimal number of contingent responses to obtain the maximum level of reinforcing activities. This approach assumes that the economic principles that apply to purchasing products tell us about the level of response in an operant conditioning setting.

Viken and McFall (1994) have pointed to a potential downside to the use of contingencies. We normally think of contingencies as serving to increase the response rate. While this is generally true, it is not always true. Consider the following example from Viken and McFall to illustrate potential pitfalls of using contingencies. Suppose that a child's blisspoint for prosocial behavior and parental rewards is 1 to 11; that is, the child's baseline level is 1 prosocial behavior for every 11 parental rewards (see Figure 8.3). What if the parent wants to increase the level of prosocial behavior and establishes a 1:2 contingency, with 1 parental reward for every 2 prosocial behaviors? As Figure 8.3 indicates, the closest point on the contingency line to blisspoint is 40 prosocial behaviors and 20 parental rewards. Perhaps the parent wants to increase the number of prosocial behaviors and changes the contingency to 1:1, or 1 parental reward for every prosocial behavior. Intuitively, this change in contingency should result in a higher level of prosocial behavior. But as Figure 8.3 shows, blisspoint is now 30 prosocial behaviors for 30 parental rewards. Thus, the effect of changing from a 1:2 to 1:1 contingency schedule has the opposite to the desired effect: Rather than increasing the level of prosocial behavior, the new contingency actually decreases it. More telling is that establishing an even more lenient 2:1 contingency results in an even further decline in the level of prosocial behavior (also illustrated in Figure 8.3).

Figure 8.3 This graph shows the blisspoint (open circle) for prosocial behavior and social reward, as well as the contingency lines for the 2:1, 1:1, and 1:2 social rewards-prosocial behavior contingencies. The closed circles show the equilibrium point on each contingency line.

Richard J. Herrnstein (1930–1994)

Herrnstein received his doctorate from Harvard University under the direction of B. F. Skinner. He taught at Harvard University for 36 years, where he served chair of the Department of Psychology. At 64, he died of lung cancer. His research contributed to the development of the field of behavior economics. His controversial book the *Bell Curve,* with political scientist Charles Murray, argues that intelligence is both fixed by genetics and related to economic success.

These observations suggest that the establishment of a contingency must recognize the blisspoint in order for the contingency to have its desired effect.

Choice Behavior

There are many circumstances in which a simple contingency is not operative; instead, the animal or person must choose from two or more contingencies. To illustrate this type of situation, suppose that an operant chamber has two keys instead of one, and a pigeon receives reinforcement on a VI 1-minute schedule on one key and a VI 3-minute schedule on the other key. How would the pigeon respond on this task? Richard Herrnstein's **matching law** (Herrnstein, 1961; Herrnstein & Vaughn, 1980) describes how the animal would act in this two-choice situation.

Matching Law. Herrnstein's matching law assumes that when an animal has access to different schedules of reinforcement, the animal allocates its response in proportion to the level of reinforcement available on each schedule. In terms of our previous example, a pigeon can obtain three times as many reinforcers on a VI 1-minute schedule as on a VI 3-minute schedule. The matching law predicts that the pigeon will respond three times as much on the key with the VI 1-minute schedule as it will on the key with the VI 3-minute schedule.

The matching law can be stated mathematically to provide for a precise prediction of the animal's behavior in a choice situation. The mathematical formula for the matching law is as follows:

$$\frac{x}{x + y} = \frac{R(x)}{R(x) + R(y)}$$

In the equation, x represents the number of responses on Key x, y is the number of responses on Key y, $R(x)$ represents the number of reinforcements received on Key x, and $R(y)$ is the number of reinforcements on Key y. In our example, the animal can receive three times as many rewards on Key x as it can on Key y. The matching law shows that the animal will key peck three times as much on Key x as on Key y.

Does the matching law accurately predict an animal's behavior in a choice situation? To test the theory, Herrnstein varied the proportion of reinforcements that the pigeon could obtain on each key and then determined the pigeon's proportion of key pecks on each key. The data from this study appear in Figure 8.4. Herrnstein's results show exceptional matching; that is, the pigeon's number of responses on each key is a function of the reinforcements available on each key.

Other researchers have shown that the matching law also predicts choice behavior in humans. For example, Hantula and Crowell (1994) observed that the matching law predicted the response allocations of college students working on a computerized analogue investment task, while Mace, Neef, Shade, and Mauro (1996) reported that the matching law predicted the behaviors of special education students working on academic tasks.

D. D. Reed, Critchfield, and Martens (2006) examined whether the matching law could predict play calling (passing versus rushing) during the 2004 National Football League (NFL) season. These researchers calculated the relative ratio of passing to rushing plays as a function of the

Figure 8.4 The proportion of key pecks on *x* and *y* is proportional to the reinforcements available to Keys *x* and *y*.

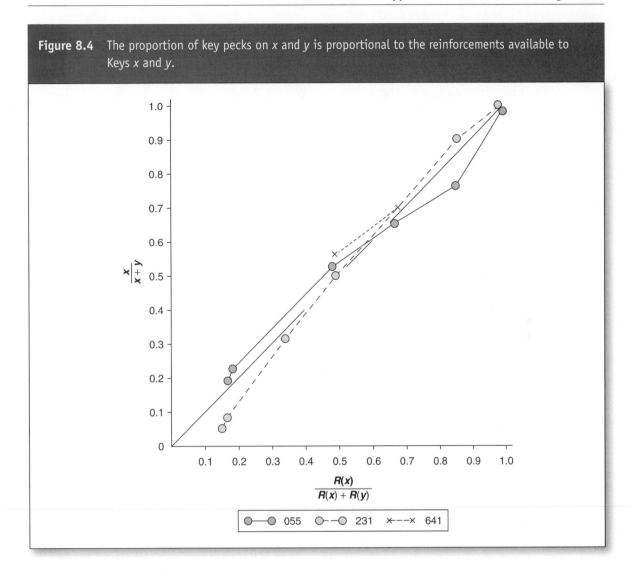

relative ratio of performance, which was defined as the yards gained from passing versus rushing. The matching law predicted the play calling of most NFL teams, except for a few that were biased toward rushing or passing. Perhaps most interesting, adherence to the matching law correlated with both team success on offense and winning percentage; that is, the teams that were sensitive to the matching law were the most successful both in terms of yards gained and winning percentage. Being sensitive to reinforcement contingencies does seem to pay off.

Our discussion indicates that the matching law assumes that an individual's choice behaviors will be divided proportionally according to the level of reinforcement available on each schedule. The matching law also predicts behavior when the choice is between two different magnitudes of reinforcement (de Villiers, 1977). For example, suppose a pigeon receives one reinforcer when key pecking on a VI 1-minute schedule and five reinforcers when pecking at a second key on the same VI schedule. How would the pigeon act? While it would seem reasonable to expect the pigeon to only peck the key associated with five reinforcements, the matching law predicts that it will actually respond to the key associated with one reinforcement for 17% of its responses.

A real-world example might be having to choose between going to one of two restaurants. While the food at one restaurant may be a greater reinforcer than the food at the other restaurant, the matching law predicts that you will visit both places and that the frequency of each choice will depend on the difference in reinforcer magnitude between the two restaurants.

The matching law also has been shown to predict the allocation of responses in humans in situations involving differential reinforcer magnitudes. One such situation involves the choice between taking a two-point shot and a three-point shot in a basketball game. Vollmer and Bourret (2000) determined that the matching law predicted the response allocation of two- and three-point shots that male and female basketball players took at a major state university. In their study, they factored into the matching law equation the fact that the magnitude of reinforcement is one and a half times higher for a three-point shot than for a two-point shot, and they found that the proportion of three-point shots taken matched the percentage of three-point shots made. Notably, the matching law only predicted the response allocation for experienced players, presumably because a basketball player needs to learn the probability of making a two- or a three-point shot before choosing how to allocate the shot selection.

In a more recent study, Alferink, Critchfield, Hitt, and Higgins (2009) reported that the matching law predicted the proportion of two- versus three-point shots taken both by college and professional basketball players. Further, the National Basketball Association in 1994 decreased the three-point shooting distance and then subsequently increased it after 3 years. Romanowich, Bourret, and Vollmer (2007) found that the matching law predicted the change in the rate of three-point shooting when the distance was first decreased and then subsequently increased.

The matching law also predicts behavior when an individual is faced with a choice between different delays of reinforcement. Again, the matching law states that the level of response to each choice will be proportional to the delay of reinforcement associated with each choice. For example, a pigeon receives reinforcement after a 1-second delay following pecking one key, while key pecking on the other key produces reinforcement after a 3-second delay. The matching law predicts that 25% of the pigeon's key pecking will be at the key with the 3-second delay and 75% at the key with a 1-second delay. Returning to our restaurant example, suppose that the usual wait is 5 minutes at one restaurant and 60 minutes at the other. The matching law predicts that you will go to the restaurant with only a 5-minute delay 91% of the time.

You might be thinking that the food in the restaurant with a long delay might be much better than the one with a short wait. How would a person behave in this choice situation? Let's suppose that the restaurant with the 60-minute delay is twice as good as the one with a 5-minute wait. Using the matching law, you would go to the restaurant with the 5-minute delay 87% of the time even though the food is much better at the other restaurant. This prediction suggests that you will usually choose a small, immediate reinforcer over a large, delayed reinforcer. In fact, pigeons and people typically select small, immediate reinforcers rather than large, delayed ones (Ainslie, 1975). To illustrate this principle, suppose you have to choose between watching a television show or studying for a test. While the reinforcer of a good grade on a test is definitely greater than the temporary enjoyment of a television show, the longer delay of reinforcement for studying will typically lead you to watch television rather than study.

There are many conditions that could lead to choosing a large, delayed reinforcer instead of a small, immediate one (Mischel, 1974; Rachlin & Green, 1972). The large, delayed reinforcer will be selected if the choice is made well in advance, that is, some time prior to the actual experience of either reinforcer. If people have to choose early in the day between watching television or studying, they are more likely to choose studying; if they make the choice just prior to the beginning of the television show, they are more likely to choose television. Similarly, the large, delayed reinforcer is more likely to be selected if the reinforcers are not visible or if there is something pleasurable to do until the large, delayed reinforcer becomes available. These observations have proven useful in developing techniques for enhancing self-control and enabling people to resist the temptations of small, immediate rewards (Mischel, 1974).

The matching law is a simple economic principle that predicts an individual's behavior in many choice situations. The student of economics soon discovers that simple principles are not always valid, and more complex models are needed to describe more complex activities. The same complexity holds true for behavioral economics. While the matching law accurately predicts behavior in a variety of situations, there are some situations in which it is not always valid. Other behavioral economic principles have been applied to explain these more complex choice behavior situations. We look briefly at one of these principles, called maximizing, next.

Maximizing Law. Suppose a pigeon has a choice between key pecking on one key on a VI 1-minute schedule and on a second key on a VI 3-minute schedule. As we learned earlier, the matching law predicts that the pigeon will peck at the VI 1-minute key three times as often as it does the VI 3-minute key. The matching law provides one explanation of the pigeon's behavior; that is, the pigeon allocates its responses according to the proportion of reinforcements available for each choice. In contrast, the **maximizing law** assumes that the aim of the pigeon's behavior will be to obtain as many reinforcers as possible.

In this example, the maximizing law argues that the pigeon switches responses because it can receive reinforcement on both keys. Instead of the pigeon gaining reinforcement on two VI schedules, suppose that responding on one key is reinforced on a FR-10 schedule and on the other key on an FR-40 schedule. How would the pigeon act in this situation? While the matching law predicts continued responding on both keys, maximizing theory assumes that the pigeon would respond only to the FR-10 key. It is illogical for the pigeon to respond 40 times for a reinforcer when it can obtain the same reinforcer by pecking only 10 times. As expected, research (Rachlin, Battalio, Kagel, & Green, 1981; Staddon & Motheral, 1978) shows that the pigeon's behavior corresponds to the maximizing law rather than the matching law.

You might think that the maximizing law provides a valid explanation for choice behavior. However, not all investigations (Savastano & Fantino, 1994; Vyse & Belke, 1992) have reported results consistent with the maximizing theory. For example, suppose that a pigeon is reinforced on a VR schedule on one key and a VI schedule on a second key. Maximizing theory predicts that the pigeon will make most of the responses on the VR key because most of the responses on the VI key are wasted. Yet, Vyse and Belke (1992) observed that the pigeon responds more on the VI key than one would predict from the maximizing theory. In an analogous situation with college students, Savastano and Fantino (1994) found that the college students spent more time on the VI schedule than the maximizing schedule predicted. Further, the college students' choices were much closer to the matching law than the maximizing law. In a more recent study, West and Stanovich (2003) observed that twice as many college students' choice behavior was based on a matching than a maximizing strategy.

While the concepts of matching and maximizing have advanced our understanding of choice behavior, other behavioral principles are needed to fully explain the economics of choice. Psychologists have proposed a number of alternative theories. For example, **momentary maximization theory** proposes that a specific choice is determined by which alternative is perceived to be best at that moment in time (Silberberg, Warren-Bolton, & Asano, 1988). According to this view, variables such as the size and quality of the reinforcer determine momentary choices, while principles such as matching law determine the overall pattern of responses. An animal may make a momentary choice that does not fit the matching law, but its overall response pattern might. **Delay-reduction theory** suggests that while overall choices are based on the matching law, individual choices depend on which choice produces the shortest delay in receiving the next reinforcer (Fantino, Preston, & Dunn, 1993). Again, an individual choice to produce a shorter delay in reinforcement might not be consistent with the matching law, but the overall pattern of response might be consistent. However, Shahan and Podlesnik (2006) reported that the pigeons' individual choice behavior in their study was not consistent with delay reinforcement theory, but instead, was predicted by the matching law. Research continues to investigate the economics of choice behavior, with the goal of fully understanding both immediate and long-term choices.

BEFORE YOU GO ON

- What might Premack's probability-differential theory suggest that Julia do to motivate her son to do his homework?

- Would Timberlake and Allison's response deprivation hypothesis make the same or a different suggestion?

SECTION REVIEW

- Premack's probability-differential theory indicates that activities can serve as reinforcers, with high-probability activities reinforcing lower-probability activities.

- Timberlake and Allison's response deprivation hypothesis states that an activity will become a reinforcer if access to that activity is restricted, with a subsequent increase in the operant response that restores access to the restricted activity.

- The behavioral allocation view suggests that an animal emits the number of contingent responses needed to come as close as possible to blisspoint, or the free operant level of two responses.

- The matching law states that the rate of responding of two operants is in direct proportion to the level of reinforcement available through each operant.

- The maximizing law states that an individual responding in choice situations attempts to obtain as much reinforcement as possible.

- Momentary maximization theory argues that a specific choice is determined by the perception of which alternative is best at that moment in time.

- Delay-reduction theory proposes that while overall choices are based on the matching law, individual choices are determined by which choice produces the shortest delay in gaining the next reinforcement.

THE PAIN OF FAILURE

Edmond is dreading next week. He has a major project due at work, and he is not anywhere near finished. His boss gave him the assignment three weeks ago. It is a difficult task that requires a lot of effort. But Edmond has not been able to focus his attention on the project. He spent much of his time worrying about being fired. Edmond joined the accounting firm three months ago, just after graduating from college. After four years of school, he was very excited about working. Edmond enjoyed the first few weeks at the job. Everything was new, and people willingly answered all his questions. Edmond was pleased with his job until last month.

His anxiety began when he made a major mistake on a report. The error was caught by a senior officer at the firm, who was furious with Edmond. Edmond received very strong criticism from his boss, and this had an extremely adverse effect on Edmond. Edmond did not sleep well that night and was anxious the next day at work. Edmond tried to stay away from his boss, but Edmond could not avoid him. His boss looked angry even a week after the reprimand. By the end of each day, Edmond was so nervous that he began frequenting a bar on his way home. Several beers eased his pain. Edmond was anxious again by the time he got home, so he had several more beers before dinner and a few more while watching television. He did not like to drink a lot, but at least he could sleep. When his boss gave him the new project three weeks ago, Edmond knew he was in trouble. The boss told him that the project was extremely important and that he had better not make any mistakes. This threat made him extremely nervous, and he got very drunk that night. As the project's due date approached, his nervousness increased, as did his drinking. Edmond is sure he is going to get fired next week, when his boss will find out the project has not been completed. His world is falling apart, and he does not know what to do to prevent its collapse.

Edmond's fear is a conditioned response to his boss's reprimand. Edmond responded to the situation by drinking. The alcohol dulled his nervousness, and his increased drinking became a habitual way to cope with fear. Some people who find themselves in unpleasant circumstances may drink to reduce their distress; others may respond in more constructive ways. Chapter 7 detailed the principles that determine whether people learn to avoid aversive events as well as how rapidly they learn that behavior. This section discusses the processes that enable a person to learn to avoid aversive events.

THEORIES OF AVERSIVE CONDITIONING

The Nature of Avoidance Learning

We learned in the last chapter that animals and people can readily learn to avoid unpleasant events. What processes enable animals or people to prevent aversive events? The observation that animals can act to avoid unpleasant events suggests a cognitive process; that is, behaving in order to prevent an aversive event. Yet the Hullian drive theory described in Chapter 2 argued that mechanistic rather than cognitive processes govern behavior. O. H. Mowrer (1939, 1947, 1956) developed a drive-based view of avoidance behavior, an approach regarded as an accurate explanation of avoidance behavior until problems with this theory became apparent during the 1960s. We begin by describing O. H. Mowrer's **two-factor theory of avoidance learning**, followed by a discussion of the problems with two-factor theory of avoidance learning. This section also describes how the theory was modified to address these problems. A cognitive theory of avoidance behavior will be presented in Chapter 11.

Two-Factor Theory of Avoidance Learning

Mowrer (1939, 1947, 1956) proposed that we learn to avoid aversive events in two stages. In the first stage, fear is conditioned to the environmental conditions that precede an aversive event. In the second stage, we learn an instrumental or operant behavior that successfully terminates the feared stimulus. In Mowrer's view, although it appears that we are avoiding painful events, we are actually escaping a feared stimulus. Consider Neal Miller's (1948) classic study to illustrate Mowrer's view of avoidance behavior.

**Orval Hobart Mowrer
(1907–1982)**

Mowrer received his doctorate from Johns Hopkins University under the direction of Knight Dunlap. After receiving his doctorate, he was at Yale University for 6 years, where he published, with John Dollard and Neal Miller, *Frustration and Aggression*. While at Yale, he and his wife Willie Mae (Molly) developed the first bedwetting alarm system while serving as houseparents at a residential home for infants and children. He then taught at Harvard University for 8 years before accepting a research position at the University Of Illinois at Urbana in 1948, where he remained for the next 27 years. His research contributed greatly to understanding the process responsible for the development of avoidance behavior. He was president of the American Psychological Association in 1953.

In Miller's (1948) study, rats were shocked in a white chamber and learned to avoid shock by running from the white chamber through a doorway into a nonshocked black chamber. According to Mowrer (1939, 1947, 1956), the rats were simply escaping the feared white compartment and were not behaving to avoid being shocked. In his view, the fear reduction that resulted from the termination of the feared stimulus (the white compartment) rewarded the rats' behavior.

Recall our discussion of Edmund's drinking behavior in the section opening vignette. Mowrer's two-factor theory would explain Edmund's drinking behavior as developing in two stages: in the first stage, Edmund became afraid of his boss as a result of being severely reprimanded for a mistake on a report, while in the second stage, stopping at a bar and drinking a beer reduced his fear.

Initial research evaluating Mowrer's theory was positive. Several studies reported that once fear of a distinctive cue was established, an animal learned a new response to escape from the feared stimulus (J. S. Brown & Jacobs, 1949; N. E. Miller, 1948). Neal Miller (1951) suggested that psychologists had discovered how avoidance behavior is learned. However, some problems with Mowrer's view became evident during the 1950s and 1960s.

Criticisms of Two-Factor Theory

Several problems exist with Mowrer's two-factor theory of avoidance learning. First, although exposure to the conditioned stimulus without the unconditioned stimulus should eliminate avoidance behavior, avoidance behavior is often extremely resistant to extinction. For example, Solomon and Wynne (1953) reported that their dogs, even after receiving over 200 extinction trials, continued to perform a previously established avoidance response. The apparent failure of extinction represents a problem for the two-factor theory: If fear is acquired through classical conditioning and is responsible for motivating the avoidance behavior, then the presentation of the CS during extinction should cause a reduction in fear and the avoidance behavior should cease.

Levis and Boyd (1979) offered one answer to this problem: It is not the number of extinction trials, but rather the duration of exposure to the CS that determines the fear reduction and thus the elimination of an avoidance response. Levis and Boyd found that the persistence of avoidance behavior depends on the duration of exposure to the feared stimulus: The longer the exposure, the weaker the avoidance response. For example, for a person with a fear of heights, the time spent on the top of a high ladder, and not the number of times the person climbs the ladder, determines the amount of extinction.

Levis (1989) also suggests that the rapid acquisition of an avoidance response prevents the extinction of cues experienced close to the time of the UCS. Suppose that the aversive event (UCS) does not occur until 10 seconds after the CS begins. If the animal avoids after 2 seconds, the short latency cues will extinguish but not the longer latency ones. When the avoidance response slows, the long latency cues will elicit fear, which will act to recondition fear to the short latency cues. In support of this view, Levis (1989) found that extinction of the avoidance response is much slower if there are separate cues associated with short and long latency than if a single cue is present during the entire CS-UCS interval.

A second problem for the two-factor theory concerns the apparent absence of fear in a well-established avoidance response. For example, Kamin et al. (1963) observed that a CS for a well-learned avoidance behavior did not suppress an operant response for food reinforcement. The failure to suppress the response is thought to reflect an absence of fear because one indication of fear is the suppression of appetitive behavior. However, it is possible that the absence of suppression does not indicate that an animal is experiencing no fear in response to the CS, but rather that the animal's motivation for food is stronger than the fear induced by the CS. Further, strong fear is not necessary to motivate a habitual avoidance response—an observation that is consistent with Hull's idea that the tendency to respond is a joint function of drive and habit strength.

The Sidman avoidance procedure represents a third problem for two-factor theory. In the **Sidman avoidance** task, an animal experiences periodic aversive events unless it responds to prevent them. The avoidance response delays the occurrence of the next aversive event for a specific period of time. The interval between aversive events is the S-S interval, while the time that the aversive event is delayed is the R-S interval. If an animal responds consistently prior to the end of the R-S interval, it will not experience an aversive event. There is no external warning stimulus in the Sidman avoidance procedure. This should prevent avoidance learning, because there is no external conditioned stimulus to arouse fear prior to the avoidance behavior, nor is there any external conditioned stimulus terminating after the avoidance response and producing fear reduction. Yet, animals can learn to avoid aversive events with the Sidman avoidance procedure (Sidman, 1953; Weisman & Litner, 1972).

Kamin's (1956) experiment, which demonstrates that preventing an aversive event is necessary to learn an avoidance response, provides perhaps the most damaging evidence against Mowrer's two-factor theory. Kamin compared avoidance learning in four groups of rats: (1) rats whose response both terminated the CS and prevented the UCS (Normal condition), (2) rats who were presented with the UCS at a predetermined time but whose behavior could terminate the CS (Term CS condition), (3) rats who could avoid the UCS but not escape the CS (Avoid UCS condition), and (4) rats who were exposed to both the CS and UCS but who could not escape the CS or avoid the UCS (Classical Conditioning Control condition). Mowrer's two-factor theory predicts that subjects in the Term CS condition would learn to avoid because that response terminated the CS even though it did not prevent the UCS from occurring. Mowrer's two-factor theory also predicts that subjects in the Avoid UCS condition would not learn to avoid the UCS because the CS remained on after the avoidance response, even though the response actually prevented the UCS.

The results of Kamin's (1956) study did not match these predictions. Kamin found that the level of avoidance response was lower in both the Term CS and Avoid UCS conditions than in the Normal condition, in which the responses both terminated the CS and avoided the UCS. Also, subjects in both the Term CS and Avoid UCS groups demonstrated greater avoidance than the subjects in the Classical Conditioning Control condition, whose responses neither terminated the CS nor avoided the UCS. Further, the Avoid UCS subjects responded as often as the rats in the Term CS group. Figure 8.5 presents the results of Kamin's study, which indicate that two factors—termination of the CS and avoidance of the UCS—play an important role in avoidance learning.

D'Amato's View of Avoidance Learning

Michael D'Amato (1970) developed an acquired motive theory to explain why prevention of the aversive event is important in learning avoidance behavior. According to D'Amato, an aversive event, such as a shock, elicits an unconditioned pain response (R_p), and the stimulus consequences of the painful event (S_p) motivate escape behavior. As the result of conditioning, the environmental cues present during shock can eventually produce an **anticipatory pain response** (r_p). The anticipatory pain response also produces distinctive stimulus aftereffects (s_p), which act to motivate an escape behavior.

Figure 8.5 The percentage of avoidance responses as a function of the rats' ability to terminate the CS, avoid the UCS, or both. The level of avoidance behavior was greatest when the rats could both terminate the CS and avoid the UCS.

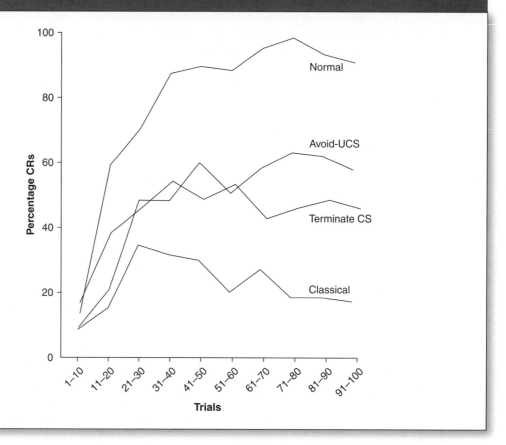

D'Amato's (1970) r_P-s_P mechanism motivates escape from the conditioned stimulus. The termination of an aversive event (e.g., shock) produces an unconditioned relief response (R_R). The stimulus consequences (S_R) of the relief response are rewarding. According to D'Amato, the stimuli associated with the termination of the aversive event develop the ability to elicit an **anticipatory relief response** (r_R). The stimulus aftereffects (s_R) of this anticipatory relief response are also rewarding. Furthermore, the cues associated with anticipatory relief motivate approach behavior in a manner similar to Spence's (1956) description of the approach response to goal-related cues that was discussed in Chapter 2. This idea suggests a second motivational basis of avoidance behavior. The animal or human is not only escaping from an aversive situation; it is approaching a rewarding one. According to D'Amato, the avoidance of the aversive event is important because if the animal does not avoid, the r_R-s_R mechanism will not develop, and the avoidance response will not be rewarded.

Let's consider how D'Amato's theory would explain why some children avoid dogs. Being bitten by a dog is an aversive event that produces an unconditioned pain response and causes the child to associate the dog with pain. Through this conditioning, the dog produces an anticipatory pain response (r_P). The r_P-s_P mechanism motivates a child who has been bitten to get away from a dog when he or she sees one; this escape produces an unconditioned relief response. Suppose that such a child runs into a house to escape a dog. The house then becomes associated with relief and is able to produce an anticipatory relief response. Thus, if the dog is seen again, the sight of the house produces the r_R-s_R complex, which motivates the child to run into the house. Therefore, the anticipation of both pain and relief motivate the child to avoid the dog.

Another problem for Mowrer's two-factor theory is that an avoidance response is not learned when a trace conditioning procedure is used. With trace conditioning, the CS terminates prior to the UCS presentation, which is a procedure that should lead to avoidance learning according to Mowrer's two-factor theory. D'Amato, Fazzaro, and Etkin (1968) suggested that avoidance learning is not learned with a trace conditioning procedure because no distinctive cue is associated with the absence of the UCS. If a cue were present when the aversive event ended, an avoidance response would be learned. To validate this idea, D'Amato et al. presented a second cue (in addition to the CS) when their subjects exhibited an avoidance response. Although learning was slow—only reaching the level observed with the delayed-conditioning procedure (the CS and UCS terminated at the same time) after 500 trials—these subjects performed at a higher level than when the second cue was not present (see Figure 8.6). According to D'Amato et al., once the second cue was associated with the termination of shock, the r_R-s_R mechanism was acquired, and it then acted to reward avoidance behavior.

The importance of a discriminative cue signaling the absence of an aversive event can be used to explain avoidance learning with the Sidman avoidance task. Recall that there is no external warning stimulus with the Sidman avoidance task. According to Levis (1989), the periodic aversive events experienced early in learning condition high levels of fear to the training environment. This fear produces high levels of activity, which motivates the avoidance

Figure 8.6 The percentage of avoidance responses during 700 trials for standard delayed-conditioning group (Group C), trace conditioning group (Group T), and group receiving a cue for 5 seconds after each avoidance response (Group TS). The feedback stimulus overcame the poor performance observed with the trace conditioning procedure. The break indicates that a 24-hour interval elapsed between the fifth and sixth blocks of trials.

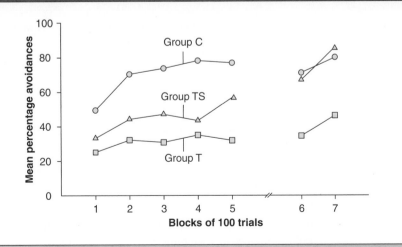

response, and response-produced cues predict the absence of the aversive event. The relief experienced following the avoidance response reinforces the avoidance behavior and results in effective learning.

D'Amato's (1970) view asserts that we are motivated to approach situations associated with relief as well as to escape events paired with aversive events. Furthermore, the relief experienced following avoidance behavior rewards that response. Denny (1971) demonstrated that relief has both a motivational and rewarding character. Let's examine Denny's evidence, which validates both aspects of D'Amato's view.

Denny and Weisman (1964) demonstrated that animals anticipating pain will approach events that are associated with relief. The researchers trained rats to escape or to avoid shock in a striped shock compartment within a T-maze by turning either right into a black chamber or left into a white chamber. One of the chambers was associated with a 100-second delay before the next trials, the other chamber with only a 20-second delay. The rats learned to go to the compartment associated with the longer intertrial interval. These results suggest that when the rats anticipated experiencing an aversive event, they were motivated to seek the environment associated with the greatest relief.

Denny (1971) argued that the amount of relief depends upon the length of time between aversive events: The longer the nonshock interval (or intertrial interval, ITI), the greater the conditioned relief. In Denny's view, the greater the relief, the faster is the acquisition of an avoidance habit. To test this idea, Denny and Weisman (1964) varied the time between trials from 10 to 225 seconds. They observed that acquisition of an avoidance response was directly related to the intertrial interval: Animals that experienced a longer interval between trials learned the avoidance response more readily than those given a shorter time between trials. These results show that the longer the period of relief after an aversive event, the more readily the rats learned to avoid the aversive event.

BEFORE YOU GO ON

- What circumstances made Edmund anxious and caused him to drink?

- What reinforced Edmund's drinking behavior?

SECTION REVIEW

- Mowrer suggested that fear is conditioned during the first phase of avoidance learning.

- Mowrer proposed that in the second stage of avoidance learning, fear motivates any behavior that successfully terminates the fear.

- In Mowrer's view, the behavior that terminates the feared stimulus will be rewarded by fear reduction and elicited upon future exposure to the feared stimulus.

- According to Mowrer, the aversive event will be avoided only if the avoidance response also results in escape responses to the feared stimulus.

- D'Amato suggested that the classical conditioning of the anticipatory pain response mechanism (r_p-s_p) to the environmental cues associated with an aversive event motivates escape from these cues.

- In D'Amato's view, the termination of pain produces an unconditioned relief response (R_R) and the establishment of the anticipatory relief response mechanism (r_R-s_R) provides motivation to approach the cues associated with relief.

The Nature of Punishment

Thorndike's Negative Law of Effect

Edward Thorndike (1913) suggested that punishment weakened the strength of an S-R bond. The recovery of responding shortly after exposure to a mild punishment clearly contradicts this view of punishment (Estes, 1944; Estes & Skinner, 1941; Skinner, 1938). If punishment acted to weaken S-R strength, the effect would be permanent, not temporary. Clearly, the effect of punishment on behavior must be caused by a process other than weakening S-R strength.

Guthrie's Competing Response View

Edwin Guthrie (1934; see Chapter 2) suggested that an aversive event can elicit a number of unconditioned responses (e.g., flinching, jumping, or freezing). These unconditioned responses will then be conditioned to the environment present during the aversive event. According to Guthrie, the punished response will be suppressed only if the response conditioned to the cues associated with the aversive event is incompatible with the punished response. For example, punishment will suppress bar pressing, in Guthrie's view, if a response incompatible with bar pressing has been conditioned to the operant chamber.

Fowler and Miller's (1963) classic study provides support for Guthrie's view of punishment. In their study, rats were initially trained to run down an alley for food reward. In one group, the rats were then shocked when their forepaws touched the metal rods in front of the goal box. Electric shock applied to the forepaw elicits a flinching reaction, a response that is incompatible with forward running; shock, therefore, should result in rapid suppression of the running response, according to Guthrie. A second group of rats was shocked on the hind paw; this elicits a lurching response, a behavior that is compatible with the running response. Lurching, again according to Guthrie, should therefore increase the speed of the rats' response toward reward. A third group of rats was not shocked. Fowler and Miller reported that running was suppressed by forepaw shock but was facilitated by hind paw shock. Apparently, the response elicited by punishment does influence the effectiveness of punishment.

Other studies also support Guthrie's view of punishment. Morse, Mead, and Kelleher (1967) punished monkeys for struggling on a leash by shocking them. However, punishment increased rather than suppressed struggling, presumably because the shock elicited struggling rather than a behavior that would have competed with struggling. Also, when Walters and Glazer (1971) punished gerbils for standing in an upright posture, they discovered that punishment increased, rather than decreased, the occurrence of the punished response.

Our discussion suggests that to be effective, punishment must elicit a behavior incompatible with the punished response. However, other research indicates that response competition alone is insufficient to make punishment effective. Quite a few studies (Azrin, 1956; Camp et al., 1967; R. Schuster & Rachlin, 1968) show that the suppression of a response is significantly greater when an aversive event is contingent on the occurrence of the response than when the aversive event occurs independently of behavior. Guthrie's view suggests that contingent and noncontingent aversive events have an equal effect on behavior: Conditioning a competing response should occur regardless of whether the presentation of the aversive event depends on the occurrence of a response. The observation that contingency influences the level of response suppression shows that response competition alone is insufficient to suppress a response. Mowrer's two-factor theory provides another explanation of the influence of punishment on behavior.

Two-Factor Theory of Punishment

Mowrer's (1956) view of the process responsible for the effect of punishment on behavior is similar to his theory of avoidance learning described earlier. According to Mowrer, the suppressive influence of punishment occurs in two stages. In the first stage, fear is classically conditioned to the environmental events present during punishment. Fear is elicited when an animal or person experiences the environmental events preceding punishment; this fear acts to motivate the animal or person to escape from the feared stimulus. Any behavior, either overt response or failure to respond, that terminates the feared stimulus will be acquired through instrumental conditioning in the second stage. The reinforcement of the escape response causes the animal or person to exhibit the escape response rather than the punished response in the punishment situation. Thus, the suppressive effect of punishment results from elicitation of a behavior other than the punished behavior.

You may have noticed the similarity between Mowrer's view of avoidance learning and his **two-factor theory of punishment**. In fact, Mowrer is describing two aspects of the same process: Fear motivates an avoidance behavior, which enables an animal or person to prevent punishment. Also, the occurrence of the avoidance behavior causes an animal or person not to exhibit the punished response, which is thus responsible for the suppressive effect of punishment.

There is evidence supporting Mowrer's idea that fear is involved in the suppression of punished behavior. Chapter 4 detailed a number of studies in which a stimulus that had been classically conditioned to elicit fear in one situation suppressed an appetitive instrumental behavior when experienced in an entirely different situation. Further, a feared stimulus also increased the level of avoidance responding.

However, learning theorists (Estes, 1969) have pointed to a weakness in Mowrer's view of punishment: The overt behavior that fear motivates and that prevents an animal from exhibiting the punished response is often difficult to identify. Estes's motivational view of punishment explains why an overt response is not essential.

Estes's Motivational View of Punishment

According to Estes (1969), when a behavior is reinforced, the motivational system that is present prior to reward and the response become associated. When this motivational system is activated again, the response is elicited. For example, if a hungry rat is reinforced for bar pressing, the bar-pressing response and hunger become associated. The presence of hunger in the future will act to elicit bar pressing in this rat. Similarly, when a child seeking approval of peers is disruptive in school and obtains approval for these actions, the disruptive response and the approval of peers become associated. When the child wants approval again, the child will be disruptive.

In Estes's view, the primary mechanism underlying the influence of punishment on behavior is the competition of motives. If a stimulus precedes punishment, it develops the ability to inhibit the motive associated with the punished behavior. Thus, Estes asserts that punishment works because an animal or person is no longer motivated, and therefore, the punished response is no longer elicited.

Let's see how Estes's view of punishment would explain the suppression of rats' bar pressing or of children's disruptive classroom behavior. According to Estes's approach, punishment does not directly suppress rats' bar pressing or children's disruptive behavior; instead, punishment inhibits the rat's hunger or the child's need for approval. Therefore, since the punished rat or child is no longer motivated, the punished responses of bar pressing or disruptive behavior will no longer be elicited.

There is evidence (Walters & Grusec, 1977) supporting Estes's view. Wall, Walters, and England (1972) trained water-deprived rats to bar press for water and to "dry lick" for air; these behaviors were displayed on alternate days. The rate of both responses increased to a stable level after 62 days of training. Although each behavior was then punished, the rats showed greater suppression of the dry-licking response than of the bar-pressing response. According to Walters and Grusec, the internal stimuli associated with dry licking are more closely tied with the thirst motivational system than are the internal stimuli associated with bar pressing. Therefore, if punishment acts to decrease the thirsty rats' motivation for water, it should have more influence on dry licking than on bar pressing. Wall et al.'s results support this view: Punishing thirsty rats suppresses dry licking more effectively than bar pressing. However, punishing hungry rats does not suppress dry licking more than bar pressing for food. According to Walters and Grusec, dry licking is not more closely associated with the hunger system than is bar pressing, and thus reducing animals' motivation for food will not suppress dry licking any more than it suppresses bar pressing.

Thus, punishment suppresses behavior by inhibiting the motivational system responsible for eliciting the punished response. Note that external stimuli present during punishment can become conditioned to produce fear, and this emotional response of fear represents a general motivational response, capable of suppressing any reward-seeking behavior or arousing any avoidance response (see Chapter 4). However, the desired effect of punishment is to suppress a specific behavior, and the evidence indicates that punishment works best when it inhibits the specific motivational state that has been associated with the punished response.

BEFORE YOU GO ON

- What behavior was Edmund's boss punishing?

- Did the punishment have the desired effect? Why or why not?

SECTION REVIEW

- Guthrie proposed that punishment elicits a specific behavior.

- According to Guthrie, if the response elicited by punishment is antagonistic to the punished behavior, punishment will suppress the undesired behavior, but punishment may increase the behavior if it elicits a compatible response.

- Mowrer believed that fear is conditioned by the use of punishment and that it is this fear that motivates escape behavior.

- In Mowrer's view, the escape behavior prevents the punished response.

- Estes's motivational view suggests that punishment reduces the motivational level; the absence of motivation suppresses the undesired response.

CRITICAL THINKING QUESTIONS

1. Corlisha would like for her 6-year-old daughter to be able dress herself, but so far her efforts to establish the behavior have been unsuccessful. Using the Premack principle, suggest a way that Corlisha can accomplish her goal.

2. Nikki is saving her money to buy a car. Vernon goes out every Friday night and never has any money by Saturday morning. How would the matching law explain Nikki's and Vernon's actions? What factors might lead Nikki to spend some of her money on a new dress or Vernon to save his money for a trip to Florida over spring break?

3. Angeline becomes very nervous when she eats fattening foods, yet she impulsively eats large quantities before forcing herself to vomit. Discuss Angeline's avoidance behavior using Mowrer's two-factor theory.

KEY TERMS

anticipatory pain response

behavioral allocation view

delay-reduction theory

maximizing law

probability-differential theory

Sidman avoidance

two-factor theory of punishment

anticipatory relief response

blisspoint

matching law

momentary maximization theory

response deprivation theory

two-factor theory of avoidance learning

CHAPTER 9

Biological Influences on Learning

A NAUSEATING EXPERIENCE

For weeks, Sean looked forward to spending his spring break in Florida with his roommate Tony and Tony's parents. Since he had never visited Florida, Sean was certain his anticipation would make the 18-hour car ride tolerable. When he and Tony arrived, Sean felt genuinely welcome; Tony's parents had planned many sightseeing tours for them during the week's stay. Tony had often mentioned his mother was a gourmet cook. He especially raved about her beef bourguignon, which Tony claimed melted in your mouth. Sean was certainly relishing the thoughts of her meals, especially since his last enjoyable food had been his own mother's cooking, months earlier. Sean was also quite tired of the many fast-food restaurants they had stopped at during their drive. When Tony's mother called them to dinner, Sean felt very hungry. However, the sight of lasagna on the dining table almost immediately turned Sean's hunger to nausea. As he sat down at the table, the smell of the lasagna intensified his nausea. Sean began to panic; he did not want to offend his hosts, but he hated lasagna. Although he had stopped Tony's mother after she had served him only a small portion, Sean did not know whether he could eat even one bite. When he put the lasagna to his mouth, he began to gag and the nausea became unbearable. He quickly asked to be excused and bolted to the bathroom, where he proceeded to vomit everything he had eaten that day. Embarrassed, Sean apologetically explained his aversion to lasagna. Although he liked most Italian food, he had once become intensely ill several hours after eating lasagna, and now he could not stand even the sight or smell of lasagna. Tony's mother said she understood: She herself had a similar aversion to seafood. She offered to make Sean a sandwich, and he readily accepted.

This chapter explores the learning process that caused Tony to develop an affinity for his mother's beef bourguignon or Sean to develop his aversion to lasagna. We will discover that Tony's and Sean's experiences affected their instinctive feeding systems, which was modified to release insulin at the thought of beef bourguignon or become nauseous at the sight of lasagna. The insulin release motivated Tony to ask his mother to cook beef bourguignon while he was home, while a nauseous feeling caused Sean to be unable to eat lasagna.

A person's biological character also affects other types of learning. Examples include developing an attachment to one's mother and learning to avoid aversive events. In this chapter, we examine several instances in which biological character and the environment join to determine behavior. But before examining these situations, we discuss why psychologists initially ignored the influence of biology on learning.

GENERALITY OF THE LAWS OF LEARNING

Why do psychologists train rats or monkeys to press a bar for food, or present a buzzer prior to food presentation for cats or dogs, when these situations bear little resemblance to the real world? (In natural settings, rats and monkeys do not have to bar press for food, and cats and dogs do not usually hear a buzzer before they eat.) The answer to this question lies in the belief that there are some general laws of learning. These laws reveal themselves in the study of any behavior, even behaviors not exhibited in natural settings.

Psychologists investigating operant conditioning use the bar-press response because many different species acquire it easily. But the same rules governing the acquisition or extinction of an operant response could be demonstrated by using a maze or alley to study the instrumental conditioning process. Actually, the unnaturalness of bar pressing is thought to be desirable because the animal comes into the conditioning situation without any past experience that may affect its behavior. The following statement by Skinner (1938) illustrates the belief that the study of any behavior reveals specific laws governing operant conditioning: "The general topography of operant behavior is not important because most if not all specific operants are conditioned. I suggest that the dynamic properties of operant behavior may be studied with a single reflex" (pp. 45–46).

Although Skinner studied operant conditioning using the bar-press response, the observations reported in Chapter 6 show that the rules Skinner detailed governing the acquisition and extinction of the bar-pressing response control the operant conditioning process with many different behaviors and in many species. Also, research demonstrates that many varied reinforcers can increase the rate of bar pressing and that the rules Skinner described have been found to operate in both laboratory and real-world settings. It is not surprising that psychologists have felt confident that training rats and animals to bar press for food reveals the general laws of operant conditioning.

Similarly, psychologists who present a buzzer prior to food assume that any rules they uncover governing the acquisition or extinction of a conditioned salivation response will represent the general laws of classical conditioning. The choice of a buzzer and food is arbitrary: Cats or dogs could be conditioned to salivate as readily to a wide variety of visual, auditory, or tactile stimuli. The following statement by Pavlov (1928) illustrates the view that all stimuli are capable of becoming conditioned stimuli: "Any natural phenomenon chosen at will may be converted into a conditioned stimulus . . . any visual stimulus, any desired sound, any odor, and the stimulation of any part of the skin" (p. 86).

The specific UCS used also is arbitrary: Any event that can elicit an unconditioned response can become associated with the environmental events that precede it. Thus, Pavlov's buzzer could have as easily been conditioned to elicit fear by pairing it with shock as it was conditioned to elicit salivation by presenting it prior to food. Pavlov (1927) described the equivalent associability of events in the following statement: "It is obvious that the reflex activity of any effector organ can be chosen for the purpose of investigation, since signaling stimuli can get linked up with any of the inborn reflexes" (p. 17). Pavlov found that many different stimuli can become associated with the UCS of food. Other psychologists documented the conditioning of varied stimuli with a multitude of UCSs. Also, the literature points out that different CSs and UCSs can become associated in both laboratory and natural situations. The idea that any environmental event can become associated with any unconditioned stimulus seemed a reasonable conclusion, based on the research conducted on classical conditioning.

A BEHAVIOR SYSTEMS APPROACH

All organisms inherently possess the basic behavioral patterns that enable them to survive in their niches, but learning provides the fine tuning necessary for successful adaptation.

—Garcia and Garcia y Robertson (1985, p. 197)

The "general laws of learning" view we just described assumes that learning is the primary determinant of how an animal acts. According to this approach, learning functions to organize reflexes and random responses so that an animal can effectively interact with the environment. The impact of learning is to allow the animal to adapt to the environment and thereby survive. However, the quote presented at the beginning of this section provides a different perspective on the impact of learning on behavior. Rather than proposing that learning organizes behavior, Garcia and Garcia y Robertson (1985) argued that the function of learning is to enhance existing organization rather than to create a new organization. Many psychologists (Garcia & Garcia y Robertson, 1985; Hogan, 1989; Timberlake, 2001) have suggested that learning modifies preexisting instinctive systems rather than constructs a new behavioral organization; we look at this idea next.

William Timberlake's **behavior systems approach** (Timberlake, 2001; Timberlake & Lucas, 1989) offers an alternative to the general laws of learning view. According to Timberlake, an animal possesses instinctive behavior systems such as feeding, mating, social bonding, care of young, and defense. Each instinctive behavior system is independent and serves a specific function or need within the animal. Figure 9.1 shows the predatory subsystem of the feeding system in rats.

Figure 9.1   Illustration of the basic components of the rat's feeding system. The predatory subsystem can activate one of three modes (general, focal, or handle/consume), which in turn activates one or more modules appropriate to that mode. The arousal of a specific module then leads to one or more specific behaviors, each directed toward the consumption of needed nutrients.

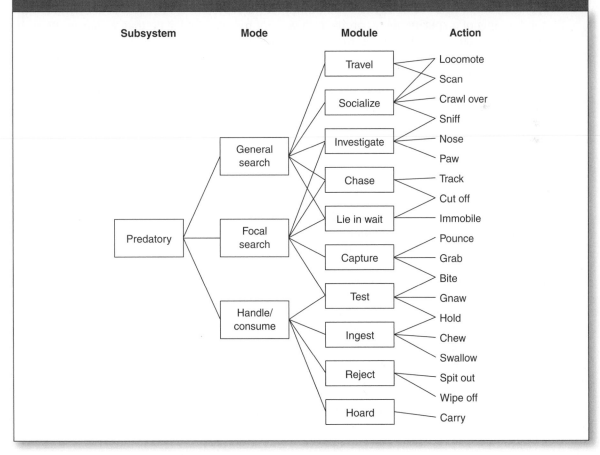

As the figure shows, there are several components of the animal's predatory response. The predatory sequence begins with the rat in a general search mode. The search mode causes the rat to show enhanced general searching, which leads to greater locomotion and increased sensitivity to spatial and social stimuli that are likely to bring the rat closer to food. The increased locomotion and greater sensitivity to the environment lead the rat to notice a small moving object in the distance as its prey. Once the prey is close, the rat shifts from a general search mode to a focal search mode. The focal search mode causes the rat to engage in a set of perceptual-motor modules related to capturing and subduing its prey. Once the prey is captured, the rat shifts to a handle/consume mode, which elicits the biting, manipulating, chewing, and swallowing involved in the consumption of the prey. This complex instinctive predatory behavior system allows the animal to find and consume the nutrients it needs to survive.

Timberlake's (2001) behavior systems approach suggests that learning evolved as a modifier of existing behavior systems. According to Timberlake, the impact of learning is to change the integration, tuning, instigation, or linkages within a particular behavior system. For example, a new environmental stimulus could become able to release an instinctive motor-response module as a result of a classical conditioning experience. Learning can also alter the intensity of a simple motor response due to repetition, or improve the efficiency of a complex behavior pattern as a result of the contingent delivery of a reinforcer.

Activation of a mode can also be conditioned to cues that signal the receipt of reinforcers. For example, the search modes that bring the rat into contact with its prey can be conditioned to cues associated with the prey. However, the conditioning of modes is different from the conditioning of perceptual-motor modules (Timberlake, 2001). Specific motor responses are conditioned to specific stimuli as a result of the conditioning of perceptual-motor modules. By contrast, the conditioning of a specific mode produces a general motivational state that sensitizes all of the perceptual-motor modules in that mode. For example, activation of the general search mode of the predatory subsystem sensitizes the rat to engage in the travel, socialize, investigate, chase, and lie-in-wait perceptual-motor modules (see Figure 9.1).

One important aspect of Timberlake's behavior systems approach is that different stimuli can be conditioned to different modes. For example, distal cues are relevant to a general search mode—the rat must locate distant prey. By contrast, proximal cues are relevant to a focal search mode—the rat must capture and subdue its prey.

The following study illustrates the conditioning of the general search mode to distal cues and the focal search mode to proximal cues. Akins, Domjan, and Gutierrez (1994) presented a light CS for either 30 seconds or 1,200 seconds to a male quail. The light CS predicted access to a receptive female quail. The male quail approached the alcove where the female quail would appear when the 30-second CS was presented, but not when the 1,200-second CS was presented. Instead, the male quail showed increased locomotion in response to the CS presented for 1,200 seconds. Why the difference in the quail's response to the same CS presented for different durations? The 30-second CS is proximal (near) to the reinforcer (female quail), and thus, a focal search—leading the male to approach the alcove—was conditioned to the 30-second CS. The 1,200-second CS is distal (far) from the reinforcer (female quail); thus, a general search—leading the male to increase locomotion—was conditioned to the 1,200-second CS.

One of the functional features of the behavior system approach is that variations in learning occur between species (Timberlake, 2001). In Timberlake's view, different species of animals learn a particular behavior at different rates. Different species also learn different ways to respond to a particular situation. Considerable variation also occurs within a species. Timberlake suggests that some behaviors are learned more rapidly than others within a given species. Further, there may be different rates of learning of a particular behavior between different members of a species.

What causes these variations between and within animal species? Timberlake (2001) suggests that the variations are due either to predispositions or constraints on what an animal can learn. A **predisposition** refers to instances in which an animal learns more rapidly or in a different form than expected. Timberlake suggests that predispositions occur when environmental circumstance easily modifies the instinctive behavior system that the animal brings into the situation. Recall our discussion of Tony's affinity for beef bourguignon and Sean's aversion to lasagna described in the chapter-opening vignette. A predisposition undoubtedly contributed both to Tony's affinity for beef bourguignon and Sean's aversion to lasagna.

Variations in learning also can reflect the impact of a **constraint** on learning; a constraint occurs when an animal learns less rapidly or less completely than expected. According to Timberlake, constraints on learning occur when environmental circumstance is not suited to the animal's instinctive behavior system. In the next five sections, we examine examples of predispositions and constraints on learning.

ANIMAL MISBEHAVIOR

Several summers ago, my family visited Busch Gardens. We observed some unusual behaviors among birds during our visit; they walked on a wire, pedaled a bicycle, pecked certain keys on a piano, and so on. The birds had been trained to exhibit these behaviors using the operant conditioning techniques detailed in Chapter 6. Keller Breland and Marian Breland (1961) initiated the use of operant procedures to teach exotic behaviors to animals. They conducted their research at Animal Behavior Enterprises in Hot Springs, Arkansas, to see whether the techniques Skinner described could be used in the real world.

The Brelands trained 38 species, including reindeer, cockatoos, raccoons, porpoises, and whales. In fact, they trained over 6,000 animals to emit a wide range of behaviors, including teaching hens to play a five-note tune on a piano and perform a "tap dance," pigs to turn on a radio and eat breakfast at a table, chicks to run up an inclined platform and slide off, a calf to answer questions in a quiz show by lighting either a yes or no sign, and two turkeys to play hockey. Established by the Brelands and many other individuals, these exotic behaviors have been on display at many municipal zoos and museums of natural history, in department store displays, at fair and trade convention exhibits, at tourist attractions, and on television. These demonstrations have not only provided entertainment for millions of people; they have documented the power and generality of the operant conditioning procedures Skinner outlined.

Although Breland and Breland (1961, 1966) were able to condition a wide variety of exotic behaviors using operant conditioning, they noted that some operant responses, although initially performed effectively, deteriorated with continued training despite repeated food reinforcements. According to Breland and Breland, the elicitation of instinctive food-foraging and food-handling behaviors by the presentation of food caused the decline in the effectiveness of an operant response reinforced by food. These instinctive behaviors, strengthened by food reinforcement, eventually dominated the operant behavior. Breland and Breland called the deterioration of an operant behavior with continued reinforcement **instinctive drift**, and the instinctive behavior that prevented the continued effectiveness of the operant response an example of **animal misbehavior**. One example of animal misbehavior is described next.

Breland and Breland (1961) attempted to condition pigs to pick up a large wooden coin and deposit it in a piggy bank several feet away. Each pig was required to deposit four or five coins to receive one reinforcement. According to Breland and Breland, "pigs condition very rapidly, they have no trouble taking ratios, they have ravenous appetites (naturally), and in many ways are the

Keller Bramwell Breland (1915–1965)

Keller Breland worked with B. F. Skinner at the University of Minnesota. During World War II, he and his wife Marion assisted Skinner in the training of pigeons to guide bombs for the U.S. Navy. He left the University of Minnesota prior to completing his degree to start, with Marion, the first commercial application of operant conditioning, Animal Behavior Enterprises, on a small farm in Mound, Minnesota. Their first contract was with General Mills to train animals for farm feed promotions. In 1955, Animal Behavior Enterprises moved to larger quarters in Hot Springs, Arkansas, where they continued to develop shows and training methods for oceanariums and theme parks that are used to this day.

Marion Breland Bailey (1920–2001)

Marion Breland Bailey worked with B. F. Skinner at the University of Minnesota, first as an undergraduate and later as his second graduate student. She left the University of Minnesota prior to completing her degree to start, with Keller, the first commercial application of operant conditioning, Animal Behavior Enterprises. Animal Behavior Enterprises help establish humane ways to teach animals. She also worked with Canine Companions for Independence to train dogs to assist individuals with disabilities. She received her doctorate from the University of Arkansas in 1978 and taught at Henderson State University for 17 years.

most trainable animals we have worked with" (p. 683). However, each pig they conditioned exhibited an interesting pattern of behavior following conditioning (see Figure 9.2). At first, the pigs picked up a coin, carried it rapidly to the bank, deposited it, and readily returned for another coin. However, over a period of weeks, the pigs' operant behavior became slower and slower. Each pig still rapidly approached the coin, but rather than carry it immediately over to the bank, the pigs "would repeatedly drop it, root it, drop it again, root it along the way, pick it up, toss it up in the air, drop it, root it some more, and so on" (p. 683).

Why did the pigs' operant behavior deteriorate after conditioning? According to Breland and Breland (1961), the pigs merely exhibited the instinctive behaviors associated with eating. The presentation of food during conditioning not only reinforces the operant response; it also elicits instinctive food-related behaviors. The reinforcement of these instinctive food-gathering and food-handling behaviors strengthens the instinctive behaviors, which results in the deterioration of the pigs' operant responses (depositing the coin in the bank). The more dominant the instinctive food-related behaviors become, the longer it takes for the operant response to occur. The slow deterioration of the operant depositing response provides support for Breland and Breland's instinctive drift view of animal misbehavior.

Breland and Breland have reported many other instances of animal misbehavior, for example, the porpoises and whales that attempted to swallow balls or inner tubes instead of playing with them to receive reinforcement or cats that refused to leave the area around the food dispenser. Breland and Breland also reported extreme difficulty in conditioning many bird species to vocalize to obtain food reinforcement. Breland and Breland (1961) suggested that the strengthening of instinctive food-related behaviors during operant conditioning is responsible for animal misbehavior.

Boakes, Poli, Lockwood, and Goodall (1978) proposed that animal misbehavior is produced by classical conditioning rather than by operant conditioning. The association of environmental events with food during conditioning causes these environmental events to elicit species-typical foraging and food-handling behaviors; these behaviors then compete with the operant behavior. Consider the misbehavior of the pig detailed earlier. According to Breland and Breland (1961), the pigs rooted the tokens because the reinforcement presented during operant conditioning strengthened the instinctive food-related behavior; in contrast, Boakes et al. suggested that the association of the token with food caused the token to elicit the rooting behavior.

Timberlake, Wahl, and King (1982) conducted a series of studies to show that both operant and classical conditioning contribute to producing animal misbehavior. In their view, misbehavior

Figure 9.2   Breland and Breland attempted to train this pig to deposit the wooden disk into a piggy bank. Unfortunately, the pig's operant response deteriorated with repeated food reinforcements due to the elicitation of the instinctive foraging and rooting responses.

represents species-typical foraging and food-handling behaviors that are elicited by pairing food with the natural cues controlling food-gathering activities. Also, the instinctive food-gathering behaviors must be reinforced if the misbehavior is to dominate the operant behavior. Animal misbehavior does not occur in most operant conditioning situations because (1) the cues present during conditioning do not resemble the natural cues eliciting instinctive foraging and food-handling behaviors and (2) these instinctive behaviors are not reinforced.

Timberlake and his colleagues (1982) assessed the contribution of classical conditioning to animal misbehavior by pairing a ball bearing with food in experimental subjects. In one study, experimental animals received food after the ball bearing had rolled out of a chute. (In this condition, animal misbehavior is found as rats will repeatedly mouth, paw, and retrieve the ball bearing.) Also, this study used two control conditions to evaluate the importance of pairing the ball bearing and food: Animals in one control condition were given random pairings of the ball bearing and food (random group); subjects in the second control condition received only the ball bearing (CS-only group). They reported that experimental group exhibited a significant amount of misbehavior toward the ball bearing: They touched it, carried it about the cage, placed it in their mouths, and bit it while holding it in their forepaws. In contrast, infrequent misbehavior occurred in the two control groups. These observations show that the ball bearing and food must be paired for a high level of misbehavior to occur.

Timberlake et al. (1982) also determined the importance of operant conditioning to the establishment of animal misbehavior. In a second study, contact with the ball bearing caused food to be omitted. The researchers assumed that if reinforcing contact with the ball bearing is necessary for animal misbehavior, the contingency that contact with the ball bearing would prevent reinforcement would lead to an absence of animal misbehavior. The results of this study show that if contact with the ball bearing prevents reinforcement, then the animals did, indeed, exhibit no contact with the ball bearing. The experimenters then reinforced contact with the ball bearing in a third study. If the animal did not touch the ball bearing, it received no food on that trial. Timberlake et al. reported that reinforcement of contact with the ball bearing produced a rapid increase in the level of animal misbehavior. These studies suggest that for misbehavior to develop, stimuli (e.g., ball bearings) resembling the natural cues controlling food-gathering activities must be consistently paired with food (classical conditioning), and the presentation of food must reinforce the occurrence of species-typical foraging and food-handling behaviors elicited by the natural cues (operant conditioning).

Does animal misbehavior occur in humans? Many children play with their food, but is this an example of misbehavior? Should a child play with food like the Brelands' pigs, the child's parents would not allow misbehavior to continue (e.g., remove the child's plate if dinner is not finished in a certain period of time). In other words, eating is reinforced on a differential reinforcement of high responding (DRH) schedule (see Chapter 6). But what if a parent would not stop misbehavior from occurring? If this was the case, misbehavior may well occur. Many years ago, I watched a young girl spend over an hour eating (playing) with her spaghetti at my middle son's football banquet. The child's parents allowed their daughter to take as long as she wanted to finish a meal. They reported that it took her so long to eat her cake at her last birthday party, that the other children opened her presents. Her parents also said that their son took a long time to eat, but not as long as his sister.

BEFORE YOU GO ON

- What predisposition allowed Sean to develop an aversion to Tony's mother's lasagna?

- What constraint prevented Sean from learning an aversion to his own mother's cooking?

SECTION REVIEW

- The view that some laws govern the learning of all behaviors has allowed psychologists to study behaviors in the laboratory that animals do not exhibit in natural settings and propose that learning functions to organize reflexes and random responses.

- Timberlake's behavior systems approach suggests that animals possess highly organized instinctive behavior systems that serve specific needs or functions in the animal.

- In Timberlake's view, learning modifies instinctive behavior systems and intensifies a motivational mode or changes the integration or sensitivity in a perceptual-motor module.

- Variations in learning are due either to predispositions, when an animal learns more rapidly or in a different form than expected, or constraints, when an animal learns less rapidly or completely than expected.

- Breland and Breland trained many exotic behaviors in a wide variety of animal species; however, they found that some operant responses, although initially performed effectively, deteriorated with continued training despite repeated food reinforcements.

- Animal misbehavior occurs when (1) the stimuli present during operant conditioning resemble the natural cues controlling food-gathering activities, (2) these stimuli are paired with food reinforcement, and (3) the instinctive food-gathering behaviors the stimuli elicit during conditioning are reinforced.

SCHEDULE-INDUCED BEHAVIOR

B. F. Skinner (1948) described an interesting pattern of behavior that pigeons exhibited when reinforced for key pecking on a fixed-interval schedule. When food reinforcement was delivered to the pigeons on a fixed-interval, 15-second schedule, they developed a "ritualistic" stereotyped pattern of behavior during the interval. The pattern of behavior differed from bird to bird: Some walked in circles between food presentations; others scratched the floor; still others moved their heads back and forth. Once a particular pattern of behavior emerged, the pigeons repeatedly exhibited it, with the frequency of the behavior increasing as the birds received more reinforcement. Skinner referred to the behaviors of his pigeons on the interval schedule as examples of **superstitious behavior**.

Why do animals exhibit superstitious behavior? One reasonable explanation suggests that animals have associated the superstitious behavior with reinforcement, and this association causes the animals to exhibit high levels of the superstitious behavior. However, Staddon and Simmelhag's (1971) analysis of superstitious behavior indicates it is not an example of the operant behavior Chapter 6 described. They identified two types of behavior produced when reinforcement (e.g., food) is programmed to occur on a regular basis: terminal behavior and interim behavior. **Terminal behavior** occurs during the last few seconds of the interval between reinforcer presentations, and it is reinforcer oriented. Staddon and Simmelhag's pigeons pecked on or near the food hopper that delivered food; this is an example of terminal behavior. **Interim behavior**, in contrast, is not reinforcer oriented. Although contiguity influences the development of terminal behavior, interim behavior does not occur contiguously with reinforcement. Terminal behavior falls between interim behavior and reinforcement but does not interfere with the exhibition of interim behavior.

According to Staddon and Simmelhag (1971), terminal behavior occurs in stimulus situations that are highly predictive of the occurrence of reinforcement; that is, terminal behavior is typically emitted just prior to reinforcement on a fixed-interval schedule. In contrast, interim behavior occurs during stimulus conditions that have a low probability of the occurrence of reinforcement; that is, interim behavior is observed most frequently in the period following reinforcement. When fixed-interval schedules of reinforcement elicit high levels of interim behavior, we refer to it as **schedule-induced behavior**.

Schedule-Induced Polydipsia

The most extensively studied form of schedule-induced behavior is the excessive intake of water (polydipsia) when animals are reinforced with food on a fixed-interval schedule. John Falk (1961) was the first investigator to observe **schedule-induced polydipsia**. Falk deprived rats of food until their body weight was approximately 70% to 80% of their initial weight and then trained them to bar press for food reinforcement. When water was available in an operant chamber, Falk found that the rats consumed excessive amounts of water. Even though Falk's rats were not water deprived, they drank large amounts of water; in fact, under certain conditions, animals provided food reinforcement on an interval schedule will consume as much as one-half their weight in water in a few hours. Note that water deprivation, heat stress, or providing a similar amount of food in one meal cannot produce this level of excessive drinking. Apparently, some important aspect of providing food on an interval schedule can elicit excessive drinking.

Is schedule-induced polydipsia an example of interim behavior? Recall Staddon and Simmelhag's (1971) definition: Interim behavior occurs in stimulus situations that have a low probability of reinforcement occurrence. Schedule-induced drinking does fit their definition: Animals reinforced on an interval schedule typically drink during the period following food consumption. In contrast, drinking usually does not occur in the period that precedes the availability of food reinforcement.

Researchers have consistently observed schedule-induced polydipsia in rats given food on an interval schedule (Wetherington, 1982). A variety of different interval schedules of reinforcement have been found to produce polydipsia. For example, Falk (1966) observed polydipsia in rats on a fixed-interval schedule, and Jacquet (1972) observed polydipsia on a variety of compound schedules of reinforcement. Schedule-induced polydipsia has also been found in species other than rats. For example, Shanab and Peterson (1969) reported this behavior in pigeons on an interval schedule of food reinforcement, and Schuster and Woods (1966) observed it in primates.

Other Schedule-Induced Behaviors

Several other instinctive behaviors are observed in animals on interval schedules. A number of psychologists (King, 1974; Staddon & Ayres, 1975) have reported that interval schedules of reinforcement produce high levels of wheel running. These researchers observed schedule-induced wheel running using both food and water reinforcement. Furthermore, Levitsky and Collier (1968) found that the highest rate of wheel running occurs in the time immediately following reinforcement and then decreases as the time for the next reinforcement nears. Moreover, Staddon and Ayres (1975) reported that as the interreinforcement interval increases, the intensity of wheel running initially increases and then declines.

Animals receiving reinforcement on an interval schedule will attack an appropriate target of aggressive behavior. For example, Cohen and Looney (1973) reported that pigeons will attack another bird or a stuffed model of a bird present during key pecking for reinforcement on an interval schedule. Similar schedule-induced aggression appears in squirrel monkeys (Hutchinson, Azrin, & Hunt, 1968) and rats (Knutson & Kleinknecht, 1970). Further, Knutson and Kleinknecht (1970) reported that the greatest intensity of aggressive behavior occurred in the immediate postreinforcement period.

The Nature of Schedule-Induced Behavior

Riley and Wetherington (1989) proposed that schedule-induced behavior is an instinctive behavior elicited by periodic reinforcement. The elicited nature of schedule-induced behavior is evident from the fact that animals continue to drink a flavor that was previously paired with illness. (Recall that an aversion to a flavor is established when the flavor is paired with illness.) The relative insensitivity of schedule-induced polydipsia to flavor aversion learning provides the strongest evidence that reinforcement elicits schedule-induced behavior.

Riley, Lotter, and Kulkosky (1979) provide evidence of this insensitivity. They gave two groups of animals spaced food sessions with water available for 13 days. This procedure resulted in schedule-induced polydipsia, or substantial water intake (see Figure 9.3). On Day 14, animals in Group P received an injection of lithium chloride (LiCl) after experiencing saccharin during the training session; this procedure paired saccharin consumption and illness and led to the establishment of an aversion to saccharin. Evidence of the aversion to saccharin in the Group P animals was the significant reduction in saccharin intake on the first test day (Day 16). The rats in Group S received saline after the training session with saccharin. These animals did not have saccharin paired with illness and developed no aversion to saccharin.

Figure 9.3 The mean consumption of water during the first 12 days of polydipsia acquisition followed by saccharin and water presentations on alternating days. The animals in Group P received a lithium chloride injection following saccharin consumption on Day 14, while saline followed saccharin in Group S animals. The rapid extinction of the saccharin aversion suggests an insensitivity to an aversive flavor in a schedule-induced polydipsia situation.

A different result was obtained on the third test day. The saccharin intake in Group P was equal to saccharin intake in Group S by the third test day (Day 20; see Figure 9.3). The rapid extinction of a saccharin aversion in Group P was much faster than we would generally see with flavor aversions (Elkins, 1973). This rapid extinction suggests an insensitivity of schedule-induced polydipsia to an aversive flavor. It is possible, however, that only a weak aversion was established when saccharin was paired with illness in the schedule-induced polydipsia paradigm.

Hyson, Sickel, Kulkosky, and Riley (1981) evaluated the possibility that the rapid extinction of the saccharin aversion was due to a weak flavor aversion established in a schedule-induced polydipsia situation. These researchers initially established a flavor aversion by pairing saccharin with illness in the animals' home cages. These animals were given either one, two, or four saccharin-illness pairings. After flavor aversion conditioning, animals received either a single meal or periodic meals in the training situation outside the home cage. The periodic meals (SIP treatment) produced excessive fluid consumption, while the single meal (PD treatment) did not. The researchers found greater suppression of saccharin intake in the PD treatment than the SIP treatment during the entire extinction period procedure (see Figure 9.4). The suppression over the course of extinction trials in the PD treatment indicates a strong flavor aversion to saccharin. Yet, the animals in the periodic meals treatment drank significantly more saccharin than did animals in the massed feeding treatment. The increased consumption in the SIP treatment was found even with four saccharin-illness pairings. This result provides strong support for the view that schedule-induced polydipsia is relatively insensitive to a flavor

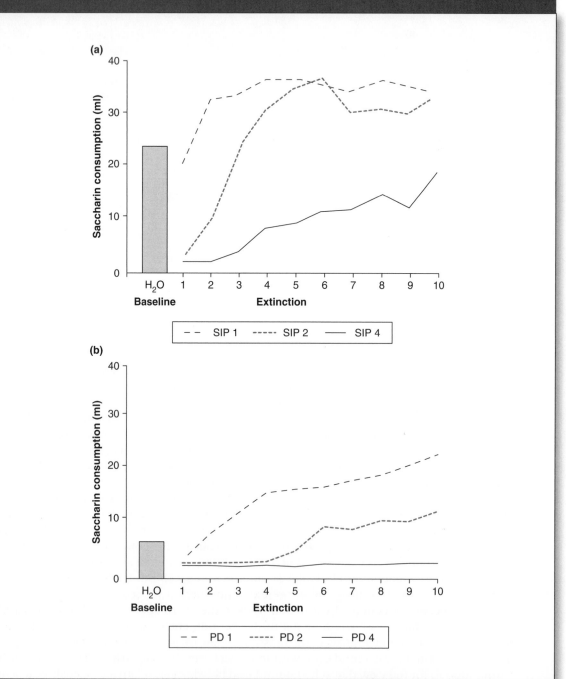

Figure 9.4 The mean consumption of saccharin for groups SIP-1, SIP-2, and SIP-4 (top graph) and for groups PD-1, PD-2, and PD-4, (bottom graph). The intake of saccharin was much higher for animals receiving periodic food reinforcements in the training environment (SIP groups) than for animals receiving food in a single meal (PD groups). Also, the greater the number of saccharin-lithium chloride pairings, the stronger the suppression of saccharin intake.

aversion. Further, the continued consumption of saccharin despite its aversion in the SIP treatment indicates that food elicits drinking.

Does Schedule-Induced Behavior Occur in Humans?

In many situations in our society, reinforcement is programmed to occur on an interval schedule. Furthermore, excessive levels of instinctive appetitive behaviors do often occur in humans. Gilbert (1974) suggested that interval schedules could be responsible for some people's excessive consumption of alcohol. Gilbert's demonstration that rats on an interval schedule consume excessive levels of ethanol supports his view. Animals do not normally drink any ethanol, and the use of an interval schedule of reinforcement is one of the few ways of inducing them to drink alcohol. Other researchers (Colotla, 1981; Samson & Pfeffer, 1987; Tang, Kenny, & Falk, 1984) also have found that intermittent schedules of reinforcement produce excessive consumption of alcohol.

There is considerable evidence that schedule-induced polydipsia is a good animal model of human alcoholism (Riley & Wetherington, 1989). Animals on an intermittent schedule of reinforcement exhibit behaviors characteristic of human alcoholism: They drink alcohol excessively and chronically on an intermittent schedule of reinforcement (Falk, Samson, & Tang, 1973), consume sufficient alcohol to produce blood alcohol levels analogous to that seen in human alcoholics (Leander, McMillan, & Ellis, 1976), show tolerance to the effects of alcohol (Samson & Falk, 1974), experience withdrawal (e.g., audiogenic seizures) from the effects of alcohol consumption (Falk & Samson, 1976), come to prefer alcohol over a sucrose solution (Falk, Samson, & Winger, 1976), and emit an operant response to obtain access to alcohol (Meisch & Thompson, 1974).

If schedule-induced polydipsia is a good animal model of human alcoholism, it is important to show that intermittent schedules of reinforcement produce excessive alcohol consumption in humans. Doyle and Samson (1988) provide evidence that intermittent schedules can produce excessive alcohol consumption in humans. They allowed human subjects access to beer while they played a gambling game for monetary reinforcements. Doyle and Samson reported that subjects assigned to a FI 90-second schedule of reinforcement drank significantly more beer than did subjects assigned to a FI 30-second schedule of reinforcement. The increased beer consumption with a longer intermittent schedule of reinforcement is consistent with the literature showing that polydipsia increases in animals with longer schedules of reinforcement (Flory, 1971).

Falk (1998) suggests that alcoholism is not the only addictive behavior produced by exposure to an intermittent schedule of reinforcement. Lau, Neal, and Falk (1996) found that rats drank significant amounts of a cocaine solution on an interval schedule, while Nader and Woolverton (1992) reported that cocaine self-administration in primates was higher on a fixed-interval than a fixed-ratio schedule. Further, Nader and Woolverton found that the amount of cocaine self-administered increased as the fixed-interval schedule increased. Addictive behaviors such as excessive smoking and eating have been observed in the interval following reinforcement in real-world settings (Cantor & Wilson, 1984; Cherek, 1982).

While there have been a number of demonstrations of schedule-induced behavior in humans, some important distinctions exist between research with animals and humans (Sanger, 1986). Unlike the consistently powerful demonstration of schedule-induced behavior in animals, evidence indicates that schedule-induced behavior in humans is often weak and variable. Also, schedule-induced behavior develops slowly in animals but is seen on the first trial in humans. The reasons for differences between animals and humans await future investigation. Further, the real-world relevance of the findings of human schedule-induced behavior is unclear. Schedule-induced behavior in humans decreases even with very short intervals (approximately 240 seconds) between reinforcements. As reinforcers typically occur farther apart in the real world, it is speculative whether interval reinforcement schedules lead to excessive consummatory behavior in humans.

FLAVOR AVERSION LEARNING

I have a friend who refuses to walk down an aisle in a supermarket where tomato sauce is displayed; he says that even the sight of cans of tomatoes makes him ill. My oldest son once got sick after eating string beans, and now he refuses to touch them. I once was very nauseated several hours after eating at a local restaurant, and I have not returned since. In the chapter-opening vignette, we learned that Sean became ill several hours after eating lasagna and now the sight or smell of lasagna makes him nauseous. Almost all of us have some food that we will not eat or a restaurant we avoid. Often the reason for this behavior is that at some time we experienced illness after eating a particular food or in a particular place, and we associated the event with the illness through classical conditioning. Such an experience engenders a **flavor aversion** to the taste of the food or the place itself. Subsequently, we avoid it.

In Chapter 4, we learned that contiguity plays a critical role in the acquisition of a conditioned response: Little conditioning occurs if the CS precedes the UCS by several seconds or minutes. However, animals will develop aversions to taste cues even when the taste stimulus precedes illness by several hours. This indicates that, unlike other conditioned responses, the flavor aversion does not depend on contiguity. The association of a flavor with illness is often referred to as **long-delay learning**; this term suggests a difference between flavor aversion learning and other examples of classical conditioning.

The Selectivity of Flavor Aversion Learning

We also discovered in Chapter 4 that stimuli differ in salience; that is, some stimuli are more likely than others to become associated with a particular UCS. Garcia and Koelling's (1966) classic study shows that a taste is more salient when preceding illness than when preceding shock, whereas a light or a tone is more salient when preceding shock than when preceding illness. In Garcia and Koelling's study, rats were exposed to either a saccharin taste cue or a light and tone compound stimulus. Following exposure to one of these cues, animals received either an electric shock or irradiation-induced illness. Figure 9.5 presents the results of the study. The animals exhibited an aversion to saccharin when it was paired with illness but not when it was paired with shock. In addition, they developed a fear of the light and tone stimulus when it was paired with shock but not when paired with illness.

On the basis of the Garcia and Koelling study, Seligman (1970) proposed that rats have an evolutionary preparedness to associate tastes with illness. Further support for this view is the observation that adult rats acquire an intense aversion to a flavor after a single taste-illness pairing. Young animals also acquire a strong aversion after one pairing (S. B. Klein, Domato, Hallstead, Stephens, & Mikulka, 1975). Apparently, taste cues are very salient in terms of their associability with illness. The salience of lasagna undoubtedly was responsible for the fact that Sean, described in our chapter-opening vignette, developed an aversion to lasagna after a single experience of becoming ill after eating lasagna.

Seligman (1970) also suggested that rats are contraprepared to become afraid of a light or tone paired with illness. However, other research (S. B. Klein, Freda, & Mikulka, 1985) indicates that rats can associate an environmental cue with illness. Klein et al. found that rats avoided a distinctive black compartment previously paired with an illness-inducing apormorphine or lithium chloride injection, while Revusky and Parker (1976) observed that rats did not eat out of a

Figure 9.5 Effects of pairing a gustatory cue or an auditory cue with either external pain or internal illness. In this study, animals readily associated flavor with illness and a click with electric shock, but they did not associate food with electric shock and a click with illness.

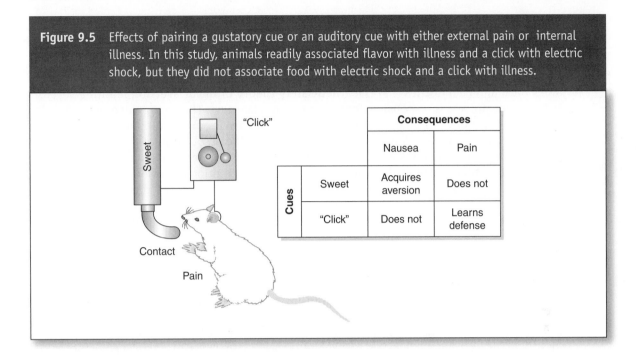

container that had been paired with illness induced by lithium chloride. Although animals can acquire environmental aversions, more trials and careful training procedures are necessary to establish an environmental aversion than a flavor aversion (Riccio & Haroutunian, 1977).

Although rats form flavor aversions more readily than environmental aversions, other species do not show this pattern of stimulus salience. Unlike rats, birds acquire visual aversions more rapidly than taste aversions. For example, Wilcoxin, Dragoin, and Kral (1971) induced illness in quail that had consumed sour blue water. They reported that an aversion formed to the blue color, but not to the sour taste. Similarly, Capretta (1961) found greater salience of visual cues than taste cues in chickens.

Why are visual cues more salient than taste stimuli in birds? According to Garcia, Hankins, and Rusiniak (1974), this salience hierarchy is adaptive. Since birds' seeds are covered by a hard, flavorless shell, they must use visual cues to assess whether food is poisoned; thus, visual cues enable birds to avoid consuming poisonous seeds. Although this view seems reasonable, it does not appear to be completely accurate. According to Braveman (1974, 1975), the feeding time characteristic of a particular species determines the relative salience of stimuli becoming associated with illness. Rats, which are nocturnal animals, locate their food at night and therefore rely less on visual information than on gustatory information to identify poisoned food. In contrast, birds search for their food during the day, and visual information plays an important role in controlling their food intake. Braveman evaluated this view by examining the salience hierarchies of guinea pigs, which, like birds, seek their food during the day. Braveman found visual cues to be more salient than taste stimuli for guinea pigs.

Nature of Flavor Aversion Learning

Why do animals and people develop aversions to a specific food consumed prior to illness, despite a delay of several hours between consumption of the food and illness? Two very different theories attempt to explain long-delay flavor aversion learning: Kalat and Rozin's (1971) learned-safety theory and Revusky's (1977) concurrent interference theory. Research suggests that each process contributes to flavor aversion learning.

Learned-Safety Theory

James Kalat and Paul Rozin's (1971) **learned-safety theory of flavor aversion learning** suggests that a unique process is responsible for flavor aversion learning. The contiguity process detailed in Chapter 4 has obvious adaptive significance for most Pavlovian conditioning situations. For example, a child touches a flame and experiences pain. The association of the flame with pain produces the conditioned response of fear; fear elicited on subsequent exposure to the flame motivates this child to avoid pain. However, since the consumption of poisoned food rarely produces immediate illness, the contiguity process characteristic of other classical conditioning situations will not enable an animal to associate food and illness. In Kalat and Rozin's view, a mechanism unique to learning a flavor aversion evolved to allow animals to avoid potentially lethal foods.

An animal exposed to a new food consumes only a small portion of it. This low intake of a novel food, called **ingestional neophobia**, has adaptive significance: It prevents animals from consuming large quantities of a potentially poisonous food, so that if the food is poisonous, the animals will become sick but not die. According to Kalat and Rozin (1971), if an animal becomes sick within several hours after food consumption, it will associate the food with illness and develop an aversion to that food. However, if illness does not occur, the animal learns the food is not poisonous and that it can safely consume the food again. Learned safety overcomes an animal's reluctance to eat new foods, enabling it to eat foods that enhance its survival.

Kalat and Rozin (1973), seeking to provide support for their learned-safety view, gave animals one of three treatments. One group of rats received a novel flavor 4 hours before being made sick (4-P treatment). A second group was made sick half an hour after receiving the novel food (1/2-P treatment). A third group was given access to the novel flavor and was again exposed to it 3.5 hours later; illness followed half an hour later (3 1/2–1/2-P treatment). A contiguity view of classical conditioning predicts the flavor aversion will be equally strong in the second and third groups because a half-hour interval separated the flavor and illness in both groups, and the aversion should be weaker in the first group because a 4-hour interval separated the flavor and illness. In contrast, the learned-safety view assumes a strong aversion in the second group and a weak aversion in the first and third groups because the rats in both the first and third groups had 4 hours after consumption of the novel flavor to learn it was safe. As Figure 9.6 demonstrates, the results of Kalat and Rozin's study support a learned-safety view of flavor aversion learning.

Concurrent Interference View

Sam Revusky (1971) argues that associative processes influence flavor aversion learning. Pavlovian conditioning reflects the association of a CS with a UCS. However, what happens when an animal experiences several stimuli prior to the UCS? According to Revusky, proximity is a critical factor in conditioning; the stimulus occurring closest to the UCS will become able to elicit the CR. If another stimulus intervenes between the CS and UCS, it will produce **concurrent interference**, or the prevention of the CS becoming associated with the UCS and able to elicit the CR. After eating a food, an animal is unlikely to consume another food for several hours. Thus, long-delay learning occurs in flavor aversion learning as a result of the absence of concurrent interference.

Revusky (1971) conducted a number of studies showing that the presence of other taste cues can interfere with the establishment of a flavor aversion. In a typical study, rats received initial exposure to saccharin (CS) followed by illness 75 minutes later. A second flavor was introduced

Figure 9.6 Mean casein hydrolysate consumption for 1/2-P, 3 1/2-1/2-P, and 4-P treatment conditions. The results of this study showed that a significantly stronger aversion to casein hydrolysate developed in the 1/2-P treatment animals than in either the 3 1/2-1/2-P or 4-P treatment animals.

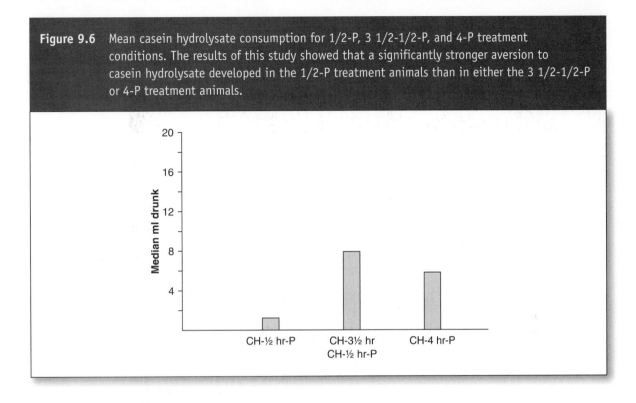

15 minutes after the CS and 1 hour before the UCS. For some subjects, tap water was the second solution; for others, it was vinegar. Revusky reported a weaker aversion to saccharin when vinegar rather than water was used as the second solution, indicating that the presentation of vinegar interfered with the establishment of the saccharin aversion. Furthermore, the amount of concurrent interference was related to the intensity of the vinegar: the stronger the vinegar, the weaker the aversion to saccharin.

Flavor Aversion Learning in Humans

We learned in Chapter 4 that many people report acquiring a flavor aversion as the result of illness after ingesting a particular food or drink. Research (Logue, 1985) has documented the establishment of food aversions in people. In one study, Bernstein (1978) found that children in the early stages of cancer acquired an aversion to a distinctively flavored Mapletoff ice cream (maple and black walnut flavor) consumed before toxic chemotherapy that affects the gastrointestinal (GI) tract. Instead of eating Mapletoff ice cream, these children now preferred either to play with a toy or to eat another flavor of ice cream. In contrast, both children who had previously received the toxic therapy to the GI tract without the Mapletoff ice cream and children who had been given the Mapletoff ice cream before toxic chemotherapy without GI-tract involvement continued to eat the Mapletoff ice cream. Bernstein and Webster (1980) reported similar results in adults.

Both adult and child cancer patients receiving radiation therapy typically lose weight (Bernstein, 1991). These cancer patients also show an aversion to foods eaten prior to chemotherapy (Bernstein & Webster, 1980; Carrell, Cannon, Best, & Stone, 1986). The association of hospital food with illness is a likely cause of the weight loss seen in cancer patients. Can this weight loss be prevented? Experiencing the hospital food without illness prior to the introduction of chemotherapy might work, or experiencing illness without the hospital food might also work. (Refer back to the discussion of the CS preexposure and UCS preexposure effects for an explanation of why these two procedures might reduce the weight loss that occurs with chemotherapy.) Can you think of any other possibilities?

BEFORE YOU GO ON

- Would the presence of an interval schedule at work cause Sean to eat lasagna at home? At work?

- How would Kalat and Rozin's learned-safety theory explain Sean's aversion to lasagna?

SECTION REVIEW

- A wide variety of instinctive behaviors occur at excessive levels with an interval schedule of reinforcement; the highest levels occur in the time period following reinforcement.

- Schedule-induced behavior appears to reflect the elicitation of instinctive consummatory behavior by periodic reinforcements.

- When an animal or person experiences illness after eating a particular food, an association develops between the food and the illness.

- Nocturnal animals, like rats, associate flavor more readily with illness than with environmental events; in contrast, visual stimuli are more salient than flavor cues in diurnal animals like birds or guinea pigs.

- Kalat and Rozin's learned-safety view assumes that when an animal eats a food and no illness results, it learns that the food can be safely consumed; however, if the animal becomes ill after eating, the animal will learn to avoid that food.

- Revusky's concurrent interference theory proposes that an aversion may not develop if other foods are experienced between the initial food and the illness.

IMPRINTING

Infant Love

You have undoubtedly seen young ducks swimming behind their mother in a lake. What process is responsible for the young birds' attachment to their mother? Konrad Lorenz (1952) investigated this social attachment process, calling it **imprinting**. Lorenz found that a newly hatched bird approaches, follows, and forms a social attachment to the first moving object it encounters. Although typically the first object that the young bird sees is its mother, birds have imprinted to many different and sometimes peculiar objects. In a classic demonstration of imprinting, newly hatched goslings imprinted to Konrad Lorenz and thereafter followed him everywhere (see Figure 9.7). Birds have imprinted to colored boxes and other inanimate objects as well as to animals of different species. After imprinting, the young animal prefers the imprinted object to its real mother; this shows the strength of imprinting.

Although animals have imprinted to a wide variety of objects, certain characteristics of the object affect the likelihood of imprinting. For example, Klopfer (1971) found that ducklings imprinted

Figure 9.7   The newly hatched greylag goslings imprinted on Konrad Lorenz and followed him wherever he went.

more readily to a moving object than a stationary object. Also, ducks are more likely to imprint to an object that (1) makes "lifelike" rather than "gliding" movements (Fabricius, 1951); (2) vocalizes rather than remains silent (Collias & Collias, 1956); (3) emits short, rhythmic sounds rather than long, high-pitched sounds (Weidman, 1956); and (4) measures about 10 centimeters (cm) in diameter (Schulman, Hale, & Graves, 1970).

Harry Harlow (1971) observed that baby primates readily became attached to a soft terry cloth surrogate mother but developed no attachment to a wire mother. Harlow and Suomi (1970) found that infant monkeys preferred a terry cloth mother to a rayon, vinyl, or sandpaper surrogate; liked clinging to a rocking mother rather than to a stationary mother; and chose a warm (temperature) mother over a cold one. Mary Ainsworth and her associates (Ainsworth, 1982; Blehar, Lieberman, & Ainsworth, 1977) reported that human infants also need a warm, responsive mother for social attachment; they found a strong attachment to mothers who were responsive and sensitive to their children's needs. In contrast, infants showed little attachment to anxious or indifferent mothers.

Age plays an important role in the imprinting process. Imprinting occurs readily during certain sensitive periods and is less likely to occur following this sensitive period. Illustrating the importance of age in imprinting, Jaynes's (1956) study exposed newly hatched New Hampshire chicks to cardboard cubes at different times. Jaynes reported that five-sixths of the chicks imprinted within 1 to 6 hours after hatching. However, only five-sevenths of the chicks imprinted when exposed to a cardboard cube 6 to 12 hours after hatching. The percentage declined to three-fifths at 24 to 30 hours, two-fifths at 30 to 36 hours, and only one-fifth at 48 to 54 hours.

However, the sensitive period merely reflects a lesser degree of difficulty in forming an attachment; when sufficient experience is given, imprinting will occur after the sensitive period has lapsed. For example, J. S. Brown (1975) trained ducklings ranging in age from 20 to 120 hours to follow an object. Brown found that although the older the duckling, the longer the time required for it to follow the imprinted object, all the ducklings with sufficient training showed an equal degree of attachment to the imprinted object.

The sensitive period for social attachment differs among species; in sheep and goats, it is 2 to 3 hours after birth (Klopfer, Adams, & Klopfer, 1964); in primates, 3 to 6 months; and in humans, 6 to 12 months (Harlow, 1971).

A young animal's attachment to "mother" is not the only form of imprinting. In the next section, we examine sexual preference as another instance of imprinting.

Sexual Preference

Konrad Lorenz (1952) reported an interesting behavior in one of his male jackdaws. The bird attempted courtship feeding with him: It finely minced worms, mixed them with saliva, and attempted to place the worms in Lorenz's mouth. When Lorenz did not open his mouth, he got an earful of worm pulp. Lorenz suggested that the male jackdaw had sexually imprinted to him. The sexual preference of many birds is established during a sensitive period (Eibl-Eibesfeldt, 1970; Lorenz, 1970). Also, the birds' sexual preference does not have to be for their own species; that is, a sexual preference can be established to another species if exposure occurs during the sensitive period. Since sexual preference develops in immature birds when copulation is impossible, the establishment of the birds' sexual preference does not depend upon sexual reinforcement. Further, the imprinted bird's sexual preference is not modified even after sexual experience with another bird species.

Nature of Imprinting

What process allows animals to develop a social attachment (or sexual preference) during a specific developmental period? Two different views of imprinting have been offered: One suggests that associative learning is responsible for imprinting, and the other proposes that genetic programming produces imprinting. The evidence indicates that both instinctive and associative processes contribute to the imprinting process.

An Associative View of Imprinting

Moltz (1960, 1963) proposed that classical and operant conditioning are responsible for social imprinting. Consider the imprinting of a chick to its mother to illustrate the **associative learning view of imprinting**. When the chick is old enough to move around in its environment, any large object (e.g., mother) in the environment attracts the chick's attention, and it orients toward the object. The chick at this developmental age has little fear of new objects in its environment; therefore, only a low level of arousal will be conditioned to these objects. When the chick's fear system does emerge, new objects will elicit high levels of arousal. Since familiar objects produce only low levels of arousal, their presence elicits relief. This relief reduces the chick's fear and enables it to reach the familiar object. Thus, the chick develops an attachment to mother (or any other object) because her presence elicits relief and reduces fear. A considerable amount of literature indicates that the imprinted object does have fear-reducing properties. For example, Bateson (1969) and Hoffman (1968) noted that the imprinting object's presence reduced distress vocalizations in birds. Harry Harlow's (1971) classic research with primates clearly shows the fear-reducing properties of "mama."

Harlow (1971) observed that young primates up to 3 months old do not exhibit any fear of new events; after 3 months, a novel object elicits intense fear. Young primates experience a rapid reduction in fear when clinging to their mother. For example, 3-month-old primates are extremely frightened when introduced to a mechanical monster or plastic toy and will run to their mother; clinging to her apparently causes the young primates' fear to dissipate. Human children show a similar development of fear at approximately 6 months of age (Schaffer & Emerson, 1964). Before this time, they exhibit no fear of new objects. An unfamiliar object elicits fear after children are 6-months-old, with children reacting by running to mother and clinging to her, which causes their fear to subside.

Is this fear reduction responsible for the young primate's or human's attachment to "mother"? Harlow (1971) developed two inanimate surrogate mothers to investigate the factors that influence attachment to the mother (see Figure 9.8). Each "mother" had a bare body of welded wire; one had only the wire body, and the other was covered with soft terry cloth. In typical studies, primates were raised with both a wire and a cloth-covered surrogate mother. While both the wire and cloth surrogate mothers were equally unresponsive, frightened young primates experienced fear reduction when clinging to the cloth mother but showed no reduction in distress when with their wire mother. When aroused, the infants were extremely motivated to reach their cloth mother, even jumping over a high Plexiglas barrier to get to it. In contrast, the frightened young primates showed no desire to approach the wire mother. Also, the young primate preferred to

Figure 9.8   Cloth and wire surrogate mothers.

remain with the cloth mother in the presence of a dangerous object rather than to run away alone; however, if the wire mother was present, the frightened primate ran away.

Mary Ainsworth and her colleagues (Ainsworth, 1982; Blehar et al., 1977) reported a similar reaction in human infants. Consider the Blehar et al. (1977) study to illustrate this maternal attraction. They initially observed the maternal behavior of white middle-class Americans feeding their infants from birth to 54 weeks of age. They identified two categories of maternal care: One group was mothers who were attentive to their children during feeding; the other mothers were indifferent to their infants' needs. During the second stage of their study, Blehar et al. examined the behavior of these infants at 1 year of age in a strange environment. In the unfamiliar place, the interested mothers' children occasionally sought their mothers' attention; when left alone in a strange situation, these children were highly motivated to remain with the mother when reunited. In addition, once these children felt secure in the new place, they explored and played with toys. The researchers called this type of mother–infant bond a **secure relationship**. The behavior of these secure children strikingly resembles the response of Harlow's monkeys to the cloth mother. In contrast to this secure relationship, children of indifferent mothers frequently cried and were apparently distressed. Their alarm was not reduced by the presence of the mother. Also, these children avoided contact with their mothers, either because the mothers were uninterested or because the mothers actually rejected them. The researchers labeled this mother–infant interaction an **anxious relationship**. The failure of the mothers of these anxious children to induce security certainly parallels the infant primates' response to the wire surrogate mother.

Moltz's (1960, 1963) associative view of imprinting suggests that initial conditioning of low arousal to the imprinting object develops because the object is attention provoking, orienting the animal toward the imprinting object. Chicks imprint more readily to objects moving away than to objects moving toward them. One would assume that advancing objects would be more attention provoking than retreating objects. Chicks' greater imprinting to objects moving away argues against an explanation of imprinting based only on simple associative learning. This observation also points to another problem with an associative learning view: Some objects are more likely than others to become imprinting objects. For example, animals imprint more readily to objects having characteristics of adult members of their species.

A simple associative explanation of imprinting would not assume that the characteristics of the imprinting object are important: Any object attracting the animal's attention prior to the development of fear should become able to provide relief, and therefore, a strong attachment should ensue. The fact that the specific attributes of the object are important in the formation of a social attachment argues against a purely associative explanation of imprinting.

An Instinctive View of Imprinting

Konrad Lorenz (1935) suggested that imprinting is a genetically programmed form of learning. Hess (1973) eloquently describes the role of instinct in the social attachment of the young mallard to its mother:

> We must consider that young ducks innately possess a schema of the natural imprinting object, so that the more a social object fits this schema, the stronger the imprinting that occurs to the object. This innate disposition with regard to the type of object learned indicates that social imprinting is not just simply an extremely powerful effect of the environment upon the behavior of an animal. Rather, there has been an evolutionary pressure for the young bird to learn the right thing—the natural parent—at the right time—the first day of life—the time of the sensitive period that has been genetically provided for. (p. 380)

Several observations support an **instinctive view of imprinting** (Graham, 1989). The animal's response to the imprinting object is less susceptible to change than is an animal's reaction to events acquired through conventional associative learning. For example, conditioned stimuli that elicit saliva quickly extinguish when food is discontinued. Similarly, the absence of shock produces a rapid extinction of fear. In contrast, the elimination of reinforcement does not typically lead to a loss of reaction to an imprinting object.

While punishment quickly alters an animal's response to conditioned stimuli associated with reinforcement, animals seem insensitive to punishment from an imprinting object. Kovach and Hess (1963) found that chicks approached the imprinting object despite its administration of electric shock. Harlow's (1971) research shows how powerful the social attachment of the infant primate is to its surrogate mother. Harlow constructed four abusive "monster mothers." One rocked violently from time to time; a second projected an air blast in the infant's face. Primate infants clung to these mothers even as they were abused. The other two monster mothers were even more abusive: One tossed the infant off her, and the other shot brass spikes as the infant approached. Although the infants were unable to cling to these mothers continuously, they resumed clinging as soon as possible after the abuse stopped.

THE AVOIDANCE OF AVERSIVE EVENTS

Species-Specific Defense Reactions

We discovered earlier in the chapter that animals possess instinctive responses enabling them to obtain reinforcement (e.g., food, water, mate). Robert Bolles (1970, 1978) suggested that animals also have **species-specific defense reactions** (SSDR) that allow them to avoid dangerous events. According to Bolles, animals have little opportunity to learn to avoid danger: They either possess an instinctive means of keeping out of trouble, or they perish. For example, a deer does not have time to learn to avoid its predator. Unless the deer possesses an instinct for avoiding predators, it will probably wind up as a predator's meal.

The instinctive responses that enable animals to avoid aversive events differ. An animal's evolutionary history determines which behaviors will become SSDRs: Responses that enable animals to avoid aversive events will remain in their genetic programming, whereas nonadaptive responses will not be passed on to future generations. Since evolution has proved the species-specific defense reactions to be effective and other behaviors likely to produce failure, behaviors other than the species-specific defense reactions probably would be nonadaptive. Thus, animals limit their reactions to SSDRs as they attempt to avoid danger.

Rats employ three different species-specific defense reactions: running, freezing, and fighting. They attempt to run from a distant danger; a close danger motivates freezing. When these two responses fail, rats use aggressive behavior to avoid aversive events. Other animals employ different instinctive responses to avoid danger: The mouse, as Bolles (1970) suggests in a quote from Robert Burns's "To a Mouse," is "a wee timorous beastie" when experiencing danger because this is the only way this small and relatively defenseless animal can avoid danger. In contrast, the bird flies away.

A study by Bolles and Collier (1976) demonstrates that the cues that predict danger not only motivate defensive behavior but also determine which response rats will exhibit when they expect danger. Bolles and Collier's rats received shock in a square or a rectangular box. After they experienced the shock, the rats either remained in the dangerous environment or were placed in another box where no shocks were given. The researchers found that defensive behavior occurred only when the rats remained in the compartment where they had been shocked.

Also, Bolles and Collier found that a dangerous square compartment produced a freezing response, while a dangerous rectangular box caused the rats to run. These results suggest that the particular SSDR produced depends on the nature of the environment.

Psychologists have found that animals easily learn to avoid an aversive event when they can use an SSDR. For example, rats readily learn to run to avoid being shocked. Similarly, pigeons easily learn to avoid shock by flying from perch to perch. In contrast, animals have difficulty learning to avoid an aversive event when they must emit a behavior other than an SSDR to avoid the aversive event. D'Amato and Schiff's (1964) study provides an example of this difficulty. Trying to train rats to bar press to avoid electric shock, D'Amato and Schiff reported that over half their rats, even after having participated in more than 7,000 trials over a 4-month period, failed to learn the avoidance response.

Bolles (1969) provided additional evidence of the importance of instinct in avoidance learning. He reported that rats quickly learned to run in an activity wheel to avoid electric shock, but he found no evidence of learning when the rats were required to stand on their hind legs to avoid shock (see Figure 9.9). Although Bolles's rats stood on their hind legs in an attempt to escape from the compartment where they were receiving shock, these rats did not learn the same behavior to avoid shock. According to Bolles, the rats' natural response in a small compartment was to freeze, and this innate SSDR prevented them from learning a response other than a species-specific defensive reaction as the avoidance behavior.

Figure 9.9 Percentage of avoidance responses during training in animals that could avoid shock by running or standing on their hind legs. The results of this study show that avoidance learning was significantly greater if the rats could run to avoid shock.

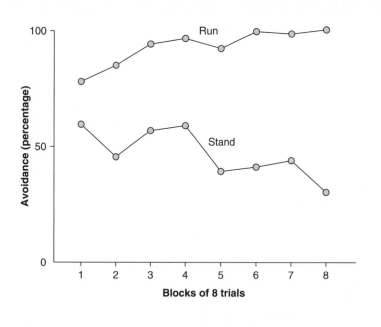

Predispositions and Avoidance Learning

Bolles (1978) suggested that aversive events elicit instinctive species-specific defensive responses. The environment present during aversive events becomes able to produce these instinctive defensive reactions as a conditioned response. Whereas instinctive CRs to cues associated with reinforcement elicit approach and contact behavior that enables an animal to obtain reinforcement, stimuli associated with aversive events produce instinctive defensive responses that allow the animal to avoid aversive events. Bolles's approach suggests that classical conditioning, rather than operant conditioning, is responsible for avoidance learning.

Bolles and Riley's (1973) study shows that reinforcement is not responsible for the rapid acquisition of avoidance behavior. In their study, some animals could avoid being shocked by freezing. Bolles and Riley reported that after only a few minutes of training, their animals were freezing most of the time. Two additional groups were included in their study: One group was punished for freezing and could avoid shock by not freezing; the other group was shocked regardless of their behavior. Bolles and Riley observed that the rats punished for freezing still froze much of the time. Furthermore, rats punished for freezing froze as much as the rats shocked regardless of their behavior.

Bolles (1978) suggested that when an animal is in a small, confined area and anticipates an aversive event, it freezes. The animals punished for freezing would still have frozen all the time, in Bolles's view, had frequent shocks not disrupted their freezing. Yet, as soon as the shock ended, the anticipation elicited the instinctive freezing response. Thus, with the exception of shock-induced disruption of freezing in animals punished for freezing, animals either reinforced or punished for freezing showed equivalent levels of freezing behavior. These results suggest that the contingency between the freezing response and the aversive event did not affect these animals' behavior.

BEFORE YOU GO ON

- Can imprinting explain Sean's preference for his mother's cooking?
- Is an SSDR involved in Sean's avoidance of lasagna?

SECTION REVIEW

- Young animals develop strong attachments to their mothers through the imprinting process.
- Animals are most likely to imprint during a specified period of development called a sensitive period.
- The animal's attachment to the imprinted object reflects both associative and instinctive processes.
- Sexual preference is another form of imprinting.
- Animals possess instinctive responses called species-specific defense reactions (SSDRs) that allow them to avoid dangerous events.
- Once animals anticipate danger, they will readily learn to avoid it if a species-specific defense reaction is effective.

James Olds (1922–1976)

Olds received his doctorate from Harvard University in the Department of Social Relations under Talcott Parsons. He then did postdoctoral work at McGill University in Canada with Donald Hebb. While at McGill, he discovered, while working with Peter Milner, the reinforcing effect of brain stimulation. Olds taught at the University of Michigan for 12 years and at the California Institute of Technology for 7 years until his untimely death from a swimming accident. He was awarded the Distinguished Scientific Contribution Award by the American Psychological Association in 1967.

THE BIOLOGY OF REINFORCEMENT

People's responses to reinforcement differ considerably. Some people are intensely motivated to obtain reinforcement; others show a lack of interest. Although psychological factors clearly can affect sensitivity to reinforcement, the evidence indicates that several brain systems also are significantly involved in the response to reinforcement.

Electrical Stimulation of the Brain

James Olds and Peter Milner (1954) found that stimulation of some areas of the brain is reinforcing. Interestingly, they made their classic observations accidentally, while trying to determine the effects of activating the reticular formation. Their electrode placement mistakenly swung forward into the hypothalamus. When this area was aroused, their rats behaved as if the stimulation was reinforcing. For example, the rats strongly preferred the place on the long table where they received the stimulation.

To evaluate their findings further, Olds and Milner (1954) made the electrical stimulation contingent on pressing a bar in an operant chamber (see Figure 9.10). They found that the rats pressed a bar to receive brain stimulation. The animals' behavior to obtain brain stimulation is called either **electrical stimulation of the brain** (ESB) or intracranial self-stimulation (ICSS). Many species, including pigeons (Goodman & Brown, 1966), rats (Olds & Milner, 1954), dogs (Wauquier & Sadowski, 1978), primates (Aou, Oomura, Woody, & Nishino, 1988), and humans (Ervin, Mark, & Stevens, 1969) have demonstrated that brain stimulation can be reinforcing.

The Influence of the Medial Forebrain Bundle

Larry Stein and his associates (Stein & Wise, 1973) presented evidence suggesting that a group of nerve fibers, the **medial forebrain bundle** (MFB) located in the limbic system, is the brain's reinforcement center. Stimulation of the MFB has four characteristics: (1) It is highly reinforcing; (2) it motivates behavior; (3) its functioning is stimulated by the presence of reinforcers; and (4) its reinforcing effects are enhanced by deprivation. We discuss each of these characteristics in the following sections.

The Reinforcing Effect of MFB Stimulation

You place a dollar in a video poker machine and pull the lever. When the machine stops spinning, you get four aces and win $200. Not surprisingly, you shout with joy. Why are you so overjoyed after winning $200? The research on MFB stimulation provides a likely answer.

Valenstein and Beer's (1964) study of the reinforcing properties of brain stimulation in rats found that for weeks, rats would press a bar that delivered stimulation of the MFB up to 30 times per minute, stopping for only a short time to eat and groom. These rats responded until exhausted, fell asleep for several hours, and awoke to resume bar pressing. But would electrical

Figure 9.10 (a) A rat presses a bar for electrical brain stimulation (ESB). (b) A sample cumulative record. Note the extremely high rate of responding (over 2,000 bar presses per hour) that occurred for more than 24 hours and was followed by a period of sleep.

stimulation of the brain (ESB) have a more powerful effect on behavior than conventional rein-forcers such as food, water, or sex? Routtenberg and Lindy (1965) constructed a situation in which pressing one bar initiated brain stimulation and pressing another bar produced food. The rats in this experiment were placed in this situation for only one hour a day and had no other food source. Still, all of the rats spent the entire hour pressing for brain stimulation, eventually starving themselves to death.

The pleasurable aspect of brain stimulation has also been demonstrated in humans. For example, Ervin et al. (1969) reported that MFB stimulation not only eliminated pain in cancer patients but also produced a euphoric feeling (approximately equivalent to the effect of two strong alcoholic drinks) that lasted several hours. Sem-Jacobson (1968) found that patients suffering intense depression, fear, or physical pain found brain stimulation pleasurable; patients who felt well prior to ESB experienced only mild pleasure.

The Motivational Influence of MFB Stimulation

You go to the bank and cash a $50 check that you received for your birthday. The cashier hands you two $20 and one $10 bill. How does this make you feel? In all likelihood, you would experience a little pleasure from feeling the bills in your palm. Now, what might you do next? You could set the money in a drawer for a rainy day or take it to the music store and buy the latest CD. You probably go to the store. This demonstrates that reinforcers have both pleasurable and motivating properties. The pleasurable property is the feeling that you experience when you receive the reinforcer (money). The motivating property is that, upon receipt of the reinforcer, you are motivated to perform another behavior (spend it).

The research of Elliot Valenstein and his associates (Valenstein, Cox, & Kakolewski, 1969) demonstrated that activation of the medial forebrain bundle motivates behavior. The researchers found that the specific response that brain stimulation motivates depends upon the prevailing conditions: Brain stimulation motivates eating when food is available and drinking when water is present. This phenomenon is called **stimulus-bound behavior**.

To this point, we have discussed the reinforcing and motivational effects of direct MFB stimulation. Yet, we do not have electrodes implanted in our MFBs; naturally occurring processes must activate this brain area. The next two sections explain how reinforcement and deprivation naturally stimulate the MFB and increase our search for reinforcement.

The Influence of Reinforcers on MFB Function

Many people report finding sexual intercourse more pleasurable after watching an erotic film. Based on our discussion to this point, do you think it is possible that the movie activates the MFB, which then increases the reinforcing quality of sex? A number of studies have demonstrated that a reinforcing activity (e.g., sexual activity) or stimuli associated with a reinforcing activity (e.g., an erotic film) enhances the functioning of the MFB.

Mendelson (1967) demonstrated the effect of water on the reinforcement value of electrical brain stimulation. Mendelson compared how often rats in his study pressed a bar to obtain brain stimulation when water was available and when it was not. His results showed that rats exhibited a significantly higher rate of bar pressing when water was present than when it was absent. Coons and Cruce (1968) found that the presence of food increased the number of attempts to obtain brain stimulation, and Hoebel (1969) reported that a peppermint odor or a few drops of sucrose in the mouth had the same effect. These results suggest that the presence of reinforcement enhances the functioning of the MFB. The effect of this enhanced functioning is an increased response to reinforcers. Returning to our example, watching an erotic film activates the MFB, which motivates people to engage in sexual activity, which they find highly reinforcing.

The Influence of Deprivation on the MFB

You go the ballpark on a very hot day and drink several beers. It is cold the next time you go to the ballpark, and you drink only one beer. Why do you drink more beers on a hot day than a cold day? The effect of deprivation on MFB functioning gives us an answer to this question.

Drinking ice water is very satisfying on a hot day, yet on a cold day, ice water has little incentive value. This illustrates one characteristic of deprivation: A physiological need increases the incentive value of reinforcers. In this example, thirst on a hot day (a physiological need) enhances the reinforcement value of ice water. Increased activity in the brain's reinforcement system is one probable mechanism behind this enhancement.

Brady (1961) showed that the rate of a rat's self-stimulation varies depending on its level of hunger; the longer the rats were deprived of food, the more intensely they pressed the bar to obtain brain stimulation. Similarly, Olds (1962) found that rats that had been deprived of water responded more intensely for brain stimulation than nondeprived rats did.

Recall our discussion of Tony's affinity for his mother's beef bourguignon described in the chapter-opening vignette. The thought of beef bourguignon activated his medial forebrain bundle, which motivated him to ask his mother to cook his favorite meal whenever he was home from college. The relative deprivation caused by eating college cafeteria food aroused his medial forebrain bundle and intensified both the motivation to eat beef bourguignon and the pleasure derived from his mother's cooking.

Mesolimbic Reinforcement System

In the late 1980s, Wise and Rompre (1989) concluded that the medial forebrain bundle is only part of the brain's reinforcement system. Wise and Rompre suggested that the **mesolimbic reinforcement system** contains two neural pathways. One is the **tegmentostriatal pathway**, which begins in the lateral and preoptic areas of the hypothalamus (see Figures 9.11 and 9.12). Neurons in these areas of the hypothalamus detect reinforcement-related stimuli (e.g., food or stimuli associated with food) and transmit the information through the MFB to the **ventral tegmental area (VTA)**. Neural impulses from the VTA then move to the **nucleus accumbens (NA)**, septum, and prefrontal cortex, the brain area that plans the response to reinforcement-related stimuli. The second pathway is the **nigrostriatal pathway** (see again Figures 9.11 and 9.12). This pathway begins in the substantia nigra and projects to the basal ganglia (the caudate nucleus and putamen).

Function of the Two Reinforcement Systems

Why would the brain have two separate reinforcement systems? It is likely that the two pathways regulate two different aspects of reinforcement (Vaccarino, Schiff, & Glickman, 1989). The tegmentostriatal pathway detects whether sufficient motivation is present for voluntary behavior to occur. For example, a rat will not bar press for food if it is not deprived or if the value of the reinforcer is insufficient. In this context, deprivation and reinforcer value are called motivational variables.

Motivational variables also influence the behavioral effects of stimulating structures in the tegmentostriatal pathway other than the MFB (Evans & Vaccarino, 1990). In contrast, motivational

Figure 9.11   A view of the mesolimbic reinforcement system. The tegmentostriatal pathway begins in the lateral and preoptic area of the hypothalamus and goes through the medial forebrain bundle to the ventral tegmental area. Fibers from the ventral tegmental area then go to the nucleus accumbens, septum, and prefrontal cortex. The nigrostriatal pathway begins in the substantia nigra and projects to the neostriatum.

variables do not influence the behavioral effects of stimulation of structures in the nigrostriatal pathway (Winn, Williams, & Herberg, 1982).

In addition to motivating behavior, reinforcers facilitate the storage of experiences, commonly known as memory. Memory allows past experiences to influence future behavior—the rat has to be able to remember that it was the bar press that delivered the electrical brain stimulation. While structures in the nigrostriatal pathway are not involved in the motivational aspect of reinforcement, they do play a role in the storage of a memory. Evidence for this influence is that memory is significantly enhanced when an animal is exposed to a positive reinforcer for a short time following training (Coulombe & White, 1982; Major & White, 1978). Other studies have shown that stimulation of the nigrostriatal pathway, but not the tegmentostriatal pathway, increases the memory of a reinforcing experience (Carr & White, 1984).

Let's return to Tony from our chapter-opening vignette. The sight and smell of his mother's beef bourguignon activated the tegmentostriatal pathway, which motivated Tony to eat his mother's cooking. Activation of the nigrostriatal pathway when eating his mother's nigrostriatal pathway will lead to an even stronger memory of a very reinforcing meal.

Dopaminergic Control of Reinforcement

The neurotransmitter dopamine plays a significant role in regulating the behavioral effects of reinforcement (Schultz, 2002; Wise, 2004). Dopamine governs the activity of the neurons that connect the VTA to the NA, septum, and prefrontal cortex, and several lines of evidence indicate that dopamine plays an important role in mediating the effect of reinforcement on behavior.

Figure 9.12   The mesolimbic reinforcement system consists of two brain pathways. The tegmentostriatal pathway mediates the influence of motivation on reinforcement, and the nigrostriatal pathway is involved in memory consolidation.

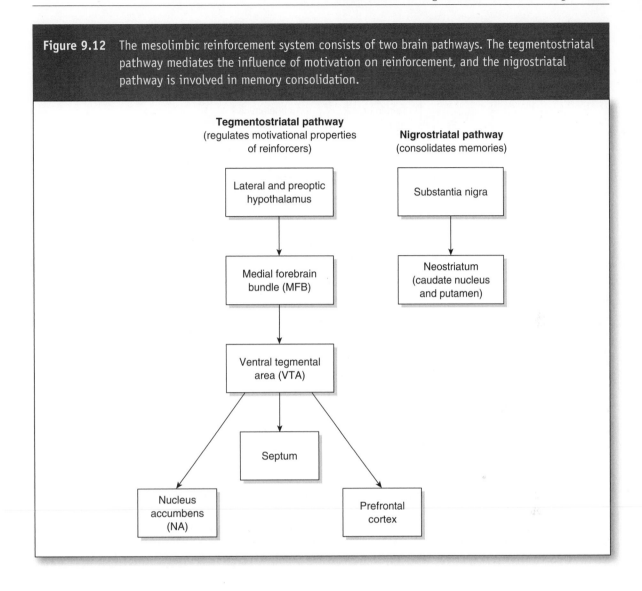

One indication of dopaminergic influence is the powerful reinforcing properties of amphetamine and cocaine, which increase the level of activity at dopaminergic receptors (see Figure 9.13). Some people are highly motivated to obtain substances such as amphetamine or cocaine. The reinforcing properties of these drugs come, in part, from their ability to activate the dopaminergic tegmentostriatal pathway.

Many researchers have shown that animals will quickly learn a behavior that enables them to self-administer amphetamine (Bush, DeSousa, & Vaccarino, 1999) and cocaine (Norman, Norman, Hall, & Tsibulsky, 1999). Animals also will emit, at a high rate, a behavior that triggers injections of cocaine or amphetamine into the NA (Carr & White, 1986). Further, dopamine levels in the NA elevate after the administration of amphetamine or cocaine (Carboni, Silvagni, Rolando, & Di Chiara, 2000; Y. Zhang, Loonam, Noailles, & Angulo, 2001).

Figure 9.13   Diagram showing the separate mechanisms by which opioid agonists (heroin, morphine) and dopamine agonists (amphetamine, cocaine) activate the nucleus accumbens.

Reinforcers other than cocaine and amphetamine also trigger dopamine release, providing support for dopaminergic involvement in the neural control of reinforcement. When animals perform a behavior in order to receive stimulation of the MFB or VTA, dopamine is released. Natural reinforcers, such as food and water, also elicit release of dopamine in the NA (Bassareo & Di Chiara, 1999). In addition, stimuli associated with a natural reinforcer increase dopamine levels in the NA (Datla, Ahier, Young, Gray, & Joseph, 2002). Researchers have found increased dopamine levels following the administration of alcohol (Melendez et al., 2002), cannabis (Mechoulam & Parker, 2003), and nicotine (Fadda, Scherma, Fresu, Collu, & Fratta, 2003).

Dopamine release into the nucleus accumbens also can be elicited by stimuli that are associated with drugs that induce dopamine from the nucleus accumbens (Bassareo et al., 2007). This research paired a Fronzies-filled box conditioned stimulus with nicotine injections (Fronzies is a snack food from Germany that is a highly palatable food made of corn flour, hydrogenated vegetable fat, cheese powder, and salt). Bassareo, De Luca, and Di Chiara (2007) found that presentation of the conditioned stimulus elicited dopamine release into the nucleus accumbens.

Recall that Tony found his mother's beef bourguignon highly reinforcing. When Tony eats his mother's beef bourguignon, dopamine is released from the ventral tegmental area into the nucleus accumbens. As a result of Tony's experiences with his mother's beef bourguignon, dopamine is released into the nucleus accumbens by the sight and smell of beef bourguignon. Even the thought of beef bourguignon elicits a dopamine release, which is why Tony asks his mother to cook beef bourguignon when he comes home from college.

Studies of animals with impaired functioning of dopaminergic neurons in the mesolimbic pathway provide further support for the dopaminergic control of reinforcement. For example, destruction of dopaminergic neurons in this pathway weakens the reinforcing properties of both electrical stimulation and dopamine agonists such as amphetamine and cocaine (Gerrits & Van Ree, 1996). In addition, drugs that block dopamine receptors cause animals to reduce or stop behaviors they have been using to obtain cocaine or amphetamine (Fletcher, 1998) or alcohol (Files, Denning, & Samson, 1998).

Opiate Activation of the Tegmentostriatal Pathway

Opiate drugs also stimulate the tegmentostriatal pathway (Vaccarino et al., 1989). Animals will learn to self-administer opiate drugs such as heroin or morphine just as they learn to self-administer amphetamine and cocaine (Li, He, Parrish, Delich, & Grassing, 2003). Animals will also bar press to receive injections of morphine into the VTA (Devine & Wise, 1994) or NA (Goeders, Lane, & Smith, 1984). Injection of drugs that suppress opiate activity in the VTA or NA causes rats to stop bar pressing (Britt & Wise, 1983).

Do opiates stimulate the same dopaminergic receptors in the VTA or NA as amphetamine and cocaine? Studies suggest that the opiate drugs activate opiate-sensitive receptors and not dopaminergic receptors (see Figure 9.13). For example, drugs that block dopamine receptors reduce the self-administration of amphetamine or cocaine but do not affect self-administration of opiate drugs (Ettenberg, Pettit, Bloom, & Koob, 1982). Also, destruction of the dopamine receptors in the NA decreases intake of cocaine intake but not heroin (Gerrits & Van Ree, 1996). An opposite pattern is found when opiate receptors are blocked: Walker, Ahmed, Gracy, and Koob (2000) reported that the administration of opiate antagonists causes animals to stop self-administering morphine but not cocaine.

Koob (1992) suggested that the tegmentostriatal pathway contains two separate types of receptors, dopamine receptors and opiate receptors, that produce the same result—activation of the NA (see again Figure 9.13). In support of this idea, Gianoulakis (2004) reported that stimulation of opioid receptors in either the VTA or the NA increased release of dopamine in the NA. Recall the discussion of the Bassareo, De Luca, and Di Chiara (2007) study showing that a conditioned stimulus associated with nicotine caused the release of dopamine into the nucleus accumbens. These researchers also found that a conditioned stimulus paired with morphine also elicited dopamine release into the NA.

Individual Differences in Mesolimbic Reinforcement System Functioning

Some people find gambling highly reinforcing, while others seem totally disinterested. While such a difference could be due to differential reinforcement experiences (people who like gambling have been reinforced, and people who dislike gambling have not), individual differences in the functioning of the mesotelencephalic reinforcement system might also influence whether a person finds gambling reinforcing. Individual differences in responses to other reinforcers might similarly reflect differences in the functioning of the brain's reinforcement system.

DeSousa and Vaccarino (2001) suggested that the motivational and reinforcing effects of reinforcers are positively correlated with the level of activity in the mesotelencephalic reinforcement system. How has this positive correlation been documented? One way is to compare animals who respond differently to various reinforcers. For example, some rats consume high levels of sucrose (high sucrose feeders, or HSFs), while other rats consume low levels of sucrose (low sucrose feeders, or LSFs). Sills, Onalaja, and Crawley (1998) found greater dopamine release in the NA when HSFs were given access to sucrose than when LSFs were given access to sucrose. One interpretation of these results is that HSFs find sucrose more reinforcing than do LSFs (and thus consume more sucrose) because their mesotelencephalic reinforcement systems are more responsive to sucrose.

If the greater response of HSFs to sucrose is due to the greater response of the mesotelencephalic reinforcement system, the HSFs should also be more responsive to other reinforcers than are LSFs. Amphetamine is a powerful reinforcer that causes the release of dopamine in the NA. And consistent with the prediction, self-administration of amphetamine is significantly higher in HSFs than LSFs (DeSousa, Bush, & Vaccarino, 2000).

Animals also differ in terms of their response to novel environments: Low responders (LRs) show much less locomotor response in a novel environment than do high responders (HRs). Perhaps not surprising, HRs self-administer amphetamine more than do LRs (Cain, Smith, & Bardo, 2004). Further, dopamine release in response to amphetamine was significantly higher in HRs than LRs (Hooks, Colvin, Juncos, & Justice, 1992).

Reconsider our example of gambling. Our discussion suggests that reinforcement (winning) releases more dopamine in the NA of gamblers than it does in nongamblers. And the greater release of dopamine is one reason why some people gamble and others do not. It also may well be a reason why some people smoke cigarettes and others do not and why gamblers seem more likely to smoke cigarettes.

BEFORE YOU GO ON

- What is the role of the nucleus accumbens in Tony's liking of his mother's cooking?

- How would cocaine influence Sean's aversion to lasagna?

SECTION REVIEW

- The mesolimbic reinforcement system includes the tegmentostriatal pathway, which governs the motivational properties of reinforcers, and the nigrostriatal pathway, which governs memory consolidation.

- The reinforcing effects of both amphetamine and cocaine result from the activation of dopaminergic receptors in the tegmentostriatal pathway.

- The reinforcing effects of opiate agonists such as heroin and morphine result from the stimulation of opiate receptors in the tegmentostriatal pathway.

- Opiate agonists and dopamine agonists activate different receptors in the tegmentostriatal pathway, with the same end result: activation of the nucleus accumbens.

- Individual differences in response to reinforcement are positively correlated with the level of dopamine release in the nucleus accumbens.

CRITICAL THINKING QUESTIONS

1. Jeffrey has a drinking problem. He consumes some alcohol every day and often drinks more than he had planned. How would schedule-induced polydipsia explain Jeffrey's problem? Does the schedule-induced polydipsia paradigm suggest an approach to reduce Jeffrey's alcohol consumption?

2. Early social experience has a profound impact on adult emotionality. Discuss the relevance of Harlow's research to human emotional development.

3. Anita finds cocaine extremely pleasurable. In fact, she prefers it to anything else; she says it is even better than a sexual orgasm. Describe the neural system that allows Anita to experience pleasure from cocaine. Explain why cocaine is such a powerful reinforcer.

KEY TERMS

animal misbehavior

associative learning view of imprinting

concurrent interference

electrical stimulation of the brain (ESB)

imprinting

instinctive drift

interim behavior

long-delay learning

mesolimbic reinforcement system

nucleus accumbens (NA)

schedule-induced behavior

secure relationship

stimulus-bound behavior

tegmentostriatal pathway

ventral tegmental area (VTA)

anxious relationship

behavior systems approach

constraint

flavor aversion

ingestional neophobia

instinctive view of imprinting

learned-safety theory of flavor aversion learning

medial forebrain bundle (MFB)

nigrostriatal pathway

predisposition

schedule-induced polydipsia

species-specific defense reaction (SSDR)

superstitious behavior

terminal behavior

Stimulus Control of Behavior

A CASE OF MISTAKEN IDENTITY

Walking to the grocery store, Miguel was approached by a tall man who suddenly jumped directly in front of him and drew a large knife. The stranger grabbed Miguel's arm and demanded his money. Frightened, Miguel surrendered the $25 he had planned to use to buy food. After grabbing the money, the thief bolted down the street, disappearing into an alley. Miguel began yelling, "I've been robbed! I've been robbed!" But the criminal had fled, and the several people who had witnessed the robbery had dispersed. A merchant hearing Miguel's screams did call the police, who arrived within 5 minutes. The police first questioned Miguel, asking him to describe the robber. The merchant, upon questioning, denied witnessing the crime and attested only to hearing Miguel's screams. Several weeks passed before the police contacted Miguel, informing him that they had a suspect who met Miguel's description and had a record of attacks similar to the one on Miguel. The police asked Miguel to come to the police station to try to identify his assailant in a lineup. The lineup was a cinch; Miguel immediately recognized his attacker. On the basis of his criminal record and Miguel's identification, the suspect was charged with assault and robbery. However, the person Miguel identified was not his assailant. Two weeks after the lineup, another man was apprehended while attempting to rob a woman on her way home from work. During his interrogation, the man confessed not only to this crime but also to robbing Miguel.

Since Miguel had a close view of his assailant, why did he identify the wrong man? To answer, we must consider the five individuals in the lineup. Although five men were in the lineup, only two were as tall as Miguel's assailant. Of these two men, one was thin, the other, fat. Since his attacker was tall and thin, Miguel's choice seemed obvious, and he picked the man he believed had robbed him. Miguel's behavior illustrates discrimination learning: He had recognized several important attributes of his assailant, and he used this knowledge to discriminate his assailant from the other men in the lineup. However, his discrimination was not perfect; although Miguel's assailant and the man he identified in the lineup shared two attributes—they were both thin and tall—their facial characteristics differed significantly. But Miguel had not attended to facial attributes; instead, he had responded only to size characteristics.

This chapter discusses the impact of the stimulus environment on behavior. An individual may respond in the same way to similar stimuli, a process called **stimulus generalization**. In the chapter-opening vignette, Miguel responded in the same manner to both the assailant and the tall, thin man in the lineup. Individuals may also learn to respond in different ways to different stimuli; the process of responding to some stimuli but not others is called **discrimination learning.** Miguel discriminated between his assailant and four of the five men in the lineup.

To begin our discussion of stimulus control of behavior, we examine stimulus generalization, or responding to stimuli similar to the conditioning stimulus. We address other aspects of stimulus control later in the chapter.

THE STIMULUS GENERALIZATION PROCESS

On September 11, 2001, two airplanes crashed into the twin towers of the 110-story World Trade Center in New York. The collapse of the twin towers killed almost 3,000 people. An investigation by the FBI and the New York City Police revealed that 10 Arab Moslem individuals were responsible. Extensive media coverage of this and similar acts of violence has aroused the belief in some Americans that many Arab Moslems are terrorists. Why do some Americans dislike Arab Moslems? Stimulus generalization may be responsible for their strong, negatively conditioned emotional response toward Arab Moslems.

Stimulus generalization occurs frequently in the real world. Sometimes, stimulus generalization is undesirable, as when some Americans choose to dislike all Arab Moslems. Racial, ethnic, and religious prejudices are examples of an undesirable stimulus generalization that occurs when someone who has had an unpleasant experience with one member of a racial, ethnic, or religious group generalizes this dislike to other members of that group.

Recall our discussion of Miguel in the chapter-opening vignette. Miguel picked a man out of the police lineup who looked like his assailant. Miguel's stimulus generalization from his assailant to the man in the lineup could have resulted in a man falsely accused of a felony assault. Unfortunately, there are too many cases where stimulus generalization causes wrongly convicted individuals to spend significant time in prison.

However, stimulus generalization is often adaptive. For example, if a parent reads a book to a child and the child enjoys it, a positive emotional experience is conditioned to the book. The child then generalizes this positive emotional response to other books. The child's stimulus generalization even extends to liking books not yet read. To use another example, preschool children may enjoy playing with other neighborhood children; this enjoyment reflects a conditioned response acquired through past experience. When these children attend school, they generalize their conditioned social responses to new children and are motivated to play with them. This stimulus generalization enables children to socialize with new children; otherwise, children would have to learn to like new acquaintances before they would want to play with them. Thus, stimulus generalization allows people to respond positively to strangers.

Stimulus generalization causes us to respond in basically the same way to stimuli similar to the stimulus present during prior experience. However, different degrees of stimulus generalization occur. In some instances, we respond the same to all stimuli resembling the stimulus associated with conditioning. For example, people who become ill after eating in one restaurant may generalize their negative emotional experiences and avoid eating out again. In other situations, less stimulus generalization occurs as the similarity to the conditioned stimulus lessens. Suppose that a college student drinks too much vodka and becomes quite ill. This student may show an intense dislike of all white alcohol (e.g., gin), experience a moderate aversion to wine, and feel only a slight dislike of beer. In this case, the greater the difference in the alcohol content of the drink, the less the generalization of dislike. Or the person might have an aversion to only straight alcohol; if so, only stimuli very similar to the conditioning stimulus, such as gin, will elicit dislike.

To study the level of stimulus generalization, psychologists have constructed generalization gradients. A **generalization gradient** is a visual representation of the strength of each response produced by stimuli of varying degrees of similarity to the stimulus present during training; these gradients show the level of generalization that occurs to any given stimulus similar to the one present during conditioning. A steep generalization gradient indicates that people or animals respond very little to stimuli that are not very similar to the training stimulus, while a flat generalization gradient shows that response occurs even to stimuli quite unlike the conditioning stimulus.

Generalization Gradients

Most generalization studies have investigated the generalization of excitatory conditioning. Recall from Chapter 4 that in excitatory conditioning, a specific stimulus is presented prior to the unconditioned stimulus. Following acquisition, the stimulus (S+) that was paired with the unconditioned stimulus is presented again, along with several test stimuli varying from very similar to very dissimilar to the S+. A comparison of the levels of response to the test stimulus and the training stimulus indicates the level of generalization of excitatory conditioning. A graph of the response to each stimulus visually displays the level of excitatory generalization.

Some research has studied the generalization of inhibitory conditioning. Remember that inhibitory conditioning develops when one stimulus is presented with either reward or punishment and another stimulus with the absence of the event (see Chapter 4). Conditioning of inhibition to the second stimulus (inhibitory stimulus, S–) will cause it to suppress the response to the first stimulus (excitatory stimulus, S+). After training, the second stimulus (S–) and several test stimuli, varying from very similar to very dissimilar to the inhibitory stimulus, are presented before the excitatory stimulus (S+). The level of response suppression produced by the inhibitory stimulus, compared with that produced by the test stimuli, indicates the amount of generalization of inhibition. A graph of the level of suppression produced by each stimulus can provide a visual display of the level of inhibitory generalization.

We first discuss excitatory-conditioning generalization gradients, followed by a discussion of inhibitory-conditioning generalization gradients. A discussion of the nature of stimulus generalization follows the discussion of generalization gradients.

Excitatory-Conditioning Generalization Gradients

Much of the research on **excitatory generalization gradients** has been conducted using pigeons as subjects. Pigeons have excellent color vision, and it is easy to establish their generalization to stimuli that are similar to the color used in training. Guttman and Kalish's (1956) classic experiment trained hungry pigeons to peck a small illuminated disk to obtain food reinforcement. Four groups of pigeons were shown one of four colors (530, 550, 580, and 600 nanometers [nm or one billionth of a meter]), ranging from yellowish-green to red, as the training stimulus. The key was illuminated for 60-second periods, and these periods alternated with 10-second periods of no illumination. The pigeons were reinforced on a VI 1-minute schedule when the key was illuminated; reinforcement was unavailable when the key was not illuminated. After acquisition training, Guttman and Kalish tested for generalization of response to similarly colored stimuli. The generalization test presented the color illuminated during training and 10 other stimuli (5 were higher on the wavelength color spectrum, and 5 were lower). The researchers presented each stimulus randomly 12 times for a period of 30 seconds each time. The results showed that the pigeons made the maximum number of responses to the training stimuli (see Figure 10.1). Guttman and Kalish noted that the level of response declined as the difference between training and test stimuli increased. Furthermore, the general shape of each gradient was similar for all four subject groups, regardless of the training stimulus.

Figure 10.1 Generalization gradients obtained using four different wavelengths in separate groups of pigeons trained to key peck for food reinforcement. The results of this study showed that the amount of generalization decreased as the difference between the conditioning and the test stimuli increased.

Researchers using species other than pigeons have reported excitatory-conditioning generalization gradients similar to those Guttman and Kalish (1956) found in pigeons. J. W. Moore (1972) provides an illustration of this generalization gradient form in rabbits. Moore initially conditioned an eyeblink response to a 1200-Hz (hertz) tone. Following conditioning, the S+ and other stimuli varying from 400 Hz to 2000 Hz were presented to the rabbits. Moore reported that the highest percentage of response was to the 1200-Hz tone (S+) and that the number of responses declined as the similarity of the test and training stimuli decreased. Earlier, Razran (1949) described the results of 54 different experiments in Pavlov's laboratory, examining the generalization of salivary conditioning in dogs. The results of these experiments show a generalization gradient in which response increases as the test and training stimuli become more similar.

Generalization gradients like those Guttman and Kalish (1956) reported have been observed using a wide variety of stimuli and responses in humans (Bass & Hull, 1934; Hoveland, 1937; Razran, 1949). For example, Hoveland (1937) paired a tone (S+) with an electric shock and then investigated the generalization of the galvanic skin response (a measure of skin conductance that reflects autonomic nervous system arousal). Hoveland reported that less response occurred as the test and conditioning tones became more dissimilar (see Figure 10.2). Bass and Hull (1934), using a tactile stimulus (stimulation of the shoulder) as the S+ and electric shock as the UCS, presented the S+ and other tactile stimuli after conditioning of the electrodermal response (another measure of skin conductance). The form of the generalization gradient for tactile stimuli that Bass and Hull observed was similar to the one Hoveland found for auditory stimuli (see Figure 10.2).

Figure 10.2 Amplitude of galvanic skin response (GSR) in millimeters during generalization testing as a function of the number of just noticeable differences (JNDs) from the S+. The findings revealed that the level of generalization decreased as the just noticeable difference between the conditioning and the test stimuli increased.

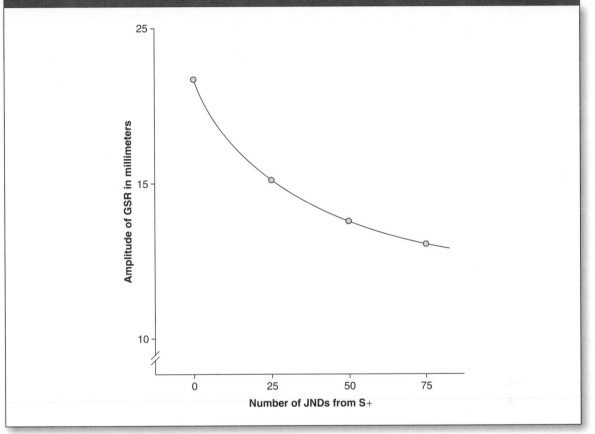

You may be wondering whether the level of stimulus generalization shown in Figure 10.1 is characteristic of all situations. Although in many circumstances an individual will respond to stimuli similar to the conditioning stimulus, in other situations, animals or people may generalize to stimuli that are both very similar and quite dissimilar to the conditioning stimulus. Consider the following example: Some people who do not interact easily with others find that being around people elicits anxiety, and, although they may be lonely, they avoid contact. These people probably experienced some unpleasantness with another person (or persons)—perhaps another person rebuked an attempted social invitation or said something offensive. As a result of a painful social experience, a conditioned anxiety about or dislike of the other person developed. Although everyone has had an unpleasant social experience, most people limit their dislike to the person associated with the pain, or perhaps to similar individuals. Individuals with social anxiety generalize their anxiety or dislike to all people, and this generalization makes all interactions difficult.

Many studies have reported flat excitatory-conditioning generalization gradients; that is, an animal or person responds to stimuli quite dissimilar to the conditioning stimulus. The Jenkins and Harrison (1960) study is one example. H. M. Jenkins and Harrison trained two groups of pigeons to key peck for food reinforcement. A 1000-Hz tone was present during the entire conditioning phase in the control group. In contrast, animals in the experimental group received some training periods that made reinforcement contingent on key pressing, with a 1000-Hz tone present; reinforcement was unavailable despite key pecking during other training periods, and no tone was present when the reinforcement was not available. Thus, control group animals heard the 1000-Hz tone for the entire period, while the experimental group animals heard the tone only when reinforcement was available.

Generalization testing followed conditioning for both groups of pigeons. Seven tones (300, 450, 670, 1000, 1500, 2250, and 3500 Hz) were presented during generalization testing. Jenkins and Harrison's results, presented in the bottom panel of Figure 10.3, show that experimental animals exhibited a generalization gradient similar to the one Guttman and Kalish (1956) reported, and control animals responded to all tones equally, presented in the top panel of Figure 10.3.

Inhibitory-Conditioning Generalization Gradients

In all likelihood, you are apprehensive when you start dating a person. If this is your initial date with this person, you did not acquire your fear directly. Instead, your fear could be caused by one of several other factors, such as excitatory generalizations from a negative experience with another person. Suppose your fears are unfounded and you have an enjoyable time. As the result of your experience, you will associate your date with the absence of an aversive event, the occurrence of a reinforcing experience, or both. This conditioning will diminish your apprehension about dating this person again. Fortunately, the inhibition of fear not only reduces your apprehensiveness about dating this particular person but also generalizes to dating other new people. Thus, the generalization of inhibition allows you to be less fearful of dating others.

Weisman and Palmer's (1969) study illustrates the generalization of inhibition. In their study, pigeons learned to peck at a green disk (S+) to receive reinforcement on a VI 1-minute schedule. When a white vertical line (S–) was presented, the pigeons were not reinforced for disk pecking. After conditioning, the pigeons received a conditioned inhibition generalization test. In this phase of the study, the white vertical line (S–) plus six other lines that departed from the vertical line by 290, 260, 230, 130, 160, and 190 degrees were presented to the subjects. As Figure 10.4 indicates, the presentation of the vertical line (S–) inhibited pecking. Furthermore, the amount of inhibition that generalized to other lines differed depending on the degree of similarity to the S–: the more dissimilar the line to the S–, or the greater the extent to which the orientation of the line deviated from vertical, the less inhibition of responding.

As is true of excitatory generalization, in certain circumstances, inhibition generalizes to stimuli quite dissimilar to the training stimulus. Even dissimilar stimuli can sometimes produce responses equivalent to those elicited by the conditioning stimulus. The generalization of inhibition to stimuli quite dissimilar to the training stimulus is apparent in a study Hoffman (1969) did. In his study, pigeons first learned to key peck for food reinforcement. Following this initial training phase, the birds were exposed to 24 conditioning sessions. During each session, a 2-minute, 88-decibel (dB) noise followed by an electric shock was presented three times, and a 2-minute, 88-dB, 1000-Hz tone not followed by electric shock was presented three times.

Hoffman's procedure established the 88-dB noise (S+) as a feared stimulus, and the presentation of the 88-dB noise suppressed key pecking. In contrast, little suppression was noted when the 88-dB, 1000-Hz tone (S–) was presented. Furthermore, the presence of the tone inhibited fear of the noise. Generalization-of-inhibition testing consisted of presenting the noise (S+) and several test tones. The tones varied in pitch from 300 to 3400 Hz. Hoffman reported that each tone

Figure 10.3 Percentage of total responses to S+ (1000-Hz tone) and other stimuli (ranging in loudness from 300 to 3500 Hz) during generalization testing for control group subjects receiving only the S+ in acquisition (top graph) and for experimental group animals given both S+ and S– in acquisition (bottom graph). A steep generalization gradient characterized the responses of experimental subjects, while a flat gradient demonstrated the behavior of control subjects.

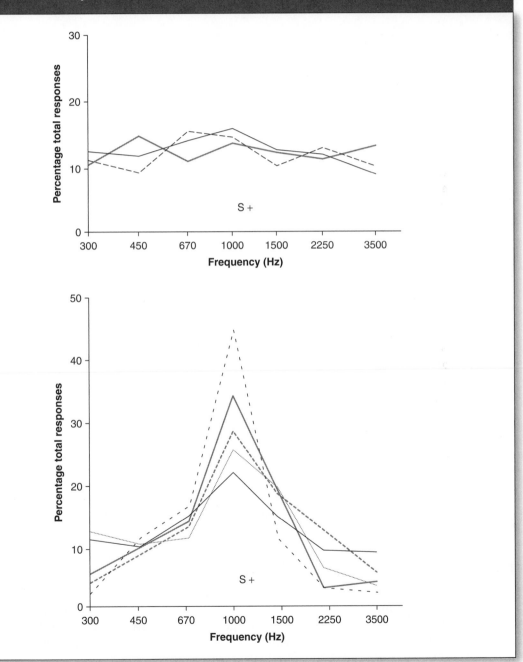

Figure 10.4 The inhibitory generalization gradients for five subjects receiving a vertical line as S–. The gradients show the number of responses to the test stimuli and S+. The study showed that the level of inhibition generalizing to the test stimuli increased as the difference between the training and the test stimuli decreased.

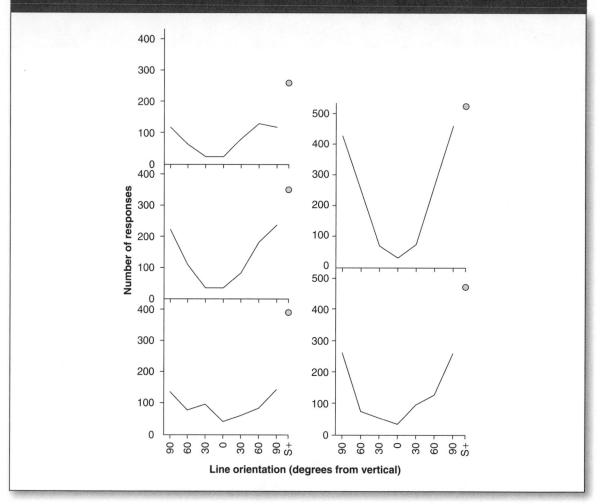

equally inhibited the fear of the noise. Almost complete generalization of inhibition had occurred; that is, tones with very dissimilar pitches produced about as much inhibition as did the S– (1000-Hz tone).

The Nature of the Stimulus Generalization Process

Why do we generalize our response to stimuli similar to the stimulus associated with conditioning at certain times, but show no generalization to similar stimuli at other times? Many theories have been proposed to explain stimulus generalization. We will examine the **Lashley-Wade theory of stimulus generalization** because it seems to best explain why stimulus generalization occurs on some occasions but not others.

**Karl Spencer Lashley
(1890–1958)**

Lashley received his doctorate in genetics from Johns Hopkins University. While at Johns Hopkins, he worked with John Watson, but he was more interested in studying the physiology of conditioned reflexes than the conditioned reflex itself. He taught at the University of Minnesota for 5 years and the University of Chicago for 6 years before spending 20 years at Harvard University. He served as president of the American Psychological Association in 1929.

Karl Lashley and M. Wade (1946) suggested that animals and people respond to stimuli that differ from the training stimulus because they are unable to distinguish between the generalization test stimulus and the conditioning stimulus. Thus, an inability to discriminate between the training and test stimuli is responsible for stimulus generalization. If people could differentiate between the conditioning stimulus and other stimuli, Lashley and Wade's view suggests that people would not show a generalized response to the other stimuli. Therefore, according to Lashley and Wade, stimulus generalization represents the failure to discriminate, discrimination prevents stimulus generalization, and a failure to discriminate leads to generalization.

Several lines of evidence support the Lashley-Wade view of stimulus generalization. First, generalization to stimuli even dissimilar to the training stimulus occurs when nondifferential reinforcement training is used. When nondifferential reinforcement is used, the conditioning stimulus is present during the entire training session. Thus, the only stimulus the subject experiences is the excitatory stimulus (S+). The Lashley-Wade view suggests that without experience with stimuli other than the S+, the subject will generalize to all similar stimuli. The H. M. Jenkins and Harrison (1960) study previously described provides an excellent example of such a generalization gradient. In their study, control group animals received nondifferential training, with the 1000-Hz tone present during the entire conditioning session. Following training, each subject was exposed to seven tones ranging from 300 to 3500 Hz and to a nontone presentation. As the top panel of Figure 10.3 shows, the pigeons responded equally to all tones.

The second line of evidence supporting the Lashley-Wade theory is that discrimination training results in generalization only to stimuli very similar to the conditioning stimulus. As discussed earlier, during discrimination training, the excitatory stimulus (S+) is present when reinforcement is available, and the inhibitory stimulus (S−) is present when reinforcement is unavailable. According to the Lashley-Wade view, an animal learns to differentiate between the S+ and other stimuli as the result of discrimination training. This experience produces responses that are almost always limited to the S+, with few or no responses to other stimuli; that is, little or no stimulus generalization occurs when an animal recognizes the specific stimulus associated with reinforcement.

A number of studies show that discrimination training leads to steep generalization gradients. We described a few of these experiments earlier in the chapter. The H. M. Jenkins and Harrison (1960) study also evaluated the influence of discrimination training on stimulus generalization gradients. Jenkins and Harrison trained pigeons to discriminate between a key that produced the S+ (a 1000-Hz tone) and resulted in reinforcement and a key associated with the S− (no tone presented) that did not lead to reinforcement. After training, stimulus generalization testing presented seven tones ranging from 300 to 3500 Hz. The bottom panel of Figure 10.3 illustrates that this discrimination training produced a steep generalization gradient.

The third line of evidence, according to Lashley and Wade, is that generalization occurs when an animal cannot differentiate between the training stimulus and generalization test stimuli. An extension of this view suggests that little generalization should occur, and that discrimination should readily form, when an animal can easily differentiate between S+ and S−. The literature (Kalish, 1969) indicates that the more able an animal is to differentiate between the S+ and S−, the easier it learns a discrimination. Furthermore, a steeper generalization gradient is observed when an animal can easily distinguish between the S+ and S−.

The final evidence supporting the Lashley-Wade theory is that perceptual experience influences the amount of stimulus generalization. The Lashley-Wade view proposes that animals learn to distinguish similarities and differences in environmental events. This perceptual learning is essential for an animal to discriminate between different stimuli yet generalize to similar stimuli. Without this perceptual experience, different environmental events appear similar, thereby making discrimination very difficult. For example, a person with little or no experience with varied colors might find it difficult to distinguish between green and red; this difficulty could result in failing to learn to observe traffic lights. Several studies have evaluated the influence of various levels of perceptual experience on the level of stimulus generalization (Houston, 1986); these results have shown that as perceptual experience increases, the generalization gradient becomes steeper.

N. Peterson's (1962) classic study illustrates the effect of perceptual experience on the amount of stimulus generalization. Peterson raised two groups of ducks under different conditions. The experimental group ducks were raised in cages illuminated by a 589-nm light and therefore experienced only a single color. In contrast, control group animals were raised in normal light and were exposed to a wide range of colors. During the initial phase of the study, Peterson trained the ducks to peck at a key illuminated by the 589-nm light. After training, both groups received generalization testing using stimuli varying from a 490-nm to 650-nm light. The top panel of Figure 10.5 illustrates that ducklings raised in a monochromatic environment showed a flat generalization gradient. These results indicate that ducks without perceptual experience with various colors generalized their response to all colors. In contrast, the ducks raised in normal light displayed the greatest response to the S+ (the 589-nm light; see bottom panel of Figure 10.5). As the result of perceptual experience with various colors, animals apparently learn to differentiate between colors and are therefore less likely to generalize to similar colors. A similar influence of restricted perceptual experience on stimulus generalization was observed in rats (Walk & Walters, 1973), in monkeys (Ganz & Riesen, 1962), and in congenitally blind humans (Ganz, 1968).

BEFORE YOU GO ON

- How would the Lashley-Wade theory explain Miguel's failure to correctly identify his assailant?

- What would the Lashley-Wade theory suggest might prevent Miguel from making a wrongful accusation?

SECTION REVIEW

- Stimulus generalization is a process in which animals or people respond in the same way to similar stimuli.

- Discrimination is a process in which animals or people learn to respond in different ways to different stimuli.

- In excitatory generalization, a cue (S+) is associated with reinforcement or punishment, and stimuli similar to the S+ will elicit the response.

- In inhibitory generalization, a cue (S−) is associated with the absence of reinforcement or punishment, and stimuli similar to the S− will inhibit responding.

- A steep generalization gradient occurs when an animal or person only responds to stimuli very similar to the S+ or the S−.

- A flat generalization gradient occurs when the animal or person exhibits the same amount of excitation or inhibition to any stimuli resembling S+ or S–.

- According to the Lashley-Wade view, animals and people generalize to stimuli quite dissimilar to the conditioning stimulus when they fail to distinguish between the S+ or S– and other stimuli.

Figure 10.5   Generalization gradients obtained with ducklings reared in monochromatic light (top graph) and in white light (bottom graph). Ducklings raised in monochromatic light exhibited flat generalization gradients, whereas those reared in white light demonstrated steep generalization gradients.

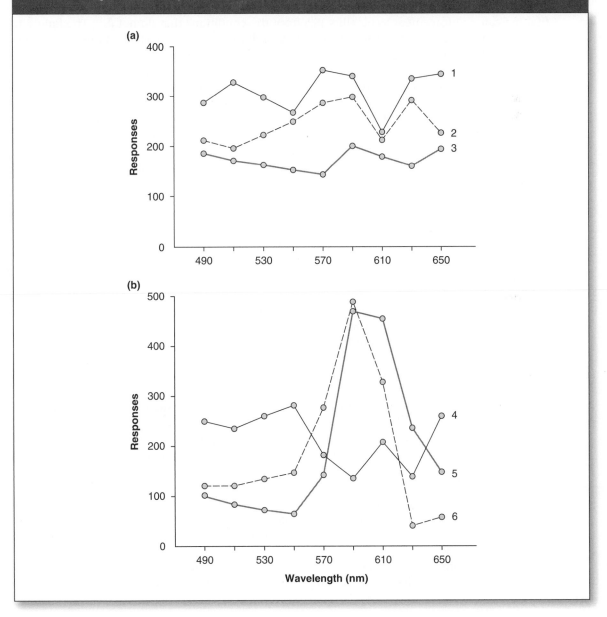

DISCRIMINATION LEARNING

We know that on some occasions, reinforcement is available and will occur contingent on an appropriate response, while on other occasions, reinforcement is unavailable and will not occur despite continued response. To respond when reinforcement is available and to not respond when reinforcement is unavailable, we must learn to discriminate; that is, we must not only discover the conditions indicating that reinforcement is available and respond when those conditions exist, we must also recognize the circumstances indicating that reinforcement is unavailable and not respond during these times. Skinner (1938) referred to a stimulus associated with reinforcement availability as an S^D (or S-dee) and a stimulus associated with the unavailability of reinforcement as an S^Δ (or S-delta). Further, Skinner called an operant behavior under the control of a **discriminative stimulus** (either an S^D or an S^Δ) a **discriminative operant**.

To interact effectively with our environment, we must learn to discriminate the conditions that indicate reinforcement availability (S^D) from the conditions that do not (S^Δ). The failure to discriminate will cause us not to respond when reinforcement is available, to respond when reinforcement is unavailable, or both. In most cases, the failure to discriminate will cause inconvenience. For example, you will lose time and effort if you go to the library when it's closed. Embarrassment may occur during some circumstances if you do not discriminate. If you go to the movies with friends, you will feel foolish if you usher them into the wrong line. In some cases, behavior pathology can result from discriminative failure. Consider a sociopath who fails to discriminate between the acceptability of violence on television and the unacceptability of violent behavior in real life.

The failure to discriminate need not occur. The following study illustrates that the ability to discriminate between stimuli merely reflects the use of differential reinforcement contingencies. Watanabe, Sakamoto, and Wakita (1995) reinforced pigeons for key pecking in the presence of the works of a certain painter (e.g., the impressionist Claude Monet). The pigeons were not reinforced in the presence of the works of another painter (e.g., the cubist Pablo Picasso). Watanabe, Sakamoto, and Wakita found that the pigeons learned to respond in the presence of Monet's paintings (S^D), but not to respond to Picasso's (S^Δ). So, the next time you think you cannot discriminate between two stimuli, remember the pigeons that learned to discriminate between the paintings of Monet and Picasso.

Discriminative stimuli are often external events, but they also can be interoceptive stimuli. In these studies, the interoceptive stimulus served as either the S^D availability of reinforcements or the S^Δ for the nonavailability of reinforcement. A wide variety of psychoactive drugs have gained stimulus control, including cocaine (Kueh & Baker, 2007), morphine (Craft, Kalivas, & Stratmann, 1996), MDMA ecstasy; Bondavera et al., 2005); nicotine (Stolerman, 1989); and pentobarbital (McMillan & Li, 2000). In fact, the level of stimulus control exerted by an interoceptive stimulus is comparable to that of an exteroceptive stimulus. For example, McMillan, Wessinger, Paule, and Wenger (1989) compared the stimulus control exerted by an interoceptive stimulus (phencyclidine, PCP) with that of an exteroceptive stimulus (blinking light). These researchers reported that the exteroceptive and interoceptive stimuli produced similar discriminative control of key pecking in pigeons.

Discrimination learning involves discovering not only when reinforcement is available or unavailable, but also when aversive events may or may not occur. For example, some conditions forecast rain, and some predict no rain. Since you will get wet (typically an aversive event) if you go out in the rain, you need to carry an umbrella to avoid becoming wet when it rains. If you fail to learn the conditions indicating impending rain, you will often become wet. Similarly, you need not carry an umbrella on a clear, sunny day. Nothing appears quite as foolish as someone carrying an umbrella when the sun is shining. However, it is difficult to learn when to carry an umbrella and when not to, because no stimuli always signal rain (the aversive event) or always indicate no rain (the absence of the aversive event). We discuss the influence of predictiveness on discrimination learning later in the chapter.

In many circumstances, the occurrence or nonoccurrence of aversive events is easily predicted. A course outline for this class indicates that an exam is impending, but the lack of a specific prior announcement means you will have no exam. If you recognize the significance of the schedule, you will study before the next exam, but you will not study if no exam is scheduled. The failure to discriminate may cause you to study even though you have no exam or to fail to prepare for a scheduled exam. Another example of discrimination involves children who misbehave for a substitute teacher but behave appropriately with their regular teacher. Their behavior is based on having learned that their regular teacher will punish them but that a substitute is not likely to do so.

You might have noticed that the abbreviations changed from S+ and S– in the stimulus generalization discussion to S^D and S^Δ in the discussion of discrimination learning. This change reflects the conventional terms used in each area of research; it does not indicate that we are talking about different stimuli but instead that we are referring to different properties of the same stimulus. Consider the following example to illustrate that a stimulus can function as both a discriminative stimulus and a conditioned stimulus. On a hot summer day, going to the beach can be quite reinforcing. The hot summer day is a discriminative stimulus indicating that reinforcement is available; it is also a conditioned stimulus that motivates the instrumental activity of going to the beach.

Perhaps you are still confused about the difference between a conditioned stimulus and a discrimination stimulus. A conditioned stimulus automatically elicits a conditioned response. In contrast, a discriminative stimulus "sets the occasion" for an operant or instrumental behavior. As an example, consider watching a favorite television show. As the time for the program nears, you become excited (a conditioned response). You also turn on the television. The time of the show both elicits the involuntary conditioned response and sets the occasion for you to perform the voluntary operant behavior of turning on the television to the appropriate channel.

Discrimination Paradigms

Sometimes, discrimination learning involves one stimulus as the S^D and another as the S^Δ. In contrast, the same stimulus can be an S^D sometimes and the S^Δ at other times. In this section, we discuss these two types of discrimination situations.

Two-Choice Discrimination Tasks

In a **two-choice discrimination learning** task, the S^D (the stimulus signaling reinforcement or punishment availability) and the S^Δ (the stimulus signaling reinforcement or punishment unavailability) are on the same stimulus dimension (e.g., the S^D is a red light and the S^Δ a green light). Responding to the S^D produces reinforcement or punishment, and choosing the S^Δ leads to neither reinforcement nor punishment.

In some cases, the S^D and the S^Δ are presented simultaneously, while in other cases, the S^D and the S^Δ are presented sequentially. It also is not unusual for there to be more than one S^D and more than one S^Δ. In some situations, the choice is between just two stimuli; in other situations, the choice is between several stimuli. Two-choice discrimination occurs in a situation in which an animal or person must choose between responding to either an S^D or an S^Δ.

Consider the following example of a two-choice discrimination task. Suppose that one of a child's parents is generous, and the other parent is conservative. Asking one parent for money to go to the video arcade will be successful; a request to the other will result in failure. The first parent, whose presence indicates that reinforcement is available, is an S^D. Because reinforcement is unavailable when the other parent is asked, the presence of this parent is an S^Δ.

Research evaluating two-choice discrimination learning shows that animals begin by responding equally to the S^D and S^Δ. With continued training, responding to the S^D increases and responding to the S^Δ declines. At the end of training, an animal responds at a high rate to the S^D and responds little or not at all to the S^Δ.

G. S. Reynolds (1961) initially trained his pigeons to peck for food reinforcement on a multiple VI 3-minute, VI 3-minute schedule. (A multiple schedule is a compound schedule consisting of two or more independent schedules presented successively; each schedule is associated with a distinctive stimulus.) In Reynolds's study, the researchers presented a red light and a green light associated with the separate components of the multiple schedule. As Figure 10.6 demonstrates, Reynolds's pigeons exhibited equal responses to the red and green lights during the prediscrimination phase of his study.

In the discrimination stage, Reynolds (1961) changed the schedule to a multiple VI 3-minute, extinction schedule. In this schedule, the red light continued to correlate with reinforcement and the green light was associated with the extinction (or nonreinforcement) component of the multiple schedule. During the discrimination phase of the study, Reynolds noted that the response rate to the red light (S^D) increased, and the response rate to the green light (S^Δ) declined (see again Figure 10.6).

To show that the response change during the discrimination phase was due to differential reinforcement, Reynolds (1961) shifted the schedule back to a multiple VI 3-minute, VI 3-minute schedule in the third phase of his study. Reynolds found that response to the red light declined and response to the green light increased during the third (nondiscrimination) phase, until an equivalent response rate occurred to both stimuli. This indicates that the differential reinforcement procedure controlled responses during the discrimination phase.

Studies using human subjects indicate that people also are sensitive to two-choice discrimination tasks. For example, Terrell and Ware (1961) trained kindergarten and first-grade children to discriminate between three-dimensional geometric forms. In one discrimination task, the children needed to distinguish between large and small cubed boxes; in the other discrimination task, the children needed to distinguish between a sphere and pyramid. A light indicated a correct response. Terrell and Ware reported that the children quickly learned to discriminate between the geometric forms.

Conditional Discrimination Task

In a **conditional discrimination** task, the reinforcement contingency associated with a particular stimulus depends on the status of a second stimulus. In other words, a specific stimulus does not always signal either the availability or nonavailability of reinforcement in a conditional discrimination task. Instead, in some circumstances, a particular cue indicates that reinforcement is contingent on the occurrence of an appropriate response, whereas under other conditions, the cue does not signal reinforcement availability. As was the case with a two-choice discrimination task, the stimuli may occur simultaneously or sequentially. Further, there may be two or more S^Ds and S^Δs in a conditional discrimination.

There are many instances of conditional discrimination in the real world. For example, a store is open at certain hours and closed at others, or a colleague is friendly sometimes but hostile at other times.

It is more difficult to learn that a particular cue signals reinforcement availability sometimes but not at other times than to learn that a specific stimulus is always associated with either reinforcer availability or nonavailability. However, we must discover when a cue signals reinforcement availability and when it does not if we are to interact effectively with our environment. Psychologists have observed that both animals and humans can learn a conditional discrimination; we look at one of these studies next.

Figure 10.6   Mean number of responses per minute during discrimination learning. The pigeons' responses to the reinforced key increased as their responses to the nonreinforced key declined.

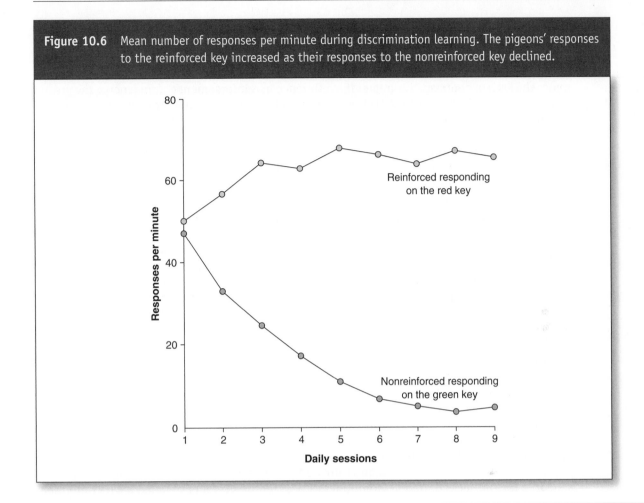

Nissen (1951) discovered that chimpanzees can learn a conditional discrimination. In Nissen's study, large and small squares were the discriminative stimuli; the brightness of the squares was the conditional stimulus. When the squares were white, the large square was the S^D and the small square was the S^Δ; when the squares were black, the small square was the S^D and the large square was the S^Δ. Nissen reported that his chimpanzees learned to respond effectively; that is, they responded to the large square when it was white but not black and to the small square when it was black but not white.

Behavioral Contrast

Recall our discussion of G. S. Reynolds's (1961) two-choice discrimination study in which pigeons learned to respond to a red light (S^D) and not to respond to a green light (S^Δ). Reynolds found that not only did the animals stop responding to the green light (S^Δ), but they also increased their response rate to the red light (S^D) during the discrimination phase of the study. The increased response to S^D and decreased response to S^Δ is called **behavioral contrast**. The increased response rate to S^D occurs despite the fact that the reinforcement schedule has not changed. Behavioral contrast has been consistently observed in differential reinforcement situations (Flaherty, 1996; B. A. Williams, 2002).

Behavioral contrast also can be produced when there is a decrease or increase in reinforcement disparity (B. A. Williams, 2002). As we learned in Chapter 6, responding increases when the reinforcer magnitude changes from low to high and decreases when the reinforcer magnitude changes from high to low. Further, the difference in relative reinforcement contingencies determines the level of contrast: The greater the difference in reinforcement contingencies, the greater the contrast (B. A. Williams, 2002). Differences in each component's duration on a discrimination task will also produce behavioral contrast (Aronson et al., 1993). In this case, responding will increase when the change is from a less valued to a more valued duration and decrease when the reinforcement duration changes from a more valued to a less valued duration. For example, B. A. Williams (1991a) found maximum contrast with a multiple VI 3-minute, VI 10-minute contingency, with the VI 10-minute schedule being the less valued duration.

Charles Flaherty (1996) has described two important aspects of the behavioral contrast phenomenon: **local contrast** and **sustained contrast**. A change in response (increase to the S^D and decrease to the S^Δ) that the switch from the S^D to the S^Δ or vice versa activates is called local contrast. This change in response fades with extended training and is due to the emotional response (elation or frustration) that a change in reinforcement contingency elicits. Thus, a pigeon becomes frustrated by the switch from S^D to S^Δ and elated by the switch from S^Δ to S^D. A change in response that occurs due to the anticipation of the impending reinforcement contingencies is called sustained contrast. This change will persist as long as the differential reinforcement contingencies exist. According to Flaherty, an animal's response to S^D or to S^Δ is determined by comparing the current reinforcement with the previous one (local contrast) and the one coming next (sustained contrast). If the animal is anticipating a shift from S^D to S^Δ, response to the S^D will be high. In contrast, if the animal is anticipating a shift from S^Δ to S^D, response to the S^Δ will be low.

B. A. Williams (1983) provides evidence that sustained contrast (which he calls **anticipatory contrast**) is due to the anticipation of a future reinforcement contingency rather than the recall of the past reinforcement contingency. Williams used a multiple VI 3-minute, VI 6-minute, VI 3-minute schedule. (In this multiple schedule, the pigeon was reinforced for key pecking on a VI 3-minute schedule for the first and third components of the schedule and on a VI 6-minute schedule for the second, middle component.) A different stimulus signaled each component of this schedule. Williams was most interested in the pigeons' response rate in the first and third components (or those components that preceded or followed the VI 6-minute duration). Williams found the VI 6-minute second component had more influence on the pigeons' responses in the first than in the third VI 3-minute component. According to Williams, these results suggest that the level of the pigeons' responses was influenced more by the impending reinforcement contingency (VI 3-minute component to VI 6-minute component) than by the preceding reinforcement contingency (VI 6-minute to VI 3-minute component).

B. A. Williams (1983) reported that response rate was higher to the stimulus that was associated with the VI 6-minute component than the VI 3-minute component. Did the higher responding to the stimulus associated with the VI 6-minute component mean that the animal had come to prefer the VI 6-minute schedule? Despite anticipatory contrast producing a high response rate to the stimulus associated with the VI 6-minute schedule, the VI 3-minute schedule is the preferred schedule. When given a choice, animals still choose a stimulus associated with the VI 3-minute schedule. According to B. A. Williams (2002), anticipatory contrast only occurs when its effect on behavior is stronger than the prevailing reinforcement contingencies; that is, a higher rate of reinforcement that can be had on a VI 3-minute than on a VI 6-minute schedule.

The behavioral contrast phenomenon points to one problem with discrimination learning: It can have negative consequences. Consider the following situation. A disruptive child's teacher decides to extinguish the disruptive behavior by no longer reinforcing (perhaps by discontinuing attention to the child's disruptive activities). But the child's parents may continue to attend to the disruptive behavior. In this case, the child will be disruptive at home (S^D) but not at school (S^Δ). In fact, the parents will probably experience an increase in disruptive behavior at home due to behavioral contrast; that is, as the rate of disruptive behavior during school declines, the child will become more disruptive at home. Parents can deal with this situation only by discontinuing reinforcement of the disruptive behavior in the home. This observation points out that one consequence of extinguishing an undesired behavior in one setting is an increase in that behavior in other situations. The solution to this problem is to extinguish an undesired behavior in all situations.

BEFORE YOU GO ON

- What stimulus was the S^D for Miguel?

- Suggest an experience that led Miguel to incorrectly identify his assailant.

SECTION REVIEW

- In discrimination learning, an individual discovers the stimuli (S^D) signaling reinforcement availability and the events (S^Δ) indicating that reinforcement is unavailable.

- Learning to discriminate results in responding when the S^D, but not the S^Δ, is present.

- Individuals must also learn to discriminate between occasions when punishment will occur and when it will not.

- There is an increased response to S^D and a decreased response to S^Δ during discrimination learning, an effect called behavioral contrast.

- The switch from the S^D to the S^Δ, or vice versa, causes an emotional response and a temporary change in response called local contrast.

- The anticipation of a change in reinforcement contingencies causes a long-lasting change in response called sustained or anticipatory contrast.

Occasion Setting

You may still have difficulty understanding the difference between a conditioned stimulus that elicits (involuntarily produces) a conditioned response and a discriminative stimulus that "sets the occasion" for emitting (voluntarily producing) an operant response. One way to appreciate the difference between the eliciting function of a conditioned stimulus and the occasion-setting function of a discriminative stimulus is to examine the properties of a Pavlovian occasion-setting stimulus.

The Properties of a Pavlovian Occasion-Setting Stimulus

A stimulus can have an excitatory property other than eliciting a conditioned response. In some circumstances, a stimulus can prepare, or set the occasion, for an animal to respond to a conditioned stimulus. In other words, an occasion-setting stimulus can create the conditions necessary for a conditioned stimulus to elicit the conditioned response. In the absence of the occasion-setting stimulus, the conditioned stimulus has no effect on behavior.

Perhaps a real-world example of occasion setting would be helpful. Many people smoke at the end of a meal. These people see a cigarette at this time and feel a need to smoke. Yet, at other times, the sight of a cigarette does not produce a craving to smoke. It could be argued that the end of the meal is the occasion setter for the cigarette to elicit craving as the conditioned response. Why would the end of the meal be an occasion setter for cigarette-induced craving? People report that smoking a cigarette is more pleasurable after a meal than at other times. Thus, a cigarette is more strongly associated with pleasure following a meal (the occasion setter) than at other times.

Holland (1992) has referred to the ability of one stimulus to enhance the response to another stimulus as **occasion setting** because one stimulus sets the occasion for another stimulus to elicit the conditioned response. Rescorla (1990) suggested that the occasion-setting stimulus facilitates the response to the conditioned stimulus.

When can a stimulus facilitate responding to another stimulus? Holland (1983, 1992) and Rescorla (1985, 1990) conducted a number of studies investigating the occasion-setting ability of a stimulus. In a typical experiment, pigeons experience Stimulus A (e.g., a localized lighted key on the wall of operant chamber) without the unconditioned stimulus on some trials (see Figure 10.7). On other trials, Stimulus A follows a diffuse Stimulus B (e.g., a 1800-Hz tone), and both stimuli are paired with the unconditioned stimulus of food. In this research, the conditioned response is the key peck to the lighted key; that is, the pigeons' conditioned response to the lighted key is the same as their unconditioned pecking response to food. The presentation of Stimulus A (the lighted key) alone elicited no response. In contrast, the presentation of Stimulus B, or the occasion-setting stimulus (a 1800-Hz tone), prior to Stimulus A (the lighted key) caused Stimulus A to elicit the conditioned key-peck response. In other words, the pigeons did not peck at the lighted key when it was presented alone, but the lighted key did elicit a conditioned key-peck response when it followed the tone.

You might think that the response to Stimulus A (lighted key) in the presence of Stimulus B (tone) is merely due to excitatory conditioning to Stimulus B. However, both Holland (1992) and Rescorla (1990) argue that conditioned excitation and facilitation are separate properties of a stimulus. Conditioned excitation refers to a stimulus eliciting a conditioned response, while facilitation represents a stimulus's occasion-setting function.

Figure 10.7 Illustration of the occasion-setting procedure. Animals receive light (Stimulus A) without a food UCS on some (X) trials. On other (Y) trials, the light stimulus follows a more diffuse tone (Stimulus B), which are both paired with the food UCS.

Several lines of evidence demonstrate the separate facilitation and excitation properties of a stimulus. Excitatory conditioning to Stimulus B does not automatically lead that stimulus to facilitate a response to Stimulus A (Rescorla, 1985). Also, the establishment of Stimulus B as a facilitator of response to Stimulus A does not result in the ability of Stimulus B to elicit a conditioned response (Holland, 1983). Further, the facilitating influence of Stimulus B may transfer to conditioned stimuli other than Stimulus A (Rescorla, 1985). These observations provide strong support for the view that facilitation and excitation represent separate learning processes.

We learned earlier in the chapter that interoceptive stimuli, as well as exteroceptive stimuli, could serve as discriminative stimuli and gain control over behavior. Interoceptive stimuli also can serve as occasion-setters for conditioned stimuli (Palmatier & Bevins, 2008). Palmatier and Bevins paired a discrete conditioned stimulus (15-second light or 15-second noise) and sucrose in a nicotine, an amphetamine, or a chlordiazepoxide (Librium) drug state. The conditioned stimulus was presented without reward when the drug state was not present. These researchers reported that the conditioned stimulus elicited a sign-tracking conditioned response, but only when the relevant drug state was present (a sign-tracking conditioned response is elicited by and oriented toward a stimulus associated with a goal or reward. The conditioned response allows the animal to approach and contact the goal stimulus). These results suggest that when the light or noise CS was paired with the sucrose UCS, the present drug state had acquired occasion-setting properties, as the light or noise CS did not elicit the sign-tracking CR in the presence of a novel drug state.

What process enables an occasion-setting stimulus to facilitate response to other stimuli? Rescorla (1986) argued that the facilitating effect of an occasion-setting stimulus is due to lowering the threshold of reaction to conditioned stimuli. He suggested that this facilitation effect is the opposite of the effect of conditioned inhibition, which raises the threshold reaction.

Support for this conclusion can be found in the observation that Stimulus B facilitates response to excitatory conditioned stimuli but not to neutral stimuli (Rescorla, 1985). Thus, the facilitating effect of a stimulus seems to be limited to stimuli possessing excitatory associative strength. An occasion setter, however, facilitates response to an excitatory conditioned stimulus only if that conditioned stimulus has previously served as a target stimulus for other occasion setters (Holland, 1992; Palmatier & Bevins, 2008). If the excitatory conditioned stimulus has not been associated with another occasion setter during conditioning, the presentation of the occasion-setting stimuli will not facilitate a response to that excitatory stimulus. The fact that an occasion setter influences the response only to those excitatory conditioning stimuli previously associated with other occasion-setting stimuli points to the importance of contingency in classical conditioning. The process by which a contingency affects classical conditioning is explored in the next chapter.

We have learned that one stimulus can facilitate the ability of a conditioned stimulus to elicit a conditioned response. In the next section, we will discover that a classical occasion-setting stimulus can also influence operant behavior.

Pavlovian Occasion-Setting Stimuli and Operant Behavior

Rescorla and his colleagues (T. L. Davidson, Aparicio, & Rescorla, 1988) have reported that a Pavlovian occasion setter can increase operant behavior. In their study, a light became a Pavlovian occasion setter after the light was presented prior to a tone (excitatory conditioned stimulus) and food (UCS) during half of the trials, with only the tone presented during the other half of the trials. After the light was established as a Pavlovian occasion setter, the subjects, rats, were given discrimination training in which bar pressing produced food reinforcement when a white noise was present (S^D), but not when the white noise was absent (S^Δ). Following discrimination training, the researchers assessed the influence of both a Pavlovian occasion setter and the discriminative stimulus (S^D) on bar pressing. T. L. Davidson et al. (1988) found that both the Pavlovian occasion setter and the discriminative stimulus (S^D) increased bar pressing (see Figure 10.8).

Figure 10.8   The mean discrimination ratio to a Pavlovian occasion setter (L), a pseudofacilitatory stimulus (L′) and an operant discriminative stimulus (S^D). (In the mean discrimination ratio, A is the mean number of responses to the stimulus and B is the mean number of responses during the time between trials.) The results show that rats bar press when presented with the Pavlovian occasion setter (L) and the operant discriminative stimulus (S^D), but not the pseudofacilitatory stimulus (L′).

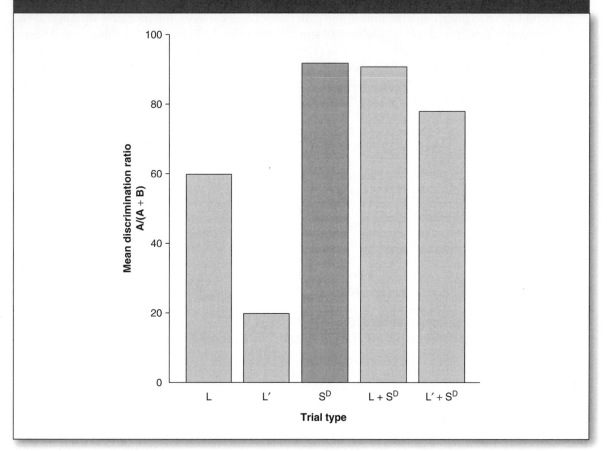

In the T. L. Davidson et al. (1988) study, the Pavlovian occasion setter signaled reinforcement. This study also examined the effect of a pseudofacilitatory stimulus, a stimulus that did not signal reinforcement. In the pseudofacilitation control treatment, the UCS (food) followed both the light and tone pairings and the tone alone. Thus, the light pseudofacilitatory stimulus provided no information about food reinforcement. Davidson et al. found that the pseudofacilitatory stimulus had no effect on the operant bar-pressing response (see Figure 10.8). This failure of the pseudo-facilitatory stimulus to influence operant responding again points to the importance of contingency in the ability of a stimulus to act as an occasion setter.

To illustrate the influence of an occasion setter on operant behavior, let's return to a previous example—the end of a meal acting as an occasion setter so that the sight of a cigarette elicits a conditioned craving response. If the person does not have a cigarette, he or she might ask a friend for one. The request is an operant behavior, and the end of the meal sets the occasion for the request.

Discriminative Stimuli and Conditioned Responses

An excitatory CS's elicitation of a CR is influenced not only by Pavlovian occasion-setting stimuli but also by discriminative stimuli (T. L. Davidson et al., 1988). In the Davidson et al. study, rats initially received food reinforcement for a bar-press response on a VI 30-second schedule in the presence of a light S^D, but they were not reinforced in the absence of the light. After operant conditioning, occasion-setting training occurred; a click (CS) was followed by food (UCS) only when a tone (occasion setter) preceded the click. Davidson et al. reported that the presence of the light S^D enhanced the head-jerk response (conditioned response) to the click (conditioned stimulus).

These findings suggest that an S^D can facilitate the response to a CS just as an occasion setter does. These findings also imply an interchangeability of Pavlovian occasion setters and discriminative stimuli, with one stimulus acting on the target behaviors of the other.

BEFORE YOU GO ON

- What Pavlovian occasion setter might cause Miguel to pick the wrong man out of the lineup?

- Could this Pavlovian occasion setter influence other aspects of Miguel's behavior?

SECTION REVIEW

- A stimulus develops occasion-setting properties when the CS and the UCS follow the occasion-setting stimulus and the CS occurs without the UCS when the occasion-setting stimulus is not present.

- Rescorla suggested that a stimulus facilitates the response to another stimulus by lowering the elicitation threshold of the conditioned response to the second stimulus.

- Pavlovian occasion setters also have an influence on operant behavior; the presence of a Pavlovian occasion setter has the same effect on an operant response as an S^D.

- An operant S^D has the same facilitatory influence on an excitatory conditioned stimulus to elicit a conditioned response as a Pavlovian occasion setter.

The Nature of Discrimination Learning

How do we learn to discriminate between the S^D and the S^Δ? Researchers have proposed several very different views of the nature of discrimination. We start by discussing the Hull-Spence theory.

Hull-Spence Theory of Discrimination Learning

Clark Hull (1943) and Kenneth Spence (1936) offered an associative explanation of discrimination learning. Although it is now believed not to be a completely accurate view of the nature of discrimination learning, the **Hull-Spence theory of discrimination learning** does describe some essential aspects of the discrimination learning process.

Development of Conditioned Excitation and Inhibition. According to the Hull-Spence view, discrimination learning develops in three stages. First, conditioned excitation develops to the S^D as the result of reinforcement. Second, nonreinforcement in the presence of the S^Δ results in the development of conditioned inhibition to the S^Δ. As we learned earlier in the chapter, conditioned inhibition suppresses the response to the S^D. Finally, the excitation and inhibition generalize to other stimuli (see Figure 10.9); the combined influence of excitation and inhibition determines the level of response to each stimuli. As Figure 10.9 indicates, the Hull-Spence model predicts a steeper generalization gradient with discrimination training than with nondiscrimination training. Also, their model proposes that maximum response occurs not to the S^D, but rather to a stimulus other than the S^D, and in the stimulus direction opposite to that of the S^A. The reason for this prediction is that although the S^D (256 in Figure 10.9) has the greatest excitatory strength, it also has accrued inhibitory strength. Although another stimulus (409 in Figure 10.9) may have less excitatory strength than the S^D, it also has accrued little inhibitory strength. Thus, the resultant strength of the S^D will be less than that of the other stimulus.

The Peak Shift Phenomenon. H. M. Hanson (1959) tested the assumptions of the Hull-Spence model of discrimination learning. In Hanson's study, pigeons received discrimination training using a 550-nm light as the S^D and either a 555-, 560-, 570-, or 590-nm as the S^A, or nondiscrimination training using a 550-nm light present during the entire training session. Following training, both groups of pigeons were given a generalization test using stimuli ranging from 480 to 620 nm. Hanson reported three important differences between the discrimination and nondiscrimination generalization gradients (see Figure 10.10). First, a steeper generalization gradient appeared with discrimination than with nondiscrimination training, a prediction in accord with the Hull-Spence model. Second, the greatest response for discrimination-training subjects was not to the 550-nm S^D, but to the 540-nm stimulus. This change, referred to as the **peak shift**, also supports the Hull-Spence view of discrimination training. In contrast, pigeons receiving nondiscrimination training responded maximally to the 550-nm stimulus. Finally, the overall level of response was higher with discrimination training than with nondiscrimination training, an observation the Hull-Spence model did not predict. The peak shift has also been observed in species other than pigeons, including rats (S. J. Weiss & Schindler, 1981) and humans (D. R. Thomas, Mood, Morrison, & Wiertelak, 1991).

Figure 10.9   Spence's theoretical view of the interaction of excitatory and inhibitory generalization gradients on discriminated behavior. During acquisition, reward is available when 256 stimulus size is present, but not when 160 stimulus size is present. Excitatory potential (solid lines) generalizes to similar stimuli, as does inhibitory potential (broken lines). The resultant reaction tendency, indicated by the value above each stimulus size, is obtained by subtracting the inhibitory from the excitatory potential.

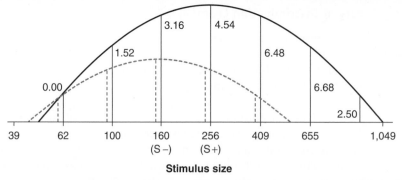

Figure 10.10   Mean number of responses on a generalization test (using wavelengths varying from 480 to 620 nm) for four experimental groups receiving prior discrimination training. The four groups received training with 550 nm as the S^D and either 555, 560, 570, or 590 nm as the S^Δ; the control group did not receive discrimination training. Experimental subjects showed a steeper generalization gradients and a greater response to stimuli similar to S^D than did control subjects. Also, the peak shift was seen in the experimental but not in control subjects.

The Aversive Character of S^Δ. Herbert Terrace (1964) suggested that behavioral contrast is responsible for the heightened response seen with discrimination training. Terrace argued that exposure to the S^Δ is an aversive event, and that the frustration produced during S^Δ periods increased the intensity of the response to other stimuli.

The effect of drugs (e.g., chlorpromazine and imipramine) that eliminate frustration-induced behavior provides support for Terrace's view of the aversiveness of S^Δ. Administration of these drugs disrupts the performance on a discrimination task (Bloomfield, 1972; Terrace, 1963a). Animals receiving chlorpromazine (an antipsychotic drug) or imipramine (an antidepressant drug) exhibit a high level of response to the S^Δ. It is thought that the reduced aversiveness of the S^Δ is responsible for the lack of inhibition of response to the S^Δ.

Errorless Discrimination Training

Can an animal acquire a discrimination without ever responding to the S^D? Although you might not think so, psychologists have discovered that a discrimination can be learned with few or no errors. Several studies conducted during the 1930s and 1940s (Schlosberg & Solomon, 1943; Skinner, 1938) showed that with sufficient care, an animal could learn a discrimination with few errors. However, the significance of these studies was not recognized until Terrace (1963a, 1963b, 1963c, 1964, 1966) conducted a detailed examination of **errorless discrimination learning**.

Training Procedure. Terrace (1963b) trained pigeons on a red-green (S^D-S^Δ) discrimination. Each pigeon was trained to peck at a red illuminated key (S^D) to receive food reinforcement on a VI 1-minute schedule. The pigeons were divided into four groups, and each group received a different combination of procedures to introduce the S^Δ. Two groups of pigeons received a progressive S^Δ introduction. During the first phase of this procedure, the presentation of the S^Δ, a dark key, lasted 5 seconds and then increased by 5 seconds with each trial until it reached 30 seconds. In the second phase of S^Δ introduction, the duration of the S^Δ was kept at 30 seconds, and the intensity of the S^Δ was increased until it became a green light. During the final phase of the study, the duration of the S^Δ was slowly increased from 30 seconds to 3 minutes. (Note that the duration of the S^D was 3 minutes during all three phases.) By contrast, for pigeons receiving constant training, the S^Δ was initially presented at full intensity and full duration. One progressive training group and one constant training group were given an early introduction to S^Δ; the S^Δ was presented during the first session that a pigeon was placed in the training chamber. The other two groups (one progressive, one constant) received late S^Δ introduction; the S^Δ was introduced following 14 sessions of key pecking with the S^D present.

Figure 10.11 presents the results of Terrace's (1963b) study. Terrace reported that pigeons receiving early progressive training did not emit many errors (a range of two to eight during the entire experiment). By contrast, the animals in the other three groups emitted many errors during S^Δ periods. Furthermore, the errors the early progressive subjects made occurred at either the beginning or the end of the S^Δ period, whereas the errors of the other three groups of pigeons occurred throughout S^Δ exposure and often came in bursts. These results show that an animal

Figure 10.11   Number of responses each bird emitted during 28 trials of training as a function of the discrimination training procedure.

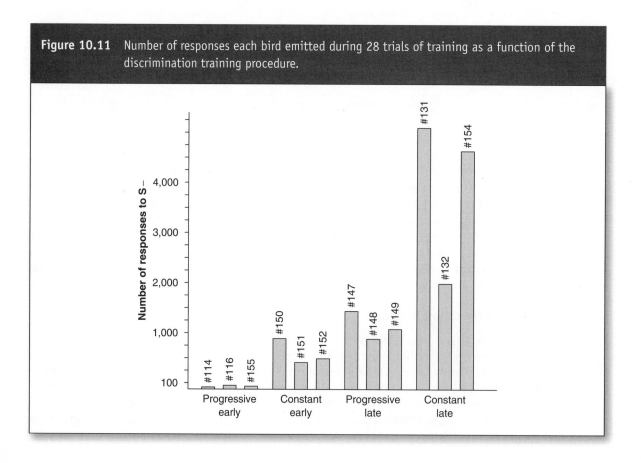

can learn a discrimination with few errors only when the S^Δ has been gradually introduced early in training. In later articles, Terrace reported completely errorless discrimination training with the use of slight variations in the early progressive procedure.

Some discriminations are more difficult to acquire than others. For example, pigeons learn a color (red-green) discrimination more readily than a line-tilt (horizontal-vertical) discrimination. Furthermore, not only are pigeons slow to acquire a horizontal-vertical discrimination, but they also make many errors in response to the S^Δ. While more difficult, Terrace (1963c) found that pigeons can learn a difficult line-tilt discrimination without errors. To accomplish this goal, Terrace first trained pigeons on a red-green color discrimination task using the early progressive errorless training technique. After training, the vertical and horizontal lines were superimposed on the colors to form compound stimuli (the red vertical line was the S^D; the green horizontal line, the S^Δ). During this segment of training, the intensity of the colors was reduced until they were no longer visible. Terrace found that this "fading" procedure helped the pigeons to learn the horizontal-vertical discrimination quickly and without making any errors. In contrast, if colors were quickly removed or never presented with the horizontal-vertical lines, the pigeons made many errors before learning the line-tilt discrimination.

Nonaversive S^Δ. The behavioral characteristics found with standard discrimination training are not observed with errorless discrimination training (Terrace, 1964). The peak shift does not appear in errorless discrimination training. Errorless discrimination training produces the same level of response to the S^D as nondiscrimination training does. Furthermore, the presentation of the S^Δ, as well as stimuli other than the S^D, inhibits responses in subjects receiving errorless discrimination training. Finally, the administration of chlorpromazine or imipramine does not disrupt discrimination performance; that is, the individual continues to respond to the S^D, but not to the S^Δ.

Terrace's observations have important implications for our understanding of the nature of discrimination learning. These data indicate that with errorless discrimination training, the S^Δ is not aversive. Also, Terrace argued that with errorless discrimination, the S^Δ does not develop inhibitory control; instead, individuals learn to respond only to the S^D. These results suggest that inhibitory control is not the only response acquired during discrimination training. In fact, inhibitory control does not seem to be essential for effective discrimination performance. How can a pigeon or person learn not to respond to the S^Δ with errorless discrimination training? Perhaps the pigeon or person learns to expect that no reinforcement will occur during S^Δ, and this expectation leads the pigeon or person to not respond to the S^Δ. The next chapter examines the evidence that expectations, as well as emotions, affect behavior.

Application: Errorless Discrimination Training in Humans. Errorless discrimination training also is possible with humans. Gollin and Savoy (1968) taught preschool children a shape discrimination using the fading technique; R. Moore and Goldiamond (1964) used this procedure to teach a pattern match; and Corey and Shamov (1972) used it to teach oral reading. In each of these studies, the children given the faded series of S^Δ stimuli made few errors, while other subjects who received standard discrimination training made many incorrect responses to the S^Δ.

The significance of Terrace's fading procedure is best seen in the research of Dorry and Zeaman (1975, 1976). Using the fading procedure, they trained children with mental retardation to identify vocabulary words. In their studies, the children initially learned picture discriminations. After picture discrimination training, words were presented with the pictures; the pictures were then slowly faded out. Dorry and Zeaman compared the effectiveness of the fading procedure with that of normal discrimination training. They reported that the children taught with the fading procedure learned more words than did the children given standard discrimination training.

Programs for children with mental retardation have successfully incorporated errorless procedures into the teaching of discriminations (Conners, 1992; Zygmont, Lazar, Dube, & McIlvane, 1992). However, not all errorless procedures have worked. R. S. Jones and Eayrs (1992) reported that children with mental retardation have difficulty generalizing their discrimination learning to new situations, while McIlvane, Kledaras, Iennaco, McDonald, and Stoddard (1995) found that such children have difficulty learning discriminations in which the consequences of the S^D and S^Δ are reversed.

The errorless discrimination procedure has also been used successfully with children who have difficulty detecting speech sounds. Merzenich et al. (1996) first presented sounds that had certain components exaggerated by making the sounds longer or louder. For example, the word *banana* became *baaaanana*. As the children correctly identified a sound, the sound was gradually made normal. Merzenich and his colleagues reported that these children correctly learned the sounds with few errors.

Learning without errors also has been shown to facilitate discrimination learning in adults (Mueller, Palkovic, & Maynard, 2007). For example, Kessels and de Haan (2003) reported that young adults and older adults learned face–name associations more readily with an errorless than with trial-and-error discrimination learning. Komatsu, Mimura, Kato, Wakamatsu, and Kashima (2000) found that an errorless discrimination training procedure facilitated face–name associative learning in patients with alcoholic Korsakoff's syndrome, while Clare, Wilson, Carter, Roth, and Hodges (2002) observed that face–name associations were more easily learned with an errorless discrimination procedure than trial-and-error discrimination learning in individuals in the early stage of Alzheimer's disease. Further, F. C. Wilson and Manley (2003) observed that errorless discrimination learning enhanced self-care functioning in individuals with severe traumatic brain injury, while Kern, Green, Mintz, and Liberman (2003) reported that errorless discrimination learning improved social problem-solving skills in persons with schizophrenia. Finally, Benbassat and Abramson (2002) reported that novice pilots learned to respond to a flare discrimination cue more efficiently (smoother and safer landings) with an errorless discrimination than with a control procedure involving errors.

Wolfgang Köhler (1887–1967)

Kohler received his doctorate from the University of Berlin under the direction of Max Planck and Carl Stumpft. After receiving his doctorate, he spent 3 years at the Psychological Institute in Frankfurt, Germany, working with Max Wertheimer and Kurt Koffka and helping to develop Gestalt psychology. He spent the next 6 years as director of the Prussian Academy of Sciences in the Canary Islands, where he wrote *The Mentality of Apes,* describing his observations of problem solving in chimpanzees. He then returned to Germany and was director of the Psychological Institute at the University of Berlin for 15 years. He objected to the dismissal of his Jewish colleagues by the Nazis and, in 1935, left for the United States. He taught at Swarthmore College for 20 years and served as president of the American Psychological Association in 1959.

The Transposition Effect

Although the peak shift phenomenon appears to support the Hull-Spence view, the noted Gestalt psychologist Wolfgang Kohler (1939) provides an alternative view of discrimination learning that can also explain the peak shift. According to Kohler, we do not evaluate stimuli in absolute terms, but instead in relation to other stimuli. For example, a 75-dB tone may seem loud in a quiet room but soft in a noisy room. Thus, when we say that a noise is loud or soft, the perceived loudness depends on the context in which the noise is heard.

Kohler's (1939) view is important when applied to discrimination learning. For example, suppose that a rat learns to discriminate between an 80-dB S^D and a 60-dB S^Δ. Has the rat learned to respond to the 80-dB tone and not to the 60-dB tone? In Kohler's view, the animal has merely learned to respond to the louder of the two tones. How would the rat react to a 90-dB tone? Kohler's theory predicts that because the rat learned to respond to the louder tone, the rat would react more intensely to the 90-dB than the 80-dB tone. To evaluate this view, Kohler trained chickens and chimpanzees to respond to the brighter of two stimuli (the S^D). When he tested his subjects with the S^D and a still brighter light stimulus, the animals chose the brighter of the two lights. Kohler called this phenomenon **transposition**, a term drawn from the idea that the relation among notes composing musical compositions does not change when the melodies are transposed to a different key.

Which view of discrimination learning is accurate: the Hull-Spence absolute view or the Kohler relational view? According to Schwartz and Reisberg (1991), there is evidence supporting both views. Studies that give animals the choice between two stimuli support the relational or transposition view; that is, the animals respond to the relative rather than absolute qualities of the stimuli. One study providing support for the relational view was conducted by Lawrence and DeRivera (1954). Lawrence and DeRivera initially exposed rats to cards that were divided in half. During training, the bottom half of the card was always an intermediate shade of gray, and the top half was one of three lighter or one of the three darker shades of gray. A darker top half meant that the rats needed to turn left to obtain reward; a lighter top half signaled a right turn for reward. Figure 10.12 presents a diagram of this procedure.

During testing, Lawrence and DeRivera (1954) no longer presented the intermediate shade of gray; instead, two of the six shades of gray presented on top during training were shown (one on the top, the other on the bottom). Although a number of combinations of these six shades were used, only one combination is described here to illustrate how this study supports a relational view. On some test trials, two of the darker shades were used, with the lighter of the two on top (see again Figure 10.12). If the animals had learned based on absolute values, they would turn left because during training the dark shade on the top meant "turn left." However, if the animals had learned based on the relation between stimuli, they would turn right during testing because the darker stimulus was still on the bottom. Lawrence and DeRivera reported that on the overwhelming majority of such test trials, the animals' responses were based on the relation between stimuli rather than on the absolute value of the stimuli. Thus, in our example, most of the animals turned right because the darker shade of gray was on the bottom half of the card.

Although some studies support a relational view of discrimination, other experiments support the Hull-Spence absolute stimulus view. Hanson's (1959) study provides support for the Hull-Spence theory. Hanson trained pigeons to peck at a 550-nm (S^D) lighted key to receive reinforcement; pecking at a 590-nm (S^Δ) light yielded no reinforcement. On generalization tests, the pigeons were presented with a range of lighted keys varying from 480 to 620 nm. According to the Hull-Spence view, at a point on the stimulus continuum below the S^D, the **inhibitory generalization gradient** does not affect excitatory response. At this point on the gradient, response to the S^D should be greater than the response occurring at the lower wavelength test stimuli. In contrast, the relational view suggests that a lower wavelength of light will always produce a response greater than the S^D does. Hanson's results showed that while greater response did occur to the 540-nm test light than to the 550-nm S^D, less response occurred to the 530-nm light than to the S^D (refer to Figure 10.10). Thus, on generalization tests, greater response occurs only to stimuli close to the S^D.

You might wonder why some results support the Hull-Spence absolute-value view and others suggest that Kohler's relational approach is more correct. As Schwartz and Reisberg (1991) pointed out, a choice test supports the relational view; that is, subjects must choose to respond to one of two stimuli. In contrast, on a generalization test in which a subject responds to one stimulus, results support the Hull-Spence approach. In Schwartz and Reisberg's view, it is not unreasonable for both approaches to be valid; animals could learn both the relationship between stimuli and the absolute characteristics of the stimuli. In choice situations, the relationship

Figure 10.12 Diagram showing the procedure used by Lawrence and DeRivera (1954) in their analysis of the absolute versus the relational view of discrimination learning. The numbers indicate darkness of gray used in the study. A left turn in response to the test stimulus shown in this illustration indicates absolute control of response, and a right turn indicates relational control of response.

between stimuli is important, and the animal responds to the relational aspects it has learned. In contrast, when only a single stimulus is presented, the absolute character of a stimulus determines the level of response.

Sutherland and Mackintosh's Attentional View

Norman Sutherland and Nicholas Mackintosh (1971) suggested that discrimination learning occurs in two stages. During the first stage, an individual's attention to the relevant dimension strengthens. The second phase involves the association of a particular response to the relevant stimulus.

The Recognition of the Relevant Dimension. Suppose that the S^D and the S^Δ are multidimensional; that is, each consists of several different stimulus dimensions. For example, perhaps the S^D is a bright, green, striped light, while the S^Δ is a dull, red, solid light. How would a pigeon respond in this situation? When a stimulus consists of more than one dimension, one of the stimulus dimensions generally gains control of responding. Why? According to Sutherland and Mackintosh (1971), each stimulus dimension can activate an analyzer. The analyzer detects the presence of the salient or relevant aspect of a stimulus, and the arousal of a particular analyzer causes an animal to attend to that dimension. Thus, the presentation of a compound stimulus arouses the analyzer of the relevant dimension, but not the analyzers of the other stimulus dimensions.

Consider the following example to illustrate the **Sutherland-Mackintosh attentional theory**. A person viewing a 5-inch red horizontal bar projected onto a gray background could attend to several dimensions—for example, the color, brightness, length, or orientation of the bar. However, this person notices only the color of the bar. In Sutherland and Mackintosh's (1971) view, the reason for this phenomenon is that the analyzer for the color dimension is aroused, but the analyzers for the other dimensions are not.

What determines which analyzer will be aroused? Initially, the level of arousal of a particular analyzer relates to the intensity and salience of the stimulus dimension; the greater the strength and salience of a particular stimulus dimension, the more likely that dimension will activate the analyzer sufficiently to arouse attention. With certain types of experiences, the ability of analyzers to attract attention changes. According to Sutherland and Mackintosh (1971), the predictive value of a particular stimulus dimension influences the amount of attention the analyzer of that stimulus dimension arouses. The analyzer will arouse more attention if the stimulus dimension predicts important events. However, an analyzer will arouse less attention if the stimulus dimension for that analyzer is not predictive of future events.

Association of the Analyzer With a Response. In the second phase of discrimination learning, the activity of the analyzer attaches to a particular response. The connection between the analyzer and the response strengthens as the result of reinforcement. Thus, in Sutherland and Mackintosh's (1971) view, reinforcement increases both the attention to a particular dimension and the ability of a particular stimulus to elicit the response.

Predictive Value of Discriminative Stimuli

Research indicates that predictiveness has an important influence on discrimination learning. Recall from Chapter 4 that the predictive value of the CS determines whether it becomes able to elicit a CR. Similarly, the ability of the S^D to predict reinforcement is important. Only if the S^D is predictive of reinforcement will it control the response.

Wagner, Logan, Haberlandt, and Price (1968) investigated the influence of the S^D's predictiveness on its control of operant response. Two groups of rats were trained to bar press for reinforcement. Subjects in the first group were reinforced on 50% of the trials in which the light-with-the-first-tone compound stimulus was presented and on 50% of the trials in which the light-with-the-second-tone compound stimulus was presented (see Figure 10.13). The rats in the second group received the light-with-the-first-tone stimulus paired with reinforcement 100% of the time; the light-with-the-second-tone stimulus was presented 0% of the time.

Wagner and his colleagues were interested in the degree of control the light cue would gain. For subjects in the first group, the light cue was present when reinforcement was available on 50% of the trials. For the second group, the first tone was much more predictive of reinforcement than the light cue; for these subjects, the first tone was present during 100% of the trials on which reinforcement was available, but the light was paired with reinforcement on only 50% of the trials. Although the light was paired with reinforcement availability on 50% of the trials in both groups, the light was a better predictor in the first group than in the second: No cue in the first group predicted reinforcement more reliably than did the light, whereas in the second group, the first tone predicted reinforcement better than the light. Wagner et al. reported that the light better controlled responses for subjects in the first group than in the second group. These results indicate that it is the relative predictiveness of an S^D that determines its ability to control response.

Continuity Versus Discontinuity

The Hull-Spence view asserts that excitation and inhibition gradually increase during the acquisition of a discrimination. This position is referred to as a **continuity theory of discrimination learning**

Figure 10.13 Two treatment conditions in the Wagner, Logan, Haberlandt, and Price (1968) study. For subjects in Group 1, the light was equally predictive of reinforcement as either tone, but for Group 2, the light was a worse predictor than Tone 1 and a better predictor than Tone 2.

because it proposes that the development of a discrimination is a continuous and gradual acquisition of excitation to the S^D and inhibition to the S^Δ. Krechevsky (1932) and Lashley (1929) presented a view of discrimination learning that differs substantially from the Hull-Spence approach. According to Krechevsky and Lashley, the learning of a discrimination is not a gradual, continuous process. Instead, they believed that an animal acquires a discrimination by establishing a hypothesis about which stimulus is associated with reinforcement. While testing this hypothesis, the animal attends to the stimulus relevant to its hypothesis and learns nothing about other stimuli. The view is referred to as a **noncontinuity theory of discrimination learning** because it assumes that once an animal focuses its attention on the relevant stimuli, it will rapidly acquire the discrimination.

A considerable amount of research has attempted to evaluate the continuity and noncontinuity views. Some studies support the continuity approach of Hull and Spence, and other research has agreed with the noncontinuity approach Krechevsky and Lashley take. It is not surprising that research exists to validate both points of view because discrimination learning reflects both the acquisition of excitatory and inhibitory strength and the development of attention to predictive events in the environment. It seems reasonable that continuity theory explains how the emotional components of a discrimination are learned and that noncontinuity theory describes the attentional aspects of discrimination learning.

BEFORE YOU GO ON

- How would the Hull-Spence theory explain Miguel's failure to correctly identify his assailant?

- How would the Sutherland-Mackintosh attentional view explain Miguel's failure to correctly identify his assailant?

SECTION REVIEW

- The Hull-Spence view proposes that conditioned excitation develops to the S^D as the result of reward.

- After conditioned excitation is established, nonreward in the presence of the S^Δ results in the development of conditioned inhibition to the S^Δ.

- Discrimination training causes a steeper generalization gradient than nondiscrimination training.

- With traditional discrimination learning, the greatest response for discrimination-training subjects is not to the S^D, but to a similar stimulus, a phenomenon referred to as the peak shift.

- Terrace argued that exposure to the S^Δ is an aversive event and that frustration produced during S^Δ periods increases the intensity of response to other stimuli.

- The early progressive introduction of S^Δ leads to a discrimination being learned without a response to the S^Δ.

- Errorless discrimination training produces the same level of response to the S^D as is found with nondiscrimination training and no peak shift.

- Kohler's relational or transposition view assumes that animals or people learn the relative relationship between the S^D and the S^Δ.

- Sutherland and Mackintosh suggested that during discrimination learning, an animal's attention to relevant dimensions strengthens.

- According to the Sutherland-Mackintosh view, after an animal attends to the relevant dimension, the association between the operant response and the relevant stimulus strengthens.

- The continuity view of discrimination learning assumes that excitation and inhibition gradually increase during the acquisition of a discrimination.

- The noncontinuity approach asserts that there is an abrupt recognition of the salient features of a discrimination.

CRITICAL THINKING QUESTIONS

1. Generalization can lead to effective coping, or it can cause behavioral problems. Discuss the positive and negative aspects of the generalization process. What can be done to prevent unwanted generalization?

2. Shameca is very selective about the clothes she buys. She will shop in some stores, but not in others. Explain one possible basis for Shameca's selectivity.

3. Natalie becomes sexually aroused by her husband when they are alone with the lights dimmed and soft music playing. By contrast, she is not physically aroused by him when they are shopping in a mall. Describe how occasion setting can explain Natalie's different responses to her husband.

KEY TERMS

anticipatory contrast

conditional discrimination

discrimination learning

discriminative stimulus

excitatory generalization gradient

generalization gradient

inhibitory generalization gradient

local contrast

occasion setting

S^D

stimulus generalization

sustained contrast

transposition

behavioral contrast

continuity theory of discrimination learning

discriminative operant

errorless discrimination learning

Hull-Spence theory of discrimination learning

Lashley-Wade theory of generalization

noncontinuity theory of discrimination learning

peak shift

S^Δ

Sutherland-Mackintosh attentional theory

two-choice discrimination learning

Cognitive Control of Behavior

THE INSURMOUNTABLE BARRIER

Math has always been an obstacle for Martha. Even in elementary school, her distaste for arithmetic was evident. She dreaded working with numbers, and her lowest grades were always in math. Martha's high marks in her other classes came without much effort, but she always had to struggle to earn an acceptable grade in her math courses. In college, she avoided the high-level math courses and chose only the ones other students said were easy. She did okay in these courses because they were not much different from her high school math classes. During the summer before her sophomore year in college, Martha decided to major in psychology. One C in college math was the only mark to mar her superior grade record. To earn her psychology degree, Martha should have completed a statistics course during the fall semester of her sophomore year, but she did not. The hour was not right that fall, and she did not like the professor who taught the course the following spring. Determined to complete her degree, Martha enrolled in the statistics course this past fall—only to drop out three weeks later. She could not comprehend the material and failed the first exam. Martha knows that she cannot finish her psychology degree without the statistics class, and now only three semesters remain until she is scheduled to graduate. However, she does not believe she can pass the course. She has discussed her problem with her parents and friends, and they regularly offer encouragement. Unfortunately, their good wishes cannot make her problem go away. Yesterday, Martha learned from a friend that he had a similar problem with chemistry and that a psychologist at the university's counseling center helped him overcome his "chemistry phobia." This friend suggested to Martha that the center might help her, too. Martha has never considered her math aversion a psychological problem and is reluctant to acknowledge any need for clinical treatment. She knows that she must decide before next week's registration whether to seek help at the center.

If Martha goes for help, she may learn several things: Her fear of the statistics course results from her belief that her failure on the first statistics exam reflects a lack of ability in math and her feeling that she cannot endure taking the statistics course. On the basis of these beliefs, Martha expects to fail the course. Later in the chapter, a cognitive explanation for Martha's math phobia is described, as well as a treatment that has successfully modified the expectations that maintain the phobic behavior of people like Martha.

The term **cognition** refers to an animal's or person's knowledge of the environment. Psychologists investigating cognitive processes have focused on two distinctively different areas of inquiry. Many psychologists have evaluated an individual's understanding of the structure of the psychological environment (i.e., when events occur and what has to be done to obtain reward or avoid punishment) and how this understanding, or expectation, acts to control the animal's or person's response. In this chapter, we discuss the role of cognition in governing behavior. Other psychologists have evaluated the processes that enable an individual to acquire knowledge of the environment. This research has investigated learning processes such as concept formation, problem solving, language acquisition, and memory. These processes provide the mental structure for thinking; we discuss these in later chapters.

TOLMAN'S PURPOSIVE BEHAVIORISM

Edward Tolman proposed a cognitive view of learning during the 1930s and 1940s. At this time, this approach was not adopted by most psychologists. The S-R associative approach was the accepted view of learning during that period. As we discussed in Chapter 2, the cognitive view gained some acceptance during the 1950s and 1960s as other psychologists expanded Tolman's original cognitive approach, but only in the past few decades have psychologists recognized the important contribution of cognition in the learning process. We briefly discussed Tolman's view in Chapter 2. Our discussion in this chapter begins with a more detailed look at Tolman's work; later in the chapter, we look at the ideas and research of contemporary cognitive psychologists.

Learning Principles

Tolman's (1932, 1959) view of learning contrasts with the associative view described in Chapter 2. Tolman did not envision that behavior reflects an automatic response to an environmental event due to an S-R association; rather, he thought that human behavior has both direction and purpose. According to Tolman, our behavior is goal oriented because we are motivated either to approach a particular reward or to avoid a specific aversive event. In addition, we are capable of understanding the structure of our environment. There are paths leading to our goals and tools we can employ to reach these goals. Through experience, we gain an expectation of how to use these paths and tools. Although Tolman used the terms *purpose* and *expectation* to describe the process that motivates our behavior, he did not mean that we are aware of either the purpose or the direction of our behavior. He theorized that we act *as if* we expect a particular action to lead to a specific goal.

According to Tolman (1932, 1959), not only is our behavior goal oriented, but we also expect a specific outcome to follow a specific behavior. For example, we expect that going to a favorite restaurant will result in a great meal. If we do not obtain our goal, we will continue to search for the reward and will not be satisfied with a less-valued goal object. If our favorite restaurant is closed, we will not accept just any restaurant, but will choose only a suitable alternative. Also, certain events in the environment convey information about where our goals are located. According to Tolman, we are able to reach our goals only after we have learned to recognize the signs leading to reward or punishment in our environment. Thus, we know where our favorite restaurant is, and we use this information to guide us to that restaurant.

Tolman (1932, 1959) suggested that we do not have to be reinforced to learn. However, our expectations will not translate into behavior unless we are motivated. Tolman proposed that motivation has two functions: (1) it produces a state of internal tension that creates a demand for the goal object, and (2) it determines the environmental features we will attend to. For example, if we are not hungry, we are less likely to learn where food is than if we are starving. However, tension does not possess the mechanistic quality it did in Hull's (1943, 1952) theory. According to Tolman, our expectations control the direction of our drives. Therefore, when we are motivated, we do not respond in a fixed, automatic, or stereotyped way to reduce our drive; rather, our behavior will remain flexible enough to enable us to reach our goal.

While much research has been conducted to evaluate the validity of Hull's mechanistic approach, the research effort to validate Tolman's cognitive view has been modest, although Tolman and his students conducted several key studies that provide support for this approach. The next sections examine these studies and describe what they tell us about learning.

Place-Learning Studies

Tolman (1932, 1959) suggested that people expect reward in a certain place, and they follow the paths leading to that place. In contrast, Hull (1943, 1952) proposed that environmental cues elicit specific motor responses that have led to reward in the past. How do we know which view is valid? Under normal conditions, we cannot determine whether our expectations or our habits will lead us to reward. Tolman designed his place-learning studies to provide us with an answer.

T-Maze Experiments

Tolman, Ritchie, and Kalish (1946) designed several experiments to distinguish behavior based on S-R associations from behavior based on spatial expectations. In their studies, rats were placed for half of the trials in location S_1 in the apparatus shown in Figure 11.1. For the other half of the trials, the rats began in location S_2. For the place-learning condition, the reward was always in the same location (e.g., F_1), but the turning response needed to reach the reward differed for each trial, depending on whether the rat started at S_1 or S_2. For the response-learning condition, the rats received the reward in both locations, but only one response—either right or left—produced the reward. Tolman et al. found that all the place-condition animals learned within 8 trials and continued to behave without errors for the next 10 trials. None of the rats in the response-learning condition learned this rapidly; even after responding correctly, they continued to make errors. Tolman et al.'s results illustrate that superior learning occurs when we can obtain reward in a certain place rather than by using a certain response.

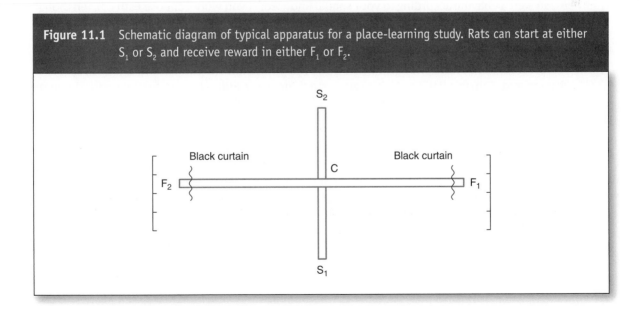

Figure 11.1   Schematic diagram of typical apparatus for a place-learning study. Rats can start at either S_1 or S_2 and receive reward in either F_1 or F_2.

In a second study, Tolman et al. (1946) demonstrated that a rat will go to a place associated with reward even when an entirely new motor response is required to reach the place. During the first phase of their study, the researchers placed the rats in location S_1 and the reward placed in F_1. In this phase of the study, both a habit (right turn) and an expectation (where food is) could lead to reward. During the second phase of the study, the researchers placed the rats at location S_2. In this stage, the rats reached the goal only by turning left toward F_1; the habitual right response led to an empty goal box. Tolman et al. reported that their subjects turned left and went to F_1, the place associated with reward. These results suggest that expectations, not S-R associations, controlled behavior in this study.

Many studies have compared place versus response learning. However, the results of some indicate that response learning is superior to place learning. Fortunately, there are several likely explanations for these different results. One cause of the conflicting results is the presence of cues to guide behavior (Blodgett & McCutchan, 1947, 1948). For example, place learning is superior to response learning when extra maze cues (e.g., the ceiling lights in the laboratory) are present, allowing a spatial orientation to guide the rats to the correct location. Without extra maze cues, the animals are forced to rely on motor responses to produce reward.

The degree of experience with the task is another reason for the different results. For example, I have sometimes experienced the following situation while driving home. Instead of turning from my typical path to run a planned errand, I continue past the turn and arrive home. Why did I drive my usual route home rather than turn off on the route necessary to do my errand? One likely answer is that I have driven home so often that the response has become the habitual route home. Kendler and Gasser's (1948) study indicates that well-learned behavior is typically under the control of mechanistic, rather than cognitive, processes. They found that with fewer than 20 trials, animals responded to place cues, whereas with greater training, the rats exhibited the appropriate motor response.

Alternate-Path Studies

To begin an understanding of alternate-path studies, examine the map in Figure 11.2. Pretend that these paths represent routes to school. Which path would you choose? In all likelihood, you would use Path A, the shortest. However, what would you do if Path A were blocked at Point Y? If you were behaving according to your spatial knowledge, you would choose Path C. Even though Path C is longer than B, your **cognitive map**, or your spatial representation of the physical environment, would produce the expectation that B is also blocked and thus would motivate you to choose C. In contrast, an S-R associative interpretation predicts that you would choose B because it represents the second strongest habit. Path C is your choice if you behave like the rats did in Tolman and Honzik's (1930a, 1930b) study. In their study, animals were familiar with the maze but usually chose Path A to reach the goal. If Path A were blocked at Point Y, however, most rats chose Path C. These results suggest that knowledge of our environment, rather than "blind habit," often influences our behavior.

Other psychologists have attempted to replicate the results of Tolman and Honzik's study. However, animals in these studies have not always chosen Path C. For example, Keller and Hull (1936) discovered that changing the width of the alleys caused their rats to respond according to habit and choose the blocked path. Unfortunately, there has been no definitive evaluation of why the rats sometimes choose the blocked path. We can conclude from our previous discussion that the salience of cues leading to the goal and the degree of experience with the paths probably determine the processes controlling behavior. Thus, if we attend to paths leading to reward and the paths have not been employed frequently, our expectations, rather than our habits, will determine our action.

Figure 11.2   Apparatus used in Tolman and Honzik's alternative-path experiment. Obstacle Y blocks not only the shortest path (A) but also the middle-length path (B). With Paths A and B blocked, the only available route to the goal is the longest route, Path C.

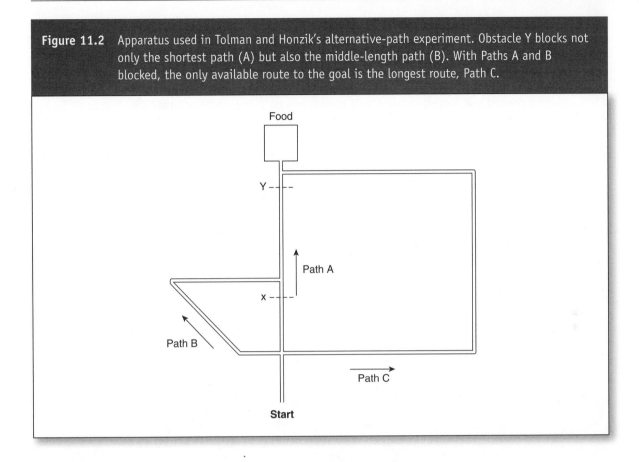

Is Reward Necessary for Learning?

Recall our discussion of the law of effect in Chapter 1. According to Thorndike (1898), S-R associations are established when the response leads to a satisfying state of affairs. As we discussed in Chapter 2, Hull (1943) expanded Thorndike's early view and asserted that associative or habit strength increases when a particular response decreases the drive state. Tolman (1932) thought that reward is not necessary for learning to occur, that the simultaneous experience of two events is sufficient. The incentive motivation process, which we explored in Chapter 2, was initially detailed by Hull in 1952 and then later described by Spence in 1956. The research of Tolman and his students strongly influenced the nature of the incentive motivation concept.

Latent-Learning Studies

Tolman (1932) believed that we can acquire a cognitive map, or knowledge of the spatial characteristics of a specific environment, merely by exploring the environment. Reward is not necessary for us to develop a cognitive map; reward influences behavior only when we must use that information to obtain reward. To distinguish between learning and performance, Tolman suggested that reward motivates behavior but does not affect learning.

Tolman and Honzik's (1930b) classic latent learning study directly assessed the importance of reward in learning and performance. Tolman and Honzik assigned their subjects to one of three conditions: (1) hungry rats in the R group always received reward (food) in the goal box of a 22-unit maze; (2) rats in the NR group were hungry but never received reward in the goal box; and (3) hungry rats in the NR-R group did not receive reward on the first 10 days of conditioning, but did for the last 10 days. Tolman and Honzik found that the animals that received a reward on each trial (R group) showed a steady decrease in number of errors during training, whereas animals not given a reward (NR group) showed little improvement in their performance (see Figure 11.3).

Does the failure of the unrewarded rats to perform indicate a failure to learn? Or have the unrewarded rats developed a cognitive map that they are not motivated to use? The behavior of those animals that did not receive reward in the goal box until the eleventh trial answers this question. Since Hull (1943) had envisioned the development of a habit as a slow process, animals in the NR-R group should have shown a slow decline in errors when rewarding began. However, if learning has already occurred by Day 11 and all these rats needed is motivation, they should have performed well on Day 12. The results indicate that on Day 12 and all subsequent days, animals in the R group (which were always rewarded) performed no differently from those in the NR-R group (which were only rewarded beginning with Day 11). These results suggest that NR-R animals were learning during the initial trials even though they did not receive any food reward.

While Tolman and Honzik's results suggest that learning can occur without reward, not all studies have found **latent learning**. MacCorquodale and Meehl (1954) reported that 30 of 48 studies replicated the latent-learning effect. Although latent learning appears to be a real phenomenon, under some conditions, it is likely, and in other circumstances, it is not. MacCorquodale and Meehl observed that when reward was present for nondeprived animals during the initial trials and motivation was introduced during later experience with the same reward, latent learning was

Figure 11.3   Results of Tolman and Honzik's latent-learning study. Animals in the NR group received no reward during the experiment; those in the R group received reward throughout the study; those in the NR-R group received reward from Day 11 to Day 20. The results show that adding reward on Day 11 led to a rapid decline in the number of errors subjects in Group NR-R made, to the level seen in animals receiving reward from the first trial (Group R).

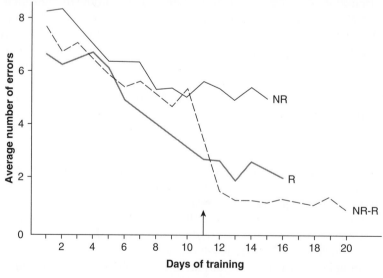

typically found. However, latent learning did not typically appear in studies in which the rewards present during the initial trials were irrelevant to the motivation existing at that time and reward only became relevant during later trials. (The presence of water in a hungry rat's goal box would be an example of an irrelevant reward.) These results suggest that a motivated animal will ignore the presence of a potent but irrelevant reward; this agrees with Tolman's belief that motivation narrows an animal's attention to those cues that are salient to its motivational state.

The Drive Response

The most consistent observation of latent learning occurs when animals are not deprived when initially exposed to reward. The anticipatory goal response (r_G-s_G) mechanism described in Chapter 2 was developed to explain the results of these latent-learning studies. The r_G-s_G develops during initial exposure to reward but is not apparent until the motivating influence of deprivation is added. However, some latent-learning studies—the original Tolman and Honzik study is one example—employ no obvious reward, yet the nonrewarded animals in those studies do show a slight improvement in their performance. This improvement indicates, according to drive view (Kimble, 1961), that these animals did experience some reward. Presumably handling or removing the animals from the strange maze to the familiar home cage sometimes represented sufficient reward to establish the r_G-s_G during initial nonreward. Although the strength of the r_G-s_G was not intense enough to motivate behavior, additional arousal produced by the introduction of reward resulted in rapid improvement in performance.

BEFORE YOU GO ON

- What expectations might have caused Martha's math phobia?

- Could these expectations have been learned many years earlier, remaining latent until she enrolled in the statistics class?

SECTION REVIEW

- Tolman proposed that our behavior is goal oriented; we are motivated to reach specific goals and continue to search until we obtain them.

- Tolman assumed that our behavior remains flexible enough to allow us to reach our goals.

- According to Tolman, we expect that behaving in a particular way will enable us to obtain reward or avoid aversive events.

- In Tolman's view, environmental events guide us to our goals.

- Tolman theorized that although we may know both how to obtain our goals and where these goals are, we will not behave unless we are motivated.

THE CONCEPT OF AN EXPECTATION

A Mental Representation of Events

What is an **expectation**? Several psychologists have suggested that an expectation is a mental representation of event contingencies (Balleine, 2001; Dickinson, 2001; Wasserman, 1993).

According to this view, an internal or mental representation of an experience develops when an animal or person experiences an event. This representation contains information about the relations among previously experienced events and also about the relations between behavior and the consequences of this behavior.

Types of Mental Representations

Anthony Dickinson (1989) proposed that there are two types of expectations and that the knowledge contained in each type of expectation differs. The first type of expectation is an **associative-link expectation**, which contains knowledge of the contiguity between two events. The learning of an associative-link expectation establishes a link between the mental representations created by two events, which allows the experience of one event to excite or inhibit the mental representation of the other event. For example, suppose a person eats a great steak in a particular restaurant. In Dickinson's view, the person's expectation would contain knowledge of the restaurant and the steak. Seeing the restaurant would cause the person to expect a great steak.

Anthony Dickinson (1944–   )

Dickinson received his doctorate from the University of Sussex. He was a postdoctoral research fellow at the University of Sussex before joining the faculty at the University of Cambridge, where he has taught for the last 33 years. His research has significantly contributed to the recognition of cognitions in animals. In 2000, he received the F. A. Beach Comparative Psychology Award from the American Psychological Association.

According to Dickinson, associative-link expectations mediate the impact of classical conditioning experiences. An excitatory associative-link expectation between a CS and a UCS allows the CS to activate the mental representation of the UCS and, thereby, elicit the conditioned response. In terms of our example, seeing the restaurant would excite the mental representation of the great steak and, thereby, would elicit hunger. In contrast, an inhibitory associative-link expectation allows a conditioned stimulus to inhibit a conditioned response.

A **behavior-reinforcer belief** is the second type of expectation, which contains knowledge of the consequences of a specific action. This knowledge is represented in propositional form as a belief that Action A causes Reinforcer B. For example, the person in our example would undoubtedly learn to go back to the restaurant serving the great steak. According to Dickinson's (1989) view, this individual's expectation would contain the knowledge that going to that restaurant yields a great steak. Dickinson suggested that the representation of behavior and outcome controls instrumental or operant activity. The intent of an animal's or person's behavior is to obtain desired reinforcement, and activation of the relevant behavior-reinforcer belief enables the animal or person to obtain reinforcement.

In Dickinson's (1989) view, the existence of two classes of mental representations explains some important differences between classical and instrumental or operant conditioning. As we discovered in Chapter 4, classical conditioning involves the acquisition of CS-UCS associations. Dickinson suggested that CS-UCS associative-link expectations operate mechanistically; this mechanistic expectation process causes the CS to involuntarily elicit the CR. In contrast, operant or instrumental conditioning involves the acquisition of behavior-outcome beliefs. According to Dickinson, intentionality is a property of belief expectations. An animal or person engages in operant or instrumental behavior based on beliefs about the consequences of specific actions.

Dickinson (1989) proposed that expectations contain knowledge of environmental circumstances. How can the idea that expectations contain representation of stimuli, actions, and reinforcers be validated? According to Dickinson, research must show that a representation of the training stimulus and reinforcer is stored during classical conditioning. Research also must demonstrate that during operant or instrumental conditioning, knowledge contained in the expectation stands in declarative relation to the conditioning contingency; that is, the knowledge in the expectation represents a belief about the impact of a behavior on the environment. Dickinson presents a number of studies supporting his expectation view; we examine several of them next.

Associative-Link Expectations

Suppose that one group of thirsty rats was trained to bar press for a sodium solution, and another group of thirsty rats was reinforced with a potassium solution. After this initial training, both groups of rats were sodium deprived as their operant response was extinguished. How would these two groups of rats act if the drive state was switched from water deprivation to sodium deprivation during extinction? Dickinson and Nicholas (1983) conducted such a study. They trained water-deprived rats to bar press for either sodium chloride or potassium chloride. The experimenters then extinguished the bar-press response under a sodium deprivation condition and found that the rats reinforced for bar pressing with sodium showed a higher response rate during extinction than did the animals reinforced with potassium. Dickinson and Nicholas also reported there was no extinction differences between animals if the animals were extinguished either when satiated or water deprived (see Figure 11.4). These results show that rats reinforced with sodium during training responded at a higher level during extinction than rats reinforced with potassium, but only when the motivational state was more relevant to sodium than potassium.

What process was responsible for the **irrelevant incentive effect**, or the higher rate of response during extinction in a sodium drive state in animals deprived of water and reinforced with sodium than in animals reinforced with potassium? According to Dickinson, an excitatory-link association developed during training between the contextual cues and the irrelevant incentive (either sodium or potassium). When the animals were later deprived of sodium, activation of this excitatory-link association led to a general enhancement of response, but only when the expectation contained knowledge that the incentive was relevant. In other words, arousing the associative-link expectation in sodium-deprived animals increased response for sodium because the incentive was relevant to the drive, while the response was low in the animals previously reinforced with potassium because the incentive experienced during training was irrelevant to the drive state experienced during extinction. Since both groups received equivalent training, and the response rate during extinction under a water deprivation condition (where the drive state was the same for both groups) was also equal for both groups, Dickinson concluded that the animals gained knowledge about the incentive experienced during initial training. Further, knowledge of the incentive was contained in an excitatory-link association; activation of this association under relevant drive conditions enhanced responding..

Taking this further, Dickinson and Dawson (1987) conducted a study to determine whether the irrelevant incentive effect was due to the development of a Pavlovian excitatory-link association or an operant behavior-reinforcer belief. Animals received four experiences during initial training in the hunger state. Two experiences involved classical conditioning: Cue A was paired with a sucrose solution, and Cue B was paired with food. Animals also received two operant conditioning experiences: They were reinforced with sucrose with Cue C present and with food with Cue D present. The drive state was then switched from hunger to thirst during extinction. Dickinson and Dawson found that responding during extinction was greater to Cues A and C

Figure 11.4 Graph illustrating the mean rate of bar pressing during extinction for animals reinforced for bar pressing with either sodium or potassium and tested while sodium deprived, water deprived, or satiated for water. The results show that animals receiving sodium during training exhibited a higher response rate when deprivation was shifted from water to sodium than did animals given potassium during training.

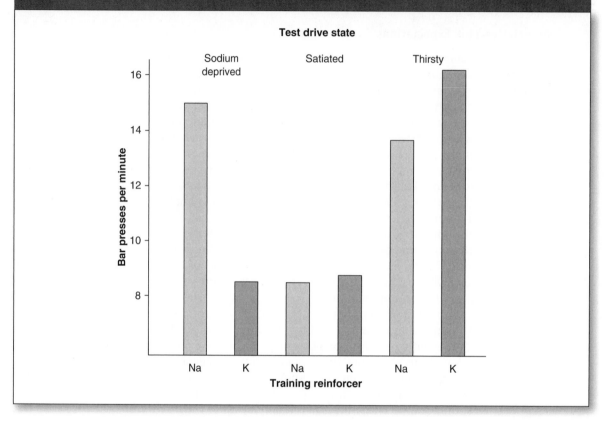

than to Cues B and D (see Figure 11.5). This means that responses were greater to stimuli paired with sucrose than stimuli paired with food. Since these animals were now thirsty, only an expectation containing knowledge of sucrose would be relevant to the thirst state. The researchers also found equal responses to Cues A and C. This indicates that a Pavlovian excitatory-link representation controlled the response because Cue A was paired with sucrose in a Pavlovian conditioning paradigm but was not associated with any operant contingency.

Behavior-Reinforcer Beliefs

According to Dickinson (1989), animals also develop behavior-reinforcer beliefs; that is, an expectation can contain knowledge that performing a specific behavior will result in the occurrence of a specific reinforcer. How can we validate the existence of a behavior-reinforcer belief? Dickinson used the **reinforcer devaluation effect** to demonstrate such an expectation.

Suppose that animals are first trained to bar press for sucrose reinforcement, and then the value of the sucrose reinforcer is devalued by pairing sucrose with illness. How would an animal respond following reinforcer devaluation? Adams and Dickinson (1981) investigated the effects

Figure 11.5   Graph illustrating the mean rate of bar pressing during extinction under water deprivation (1) in the presence of a Pavlovian-conditioned stimulus paired with sucrose solution (Suc) or food pellets (Pel) during training or (2) in the presence of an operant discriminative stimulus signaling either sucrose or food availability during training. The results show that the level of response during extinction under water deprivation was equal for both a Pavlovian-conditioned stimulus associated with sucrose and a discriminative stimulus for sucrose availability.

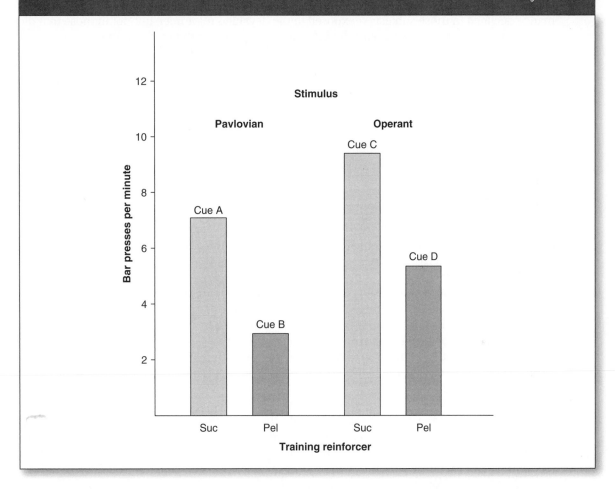

of reinforcer devaluation. They presented sucrose and food to two groups of animals. One group received sucrose for bar pressing and food no matter what the response; the other group had to bar press for food but received sucrose noncontingently. Adams and Dickinson observed that bar pressing during extinction was significantly lower for animals receiving behavior-contingent sucrose devaluation than animals receiving behavior-noncontingent sucrose devaluation. In other words, the animals whose reinforcer was devalued responded much less during extinction than did animals whose reinforcer was not devalued. This observation suggests that animals develop a belief that a specific behavior yields a specific reinforcer, and this expectation will control their response unless the reinforcer is no longer valued.

We have discovered that reinforcer devaluation can lead to a reduction in operant response. Garcia (1989) proposed that while flavor aversion alters the incentive value of a specific flavor, this learning remains latent until the animal reexperiences the flavor stimulus. In Garcia's view, flavor aversion learning establishes an association between the flavor and the gastric effects of illness. When the animal reexperiences the flavor, certain gastric reactions are elicited, and the incentive value of the flavor changes.

The idea that reexperience is necessary to alter incentive value suggests that reexposure to the flavor should be necessary to produce the reinforcer devaluation effect. Balleine and Dickinson (1991) tested this prediction by reexposing some animals to the devalued flavor. Other animals were not reexposed to the devalued flavor. Balleine and Dickinson reported that operant performance declined in those subjects reexposed to the devalued reinforcer, but not in those that did not reexperience the devalued reinforcer. These results support the idea that the incentive for a flavor paired with illness will only diminish if the animal reexperiences the flavor.

How does associating a flavor with illness cause a decrease in the level of operant behavior for that flavor? Balleine and Dickinson (Balleine, 2001; Dickinson & Balleine, 1994, 1995) provided an answer to this question. According to Dickinson and Balleine, pairing the flavor and illness causes a representation of the sensory properties of the flavor to become associated with a mental "structure" sensitive to the effects of illness. Dickinson and Balleine referred to this structure as *disgust*. Subsequently experiencing the flavor activates the disgust structure. Reexperiencing the flavor in the operant setting activates the mental representation of the flavor, which stimulates the disgust structure. Activity in the disgust structure leads to a devalued evaluation of the outcome (flavor) of the operant response. And it is the devaluation of the outcome that leads to a reduced operant behavior.

Balleine, Garner, and Dickinson (1995) provide evidence that devaluation is a two-stage process. These researchers first administered ondansetron to rats prior to pairing one flavor (either sucrose or saline) and LiCl, an illness-inducing drug. Ondansetron, a drug with strong antiemetic, or antivomiting, effects, should suppress activity in the disgust system. Animals then received the other flavor (either saline or sucrose) and LiCl without ondansetron. Despite the fact that both flavors were paired with LiCl, the animals preferred the flavor paired with LiCl under ondansetron. Why? According to Balleine et al., the disgust system must be active to establish an association between the representation of the flavor and the disgust system. Since ondansetron suppresses the disgust system, the association between the representation of the flavor and the disgust system does not form, despite the pairing of the flavor and LiCl. These rats will subsequently consume the poisoned flavor.

Suppose an aversion to a flavor was established, but ondansetron was given prior to reexposure to that flavor in the operant setting? Would the flavor be devalued in the operant setting? Balleine et al. (1995) conducted such an experiment. In their study, performing one behavior (pressing a bar) produced one outcome (sucrose or saline), while performing another behavior (pulling a chain) produced the other outcome. Both flavors were then paired with LiCl. Ondansetron was injected before the rats reexperienced one flavor, but not the other. During subsequent extinction testing, the rats showed a higher level of response to the flavor reexperienced under ondansetron. According to Balleine et al., reexperiencing the flavor under ondansetron caused the suppression of the disgust system, which prevented the devaluation of the outcome. If the outcome is not devalued, the rat will continue to perform the operant behavior.

Some illness-inducing treatments also produce somatic discomfort. Somatic discomfort following an illness-inducing treatment is immediate, rather than delayed. Balleine and Dickinson (1992) observed that reexposure is not necessary for reinforcer devaluation when illness-inducing treatments also leads to somatic discomfort. According to Balleine and Dickinson, the ability of the flavor to predict somatic discomfort is merely dependent upon the pairing of the flavor and somatic discomfort, and reexperiencing the flavor is not necessary for operant performance to be suppressed. These results also suggest that avoidance of a flavor can be based either on its perceived unpalatability or on anticipated discomfort. Perceived unpalatability can only be established with reexposure, while anticipated discomfort does not depend upon reexperience of the flavor.

We learned in Chapter 4 that the basolateral region of the amygdala appears to be responsible for the association of environmental events with foods (Petrovich & Gallagher, 2007). Damage to the basolateral region of the amygdala has been found to prevent the conditioning of feeding in satiated rats when the damage occurs prior to conditioning and to abolishing it when it occurs following training (Holland & Petrovich, 2005; Petrovich & Gallagher, 2007).

The basolateral amygdala also contributes to the formation of behavior-outcome representations (A. W. Johnson, Gallagher, & Holland, 2009; Ostlund & Balleine, 2008). These researchers discovered that reinforcer devaluation does not result in lowered performance in animals with basolateral amygdala damage. The continued instrumental responding after the reinforcer is devalued in basolateral amygdaloid–lesioned animals suggests an insensitivity to reinforcer outcomes as a result of damage to the basolateral amygdala. It would appear that the basolateral amygdala plays a critical role in the association of environmental events with food and the establishment of operant behavior–food reinforcer outcome representations.

The Importance of Habits

Some learning theorists (Levis, 1976; Rescorla & Wagner, 1972) reject the idea that mental representations of event contingencies form. Instead, they argue that stimulus-response associations, rather than expectations, form as the result of experience and that concrete environmental events, rather than subjective representations, motivate behavior.

Dickinson (2001) does not reject the idea that habits exist; instead, he argued that habits as well as expectations can control responding. In Dickinson's view, continued training leads to habits, rather than expectations, to govern behavior. A number of studies have shown that extended training lessens the effect of reinforcer devaluation (Adams, 1982; Adams & Dickinson, 1981; Dickinson, Balleine, Watt, Gonzalez, & Boakes, 1995). Let's look at the Adams (1982) study to demonstrate how habits can control operant behavior. Adams trained two groups of rats to bar press for sucrose reinforcement on a FR-1 schedule. One group received 100 reinforcements (50/day); the other group received 500 reinforcements (50/day). A third group of animals had to bar press 500 times to receive 100 reinforcements (FR-5 schedule; 50 reinforcements/day). After training, the sucrose was devalued for half of the animals in each group. Adams found that devaluation reduced responding in the groups receiving 100 reinforcements but had no effect on animals that received 500 reinforcements.

According to Dickinson's view, operant behavior initially is under the control of behavior-reinforcer beliefs. With more training, S-R habits develop, and habits—rather than expectations—control behavior. The behavior of the animals receiving 500 reinforcements supports this view; that is, these animals continued to respond despite the fact that their actions produced a devalued reinforcer. Dickinson referred to the control of response by habit rather than expectation as **behavioral autonomy**.

Habit or Expectation?

At this point, you might have the impression that expectations govern behavior early in training and that with continued training, behavior is controlled by habit. The influence of reinforcers on behavior is not quite this simple. Colwill and Rescorla (1985) observed that reinforcer devaluation does not lead to a total absence of response; that is, animals respond to some degree despite reinforcer devaluation. This observation suggests that habits develop even when expectations are controlling responses. When reinforcer devaluation eliminates the influence of expectations, responding continues to some degree, due to the control of S-R habits.

Dickinson, Wood, and Smith (2002) suggested that some behaviors may only be governed by habit rather than expectation. If this is so, some behaviors may be immune to reinforcer devaluation. One such behavior, according to these researchers, is responding for alcohol. To test this idea, Dickinson et al. (2002) trained 24 rats to bar press on one bar for a 10% ethanol solution and on another bar for a food reinforcer. These researchers provided the rats with an equivalent amount of training for both the food and ethanol reinforcers prior to pairing of one of the reinforcers with LiCl. Devaluing the food by pairing it with LiCl decreased the number of bar presses during extinction compared with rats receiving ethanol paired with LiCl or control animals receiving LiCl not paired with either food or ethanol. By contrast, devaluing the ethanol by pairing it with LiCl did not reduce responses during extinction compared with rats receiving food paired with LiCl or control animals receiving LiCl not paired with either food or ethanol. These results suggest that reinforcer devaluation does not affect operant responding for ethanol, unlike for food. Dickinson et al. proposed that while outcome expectations mediate responding for food, stimulus-response habits control responding for ethanol, which may be one reason why treating alcohol abuse in humans is so difficult.

We learned in Chapter 9 that the nigrostriatal pathway plays a role in the memory storage of reinforcing events. Memory of a reinforcing event is significantly enhanced when an animal is exposed to a positive reinforcer for a short time following training (Coulombe & White, 1982), while stimulation of the nigrostriatal pathway increases the memory of a reinforcing experience (Carr & White, 1984). Damage to the nigrostriatal pathway disrupts the formation of stimulus-response habits (Faure, Haberland, Conde, & Massiouri, 2005). These researchers concluded that lesions of the nigrostriatal pathway prevented the development of behavioral autonomy. Reward devaluation following overtraining in rats with damage to the nigrostriatal pathway significantly reduced operant responding. In contrast, control rats without damage to the nigrostriatal pathway given overtraining continued to respond at a high rate despite reinforcer devaluation.

BEFORE YOU GO ON

- What associative-link expectation was responsible for Martha's feelings toward math in high school?

- What behavior-reinforcer beliefs might have been operative when Martha took math in high school?

SECTION REVIEW

- Dickinson suggested that mental representations (expectations) contain knowledge gained through experience and that these expectations guide an animal's behavior.

- An associative-link expectation contains mental representations of two events, which allows one event to excite or inhibit the representation of the other event.

- In Dickinson's view, associative representations mediate the impact of Pavlovian conditioning experiences.

- A behavior-reinforcer belief contains an understanding of the consequences of a specific action, which is represented in propositional form as a belief that Action A causes Reinforcer B.

- According to Dickinson, the mental representation of behavior and outcomes controls instrumental or operant activity.

- In Dickinson's view, instrumental or operant behavior is initially under the control of behavior-reinforcer beliefs, while with more training, S-R habits develop, and behavior can fall under the control of habit rather than expectation.

- Dickinson referred to the control of responding by habit rather than expectation as behavioral autonomy.

What happens when an animal or a person discovers that behavior and outcomes are unrelated? In the next section, we will discover that the acquisition of a belief that events are unrelated can lead to the behavior pathology of depression.

Martin E. P. Seligman (1942–   )

Seligman received his doctorate from the University of Pennsylvania under the direction of Richard Solomon. He then taught at Cornell University for 3 years before joining the faculty of the University of Pennsylvania, where he has taught for the last 40 years. While at Penn, he has served as director of the Positive Psychology Center. His research has contributed greatly to understanding the process responsible to the development of learned helplessness and learned optimism. He was president of the American Psychological Association in 1998 and received the Distinguished Scientific Contribution Award from the American Psychological Association in 2006.

A COGNITIVE VIEW OF DEPRESSION

Martin Seligman (1975) described depression as the "common cold of psychopathology." No one is immune to the sense of despair indicative of depression; each of us has at some time become depressed following a disappointment or failure. For most, this unhappiness quickly wanes, and normal activity resumes. For others, the feelings of sadness last for a long time and impair the ability to interact effectively with the environment.

Why do people become depressed? According to Seligman (1975), depression is learned. It occurs when individuals believe their failures are due to uncontrollable events and expect to continue to fail as long as these events are beyond their control. Depression develops because these people believe that they are helpless to control their own destinies. Seligman's learned helplessness theory forms the basis for his view of depression.

Learned Helplessness Theory

Imagine that none of the medical schools to which you applied admitted you. Given that your dream since childhood has been to be a physician, you certainly would feel distressed for a while. If you are like most who are at first rejected, you might decide to enroll in some additional courses, study harder, and apply again. Or you could search for an alternative future occupation. However, these rejections might also cause you to become severely depressed. According to Seligman (1975), if you fall prey to this last alternative, you might not only believe you are capable of succeeding in medical school but also think that continued rejection is inevitable. You believe that no matter what you do, you will be rejected. This belief leads you to become depressed. Depression, according to Seligman, occurs when individuals learn that events will occur independently of the individuals' behavior. Seligman labeled the expectation that events are uncontrollable **learned helplessness**.

Original Animal Research

Seligman developed his learned helplessness theory of depression from his animal studies. The original studies (Overmier & Seligman, 1967; Seligman & Maier, 1967) used dogs as subjects. Some of these dogs were strapped in hammocks and then exposed to a series of 64 intense, inescapable shocks. Other dogs received a series of 64 escapable shocks; the shocks terminated when the dogs pressed a panel with their heads. The amount of shock the dogs received in both the inescapable and escapable condition was equal: The shocks ended for the dogs that received inescapable shock when the dogs in the escapable treatment successfully terminated their shock. A third group of dogs did not receive any shock during the initial stage of these studies.

Seligman and his colleagues placed each of the dogs in the three groups into a shuttle box 24 hours after the first stage of the study. After being placed in the shuttle box, each dog received 10 trials of signaled escape-avoidance training (see Chapter 7). Once the CS was presented, each dog had 10 seconds to jump over the hurdle to avoid shock. At the end of the 10-second interval, the shock was presented, and the dogs could terminate (escape) the shock by jumping the hurdle. The shock remained on for 50 seconds or until the dog escaped. The experimenters reported that two-thirds of the animals that had received inescapable shocks 24 hours earlier did not learn either to escape or to avoid the intense electrical shock in the shuttle box (see Figure 11.6). The dogs appeared helpless: They sat in the box and endured the shock for the entire 50-second interval. A few of the helpless dogs occasionally jumped the hurdle and either escaped or avoided shock. However, these dogs again acted helpless on the next trial; apparently, they did not benefit from their successful experiences. In contrast, the dogs that had been given either escapable shock or no shock quickly escaped shock during initial trials in the shuttle box, and in later trials, they learned to respond to the signal and avoid shock altogether.

A wide range of animal species is susceptible to the negative impact of uncontrollable experiences. Psychologists have observed the helplessness phenomenon in cats (E. Thomas & DeWald, 1977), rats (Jackson, Alexander, & Maier, 1980), and humans (Hiroto & Seligman, 1975; S. Roth & Kubal, 1975). Although the human studies have demonstrated that uncontrollable experiences do have an influence, the effects are small when compared to those found in other animals. Because exposing humans to a treatment sufficiently intense to induce helplessness is unethical, these results are not surprising; the aversive stimuli used are considerably less unpleasant in the human than in the nonhuman studies. Thus, human experiments in this area are primarily intended to demonstrate that uncontrollable experiences exert a similar influence in animals and humans.

Helplessness in Human Subjects

Hiroto's (1974) experiment with human subjects provides a good approximation of the original helplessness studies with dogs. Hiroto also employed a three-group design. College students who volunteered to participate in the study were assigned to one of three treatment groups. Some subjects could terminate an unpleasant noise by pushing a button four times. Subjects in the uncontrollable group were told that their correct response would end the noise, but there was actually no response that would terminate the noise. Parallel to the animal studies, the noise ended for the uncontrollable condition subjects when a comparable subject in the controllable-condition group successfully terminated the noise. A third group of subjects did not receive either of the noise treatments during the first stage of the study.

Following the initial part of the study, Hiroto trained all subjects to avoid or escape noise in a finger shuttle box. The noise ended when a subject moved his or her finger from one side of the shuttle box to the other. Hiroto reported that subjects in the uncontrollable-noise condition failed

Figure 11.6   Percentage of trials in which dogs failed to escape shock in the shuttle box after receiving escapable shock, inescapable shock, or no shock. The mean percentage failures to escape were significantly greater for animals exposed to inescapable shock than either escapable or no shock.

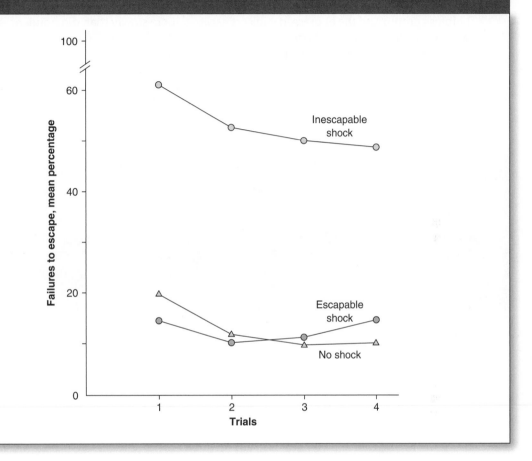

to learn either to escape or avoid the noise in the shuttle box and listened passively until the noise terminated at the end of a trial. In contrast, the group that received the controllable noise, as well as the group that did not receive any initial trials, quickly learned to escape and then to avoid noise in the shuttle box. These results suggest that uncontrollable experiences produce similar negative effects on learning in both animals and humans.

Similarities of Helplessness and Depression

The importance of the learned helplessness phenomenon lies in its proposed relation to the clinical disorder of depression. Although no one can ethically conduct a direct causal test, the similarity of the behavior of helpless subjects and depressed persons support Seligman's (1975) statement that the expectation of an inability to control events produces human depression.

Recall that Hiroto (1974) reported that college students who had previously received uncontrollable noise failed to learn to escape noise in the finger shuttle box. D. C. Klein and Seligman's (1976) depressed subjects similarly failed to escape noise in the shuttle box. Their studies contained four groups of subjects: One group contained individuals classified as depressed according to the Beck Depression Inventory, and the other three groups contained nondepressed subjects. Klein and Seligman exposed one group of nondepressed subjects to uncontrollable noise—a procedure that produces helplessness. The second nondepressed group received escapable noise; the last nondepressed group and the depressed group received no noise treatment. The study's results showed that the nondepressed subjects who were exposed to inescapable noise (the helpless group) and the depressed subjects escaped more slowly than did nondepressed subjects who received either the escapable noise or no noise treatment (see Figure 11.7). Evidently, these nondepressed subjects, as a result of uncontrollable laboratory experiences, behaved as the clinically depressed persons did. We should not assume that this treatment produced clinical depression, but rather that both groups expected they would not be able to control laboratory noise. People suffering from depression have a generalized expectation of no control; their failure to escape in the study merely reflects this generalized expectation.

Figure 11.7   Escape latency to terminate noise for four groups. Group D-NN includes depressed subjects (on Beck Depression Inventory) who were not previously exposed to noise; Group ND-NN contains nondepressed subjects who were not previously exposed to noise; Group ND-IN contains nondepressed subjects who were previously exposed to inescapable noise; and Group ND-EN includes nondepressed subjects who were previously exposed to escapable noise. The escape latency was greater for nondepressed subjects exposed to inescapable noise (ND-IN) and depressed subjects not exposed to noise (D-NN) than for nondepressed subjects exposed to escapable noise (ND-EN) or nondepressed subjects exposed to no noise (ND-NN).

Criticism of the Learned Helplessness Approach

Seligman's (1975) original learned helplessness model generated interest in the influence of the cognitive processes in depression. However, his theory encountered difficulties; it was too simplistic and did not precisely reflect the process that produces depression. We next look at these problems with the original learned helplessness theory.

One problem with the original learned helplessness model is that some other studies have not observed performance deficits following uncontrollable experiences. In fact, several studies (S. Roth & Kubal, 1975; Tennen & Eller, 1977) have demonstrated improved subject performance after exposure to insoluble problems; their human subjects exposed to insoluble problems actually scored higher on subsequent tasks than did those who were exposed to solvable problems. This facilitation of performance after exposure to uncontrollable tasks is inconsistent with Seligman's original model of helplessness, which maintains that uncontrollable experiences should create expectations that impair—not improve—later behavior.

Rizley's study (1978, Experiment 1) illustrates another problem with Seligman's original learned helplessness theory. Rizley presented depressed and nondepressed subjects with a series of 50 digits (either 0 or 1) and then instructed the subjects to guess the next digit. Although there was no pattern to the digits, Rizley told his subjects that there were number-order trends and tendencies and that their score would be above chance if they were aware of these trends. The subjects were told after the digit presentations whether they had succeeded (passed the test) by scoring 26 or more or had failed by scoring 25 or less. (Since there were only two choices, a score of 25 meant chance-level performance.) The subjects then indicated the reason for their score from a list of several possibilities—luck, task difficulty, effort, or ability.

Rizley's results demonstrated that depressed people attributed their success to the external factors of luck and task ease and their failure to internal factors of lack of effort and ability. In contrast, nondepressed people thought that internal factors accounted for their success and that external factors caused their failure. Thus, people who are depressed attribute their failure to internal processes, but they also feel helpless because they can do nothing to prevent future failures. Seligman's learned helplessness theory could not explain Rizley's observations. Responding to such difficulties, Seligman developed the attributional model of helplessness. This model provides answers to the problems inherent in the original learned helplessness theory.

An Attributional Theory of Helplessness

Seligman and his associates (Abramson, Garber, & Seligman, 1980; Abramson, Seligman, & Teasdale, 1978) proposed that the attributions people make for their failures determine whether they become depressed. An attribution is the perceived cause of an event. **Causal attributions** of failure can be made on three dimensions: personal-universal (internal-external), global-specific, and stable-unstable. An **internal attribution** is the belief that internal characteristics cause the outcome; an **external attribution** is the view that environmental forces determine success (reward) or failure (aversive event). A **stable attribution** is the belief that the perceived cause of past success or failure will determine future outcomes; an **unstable attribution** represents the belief that new factors may determine success or failure in the future. A **specific attribution** reflects the view that the cause of an outcome relates only to a specific task; a **global attribution** is the belief that the cause of the outcome in this task will determine outcomes in diverse situations. The combination of these three dimensions produces eight possible attributional outcomes (see Table 11.1). The specific attribution will determine whether (1) depression occurs, (2) depression generalizes to other situations, and (3) the depression is temporary or ongoing.

Consider, then, the examples Table 11.1 presents. If the woman attributes her rejection to an internal, stable, global factor ("I'm unattractive to all men"), she will become depressed. In contrast,

Table 11.1	The Attributional Model of Depression: A Woman Rejected			
	Internal		External	
Dimension	Stable	Unstable	Stable	Unstable
Global	I'm unattractive to men.	My conversation sometimes bores men.	Men are overly competitive with intelligent women.	Men get into rejecting moods.
Specific	I'm unattractive to him.	My conversation bores him.	He's overly competitive with women.	He was in a rejecting mood.

Note: The attribution of uncontrollability to internal causes produces personal helplessness, whereas an external causal attribution results in universal helplessness.

the woman will not become depressed if she attributes rejection to an external, unstable, specific factor ("He was in a rejecting mood"). This attributional model, while complex, provides us with an explanation for people's varied responses to uncontrollable experiences.

Personal Versus Universal Helplessness

The attributional theory proposes two kinds of helplessness: personal and universal. **Personal helplessness** occurs when an internal factor is perceived to be the cause of an undesired outcome; for example, a student perceives incompetence to be the reason he failed a test. In contrast, **universal helplessness** occurs when the environment is structured so that no one can control future events; for example, the student perceives that a test is so difficult that no one could pass the test.

Abramson (1977) ascertained from her experiments that both personal and universal helplessness produced the expectations of an inability to control future events and a lack of an ability to initiate voluntary behavior, which are characteristic of depression. In addition, Abramson and Sackeim (1977) examined the attributions of depressed people and found that those who were personally depressed made internal attributions for failure, whereas those who were universally depressed made external attributions.

The nature of the helplessness determines whether loss of esteem occurs. People who attribute their failure to external forces—universal helplessness—experience no loss of self-esteem because they do not consider themselves responsible for their failure. However, the attribution of failure to internal factors—personal helplessness—causes a loss of self-esteem; these individuals believe their incompetence causes their failure. In support of this view, Abramson (1977) found that lowered self-esteem only occurs with personal helplessness.

Global Versus Specific Causal Attributions

People exposed to uncontrollable events may not become depressed; they could make a specific attribution for their failure, and thus not experience helplessness in other circumstances. Others might make a global attribution, believing their failure will happen at other times, and become depressed. For instance, a student may come to believe that she will fail all tests and drop out of school. In contrast, the student who attributes failure to a specific instructor will drop the class and take it again next semester from a different instructor. Thus, the attribution of a lack of control to global factors will produce helplessness that will generalize to new situations, but the attribution to a specific situation will limit helplessness to that situation.

S. Roth and Kubal's (1975) experiment supports the idea that global-specific attributions are important in determining whether people feel helpless in new situations. In the study, first-year college
students volunteered to participate in two separate, very different experiments on the same day and
in the same building. The first experiment was designed to fail all students. Subjects in one group
(important condition) of this first experiment were told that the failed task was a "good predictor of
college grades"; those in the other group (unimportant condition) were informed that they were participating in "an experiment in learning." Following the first experiment, all subjects proceeded to the
second study. Since both groups experienced failure on the first experiment, the original helplessness
model predicted that both groups would fail to perform well in the second study. However, the subjects who were told that the first test was a learning experiment did significantly better on the second
test than did the subjects who thought the first experiment was a predictor of future success. According to the attributional model, the subjects in the important condition attributed their failure to a more
global factor, a lack of ability to succeed in college, while subjects in the unimportant condition attributed their failure to a single task. As a result, the helplessness generalized to the new situation for
subjects in the important condition, but not for the subjects in the unimportant condition.

Stable Versus Unstable Causal Attributions

Seligman (1975) proposed that a person's attribution of helplessness to a stable or unstable factor
also influences the effect an uncontrollable experience has on behavior. Ability is considered a
stable factor; effort is an unstable one. If someone attributes failure in an uncontrollable experience to lack of effort, this attribution will increase this person's subsequent effort. However, the
attribution of failure to the stable factor of lack of ability will lead to helplessness because people
can change their effort but not their innate ability. A test of this view appears in S. Roth and
Kubal's study (1975). Roth and Kubal gave their subjects one or two learned helplessness training
tasks and found that those who failed at one task showed more motivation than control subjects
did, but those who failed at two tasks exhibited helplessness.

The idea that the stability or instability of the perceived cause influences helplessness also
explains why depression is temporary in some situations and more enduring in other situations.
For example, suppose that only one instructor teaches the class the student failed. If so, the student will remain depressed. But the depression will be temporary if another instructor is scheduled to teach the course next semester.

Severity of Depression

Helplessness can apparently follow several different types of uncontrollable experiences. However, severe depression typically appears when individuals attribute their failure to internal,
global, and stable factors (C. Peterson & Seligman, 1984). Their depression is intense because
they perceive themselves as incompetent (internal attribution) in many situations (global attribution), and they believe their incompetence is unlikely to change (stable attribution). In support
of this notion, Hammen and Krantz (1976) found that depressed women attributed interpersonal
failure (e.g., being alone on a Friday night) to internal, global, and stable factors. In contrast, nondepressed women blamed their failure on external, specific, and unstable factors. Other researchers (Robins, 1988; Sweeney, Anderson, & Bailey, 1986) have observed a similar difference in the
attribution of failure between depressed and nondepressed people.

Hopelessness Theory of Depression

Lauren Alloy and Lyn Abramson (Abramson, Metalsky, & Alloy, 1989; Alloy, Abramson, Safford, &
Gibb, 2006; Gibb, Alloy, Abramson, & Marx, 2003) proposed a hopelessness theory of depression

that suggests that attributional style and environmental circumstance together contribute to hopelessness and hopelessness depression. We next look at the hopelessness theory of depression.

Negative Life Events and Hopelessness

Alloy, Abramson, and their colleagues suggested that some cases of depression, called hopelessness depression, are caused by a state of hopelessness. **Hopelessness** occurs when a negative life event is attributed to stable (or enduring) and global (likely to affect many) factors. Making this attribution causes the individual to believe that future negative outcomes are inevitable and that he or she is deficient or unworthy. These negative attributions also cause the symptoms of hopelessness depression, which include sadness, apathy, a retarded initiation of voluntary behavior, psychomotor retardation, and suicidality.

The **hopelessness theory of depression** proposes that whether a person will become hopeless and develop the symptoms of hopelessness depression depends upon both the likelihood that the person will make a negative attribution and the severity of the negative life event. If the individual makes a very negative attribution, even a minor stressor could lead to hopelessness depression. By contrast, a series of major negative events could cause hopelessness depression even in an individual who does not make very negative attributions. In other words, some people are cognitively vulnerable (consistently make negative attributions) to developing hopelessness depression when encountering negative life events while other people will only develop hopelessness depression when they are confronted with a sufficient number or magnitude of negative life events.

A Negative Attributional Style and Vulnerability to Depression

The hopelessness theory of depression (Alloy et al., 2006) assumes that a **negative attributional (or explanatory) style** makes one vulnerable to becoming hopeless when exposed to a negative life event. There are obviously many negative life events that a person can experience. Certainly, not doing well on an examination or a paper in college are examples of negative events in the life of a student. If the hopelessness theory of depression is valid, students making stable and global attributions following those events are more likely to become hopeless and experience symptoms of hopelessness depression than students not making stable and global attributions for those negative life events.

Gibb, Beevers, Andover, and Holleran (2006) conducted a test of the relationship between attributional style and vulnerability to hopelessness depression. These researchers assessed attributional style at the beginning of a 6-week longitudinal study with undergraduate students and then assessed the incidence of negative events and depressive symptoms over the course of the study. Gibb et al. found that attributional style and negative life events jointly determined the levels of depressive symptoms. Students with the most negative attributional style who experienced the highest severity of negative life events showed the greatest increases in depressive symptoms during the week that followed the negative life events.

Other researchers have reported that negative attributional style is associated with depression when people encounter such additional stressors as unemployment or illness. Let's consider several other negative life events to illustrate the validity of the hopelessness theory of depression. Losing one's job is another life stress. Lynd-Stevenson (1996) found that in unemployed young adults, a negative attributional style was associated with hopelessness depression.

Research shows that becoming ill is another negative life event in which a negative attributional style makes one vulnerable to hopelessness depression. Kneebone and Dunmore (2004) found that negative attributional style was positively correlated with symptoms of hopelessness depression in 495 persons with multiple sclerosis. Similarly, J. G. Johnson, Metalsky, Rabkin,

Williams, and Remien (2000) reported that a negative attributional style made males infected with human immunodeficiency virus (HIV) vulnerable to hopelessness depression compared with HIV-infected males who did not have a negative attributional style or males who did not have HIV but had a negative attributional style.

A Positive Attributional Style and Hopelessness Depression

Ellen Langer (1983) suggested that "perceived control is basic to human functioning" (p. 14). According to Langer, individuals strive to acquire feelings of competence and to master life's circumstances. Optimists feel they are able to control external events; pessimists believe they have no control. An optimistic (positive) attributional style leads to greater successes than a pessimistic (negative) attributional style. For example, Seligman and Schulman (1986) reported that new insurance salespersons who were optimists sold more policies and were 50% less likely to quit within one year than salespersons who habitually explained failures as uncontrollable ("I always fail" or "This is impossible").

The evidence indicates that a **positive attributional style** creates expectations of **hopefulness,** rather than hopelessness, when encountering negative life events. For example, Tripp, Catano, and Sullivan (1997) found that a positive attributional style was associated with hopefulness, while a negative attributional style was associated with hopelessness. Further, hopelessness was associated with depression, while hopefulness was not. These findings suggest that people with a negative attributional style are likely to become depressed when experiencing a negative life event, while people with a positive attributional style are not. In support of this conclusion, Rogers, Hansen, Levy, Tate, and Sikkema (2005) found that following the loss of a loved one from HIV/AIDS, optimism or hopefulness was negatively correlated with hopelessness and depression. Similarly, Roehrig (1997) reported that hopefulness was negatively correlated with depression in adolescents.

Does a change in attributional style influence depression? As predicted from an attributional model, many studies (Han, 1996; Voelz, Haeffel, Joiner, & Wagner, 2003) have found that enhancing positive attributional style in depressed patients increased their hopefulness and decreased their depressive symptoms. Seligman, Schulman, and Tryon (2007) even found that changing the attributional style of college students could serve to prevent the development of depressive symptoms. In their study, college students who were identified as at risk for depression received a workshop that was designed to reduce negative attributions and enhance positive attributions once a week for 2 hours for the first 8 weeks of the fall semester. For the remainder of the fall semester, these subjects were contacted both in person and via e-mail by workshop coaches to reinforce what they had learned in the workshop. Control subjects received neither the workshop nor the follow-up contacts.

Seligman et al. (2007) measured both attributional style and depressive symptoms in both the workshop and control subjects during each of the next six semesters. These researchers found that subjects receiving the workshop and follow-up experiences showed a significant increase in optimistic or positive attributional style and fewer depressive symptoms from pretest to posttest than did control subjects. Seligman et al. concluded that individuals with negative attributional styles are at risk to become depressed following negative life events that normally occur during college but that certain kinds of experiences can prevent depression by changing negative attributions into positive attributions for negative life events.

Biological Influences on Learned Helplessness

Although our discussion indicates that cognitions influence the development of depressive symptoms, it is important to recognize that other factors are also involved in depression. Several lines of research suggest that biology, either alone or in combination with pessimistic or negative attributions, produces depression.

The research of Jay Weiss and his associates (Weiss et al., 1981; Weiss, Simpson, Ambrose, Webster, & Hoffman, 1985) has suggested that repeated exposure to uncontrollable events may produce the biochemical, as well as the behavioral, changes observed in people who are depressed. This research has found that when rats are exposed to a series of inescapable shocks, they show a pattern of behavior that includes early-morning wakefulness, decreased feeding and sex drive, decreased grooming, and a lack of voluntary response in a variety of situations—all symptoms of clinical depression.

What are the biochemical changes that occur following uncontrollable stress such as that experienced by the rats in Weiss's experiment? Several studies (Hughes et al., 1984; Lehnert, Reinstein, Strowbridge, & Wurtman, 1984) have observed isolated decreases in norepinephrine in the locus coeruleus following prolonged exposure to inescapable shocks. (The locus coeruleus is a central nervous system structure that has widespread connections throughout the brain and that plays a key role in arousal and wakefulness.) According to Jay Weiss, Simpson, Hoffman, Ambrose, Cooper, and Webster (1986), a localized decrease in norepinephrine increases locus coeruleus activity (because of the inhibitory effect of the norepinephrine-containing neurons on the activity of the locus coeruleus); that is, a decrease in norepinephrine releases the inhibitory action of these neurons, which increases overall neural activity in the locus coeruleus and thereby produces depression. In support of this view, M. M. Grant and Weiss (2001) reported that antidepressant drugs decreased locus coeruleus activity and eliminated behavioral deficits following exposure to inescapable shock. These results suggest that uncontrollable events produce heightened activity in the locus coeruleus, which then produces the behavioral changes associated with depression.

The neurotransmitter glutamate appears to play an important role in learned helplessness (Hunter, Balleine, & Minor, 2003; Zink, Vollmayr, Gebicke-Haerter, & Henn, 2010). Zink et al. (2010) reported increased glutamate levels in rats demonstrating learned helplessness, while Hunter, Balleine, and Minor (2003) found that glutamate injections produced deficits in escape performance that is characteristic of learned helplessness. Further, Hunter, Balleine, and Minor observed that an administration of a glutamate antagonist during inescapable shock prevented the shock-induced learned helplessness effect.

Glutamate also has been found to play an important role in clinical depression (Hashimoto, 2009). Glutamate levels are elevated in individuals with major depression (Mitani et al., 2006). Mitani et al. also found that there was a positive correlation between plasma glutamate levels and the severity of depression. Further, ketamine, a glutamate antagonist due to its blockade of the N-methyl-D-asparate (NMDA) receptor, has a rapid antidepressant effect (Aan het Rot, Charney, & Mathew, 2008). While antidepressant drugs typically take at least 2 weeks for the depressive mood to improve, the antidepressant response to ketamine occurs within hours.

We have observed that learned helplessness is associated with increased activity in the locus coeruleus and increased glutamate levels. Not surprisingly, Karolewicz et al. (2005) observed that glutamatergic activity in the locus coeruleus was increased in individuals diagnosed with major depression.

BEFORE YOU GO ON

- Could Martha's experiences with statistics lead to hopelessness and depression?

- What might prevent Martha from becoming hopeless?

SECTION REVIEW

- The learned helplessness theory assumes that exposure to uncontrollable events leads to an expectation of no control of events, which leads to helplessness.

- The attributional theory of helplessness states that the attributions that are made for aversive events determine whether or not helplessness occurs.

- An internal attribution may lead to personal helplessness, while an external attribution may lead to universal helplessness.

- A stable attribution leads to long-lasting helplessness, while an unstable causal attribution results in short-lived helplessness.

- Helplessness is restricted to a particular circumstance following a specific attribution, but a global attribution leads to helplessness and depression in many situations.

- Hopelessness occurs when a negative life event is attributed to stable (or enduring) and global (likely to affect many) outcomes.

- Making a negative attribution can lead to the symptoms of hopelessness depression.

- A positive attributional style is associated with hopefulness and resilience to depression.

- Producing a positive attributional style in individuals at risk can serve to prevent the onset of depression.

- Decreases in brain norepinephrine levels that are produced by exposure to uncontrollable events also have caused the behaviors associated with depression.

A COGNITIVE VIEW OF PHOBIC BEHAVIOR

All of us have fears. In most cases, these fears are realistic and enable us to avoid aversive events. For example, people are afraid to cross a street when cars are approaching; their fear motivates them to avoid walking in front of moving cars, thereby avoiding injury or death. However, some people's fears are unrealistic. These individuals have a phobia, a fear that might once have been appropriate (if an aversive event did occur) but is no longer realistic. This fear motivates avoidance behavior, which prevents the person from learning that the phobia is unrealistic. In many situations, the original aversive event may not be readily apparent. An individual may have forgotten the unpleasant event, or the phobic response may have developed through high-order conditioning or vicarious conditioning (see Chapter 4). The phobic response also may result from stimulus generalization; for example, a child attacked by a peer may generalize this fear to all children. We next examine research indicating that cognitive processes also affect the development of phobias.

Phobias and Expectations

Recall our description of Martha's math phobia from the chapter's opening vignette. Albert Bandura (1977, 1982, 1986) presented a cognitive theory of phobias in which two classes of expectations—outcome and efficacy—maintain Martha's phobia. **Outcome expectations** reflect the perceived consequences of either a behavior and/or an event. Martha expects a statistics class to be aversive—a **stimulus-outcome expectation**—and she believes she cannot pass the course—a **response-outcome expectation**. Also, Martha knows she can prevent the aversive experience by not enrolling in the statistics course; this response-outcome expectation motivates her behavior.

Albert Bandura (1925–   )

Bandura received his doctorate from the University of Iowa under the direction of Arthur Benton. After receiving his doctorate, he joined the faculty at Stanford University, where he has taught for the last 57 years. His research has contributed greatly to understanding the role of cognitive and social influences on aggression and human phobias. A 2002 survey found that he was the fourth most cited psychologist behind B. F. Skinner, Sigmund Freud, and Jean Piaget. He was president of the American Psychological Association in 1974 and received the Distinguished Scientific Contribution Award from the American Psychological Association in 1980.

Martha's phobia presents her with a dilemma typical of phobic situations. Although her phobic behavior enables her to avoid the course, her phobic actions have definite negative consequences. She realizes she must pass this course to graduate, but her phobic behavior prevents her from obtaining her desired goal. Thus, she continues to avoid the course even though she cannot graduate without it.

Bandura's theory suggests that a second type of expectation is involved in motivating Martha's phobic behavior. According to Bandura's approach, Martha feels incapable of enduring the aversive statistics class. Bandura labeled this belief that one can or cannot execute a particular action an **efficacy expectation**. In Bandura's view, Martha's lack of self-efficacy causes her either to fail to register for the course or to withdraw from the course shortly after it begins.

Self-Efficacy and Phobic Behavior

Bandura and Adams's (1977) study demonstrates that efficacy expectations play a role in phobic behavior. Snake-phobic clients received the systematic desensitization therapy described in Chapter 4. Bandura and Adams discovered that even when patients no longer became emotionally disturbed by an imagined aversive scene, differences still existed in their ability to approach a snake. In contrast, the clients' self-efficacy expectation corresponded closely with their ability to interact with the snake: The greater the patients' perceived efficacy, the more able they were to inhibit phobic behavior and approach the snake (see Figure 11.8). Thus, these clients believed they could hold the snake, and this belief allowed them to overcome their phobia. This relation between self-efficacy and an absence of phobic behavior held true even after therapy, when a new snake, different from the one used before the therapy and during desensitization training, was employed. These results demonstrate that if we believe we are competent, we will generalize our self-efficacy expectations to new situations.

I have found that many of my students are frightened of talking a course in public speaking. For them, taking a public speaking course elicits much anxiety and is avoided until the last possible moment. The literature (Rodebaugh, 2006) clearly shows not only that low self-efficacy was associated with high speech anxiety, but also self-efficacy was the best predictor of whether or not a person would give a speech on a familiar topic. Other phobias have also been found to be associated with low self-efficacy (S. L. Williams, 1995). For example, Mcilroy, Sadler, and Boojawon (2007) observed that many undergraduate college students have a computer phobia, which leads them to avoid using university computer facilities. Not surprisingly, low self-efficacy was associated with high computer phobia and avoidance of university computer resources. Similarly, Gaudiano and Herbert (2007) found that many adolescents have a generalized social anxiety disorder and avoid social situations. These researchers also observed that persons with social anxiety disorder have low self-efficacy.

The Importance of Our Experiences

What factors account for Martha's outcome and efficacy expectations? Martha's outcome expectation that she will fail the statistics course could have developed through direct personal experience, through observations of the experiences of other people, or through information others have

Figure 11.8   Influence of desensitization therapy on the subject's level of self-efficacy and his or her ability to approach a snake. The success of therapy on the posttest was evaluated using both the same snake used in therapy ("similar threat") and a different snake ("dissimilar threat"). The results of this study showed that desensitization therapy increased a person's perceived self-efficacy and interaction with either the same or a different snake.

provided. Since Martha has not failed this course or any other course, her outcome expectations cannot reflect any direct personal experience. Possibly Martha has observed others, whom she perceived as similar to herself, fail the course. In addition, she has received information from other people that the course is difficult.

Bandura (1977, 1986) suggested that we use several types of information to establish an efficacy expectation. Personal accomplishments indicate our degree of self-efficacy. Successful experiences generally increase our expectations of mastery, and failure usually decreases our sense of self-efficacy (Bandura, Jeffrey, & Gajdos, 1975). The influence of success or failure on efficacy expectations depends on task difficulty, amount of effort expended, and the pattern and rate of success. We are more apt to feel competent if we usually succeed at a difficult task that requires considerable effort than if we succeed without trying.

Our sense of self-efficacy is also influenced by observing the successes and failures of other people whom we perceive as similar to ourselves. Seeing others successfully cope with perceived aversive events enhances our belief that we can also be effective, while observing others fail decreases our belief that we can succeed. Several factors determine the impact of a vicarious modeling experience. The success of the other person's behavior, or the model's behavior, must be clear; we cannot develop a sense of self-efficacy if the outcome of this other person's behavior is ambiguous (Kazdin, 1974a). Also, we acquire a stronger mastery expectation when we see several people, rather than a single person, cope with an aversive situation (Kazdin, 1974b). Furthermore, we develop greater self-efficacy when we see other people initially struggle with aversive events and slowly become more effective rather than succeed the first time we see them (Meichenbaum, 1972).

Emotional arousal also influences our sense of competence; we feel less able to cope with an aversive event when we are agitated or tense. Although Bandura (1977) suggested that emotional arousal plays a part in motivating phobic behavior, his view certainly differs from the drive approach outlined in Chapter 2. Bandura did not believe that fear directly causes avoidance behavior. Rather, he suggested that fear and defensive action are correlated, but not in a causal relationship. We are more likely to display avoidance behavior when we are afraid—but only because fear makes us feel less effective. However, because emotional arousal is only one source of information we use to develop a sense of self-efficacy, other information may enable us to feel competent even when we are afraid. Under these conditions, we interact with feared objects even though we are still afraid because we believe we are able to cope with aversive events.

Application: A Modeling Treatment for Phobias

Our discussion points to the critical role of outcome and efficacy expectations in causing phobic behavior. These expectations develop both through our experiences and through our observations of the experiences of others. Over the past 30 years, behavior therapists have used models interacting with feared objects to treat clients with phobias. The aim of this **modeling** treatment is to alter the clients' phobic behavior by vicariously modifying their expectations.

In a modeling treatment for phobias, clients see the model move closer and closer until the model encounters the feared object. A study by Bandura, Grusec, and Menlove (1967) shows the effectiveness of modeling in treating phobic behavior. These psychologists allowed children who feared dogs to watch a peer model interact with a dog. The children received eight 10-minute therapy sessions during a 4-day period. At first, the children saw the model pat the dog while it was in a pen. During later observations, the children watched the model walk the dog around the room. In the final sessions, the model climbed into the pen and played with the dog. Other children did not see the model but saw only the dog, which occupied the pen for the first therapy session and was leashed in the later sessions. Bandura et al. assessed the effectiveness of modeling by determining whether the children who initially feared dogs could approach and play with either the dog seen in the therapy sessions or a new dog. The results indicated that modeling reduced the children's phobic behavior and increased their interaction with the dog used in the study as well as with a new dog.

According to Bandura, the success of modeling therapy must be attributed to the vicarious modifications of a client's expectations. Support for this view is evident in a study by Bandura, Adams, and Beyer (1977). They exposed adults with a snake phobia to models interacting with a snake, and assessed the influence of this modeling treatment on the subjects' approach response to the snake and their efficacy expectation—that is, their expectation of being able to interact fearlessly with the snake. Bandura et al. found that the degree of success corresponded to the increase in the self-efficacy expectation: The more the model's action altered the client's efficacy expectation, the greater the client's approach to the snake.

Other studies have also demonstrated that modeling is an effective way to reduce unrealistic fears. For example, Melamed and Siegel (1975) and Shaw and Thoresen (1974) reported that fear of going to the dentist was reduced, in both adults and children, by watching a model. Similarly, Faust, Olson, and Rodriquez (1991) observed that participant modeling reduced the distress experienced by children faced with the prospect of having surgery. Further, Jaffe and Carlson (1972) found modeling effective in reducing test anxiety. Barber (1994) even found that students' fear of handling a laboratory rat was reduced through participant modeling. In a more recent study, Scott and Cervone (2008) reported that participant modeling was an effective way to eliminate a simple phobia and agoraphobia. Scott and Cervone also found that modeling reduced fears more quickly than did systematic desensitization or flooding.

The effectiveness of modeling to reduce fears appears to be long lasting. Ost (1989) treated 20 phobic patients with a variety of phobias including fears of dogs, cats, rats, spiders, and hypodermic needles. Not only did a 2-hour modeling session reduce the phobic patients' fears and increase their interaction with a feared stimulus immediately after the modeling treatment, but Ost reported that 90% of the patients maintained their improved behavior on a 4-year follow-up study.

An Alternative View

Not all psychologists have accepted Bandura's view of the role of cognitions in causing avoidance behavior. Some psychologists (M. W. Eysenck, 1978; Wolpe, 1978) have continued to advocate a drive-based view of avoidance behavior (see Chapter 8). According to these psychologists, anxiety elicits cognitions, but they do not affect the occurrence of avoidance response. Eysenck considers efficacy expectations to be merely "epiphenomenological" by-products of anxiety.

Other psychologists (Borkovec, 1976; P. J. Lang, 1978) suggest that three types of anxiety exist: cognitive, physiological, and behavioral. Cognitive anxiety refers to the effect of anxiety on self-efficacy, physiological anxiety affects the physiological state, and behavioral anxiety directly influences behavior. In this view, cognitions or physiological state can mediate the influence of anxiety on behavior, or anxiety can directly influence behavior. According to P. J. Lang (1978), the relative contribution of each type of anxiety differs depending on the individual's learning history and type of situation. Sometimes cognitions will mediate the effect of anxiety on behavior; under other conditions, anxiety will directly affect behavior.

Our discussion suggests that both cognitive and noncognitive processes motivate avoidance behavior. A study by Feltz (1982) supports this view. Feltz examined the variables controlling whether female college students would execute a difficult back dive. Feltz discovered that self-efficacy predicted whether the subjects executed or avoided the task on the first trial; however, the influence of self-efficacy diminished on subsequent trials, indicating an influence other than cognitive anxiety. Feltz discovered that physiological arousal also influenced whether the subjects avoided the back dive; that is, physiological measures of anxiety (i.e., heart rate) predicted behavior on Trials 1 and 3. Furthermore, Feltz's research demonstrates that anxiety can directly affect behavior. On Trial 2, the subjects' self-reported anxiety level was the only predictor of whether they completed the back dive or avoided it. Interestingly, self-efficacy and heart rate did correlate with self-reported anxiety prior to the first dive; however, self-reported anxiety did not correlate with either efficacy or heart rate on subsequent dives. On the basis of her research, Feltz suggested that anxiety can either directly or indirectly affect behavior by altering cognitive or physiological processes. Her study also provides support for the idea that both cognitive and noncognitive processes motivate avoidance behavior.

Other research (Moritz, Feltz, Fahrbach, & Mack, 2000; Vancouver, Thompson, Tischner, & Putka, 2002) suggested that past performance was a better predictor of performance than self-efficacy. Moritz, Feltz, Fahrbach, and Mack reported that the correlation between self-efficacy and sport skill performance was .38. Further, Vancouver, Thompson, Tischner, and Putka observed that self-efficacy can sometimes lead to overconfidence and increase the likelihood of logic errors in an analytic game.

Further, Bandura and Locke (2003) argued that studies examining the relationship between self-efficacy and performance underestimated the influence of self-efficacy on performance. In their view, past performance is a "conglomerate index" that includes self-efficacy. Feltz, Chow, and Hepler (2008) partialled out the influence of self-efficacy and found out that the effect of self-efficacy on performance was stronger than in prior research. Further, they observed that the relationship between self-efficacy and performance increased across trials. However, Feltz, Chow, and Hepler still observed that a significant amount of performance was not predicted by self-efficacy levels, a finding that supports the view that processes other than self-efficacy also contribute to performance.

BEFORE YOU GO ON

- What outcome expectancies cause Martha's statistics phobia?
- Could Martha successfully complete a statistics course yet still be afraid of taking another one?

SECTION REVIEW

- Phobic behavior occurs when individuals expect that (1) an aversive event will occur, (2) an avoidance behavior is the only way to prevent the aversive event, and (3) they cannot interact with the phobic object.
- Modeling has been found to be an effective means to change expectations and eliminate phobic behavior.
- Cognitive and noncognitive processes influence the likelihood of phobic behavior.

CRITICAL THINKING QUESTIONS

1. Kai Leng is going to New Orleans next week. She loves drinking coffee and eating beignets at Café du Monde. Kai Leng will assuredly stop there several times while she is in New Orleans. Identify the associative-link and behavior-reinforcer expectations responsible for Kai Leng's behavior.

2. Eric believes he will do well in his learning class, while Sidney is not so sure he will get a good grade. Using an attributional approach, suggest how Eric and Sidney might react to a poor performance on the first exam. What might be the effect of a poor outcome on the second or third exams?

3. Kasha is fearful of driving in a large city. How would Bandura's model explain Kasha's fearfulness? What approach might she take to eliminate her fear?

KEY TERMS

associative-link expectation
behavior-reinforcer belief
cognition
efficacy expectation
external attribution
hopefulness
hopelessness theory of depression
irrelevant incentive effect
learned helplessness
negative attributional style
personal helplessness
reinforcer devaluation effect
specific attribution
stimulus-outcome expectation
unstable attribution

behavioral autonomy
causal attribution
cognitive map
expectation
global attribution
hopelessness
internal attribution
latent learning
modeling
outcome expectation
positive attributional style
response-outcome expectation
stable attribution
universal helplessness

Complex Learning Tasks

A DAY AT THE BEACH

Regina thought it was a lovely summer day. The temperature was about 85 degrees, and the humidity was quite moderate. It would be hard to find a better day to go to the beach. Despite the fact that it was the middle of the summer, Regina had not been to the beach this year. She had always enjoyed the beach, but with a full-time job, Regina had not found the time to go this summer. Her two best friends, Beth and Ivana, had asked her on numerous occasions, but she always seemed to have commitments at work that prevented her from accepting their invitations. When Beth called on Monday, Regina thought she would be able to go to the beach on Saturday. She had just completed a major project and certainly could handle the minor jobs on her desk during the week. On Tuesday, Regina's boss informed her that a report was needed a week earlier than planned and would have to be on her desk by Monday morning; Regina was devastated. She wanted to go to the beach very badly, but she did not think she could get the report done if she went on Saturday. Beth probably would not ask her again if she backed out this time, but the report had to be done. What could she do? Maybe she could go to her boss, tell her about her commitment to Beth, and ask for an extension on the project. She had always handed in her work on time; maybe the boss would be agreeable. However, Regina decided not to ask for more time: It would look bad, and her boss probably would not agree, anyway. Another option would be to stay up late for the remainder of the week to get the project done. Regina did not function well on little sleep, so she dismissed this option. Could anyone else help her? Her coworker, Heath, was familiar with the project. While he was definitely busy, maybe he would help her. He would understand her social dilemma. She could make it up to him by helping him with his work at some other time. This seemed like a reasonable solution. She would talk with him after lunch.

In this vignette, Regina has a problem. She wants to find a way to go to the beach on Saturday and still complete her work project by Monday morning. In the story, Regina recognized the problem, identified her goal, and generated a number of possible solutions. After considering the possibilities and the probable success of each one, she decided on the solution she thought was most likely to be successful.

Each of us faces many problems during our lives. In some instances, we adopt a systematic strategy to solve a problem, while in other cases we use the first solution that comes to mind. In this chapter, we examine how people solve problems and consider reasons why we might or might not be able to solve a particular problem.

This chapter describes three major complex learning tasks. First, we explore how concepts form. A concept is a symbol that represents a group of objects or events with common characteristics. Recognizing the attributes that define a concept helps us organize our world and respond appropriately to the members of a particular concept. Second, we discuss problem solving. A problem exists when obstacles prevent us from attaining a desired goal. To reach the goal, we must overcome these obstacles by selecting the most effective solution to the problem. Finally, we examine the structure of language and how we learn to use it. Language is a means of communicating our thoughts, feelings, and intentions to other people.

CONCEPT LEARNING

What is an airplane? *Merriam-Webster* defines it as a "fixed-wing aircraft, heavier than air, which is driven by a screw propeller or by a high velocity rearward jet and supported by the dynamic reactions of the air against its wings." The word *airplane* is a **concept**. A concept, again, is a symbol that represents a class or group of objects or events with common properties. Thus, the concept of *airplane* refers to all objects that (1) have fixed wings, (2) are heavier than air, (3) are driven by a screw propeller or high-velocity rearward jet, and (4) are supported by the dynamic reactions of the air against the wings. Airplanes come in various sizes and shapes, but as long as they have these four properties, we can easily identify them as airplanes. As the understanding of airplane as a concept suggests, we are all familiar with many concepts. *Chair, book,* and *hat* are three such concepts: They stand for groups of objects with common properties.

Concept learning significantly enhances our ability to effectively interact with the environment. Instead of separately labeling and categorizing each new object or event we encounter, we simply incorporate it into our existing concepts. For example, suppose a child sees a large German shepherd. Even though this child may have been exposed only to smaller dogs like poodles and cocker spaniels, the child will easily identify the barking animal with four legs and a tail as a dog.

You may have noticed the similarity of concept learning to our discussion of generalization and discrimination learning in Chapter 10. If so, you have made a good observation. Concept learning, in part, involves discriminating between stimuli and then generalizing that discrimination to other stimuli that are similar to the discriminative stimulus. For example, a child may learn the concept of *dog* and discriminate between dogs and cats. But there are many kinds of dogs. Once the child has learned to discriminate between dogs and cats, the child can generalize the response to different dogs, but not to different cats. We next turn our attention to the process of learning a concept.

The Structure of a Concept

Attributes and Rules

Concepts have two main properties: attributes and rules. An **attribute** is any feature of an object or event that varies from one instance to another. For example, height, weight, and coloring differ from person to person and, therefore, are attributes of each individual.

An attribute can have a fixed value; for example, the attribute of gender can only be either male or female. In other cases, attributes have continuous values; for instance, the shade of a certain color can vary from light to dark.

For each concept, a **rule** defines which objects or events are examples of that particular concept. For the concept of *airplane*, the defining rule indicates that to be an airplane, an object must have fixed wings, be heavier than air, be driven by a screw propeller or high-velocity rearward jet, and be supported by the dynamic reactions of the air against its wings.

Types of Rules

A number of different rules may be used to define the attributes of a concept. In some instances, the rules are simple; in other cases, they are more complex. When the rule is simple, an object or event must possess only one attribute to be an example of that particular concept. Suppose that an object is green. This object belongs to the concept of *green* whether it is a green car, a green shirt, or a green pea.

The concept *green* is defined by an affirmative rule. An **affirmative rule** specifies that a particular attribute defines a concept. In Figure 12.1, the affirmative rule indicates that the concept is *large*. A **negative rule** states that any object or event having a certain attribute is not a member of the concept. Figure 12.1 shows that any object that is small is not an example of the concept *large*. Another example of a concept defined by a negative rule is blindness: Anyone who can see is not blind.

When a concept is based on the presence of two or more attributes, it is defined by the **conjunctive rule**. The conjunctive rule states that all the specified attributes must be present to be an example of the concept. Figure 12.1 shows that to be an example of the conjunctive rule, the object must be large and circular. To illustrate a real-world example of the conjunctive rule, consider the question, "What is poison ivy?" Poison ivy is a *vine* that has *three-leaf clusters;* each leaf is *pointed* and *tooth-edged,* and each vine is *red* at the base of the branch of leaves. To be *poison*

Figure 12.1   The dashed lines surround examples of the affirmative rule (large), the negative rule (not large), the conjunctive rule (large and circle), and disjunctive rule (large and/or circle).

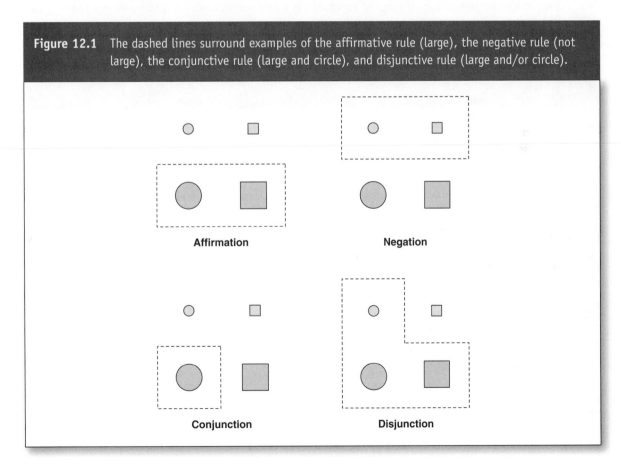

ivy, a plant must have all five of these attributes. The Virginia creeper vine is like poison ivy but has five-leaf clusters; seedlings of the box elder also look like poison ivy, but they have straight instead of vinelike stems.

A **disjunctive rule** specifies that concepts can be defined by the presence of one of two, or both, common attributes; that is, an example of the concept can possess either of the two common attributes, or it can possess both of them. In Figure 12.1, the disjunctive rule is *circle* or *large* or both. A large circle is an example of the concept, as are both a large square and a small circle. As another example of a concept defined by a disjunctive rule, consider the question, "What is schizophrenia?" Schizophrenia is characterized by persistent hallucinations and/or delusions. Thus, a person who has either or both of the attributes may suffer from schizophrenia.

Our discussion suggests that for a specific object or event to be an example of a concept, it must have all the attributes characteristic of that concept. Yet, this is not always true. Consider the concept *bird.* We know that birds can fly, are usually relatively small in size, have feathers, build nests, and head for warmer climates during the winter. But as we will see in the next section, not all birds have all the attributes of the concept *bird.*

The Prototype of a Concept

Not all examples of a concept necessarily have all the attributes characteristic of that concept (Rosch, 1975, 1978). Consider the concept of *vegetable.* How exemplary of this concept is a pea, a carrot, or a beet? Rosch found that subjects could rank the degree to which a particular item fits a certain concept. As Table 12.1 indicates, different vegetables vary in the extent to which they are examples of the concept of *vegetable.* Pea and carrot exemplify the concept to the greatest degree; cucumber and beet to the least.

Table 12.1 Rankings of Furniture and Vegetables by How Well They Exemplify Their Respective Categories

Furniture		Vegetables	
Exemplar	**Goodness-of-Example Rank**	**Exemplar**	**Goodness-of-Example Rank**
Chair	1.5	Peas	1
Sofa	1.5	Carrots	2
Couch	3.5	Green beans	3
Table	3.5	String beans	4
Easy chair	5	Spinach	5
Dresser	6.5	Broccoli	6
Rocking chair	6.5	Asparagus	7
Coffee table	8	Corn	8
Rocker	9	Cauliflower	9
Love seat	10	Brussels sprouts	10
Chest of drawers	11	Squash	11
Desk	12	Lettuce	12
Bed	13	Celery	13
Bureau	14	Cucumber	14
End table	15.5	Beets	15

Why are some objects or events better examples of a concept than are others? Rosch (1975) suggested that the degree to which a member of a concept exemplifies the concept depends on the degree of **family resemblance**: The more attributes a specific object or event shares with other members of a concept, the more the object or event exemplifies the concept. Thus, compared with cucumber and beet, pea and carrot are better examples of the concept of *vegetable* because they share more attributes with other members of the concept.

When you think of the concept of *furniture,* you are most likely to imagine a chair. Why? According to Rosch (1978), the **prototype** of a concept is the object that has the greatest number of attributes in common with other members of the concept and is, therefore, the most typical member of a category. As Table 12.1 shows, the chair is the prototype of the concept of *furniture.* Members of the concept that have many attributes in common with the prototype are considered typical of the concept; thus, table and sofa are typical of *furniture* because they share many of the same attributes as the chair. In contrast, bureau and end table are atypical of the concept because they share only a few attributes with the chair.

Perhaps another example would be helpful. Consider the concept of *dog.* When a person thinks of the concept *dog,* the person is more likely to think of a German shepherd than a miniature dachshund.

The next example provides a very different prototype of a concept. Fehr and Russell (1991) asked subjects to indicate "if maternal love is a type of love" and "if self-love is a type of love." Their subjects agreed that maternal love is a type of love more often than they agreed that self-love is a type of love, presumably because maternal love better matched their prototype of love.

The degree to which an object or event exemplifies a concept is important. To illustrate, Rosch (1978) asked subjects to indicate whether a particular object or event was a member of a specific concept. For example, subjects were asked whether it is true or false that robins and penguins are birds. Rosch reported that subjects took less time to say "true" when the object or event was a good example of the concept (robin) than when it was a poor example (penguin). Thus, the more an object or event differs from the prototype, the more difficult it is to identify it as an example of the concept.

Boundaries of the Concept

Two objects or events may share certain attributes but not be examples of the same concept. For example, although robins and bats both have wings, the robin is a bird and the bat is a mammal. Certain rules, then, define the boundaries of a concept. These rules reveal whether differences between the prototype of a concept and another object or event indicate either that the other object or event is less typical of the concept, or that it is an example of another concept. Thus, even though robins and bats both have wings, the other differences between them mean that the bat and the robin are not members of the same concept.

Sometimes boundaries between concepts are not clearly defined (Zazdeh, Fu, Tanak, & Shimura, 1975). For example, what is the difference between a river and a stream? When the boundary of a concept is vague, it is difficult to know whether an object or event is a member of that concept. Rosch (1978) reported that subjects easily answered that a stone is not a bird, but they had difficulty indicating that a bat is not a bird. In fact, many subjects thought a bat is some kind of bird. This study suggests that we do not always know the boundaries that define certain concepts.

Studying Concept Learning in Humans

Psychologists have conducted numerous experiments examining concept learning in humans. An early representative study by Smoke (1933) presented subjects with a large number of figures that differed in the shape, size, number, and location of their dots. The subjects' task was to learn the concept of *DAX*, which consisted of a circle with one dot inside and another dot outside (see Figure 12.2). The *DAX* concept uses the conjunctive rule; a figure that (1) is a circle, (2) has two dots, and (3) has one dot inside and one outside the circle is an example of the *DAX* concept. Subjects saw each figure, indicated whether they thought it was an example of the concept, and received feedback about the correctness of their response. Smoke reported that subjects readily learned the concept of *DAX*.

Studying Concept Learning in Animals

Concept learning involves identification of the properties that characterize a concept as well as those that do not. Can animals learn concepts? The research of Richard Herrnstein and his associates (Herrnstein, 1979; Herrnstein & de Villiers, 1980; Herrnstein, Loveland, & Cable, 1976) clearly shows that animals can indeed learn a concept.

Herrnstein et al. (1976) presented a series of 80 slides to a group of pigeons. Half of the slides were S^D, and pecking at these slides resulted in food reinforcement. The other 40 slides were S^Δ, and the pigeons did not receive a reinforcer for pecking at them. The S^D slides were examples of natural objects; for example, for some pigeons, the S^D slides were pictures of water, for some they were pictures of trees, and for some they were pictures of a specific woman. The S^Δ slides did not show examples of the appropriate objects. Figure 12.3 shows positive (S^D) and negative (S^Δ) instances of each concept. During each daily session, the pigeons saw each of the 80 slides briefly. Herrnstein et al. found that the pigeons quickly learned to respond to the S^D and not to the S^Δ.

Did these pigeons really learn a concept? Did they discover which stimuli contained examples of the concept and which did not? Or did they merely learn to respond to some particular stimuli but not to others? Herrnstein and de Villiers (1980) evaluated whether the pigeons had actually learned a concept in two ways. First, they presented the same 80 slides to the pigeons, but this time not just the S^D slides contained examples of the concept; that is, the example slides were randomly assigned to S^D and S^Δ. If the pigeons were just learning to respond to some stimuli but

Figure 12.2   Samples of *DAX* and non-*DAX* figures. The *DAX* concept was defined as a circle with one dot inside and one dot outside its boundary. All objects possessing these attributes are examples of the *DAX* concept.

Figure 12.3 Examples of stimuli Herrnstein, Loveland, and Cable (1976) used in their study. Figures A, C, and E are S^Ds. Figures B, D, and F are S^Δs. The concept of water is present in Figure A, but not in Figure B. The concept of trees is present in Figure C, but not in Figure D. The particular woman present in Figure E is not present in Figure F.

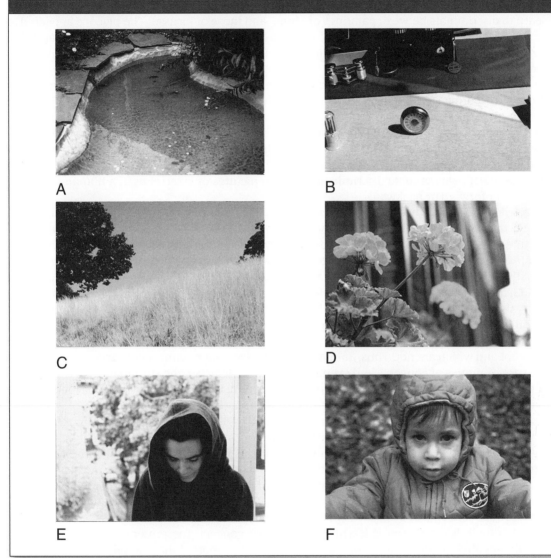

A

B

C

D

E

F

not to others, then the random assignment of slides should not affect how fast the pigeons learned the discrimination. Although the pigeons did learn the discrimination when the slides were randomly presented as S^D and S^Δ, Herrnstein and de Villiers reported that learning was much slower when no concept defined S^D and S^Δ.

Herrnstein and de Villiers (1980) also used a positive-transfer test to show that the pigeons did learn a concept. After the pigeons had learned the discrimination in which S^D contained an example of the concept and S^Δ did not, they viewed two new slides of S^D and S^Δ. According to Herrnstein and de Villiers, if the pigeons had only learned to respond to certain stimuli, then learning to discriminate new slides of S^D and S^Δ should proceed at the same rate as original learning. However, if the pigeons had learned the concept, positive transfer should occur, and the pigeons should readily learn how to respond to the new slides. Herrnstein and de Villiers observed considerable positive transfer to the new slides; the pigeons responded differentially to the new examples of S^D and S^A almost as effectively as they had to the original slides.

Pigeons have shown the ability to learn many different concepts since Herrnstein's classic studies. In Chapter 10, we described a study by Watanabe et al. (1995) showing that pigeons could learn to discriminate between paintings of Monet and those of Picasso. The pigeons appeared to learn the concept of a Monet painting, as distinguished from a Picasso painting, because the pigeons responded to new Monet paintings during testing as they had to Monet paintings (S^Ds) experienced during training.

Pigeons also have learned to discriminate between the music of Bach and the music of Stravinsky (Porter & Neuringer, 1984) and between line drawings of different objects (Kirkpatrick-Steger, Wasserman, & Biederman, 1996). Further, Nakamura, Croft, and Westbrook (2003) reported that pigeons could discriminate between photographs of individual pigeons, and Nakamura, Ito, Croft, and Westbrook (2006) found that pigeons could discriminate between photographs of male and female pigeons. Interestingly, Mui, Haselgrove, McGregor, Futter, Heyes, and Pearce (2007) observed that pigeons could discriminate between pictures of video clips of a human walking a dog either forward or backward.

Monkeys also have been able to learn concepts. For example, D'Amato and Van Sant (1988) found that monkeys could learn the concept of *humans*. In their study, monkeys were shown pictures of scenes with humans (S^D) and pictures of scenes without humans (S^A) in a simultaneous two-choice discrimination procedure. D'Amato and Van Sant reported that the monkeys rapidly learned to choose the pictures that featured humans. More recently, Vonk and MacDonald (2002) found that a female gorilla could learn to discriminate between primates and nonprimate animals, while Vonk and MacDonald (2004) reported that six orangutans could learn to distinguish between photos of orangutans and other primates.

Our discussion indicates that animals can learn which stimuli are examples of a particular concept and which are not. Thus, animals can organize their environments according to events that are examples of concepts and events that are not. However, the stimuli used in the preceding studies involved natural concepts; that is, the stimuli represented concrete aspects of the natural environment. Can animals also learn abstract concepts such as *same* or *different?* Robert Cook and his associates (Cook, 2002; Cook & Blaisdell, 2006; Cook & Brooks, 2009; Cook, Kelly, & Katz, 2003) used a successive two-item same-different discrimination to investigate whether pigeons can learn abstract concepts. The same-different discrimination task procedure involves the pigeons being reinforced for responding when two or more stimuli are identical (concept of *same*) and not reinforced for responding when one or more of the stimuli are different from each other (concept of *different*). To evaluate whether pigeons had learned the abstract concepts of *same* and *different,* the pigeons were exposed to novel same and different stimuli. If the pigeon is learning the abstract concept, the presentation of new stimuli should not affect performance. Cook and his associates reported that the pigeons continued to perform well when presented with new stimuli, which indicated that the pigeons had learned the concepts of *same* and *different.* Wasserman and his colleagues (Castro, Kennedy, & Wasserman, 2010; Wasserman & Young, 2010) also reported that pigeons could learn same-different discriminations. Similarly, A. A. Wright and Katz (2007) and Castro, Young, and Wasserman (2006) found that primates could learn to discriminate between arrays of two or more stimuli that are the same and arrays of stimuli that contain one or more of the stimuli that are different from the rest of the stimuli.

Wasserman and Young (2010) suggested that being able to discriminate the same from different collections of stimuli is central to human thought and reasoning. They argued that the ability of pigeons and baboons to be able to learn same-different discriminations without the benefit of human language suggests that thought and reasoning are not solely human qualities.

Theories of Concept Learning

There are two main theories of concept learning. One view argues that concept learning is an associative process; the other argues that concept learning is a cognitive process.

Associative Theory

Clark Hull (1920) envisioned concept learning as a form of discrimination learning (see Chapter 2). In his view, concepts have both relevant and irrelevant attributes. On each trial of a concept-learning study, a subject determines whether the object or event shown is characteristic of the concept. A subject who responds correctly receives reward by feedback (the researcher tells the subject the response was correct). As a result of reward, response strength increases to the attributes characteristic of the concept.

Consider the Smoke (1933) study described earlier. The subjects received reward when they recognized DAX figures (figures of a circle with one dot on the inside of the circle and another on the outside). As the result of reward, the stimulus (figure) and response (*DAX*) were associated. In contrast, subjects that identified figures that were not examples of the *DAX* concept did not receive reward. The result of nonreward was a diminished response to nonexamples of the concept of *DAX*.

Hull's (1920) classic study provides evidence for an associative view of concept learning. In this study, adult subjects learned six lists of 12 paired associates. The stimuli were Chinese letters containing 12 different features. The stimuli changed from task to task, but the features did not. (Six of the features appear in Figure 12.4.) The responses were nonsense syllables paired with each feature, the same feature-nonsense syllable pairs were used in all of the lists. Hull found that the subjects learned each successive list more rapidly than the preceding one. According to Hull, the subjects were able to learn later lists more quickly because they had learned the common feature of each stimulus in the category. Hull believed that subjects were not consciously aware of the association, but instead had become trained to respond to a specific stimulus event.

Hull's view that associative processes alone control concept learning was supported by most psychologists until the late 1950s, when further research revealed that cognitive processes also are involved in concept learning.

Cognitive Process in Concept Learning

Bruner, Goodnow, and Austin (1956) suggested that a concept is learned by testing hypotheses about the correct solution. If the first hypothesis is correct, the individual has learned the concept. However, if the hypothesis is incorrect, another hypothesis will be generated and tested. Hypothesis testing continues until a correct solution is discovered.

Consider again the *DAX* concept. Suppose that on the first trial (see Figure 12.5 on page 325), the individual saw a figure of a circle and a dot, and his or her first guess or hypothesis was that this figure was an example of the concept *DAX*. Since DAX is a figure with a circle and two dots, the response "DAX" to the first figure was wrong. Thus, the initial hypothesis was incorrect, and the subject needed to generate a new one. On Trial 2, the subject hypothesized that DAX was a single dot inside the circle, so his or her response was "Not DAX." The subject learned that this response was also wrong, and on Trial 3, he or she hypothesized that two dots represent the concept. Again the subject learned that this guess was wrong. The subject's next hypothesis was that the concept was any two dots and a circle. Although Trial 4 suggests that this is a possibility, Trial 5 proves it to be incorrect. The subject then hypothesized that the concept of *DAX* is one dot

Figure 12.4 The stimuli used in Hull's concept-learning study. Notice that each of the features on the left is part of the corresponding letter in each list on the right.

inside a circle and one dot outside. The subject tested this hypothesis on Trials 6, 7, and 8 and finally concluded that it was correct. Our example suggests that, in addition to forming hypotheses to learn concepts, individuals adopt a win-stay, lose-shift strategy; that is, they will stick with a hypothesis as long as it works and will generate a new one when evidence indicates that the old hypothesis is not valid.

What evidence demonstrates that concept learning involves testing hypotheses? Levine (1966) developed a blank-trials procedure to show that people learn concepts by testing hypotheses. On each trial, subjects were shown two letters. The letters differed in terms of color (black or white), identity (X or T), size (large or small), and position (left or right). Levine chose one attribute (e.g., white) as the concept and the subjects' task was to learn which attribute had been chosen. On each trial, the subjects chose one of the two stimuli and were told whether their response contained the correct attribute. After each study trial, subjects were given four blank trials. On each blank trial, two stimuli were presented and the subjects again tried to choose the one that represented the concept. However, the subjects received no feedback on these trials. The subjects' responses on the blank trials indicated whether they were testing a hypothesis about the correct attribute. If they were, a particular pattern of responses would appear. Figure 12.6 on page 326 presents several patterns of responses. Suppose that a subject hypothesized that *black* was the correct attribute. This subject's responses should match those depicted in the first column of Figure 12.6. In contrast, the responses of a subject who thought that *large* was correct should match those in the fourth column, while a random pattern of responses would develop if subjects had not been testing hypotheses to learn the concept.

Figure 12.5   A hypothetical series of eight trials of the DAX problem. Successive rows show, trial by trial, the stimulus presented, the response given, and the feedback the experimenter provided.

Trial	Figure presented	Response	Feedback
1		"DAX"	Wrong
2		"Not DAX"	Wrong
3		"DAX"	Wrong
4		"DAX"	Right
5		"DAX"	Wrong
6		"DAX"	Right
7		"Not DAX"	Right
8		"Not DAX"	Right

Levine (1966) found that subjects engaged in hypothesis testing on over 95% of the trials. Furthermore, he found that subjects adopted a win-stay, lose-shift strategy. When a hypothesis was confirmed on a feedback trial, subjects retained this hypothesis throughout the blank trials and continued to use it until they received feedback that the attribute was incorrect. When a hypothesis was found to be incorrect, subjects generated and used a new hypothesis on the four subsequent blank trials and then on study trials.

Do not assume that associative learning and hypothesis testing are mutually exclusive means of learning a concept. A concept can be learned using either method, but it is learned best when both means are employed. For example, Reber, Kassin, Lewis, and Cantor (1980) found that subjects acquired a concept most rapidly when they learned both the rules defining the concept and specific instances of the concept.

Figure 12.6 The stimuli Levine used in his blank trials are in the middle of the figure. The eight possible hypotheses are to the left and right of the stimuli. The column below each hypothesis shows the pattern of choices that test the hypothesis.

BEFORE YOU GO ON

- What concept had Regina learned about the beach?

- How can associative and cognitive theories explain Regina's concept of *beach?*

SECTION REVIEW

- A concept is a symbol that represents objects or events that have common characteristics.

- The prototype best exemplifies the concept because it possesses more attributes of the concept than the other members of the concept do.

- Boundaries specify the point at which a particular object or event is not a member of a specific concept.

- The affirmative rule is that the presence of a particular attribute defines the concept.

- The negative rule is that a member of the concept cannot possess a specific attribute.

- The conjunctive rule is that the presence of two or more attributes defines the concept.

- The disjunctive rule is that the presence of one of two or both attributes defines the concept.

- Concepts are learned by associating the concept name with specific instances of the concept.

- A concept can also be learned by testing hypotheses about the attributes of the concept or about the rules defining the concept.

PROBLEM SOLVING

The Missionaries-and-Cannibals Problem

> On one side of a river there are three missionaries and three cannibals. They have a boat on their side that is capable of carrying two people at a time across the river. The goal is to transport all six people across to the other side of the river. At no point can the cannibals on either side of the river outnumber the missionaries on that side of the river (or the cannibals would eat the outnumbered missionaries). This constraint only holds when there is at least one missionary on the side of the river where there are more cannibals. That is, it is all right to have one, two, or three cannibals on the same side of the river with zero missionaries, because they would have no missionaries to eat. (Wickelgren, 1974, p. 86)

Can you solve this problem? (Remember that someone will have to row the boat back after each trip across.) Spend several minutes trying to find a solution.

Were you able to transport the missionaries and cannibals without losing any missionaries? If you are like most people, you had great difficulty solving this problem. Figure 12.7 provides the series of trips necessary to move all the cannibals and missionaries to the other side of the river. Each box indicates where the missionaries, cannibals, and boat are after each trip. The arrows between the boxes show which people take the boat ride on each trip. The trips (arrows) following the odd numbers take the missionaries and cannibals across; the trips following the even numbers are to return the boat to the original side.

Why is this problem so difficult to solve? The difficulty lies in Trip 6. On this trip, it is *necessary* to have both a cannibal and missionary return across the river; otherwise, the cannibals will outnumber the missionaries on one side or the other. People usually pause for a long time at this point and are very likely to make an error. Why? The reason is that this choice (and the solution to the problem) appears to lead away from the solution to the problem; that is, this choice takes some of the missionaries and cannibals back to the original side of the river. Like this problem, solutions for many real-life problems do not necessarily follow a straight line toward the goal.

The Nature of the Problem

What is a problem? A **problem** is a situation in which a person is motivated to reach a goal, but some obstacle or obstacles blocks the attainment of the goal. The person's task is to find a solution to the problem, that is, to discover a way to overcome the obstacles. Recall our discussion of Regina's problem described in the chapter-opening vignette. Regina wants to find a way to go to the beach Saturday and still complete her work project by Monday morning. How she might solve this problem is described next.

Edward Thorndike (1898) proposed that animals and people solve problems by trial and error (see Chapter 1). For example, Thorndike did not believe that the cats in his famous puzzle box study were able to figure out how to open the latch to escape from the box. Instead, the cats performed a large number of responses, and those that enabled them to reach the goal were rewarded. Wolfgang Kohler (1925) suggested a different view of problem solving. According to Kohler, an animal internally or mentally explores the problem before exhibiting a specific response. The exploration involves considering and rejecting possible solutions and finally developing insight as to the correct solution.

Consider Wolfgang Kohler's (1925) classic primate studies. Kohler presented several chimpanzees with the problem of reaching a piece of fruit that was suspended over their heads in their

Figure 12.7 Solution to the missionaries-and-cannibals problem. At the starting point, the three missionaries and cannibals are on the left side of the river. On each boat ride, two people can travel across. The problem is that at no point can the cannibals outnumber missionaries on either side. The odd-numbered trips are across the river and the even numbers are return trips. The key to the solution of this problem is on Trip 6: only by returning both a cannibal and a missionary to the original side of the river can the problem be solved.

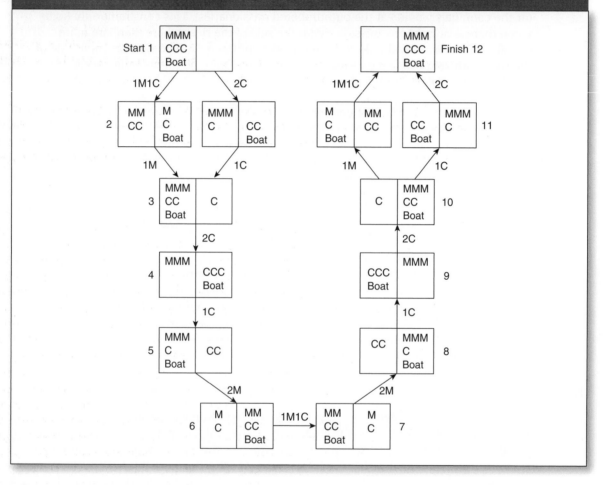

play area. The problem was structured so that the chimps could not reach the fruit even by jumping. Kohler randomly placed several boxes and sticks throughout the play area. According to Kohler, the chimpanzees initially attempted to reach the fruit by jumping. When that failed, they stopped jumping and paced back and forth. Kohler then observed that the chimps abruptly stopped pacing and, looking quite resolute, used the boxes and sticks to reach the fruit. One chimp obtained the fruit by gathering several boxes, stacking them on top of each other, and climbing up the boxes to reach the fruit. Another chimp climbed on one box and used a stick to knock down the fruit. A third chimp collected two hollow sticks and made one long stick by inserting the end of one stick into the other.

Several critical observations led Kohler to suggest that **insight** was responsible for the chimpanzees' solutions to the problem. First, the chimps solved the problem with few or no mistakes. Second, once they had solved the problem, the chimps were able to quickly solve other similar problems.

Did Regina solve her problem of wanting to go to the beach while still completing her project by insight? Or did she solve it by trial and error? We next look at the process or processes used to solve problems.

Defining the Problem

The first step in solving a problem is defining the problem, which entails identifying both the starting point, or **initial state**, of the problem and the end point, or **goal state**, of the problem. Consider the following example to illustrate this aspect of problem solving. How can you get from the store to your car without getting wet in the rain when you have no umbrella? The initial state of this problem is that you are in the store and it is raining. The goal state of this problem is being in the car without being wet.

Solving the problem involves two additional processes: First, you need to identify the operations that solve the problem. In our example, you want to be in your car and not be wet. Operations that would help you avoid getting wet include bringing along an umbrella to the store, not losing the umbrella in the store, or using some other item to cover your head. Second, restrictions limit what you can do to solve a problem. In our example, stealing another person's umbrella or parking at the door of the store are not acceptable solutions to the problem.

Well-Defined Versus Ill-Defined Problems

Some problems are well-defined: Both the initial state and the goal state of the problem are clear. Our example of being in your car and not being wet is a well-defined problem; a **well-defined problem** has an initial state and a goal state that is obvious. However, some problems are ill-defined: An **ill-defined problem** has no clear starting point or end point. Consider the problem of an instructor who wants to teach a good class. How does the instructor determine whether a class is good? Since there are not inherent definite standards to measure the success of a course, how can the instructor know that he has reached the goal state? In this example, the end point is unclear. In some cases, the starting point is unclear. For example, a person may recognize that a car must be in good working order to run smoothly, but the individual may not be able to check the condition of the car and therefore cannot identify the starting point of the problem.

Solving Ill-Defined Problems

Reitman (1965) suggested that identifying the starting point and end point is the key to bringing an ill-defined problem closer to a well-defined one, and that generating additional structures (subproblems) can accomplish this goal. Consider the following example. You are asked to write a term paper for a biology class. Your starting point is gathering and analyzing a large body of literature. The end point is a finished term paper that has a beginning, a middle, and an end; is sufficient in length and depth; and accurately discusses the topic. To narrow the definition of the problem, you must first choose a specific topic, such as genetics. You can further define the problem by identifying several subtopics of genetics and then break these subtopics down into even more specific groups.

Holyoak (1990) suggested that creating a set of manageable subproblems provides the structure for converting an ill-defined problem into a well-defined one. Wessels (1982) proposed that creating a hierarchy of clearly stated subproblems makes an ill-defined problem easier to solve. Several studies have found that using subproblems facilitates the solving of such ill-defined problems as designing a shop (J. R. Hayes, 1978), writing a fugue (Reitman, 1965), and building a warship (G. A. Simon, 1973).

A Strategy for Solving Problems

After the problem has been defined, the next step is to develop a plan of attack. There are two major strategies—algorithms and heuristics—that can be used to solve problems.

Algorithms

An **algorithm** is a precise set of rules used to solve a particular type of problem. To illustrate, consider the algorithm for subtracting: One number is deducted from another to obtain the correct answer. If the algorithm is applied correctly, the solution will be accurate; in this case, following the rules of subtraction will produce a correct calculation.

In some cases, a simple algorithm is all you need to solve the problem. The application of the subtraction algorithm, for instance, quickly leads to a correct answer. However, in many cases, the set of rules that will solve the problem is not easy to identify, and many alternatives must be tried before the correct solution is found. This process of trial and error often uses an enormous amount of time to solve a problem, as illustrated by Samuel's (1963) analysis of the use of this strategy in the game of checkers. Using an algorithm to win a checker game would involve (1) identifying all possible opening moves, (2) predicting an opponent's response to each of these moves, and (3) anticipating all the further responses of both players until all the possible outcomes of the game had been analyzed. Samuel calculated that discovering a series of moves that would guarantee a win would involve considering 10^{40} moves and take 10^{21} centuries to complete. Obviously, using an algorithm to play checkers is not very practical.

Heuristics

A **heuristic** is a "best guess" or "rule of thumb" solution to a problem. The use of a heuristic is an alternative to the exhaustive search that the algorithm strategy usually entails. Heuristics increase the likelihood but do not guarantee the problem will be solved. Suppose you are playing chess. Using an algorithm to discover a winning solution is not practical. You could decide to use a heuristic strategy such as maximizing the protection of the queen. You may not always be able to protect your queen and win (e.g., when the only way to win is to sacrifice your queen), but usually heuristics will help you find a winning approach.

Consider the following real-world example of a problem that both an algorithm and a heuristic could solve. You need a special tool to fix your car, but you do not have the tool, nor do you know which hardware store carries that tool. One way to solve your problem is to call every hardware store in the telephone book—using an algorithm to solve the problem. However, you might find this strategy time-consuming, especially if there are hundreds of hardware stores in the telephone book. An alternative would be to call the hardware stores that have large ads in the phone book, since these stores would be more likely to stock the desired tool. Solving the problem this way uses a heuristic strategy.

Many heuristics can be used to solve various problems. Some of these heuristic strategies provide a systematic method to arrive at a solution without taking as long as an algorithm, while other heuristic strategies represent cognitive shortcuts to problem solving and often lead to incorrect solutions (Medin & Ross, 1992). Two of them, working backward and means-end analysis, involve the systematic evaluation of a problem. Two other heuristics, representativeness and availability, are affected by bias from past experience and therefore sometimes lead to ineffective solutions.

Working-Backward Heuristic. Best (1995) likened many problems to a tree with many branches. The trunk of the tree is the starting point, and one of the twigs is the end point. The logical approach to solving a problem is to work forward from the starting point toward the end point.

Unfortunately, this approach can lead a person to branch off in the wrong direction. Going off on a wrong branch will make it difficult, and sometimes impossible, to solve the problem. One widely used heuristic that avoids this problem is the working-backward heuristic. In the **working-backward heuristic**, the person starts at the end point and works backward to the starting point.

The working-backward heuristic is often used in mathematics and other formal systems of analysis. In an elegant analysis of this type of heuristic, Newell, Shaw, and Simon (1958) found that computers programmed to use the working-backward heuristic rapidly generated proofs for mathematical theorems. In contrast, the computers programmed to work forward from the axioms required a great deal of time to prove even simple theorems.

The failure to use the working-backward heuristic can even be fatal. Six climbers died trying to ascend the summit of Mount Everest in 1996, in part because they did not have sufficient oxygen supplies at the highest camp. The failure to apply the working-backward heuristic contributed to these climbers' deaths. The best strategy for reaching the summit of a tall mountain is to start by determining the equipment and supplies needed at the highest camp on the night before the attempt on the summit (Krakauer, 1997). The number of people who need to be at the highest camp on the night before the summit attempt is determined next, followed by the number of people needed to supply the highest camp. This process of working backward continues until the logistics are completed for the entire expedition. Had the working-backward heuristic been followed, the climbers would have had sufficient supplies at the highest camp and likely would have survived (Krakauer, 1997).

Means-End Analysis. Another systematic heuristic used for solving problems is the **means-end analysis**, which breaks down a particular problem into a series of subproblems that are solved. These solutions, in turn, may make it possible to solve the original problem.

Newell and Simon (1972) provide a real-world example of the means-end heuristic:

> I want to take my son to nursery school. What's the difference between what I have and what I want? One of distance. What changes distance? My automobile. My automobile won't work. What is needed to make it work? A new battery. What has new batteries? An auto repair shop. I want the repair shop to put in a new battery; but the shop doesn't know I need one. What is the difficulty? One of communication. A telephone . . . and so on. (p. 416)

In this example, the starting point is an automobile that does not work; the end point is getting the child to the nursery school; the problem is how to take the child in the car to the nursery school. Creating an initial subproblem of why the automobile does not work helps solve the larger problem. Recognizing that the car needs a new battery not only solves the subproblem but also increases the probability that the overall problem will be solved.

Working backward and means-end analysis both represent systematic heuristic problem-solving strategies that seek all available information and, under most circumstances, provide accurate solutions. Other heuristics use only a limited amount of information to attempt to solve a problem. Using cognitive shortcuts that fail to use all available information can cause errors in judgment and lead to inaccurate solutions. Amos Kahneman and Daniel Tversky (Kahneman & Tversky, 1972, 1973; Kahneman, Slovic, & Tversky, 1982) have identified two types of heuristics—representativeness and availability—as cognitive shortcuts to problem solving.

Representativeness Heuristic. Representativeness is a heuristic that makes judgments based only on the obvious characteristics of the problem. Consider the following example. You are presented with the problem, "What occupation should John pursue in college?" You are told that John is shy, helpful, good with figures, and has a passion for detail. You may ask for and receive further details needed to solve this problem; however, if you use the **representativeness heuristic**, you will not seek additional information but will choose John's career based only on the facts initially given—facts that prompt you to decide that John should become an accountant. Although this strategy allows for faster choices, you may be ignoring salient information (e.g., John's preferences, his previous school grades, or the job opportunities in this field).

Kahneman and Tversky (1972, 1973) reported that the representativeness heuristic is frequently used, even when it leads to illogical solutions. In one study, Kahneman and Tversky presented their subjects with a problem similar to the last example. In addition to being given the personality sketch, subjects were told that the information was based on a psychologist's projective test given at the beginning of John's senior year of high school. Although the subjects expressed little faith in personality tests, they still based their selections on information provided by John's test results.

If, as suggested, use of the representative heuristic may lead to error, why do people use it? There are two reasons. First, this heuristic often does work. Second, the heuristic provides a quick way to make a decision. For example, suppose you are managing a convenience store and have been robbed at gunpoint several times late at night. It is now 2:00 a.m.; someone enters the store alone. This person seems anxious and nervous—just like the previous robbers. The present conditions are similar to those that existed at the time of the previous robberies. You decide that this person is a robber, and you call the police. Although you may have behaved differently had you waited to gather further information, this choice is definitely the safest one.

Availability Heuristic. Solutions selected using the **availability heuristic** are based only on information that can be readily brought to mind (Levi & Pryor, 1987). According to Levi and Pryor, people usually select the solution that is more mentally "available," much as a person chooses a sweater because it is at the top of the dresser drawer. The availability heuristic means that solutions are usually based on recent experiences, which are most likely to be on our minds. Suppose you are trying to choose whether to drive or fly to college. If you have just read about a horrible airplane crash, your fears about the dangers of flying will be greater than if you did not have this information. Employing an availability heuristic may prompt you to choose to drive, even though this solution may entail much more time and effort.

The Problem Solved

The final stage of problem solving is determining the accuracy of the solution. Although we may not always know whether we have solved a problem correctly, feedback often indicates whether our solution was effective. This information about the accuracy of the solution is important for two reasons. First, when we know we have chosen the right solution, we can then overcome the obstacles and reach our goals. If our solution is not accurate, this feedback lets us know that we need to find another way to solve the problem. At this point, we start over at the beginning of the problem-solving process. Second, the success or failure of our attempt to solve a problem can influence future problem solving by prompting us to continue to use effective approaches and to abandon ineffective ones.

However, in some cases, present problem solving can negatively affect future decisions by causing us to retain previously effective problem-solving approaches that are no longer effective and to overlook approaches that may have been ineffective in one situation but might be effective in another. We look at these effects of experience next.

The Consequences of Past Experience

Functional Fixedness

After shopping at a local mall, you walk back to your car and notice that your license plate is loose. You know that it will probably fall off if you don't tighten the screws holding the plate to the frame, but how do you tighten the screws without a screwdriver? Although you might think of using a coin as a screwdriver, many other people might fail to recognize that a coin can be used for something other than to buy things. Solving a problem often requires that we use a familiar object in a novel way. However, it is often hard to recognize these solutions.

Functional fixedness refers to the difficulty involved in recognizing novel uses for an object. In our example, because of functional fixedness, many people would not think to use a coin as a screwdriver. Prior experience using an object to solve one problem makes it difficult to recognize that the same object can be used in a different manner to solve another problem.

To study functional fixedness, H. G. Birch and Rabinowitz (1951) gave their subjects in the experimental groups two problems to solve. For the first problem, subjects were asked to complete an electrical circuit. Some of the subjects received a switch to use; others had a relay. Control subjects did not participate in this initial problem. In the second problem, subjects were then shown two strings hanging from the ceiling and told to tie the ends of the strings together. The problem was that the two strings were too far apart to hold one and reach the other. To solve this problem, subjects were given access to two heavy objects, a switch and a relay. The subjects could then tie a heavy object to the end of one string, swing that string like a pendulum, grab the end of the other string, catch the first string when it swung back to them, and then tie the two strings together.

Birch and Rabinowitz reported that subjects who had used the relay to complete the circuit in the first problem chose the switch as the weight in the pendulum problem. In contrast, subjects who had used the switch to solve the first problem chose the relay as the weight in the second problem. Control subjects used the relay and switch equally often. These results indicate that once the experimental subjects had established a function for an object (relay or switch) during the first problem, they did not think of using that object in a different manner to solve the second problem. Because control subjects had no prior experience with either object, the function of the objects had not been fixed, and these subjects chose either one to solve the pendulum problem.

Functional fixedness reflects a rigidity that can impair problem solving; however, there are ways to overcome functional fixedness. One way is to learn that objects can function in many ways. To illustrate this concept, Flavell, Cooper, and Loiselle (1958) asked subjects to use objects such as a switch and pliers in various ways before exposing them to the pendulum problem. They reported that using one of these objects in several different ways prompted subjects to use that object again as a weight in the pendulum problem. However, if a subject had used the object in only one way, the subject did not tend to use that object to solve the pendulum problem.

Set

People also have a tendency to attack new problems in the same way they have solved earlier problems: The tendency to continue to use an established problem-solving method for future tasks is referred to as a **set**. A set is a source of negative transfer only if a new problem-solving approach is needed. In fact, if the habitual approach will effectively solve the new problem, the set will actually be a source of positive transfer; that is, the set will enhance the solving of the new problem.

Luchins's (1942) classic study showed the impact of set on problem solving. Subjects were given a series of problems that involved measuring a given amount of water by using a water tap and three jars of different sizes. Table 12.2 presents the sizes of the jars and the amount of water needed to solve the 11 problems. All subjects received Problem 1, which could be solved by filling Jar A and pouring three times the water into Jar B. Subjects in the experimental group received Problems 2 through 11; control-group subjects were only given Problems 7 through 11. Most of the subjects in the experimental group learned that a single approach, B – A – 2C, could solve Problems 2 through 6. Although Problems 7 through 11 could also be solved using this approach, a simpler strategy, A + C or A – C, could be used to solve these problems. Control subjects used the shorter solution for Problems 7 through 11; in contrast, experimental subjects continued to use the longer method. This study demonstrated that the experimental group subjects established a set as they solved Problems 2 through 6, and they continued to use this approach for the remaining problems. Why did they continue to use the less efficient strategy? The reason is that the first strategy was still successful in solving the problem. According to Luchins, a set "blinded them to the possibility of a more direct and simple procedure" (p. 1), which is unproductive when other solutions are more efficient.

The Nature of Expertise

People differ in terms of their ability to solve problems: Some are extremely good at solving problems; others are not. Researchers (Charness, 1991; Gobet & Simon, 1996) have examined why by comparing chess masters with novice players. This research has shown that the chess master has learned thousands of different patterns, perhaps as many as 50,000 in some cases, and can therefore predict the effectiveness of all possible moves before choosing a particular one. In contrast, the novice player, before every move, must generate from scratch several possible responses to the opponent's last move and then try to anticipate the consequences of each

Table 12.2 Luchins's Water Measurement Problem

Problem	Given Jars of the Following Sizes:			Obtain the Amount:
	A	B	C	
1.	29	3		20
2. E1	21	127	3	100
3. E2	14	163	25	99
4. E3	18	43	10	5
5. E4	9	42	6	21
6. E5	20	59	4	31
7. C1	23	49	3	20
8. C2	15	39	3	18
9.	28	76	3	25
10. C3	18	48	4	22
11. C4	14	36	8	6

Note: E = Experimental group; C = Control group.

possible move before deciding which move to choose. Thus, an expert has more knowledge than the novice. But expertise involves more than greater knowledge; an expert also possesses more abstractions and uses more general concepts than does the novice, who is more concrete and employs specific bits of information. In terms of chess, experts have a general understanding of the utility of each piece and how each piece can move to the greatest advantage, whereas the novice has memorized some moves that, in the past, have been successful.

Other researchers have provided additional insight into the nature of expertise. Experts are more able to extract information from a problem than are novices (Shanteau, 1992). The greater perceptiveness allows the expert to recognize important information that the novice misses. Experts also are better able to perceive the similarity between new and old problems than are novices (Hardimann, Dufresne, & Mestre, 1989). The ability to recognize similarities enables the expert to use principles gained from prior experience to solve new problems. Further, experts are able to perceive the whole problem, which allows them to go forward from the initial goal state (Bedard & Chi, 1992). In contrast, the novice sees only the initial and goal states and must use a slower heuristic.

Expertise is not without its drawbacks. Experts are more likely to show functional fixedness or mental sets than are novices. The reliance on past experiences can cause the expert to be less likely than the novice to learn from mistakes (Camerer & Johnson, 1991; S. A. Hawkins & Hastie, 1990). Heuristic biases can also lead the expert to choose solutions that are no more effective than those chosen by a novice. While experience may lead experts to be more confident than novices, their choices are not always more successful in such areas as banking (Andersson, 2004), accounting (Marchant, Robinson, Anderson, & Schadewald, 1991), and pilot judgment (Wickens, Stokes, Barnett, & Hyman, 1993).

Recall our discussion of Regina's problem described in the chapter-opening vignette. The initial state of her problem was that she had an invitation to go to the beach on Saturday, but had a work assignment due on Monday. The goal state of her problem was to go to the beach and still hand in the problem on time. Regina used the availability heuristic to solve her problem; that is, she asked her coworker Keith to help her. As he has expertise to complete the assignment in a timely fashion, Regina is able to go to the beach on Saturday and turn in her assignment on Monday.

BEFORE YOU GO ON

- Was Regina facing a well-defined or ill-defined problem?
- Did past experience help or hinder Regina's search for a solution to her problem?

SECTION REVIEW

- A problem exists when an obstacle or obstacles block attainment of a desired goal.
- The first step to solve a problem is identifying both the starting point, or initial state, and the end point, or goal state, of the problem.
- Well-defined problems have clear starting and end points; ill-defined problems do not.
- Algorithms have precise rules to solve problems, while heuristics are best-guess strategies to solve problems.
- The working-backward strategy begins at the end point and works back to the starting point; the means-end strategy breaks the problem down into a series of subproblems.

- With the representative heuristic, solutions are based only on the obvious characteristics of the problem; with the availability heuristic, only information that one can remember is used to solve problems.

- Functional fixedness is an inability to recognize new uses for familiar objects; a set solves new problems with strategies that solved earlier problems.

- Experts are generally able to solve problems more readily than novices, in part due to greater knowledge and understanding.

LANGUAGE

Language serves three very important functions in our lives. First, language allows us to communicate with other people. Just imagine how difficult life would be if we could not express our ideas to family and friends. We could not, for example, complain to our friends about how much schoolwork we have this weekend or call home to ask for money. Second, language facilitates the learning process by providing a system of interrelated symbols and rules. Third, language allows us to recall information beyond the limits of our memory stores.

The Structure of Language

Phonemes

A **phoneme** is the simplest functional speech sound. For example, consider the words *pin* and *bin*. These two words have different meanings and can be distinguished only because their initial sounds, /p/ and /b/, are different phonemes. Note that these distinguishing sounds can occur anywhere in the word. The two word pairs *but* and *bet,* and *top* and *ton,* illustrate that the different phonemes occurring at various places in words enable us to distinguish the meanings of different words.

Every language has a limited number of different sounds or phonemes. English is composed of 45 basic sounds, but some languages have as few as 15 basic sounds or as many as 85 (Mills, 1980). Also, phonemes differ from one language to the next. For example, English contains the /l/-/r/ distinction (as in the words *late* and *rate*), but no such sound difference exists in Japanese. In fact, Miyawaki, Strange, Verbugge, Liberman, Jenkins, and Fujimura (1975) reported that the Japanese do not hear the difference between the two sounds. When they are learning to speak English, they have difficulty mastering the phoneme distinction between /l/ and /r/. This research indicates that we only distinguish the phonemes in the languages with which we are familiar.

Eimas and Corbit (1973) discovered that each sound has its own categorical boundaries that allow it to be distinguished from other sounds. Consider the two syllables *ba* and *pa*. Using a speech synthesizer, Eimas and Corbit slowly changed the sound from the phoneme /b/ to the phoneme /p/, thus changing the syllable *ba* to the syllable *pa*. Although the synthesizer changed the speech sound gradually, the subjects did not respond to the subtle changes. Instead, they reported hearing an abrupt change in the syllable, indicating that sharp physical boundaries delineate different phonemes.

Interestingly, Eimas, Siqueland, Jusczyk, and Vigorito (1971) used habituation (see Chapter 3) to show that even 1-month-old babies make similar categorical distinctions between phonemes. Infants from Spanish-speaking homes who had never been exposed to English react the same way as infants from English-speaking homes (Lasky, Syrdal-Lasky, & Klein, 1975). These observations suggest an innate ability to detect specific phonemes. However, experience determines which sounds gain significance. The finding that different languages use different phonemes indicates that cultural experience governs which phonemes adults will be able to recognize.

Morphemes

A **morpheme** is the smallest meaningful unit of language. Whereas phonemes are single sounds that enable us to distinguish the meanings of different words, morphemes are the simplest combinations of phonemes that can be formed and still have meaning. Some morphemes are single phonemes, such as the article *a* and the pronoun *I*. Other morphemes contain two or more phonemes: the words *fun, joy,* and *car,* for example. A morpheme does not have to be a word: Prefixes (e.g., *un-* and *re-*) and suffixes (*-er* and *-able*) are also morphemes.

Similarly, parts of words that make a noun plural (leaf to leaves) or indicate that a verb is present or past (catch, caught) are also morphemes. Consider the words *pill* and *pillow*. Adding *ow* to the word *pill* creates a word with a different meaning. The word *pill* is a **free morpheme**, because it can stand alone; *-ow* is a **bound morpheme** because it must be bound to a free morpheme to have meaning.

Sentences

Words can be combined into a **phrase**, a group of two or more related words that express a single thought, and phrases can connect to form a sentence. A **sentence** consists of two or more phrases and conveys assertion, question, command, wish, or exclamation. For example, the sentence *the couple bought the house* consists of two major phrases: the noun phrase *the couple* and the verb phrase *bought the house*.

How do we construct a sentence? Phrases cannot be randomly combined to form a sentence. Rules govern the formation of sentences, and rules determine how phonemes group to form words and how words combine to express various ideas. The rules that govern language are called **syntax**.

Syntax: The Rules of Language

Syntax is the system of rules for combining the various units of speech. These rules can form an infinite number of morphemes, phrases, and sentences. Thus, human language is generative: Syntax enables us to create an infinite number of meaningful expressions. Every language has its own syntax and, therefore, its own unique way of communicating ideas.

Phonology

Languages do not use every possible phoneme combination. For example, the two phonemes /p/ and /z/ cannot be combined to begin a word in the English language. Each language restricts the way in which phonemes can combine to produce meaningful morphemes. **Phonology** refers to the rules that dictate how phonemes can be combined into morphemes.

Grammar

Grammar rules establish the ways that words can be combined into meaningful phrases, clauses, and sentences. Words must be arranged to indicate mutual relations; they cannot be grouped haphazardly. Consider the following example provided by Noam Chomsky (1957): *Colorless green ideas sleep furiously* is a meaningful sentence, although somewhat ridiculous, whereas the same five words arranged as *furiously sleep ideas green colorless* is not even a sentence. When words are organized according to the rules of grammar, the resulting sentence conveys some kind of meaning. However, words strung together randomly do not express a coherent thought or idea.

Linguists have studied the structure of the sentence in terms of phrases. This analysis of the constituents of a sentence is called **phrase-structure grammar**. The analysis begins by dividing a sentence into a noun phrase and a verb phrase. Figure 12.8 presents a diagram of the

Figure 12.8   The phrase-structure grammar of the sentence *the couple bought the house*.

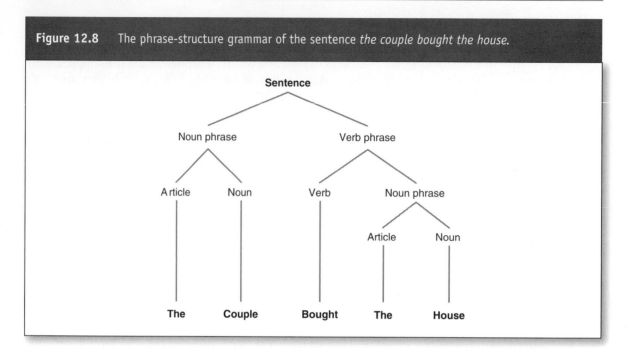

phrase-structure grammar for the sentence *the couple bought the house*. As the diagram illustrates, the noun and verb phrase can then be divided further. This detailed linguistic analysis identifies all of the constituent structures of the sentence. The phrase-structure analysis of a simple sentence can be easy; obviously, complex sentences are more difficult to diagram. In fact, I still remember my seventh-grade English class and the considerable frustration I experienced trying to construct "grammar trees."

The rules of grammar are elaborate, and we do not always follow them. However, because they are generally accepted, using these rules of grammar allows us to communicate effectively with each other.

Semantics: The Meaning of Language

Consider the following two sentences: *The boy hit the ball. The ball was hit by the boy.* As Figure 12.9 shows, the grammar trees for these two sentences are quite different, but the sentences convey the same meaning. According to Houston (1986), the fact that different sentences may have the same meaning points to one important problem of the phrase-structure grammar approach to language. Also, according to Houston, there is a second difficulty with this approach: One sentence may have two different meanings. For example, the sentence *they are growing trees* can mean either that a group of people are in the business of growing trees or that certain trees are in the process of growing. Figure 12.10 on page 340 presents the phrase-structure analyses of this ambiguous sentence.

Analyzing the grammar of a sentence is not the same as analyzing the meaning or the study of **semantics**. Chomsky (1965) recognized this difference. In Chomsky's view, the arrangement of the words in a sentence represents the sentence's **surface structure**. The meaning or idea conveyed by the sentence is its deep structure. Only by determining the **deep structure** can we understand the meaning of a sentence.

How do we figure out the meaning of a sentence? A number of psychologists have described this process (Forster, 1979; Wanner & Maratsos, 1978). The first step in the comprehension of a

Figure 12.9   The phrase-structure grammar of two sentences: *The boy hit the ball* and *The ball was hit by the boy.*

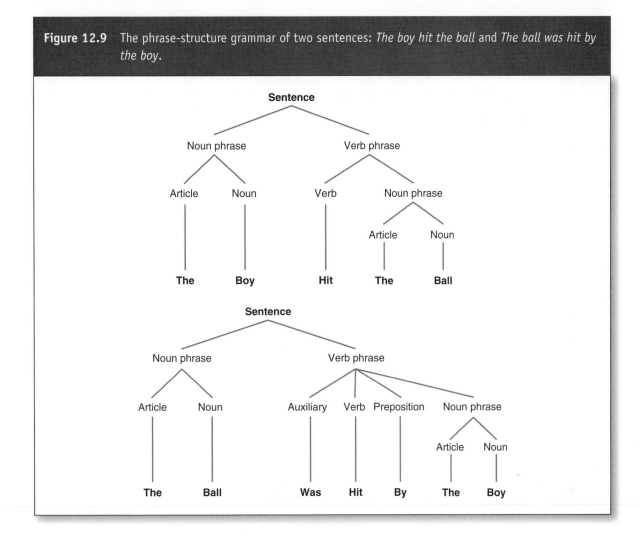

sentence is to divide it into **clauses**. For example, consider the sentence: *The pitcher threw the ball, and the batter hit it.* The sentence expresses two complete thoughts or propositions; these two thoughts are clauses. Evidence of the application of clause analysis comes from a study by Foder, Bever, and Garrett (1974) in which subjects heard a clicking sound either in the middle of the first clause or between the two clauses. Regardless of when the click was actually presented, subjects reported hearing a click between the two clauses. This study indicates that a clause is a cognitive unit that resists disruption. Thus, the click presented in the middle of the first clause "migrated" to the end of the clause, and a click presented at either point in the sentence represented a "mental comma" between the two clauses.

After we have divided a sentence into clauses, we can then determine its meaning. To illustrate this process, let's use the following sentence: *The cat chased the mouse.* To understand the sentence, the reader must determine who is the "doer" and who is "done-to." One approach is to use the "first-noun-phrase-did-it" strategy (Bever, 1970). Using this strategy, we assume the sentence is in the active voice, and we tentatively identify the first noun clause as the doer and the second noun clause as the done-to. This strategy can convey the meaning of the sentence, and of most sentences, because we use the active voice much more frequently than the passive

Figure 12.10 Two different phrase-structure grammar trees for an ambiguous sentence: *They are growing trees.*

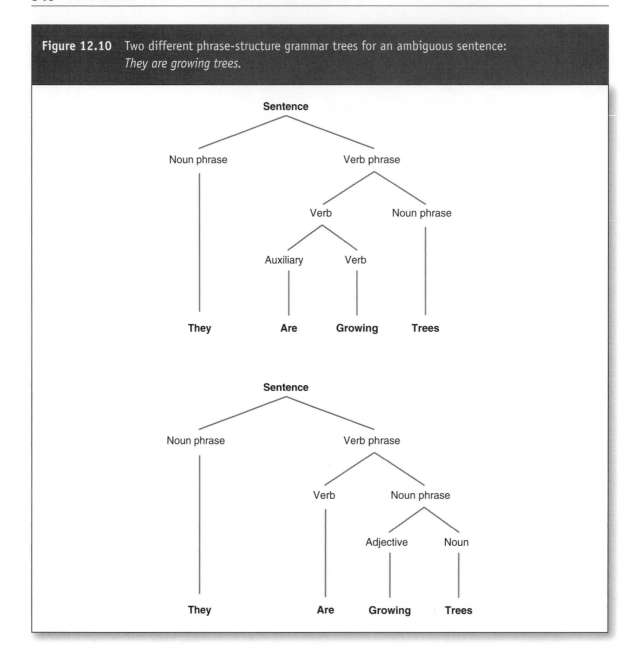

voice. However, it will communicate an incorrect meaning if the sentence is in the passive voice. Several clues indicate the use of the passive voice; for example, in the sentence *the mouse was chased by the cat,* the words *was* and *by* indicate that the first-noun-phrase-did-it strategy is invalid.

Slobin (1966) suggested that an elaborate grammatical analysis is often used to determine the deep structure of passive-voice sentences. To provide evidence for this view, Slobin asked his subjects to listen to a sentence, look at a picture, and then decide whether the sentence described the picture. Slobin reported that subjects took longer to react to passive-voice sentences than to active-voice sentences. Because the grammatical analysis was more elaborate, subjects had longer reaction times for passive-voice sentences than for active-voice ones.

Not only do we receive and interpret language, we also generate it. According to Chomsky (1965), we can express ideas in a number of ways; that is, deep structures can be transmitted through various surface structures. Chomsky suggested that transformational rules enable the same deep structure to generate many different surface structures. Each language has its own acceptable rules of transformational grammar. Individuals in particular cultures must learn these rules so that their use of language complies with accepted grammatical principles and is thus understood by other members of that culture.

Acquisition of Language

B. F. Skinner (1957) proposed that we acquire language through the operant conditioning process (see Chapter 6). According to this approach, children learn to use language because their parents and other people in their environment reinforce it. In contrast, Chomsky (1965) argued that language acquisition is innate. In his view, humans are born with certain mechanisms that enable them to learn to communicate with only a minimal amount of linguistic experience.

A Reinforcement Approach

Suppose that a mother hears her young child say "mama." In all likelihood, the mother will be pleased, and she will give the child a hug and kiss. This affection reinforces the child's behavior and increases the child's use of language.

Skinner (1957) argued that humans acquire responses, including language, according to the laws of operant conditioning (see Chapter 6). In Skinner's view, shaping is used to encourage children to learn to communicate with words. Initially, adults reinforce approximations of a desired verbal response, but eventually they expect a closer resemblance to the final behavior before providing reinforcement. Consider Anne, a baby learning to talk. When Anne first makes any sound resembling a real word, such as the *m* sound for *mama,* Anne's parents are delighted and reinforce her with praise and affection. However, as Anne continues to make nonsense sounds, her parents gradually stop responding to them. To again receive reinforcement, Anne must learn to say something closer to an actual word, such as "mama."

Words are not the only language units that we can acquire through reinforcement. Skinner argued that phrases and sentences can also be learned by the process of shaping; initially, nongrammatical phrases and sentences may be reinforced, but eventually only correct language use will be reinforced.

Many psychologists have been critical of Skinner's reinforcement view of language acquisition. There are three major aspects of this criticism. The first problem is that Skinner's view assumes that parents reinforce the correct use of language and ignore or penalize incorrect use, but observations (McNeill, 1966) show that parents reinforce and punish only the content, not the grammatical correctness, of their children's language. Thus, a parent will allow a grammatically incorrect sentence to be used as long as the content is accurate. R. Brown, Cazden, and Bellugi's (1969) description of the language of two children, Eve and Adam, provides an excellent illustration of the influence of parental approval and disapproval on a child's use of language:

> Gross errors of word choice were sometimes corrected, as when Eve said, "What the guy idea." Once in a while an error of pronunciation was noticed and corrected. More commonly, however, the grounds on which an utterance was approved or disapproved . . . were not strictly linguistic at all. When Eve expressed the opinion that her mother was a girl by saying, "She a girl," the mother answered, "That's right." The child's utterance was ungrammatical but the mother did not respond to

that fact; instead she responded to the truth . . . of the proposition the child intended to express. . . . Adam's "Walt Disney comes on Tuesday" was disapproved because Walt Disney came on some other day. It seems then to be truth value rather than syntactic well-formedness that chiefly governs explicit verbal reinforcement by parents—which renders mildly paradoxical the fact that the usual product of such [training] is an adult whose speech is highly grammatical but not notably truthful. (pp. 70–71)

Avram Noam Chomsky (1928–)

Chomsky received his doctorate from the University of Pennsylvania under the direction of linguist Zellig Harris. He conducted part of his doctoral research during 4 years as a junior fellow at Harvard University and elaborated on his thinking about transformational grammar in his best known text in linguistics, *Syntactic Structures*. He has been a vocal critic of American foreign policy beginning with the Vietnam War. Chomsky has taught in the Department of Linguistics and Philosophy at the Massachusetts Institute of Technology for the last 55 years. His work has contributed significantly to the recognition that humans have an innate knowledge, or universal grammar, of the basic grammatical structure common to all human languages that allows language to be rapidly acquired. He received the Distinguished Scientific Contribution Award from the American Psychological Association in 1984.

A second problem with the reinforcement view concerns the creative aspect of language. Children (as well as adults) frequently use original combinations of words to convey an idea. The fact that people can generate new but grammatically accurate language is difficult to explain in terms of operant conditioning principles: How can children (or adults) use a combination of words that they have never said or heard before and that therefore has never been reinforced? Consider G. A. Miller's (1965) statement to illustrate this criticism of the reinforcement theory:

> By a rough, but conservative, calculation there are 10^{20} sentences 20 words long, and if a child were to learn only these it would take him something on the order of 1000 times the estimated age of the earth just to learn them. . . . Any attempt to account for language acquisition that does not have a generative character will encounter this difficulty. . . . Since the variety of admissible word combinations is so great, no child could learn all of them. Instead of learning specific combinations of words, he learns rules for generating admissible combinations. (pp. 18, 19)

The final and perhaps strongest criticism comes from research showing that despite widely varying social conditions, most children acquire language in a relatively constant pattern. It seems reasonable to expect that children living in different cultures would show various patterns of language acquisition. Yet, Lenneberg (1969) found that nonsense sounds are always followed by one-word speech, which then develops into the use of two-word sentences, followed by telegraphic speech, and then the use of complex sentences. The observation that even children raised by deaf parents follow the same pattern of language development suggests that social reinforcement is not a critical determinant of language acquisition.

A Functionalist Approach

Noam Chomsky (1965, 1975, 1987) was very impressed with how easily young children learn their native language. He described the universal sequence of language development from nonsense sounds to the generation of complex sentences and, on the basis of these observations, suggested that children are born with a language-generating mechanism called the **language acquisition device** (LAD). The LAD "knows" the universal aspects of language. This knowledge allows children to readily grasp the syntax relevant to their native language. In Chomsky's view, however, this biological preparedness does not result in automatic language acquisition; a child must still be exposed to language to learn it. Usually, though, parents eager for their child to start talking provide more than adequate stimulation.

Only minimal exposure is necessary for language to be acquired, and the earlier the experience, the better. J. S. Johnson and Newport (1989) evaluated the ability of Korean and Chinese immigrants to accurately identify 276 sentences as being grammatically correct or incorrect. Each immigrant had been living in the United States for approximately 10 years. Even though all the immigrants had the same length of exposure to English, Johnson and Newport found that those immigrants who arrived before age 8 understood grammar as well as native speakers. The accuracy declined to approximately 80% when age at immigration was 11 to 15 years of age and approximately 75% when age at immigration was 17 to 39 years of age. While individuals who immigrate to the United States after age 8 can master basic words and how to use them, the results of Johnson and Newport's study suggest that these immigrants are unlikely to become as fluent as individuals born in the United States in producing and comprehending subtle grammatical differences.

Deaf children also appear to need only minimal exposure to learn sign language. Petitto and Marentette (1991) reported that deaf children with deaf-signing parents learn to sign at the same age that hearing children with hearing-speaking parents learn to speak. However, deaf children who are not exposed early to sign language never become as fluent in signing as do deaf children exposed at an early age. The deaf children who are not exposed to sign language at an early age also have a difficult time producing and comprehending the subtle aspects of language. These results support the view that early exposure to language is necessary for a person to become proficient in a language. Failure to attain this early language experience—either sign language in deaf children or English in immigrants—has permanent effects.

Our discussion suggests that human language acquisition is a biologically based form of learning that occurs during a sensitive period of development. Some psychologists (Elkind, 1981; Rice, 1989) argue that language acquisition is not a unique form of learning, but instead merely reflects cognitive strategies that are translated into language. If language acquisition merely reflects an extension of our cognitive abilities, then we should see a high level of correspondence between cognitive abilities and language proficiency. While a high correspondence usually does exist between cognitive and linguistic abilities, as Pinker (1999) points out, cognitive development and linguistic development can be decoupled.

Consider two case studies described by Cromer (1981) to illustrate the decoupling of cognition and language. In one case history, a 20-year-old woman was deprived of language until the age of 12. Despite extensive training, the woman's language ability never progressed beyond that of a typical 2-year-old. However, the woman did show a general cognitive ability of a 7- to 12-year-old child. The second case history involves a child who had poor cognitive ability. This child could create highly complex, grammatically correct language. Unfortunately, the content of the child's language was often nonsensical, presumably because language content depends upon cognitive ability. It would seem that humans are biologically prepared to learn language but need some cognitive ability to use it effectively.

Application: Teaching Primates Language

Primates use sounds to communicate with each other. A primate can express a variety of different emotional states in a manner that and to which other primates understand and respond. Observations of vervet monkeys in Kenya (Seyfarth, Cheney, & Marler, 1980) reveal both the sophistication of primates' vocalizations as well as the reactions of other primates to these vocalizations. For example, the vervet monkeys made distinctive alarm calls when they spotted predators. The sight of a leopard caused them to emit a series of short, tonal calls. The sight of an eagle elicited a low-pitched grunt. The reaction to a snake consisted of a series of high-pitched "chutters." Each of these calls elicited a different response from vervet monkeys nearby: They ran for cover when hearing the eagle alarm call, and they looked down when hearing the snake alarm call. These observations indicate that primates can communicate through vocalizations; however, these vocalizations are not language. Can primates learn to use language to communicate?

Early investigations suggested that primates could not learn language. Winthrop and Luella Kellogg (1933) raised the baby chimpanzee Gua in their home with their infant son Donald. Despite many attempts to teach Gua to speak, the chimp never uttered any English words, although she did learn to obey certain commands. Later, Keith and Cathy Hayes (1951) were somewhat more successful in teaching the chimpanzee Vicki to speak. Vicki learned to say three words—*papa, mama,* and *cup.* Yet she acquired these words only after a long period of training, which included manipulating the chimp's lips.

Beatrice and Allen Gardner (1971) were much more successful in teaching language to their chimpanzee, Washoe. The Gardners believed that intellectual impairment was not responsible for earlier failures to teach chimpanzees language; instead, these failures were caused by the chimpanzees' physical inability to produce the complex vocalizations necessary for speech. Instead of trying to teach Washoe to speak English, they taught her American Sign Language. Washoe lived in a trailer in the Gardners' backyard and had one or two people talking to her only in sign language during all her waking hours. After four years of training, Washoe had learned over 200 signs and was able to combine them into sentences, such as "Please tickle more" or "Give me sweet drink."

Did Washoe learn to use language to communicate? The Gardners thought so. Washoe's "language" certainly had many of the characteristics of human language. First, it made sense. For example, Washoe used the sign for *cat* to point out a cat and the sign for *dog* to identify a dog. Second, Washoe's verbalizations were in sentence form. Third, Washoe's sentences were structured according to the rules of grammar; the sentence *please tickle more* illustrates Washoe's mastery of syntax. Finally, Washoe responded to questions. For example, if the Gardners asked in sign language the question, "Who pretty?" Washoe answered, "Washoe."

Despite the fact that primates appear to use language to communicate, many psychologists do not believe that primates are capable of learning language. Herbert Terrace (1979), for example, teaching American Sign Language to a chimpanzee named Nim Chimpsky, noted some important differences between Nim's signing and human language. An intense, directed effort was required to teach Nim even very simple signs, whereas children do not need to be taught language; they learn to talk simply by being in an environment where language is used.

Terrace also found no evidence that Nim could create unique grammatically correct sentences. According to Terrace, the chimpanzee did not learn the creative aspect of language; that is, he did not know how to use rules to create an infinite number of new and complex sentences. Instead, Terrace argued that the chimpanzee's multiword sentences merely imitated the order the trainer used. Reviewing the transcripts of the communications of Washoe and several other chimpanzees, Terrace concluded that these animals were unable to generate syntactically correct, novel combinations of signs. Terrace also noted that few of Nim's statements were spontaneous; most of them came in response to a human's statement. This lack of spontaneous speech is quite different from human speech.

Other psychologists (Marx, 1980; Pate & Rumbaugh, 1983; C. R. Thompson & Church, 1980) have supported Terrace's view. They report that while their chimpanzees were able to learn the meanings

**Sue Savage-Rumbaugh
(1946–   )**

Savage-Rumbaugh received her doctorate from the University of Oklahoma. She taught at Georgia State University for 30 years, where she conducted research on primate communication in bonobo chimpanzees at the Georgia State University Language Research Center. In 2005, she joined the Great Ape Trust in Iowa to continue to investigate language acquisition in primates.

of many symbols, the chimps were unable to link them together into a meaningful sentence. Further, Duane Rumbaugh (1990) reported that while his chimpanzees would respond when symbols were arranged in a familiar order, the chimps were unable to respond correctly to a new symbol order. These observations suggest that chimpanzees, unlike humans, are unable to generate or understand new linguistic units.

You might conclude that the research shows that primates are unable to learn language. However, recent studies by Sue Savage-Rumbaugh and her colleagues (Savage-Rumbaugh, Segerdahl, & Fields, 2005; Savage-Rumbaugh, Sevcik, Brakke, & Rumbaugh, 1992; Savage-Rumbaugh, Shanker, & Taylor, 1996) suggest that the *Pan paniscus* chimpanzee may be able to learn language. The *Pan paniscus* chimpanzee, while related to the common (*Pan troglodytes*) chimpanzee, shows social behavior more typical of humans than other chimpanzees. For example, the *Pan paniscus* chimpanzee, also known as the pygmy chimpanzee or the bonobo chimpanzee, forms long-lasting attachments. Further, the female bonobo is sexually responsive throughout her menstrual cycle, and a male bonobo shares responsibility for infant care with its female mate. By contrast, for most other chimpanzee species, females are promiscuous and only responsive during estrus, and males contribute little to child rearing.

Savage-Rumbaugh and her colleagues first tried to teach a female bonobo, Mata, to respond by pressing symbols representing specific words on a board. While Mata was unable to learn to use the symbols, her infant son Kanzi quickly mastered the task. Both Kanzi and his sister Panabanisha were able to use the symbols to request objects and to describe past events (see Figure 12.11).

Perhaps most important, Savage-Rumbaugh et al. (1992) reported that Kanzi and Panabanisha were able to construct new requests using original combinations of symbols. Interestingly, Kanzi also has shown an ability to understand spoken English. He can respond even to original commands, such as "Go to the refrigerator and get out a tomato."

Why might Kanzi and Panabanisha have been able to master language when other chimpanzees apparently were not able to do so? Savage-Rumbaugh et al. (1992) suggested several reasons. First, bonobos may have better language capabilities than other chimpanzees, although Kanzi and Panabanisha's mother was not able to learn to use the symbols. Second, Kanzi and Panabanisha were exposed to language early in life, observing and then imitating language. Perhaps this early observational and imitation experience promotes better language acquisition than does the formal training researchers used with other chimpanzees.

While the behavior of Kanzi and Panabanisha seems to suggest that some primates can learn language, earlier research generated the same kind of optimism. Some researchers (Kako, 1999; Wynne, 2007) continue to express skepticism that Kanzi's and Panbanisha's communications demonstrate all of the properties of language. Recent research by Givon and Savage-Rumbaugh (2009) has addressed this issue by looking at whether primates can learn grammar.

Language in children progresses from pregrammar one-word communication to multiword grammatical language; that is, language acquisition progresses from a lexicon of nouns and verbs into a syntax or set of rules for combining words into phases and sentences. As we have noted earlier, this progression occurs early in life without any explicit training in most

Figure 12.11 Photograph of Panabanisha, a bonobo chimpanzee, pressing symbols that represent specific words. Panabanisha learned to press appropriate symbols to answer a question.

children. Panabanisha had learned a lexicon of nouns and verbs, so Givon and Savage-Rumbaugh (2009) wanted to see if Panabanisha could learn grammar. In particular, Givon and Savage-Rumbaugh wanted to determine whether Panabanisha could learn that *this* meant that an object was proximate (near) or *that* meant distal (far). In this situation, a research associate pointed to a near object (this) and then said, "Now I am going to touch this" or pointed to a far object (that) and then said, "Now I am going to point to that." The research associate then asked the primate, "Panabanisha, can you now touch this?" or "Panabanisha, can you now touch that?" Givon and Savage-Rumbaugh attempted for 4 months to teach Panabanisha the symbolic value of *this* and *that*. Unfortunately, Panabanisha gestured 100% of the time to the proximate (near) object. Givon and Savage-Rumbaugh concluded that Panabanisha could not learn the communicative value of the symbolic labels this and that. Givon and Savage-Rumbaugh also tried to teach Panabanisha several other grammatical groupings—such as one, two, three, all and in, on, under, away—but without success. They concluded, based on the work with Panabanisha, that there is little optimism for primates possession of grammatical competency.

Panabanisha has a rich vocabulary of words and phrases that she uses to communicate with Sue Savage-Rumbaugh and the other scientists at the Great Apes Trust. But having many lexicons does not mean that Panabanisha has acquired language. As we learned earlier, grammar consists of the ways that words combine into meaningful phrases, clauses, and sentences. As such, language does not exist without grammar. Future research will seek to determine if primates are limited to pregrammatical means of communication.

BEFORE YOU GO ON

- How did language assist Regina in solving her problem?

- Could she have solved her problem without the use of language?

SECTION REVIEW

- Language allows us to communicate with others, facilitates the learning process, and enables us to recall information beyond the limits of our memory stores.

- Phonemes, the simplest speech sound, are combined to form a morpheme, the smallest meaningful unit of language. Morphemes are words (free morphemes) as well as prefixes and suffixes (bound morphemes).

- Words can be combined into a phrase, which expresses a single thought, and phrases can be grouped to form a sentence, which conveys an assertion, question, command, wish, or exclamation.

- Syntax is the system of rules that govern how various units of speech can be combined.

- Phonology refers to the rules specifying how phonemes can be combined into words.

- Grammar establishes how words are combined into meaningful phrases and sentences; semantics is the study of the meaning of language.

- Skinner argued that children acquire language because they are reinforced for appropriate language use.

- Chomsky suggested that humans have an innate ability to learn language and that language can be used to communicate after only a minimal amount of linguistic experience.

- Some psychologists believe that primates communicate with language; others believe that primates are not actually using language but are merely imitating behavior that their trainers have reinforced.

CRITICAL THINKING QUESTIONS

1. Dana Carvey is Paula's favorite comedian. Explain what process allows Paula to identify Carvey as a comedian. Why does she view Carvey as a great comedian?

2. Benita does not have sufficient funds for the remainder of the month. How might she obtain, in a legal fashion, enough money to pay her bills? Explain the process that allows Benita to decide how to obtain more money.

3. Lawrence read about psychologists training primates to use sign language. He is skeptical that primates use language to communicate. Discuss the basis of this skepticism. What evidence supports the claims that primates can acquire language? Does the most recent evidence in the area provide important new information? What do you think is the likely outcome of this controversy?

KEY TERMS

affirmative rule	algorithm
attribute	availability heuristic
bound morpheme	clause
concept	conjunctive rule
deep structure	disjunctive rule
family resemblance	free morpheme

functional fixedness

grammar

ill-defined problem

insight

language acquisition device (LAD)

morpheme

phoneme

phrase

problem

representativeness heuristic

semantics

set

syntax

working-backward heuristic

goal state

heuristic

initial state

language

means-end analysis

negative rule

phonology

phrase-structure grammar

prototype

rule

sentence

surface structure

well-defined problem

The Storage of Our Experiences

A FLEETING EXPERIENCE

While working at a construction site last year, Donald was hit in the head by a piece of wood. Although the accident only left Donald unconscious for several minutes, it completely altered his life. Donald can still recall events that occurred prior to the injury, but once new thoughts leave his consciousness, they are lost. Two experiences occurred today that demonstrate Donald's memory problem. Donald and his wife were shopping when a man whom Donald could not recall ever meeting approached them with a friendly greeting: "Hello, Helen and Don." The man commented that he was looking for a sweater for his daughter's birthday but so far had had no luck finding the right sweater. Helen mentioned that the clothing store at the other end of the mall had nice sweaters, and the man said that he would try that store. After the man had walked away, Helen identified the "stranger" as a neighbor, Bill Jones, who had moved into a house down the block several months before. Don became frustrated when Helen told him he frequently talked with this neighbor. Helen, too, was frustrated; she often wished that Don would remember what she told him. She knew Don would ask her again about Bill Jones the next time they met. When they arrived home, Don received a telephone call from his aunt, informing him of his uncle's death. Don, immediately struck with an intense grief, cried for several minutes over the loss of his favorite uncle. Yet, after another phone call, Donald no longer recalled his uncle's death. Helen told him again, and he experienced the intense grief all over again.

Donald suffers from a disorder called anterograde amnesia. His memory problems are the direct result of his accident, which caused an injury to an area of the brain called the hippocampus. As the result of brain damage, Donald cannot store the experiences that have occurred since the accident.

For a person to recall an event, the brain must go through three processes. First, it must store the experience as a memory. Second, it must encode or organize the memory into a meaningful form. Third, the brain must retrieve the memory. This chapter describes the storage and encoding of our experiences, and Chapter 14 looks at the retrieval of memory. Chapter 14 also discusses forgetting as a result of retrieval failure. We examine memory losses that result from storage failure in this chapter, and we also describe the biological basis of memory storage.

MEASURES OF MEMORY

How do psychologists measure the memory of past events? There are two primary ways to test memory. Explicit methods involve overt (observable) measures of memory. Implicit methods assess memory indirectly.

There are two **explicit measures of memory**: recall and recognition. Recall measures require a subject to access a memory. With free recall, no cues are available to assist recall. An example of **free recall** might be the question, "What did you have for dinner last night?" With **cued recall**, signals are presented that can help with the recall of a past experience. The question, "What did you have at the Mexican restaurant?" is an example of a cued recall test. Under most circumstances, recall is higher with cued recall than free recall.

There are some occasions when information is presented, and the subject's task is to judge whether the information accurately reflects a previous experience. When the memory measure is a judgment of the accuracy of a memory, it is a **recognition measure** of memory. With yes–no recognition, the memory task involves deciding whether or not the information is accurate. A forced-choice recognition task involves a selection of the correct information among incorrect information. Recognition is better with a strong memory but is poorer when a person is penalized for selecting an incorrect alternative.

Do recognition measures yield better retention than recall measures? Most students would claim that they do better on a recognition measure than on a free recall test. Yet the presence of certain distractors can actually yield rather poor recognition performance (M. H. Watkins & Tulving, 1975).

There are also several **implicit measures of memory**. Ebbinghaus (1885) used the **savings score** to measure memory. To obtain a savings score, one subtracts the number of trials it takes to relearn a task from the number of trials the original learning required. If one needs fewer relearning trials, the memory was probably retained from original learning. **Reaction time** is another implicit measure of memory. A subject is presented with a stimulus, and the time it takes to react to that stimulus is recorded. If the subject reacts more readily on the second encounter than on the first, the faster reaction time is thought to be due to the memory of the prior experience.

A THREE-STAGE VIEW OF MEMORY STORAGE

Richard Atkinson and Richard Shiffrin (1971) suggested that there are three stages in the storage of information: sensory register, short-term store, and long-term store. As Figure 13.1 shows, external input is initially stored in the **sensory register** for a very brief time, usually 0.25 to 2 seconds. The information contained in the sensory register is an initial impression of the external environment; this impression decays rapidly after leaving the sensory register and will be lost unless it is processed into the short-term store. The **short-term store** is a temporary, limited-capacity facility for our experiences. Memories can

Richard C. Atkinson (1929–   )

Atkinson received his doctorate in psychology and mathematics from Indiana University. He taught at Stanford University for 16 years and University of California–Los Angeles for 3 years before becoming director of the National Science Foundation for 3 years. His research contributed to the understanding of memory processes. He served as chancellor of the University of California–San Diego for 15 years and president of the University of California System for 8 years. While president of the University of California system, he advocated eliminating the SAT as a requirement for admission and argued that admission should be based on academic accomplishments. He was awarded the Distinguished Scientific Contribution Award by the American Psychological Association in 1977.

Figure 13.1   A diagram illustrating the Atkinson-Shiffrin three-stage model of memory storage. Initially, experiences are stored in the sensory register. In the second stage of memory storage, or the short-term store, experiences are interpreted and organized. The final stage, or long-term store, represents the site of permanent (or almost permanent) memory storage.

remain in the short-term store for 5, 10, 15 seconds, or even longer. The length of time information remains in short-term store depends upon whether the experience is being rehearsed or repeated. Without rehearsal, information can be lost from the short-term store before it is stored in a meaningful way. Some information contained in the short-term store is then transferred to the **long-term store**, the site of permanent memory storage.

Storage of a memory in the long-term store does not guarantee the ability to recall that particular memory. The presence of other memories may interfere with the recollection of a particular experience; this failure to recall a specific memory because of the presence of other memories is called **interference.** The failure to recall a memory also may result from the absence of a specific stimulus that can retrieve the memory. People can use salient aspects of an event, called **memory attributes,** to remember the event. The absence of these environmental events can cause memory failure. Atkinson and Shiffrin suggested that the short-term store organizes experiences in meaningful ways, facilitating later retrieval. The organization of experience can occur even after a memory moves to long-term store, where it can receive additional processing. This processing may facilitate later recall. It can also alter the memory, making the memory more logical or appealing.

We use the **Atkinson-Shiffrin three-stage model** to organize our discussion of the storage of an experience. We address an alternative to this view of memory storage later in this chapter.

SENSORY REGISTER

How are memories stored? Several lines of evidence suggest that a copy of an experience is stored in the sensory register. However, the copy lasts for only a very short time (usually 0.25 to 2 seconds). Research on the sensory store has focused on two sensory systems: the visual system and the auditory system. The visual copy contained in the sensory store is referred to as an **icon**, and the copy is stored in **iconic memory**. The auditory experience contained in the sensory store is referred to as an **echo** and is stored in **echoic memory**.

Iconic Memory

In Search of an Icon

The classic research of George Sperling (1960, 1963) examined the storage of visual information in the sensory register. Sperling's findings demonstrated that (1) an icon is a copy of a visual experience and (2) an iconic memory lasts for only a very brief time following the event. Sperling presented to subjects an array of letters arranged in three horizontal rows of four letters each (see Figure 13.2). An apparatus called a tachistoscope was used to present the letters on a screen for 0.05 seconds. The screen was then blank for a specified retention interval of 0 to 1 second.

Some of Sperling's subjects received a **partial report technique**; they were asked at the end of the interval to recall all the letters in one of the three rows. The subjects were not informed before the end of the retention interval which line they were to recall. A tone presented at the end of the retention interval indicated which line should be recalled: A high pitch indicated the top row; a medium-pitched tone, the middle row; and a low-pitched tone, the bottom row. Presenting the tone very soon after the presentation of the array of letters enabled the subjects to remember most of the letters. However, if the retention interval was greater than 0.25 seconds, the subjects' performance declined significantly, and they could remember only about one letter per line (see Figure 13.3). The fact that retention is high on an immediate but not on a delayed retention test indicates that even though subjects have access to all information contained in the sensory store, the visual copy fades quickly following entry into the sensory register.

Other subjects received the **whole report technique**. In this procedure, subjects were asked to recall as many letters in the array as possible. When recall occurred immediately after the stimulus presentation, subjects were only able to remember about 4.5 letters (see Figure 13.3). Results with the partial report technique indicated that all 12 letters were encoded into the sensory store; why, then, could subjects receiving the whole report technique remember only about one-third

Figure 13.2   Sperling's procedure for investigating the visual sensory memory. This illustration shows one trial using the partial report technique. In this procedure, subjects see 12 letters for 1/20 second. A tone is presented at the appropriate time to indicate which row of letters the subjects should attempt to recall. A high-pitched tone means the top row; a medium-pitched tone, the middle row; and a low-pitched tone, the bottom row.

Phase 1 Experimenter presents array for 1/20 second.	Phase 2 Tone signals which row subject is to recall.	Phase 3 Subject tries to recall correct row.
X G O B T M L R V A S F	High tone means recall top row. Medium tone means recall middle row. Low tone means recall bottom row.	For example: High tone signals subject to recall X G O B.

Figure 13.3   Performance level in Sperling's investigation of visual sensory memory. The solid line on the graph shows the number of letters recalled (left axis) and the percentage recalled (right axis) for subjects given the partial report technique as a function of the delay between signal and recall. The bar at the right presents the number and percentage correct for the whole report technique. As the graph shows, a subject can report most of the letters immediately after the stimulus ends; however, the recall of letters declines rapidly following stimulus presentation.

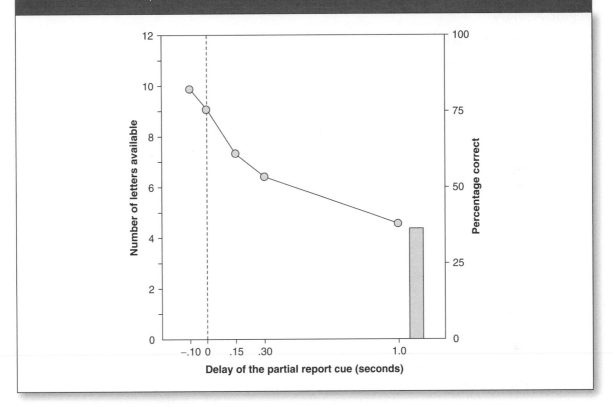

of them? Since experiences stored in the sensory register decay rapidly, the image fades before the subjects can recall more than 4 or 5 of the letters.

Note that when the retention interval was longer than 0.25 seconds, subjects were able to recall approximately 4.5 of the letters, or 1.5 of the letters in a particular row. As we learned earlier in this chapter, only a limited amount of information can be transferred from the sensory register to short-term memory. The ability of Sperling's subjects to recall only 4.5 of all 12 letters, or 1.5 of the 4 letters in a particular row, after a 0.5- or 1-second delay suggests that only these letters were transferred from the sensory store to short-term memory, and that decay caused the rest to be lost.

The Duration of an Icon

Sperling's (1960) study suggests that visual images are stored in the sensory register for 0.25 seconds. However, depending on conditions, icons may persist for as long as a second or for less than 0.25 seconds. The intensity of the visual events appears to affect the duration of an icon.

For example, Keele and Chase (1967) reported that iconic memory is longer when a bright rather than dim display of letters is used. Similarly, if the preletter and postletter exposure displays are very bright, Averbach and Sperling (1961) observed that the icon may last less than 0.25 seconds, whereas the icon may persist for more than a second when the displays following a visual event are very dark. These results suggest that an intense stimulus produces a long-duration iconic memory, and a strong second visual experience can reduce the duration of the visual image of the first stimulus.

Echoic Memory

In Search of an Echo

The sensory register can also contain a record of an auditory experience. Moray, Bates, and Barnett (1965) conducted an evaluation of echoic memory comparable to Sperling's (1960) study of iconic memory. Each subject sat alone in a room containing four high-fidelity loudspeakers placed far enough apart so that subjects could discriminate the sounds coming from each speaker. At various times during the study, each speaker emitted a list of spoken letters. The list ranged from one to four letters, transmitted simultaneously from each loudspeaker. For example, at the same instant, the first loudspeaker produced letter *e;* the second loudspeaker, letter *k;* the third loudspeaker, letter *g;* and the fourth loudspeaker, letter *t.*

For some trials, each subject was required to report as many letters as possible, a procedure analogous to Sperling's (1960) whole report technique. Moray et al. (1965) reported that subjects remembered only a small proportion of the letters presented from the four loudspeakers. On other trials, subjects were asked to recall the letters coming from only one of the four loudspeakers. In this procedure, analogous to Sperling's partial report technique, subjects recalled the letters on most of the trials.

The Duration of an Echo

Although you might anticipate that an echo would have the same duration as an icon, Wingfield and Byrnes (1981) suggested that the typical duration of an echo is 2 seconds. To examine why the sensory register stores an auditory event for a longer period than a visual event, consider this example. Suppose you look at a chair. All the information needed to detect that the object is a chair is contained in your visual snapshot of the chair. Thus, examining a single visual image of an event from a particular moment can detect salient physical characteristics of visual events. However, suppose that someone says the word *chair* to you. Five separate sounds, or phonemes, are contained in this word (see Chapter 12 for a discussion of phonemes). To detect that the word is *chair,* you must combine the five sounds into one word. Although this combining of sounds into a word occurs in the short-term store, the detection of phonemes occurs in the sensory register.

Crowder and Morton (1969) used a serial learning procedure to estimate the duration of echoic memory. In the typical serial learning study, subjects are presented a list of items to learn. Each subject's task is to learn the items in the exact order in which they are presented. Experiments on serial learning demonstrate that subjects do not learn each item on the list at the same rate. Instead, they learn items at the beginning and at the end of the list more readily than items in the middle of the list. This difference in the rate of learning is called the **serial position effect**.

Crowder and Morton presented to subjects several lists of random digits; each list contained seven digits presented at a rate of 100 milliseconds per digit. After each list, a brief, 400-millisecond delay ensued. Subjects then recalled as many of the seven digits as possible. Although all the digits were presented visually, some subjects were told to look at the digits and remain silent until the time for recall. Other subjects were instructed to say the name of each digit aloud when it was presented. The rate of recall did not differ for items early in the list using either the visual (silent) or auditory (aloud) presentations, while the retention of the last few digits was greater with auditory than with visual presentation (see Figure 13.4). Thus, more errors were made on the last few digits when the subject remained silent and relied on visual presentation alone.

The Nature of a Sensory Memory

Psychologists initially thought that a sensory memory is an exact replica of an event; that is, an icon is an exact copy of a visual stimulus and an echo is an exact duplicate of a sound (Posner, 1982). However, more recent research suggests that some processing of an event occurs in the sensory register (Leahey & Harris, 2001). For example, Merikle (1980) modified Sperling's (1960) partial report procedure by presenting mixed arrays of numbers and letters. Recall that Sperling presented different pitches to indicate the specific line of letters to be recalled. Merikle found that a cue to recall a specific set of numbers, which requires some processing of the stimulus array, was as effective as a cue to recall a particular line. These results support the view that some categorization occurs in the sensory register and that a sensory memory may not be an exact copy of a sensory experience.

We have examined the nature of iconic and echoic sensory memories. While auditory and visual memories are quite important, memories exist for all the senses. The memory of the fragrance of

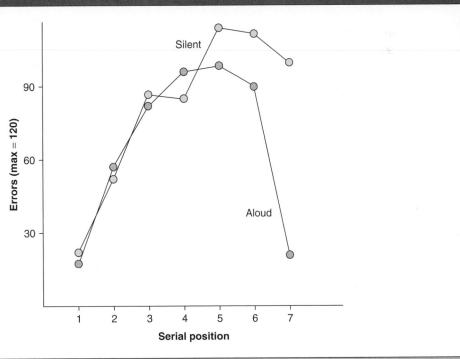

Figure 13.4   The number of errors as a function of the serial position of the letters for subjects who received stimuli that were either silent or aloud. The recall of the letters at the end of the list was significantly better (there were fewer errors) when the letters were read aloud rather than silently.

perfume certainly lingers after the odor is gone. Similarly, taste and tactile experiences last beyond the end of stimulation. Thus, the memory of spicy food remains after the food is swallowed, and the memory of stepping on a pebble while walking barefoot on the beach definitely lasts for a while.

BEFORE YOU GO ON

- Can Donald store his experiences in his sensory register?

- If so, do his immediate recollections differ from those of his wife, Helen?

SECTION REVIEW

- The Atkinson-Shiffrin three-stage model proposes that memory is stored in three successive stages.

- The sensory register is the first stage of memory storage.

- A visual copy contained in the sensory store is referred to as an icon; an auditory experience in the sensory store is called an echo.

- Echoes last longer than icons because while a visual experience conveys all the information needed to detect salient characteristics, recognition of an auditory event requires that individual sounds be retained in the sensory store until the whole event is detected.

- Information in the sensory register decays rapidly and is lost unless it is transferred to the short-term store.

SHORT-TERM STORE

The short-term store is thought to have five major characteristics: (1) it has a brief storage span; (2) the memories it contains are easily disrupted by new experiences; (3) its storage capacity is limited—it can maintain only a small amount of information; (4) its main function is to organize and analyze information; and (5) it has a rehearsal function; that is, the short-term store can rehearse or replay memories of prior experiences. We next examine these five characteristics of the short-term store.

The Span of Short-Term Memory

Say the nonsense syllable *txz*, and then start counting backward by threes, beginning with the number 632 and continuing with 629, 626, 623, 620, 617, 614, 611, 608, 605, 602, 599, 596, 593, 590, 587, 584, 581, 578, and 575. Do you remember the nonsense syllable? In all likelihood, you do not. The sensory receptors detected the nonsense syllable, and the memory of the syllable was registered in the sensory register and entered into the short-term store. Yet, the memory of the nonsense syllable was lost as the result of the counting-backward task. Because this task required only approximately 20 seconds to complete, it appears that the memory of the non-sense syllable is rapidly forgotten.

This example is modeled after the classic L. R. Peterson and Peterson (1959) study. In this study, subjects were presented with a number of three-consonant trigrams. After saying the three letters of each trigram, the subjects were given a number and required to start counting backward by threes. The numbers used were different following each trigram. The subjects were given a signal to designate when to stop counting backward and to recall the trigram; the signal was presented at different retention intervals varying from 3 to 18 seconds. Figure 13.5 presents the level of recall of a trigram as a function of the interval between presentation of a trigram and testing. As the figure shows, recall declines rapidly: The likelihood that a subject can remember the trigram is about 54% with a 3-second recall interval, compared with only about a 6% recall of the trigrams with an 18-second interval. Peterson and Peterson's study illustrates the brief retention of an item after leaving the short-term store.

Disrupting Short-Term Memory

Consider the following series of events to illustrate how easily a memory contained in the short-term store can be disrupted. After locating a number in the telephone book, you begin dialing; then your roommate says something to you, and you stop dialing to respond. After responding, you begin to dial the number again, but now you cannot remember it.

Evidence of the disruption of short-term memories comes from the memory-span studies discussed earlier. Recall that L. R. Peterson and Peterson (1959) found that subjects asked to count backward after the presentation of a trigram were unable to recall the trigram just 18 seconds after it was presented. Waugh and Norman (1965) suggested that the numbers had replaced the

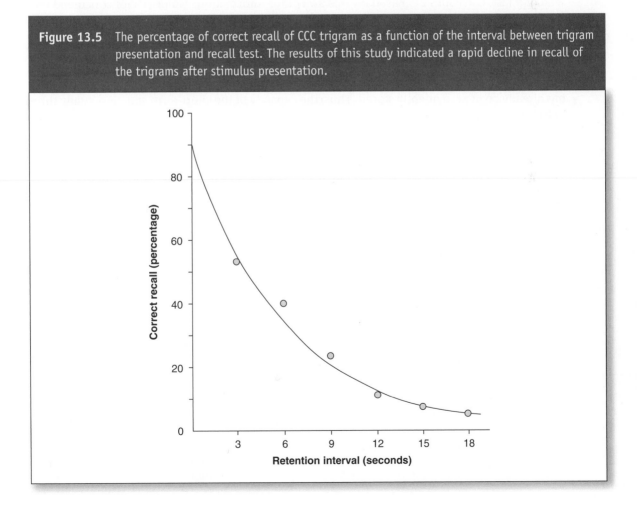

Figure 13.5   The percentage of correct recall of CCC trigram as a function of the interval between trigram presentation and recall test. The results of this study indicated a rapid decline in recall of the trigrams after stimulus presentation.

trigram in the short-term store, and, thus, Peterson and Peterson's subjects were unable to recall the trigram.

Memories in the short-term store are easily disrupted because the storage capacity of this store is so limited. As the capacity is reached, new memories automatically replace older ones. And unless they are stored in a meaningful way, the events will be lost forever. Thus, you forget a telephone number when your roommate distracts you; your roommate's words displace the memory of the number. You must look up the number again because it has not been stored in a retrievable way in the long-term store.

Limited Storage Capacity

Have you ever wondered why telephone numbers are split into three sequences of three or four numbers (e.g., 800–755–2734)? George Miller's research at Bell Labs was the reason.

In 1956, Miller published a classic paper titled "The Magic Number Seven, Plus or Minus Two: Some Limits on Our Capacity for Processing Information." Miller presented evidence that people can hold approximately five to nine items at a time in short-term store. An item may be a single letter or number; it can also be a word or an idea. A number of studies suggested that the capacity of the short-term store is seven plus or minus two items of information. For example, Pollack (1953) found that listeners recalled only six or seven items from a list of words, letters, or digits read at a fast, constant rate. Based on this and other information, Miller (1956) concluded that the short-term store is limited to seven plus or minus two items.

However, M. J. Watkins (1974) proposed that the true capacity of the short-term store may be only three to four items. According to Watkins, although the capacity of the short-term store appears to be seven plus or minus two items, some recall actually reflects information stored in the long-term store; that is, Watkins argued that information presented early in an experience has already been permanently stored. Thus, the capacity of the short-term store is actually three to four items.

The Organization of Our Experiences

The main function of the short-term store is to organize information arriving from the sensory register. The experience then is retained in the long-term store until it is recalled in the organized form. Types of organization the short-term store accomplishes include chunking, coding, and the formation of associations.

The short-term store's organization of information provides some significant advantages. People can dramatically increase the capacity of short-term memory by organizing incoming information from the sensory register. As a result of this organization, an event can become more significant or meaningful and thus become more likely to be remembered. We describe the short-term store's organizational processes next.

Chunking

Suppose you hear the three letters *b, a, t*. You undoubtedly will "hear" the word *bat*. The combining of the three letters into a single word reflects a short-term store process called **chunking**. Chunking is an automatic organizational process of the short-term store. It also significantly enhances our ability to recall past experiences.

The Short-Term Store and Chunking. People automatically chunk information contained in the short-term store. For example, in presenting six-digit numbers for subjects to memorize, Bower and Springston (1970) found that most people chunked the six digits into groups of three digits, separated by a pause and in a distinct melodic pattern. Thus, the six-digit number 427316 became 427–316. The division of a seven-digit telephone number into two separate chunks is another example of chunking.

The Effect of Chunking on Recall. Murdock's 1961 study evaluated the role of chunking in the short-term recall of our experiences. Murdock presented to his subjects a three-consonant trigram, a three-letter word, or three three-letter words and then required them to count backward for 0, 3, 6, 9, 12, 15, or 18 seconds. As Figure 13.6 indicates, the retention of the three-consonant trigram was identical to what L. R. Peterson and Peterson (1959) observed; recall of the trigram declined dramatically over the 18-second retention interval. However, Murdock's subjects, after 18 seconds, exhibited a high level of recall of the three-letter, one-word unit. Furthermore, on the 18-second recall test, the retention of the three-word unit containing nine total letters equaled the lower level of the three-letter trigram.

Chunking does not merely improve recall; instead, it causes the information to be recalled in a specific order. Suppose that a subject receives the following list of items:

tea	milk	cow	apple
cabbage	seal	spinach	pear
lion	potato	lemon	soda
coffee	orange	elephant	carrot

Figure 13.6 The percentage of correct recall as a function of the type of stimulus material and the length of the retention interval. The results show that the recall of a three-letter word is greater on an 18-second test than the recall of either three consonants or three words.

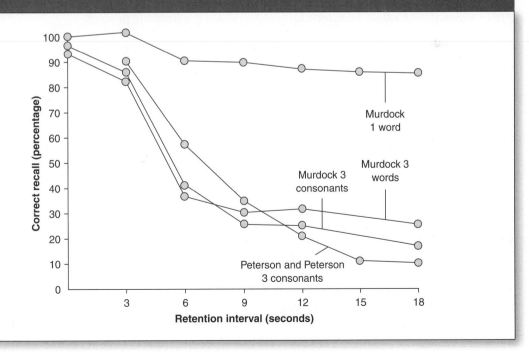

This list contains four categories of items: beverages, animals, vegetables, and fruit. How would subjects recall the items on the list? Subjects receiving the list will recall the items in each category together, even though the items were presented separately. The recall of material in terms of categories is called **clustering**. The organization of material allows us to relate similar events and contributes to a structured and meaningful world.

Coding

We have discovered that the short-term store combines information into smaller units. The short-term store can also code information; that is, it can transform an event into a totally new form. For example, visual experiences can be coded into an acoustic (auditory) code, and words or ideas can become an image or a visual code. While the transformation, or **coding**, of experiences is a natural property of the short-term store, most people do not use the coding properties of the short-term store effectively. Yet, people can learn to effectively transform their experiences; we discuss the use of coding systems in mnemonic or memory enhancement techniques in the next chapter.

Acoustic Codes. Suppose you see the word *car* on a sign. In all likelihood, your short-term store will transform the visual image of the word *car* into the sound of the word. This observation suggests that we encode a visual experience as a sound or as an **acoustic code**.

R. Conrad's study (1964) illustrates the acoustical coding of visual information. He presented a set of letters to his subjects visually and then asked them to recall all the letters. Analyzing the types of errors subjects made on the recall test, Conrad found that errors were made based on the sounds of the letters rather than on their physical appearance. For example, subjects were very likely to recall the letter *p* as the similar sounding *t*, but they were unlikely to recall it as the visually similar *f*.

Why does the short-term store transform visual events into an acoustic representation? According to Howard (1983), the short-term store not only retains specific information; it represents a space for thinking. Since language plays a central role in thinking, it seems logical that visual events would be acoustically coded to aid the thinking process.

Visual Codes. Look at, but do not name, the objects in Figure 13.7 for 30 seconds. Now close your book and see how many of these objects you can name. How many were you able to remember? If you have a good visual memory, you probably were able to recall most of the objects. In fact, most people would be able to recall more of the objects seen in a picture than objects presented verbally (Paivio, 1986). This indicates that encoding objects as images in a **visual code** can be more effective than storing them as words.

The memory of some experiences can be quite vivid. For instance, I remember quite clearly where I was and what I was doing when my aunt called to tell me that my father had died. I often remember that experience and still feel its pain. My memory of the circumstances that existed when I learned of my father's death is an example of a **flashbulb memory**, which is the vivid, detailed, and long-lasting memory of a very intense emotional experience.

Research has suggested that three separate elements make up a flashbulb memory (Burke, Heuer, & Reisburg, 1992). First, information is stored that is central to the event (e.g., learning that my father had died). Second, peripheral details are associated with the event (e.g., my aunt calling me to tell me of my father's death). Finally, personal circumstances surrounding the event are stored as part of the memory (e.g., I was watching a football game on a Sunday afternoon when my aunt called). Not all our experiences are recalled in such vivid detail. Flashbulb memories occur primarily when an event has many consequences for the person (McCloskey, Wible, & Cohen, 1988).

Figure 13.7   How good is your memory? Look at this photograph for 30 seconds, but do not name the objects. Close the book and try to recall as many of the objects as you can.

Some questions have been raised about the accuracy of flashbulb memories (Neisser, 1982). Many people believe they have a vivid memory of the space shuttle Challenger explosion. Do they have an accurate memory? McCloskey et al. (1988) interviewed 29 subjects both 1 week and 9 months after the Challenger accident. While their subjects still believed they had a vivid memory of the explosion nine months later, they had forgotten much of the detail of the event, and their recollections were distorted. A similar forgetting following the assassination attempt on President Reagan (Pillimer, 1984) and the terrorist attacks of September 11, 2001 (Talarico & Rubin, 2003).

Palmer, Schreiber, and Fox (1991) found that firsthand knowledge of the event plays an important role in accuracy of flashbulb memory. They compared the recollections of the 1989 San Francisco earthquake by those who had actually experienced the earthquake with those who merely learned about it on television. Persons who directly experienced the earthquake had more accurate recall of the earthquake than did persons who merely watched it on television. Similarly, a more accurate recall for the events of September 11, 2001, was found in college students living in Manhattan than in college students from California or Hawaii (Pezdek, 2006).

Association of Events

If someone asks you to respond to the word *day,* in all likelihood you will think of the word *night.* Your response indicates you have learned an association between the words *day* and *night.*

One organizational function of the short-term store is to form associations between concepts or events. The short-term store forms two basic kinds of associations. One form, episodic associations, are based on temporal contiguity. For example, if someone insults you, you will associate this person with the verbal abuse. The other form, semantic associations, are based on the similarity of the meanings of events. For example, the association of day and night is a semantic association because both represent times of day.

Associations appear to be made in a logical, organized fashion, for example, episodic associations are organized temporally. Consider our encoding of the 12 months of the year. We do not merely associate the months, but rather learn the months in temporal order. However, we do not associate the months in alphabetical order. While recall of the months in temporal order is easy, you would have difficulty remembering the months in alphabetical order.

Semantic memories seem to be organized hierarchically. This hierarchical structure is from general to specific concepts. Examine the hierarchy of the concept of *minerals* presented in Figure 13.8. As the illustration shows, there are four levels in the hierarchy. The concept of *minerals* contains two types: metals and stones. Similarly, there are three types of metals: rare, common, and alloys. A number of psychologists have discussed the organizational structure of semantic memories; we begin with Collins and Quillian's hierarchical approach.

A Hierarchical Approach. Collins and Quillian (1969) suggested that semantic memory consists of hierarchical networks of interconnected concepts. According to Collins and Quillian's **hierarchical approach,** a node represents each concept, and an associative link connects two nodes or concepts. At each node are paths to information about that concept. Figure 13.9 presents one of these associative networks. The superordinate concept *animal* is connected to its

Figure 13.8 Illustration showing four levels of the hierarchy of the concept *minerals*. Minerals can be grouped into two types: metals and stones. In turn, metals can be classified as rare, common, and alloys; stones as precious or masonry. In the fourth level, *platinum* is an example of a rare metal, *diamond* of a precious stone.

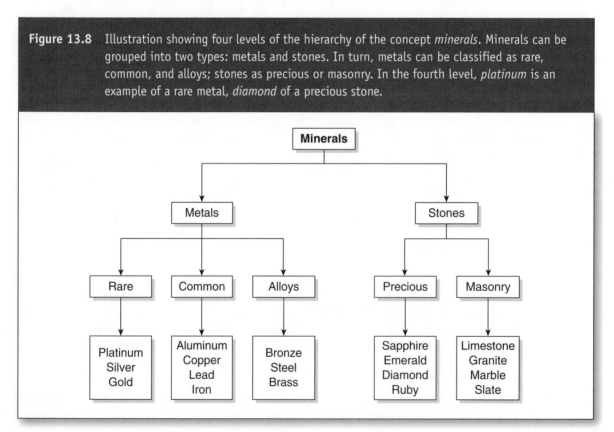

Figure 13.9   Illustration of the Collins and Quillian hierarchical model of semantic memory for the concept *animal.* The animal concept node contains four properties and is associated with the nodes of *bird* and *fish,* which also have associated properties.

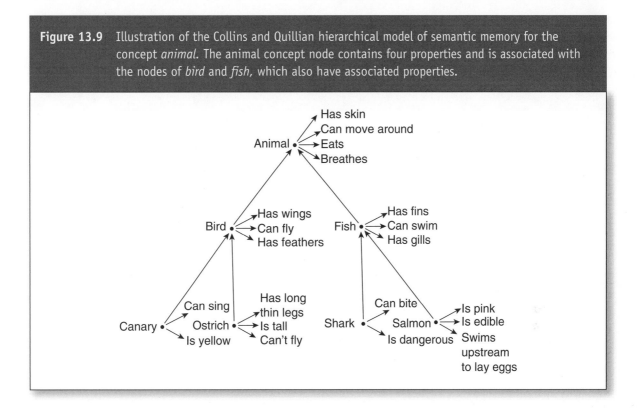

subordinate network *bird,* which then is linked to its subordinate, *canary.* The illustration also shows that each node has associated concept information; for example, the node *canary* contains the information that the canary can sing and is yellow.

How did Collins and Quillian verify that semantic memory contains networks of interconnected associations? They reasoned that the response time for accessing information contained in a network would depend upon the number of links separating the information. According to Collins and Quillian, the greater the separation was, the longer the reaction time. Consider these two questions: Can a canary sing? Does a canary have skin? The first question you probably answered more readily, since the information about singing is contained in the node *canary.* The information about skin is located in the animal node, which is separated from the node *canary* by two associative links. Verifying that a canary has skin should take longer than verifying that a canary can sing due to the greater separation of information between the node and the links in the former than in the latter statement.

Collins and Quillian investigated how the number of linkages separating the information affects the reaction time to verify statements. They observed that reaction time to verify statements was positively related to the number of nodes separating information (see Figure 13.10). As the figure shows, subjects could respond more rapidly to the statement that *a canary can sing* than *a canary has skin.*

Our discussion suggests that concepts are stored in a hierarchy of interconnected nodes. While considerable evidence supports this view, some researchers have found it too simplistic. Three main problems have been identified with the Collins and Quillian hierarchical approach (Glass & Holyoak, 1986). First, this theory assumes that concepts are stored in semantic memory in a logical hierarchy. Yet, research suggests that this may not always be true. Consider the two statements: *The collie is an animal* and *the collie is a mammal.* Quillian and Collins's view would

Figure 13.10 Reaction time and the levels separating associated concepts. This study showed that a person's reaction time to verify a statement was positively related to the number of nodes separating the information; that is, the greater the separation of the nodes, the longer the period needed to verify the concept.

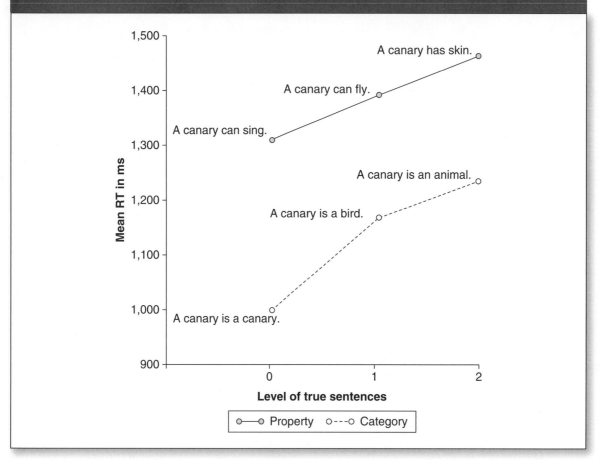

suggest that reaction time would be longer for the first than the second statement. The reason is that the concept node *mammal* is closer than the concept node *animal* to the node *collie* (the concept *animal* is superordinate to the concept *mammal*). Yet, Rips, Shoben, and Smith (1973) observed that subjects could verify the statement that *the collie is an animal* more readily than *the collie is a mammal*. Thus, the speed of reaction time does not always relate to the number of levels of concepts separating information.

A second problem involves the idea that information is stored at only one node. For example, the information that animals breathe is only stored at the concept node for *animal*. If this assumption is valid, it should take longer to verify the statement that *an ostrich can breathe* than *an animal can breathe*. Yet, C. Conrad (1972) reported no difference in reaction time for these types of sentences. This result suggests that information is stored at more than one node.

Finally, the Collins and Quillian view assumes that all subordinates of a concept are equally representative of that concept. This approach assumes that a canary and an ostrich are equally representative of the concept *bird*. We discovered in Chapter 12 that all members of a particular concept are not equally representative of the concept; that is, members vary in how closely they resemble the prototype of the concept. A canary is more representative than is an ostrich of the concept *bird*. This means a person can verify that *a canary is a bird* more readily than *an ostrich is a bird* (E. M. Roth & Shoben, 1983).

Spreading Activation Theory. Collins and Loftus (1975) revised two main aspects of the Collins and Quillian model. First, they suggested that properties can be associated with more than one concept. For example, the property *red* can be associated with a number of concepts like *fire engine, apple, roses,* and *sunsets* (see Figure 13.11). Second, a particular property can be more

Figure 13.11   Illustration of spreading activation theory. According to Collins and Loftus, a property such as *red* can be associated with several concepts. Also, each concept can have associated properties. A particular property may be more closely associated with some concepts than others.

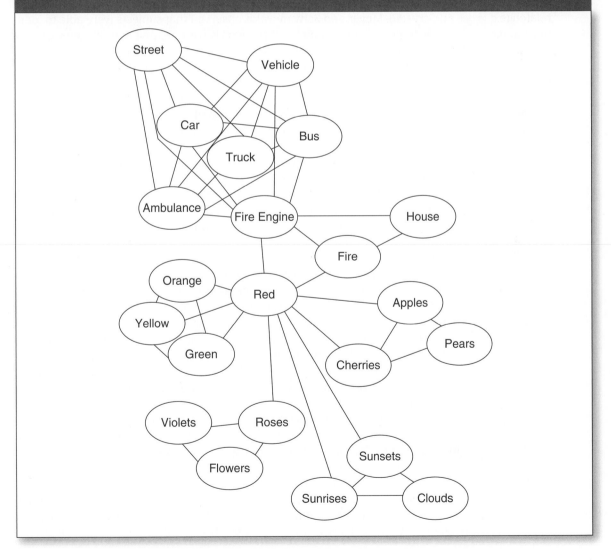

closely associated with some concepts than with others. As Figure 13.11 demonstrates, the property *red* is more closely associated with a fire engine than a sunset.

The **spreading activation theory** proposes that once a concept is activated, activation spreads to associated concepts. For example, if you heard the word *red,* you would think of associated concepts such as *fire engines* and *sunsets.* According to Collins and Loftus (1975), the activation spreads until even more distant associations can be recalled. For example, the activation of the *fire engine* concept could activate the associated concept of *vehicle.*

The difference in the lengths of association between properties and concepts explains the differences in reaction time needed to verify various statements. The greater length of association between *red* and *sunset* than *red* and *fire engine* means most people can more rapidly verify the statement that *fire engines are red* than *sunsets are red.*

The spreading activation theory can also explain the priming phenomenon, or the facilitation of recall of specific information following exposure to closely related information. To show the effect of **priming,** Meyer and Schvaneveldt (1971) asked subjects to indicate as rapidly as possible when two items were both words (e.g., *first* and *truck*) or were not both words (e.g., *roast* and *brive*). Some of the word pairs were related (e.g., *bread* and *butter*), and other word pairs were not related (e.g., *rope* and *crystal*). Meyer and Schvaneveldt observed that subjects were able to identify the pairs as both being words more quickly if the words were related than if they were not related. According to the spreading activation theory, the prime word activates related words, which leads to a rapid identification of both as words. The lack of priming slows the identification of the second string of letters as a word.

The spreading activation model suggests that semantic memory is organized in terms of associations between concepts and properties of concepts. Rumelhart and McClelland proposed a different theory of encoding in 1986; we next examine their parallel distributed processing model.

Parallel Distributed Processing Model. David Rumelhart and James McClelland (1986) suggested that memory is composed of a series of interconnected associative networks. Their **parallel distributed processing model** proposes that memory consists of a wide range of different connections that are simultaneously active. According to their theory, thousands of connections are possible. A connection can either be excitatory or inhibitory. Experience can alter the strength of either an excitatory or inhibitory connection.

The parallel distributed processing model assumes that "knowledge" is not located in any particular connection. Instead, knowledge is distributed throughout the entire system; that is, the total pattern and strength of connections represents the influence of an experience. With each individual training experience, the strength of individual connections changes. With continued training, the strength of the connections changes until the desired pattern is reached.

Suppose a person sees and smells a rose. How is this experience encoded? According to Rumelhart and McClelland (1986), the sight of the rose (visual input) arouses a certain pattern of neural units, and the smell of the rose (olfaction input) activates a different pattern of neural units. Figure 13.12 presents a hypothetical pattern in which a rose activates four neural visual units and four neural olfactory units.

As Figure 13.12 illustrates, the pattern of neural A units that the sight of a rose activates is $+1$, $-1, -1$, and $+1$, and the pattern of neural B units activated by the smell of a rose is $-1, -1, +1$, and $+1$. (A positive value indicates excitation of a neural unit, and a negative value indicates inhibition of a neural unit.) Rumelhart and McClelland proposed that the neural A units stimulated by the sight of a rose become associated with the neural B units activated by the smell of a rose.

Perhaps you see a rose in a vase on a table. This visual image likely causes you to recall the smell of a rose. Rumelhart and McClelland's parallel distributed processing model can explain how the sight of a rose causes you to remember the smell of the rose. According to

Figure 13.12   Hypothetical illustration of pattern associator matrix of visual and olfactory units activated by the sight and smell of a rose. The sight of a rose activates four A units in a +1, −1, −1, and +1 pattern, whereas the smell of a rose activates four B units in a −1, −1, +1, and +1 pattern. The interconnection of all visual A units with all olfactory B units allows the sight of a rose to elicit the recall of a rose's smell.

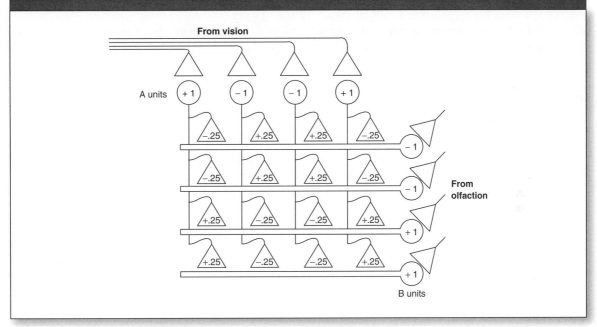

Rumelhart and McClelland, each neural unit activated by the sight of a rose is associated with each neural unit activated by the smell of a rose. They suggested that the specific neural units stimulated by the sight of the rose will arouse the pattern of neural units normally activated by smell of a rose. Stimulation of these olfactory neural units will produce the perception of the smell of a rose.

How does activating the visual units arouse the memory of a rose's smell? Using matrix algebra methods, Rumelhart and McClelland were able to construct a matrix of interconnected elements, or a pattern associator. This pattern associator matrix forms during the associations of two events and enables the presentation of one event to elicit the recall of the other event. The association of the sight and smell of a rose establishes the pattern associator matrix in Figure 13.12 and allows the sight of the rose to activate the pattern of neural activity produced by the smell of a rose. Similarly, the smell of the rose can activate the pattern produced by the sight of the rose and cause us to remember the visual image of a rose.

The main idea of the parallel distributed processing approach is that knowledge is derived from the connections rather than from the nodes. The extensive synaptic connections in the nervous system are consistent with a parallel rather than serial processing model of memory. Karl Lashley's (1950) classic examination of the location of memory provides additional support for a parallel distributed processing view. Lashley trained rats in a simple discrimination and then destroyed a small part of each animal's brain. The intent of this destruction was to locate the site of the animal's memory of the discrimination. Lashley discovered that the animals still showed retention of the discrimination despite the absence of the brain tissue. He continued the search for the engram by destroying other brain areas, but the rats remained able to recall their past learning. On the basis of his observations, Lashley stated,

> It is not possible to demonstrate the isolated localization of a memory trace anywhere within the nervous system. Limited regions may be essential for learning or retention of a particular activity, but within such regions the parts are functionally equivalent. The engram is represented throughout the region. (p. 733)

Lashley's statement suggests that knowledge is distributed throughout an entire region of the nervous system. Interestingly, the parallel distributed processing model came to the same conclusion almost a half a century later.

The Rehearsal Function of the Short-Term Store

Suppose you are trying to learn the French word for *door*. To learn that the French phrase for door is *la porte*, you must form an association between the words *door* and *la porte*. In an attempt to learn the association, you repeat the two words to yourself several times. This process, called **rehearsal**, keeps the memories in the short-term store. Rehearsal has two main functions. First, it keeps information in the short-term store so that you don't forget it. Second, rehearsal can provide the opportunity to make information more meaningful.

There is an important difference between these two functions of rehearsal. We can merely repeat information contained in the short-term store. When we simply repeat material we have experienced, we use **maintenance rehearsal**. This form of rehearsal will keep information in the short-term store and can lead to establishment of some associations. However, the likelihood of later recall of our experiences is greatly enhanced by **elaborative rehearsal**. With elaborative rehearsal, we alter information to create a more meaningful memory. We may attempt to relate the experience to other information, form a mental image of the experience, or organize the experience in some new way.

The evidence indicates that rehearsal can enhance the recall of an event (Rundus, 1971; Rundus & Atkinson, 1970). In one of Rundus's studies, subjects received a list of words to recall; the words were presented at a rate of one word every 5 seconds. Subjects were instructed to study the list by repeating the words during the 5-second interval between the presentation of the words. After the entire list had been presented, the subjects were required to recall as many words as possible from the list. Rundus observed that the more times a word is rehearsed, the higher the likelihood a subject will be able to recall the word.

You may think that rehearsal always increases the level of recall. However, evidence indicates that this is not so (Craik & Watkins, 1973); in fact, unless rehearsal leads to the organization of an event, rehearsal will not improve recall. Craik and Watkins (1973) presented subjects with a list of 21 words and instructed them to repeat the last word that began with a given letter until the next word beginning with that letter was presented, then rehearse the second word until another word beginning with that letter was presented, and so on. For example, suppose the given letter was *g* and the list of words was *daughter, oil, rifle, garden, grain, table, football, anchor,* and *giraffe*. The subjects rehearsed *garden* until the word *grain* was presented, and then *grain* until *giraffe* was presented. Using this procedure, Craik and Watkins varied the amount of time words were rehearsed. Thus, in this list, *garden* was rehearsed for less time than *grain*. Each subject received 27 lists, and the number of words between critical words varied in each list. After completing the 27 lists, each subject was asked to recall as many words as possible from any of the lists. Craik and Watkins found that the amount of time a word was rehearsed had no impact on the level of recall.

Why did rehearsal affect recall in the Rundus study but not in the Craik and Watkins study? The answer may lie in one of the differences between their studies: subjects in the Craik and Watkins experiment rehearsed only a single word (the last word beginning with a specific letter), whereas subjects in Rundus's study rehearsed several words. Thus, subjects could organize the information in the Rundus study, but not in the Craik and Watkins study. This suggests that rehearsal enhances recall only if the subject organizes the information during rehearsal.

BEFORE YOU GO ON

- What is the span of Donald's short-term store?

- Does Donald's short-term store seem more susceptible to disruption than Helen's?

SECTION REVIEW

- Information remains in the short-term store for approximately 15 to 20 seconds, and during this time an event is analyzed and organized to create a more meaningful memory.

- The short-term store is thought to have a limited storage capacity; it can retain only three or four units of information at one time.

- Chunking combines bits of information and is recalled in categories of chunked material.

- Coding transfers a visual experience into an acoustic code and words or ideas into an image or visual code.

- Another organizational function of the short-term store is the association of events.

- Spreading activation theory assumes that a property can be associated with more than one concept, but any particular property will be more closely associated with some concepts.

- The parallel distributed model assumes that knowledge is not contained in any particular location, but instead is distributed throughout the entire system.

- The short-term store can rehearse or replay prior experiences, which can help retain information in the short-term store for a longer period (maintenance rehearsal).

- Increased rehearsal also enhances the organization of the memory (elaborative rehearsal), improving the likelihood that the memory will later be available for recall.

The Atkinson-Shiffrin three-stage model, introduced earlier, assumes that memories are held for a brief time in the short-term store prior to being transferred to the permanent or long-term store. An alternative to the Atkinson-Shiffrin model is described next.

A REHEARSALS SYSTEMS APPROACH

Alan Baddeley (Baddeley, 1990; Gathercole & Baddeley, 1993) proposed an alternative to the Atkinson-Shiffrin three-stage model. Baddeley's **rehearsal systems approach** argued that while memories are retained in the sensory systems, those memories are analyzed by a process that he called **working memory**. According to Baddeley, working memory acts to enhance the organization and increase the retrieval of our experiences.

Phonological Loop

Baddeley suggested that two sensory systems hold information for rehearsal in working memory. One rehearsal system is the **phonological loop**. According to Baddeley, the phonological loop evolved to facilitate the acquisition of language. The phonological loop retains information in the verbal sensory system for a brief time (approximately 2 seconds), unless rehearsal keeps the input in working memory. Baddeley proposed that there are two components of the phonological loop: One component holds speech-based information; the other contains subvocal speech, or speech to oneself. Support for the existence of the phonological loop is provided by the observation that factors such as articulatory suppression and phonological similarity that disrupt the phonological loop also impair the learning of a foreign language, but do not impair learning associated pairs of unrelated native language words (Papagno, Valentine, & Baddeley, 1991).

Visuospatial Sketchpad

While the phonological loop facilitates language learning, the **visuospatial sketchpad** allows people to acquire knowledge of the appearance of objects and how to use those objects, as well as spatial orientation and geographical knowledge. According to Baddeley (1990), the visuospatial sketchpad acts to rehearse visual or spatial experiences, maintaining visual or spatial information by creating a mental image of an experience. For example, while listening to a radio announcer describe a basketball game, a person can visualize the action taking place. Support for existence of the visuospatial sketchpad is the fact that the ability to hold and manipulate visuospatial representations of objects in the environment is highly correlated with success in fields such as architecture and engineering (Purcell & Gero, 1998).

The Central Executive

According to Baddeley (1990), a **central executive** coordinates the phonological loop and visuospatial sketchpad. The central executive determines in which rehearsal system a specific event is placed. It also can retrieve information from any rehearsal system as well as transfer information among rehearsal systems or between permanent memory and rehearsal systems. The central executive can rely on habits guided by cues in the environment to control behavior. Or the central executive can switch to an attention supervisory control when routine automatic control is insufficient. For example, driving an automobile to school can be an automatic process, unless there is a lot of traffic and close attention to the cars around you is important.

The central executive is assumed to be a function of the frontal lobes. Support for the divided control function of the central executive and the frontal lobes can be found in the behavior of individuals with frontal lobe damage (Shallice, 2002). Shallice found that on some occasions, people with frontal lobe damage showed inappropriate perseveration, or not switching away from ineffective habits. On other occasions, these same people would show excessive distractibility, which is indicative of too much attentiveness.

Mohr, Goebel, and Linden (2006) found that the anterior middle frontal gyrus and the inferior prefrontal gyrus, which are parts of the prefrontal cortex, as well as the inferior parietal cortex as being activated during the manipulation of visual events (executive function), while Osaka et al. (2004) observed activation of the left inferior frontal gyrus and anterior cingulated cortex during a central executive task. It would appear that central executive functions involve several brain structures, in addition to the prefrontal cortex, which explains why Andres (2003) found central executive function deficits in some patients with no evidence of frontal damage, and no central executive function deficits in some patients with frontal lesions.

Episodic Buffer

Baddeley (Baddeley, 2003, Repovs & Baddeley, 2006) has more recently introduced a fourth component to his theory of working memory. According to Baddeley, the **episodic buffer** is a system that binds together events to form integrated episodes; that is, it possesses the ability to combine bits of information prior to storage in long-term memory (see Figure 13.13). As we discussed earlier, chunking is an important attribute of the short-term store, and its absence from Baddeley's original conception of working memory was a serious omission. Baddeley assumed that the episodic buffer serves as a workbench for assembling unitary multidimensional representations in different codes (visual, phonological, semantic) from different perceptual sources (visual, auditory, tactile). For example, the episodic buffer can bind visual and auditory input into a visual code. Furthermore, the episodic buffer temporarily stores these representations until they are stored in long-term memory.

Baddeley and Wilson (2002) provide support for the formation of unitary multidimensional representations by the episodic buffer. These researchers evaluated the ability of two amnesic patients with severely impaired long-term memory to recall long prose passages. As the number of words in the passage exceeded normal short-term memory capacity, good recall required the binding (or chunking) of the words. Baddeley and Wilson found that the amnesic subjects had good immediate recall but were unable to recall the prose passage after the delay. The results indicated that the processing of the prose passage was occurring in the episodic buffer of working memory.

Figure 13.13   An illustration of Baddeley's memory system. The central executive coordinates the phonological loop, the visuospatial sketchpad, the episodic buffer (fluid systems), and long-term memory (crystallized systems).

The binding of events by the episodic store can occur independently of the central executive, although the central executive can be engaged if the episodic buffer is overtaxed. To provide evidence for the independence of the episodic buffer and central executive, Allen, Baddeley, and Hitch (2006) visually presented bound or unbound colors and shapes following by an attention-demanding distracter task. If the central executive played a major role, the distracting task should have produced greater recall of unbound than bound stimuli. These researchers found that the distracting task equally affected recall of bound and unbound shapes and colors, suggesting that the central executive does not play a major role in the episodic buffer's maintenance of unified multidimensional representations of events.

Researchers have used neuroimaging to determine the brain structures activated when unitary multidimensional representations are formed and maintained by the episodic buffer (Wolters & Raffone, 2008; D. Zhang et al., 2004). D. Zhang et al. (2004) found that the right prefrontal cortex was activated when the order of auditory digits and visual locations were being stored and the unified multidimensional representations of the auditory and visual stimuli were being maintained until recall. Similarly, Wolters and Raffone (2008) found that the prefrontal cortex was activated when bound stimuli were being maintained in the episodic buffer.

Recall that Osaka et al. (2004) reported that the left frontal gyrus and anterior cingulate gyrus were activated when subjects were engaged in central executive functions. As Rudner and Ronnberg (2008) note, the left frontal gyrus and anterior cingulate gyrus are not activated while a subject is doing episodic buffer functions, which supports the view that separate areas of the brain are involved in the central executive and episodic buffer. Gooding, Issac, and Mayes's (2005) observation that amnesic patients with poor executive control generally have good immediate recall (episodic buffer) further supports the dissociation the central executive and episodic buffer.

Is There a Short-Term Memory?

Not all psychologists accept the idea that there is no separate short-term store. Cowan (1994) advocated a separate facility to store immediate memories, that is, a short-term store that is separate from the sensory register and the long-term store. Let's examine one study that supports this view.

The Cowan, Day, Saults, Keller, Johnson, and Flores (1992) study provides support for the existence of a short-term store. In their study, subjects were shown two lists of words: Some subjects saw a list of printed words that began with shorter words and ended with longer words, while other subjects saw a list that started with longer words and ended with shorter words. At the end of each list, the subjects saw a cue indicating whether to report the words in forward or backward order. These investigators found that the recall of the shorter words was low when the shorter words appeared early in the list and the cue called for backward recall. Similarly, the recall of the shorter words was low when the shorter words appeared late in the list and the cue called for forward recall. In contrast, recall of the shorter words was high when the shorter words were recalled first. As rehearsal time for the shorter words was constant in both lists, the order of recall seemed to determine the level of recall of the shorter words; that is, recall of the shorter words was high if they were recalled first and was poor if they were reported later. Cowan and his colleagues interpreted these results to mean that because time was needed to report the longer words, the shorter words were lost from the short-term store during the time used to recall the longer words. Therefore, the shorter words were unavailable for recall.

How can the Atkinson-Shiffrin three-stage model and Baddeley's rehearsal systems approach be reconciled? A likely possibility is that the properties of working memory in Baddeley's rehearsal systems approach reflect the functioning of the sensory register and short-term store in the Atkinson-Shiffrin three-stage model.

BEFORE YOU GO ON

- Does Donald's poor recall reflect a deficit in his working memory?

- How would the rehearsal systems approach explain Donald's poor recall of recent events?

SECTION REVIEW

- Baddeley's rehearsal systems approach argues that information is retained in several sensory registers for the working memory to analyze.

- Rehearsal systems hold information in working memory so that it can be processed into a more organized memory.

  - The central executive places information into a rehearsal system, transfers information among rehearsal systems and between permanent memory and rehearsal systems, and retrieves information from any rehearsal systems.

  - The episodic buffer binds together events to form integrated episodes.

Endel Tulving (1927–   )

Tulving received his doctorate from Harvard University under the direction of Eric Heinemann. He was born in Estonia, but left when the Soviet Army invaded Estonia at the end of World War II. He has taught at University of Toronto, Canada for the last 54 years. His research contributions enhanced the understanding of the nature of long-term memory processes. In 2005, he received the Gairdner Foundation International Award, Canada's leading award in biology and medicine, and, in 1983, the Distinguished Scientific Contribution Award from the American Psychological Association.

LONG-TERM STORE

Memories are permanently (or relatively permanently) encoded in the long-term store. We will explore two aspects of the long-term storage of experiences. First, we examine evidence that there are several different types of long-term memories. Second, we discuss the physiological processes governing the long-term storage of an event, as well as the psychological and physiological circumstances that can result in the failure to store an experience. A memory may be permanently stored yet still not be recalled; in the next chapter, we describe the processes that result in the failure to recall a prior event.

Episodic Versus Semantic Memories

Endel Tulving (1972, 1983) suggested that there are two types of long-term memories: episodic and semantic.

An **episodic memory** consists of information about events associated with a particular time and place, whereas a **semantic memory** contains knowledge associated with the use of language. For example, remembering that you had bacon and eggs for breakfast at the local diner is an example of an episodic memory, while remembering that a sentence contains a noun phrase and a verb phrase is an example of a semantic memory. Tulving proposed that the difference between episodic and semantic memory is greater than just the different types of information stored in each memory; he argued that the episodic memory system is functionally distinct from the semantic memory system. Table 13.1 presents a list of the differences between episodic and semantic memory.

Table 13.1 Characteristics of Episodic and Semantic Memory

Diagnostic Feature	Episodic	Semantic
Information		
Source	Sensation	Comprehension
Units	Events; episodes	Facts; ideas; concepts
Organization	Temporal	Conceptual
Reference	Self	Universe
Veridicality	Personal belief	Social agreement
Operations		
Registration	Experiential	Symbolic
Temporal coding	Present; direct	Absent; indirect
Affect	More important	Less important
Inferential capability	Limited	Rich
Context dependency	More pronounced	Less pronounced
Vulnerability	Great	Small
Access	Deliberate	Automatic
Retrieval queries	Time? Place?	What?
Retrieval consequences	Change system	System unchanged
Retrieval mechanisms	Synergy	Unfolding
Recollective experience	Remembered past	Actualized knowledge
Retrieval report	Remember	Know
Developmental sequence	Late	Early
Childhood amnesia	Affected	Unaffected

Separate Operations

The processes involved in the storage and retrieval of episodic and semantic memories differ. According to Tulving (1983), the episodic memory system registers immediate sensory experiences, while the semantic memory system records knowledge conveyed by language. The episodic memory system detects the temporal order of events; problems of temporal order can be solved only by inference in the semantic memory system. Tulving assumed that the episodic memory system has limited inferential capacity; that is, information stored in the episodic memory system is based mainly on direct sensory impressions. In contrast, the semantic memory system has a rich inferential capacity and can, therefore, discover the rules of a language merely from experience with that language.

Tulving (1983) has found that the recollection of memories from the episodic system is deliberate and often requires conscious effort, whereas recall of information contained in the semantic system is automatic and can occur without conscious knowledge. Although we can be aware of knowledge contained in both memory systems, we interpret episodic memories as part of our personal past and semantic memories as part of the impersonal present. Thus, we use the term *remember* when referring to episodic memories and the term *know* to describe semantic memories. According to Tulving, when we retrieve information from episodic memory, it is often changed, but memories we recall from the semantic memory are not altered. Thus, the episodic memory system is much more vulnerable to distortion than are memories contained in the semantic system.

Two Functionally Different Memory Systems

Tulving (1983) detailed the results of many experiments documenting the existence of separate episodic and semantic memory systems. Let's briefly examine one study supporting the distinction.

A study by Wood, Taylor, Penny, and Stump (1980) provides strong support for separate episodic and semantic memory systems. These researchers compared the regional cerebral blood flow of two groups of subjects: One group was involved in a semantic memory task; the other in an episodic memory task. The authors observed differences in the regional cerebral blood flow in each of the two groups and suggested that their results indicate "an anatomical basis for the distinction between episodic and semantic memory" (p. 122).

A number of psychologists (Kintsch, 1980; Naus & Halasz, 1979) disagreed with the idea that the episodic and semantic memory systems represent two separate systems. Instead, they suggested that there is a single memory system and that its content varies from highly context-specific episodes to abstract generalizations. Tulving (1983) asserted that the dissociation studies provide convincing evidence that there are, in fact, two separate memory systems. However, Tulving does recognize that the episodic and semantic memory systems are highly interdependent. Thus, an event takes on more meaning if both semantic and episodic knowledge are involved in its storage. Yet, Tulving believes that these two memory systems can also operate independently. For example, a person can store information about a particular temporal event that is both novel and meaningless, a result that can occur only if the episodic memory system is independent of the semantic memory system.

Tulving and Markowitsch (1997) proposed that the hippocampus is necessary for episodic memory, but not necessary for semantic memory. The important role that the hippocampus plays in memory, especially episodic memory, is explored later in this chapter.

Procedural Versus Declarative Memories

I have not been on a bicycle in several years. Yet, I would certainly remember how to ride a bicycle. As a child, I had many experiences riding bicycles. The storage of these past experiences of riding bicycles would allow me to ride a bicycle. My storage of memories of bicycle riding is an example of a procedural memory.

According to Squire (1986), **procedural memory** is skill memory. Procedural memories are not accessible to conscious awareness; instead, evidence of a procedural memory can only be gained through observations of performance. These memories represent knowledge of how to do things like tie shoelaces or play the piano. These behaviors are stored as a result of instrumental or operant conditioning experiences. Procedural memories can also represent emotional reactions to environmental events, such as becoming hungry when arriving at the movie theater or feeling fearful before driving over a bridge, that are stored as a result of classical conditioning.

Procedural memories are acquired slowly, through repeated experience. The extensive practice required to learn how to play the piano is one example of the importance of repeated experience for the storage of procedural memories. Evidence of the existence of a procedural memory lies in how well or poorly the animal or person responds. For example, the intensity of a person's fear when driving over a high bridge indicates the strength of the person's procedural memory. Similarly, the quality of piano playing documents the strength of this procedural memory.

Suppose your favorite television show is on at 8:30 p.m. on Tuesday evenings. Remembering the day and time that your favorite show airs is an example of **declarative memory** (see Table 13.2).

Table 13.2 Characteristics of Procedural and Declarative Memory

Procedural Memory	Declarative Memory
Stores skills and procedures	Stores faces, episodes, and data
Is learned over many trials	Can be learned in a single trial
Contained within processing systems	Available to many processing systems
Information is modality specific	Information is modality general
Develops early	Develops late
Preserved in amnesia	Impaired in amnesia
Inaccessible to conscious recollection	Accessible to conscious recollection

Squire (1986) refers to declarative memory as factual memory. The time and day of the television show is a fact, and you stored this information as a declarative memory. Other examples of declarative memory include remembering the route to school or recognizing a familiar face.

Recall our discussion of the interdependence of episodic and semantic memories. A similar interdependence exists between procedural and declarative memory. For example, tying a shoe can be a declarative memory; that is, you can have knowledge of how a shoe is tied, which is a declarative memory. Yet, tying one's shoe also exists as a procedural memory. Similarly, repeated practice can transform the conscious knowledge (or declarative memory) of the route to school into an unconscious habit (or procedural memory).

We have been discussing several types of long-term memories. But what physical changes provide the basis for the permanent record of an event? We address this question next.

Cellular Modification Theory

Many scientists (G. Lynch, 1986; Rosenzweig, 1984) have proposed that permanent memory represents changes in neural responsiveness. This view, referred to as **cellular modification theory**, suggests that learning either enhances the functioning of existing neural circuits or establishes new neural connections.

Learning in the Aplysia Californica

Recall our discussion of the research of Eric Kandel and his associates in Chapter 3. We learned that the habituation of the defensive reaction is caused by a depression of synaptic responsivity in the sensorimotor neurons in the defensive reflex of the sea snail *Aplysia californica,* while sensitization is caused by an increased synaptic responsivity.

The defensive reaction of the *Aplysia* also can be conditioned. For example, Carew, Hawkins, and Kandel (1983) paired a light touch to the mantle or siphon (CS) with a strong electric shock to the tail (UCS). These investigators reported that following repeated pairings of the light touch (CS) with electric shock (UCS), the light touch alone elicited the withdrawal response (CR).

Classical conditioning also enables the light touch CS to increase neurotransmitter release onto the motor neuron controlling the withdrawal CR. For example, Hawkins et al. (1993) found that the CS produces the same increase in synaptic responsivity as a sensitizing stimulus does. The increased synaptic responsivity produced by the CS causes an increased neurotransmitter release and the elicitation of the defensive conditioned response.

Structural Changes and Experience

The research of Gary Lynch (1986) showed that conditioning can lead not only to increased neurotransmitter release, but also to an increased number of synaptic connections. Lynch found that experience enhances the level of calcium ion entry into the cell. This influx of calcium ions into the cell activates the enzyme calpain. Calpain breaks down fodrin, a protein that coats the dendrites . The breakdown of the dendrite's coating exposes more of the dendrite to stimulation from other neurons; that is, as the coating breaks down, the neuron becomes more sensitive. With continued experience, the breakdown process continues, resulting in even greater neural sensitivity.

G. Lynch (1986) also suggested that the breakdown of cellular coating allows the dendrites to change shape and spread out, much like the increasing number of branches as a tree grows (see Figure 13.14). The increased arborization of the dendrites leads to the establishment of even more new neural connections.

G. Lynch and Baudry (1984) provided support for the view that the establishment of new neural connections represents the biological basis of learning and memory. They trained rats to find food in an eight-arm radial maze (see Figure 13.15). The procedure used in this study involved placing food reward in all eight arms. The rats' task on each trial was to visit each of the arms only once. When a rat returned to a previously visited arm, it received no food. The rats quickly learned the task; they remembered which arms they had visited and which arms they still could visit to receive reward. Lynch and Baudry then implanted a pump in the rat's brain that could infuse a chemical called leupeptin into the lateral ventricle. This chemical inhibits the breakdown of fodrin, thereby preventing the establishment of new neural connections. These researchers found that the animals that received leupeptin entered the arms of the radial maze randomly, recalling nothing of their past learning experience, whereas control animals that did not receive leupeptin showed good recall of the prior experiences.

Figure 13.14   Aborization of dendrites. Continued experience increases the number of neural connections because of the breakdown of the dendritic coating.

Before   After

Figure 13.15 Eight-arm radial maze used to study spatial memory. In studies of spatial memory, the researchers place reward (food) in the arms of the maze, and rats are required to visit each of these arms without returning to a previously visited arm.

ANATOMICAL BASIS OF MEMORY STORAGE

Research has indicated that two brain structures—the **medial temporal lobe** and the **mediodorsal thalamus**—are critical to the storage of the memory of events. Larry Squire and his colleagues (Squire, 1998, 2004; Squire, Stark, & Clark, 2004; Zola-Morgan & Squire, 1993) provided a model detailing the biological structures involved in memory (see Figure 13.16). In this view, an event is first detected in the sensory areas of the cortex and then sent to structures in the medial temporal lobe for analysis. Key structures in the medial temporal lobe include the hippocampus and surrounding cortical areas. Projections from these medial temporal lobe structures then convey memory to the mediodorsal thalamus, where the experience receives still further processing. Following analysis by the mediodorsal thalamus, information is relayed to the frontal lobe.

Medial Temporal Lobe

The Case of H. M.

In 1953, patient Henry Gustav Molaison (1926–2008), better known as H. M., had his medial temporal lobe (including the hippocampus, amygdala, and surrounding cortical tissue) removed as a treatment for epilepsy. Although the operation successfully treated his severe epilepsy, this success proved costly. While H. M. remained pleasant and good-humored after the operation, he suffered from a severe memory deficit. H. M. was very cooperative, and many researchers

> **Figure 13.16** A view of the key structures for memory storage and retrieval. Information is sent from sensory areas of the cortex to the medial temporal lobe (hippocampus and adjacent areas), then to the mediodorsal thalamus for further analysis. Connections from the medial temporal lobe and the mediodorsal thalamus to the frontal lobe allow memory to influence behavior.

(Gabrieli, Cohen, & Corkin, 1988; Milner, 1970; O'Kane, Kensinger, & Corkin, 2004; Scoville & Milner, 1957) have examined the details of his memory disorder.

The most profound deficit was H. M.'s **anterograde amnesia**, or the inability to recall events that have occurred since the operation. For example, on each visit to the hospital, H. M. had to be reintroduced to his doctors. His inability to recall events that occurred following his surgery resulted from his failure to permanently store those experiences. H. M. also showed **retrograde amnesia** for events that took place only a few years prior to his operation. He could recall memories more than several years old, though, and he could carry on a conversation about those events. H. M. was fully aware of the extent of his memory impairment:

> Every day is alone in itself, whatever enjoyment I've had, and whatever sorrow I've had. . . . Right now, I'm wondering. Have I done or said anything amiss? You see, at this moment everything looks clear to me, but what happened just before? That's what worries me. It's like waking from a dream; I just don't remember. (as cited in Milner, 1970, p. 37)

While H. M. suffered severe memory impairment, some areas of his memory did remain intact. Squire (1987) suggested that although H. M. could not store episodic memories, he could store and recall procedural memories. Brenda Milner's (1965) research clearly showed that H. M. could acquire new skills (procedural memories). In one study, H. M. participated in a mirror-drawing task (see Figure 13.17a). The task involved tracing an object while looking at it in a mirror. This task is difficult and requires practice. On this task, H. M.'s performance improved over a series of trials; he made fewer errors as he learned the task (see Figure 13.17b). Further,

Figure 13.17 The mirror drawing task. (a) In this illustration, H. M. traces a star seen in a mirror. (b) H. M. made fewer errors each day of training, and his improvement was retained over 3 days of training.

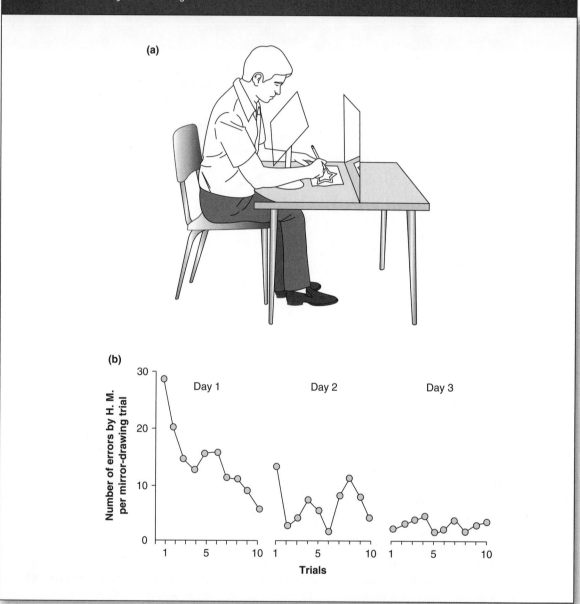

(a)

(b)

his improvement was maintained over several days of training. This indicates that a memory of the task has formed. While H. M.'s performance did improve, he could not remember having participated in the task from day to day (episodic memory).

How was H. M. able to become increasingly adept at tracing the figure but have no recollection of having previously drawn it? Tracing the figure is a visuomotor skill and involves procedural memory. Procedural memories appear to be unaffected by damage to the medial temporal lobe.

In contrast, recollection of having traced the figure is an episodic memory. Damage to the medial temporal lobe does appear to adversely affect the storage of episodic memories. Another example should clarify the kind of memory loss H. M. experienced. After his father died, H. M. could not remember it (an episodic memory), but he felt a little sad when he thought about his father (a procedural memory).

While H. M. lost recent episodic memories, his semantic memories were not affected by medial temporal lobe damage. H. M.'s language ability was not affected by the operation, and he could still read and write (Gabrieli et al., 1988). More recent work with H. M. indicated that he was able to acquire some semantic knowledge of the world in the half-century following his surgery. Researchers have used forced-choice and cued-recall recognition tasks to determine whether H. M. had any knowledge of people who have become famous since the onset of his amnesia (O'Kane et al., 2004). With first names as cues, H. M. recalled the corresponding famous last name for more than a third of postoperatively famous personalities. H. M. did even better on a task in which he was asked to identify the famous person of a pair that included a name selected from the Baltimore telephone directory. He correctly chose 88 % of the names of people who had become famous after his surgery, which is a recognition score comparable to aged-matched controls. The researchers concluded that this latest work with H. M. showed that some semantic learning can occur, presumably through the use of structures beyond the hippocampus.

The Importance of the Hippocampus

The evidence indicates that the **hippocampus** is the key memory structure in the medial temporal lobe (Squire, Stark, & Clark, 2004). Studies using animals have shown that lesions to the hippocampus and surrounding areas (perirhinal, entorhinal, and parahippocampal cortices) produce memory deficits on a simple object discrimination (Squire et al., 1988) and on a delayed matching to sample task (Alvarez-Royo, Clower, Zola-Morgan, & Squire, 1991). Zola-Morgan, Squire, and Ramus (1994) found that the memory impairment was mild when the damage was limited to the hippocampus, but was increasingly more severe when damage was first extended to the adjacent entorhinal and parahippocampal cortices and then extended forward to include the anterior entorhinal cortex and the perirhinal cortex.

Damage to the hippocampus has also been shown to produce profound and long-lasting memory impairments in humans. Zola-Morgan, Squire, and Amaral (1986) studied the memory of patient R. B., a 52-year-old man with a history of coronary disease. R. B. suffered a cardiac arrest, which caused a temporary loss of blood to the brain (hypoxia) and resulted in brain damage. The brain damage produced profound anterograde amnesia. Five years after his cardiac arrest, patient R. B. died. Histological examination of his brain revealed a significant amount of degeneration of the hippocampal tissue (see Figure 13.18). Damage to the hippocampus has also been linked to memory deficits in other patients. Squire, Amaral, and Press (1990) performed a high-resolution MRI on several patients with severe memory impairments and observed a significant reduction in the size of the hippocampus in each case. More recent MRI scans on H. M. also showed the bilateral absence of most of the hippocampus and all of the entorhinal and parahippocampal cortices (Corkin, Amaral, Gonzalez, Johnson, & Hyman, 1997; see Figure 13.19 on page 383).

H. M. was unable to store new episodic memories, but he was able to retrieve episodic memories acquired prior to his surgery, an observation that supports the idea that the hippocampus is involved in the storage of episodic memories but is not the site where those memories are stored. Several researchers (Gabrieli, 1998; Tulving, 1998) point to the frontal and temporal lobes as the storage site for episodic memories. In support of this view, PET scan studies (Tulving & Markowitsch, 1997) reveal that the frontal and temporal lobes become active during the retrieval of past events.

Figure 13.18 Two different photographs of the hippocampus. Normal hippocampal structures are visible in the top photograph; the degeneration of hippocampal pyramidal cells of field CA1 caused by anoxia in patient R. B. is evident in the bottom photograph.

Mediodorsal Thalamus

Damage to the mediodorsal thalamus also has been associated with profound memory impairment (Van der Werf, Jolles, Witter, & Uylings, 2003). Horel and Misantone (1976) observed that destruction of the mediodorsal thalamus affected the ability of primates to distinguish new from familiar objects. However, mediodorsal thalamic lesions had no influence on the retention of a simple visual discrimination. These observations suggest that, like medial temporal lobe damage, lesions of the mediodorsal thalamus affect declarative but not procedural memories. Further, Isseroff, Rosvold, Galkin, and Goldman-Rakic (1982) found impaired spatial memory following lesions of the mediodorsal thalamus in rhesus monkeys.

Memory impairments have also been observed in humans following damage to the mediodorsal thalamic nuclei (Kishiyama et al., 2005; Zoppelt, Koch, Schwarz, & Daum, 2003). For example,

Figure 13.19   The hippocampus (H) and entorhinal cortex (EC) are present in the brain of a normal subject (right) but are absent bilaterally in the brain of H. M. (left).

people with thalamic lesions with or without involvement of the mediodorsal nucleus were assessed on a word list discrimination task for their recollection of the material. Lesions that included the mediodorsal thalamus produced recollection deficits.

Severe memory impairment can occur as a result of chronic consumption of alcohol. This memory loss was first described by the Russian neurologist Sergei Korsakoff in 1889. His alcoholic patients were unable to recall past events. This disorder is now called **Korsakoff's syndrome**. The memory loss characteristic of Korsakoff's syndrome is clearly associated with damage to the mediodorsal thalamus (Gold & Squire, 2006). Gold and Squire observed impaired recollection of words (anterograde amnesia) and past events (retrograde amnesia). In fact, most of the autobiographical recollections in the patients with Korsakoff's syndrome were from the very distant past. By contrast, Gold and Squire did not observe any memory impairment of nondeclarative memories in their patients with Korsakoff's syndrome.

Although patients with damage to the mediodorsal thalamic nuclei show memory deficits similar to those seen in medial temporal lobe patients, individuals with damage to the medial temporal lobe differ in some ways. Patients like H. M., with medial temporal lobe damage, are aware of their memory deficits. In contrast, Korsakoff's syndrome patients, and others with mediodorsal thalamic nuclei damage, are unaware of their memory loss. These individuals will confabulate, or make up stories, to fill in the gaps in their memories. The confabulation and lack of insight in patients with Korsakoff's syndrome are probably due to damage to the prefrontal cortex (M. Moscovitch, 1992). The mediodorsal thalamus projects to the prefrontal cortex, and individuals with Korsakoff's syndrome show impairments like those seen following damage to the prefrontal cortex.

BEFORE YOU GO ON

- What areas of Donald's brain were probably damaged in his accident?

- Is he likely to be able to store any long-term memories? If so, what kinds of memories?

SECTION REVIEW

- The long-term store is the site of permanent memory.

- An episodic memory consists of information associated with a particular time and place, whereas a semantic memory contains knowledge necessary for language use.

- An episodic memory is easy to store but difficult to retrieve; in contrast, a semantic memory is difficult to store but easy to retrieve.

- Procedural memories contain information about the performance of specific skills, while declarative memories contain knowledge about the environment.

- Experience increases synaptic responsivity of existing neural connections as well the establishment of new connections between neurons.

- Damage to the medial temporal lobe causes anterograde amnesia, or an inability to recall events subsequent to the damage, limited to episodic and declarative memory.

- Damage to the mediodorsal thalamus is also associated with anterograde amnesia and with Korsakoff's syndrome.

- The mediodorsal thalamus projects to the prefrontal cortex, and individuals with damage to the mediodorsal thalamus confabulate and show a lack of insight.

CRITICAL THINKING QUESTIONS

1. In his American literature class, Salman learned that William Faulkner was an important twentieth-century American writer. Salman will need to remember that Faulkner was a twentieth- and not a nineteenth-century author on his next test. Using spreading activation theory, explain how he will store the information and how he will identify Faulkner as a twentieth-century writer.

2. Jondrea was in an automobile accident but has no recollection of it. What process was likely to be responsible for Jondrea's inability to recall the accident?

3. John recently suffered a stroke and now has trouble remembering recent events. He can remember an event for a brief time, but he quickly forgets it. What areas were damaged by his stroke? What are the functions of these areas, and why did damage to them cause his memory deficits?

KEY TERMS

acoustic code

Atkinson-Shiffrin three-stage model

central executive

clustering

cued recall

echo

elaborative rehearsal

episodic memory

flashbulb memory

hierarchical approach

icon

implicit measure of memory

Korsakoff's syndrome

maintenance rehearsal

mediodorsal thalamus

parallel distributed processing model

phonological loop

procedural memory

recognition measure

rehearsal systems approach

savings score

sensory register

short-term store

visual code

whole report technique

anterograde amnesia

cellular modification theory

chunking

coding

declarative memory

echoic memory

episodic buffer

explicit measure of memory

free recall

hippocampus

iconic memory

interference

long-term store

medial temporal lobe

memory storage

partial report technique

priming

reaction time

rehearsal

retrograde amnesia

semantic memory

serial position effect

spreading activation theory

visuospatial sketchpad

working memory

CHAPTER 14

Memory Retrieval and Forgetting

A LOOK INTO THE PAST

Steve's grandfather died yesterday. He was very surprised to learn this. Although he was 90 when he died, Steve's grandfather had been in relatively good health. He was riding in Steve's mother's automobile when he had a massive coronary. He died immediately, and Steve was glad he did not suffer. The plane ride home to his grandfather's funeral was long, and during the trip, Steve had a lot of time to reminisce about childhood experiences with his grandfather. His grandparents had lived in Brooklyn when he was young, and Steve would stay with them for one week every summer. He remembered those visits with his grandparents as being quite wonderful. His grandfather would take him to see the Dodgers play at Ebbets Field at least twice during each visit. He could still remember seeing Jackie Robinson, Roy Campanilla, and Duke Snider play for the Dodgers. Steve was sure that his passion for baseball began during those trips to see the Dodgers play. Steve also had gone to Coney Island with his grandparents. He remembered fondly the arcade where his grandfather would give him money to play the games. Visits to Coney Island also meant eating at Nathan's restaurant. Steve can still taste one of Nathan's hot dogs and is sure they are one of life's greatest treats. Remembering Nathan's hot dogs also reminded him of becoming very ill after riding a roller coaster at Coney Island. Not surprisingly, Steve no longer enjoys riding on roller coasters. He continued to remember his childhood experiences with his grandfather throughout the plane ride. Toward the end of the flight, Steve realized that his grandfather would always be with him. His survival past death was possible because of Steve's ability to remember the past.

Remembering is a very important part of all of our lives. It allows us to recall a first love, or a special vacation with our parents. Yet we do not remember all of the events that happen to us. People often forget where they left their car in the parking lot of a large shopping mall or where they put the car keys when they are late for an appointment. In this chapter, we discuss why sometimes we are able to recall events from the past, but at other times we are unable to remember past experiences.

MEMORY RETRIEVAL

While we remember some events in our lives, we forget other experiences. Steve, described in the chapter-opening vignette, could recall his grandfather taking him to a Brooklyn Dodgers game at Ebbets Field. At the funeral, Steve's aunt told him about the time his grandfather took him to a ball game, and he ate a whole pizza and got sick. Fortunately, Steve did not recall that unfortunate happening, but now knows why he dislikes pizza. The process of retrieving the memory of a past experience is discussed next. Why we forget is described later in the chapter.

Attributes of Memory

Benton Underwood (1983) suggested that memory can be conceptualized as a collection of different types of information. Each type of information is called a **memory attribute**. For example, the memory of an event contains information regarding the place where the event occurred. This is referred to as the spatial attribute of that memory. A memory also contains information about the temporal characteristics of an event; Underwood calls this the temporal attribute. According to Underwood, the presence of the stimulus contained in the memory attribute can act to retrieve a memory. When we encounter a stimulus that is a salient aspect of a past event, the presence of that stimulus causes us to recall the memory of that event.

Underwood (1983) proposed that there are 10 memory attributes: acoustic, orthographic, frequency, spatial, temporal, modality, context, affective, verbal associative, and transformational. Not every memory contains information about each attribute. Even though a stimulus may characterize a particular aspect of a past experience, if it is not a memory attribute of that experience, it will not lead to the recall of the event. For example, you have a traffic accident on a particular day. If the day of the accident is not an attribute of the memory, the anniversary of the accident will not remind you of this misfortune. The one or two most salient aspects of an experience generally become memory attributes of the event, and **retrieval** is based solely on the presence of these stimuli. We next look more closely at three attributes that have an important influence on memory retrieval.

Temporal Attribute

On September 15th, I know it's my birthday. The knowledge of my birth date is the **temporal attribute** of that event. Almost everyone knows the date of his or her birthday as well as the dates of other significant events. These observations indicate that time can be a very important part of a memory. Even so, research shows that only *significant* temporal information is used to recall an experience.

Underwood (1977) presented to college students a list of eight events; the events occurred approximately a year apart, and Underwood made certain the subjects were familiar with the details of these events. The students were asked to rank the events in the order they had taken place. Underwood reported that of 108 students, only 2 did so correctly. Apparently, the temporal attribute does not always contain sufficient information for retrieval; a person may know that an event occurred but may not know exactly when. For example, you may have received an excellent grade on a test on a particular date last year, but that date this year does not remind you of the test or grade. Only when the date becomes associated with the event will the temporal attribute enhance retrieval of the memory of the event.

Context Attribute

The event's background can become an attribute of memory, and reexposure to that background context can prompt the retrieval of the memory of that event. For example, in the classic movie *Casablanca,* when Sam (the piano player) played the song "As Time Goes By," Ilsa (played by Ingrid Bergman) was reminded of a love affair that she had with Rick (played by Humphrey Bogart) many years before. The song was part of the context in which their love affair had taken place, and thus, the song was a memory attribute of the affair. Hearing the song retrieved the memory of their romance and caused her to remember the events surrounding her affair. The experience Ingrid Bergman's character had is not unique. You have undoubtedly been reminded of a past event by reexperiencing some aspect of the context in which that event occurred.

Underwood's (1983) view suggests that context serves as an important memory attribute. Research investigating the **context attribute** has involved both humans (Glenberg, Schroeder, & Robertson, 1998; S. M. Smith & Vela, 2001) and animals (Gordon & Klein, 1994; Morgan & Riccio, 1998). Both types of research show that context can be an important memory attribute.

How can we know whether context has become a memory attribute? One way to demonstrate the influence of context on memory retrieval is to learn a response in one context and then see whether a change in context produces a memory loss. In 1975, Gooden and Baddeley conducted an interesting study showing the importance of context to memory. These investigators had scuba divers listen to a list of words. The divers were either 10 feet underwater or were sitting on the beach when they heard the words. The divers were then tested either in the same context or in the other context. Gooden and Baddeley observed better recall when the scuba divers were tested in the same context where they first heard the words than when they were tested in the opposite context (see Figure 14.1).

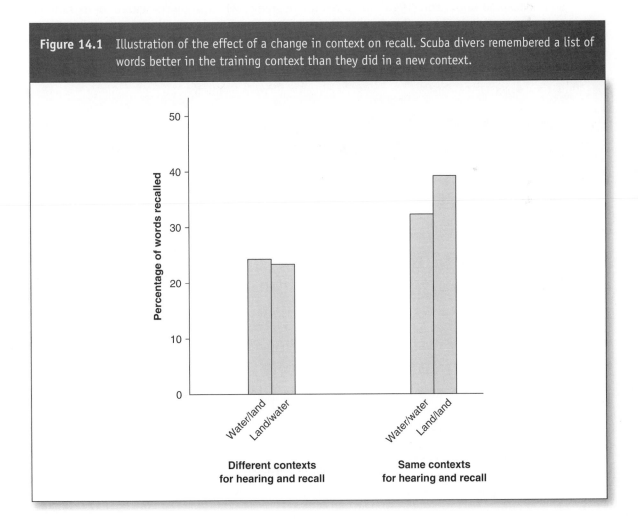

Figure 14.1 Illustration of the effect of a change in context on recall. Scuba divers remembered a list of words better in the training context than they did in a new context.

Gordon, McCracken, Dess-Beech, and Mowrer (1981) demonstrated the influence of context in animals' memory retrieval. Gordon and his colleagues trained rats in a distinctive environment to actively respond to avoid shock in a shuttle box. Forty-eight hours later, the rats were placed either in the shuttle box in the original training room or in an identical shuttle box located in another room that differed in size, lighting, odor, and ambient noise level. The researchers reported high retention when the rats were tested in the training context and significantly poorer performance when testing occurred in a novel context (see Figure 14.2).

Perhaps you are now concerned about taking an examination in a new context. Not all studies have shown that a change in context leads to forgetting. For example, Saufley, Otaka, and Bavaresco (1985) told approximately 5,000 college students during the semester that some would be taking their final exams in other rooms both to relieve overcrowded classrooms and to assist in proctoring. The results showed that the average examination grades did not differ for students taking their exam in a different classroom than for those students taking the exam in their regular classroom.

The fact that a context is a memory attribute may not always be a good thing. Glenberg (1997) suggested that when an extraneous contextual cue becomes a memory attribute capable of retrieving a previously experienced event, attention will divert from the learning process. The result of attention diversion might be less learning and poorer recall, especially if the learning task is difficult and requires a lot of attention for learning to occur. In support of this view, Glenberg, Schroeder, and Robertson (1998) measured the degree to which subjects "gazed" at extraneous environmental stimuli (e.g., floor, wall, ceiling) that was unrelated to the learning situation. These researchers found that the frequency of gazing decreased as the task difficulty increased.

Figure 14.2 The mean latencies to cross to the black chamber on the retention test for groups A-A and B-B (trained and tested in the same environment) and groups A-B and B-A (trained in one environment and tested in another). The results show that retention of past avoidance training is greater when rats are tested in the original rather than in the new context.

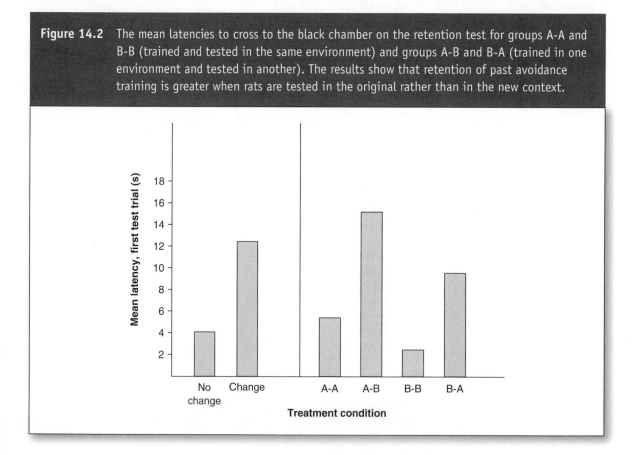

Glenberg, Schroeder, and Robertson (1998) also observed that the degree of diverting attention away from the context was related to recall and that the more a subject diverted his or her gaze, the better the recall. In fact, Glenberg, Schroeder, and Robertson found that forcing subjects to attend to irrelevant environmental events led to poor recall. Why might a person divert his or her attention away from environment? According to Glenberg (1997), averting one's gaze away from the extraneous environment allows the subject to disengage from the environment and devote all of the subject's resources to learning.

Underwood (1983) argued that although context is one attribute of memory, a memory also contains information about other characteristics of an event. The significance and availability of other attributes influence whether a memory is recalled in another context. If the context is the most unique or significant aspect of a memory, retrieval will depend on the presence of the context; however, if other attributes are important and available, retrieval will occur even in a new context.

The reminder-treatment studies (Gordon, 1983) demonstrate that retrieval can occur in a new context when other attributes are able to produce recall. The reminder treatment involves presenting subjects during testing with a subset of the stimuli that were present in training. Although this reminder treatment is insufficient to produce learning, it can induce retrieval of a past experience, even in a novel context.

The Gordon, McCracken, Dess-Beech, and Mowrer (1981) study shows this influence of the reminder treatment. Recall that in this study, changing the context caused rats to forget their prior active-avoidance responses. Another group of animals in the study received the reminder treatment 4 minutes before they were placed in the novel environment. The reminder treatment involved placing animals for 15 seconds in a cueing chamber—a white, translucent box identical to the white chamber of the avoidance apparatus where they had received shock during training. Following the reminder treatment, the rats were placed in a holding cage for 3.5 minutes and then transferred to the shuttle box in the novel context. Gordon, McCracken, Dess-Beech, and Mowrer found that animals receiving the reminder treatment performed as well as the animals that had been tested in the training context. Exposure to the cueing chamber prevented the forgetting that normally occurs in a novel context.

S. M. Smith (1982) discovered that a reminder treatment could be used with human subjects to reduce the forgetting that occurs when the context changes from training to testing. In Smith's studies, one group of subjects received a list of 32 words to learn in one context and then was asked to recall the list in the same context; a second group was asked to recall the list in a new context. A third group of subjects was exposed to a context-recall technique prior to testing in a new context. The context-recall technique involved instructing subjects to think of the original training context and ignore the new context when trying to recall the list of words. Smith reported that subjects in the context-recall technique group remembered as many words in a new room as did subjects tested in their original learning room. In contrast, subjects who were tested in a new context but did not receive the reminder treatment showed poor recall of their prior training.

Why might reminder treatments enhance recall in a new context? According to S. M. Smith and Vela (2001), the reminder treatment suppressed the context as an effective memory attribute and thereby allowed noncontextual cues to serve as an effective memory attribute. One of those nonenvironmental cues might be emotional state.

Affective Attribute

Underwood (1983) asserted that the emotional responses produced by various events can be attributes of memories. Some events are pleasant; others are unpleasant. The memory of an event contains much information regarding the emotional character of that event. This **affective attribute** enables a person to distinguish among various memories as well as to retrieve the memory of a particular event.

Underwood (1983) theorized that the affective attribute could be viewed as an internal contextual attribute; that is, it contains information about the internal consequences of an event. Events not only produce internal changes, they also occur during a particular internal state. Suppose you are intoxicated at a party. The next day, a friend asks you whether you had an enjoyable time, but you do not remember. This situation is an example of **state-dependent learning** (Overton, 1982). In state-dependent learning, an experience encountered during one internal state will not be recalled when the internal state changes. According to our memory attribute framework, internal state is an attribute of memory; that is, our memory of an event contains knowledge of the internal state. A change in internal state eliminates an attribute of memory, which can lead to a failure to recall the event. State-dependent learning has been found in rats, monkeys, cats, dogs, goldfish, and humans. Studies with humans have used alcohol (Goodwin, Powell, Bremer, Hoine, & Stein, 1969), amphetamine (Swanson & Kinsbourne, 1979), and marijuana (Eich, Weingartner, Stillman, & Gillin, 1975).

Events can also be experienced during a particular internal emotional state, and a change in this emotional state can lead to forgetting. Using hypnosis, Gordon Bower (1981) manipulated mood state (either happy or sad) before training and again prior to testing. Some subjects experienced the same mood prior to both training and testing, and other subjects experienced one mood state before training and the other before testing. Bower found significantly better recall when the emotional state induced before testing matched the emotional state present during training. Thus, a change in mood state, as well as drug state, can lead to forgetting. In a more recent study, Kenealy (1997) used music to induce either happiness or sadness and found that recall was better when learning and testing occurred in the same mood state.

Lang, Craske, Brown, and Ghaneian (2001) induced a fear state and a relaxation state in spider- or snake-fearful undergraduates. Fear was induced by having either a spider or a snake in a cage across the room and moving the spider or snake closer until the subject became afraid. Lang, Craske, Brown, and Ghaneian found that recall was significantly higher when the learning and testing state was the same than when it was different (see Figure 14.3).

The internal state experienced during training is one attribute of memory. Although a change in internal state can lead to retrieval failure, in some circumstances forgetting does not occur despite a change in internal state. For example, although intoxicated people do forget some events, they can clearly remember others. The attribute model of memory suggests that the presence of other memory attributes can lead to retrieval, despite the change in internal state.

Eich, Weingartner, Stillman, and Gillin (1975) demonstrated that a change in internal state does not always lead to forgetting. With the permission of appropriate government agencies, subjects smoked either a marijuana cigarette (drug condition) or a cigarette with the active ingredient THC removed (nondrug condition). Some subjects smoked the marijuana 20 minutes before learning a list of words and again before testing 4 hours after training. Other subjects were given the marijuana prior to training and the nondrug before testing; still other subjects received the nondrug before training and the marijuana before testing. A final group of subjects smoked the nondrug before both training and testing. Eich, Weingartner, Stillman, and Gillin evaluated the influence of marijuana by measuring heart rate (marijuana increases heart rate) and the subjective experience of being "high." They found that compared with the nondrug condition, marijuana produced a strong physiological and psychological effect.

The researchers tested half of the subjects using a free-recall task; the other half using category names of the words given in training as retrieval cues. In the free-recall testing, the subjects showed state-dependent learning; they remembered more words when the same

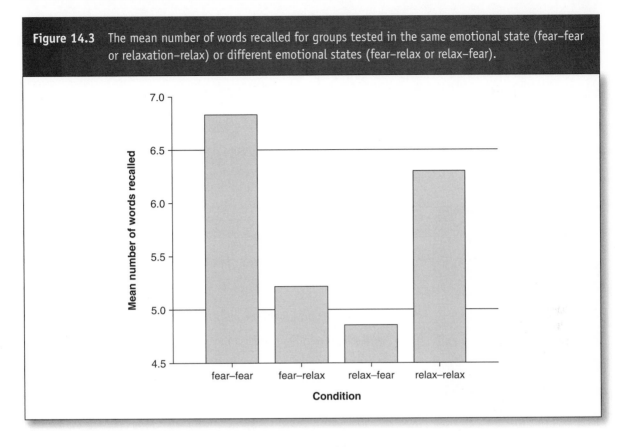

Figure 14.3   The mean number of words recalled for groups tested in the same emotional state (fear–fear or relaxation–relax) or different emotional states (fear–relax or relax–fear).

state was present during both training and testing than when the states differed (see Table 14.1). This lower recall on the free-recall test was observed whether the subjects were in a drug state during training and a nondrug state in testing or in a nondrug state during training and a drug state during testing. In contrast to the state-dependent effects with the free-recall test, subjects receiving the cued-recall test did not demonstrate state-dependent effects. When the subjects received the category words at testing, they showed a high level of recall in all four treatment conditions.

Why didn't a change in internal state cause the subjects to forget the words in the cued-recall testing procedure? Eich (1980) suggested that people typically rely on external cues. If these cues

Table 14.1   Retention of Response as a Function of Training and Testing Conditions

Training	Testing	
	Drug	**No Drug**
Drug	Good retention	Poor retention
No drug	Poor retention	Good retention

Note: The high level of retention occurred in the groups experiencing the same conditions during both training and testing.

are unavailable, they will use subtle cues associated with their physiological or mental state to retrieve memories. The cued-recall procedure provided verbal cues that eliminated the need to use internal retrieval cues for recall.

BEFORE YOU GO ON

- Can Steve remember his first date in high school? If so, why?
- What memory attribute(s) might allow him to remember that date?

SECTION REVIEW

- According to Underwood, a memory contains a collection of different types of information, called memory attributes.
- The time that at an event occurred is recorded in the temporal attribute.
- When one aspect of an event is reexperienced, the attribute of that event prompts the recall of the entire memory.
- The background in which an event took place is stored in the context attribute.
- An internal state that may either be natural reactions to the event or drug-induced can be an affective attribute.

**Hermann Ebbinghaus
(1850–1909)**

Ebbinghaus received his doctorate in philosophy from the University of Bonn, Germany. After obtaining his doctorate, he spent several years teaching in England. He became interested in psychology after reading Gustav's Fechner's *Elements of Psychophysics*. He published his most famous work *Memory: A Contribution to Experimental Psychology* in 1885, the year he joined the faculty of the University of Berlin, where he taught for 9 years. He later taught at the University of Breslau, Poland, for 15 years. His pioneering research on memory provided a procedure for objectively studying higher mental processes. He published a successful elementary psychology text shortly before he died from pneumonia at the age of 59.

FORGETTING

How Quickly We Forget

Left to itself every mental content gradually loses its capacity for being retrieved, or at least suffers loss in this regard under the influence of time. Facts crammed at examination time soon vanish, if they were not sufficiently grounded by other study and later subjected to sufficient review. (Ebbinghaus, 1885, p. 4)

This quote characterizes Hermann Ebbinghaus's view of forgetting. His work contributed to our current attention to the **forgetting** of past events. Our discussion of forgetting begins with a description of his research.

Ebbinghaus (1885) conducted an extensive study of memory, using himself as the only subject, in the latter part of the nineteenth century. To study memory, Ebbinghaus invented the nonsense syllable—two consonants separated by a vowel (e.g., *baf* or *xof*). He memorized relatively meaningless nonsense syllables because he felt that these verbal units would be uncontaminated by his prior experience. He assumed that any difference in the recall of specific nonsense syllables would be due to forgetting and not to differential familiarity with the nonsense syllables.

After memorizing a list of 10 to 12 nonsense syllables, Ebbinghaus relearned the list of non-sense syllables. (In Ebbinghaus's study, savings, the number of trials to learn the list minus the number of trials to relearn the lists, was used to indicate how much of the list was retained, with the greater the savings, the higher the recall.) He memorized over 150 lists of nonsense syllables at various retention intervals. As Figure 14.4 shows, Ebbinghaus forgot almost half of a prior list after 24 hours, and 6 days later recalled only one-fourth of the prior learning. Ebbinghaus's results show a rapid forgetting following acquisition of a list of nonsense syllables.

Why did Ebbinghaus forget so much of his prior learning? Psychologists have proposed three theories to explain why we forget previous experiences. First, some psychologists (McGeoch, 1932) have suggested that memories decay, a view which assumes that memory is lost through disuse; that is, memories that are not recalled will not survive. Second, some have proposed that interference among memories causes forgetting (McGeoch, 1932; Underwood, 1957). **Interference** refers to the inability to recall a specific event as the result of having experienced another event. The third theory is that the absence of a specific stimulus can lead to forgetting (Underwood, 1969, 1983). This view holds that a memory contains a collection of different types of information, and each type of information is an attribute of the memory. The retrieval of a memory depends on the presence of the stimulus contained in the memory attribute.

Figure 14.4 Percentage of prior learning retained as a function of the interval between training and testing. Ebbinghaus found that the recall of nonsense syllables declined rapidly as the interval between training and testing increased.

Decay of a Memory

It is generally assumed that specific physical changes take place when an event is experienced (see Chapter 13). The **engram,** or physical representation of an event, enables a person to recall the experience at a later time. A few psychologists (McGeoch, 1932) have proposed that the engram fades with disuse; that is, the physiological changes that took place during learning and that represent the record of the experience will diminish unless the memory is retrieved from time to time. Retrieval may prevent decay or strengthen a decaying memory.

In a classic study, J. G. Jenkins and Dallenbach (1924) evaluated the **decay view of forgetting** by teaching subjects a list of nonsense syllables to a criterion of one trial without errors. The retention of the nonsense syllables was evaluated 1, 2, 4, or 8 hours later. Half the subjects spent their retention interval awake; the other half of the subjects slept during the interval. If the decay view is accurate and the time between learning and recall determines the level of forgetting, an equal amount of forgetting should occur regardless of whether the subjects were asleep or awake during the retention interval. As Figure 14.5 shows, subjects who were awake actually forgot more than those asleep during the retention interval, suggesting that activities occurring while the subjects were awake contributed to the amount of forgetting.

Note that subjects who slept during the interval still forgot a considerable amount during that time. Is this forgetting the result of decay? According to Underwood (1957), the methods J. G. Jenkins and Dallenbach (1924) employed were inadequate by contemporary standards. In addition, Jenkins and Dallenbach's subjects had been in other studies; this previous participation may have produced high levels of interference, which in turn may have caused the forgetting evident in the asleep condition.

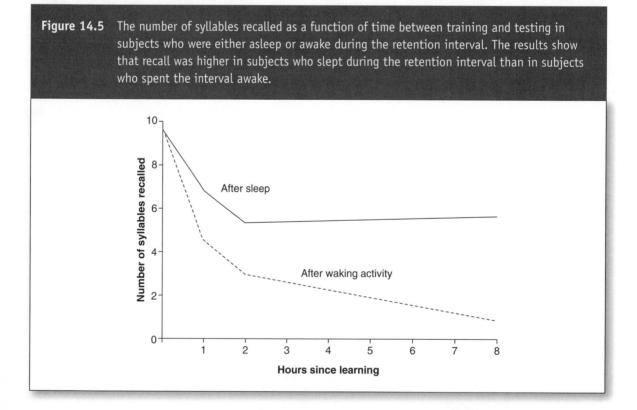

Figure 14.5 The number of syllables recalled as a function of time between training and testing in subjects who were either asleep or awake during the retention interval. The results show that recall was higher in subjects who slept during the retention interval than in subjects who spent the interval awake.

Conducting a more controlled investigation of the effects of sleep on retention, Ekstrand (1967) used subjects who had not experienced prior paired-associate tasks. One group of subjects slept during the 8-hour retention interval after learning a list of paired associates; the other group was awake during the retention interval. Ekstrand observed that subjects in the awake condition forgot 23% of the paired associates, whereas subjects in the sleep condition forgot only 11%. These observations suggest that interference, which resulted from prior experience with paired associates, caused much of the forgetting that Jenkins and Dallenbach reported in the asleep condition subjects. However, subjects in the asleep condition in the Ekstrand study did forget some material. Decay of memory may have been responsible for this forgetting. It is also feasible that extraexperimental sources of interference (interference from verbal material learned outside the laboratory) contributed to the forgetting that occurred in the asleep condition. We next examine some research supporting a decay view; we discuss interference as a cause of forgetting later in the chapter.

Rozin and Gleitman (as cited in Gleitman, 1971) used fish as their subjects and trained them to avoid shock in a shuttle box. The fish spent either a 4-week or an 8-week retention interval in either the training temperature (25°–26° C) or in a hot tank (33° C). Rozin and Gleitman reasoned that since fish are cold-blooded, heating the fish tank would accelerate their metabolic processes, thereby increasing the rate of memory decay. Rozin and Gleitman reported that the fish kept in the hot tank forgot more during the retention interval than did the fish in the training tank.

Other investigators have attempted to slow down metabolic rate to decrease the decay of memory and thereby reduce the amount of forgetting. Rensch and Ducker (1966) observed that goldfish treated with chlorpromazine, a drug that suppresses central nervous system activity, during the retention interval exhibited greater retention of a visual discrimination than did goldfish not given chlorpromazine. Ducker and Rensch (1968) observed a similar decrease in forgetting in goldfish kept in the dark during the retention interval, as did Alloway (1969) in grain beetles kept in a cold environment after training.

Gleitman (1971) points to one problem in concluding that decay is a source of forgetting. Studies evaluating the decay view have inferred that treatments such as heat or sleep affect forgetting by altering the metabolic processes that govern erosion of the memory trace. Unfortunately, no study has proved that this relationship exists; thus, decay remains only a possible source of forgetting. In contrast, considerable evidence indicates that interference is a cause of forgetting.

Interference

You are warmly greeted by someone who looks familiar, and you respond, "Hello, Bill." Unfortunately, the man's name is not Bill, but Sam. Why did you incorrectly apply the wrong name to the familiar face? Interference is one possible cause.

There are two types of interference: proactive and retroactive. **Proactive interference** (PI) involves an inability to recall recent experiences because of the memory of earlier experiences. For example, a group of subjects learns one list of paired associates (A-B list) and then learns a second list of paired associates (A-C list). (In a paired-associates learning task, subjects are presented with a list of stimuli and responses. The list usually consists of 10 to 15 pairs, and subjects are required to learn the correct response to each stimulus. In some cases, the associates are nonsense syllables; in other cases, they are words. An example of one set of pairs would be the words *book* and *shoe* in the A-B list and *book* and *window* in the A-C list.) When subjects are asked to recall the associates from the second list, they are unable to do so because the memory of the first list interferes. How do we know that these subjects would not have forgotten the response to the second list even if they had not learned the first? To show that it is the memory of the first list that caused the forgetting of the second list, a control group of subjects learned only the second list (see Table 14.2 to compare the treatments given to experimental and control subjects). Any poorer recall of the second list by the experimental subjects as compared to the control subjects is assumed to reflect proactive interference. Returning to our incorrect naming example, you may have known someone named Bill in the past who looked like the more recently met Sam. The memory of the facial attributes associated with Bill caused you to identify Sam as Bill.

Table 14.2 Design of a Proactive Interference Study			
Group	**Stage of Experiment**		
	I	**II**	**III**
Experimental	Learn first materials	Learn materials to be remembered	Test for recall
Control	Unrelated activity	Learn materials to be remembered	Test for recall

Retroactive interference (RI) occurs when people cannot remember distant events because the memory of more recent events intervenes. Retroactive interference can be observed with the following paradigm: Experimental subjects learn two lists of paired associates (A-B, A-C) and then take a retention test that asks them to recall the responses from the first list. The retention of the first list of responses among experimental subjects is compared with the retention of the list among a control group required to learn only the first list (see Table 14.3 to see the treatments given to the experimental and control subjects). If the recall of the first list is poorer for experimental subjects than for the control group subjects, retroactive interference is the likely cause of the difference. The incorrect naming of Sam as Bill could also have been due to retroactive interference. You could have recently met a man named Bill, and the memory of the facial characteristics associated with Bill caused you to be unable to name longtime acquaintance Sam.

Table 14.3 Design of a Retroactive Interference Study			
Group	**Stage of Experiment**		
	I	**II**	**III**
Experimental	Learn materials to be remembered	Learn new materials	Test for recall
Control	Learn materials to be remembered	Unrelated activity	Test for recall

Why does interference occur? We examine two theories for interference next.

Underwood's List Differentiation View

Underwood (1983) suggested that interference is caused by a failure of list (or task) differentiation. According to Underwood, subjects do remember responses from both lists but are unable to remember with which list a particular response was associated. Thus, subjects asked to recall the response learned from the first list can remember the response from both lists, but will appear to have forgotten them because the subjects cannot remember which response came from the first list. A considerable amount of research indicates that the failure of **list differentiation** is a source of forgetting. Let's briefly look at the evidence.

Underwood (1983) has found that subjects who learned one task in one environment and another task in a different environment do not display interference. According to Underwood, learning in different environments enables subjects to differentiate between memories. Although responses from the two lists are still in associative competition, interference will not occur because the subjects are able to differentiate between the two lists.

According to Underwood (1983), any treatment that increases the distinctiveness of memories will reduce the level of interference. We know that interference is reduced when the distribution of practice on the first list differs from that of the second list (Underwood & Ekstrand, 1966). Furthermore, Underwood and Freund (1968) observed less interference when 3 days separated learning of the original list and interpolated list learning, even when the two lists were acquired with the same distribution of practice. Underwood argued that each of these treatments (different distributions of practice, different times, and different environments) increased the distinctiveness of the memories, and this increased list differentiation was responsible for the reduced interference.

Postman's Generalized Competition View

Barnes and Underwood (1959) noted that the level of proactive interference (PI) increases following interpolated list learning, whereas the amount of retroactive interference (RI) declines. Postman and his associates (Postman, 1967; Postman, Stark, & Fraser, 1968) suggested that **generalized competition** is responsible for both an inability to recall first-list responses as the second list is acquired and the changes in interference after interpolated-list learning.

According to Postman (1967), generalized competition is a "set" or disposition to continue to respond in the manner learned most recently. A selector mechanism excludes from subjects' response repertoire all responses except those being learned. It is this selector mechanism that prevents a subject from being able to remember original-list responses. Postman suggested that following interpolated-list acquisition, the set to respond dissipates, or generalized competition declines; the reduced disposition to respond according to recency is responsible for the increased PI and decreased RI. Throughout the text, we have seen that recency plays an important role in determining behavior. Postman's generalized competition proposes a mechanism that ensures that recency will have a significant impact on behavior.

BEFORE YOU GO ON

- Could interference cause Steve to forget that his grandmother sometimes went to the baseball games?

- Might decay be an alternate explanation for forgetting that his grandmother went?

SECTION REVIEW

- Memories decay with the physiological changes that took place during memory formation and is one cause of forgetting.

- Proactive interference (PI) is the inability to recall recent events because of the memory of a past experience.

- Retroactive interference (RI) is the inability to remember distant events because of the memory of recent events.

- The failure to distinguish memories is one cause of interference.

- Generalized competition, a "set" to respond in the manner most recently learned, is another source of interference.

Reconstruction of the Past

How accurate is a person's recollection of an experience? Recall the chapter-opening vignette where Steve was reminiscing about going to Coney Island and eating Nathan's hot dogs. Does he really remember going? Or recall being told about going? We next discuss whether memories always are accurate recollections of the past.

Sir Fredrick Bartlett (1932) argued that a memory of an experience is often inaccurate. Sometimes details of an event are forgotten, creating an imperfect memory. To create a logical and realistic experience, people may add information to the memory during recall. Or for an experience to make sense to an individual, some information will be deleted or new information added. The alteration of a memory to be consistent with the individual's view of the world is called **memory reconstruction**. Bartlett first studied this memory reconstruction process many years ago.

Memory Reconstruction Studies

Bartlett (1932) examined the alteration of a memory during recall. In one of his classic studies, he had subjects read the folktale "The War of the Ghosts." This story contains a number of details about the experiences and eventual death of a warrior who was engaged in combat with ghosts (see Figure 14.6). The students were tested for recall of the story immediately after reading it and then several hours or days later. Bartlett noted that the subjects' memory of the stories, when tested at both time intervals, often differed from the original story. He found that some aspects of the stories were deleted; some were overemphasized; and in other cases, new information was added. According to Bartlett, the content and structure of the folktale was quite different from actual events that the subjects had experienced. Because of their unfamiliarity with the story, the subjects reconstructed their memory of it to be more consistent with their own cultural expectations. An example of a reconstructed story also appears in Figure 14.6.

To demonstrate how extensively a memory can be altered by reconstruction, Bartlett presented a figure to a subject, and then told the subject to reproduce it for a second subject. In some cases, the transmission of information continued through 10 subjects. Bartlett noted that not only did the final drawing differ from the original, but the changes were quite extensive. Also, the figure changed from subject to subject. Figure 14.7 on page 402 shows the change in each subject's recollection of the figure presented.

Bartlett's (1932) research suggests that we reconstruct memories based on inferences of what "must have happened." A study conducted by Brewer and Treyens (1981) demonstrates the inferential quality of memory reconstruction. In their study, their subjects waited in a room prior to participating in an "active study." After leaving, subjects were asked to describe the waiting room. In addition to indicating that the waiting room contained a desk, chair, and walls, a third of the subjects said that a bookcase was in the room, which was untrue. For these subjects, a bookcase "should" have been in the room, and they "remembered" it having been there.

Some memories may, in fact, reflect what actually happened. However, according to Maki (1990), when an event seems confusing or contains irrelevant details, people reconstruct the

Figure 14.6 Bartlett had subjects read stories such as "The War of the Ghosts." Subject recollections of these stories varied significantly from the original tales. An example of a reconstructed version appears here.

The War of the Ghosts

Original story

One night two young men from Egulac went down to the river to hunt seals, and while they were there it became foggy and calm. Then they heard warcries, and they thought: "Maybe this is a war-party." They escaped to the shore, and hid behind a log. Now canoes came up, and they heard the noise of paddles, and saw one canoe coming up to them. There were five men in the canoe, and they said:

"What do you think? We wish to take you along. We are going up the river to make war on the people." One of the young men said: "I have no arrows."

"Arrows are in the canoe," they said.

"I will not go along. I might be killed. My relatives do not know where I have gone. But you," he said, turning to the other, "may go with them."

So one of the young men went, but the other returned home.

And the warriors went on up the river to a town on the other side of Kalama. The people came down to the water, and they began to fight, and many were killed. But presently the young man heard one of the warriors say: "Quick, let us go home; that Indian has been hit." Now he thought: "Oh, they are ghosts." He did not feel sick, but they said he had been shot.

So the canoes went back to Egulac, and the young man went ashore to his house and made a fire. And he told everybody and said: "Behold I accompanied the ghosts, and we went to fight. Many of our fellows were killed, and many of those who attacked us were killed. They said I was hit, and I did not feel sick."

He told it all, and then he became quiet. When the sun rose he fell down. Something black came out of his mouth. His face became contorted. The people jumped up and cried.

He was dead.

Remembered story

Two men from Edulac went fishing. While thus occupied by the river they heard a noise in the distance. "It sounds like a cry," said one, and presently there appeared some in canoes who invited them to join the party on their adventure. One of the young men refused to go, on the ground of family ties, but the other offered to go.

"But there are no arrows," he said.

"The arrows are in the boat," was the reply.

He thereupon took his place, while his friend returned home. The party paddled up the river to Kaloma, and began to land on the banks of the river. The enemy came rushing upon them, and some sharp fighting ensued. Presently someone was injured, and the cry was raised that the enemy were ghosts.

The party returned down the stream, and the young man arrived home feeling none the worse for his experience. The next morning at dawn he endeavored to recount his adventures. While he was talking, something black issued from his mouth. Suddenly he uttered a cry and fell down. His friends gathered around him.

But he was dead.

memory to conform to what "must have happened." In contrast, when the event is easily understood or is distinctive or surprising, the memory will be what actually happened.

Can information received from others influence our recollections of the past? We next turn our attention to this question.

Figure 14.7   Subject 1 was shown the original drawing and asked to reproduce it after half an hour. The reproduction of the original drawing was shown to Subject 2, whose reproduction was presented to Subject 3, and so on through Subject 10. This figure presents the original drawing and the 10 reproductions. Note that the drawing changes with each successive reproduction.

Original drawing   Reproduction 1   Reproduction 2   Reproduction 3   Reproduction 4

Reproduction 5   Reproduction 6   Reproduction 7   Reproduction 8   Reproduction 9   Reproduction 10

The Accuracy of Eyewitness Testimony

Elizabeth Loftus and her colleagues (Laney & Loftus, 2009; Loftus, 1992, 2005; D. B. Wright & Loftus, 2008) recognized a significant relationship between the memory reconstruction process and the accuracy of eyewitness testimony. According to Loftus, trial witnesses recall what they think they saw or heard. The literature on memory reconstruction suggests that their recollections may not always be accurate. In all likelihood, the incident they are recalling occurred months or years earlier, and the witnesses may have forgotten some aspects of the event. To create a logical and realistic account, the witnesses will fill in information consistent with the aspects they actually remember.

Loftus (Laney & Loftus, 2009; Loftus, 1992, 2005; D. B. Wright & Loftus, 2008) contends that information received from others can also alter a memory. Because of this information, the memory of the past event is inaccurate, and the memory subsequently changes to conform to the information received from other people. Consider Loftus's 1975 study to illustrate this process. In her study, subjects first were shown a series of slides showing a red sports car headed for a collision. Two groups of subjects saw the same sequence of slides, except for one difference: Some subjects saw the car approaching a stop sign, while the other subjects saw a yield sign in the slide (see Figure 14.8 on page 404). After seeing the slides, the subjects were asked a series of questions about the accident. One question was, "Did you see the stop sign?" For half of these subjects, this question was consistent with the slides; that is, they actually saw the stop sign. For the other subjects, this question was inconsistent with their experiences because they did not see a stop sign. The other half of the subjects were asked, "Did you see the yield sign?"

Elizabeth Loftus (1944–   )

Loftus received her doctorate from Stanford University under Patrick Suppes. She taught at the University of Washington for 29 years and at the University of California, Irvine, for 8 years. Her work has contributed significantly to the understanding of the accuracy of eyewitness testimony and the memory reconstruction process. She was president of the American-Psychology Law Society in 1984 and the Society for Psychological Science in 1998. She received the Distinguished Contributions to Forensic Psychology Award from the American Academy of Forensic Psychology in 1995, the William James Fellow Award from the American Psychological Society in 2001, and Distinguished Scientific Contribution for the Applications of Psychology Award from the American Psychological Association in 2003.

A week later, all subjects were asked to recall the accident. Testing involved showing subjects pairs of slides and then asking them to identify which slide they actually saw. Loftus (1975) reported that subjects who were asked the question consistent with their actual experience correctly identified the actual slide that they had seen 75% of the time. Subjects who were asked the inconsistent question identified the correct slide only 40% of the time.

Why did the inconsistent question cause many subjects to think that the other sign was actually in the scene? According to Loftus (1975), the wording of the question implied that the other sign was present during the accident, and thus the subjects altered their memories of the accident to include the unseen sign. These results show that information received during recall can alter a memory.

The results of Loftus's study have special relevance to the reliability of eyewitness testimony. They demonstrate that a clever attorney may be able to change a witness's memory of a crime by asking leading questions, thereby altering the outcome of a trial. Other psychologists (Holliday, Reyna, & Hayes, 2002; Zaragoza, Belli, & Payment, 2007) have also found that a suggestion can alter the content of memory.

Does the memory reconstruction process permanently change the memory? The evidence (Zaragoza, McCloskey, & Jamis, 1987) suggests that the original memory still exists, but the person is uncertain whether the original or the reconstructed memory is accurate. Research on eyewitness testimony (Chandler, 1991; Schooler, Gerhard, & Loftus, 1986) also indicates that an individual witnessing an accident and then receiving misleading information cannot discriminate between the real and suggested events.

False Memory Syndrome

A depressed young woman seeks psychological help. Her therapist, discussing her past, comes to believe that her depression is caused by sexual abuse that occurred during her childhood. The therapist suggests that the depression is a result of her father's sexual abuse. The woman at first denies that she was abused, but the therapist keeps questioning her about childhood experiences. After a while, the woman begins to remember experiences of being sexually abused by her father. The therapist explains that she has repressed these painful memories and that therapy has allowed her to recall them. The young woman stops seeing and talking to her father and publicly accuses him of sexual abuse. The father is arrested and imprisoned. Has justice been served?

The vignette just described could be any one of many **repressed memory** cases that have led to litigation over the last several decades. Literally hundreds of lawsuits have been filed by adults who claim to have been victimized as children by parents, teachers, and neighbors. The legal system has often found these claims to be valid (Toufexis, 1991). For example, in 1991 a woman won $1.4 million from a church-run school in Washington. She claimed to have been repeatedly raped by a teacher at the school, to have repressed her memory of the rapes, and two decades later to have remembered the incidents. In the same year, a woman in Ohio won a $5 million settlement from her uncle, whom she claimed had sexually abused her as a child.

Figure 14.8 Did you see the stop sign? The top photo shows the car approaching a yield sign, while the bottom depicts the car approaching a stop sign. Subjects who saw the top slide sometimes altered their memories, believing they had seen the bottom one.

Can a person repress painful memories and then recall them many years later? Many psychologists (Briere & Conte, 1993; Whitfield, 1995) believe that individuals can repress the memory of extremely painful childhood experiences, even if the abuse is long lasting. It is assumed that these events are buried in the person's unconscious and are revealed only through the process of therapy. While the publicity over repressed memories suggests a real phenomenon, other psychologists (Kihlstrom, 2004; Laney & Loftus, 2005; McNally, 2003) are skeptical about the accuracy of most, if not all, of these cases.

Laney and Loftus (2005) argued that highly suggestible people with extreme emotional problems may be persuaded that their emotional problems are the result of repressed memories of sexual abuse. The therapists' suggestive questions are thought to reconstruct the patients' memories of the past and to convince the patients that they have been abused as children. In the last section, we learned that misinformation can create an inaccurate record of an event. Continued prodding by therapists could certainly create false memories of child abuse.

Perhaps one case history illustrates why many psychologists doubt the authenticity of repressed memories of sexual abuse. Loftus (1997) described a case history of a young woman who accused her minister father of sexual abuse. The woman recalled during the course of therapy with her church counselor that she was repeatedly raped by her father, who got her pregnant and then aborted the pregnancy with a coat hanger. As it turned out, subsequent evidence revealed that the woman was still a virgin and that her father had had a vasectomy years before the sexual abuse supposedly occurred.

The creation of an inaccurate record of childhood sexual abuse is now called the **false memory syndrome**. Many individuals have reported realizing that their therapists have created inaccurate memories; they then often feel that they have been victimized by their therapists. These individuals have formed a support group, called the False Memory Syndrome Foundation, to help with their recovery.

Can a suggestion create a false memory of a childhood event? Loftus, Coan, and Pickrell (1996) provided compelling evidence that it can. These researchers contacted a family member of each of the teenage subjects in their study. These family members were instructed to "remind" the subject of an incident in which the subject was lost in a shopping mall. Loftus and Coan later questioned their subjects and found that each of the subjects had created an emotionally laden memory of that event. For example, one subject, named Chris, was told by his older brother James that he had been lost in the mall when he was 5-years-old and found by a tall older man in a flannel shirt. When questioned about the incident a few days later, Chris recalled being scared, being asked by the older man whether he was lost, and being scolded later by his mother. Chris's description became even more detailed over the next few weeks when he recalled the incident in this way:

I was with you guys for a second and I think I went over to look at the toy store . . . I thought I was never going to see my family again. I was really scared, you know? And then this old man, I think he was wearing blue flannel, came up to me . . . he had like a ring of gray hair . . . he had glasses. (Loftus, Coan, & Pickrell, 1996, p. 203)

Loftus and Coan's (1994) study shows how easy it is to create a false memory. It is not hard to imagine that a therapist's suggestive questions and consistent prodding could lead a person to create a false memory of childhood abuse.

Motivated Forgetting

Sigmund Freud suggested that people can repress extremely painful memories. Repression is viewed as a process that minimizes anxiety and protects self-concept. The repressed memory is not erased, but rather is submerged in the unconscious. Painful memories that have been repressed can be retrieved during therapy.

We have learned in this chapter that people can forget previous experiences and that retrieval cues can help people access forgotten memories. Yet we have not examined whether people can deliberately forget previous experiences. Psychologists have investigated this kind of motivated forgetting using a procedure called **directed forgetting.** In this procedure, subjects are instructed to forget some information but not other information. We first describe the directed forgetting procedure and then comment again on the issue of repressed memories.

A pigeon is presented a sample stimulus; sometime later, two stimuli are presented. The pigeon is reinforced for selecting the previously viewed stimulus. With this procedure, the pigeon is on a delayed-matching-to-sample procedure. Suppose that during the interval, the pigeon is presented one of two cues: On some trials, the pigeon receives a "remember cue," while on other trials, a "forget cue" is presented. The remember cue informs the pigeon that it should remember the sample because a test will follow, and it must select the sample to receive reinforcement. The forget cue informs the pigeon that it can forget the sample because there will be no test on this trial. Will the pigeon forget the sample after receiving a forget cue? To assess directed forgetting, the pigeon receives infrequent probe trials. On a probe trial, the comparison stimuli are presented after the forget cue. A failure to respond more often to the sample than to the other stimulus presumably reflects forgetting caused by the forget cue. Figure 14.9 presents a diagram of the directed forgetting procedure.

Research (Maki & Hegvik, 1980; Stonebraker & Rilling, 1981) has consistently reported that a pigeon's performance is significantly impaired following a forget cue when compared to performance following a remember cue. In other words, the pigeon is more likely to select the sample than the other stimulus after a remember cue than following a forget cue. Directed forgetting has also been observed using the delayed-matching-to-sample procedure in primates (Roberts, Mazmanian, & Kraemer, 1984).

Studies have also investigated directed forgetting in humans (Bjork, 1989; Geiselman, Bjork, & Fishman, 1983). Directed forgetting studies with humans involve the use of either a recall measure, in which subjects are required to name either to-be-forgotten or to-be-remembered items, or a recognition task, in which subjects are merely asked to indicate whether an item has been presented. Some studies (Elmes, Adams, & Roediger, 1970; Geiselman, Bjork, & Fishman, 1983) have compared recall versus recognition measures of directed forgetting and have found that directed forgetting occurs with recall but not with recognition. This suggests that retrieval failure causes directed forgetting, because recognition but not recall would provide a retrieval cue to prevent forgetting. However, other studies (Archer & Margolin, 1970; J. C. Davis & Okada, 1971)

Figure 14.9   A diagram showing the procedure used in a directed forgetting study. During training, the pigeon sees a specific stimulus, followed by either a "remember cue" (r) or a "forget cue" (f) and then two sample stimuli. During testing, the pigeon is presented the stimulus and the sample after the forget cue to determine if the pigeon has forgotten the previously presented stimulus.

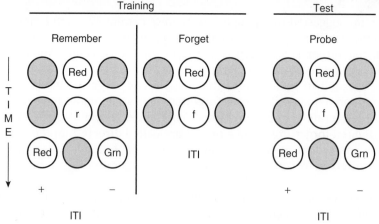

have observed directed forgetting with recognition tests, a result that points to encoding failure as a cause of directed forgetting.

What causes directed forgetting? Researchers have proposed several theories (Roper & Zentall, 1993). One theory argues that the forget cue stops the rehearsal process and thereby prevents memory elaboration. A second view, introduced previously, holds that retrieval, rather than elaboration failure, causes forgetting. According to the retrieval explanation, the memory of the sample is available, but the forget cue is a poor retrieval cue, while the remember cue is an effective retrieval cue. Many studies have attempted to evaluate the rehearsal versus retrieval theories, but they have not provided conclusive evidence for either theory (see Roper & Zentall, 1993, for a complete discussion of this issue).

We have learned that humans and animals can be directed to forget experiences. Whether people can initiate their own forgetting remains to be documented. The concept of repression requires willful forgetting of disturbing information. No convincing evidence has yet been offered that humans can repress such information for years and then remember it accurately (Holmes, 1990). In fact, most extremely negative experiences are remembered well. For example, Helmreich (1992) reported that Holocaust survivors have vivid memories of their experiences. Similarly, Malmquist (1986) found that in a group of 5- to 10-year-old children who witnessed a parent's murder, not one of the children repressed this memory. Instead, all of the children were haunted by the memory of the murder.

Can a person repress the memory of abuse and than recall it many years later? Directed memory studies suggest that voluntary processes can cause forgetting. Furthermore, retrieval cues can lead the person to recall previously forgotten information. These two findings suggest that people can repress disturbing memories and then recall them much later. Yet, extremely emotional experiences appear to be remembered, not forgotten, and memories can easily be altered at the time of retrieval. Whether repressed memories of abuse actually exist awaits future verification.

ANATOMICAL BASIS OF MEMORY RETRIEVAL

In Chapter 13, we learned that several brain areas, including the temporal lobe, the hippocampus, and the dorsomedial thalamus, are involved in memory storage. Several psychologists (Malamut, Saunders, & Mishkin, 1984; Warrington, 1985; Zola-Morgan & Squire, 1986) have suggested that damage to the hippocampus also can lead to an inability to recall past events. We next examine evidence that amnesia is caused by retrieval failure and then look at studies showing that hippocampal damage can lead to difficulty retrieving stored information.

Warrington and Weiskrantz (Warrington & Weiskrantz, 1968, 1970; Weiskrantz & Warrington, 1975) conducted a number of studies comparing the memories of amnesics with the memories of individuals who were able to recall prior events. In one study (refer to Warrington & Weiskrantz, 1968), human subjects were given a list of words to remember. The amnesics were unable to remember the words even after several repetitions; however, Warrington and Weiskrantz noted that as the amnesics had been given several lists, they began to give responses from earlier lists. In contrast, fewer prior-list intrusions were observed in nonamnesic subjects. These results indicate that the amnesics had stored the responses from earlier lists but were unable to retrieve the appropriate responses. These observations further suggest that amnesics are more susceptible to interference than are nonamnesics and that interference was responsible for the higher level of retrieval failure in amnesic subjects.

Further evidence that amnesic patients suffer from a retrieval deficit comes from Warrington and Weiskrantz's 1970 study. They used three testing procedures: recall, recognition, and fragmented words. With the recall procedure, subjects were asked to recall as many words as they could from a previously learned list. With the recognition procedure, subjects were asked to identify the words they had previously learned from an equal number of alternative words. With the fragmented words procedure, subjects were presented five-letter words in a partial form by omitting two or three of the letters. As Figure 14.10 shows, the percentage of correct responses for both amnesic and nonamnesic subjects was greater for the recognition than for the recall procedure. Further, the level of recall was equal for the amnesic and nonamnesic subjects with the fragmented words procedure. These results indicate that the amnesic subjects had stored the words but were unable to retrieve them on the recall test. According to Warrington and Weiskrantz, the recognition and fragmented word treatments provided the subjects with the cues they needed for retrieval and, therefore, enabled the amnesics to remember the words. Other studies by Weiskrantz and Warrington (1975) also showed that providing cues to amnesics at the time of testing significantly increased recall.

Our discussion suggests that retrieval failure caused the memory deficits of the amnesic subjects in Warrington and Weiskrantz's studies. Let's examine evidence that this retrieval failure results from hippocampal damage (see Squire, 1987, for a review of this literature).

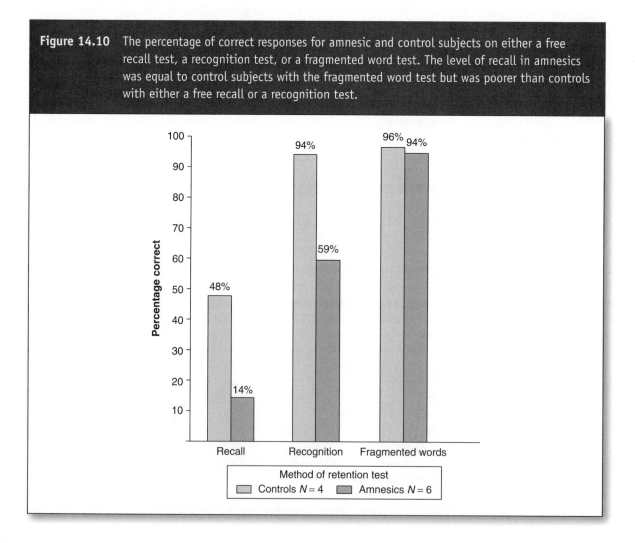

Figure 14.10 The percentage of correct responses for amnesic and control subjects on either a free recall test, a recognition test, or a fragmented word test. The level of recall in amnesics was equal to control subjects with the fragmented word test but was poorer than controls with either a free recall or a recognition test.

Malamut, Saunders, and Mishkin (1984) evaluated the effect of damage to the hippocampus on the retention of a visual discrimination task in monkeys. They found that primates with hippocampal lesions required significantly more trials to relearn the task than did nonlesioned animals. In fact, hippocampal-lesioned animals required almost as many trials to relearn the task as they did to learn the task during original training. Also, Zola-Morgan and Squire (1986) found that destruction of the hippocampus produced poor recall on a matching-to-sample task. Lesions did not affect learning but did disrupt recall of a response. These observations show that the hippocampus plays an important role in the retrieval of memories.

Zola-Morgan and Squire (1993) suggested that memories are stored by the medial temporal lobe and mediodorsal thalamus. Memories are retrieved by the hippocampus, and projections from the hippocampus to the frontal lobes provide a "route by which recollections are translated into action" (p. 557). The frontal lobes serve an important function in guiding behavior, and information from memory stores is critical to the effective functioning of the frontal lobes. The projections from the hippocampus to the frontal lobes enable us to remember the past and to use our memories to perform effectively in the present.

Recall that we learned earlier that animals and humans can be motivated to forget specific events. Michael Anderson and his colleagues (M. C. Anderson & Levy, 2006; M. C. Anderson et al., 2004) proposed that the hippocampus is activated when memories are retrieved and suppressed when unwanted memories are suppressed. M. C. Anderson et al. (2004) used a "think/nonthink" paradigm to investigate the role of the hippocampus in motivated forgetting. Subjects were instructed to recall certain stimuli on think trials, but not recall other stimuli on nonthink trials. These researchers observed that recall of stimuli was significantly higher on think than nonthink trials. They also found that the hippocampus was activated when subjects recalled a stimulus on think trials, but hippocampal activation was suppressed with stimuli were not recalled on nonthink trials.

M. C. Anderson and Levy (2009) suggested that the lateral prefrontal cortex allows for motivated forgetting by inhibiting the activity of the hippocampus on nonthink trials. These researchers found that there were individual differences in the amount of motivated forgetting; that is, some subjects are more able to forget specific stimuli on nonthink trials. Further, they found that subjects who were able to suppress unwanted memories showed significantly greater activation of the lateral prefrontal cortex than did subjects who were less able to forget previously experienced events (see Figure 14.11). As the prefrontal cortex is the executive area of the brain controlling cognitive functions (S. B. Klein & Thorne, 2007), it is not surprising that the lateral prefrontal cortex is active during motivated forgetting and is able to suppress the recall of unwanted memories by inhibiting the hippocampus.

Let's return to Steve introduced in the chapter-opening vignette. Activation of the hippocampus allows Steve to recall eating hot dogs at Coney Island with his grandfather, while inhibition of the hippocampus produced by activation of the lateral prefrontal cortex enables him to forget getting sick after eating a whole pizza at a baseball game.

APPLICATION: MNEMONICS

When my middle son was in high school, he requested that I ask him some questions for his science test. One question required him to list five items. As he recalled the list to me, it was evident that he had a system for remembering the list. He had memorized the first letter of each item and was using these letters to recall each item on the list. Although he was unaware of it, he was using a **mnemonic technique** to recall the list of items. People often unknowingly use mnemonic techniques to increase recall. For example, medical students trying to remember the bones in a

Figure 14.11 The percentage recalled for nonthink trials in a motivated forgetting task as a function of the degree of suppression of the hippocampus by the lateral prefrontal cortex. The greater the activity of the lateral prefrontal cortex, the greater the suppression of the hippocampus and the less recalled of nonthink stimuli.

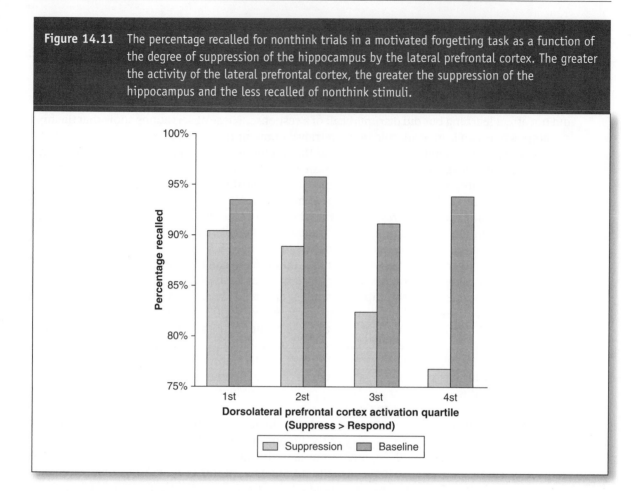

person's hand often use a mnemonic device; they take the first letter of each bone, construct a word from the letters, and use the word to recall the bones when taking a test. Other examples of mnemonics used in everyday life are "homes" for the Great Lakes (Huron, Ontario, Michigan, Erie, Superior) and "Roy G Biv" for the colors of the spectrum (red, orange, yellow, green, blue, indigo, violet).

You may have noted that the cases just described are examples of the coding process detailed in Chapter 13. Your observation is accurate. There is nothing mystical about mnemonics. Mnemonic techniques merely use the short-term store efficiently. There are a number of these techniques, each with the ability to take unorganized material and store it in a meaningful way.

The remainder of this chapter discusses several mnemonic techniques. Students in my classes using these techniques have found them an effective means of enhancing recall. Because this chapter provides only a brief discussion, interested readers should refer to *The Memory Book* by Lorayne and Lucas (2000) to master the use of mnemonics.

Method of Loci

Suppose you need to give a memorized speech in one of your classes. Trying to remember the words by rote memorization would be a time-consuming process, and you would be likely to make many mistakes. Instead, the **method of loci** is one mnemonic technique you might use to recall the speech. This method, which the Greeks developed to memorize speeches, first involves establishing an ordered series of known locations. For example, the person can take "a mental walk" through his or her home, entering the house through the living room, and so on. The individual would then separate the speech into several key thoughts, associating the key thoughts in the order corresponding to the walk through the house.

The method of loci can be used to remember any list, in either a specific or a random order. For example, you need to buy six items at the grocery store (see Figure 14.12). You could write the items on a piece of paper or use the method of loci to remember them. Perhaps one item you need is dog food. You could associate a container of dog food with your living room. Using this method to recall lists of items will help you improve your memory and will document the power of mnemonic techniques.

Remembering Names

Why do many people have such a hard time remembering other people's names? To recall a name, an individual must associate the person with his or her name, store this association, and then be able to retrieve the person's name. The main problem with remembering a person's name is that the association of a person's name with that individual is a difficult one to form. As is true with many recall problems, the association will eventually be formed with enough

Figure 14.12   A mental trip through the house provides an illustration of how one could use the method of loci to remember a shopping list of six items: butter, bread, flour, thumbtacks, sugar, and dog food. This method involves associating the mental image of the item with a familiar place, such as a room in your house.

repetition and, therefore, eventually will be recalled. Mnemonics offer a technique for enhancing the association between a name and a person; the enhanced storage of this association enables a person to recall a name after a single experience.

Lorayne and Lucas (2000) provided many examples of the use of mnemonics to recall people's names. Let's examine several of them. Suppose that you meet a person named Bill Gordon. Perhaps Bill Gordon has very bushy eyebrows. Lorayne and Lucas suggest that when you first meet him, you might visualize his eyebrows as being a *garden* with dollar *bills* growing there. The mental image you form when you first meet someone and then when you see this person again will allow you to recall the person's name.

What if you meet a woman named Ms. Pukcyva? How can you possibly use the mnemonic technique to recall her name? Perhaps she has a tall hairdo; you could see hockey *pucks shivering* as they fly out of her hair. After you have formed this association, the next time you meet Ms. Pukcyva you will remember her name. It should be mentioned that practice is required before you will be able to rapidly form a mental image of a person's name and then remember the name. The more you practice, the more efficient you will become at remembering names.

Do Mnemonics Work?

Bugelski's (1968) study provides one example of the effectiveness of mnemonics. Bugelski had an experimental group learn a list of words using the "one is a bun" peg word system, and control subjects learned the list without the aid of the mnemonic technique. (The peg word system is a mnemonic technique in which items are pegged to, or associated with, certain images in a prearranged order. *One is a bun, two is a shoe, three is a tree* is one example of a peg word system.) Bugelski then asked subjects to recall specific words; for example, he asked them, "What is the seventh word?" Bugelski reported that experimental subjects recalled significantly more words than control subjects did.

Crovitz (1971) demonstrated the effectiveness of the method of loci. He had subjects learn a list of 32 words using either the method of loci or no special techniques. Crovitz reported that experimental subjects who learned the list with the method of loci recalled 26 of the words, compared to 7 words for the control subjects who did not have the benefit of this mnemonic technique. Roediger (1980) also found that the method of loci produced significantly better recall of a list of words than did a control condition, with the greatest difference in memory when the words needed to be recalled in a specific order. Further, De Beni and Pazzaglia (1995) observed that recall of words was greater when the subject generated the loci images than when the experimenter provided the images. The method of loci has even been found to improve the recall of passages of prose (Cornoldi & De Beni, 1991; Moe & De Beni, 2005). Cornoldi and De Beni (1991) found that recall using the method of loci was better when the prose was presented orally rather than read, while Moe and De Beni (2005) observed the subjected-general loci produced better recall of prose passages than did experimenter-generated loci.

Several points are important in making effective use of mnemonics. First, Kline and Groninger (1991) reported that it is especially important to create vivid mental images. For example, imagining a person throwing a cheese hat across the living room will make the method of loci more effective. Second, the individual needs to rely on a well-learned body of knowledge (Hilton, 1986). Not knowing the rooms in a house would make using the method of loci difficult. But when used appropriately, mnemonics is an effective way to improve recall. It has been proved effective in improving face–name recall in brain-damaged adults like Donald in our chapter-opening vignette (Hux, Manasse, Wright, & Snell, 2000). Mnemonic training also improved recall of numbers (Derwinger, Stigsdotter-Neely, Persson, Hill, & Backman, 2003) and words

(R. O'Hara et al., 2007) in older adults, name recall or numerical order of U.S. presidents in junior high school children with learning disabilities (Mastropieri, Scruggs, & Whedon, 1997), and recall of music history in sixth-grade children (Brigham & Brigham, 1998).

BEFORE YOU GO ON

- Could Steve alter his memories of childhood?

- Why might Steve be motivated to forget that he rode a roller coaster at Coney Island? What mechanism(s) might enable him to do so?

SECTION REVIEW

- The memory of an experience is not always accurate: Sometimes details of an event are forgotten, creating an imperfect memory.

- Misleading information can alter a person's recollection of a witnessed event.

- Some psychologists believe that individuals can repress extremely disturbing childhood memories; other psychologists argue that suggestions create a false memory of childhood experiences that did not really occur.

- Humans and animals can be directed to forget an event.

- Encoding or retrieval failure are thought to contribute to directed forgetting.

- Repression may result in voluntary forgetting, with therapy or some other process later retrieving the memory of the event.

- A recovered memory may reflect memory alteration that leads to the "remembrance" of an event that never happened.

- There are a number of mnemonic techniques and the effectiveness of each stems from an enhanced organization of information during the storage process.

CRITICAL THINKING QUESTIONS

1. Vikas is about to write down the exam date his professor just announced when the student next to him asks for a pen. When Vikas returns to writing the exam date, he can no longer remember the date and now has to ask the professor. Why did Vikas forget the date of the exam? How common is this type of forgetting? What might Vikas do to remember the date in the future?

2. Keisha had a great time at the party last night but awoke unable to recall anything that took place. Describe state-dependent learning and how it might explain Keisha's memory loss.

3. John recently suffered a stroke and now has trouble remembering recent events. He can remember an event for a brief time, but he quickly forgets it. What areas were damaged by his stroke? What are the functions of these areas, and why did damage to them cause his memory deficits?

KEY TERMS

affective attribute

decay view of forgetting

engram

forgetting

interference

memory attribute

method of loci

proactive interference (PI)

retrieval

state-dependent learning

context attribute

directed forgetting

false memory syndrome

generalized competition

list differentiation

memory reconstruction

mnemonic techniques

repressed memory

retroactive interference (RI)

temporal attribute

Glossary

Acoustic code: The transformation of visual experiences into an auditory message.

Acquired drive: An internal drive state produced when an environmental stimulus is paired with an unconditioned source of drive.

Action-specific energy: An internal force that motivates a specific action.

Active avoidance response: An overt response to a feared stimulus that prevents an aversive event.

Affective attribute: The mood state present during an event, which can serve as a memory attribute of that experience.

Affective extension of SOP theory (AESOP): Wagner's view that a UCS elicits separate affective and sensory unconditioned response sequences.

Affirmative rule: A rule that specifies that a particular attribute defines a concept.

Algorithm: A precise set of rules to solve a particular problem.

Analgesia: A reduced sensitivity to painful events.

Animal misbehavior: Operant behavior that deteriorates, rather than improves, with continued reinforcement.

Anterograde amnesia: An inability to recall events that occur after some disturbance to the brain.

Anticipatory contrast: The long-lasting change in response due to an anticipated change in the reinforcement contingency.

Anticipatory frustration response (r_F): Stimuli associated with nonreward produce a frustration state, which motivates escape from the nonrewarding environment.

Anticipatory goal response (r_G): Stimuli associated with reward produce a conditioned arousal response, which motivates an approach to the reward.

Anticipatory pain response (r_P): Stimuli associated with painful events produce a fear response, which motivates escape from the painful environment.

Anticipatory relief response (r_R): Stimuli associated with termination of an aversive event produces relief, which motivates approach behavior.

Anxious relationship: The relationship developed between a mother and her infant when the mother is indifferent to her infant.

Appetitive behavior: Instinctive or learned response motivated by action-specific energy and attracted to a sign stimulus.

Association: The linkage of two events, usually as the result of a specific experience.

Associative learning view of imprinting: The idea that attraction to the imprinting object develops because of its arousal-reducing properties.

Associative-link expectation: A representation containing knowledge of the association of two events that occur together.

Associative shifting: The transfer of a response from one stimulus to a second stimulus when the second stimulus is gradually introduced and then the first stimulus removed.

A state: The initial affective reaction to an environmental stimulus in opponent-process theory.

Asymptotic level: The maximum level of conditioning.

Atkinson-Shiffrin three-stage model: The view that an experience is sequentially stored in the sensory register, short-term store, and long-term store.

Attribute: A feature of an object or event that varies from one instance to another.

Availability heuristic: A heuristic in which problems are solved based only on the information that can be readily remembered.

Avoidance response: A behavioral response that prevents an aversive event.

Backward blocking: Reduced conditioned response to the second stimulus (CS_2) caused when two stimuli (CS_1 and CS_2) are paired with a UCS, followed by the presentation of only the first stimulus (CS_1) with the UCS.

Backward conditioning: A paradigm in which the UCS is presented and terminated prior to the CS.

Behavioral allocation view: The idea that an animal emits the minimum number of contingent responses in order to obtain the maximum number of reinforcing activities.

Behavioral autonomy: A situation in which the continued reinforcement of a specific behavior leads to the occurrence of the response despite a devalued reinforcer.

Behavioral contrast: In a two-choice discrimination task, the increase in response to S^D that occurs at the same time as responding to S^Δ declines.

Behaviorism: A school of thought that emphasizes the role of experience in determining actions.

Behavior modification: Techniques for changing behavior that rely on the use of classical conditioning or instrumental or operant conditioning principles.

Behavior-reinforcer belief: A type of declarative knowledge that causes an animal or person to perform a specific behavior in the expectation of a specific consequence.

Behavior systems approach: The idea that learning evolved as a modifier of innate behavior systems and functions to change the integration, tuning, instigation, or linkages within a particular system.

Blisspoint: The free operant level of two responses.

Blocking: The prevention of the acquisition of a CR to a second stimulus (CS_2) when two stimuli are paired with a UCS and conditioning has already occurred to the first stimulus (CS_1).

Bound morpheme: A morpheme that must be attached to a free morpheme to have meaning.

B state: The opposite affective response that the initial affective reaction, or A state, elicits in opponent-process theory.

Cathexis: The idea that the ability of deprivation states to motivate behavior transfers to the stimuli present during the deprivation state.

Causal attribution: The perceived cause of an event.

Cause and effect: When one event produces a second event.

Cellular modification theory: The view that learning permanently alters the functioning of specific neural systems.

Central executive: The process that coordinates rehearsal systems and retrieves memory from and transfers information to permanent memory.

Chunking: The combining of several units of information into a single unit.

Classical conditioning: The association of a response with an environmental event as the result of pairing that event (CS) with a biological significant event (UCS).

Clause: A group of words containing a noun phrase and a verb phrase.

Clustering: The recall of information in specific categories.

Coding: The transformation of an experience into a totally new form.

Cognition: An understanding or knowledge of the structure of the psychological environment.

Cognitive map: Spatial knowledge of the physical environment gained through experience.

Cognitive theories: The view that learning involves a recognition of when events will occur and an understanding of how to influence those events.

Comparator theory: The theory that the ability of a particular stimulus to elicit a CR depends upon a comparison of the level of conditioning to that stimulus and to other stimuli paired with the UCS.

Complex idea: The association of sensory impressions or simple ideas.

Compound schedule: A complex contingency where two or more schedules of reinforcement are combined.

Concept: A symbol that represents a class of objects or events with common characteristics.

Concurrent interference: The prevention of learning when a stimulus intervenes between the conditioned and unconditioned stimuli or when a behavior occurs between the operant response and reinforcement.

Conditional discrimination: A situation in which the availability of reinforcement to a particular stimulus depends upon the presence of a second stimulus.

Conditioned emotional response: The ability of a CS to elicit emotional reactions as a result of the association of the CS with a painful event.

Conditioned inhibition: The permanent inhibition of a specific behavior as a result of the continued failure of that response to reduce the drive state. Alternatively, a stimulus (CS_2) may develop the ability to suppress the response to another stimulus (CS_1) when the CS_1 is paired with a UCS and the CS_2 is presented without UCS.

Conditioned reflex: The acquisition of a new S-R association as a result of experience.

Conditioned response (CR): A learned reaction to a conditioned stimulus.

Conditioned stimulus (CS): A stimulus that becomes able to elicit a learned response as a result of being paired with an unconditioned stimulus.

Conditioned withdrawal response: When environmental cues associated with withdrawal produce a conditioned craving and motivation to resume drug use.

Conjunctive rule: The simultaneous presence of two or more attributes that define a concept.

Constraint: When learning occurs less rapidly or less completely than expected.

Context attribute: The context in which an event occurred, which can be a retrieval cue.

Context blocking: The idea that conditioning to the context can prevent acquisition of a conditioned response to a stimulus paired with an unconditioned stimulus in that context.

Contiguity: The temporal pairing of two events.

Contingency: The specified relationship between a specific behavior and reinforcement.

Contingency management: The use of contingent reinforcement and nonreinforcement to increase the frequency of appropriate behavior and eliminate inappropriate behaviors.

Continuity theory of discrimination learning: The idea that the development of a discrimination is a continuous and gradual acquisition of excitation to S^D and inhibition to S^Δ.

Contrapreparedness: An inability to associate a specific conditioned stimulus and a specific unconditioned stimulus despite repeated conditioning experiences.

Counterconditioning: The elimination of a conditioned response when the conditioned stimulus is paired with an opponent or antagonistic unconditioned stimulus.

CS preexposure effect: When the presentation of a CS prior to conditioning impairs the acquisition of the conditioned response once the CS is paired with UCS.

CS-UCS interval: The interval between the termination of the CS and the onset of the UCS.

Cue-controlled relaxation: The conditioning of relaxation to a CS as a result of the association of that stimulus with exercises that elicit relaxation as a UCR.

Cue deflation effect: When the extinction of a response to one cue leads to an increased reaction to the other conditioned stimulus.

Cue predictiveness: The consistency with which the CS is experienced with the UCS, which influences the strength of conditioning.

Cued recall: A memory task that provides a stimulus that is part of the learned experience.

Debrief: An experimenter informing a subject about the nature of a study after the subject finishes participating in the study.

Decay view of forgetting: The idea that memory fades with disuse.

Declarative memory: Factual memory, or the memory of specific events.

Deep structure (of a sentence): The meaning or idea conveyed by a sentence.

Delayed conditioning: A paradigm in which the CS onset precedes the UCS, and CS termination occurs either with UCS onset or during UCS presentation.

Delay-reduction theory: The behavior economic theory that states that overall behavior in a choice task is based on the matching law, while individual choices are determined by which choice produces the shortest delay in the next reinforcer.

Depression effect: The effect in which a shift from high to low reward magnitude produces a lower level of response than if the reward magnitude had always been low.

Differential reinforcement of high responding (DRH) schedule: A schedule of reinforcement in which a specific high number of responses must occur within a specified time in order for reinforcement to occur.

Differential reinforcement of low responding (DRL) schedule: A schedule of reinforcement in which a certain amount of time must elapse without responding, with reinforcement following the first response after the interval.

Differential reinforcement of other behaviors (DRO) schedule: A schedule of reinforcement in which the absence of a specific response within a specified time leads to reinforcement.

Differential reinforcement schedule: A schedule of reinforcement in which a specific number of behaviors must occur within a specified time in order for reinforcement to occur.

Directed forgetting: The forgetting of an event following the presentation of the "forget cue."

Discrimination learning: Responding in different ways to different stimuli.

Discriminative operant: An operant behavior that is under the control of a discriminative stimulus.

Discriminative stimulus: A stimulus that signals the availability or unavailability of reinforcement.

Dishabituation: The recovery of a habituated response as the result of the presentation of a sensitizing stimulus.

Disinhibition: When the conditioned stimulus elicits a conditioned response after a novel stimulus is presented during extinction.

Disjunctive rule: When the concept is defined by the rule that the concept can possess either or both of two attributes.

Displacement: In a conflict situation, the occurrence of a behavior unrelated to that conflict.

Drive: An intense internal force that motivates behavior.

Drug tolerance: The reduced effectiveness of a drug as a result of the repeated use of the drug.

Echo: The auditory record of an event contained in the sensory register.

Echoic memory: The auditory memory of an event stored in the sensory register.

Efficacy expectation: A feeling that one can or cannot execute a particular behavior.

Elaborative rehearsal: The organization of experiences while information is maintained in the short-term store.

Elation effect: The effect in which a shift from low- to high-reward magnitude produces a greater level of responding than if the reward magnitude had always been high.

Electrical stimulation of the brain (ESB): The high levels of instrumental or operant behavior exhibited when responding leads to activation of reinforcement areas of the brain.

Engram: The physical representation of an event in a person's memory.

Episodic buffer: The system that binds visual and verbal information in the long-term store and retrieves information from the short-term store.

Episodic memory: The memory of temporally related events, or the time and place of an experience.

Equivalence belief principle: The idea that the reaction to a secondary reward is the same as the original goal.

Errorless discrimination learning: A training procedure in which the gradual introduction of S^Δ leads to responding S^D without any errors to S^Δ.

Escape response: A behavioral response to an aversive event that is reinforced by the termination of the aversive event.

Excitatory generalization gradient: A graph showing the level of generalization from an excitatory conditioned stimulus (CS_1) to other stimuli.

Excitatory potential: The likelihood that a specific event will elicit a specific response.

Expectation: A mental representation of event contingencies.

Explicit measure of memory: An observable measure of the strength of a memory.

External attribution: A belief that events are beyond one's control.

External inhibition: The presentation of a novel stimulus during conditioning suppresses response to the conditioned stimulus.

Extinction: The elimination or suppression of a response caused by the discontinuation of reinforcement or the removal of the unconditioned stimulus.

Extinction of a conditioned response: When the conditioned stimulus does not elicit the conditioned response because the unconditioned stimulus no longer follows the conditioned stimulus.

Extinction of an operant or instrumental response: When the discontinuance of reinforcement leads to response suppression.

Eyeblink conditioning: When a CS becomes able to elicit a conditioned eyeblink as a result of being paired with a puff of air or a brief electrical shock below the eye.

False memory syndrome: The creation of an inaccurate record of childhood sexual abuse.

Family resemblance: When an object or event shares many attributes with other members of the concept.

Fear: Conditioned response to stimuli associated with painful events; motivates avoidance of aversive events.

Fear conditioning: The conditioning of fear to a CS as a result of associating that CS with a painful event.

Fixed action pattern: An instinctive response that the presence of an effective sign stimulus releases.

Fixed-interval (FI) schedule: A contingency in which reinforcement is available only after a specified period of time and the first response emitted after the interval has elapsed is reinforced.

Fixed-ratio (FR) schedule: A contingency in which a specific number of responses is needed to produce reinforcement.

Flashbulb memory: A vivid, detailed, and long-lasting memory of a very intense experience.

Flavor aversion: Avoidance of a flavor that precedes an illness experience.

Flooding (or response prevention): A behavior therapy in which a phobia is eliminated by forced exposure to the feared stimulus without an aversive consequence.

Forgetting: The inability to recall a past experience.

Free morpheme: A morpheme that can stand alone and still have meaning.

Free recall: A memory task that requires recall with no cues available.

Functional fixedness: Difficulty recognizing novel uses for an object.

Functionalism: Early school of psychology that emphasized the instinctive origins and adaptive functions of behavior.

Generalization: Responding in the same manner to similar stimuli.

Generalization gradient: A visual representation of the response strength produced by stimuli of varying degrees of similarity to the training stimulus.

Generalized competition: A temporary tendency (or set) to respond with most recent learning.

Global attribution: The assumption that a specific outcome will be repeated in many situations.

Goal state: The desired end point of a problem.

Grammar: The rules that define the ways words can be combined into meaningful phrases, clauses, and sentences.

Habit: Hull's concept that a specific environmental stimulus becomes associated with a particular response when that response produces drive reduction.

Habit hierarchy: The varying level of associative strengths between a stimulus environment and the behaviors associated with that environment.

Habit strength: The strength of the connection between a particular environmental stimulus and a specific response.

Habituation: A decrease in responsiveness to a specific stimulus as a result of repeated experience with it.

Heuristic: A "best guess" solution to problem solving.

Hierarchical approach: The idea that memory consists of hierarchical networks of interconnected concepts.

Higher-order conditioning: The phenomenon that a stimulus (CS_2) can elicit a CR even without being paired with the UCS if the CS_2 is paired with another conditioned stimulus (CS_1).

Hippocampus: A brain structure in the limbic system that plays a central role in memory storage and retrieval.

Homeostasis: The tendency to maintain equilibrium by adjusting physiological or psychological processes.

Hopefulness: The belief that negative life events can be controlled and are not inevitable.

Hopelessness: The belief that negative events are inevitable and and a sense of self-deficiency or unworthiness.

Hopelessness theory of depression: The view that whether a person becomes hopeless and depressed depends upon a person making a stable and global attribution for negative life events and the severity of those negative life events.

Hull-Spence theory of discrimination learning: The idea that conditioned excitation first develops to S^D, followed by the conditioning of inhibition to S^Δ.

Hyperalgesia: An increased sensitivity to a painful event.

Hypoalgesia: A decreased sensitivity to a painful event.

Icon: The visual copy of an event contained in the sensory register.

Iconic memory: The visual memory of an event stored in the sensory register.

Ill-defined problem: A problem with no clear starting or goal state.

Implicit measure of memory: A measure that provides an indirect assessment of the strength of a memory.

Imprinting: The development of a social attachment to stimuli experienced during a sensitive period of development.

Incentive motivation: The idea that the level of motivation is affected by magnitude of reward: the greater the reward magnitude, the higher the motivation to obtain that reward.

Informed consent: A written agreement indicating that a subject is willing to participate in a psychological study.

Ingestional neophobia: The avoidance of novel foods.

Inhibition: When the presentation of the CS without the UCS suppresses the CR.

Inhibition of delay: The prevention of a response to the CS until just prior to the UCS in a trace conditioning paradigm.

Inhibitory generalization gradient: A graph showing the level of generalization from an inhibitory conditioned stimulus (CS_1) to other stimuli.

Initial state: The starting point of a problem.

Innate releasing mechanism (IRM): A hypothetical process by which a sign stimulus removes the block on the release of the fixed action pattern.

Insight: A sudden realization of how to solve a problem.

Instinct: An inherited pattern of behavior common to members of a particular species.

Instinctive drift: When operant behavior deteriorates despite continued reinforcement due to the elicitation of instinctive behaviors.

Instinctive view of imprinting: The view that imprinting is a genetically programmed form of learning.

Instrumental conditioning: A conditioning procedure in which the environment constrains the opportunity for reward and a specific behavior can obtain reward.

Interference: An inability to recall a specific memory due to the presence of other memories.

Interim behavior: The behavior that follows reinforcement when an animal is reinforced on an interval schedule of reinforcement.

Internal attribution: The assumption that personal factors lead to a particular outcome.

Interoceptive cue: An internal stimulus for an event.

Interval schedule of reinforcement: A contingency that specifies that reinforcement becomes available at a certain time after the last reinforcement.

Irrelevant incentive effect: The acquisition of an excitatory link expectation that a particular stimulus is associated with a specific reinforcer under an irrelevant drive state.

Korsakoff's syndrome: The inability of alcoholics to recall past events due to a failure to permanently store experiences.

Language: A system of words and word meanings, and a set of rules for combining the words.

Language acquisition device (LAD): Chomsky's idea of an innate mechanism that allows children to grasp the syntax of their language with minimal experience.

Lashley-Wade theory of generalization: The idea that generalization occurs when animals are unable to distinguish between the test stimulus and the conditioning stimulus.

Latent inhibition: The idea that exposure to neutral stimuli establishes an inhibitory state that later impairs excitatory conditioning to that stimulus.

Latent learning: Knowledge of the environment gained through experience but not evident under current conditions.

Law of effect: The process of a reward strengthening an S-R association.

Law of readiness: Sufficient motivation must exist in order to develop an association or exhibit a previously established habit.

Learned helplessness: The belief that events are independent of behavior and are uncontrollable, which results in behavioral deficits characteristic of depression.

Learned irrelevance: The presentation of a stimulus without a UCS leads to the recognition that the stimulus is irrelevant, stops attention to that stimulus, and impairs conditioning when the stimulus is later paired with the UCS.

Learned-safety theory of flavor aversion learning: The recognition that a food can be safely consumed when illness does not follow food consumption.

Learning: A relatively permanent change in behavior potential that occurs as a result of experience.

List differentiation: An ability to distinguish between memories, reducing the level of interference.

Local contrast: A change in behavior that occurs following a change in reinforcement contingency. The change in behavior fades with extended training.

Long-delay learning: The association of a flavor with an illness that occurred even several hours after the flavor was consumed.

Long-term store: The site of permanent memory storage.

Mackintosh's attentional view: The idea that animals attend to stimuli that are predictive of biologically significant events (UCSs) and ignore stimuli that are irrelevant.

Maintenance rehearsal: The mere repetition of information in the short-term store.

Matching law: When an animal has free access to two different schedules of reinforcement; its response is proportional to the level of reinforcement available on each schedule.

Maximizing law: The goal of behavior in a choice task is to obtain as many reinforcements as possible.

Means-end analysis: Breaking a particular problem into a series of solvable subproblems.

Medial forebrain bundle (MFB): The area of the limbic system that is part of the brain's reinforcement center.

Medial temporal lobe: A central nervous system structure, containing the hippocampus and surrounding cortical areas, that is involved in the storage and retrieval of experiences.

Mediodorsal thalamus: A central nervous system structure involved in the storage of experiences.

Memory attribute: A salient aspect of an event whose presence can lead to retrieval of the past event.

Memory reconstruction: The alteration of a memory to provide a consistent view of the world.

Mesolimbic reinforcement system: A collection of structures within the central nervous system that mediates the influence of reinforcement on behavior.

Method of loci: A mnemonic technique in which items are stored in an ordered series of known locations and a specific item is recalled by visualizing that item in an appropriate location.

Mnemonic techniques: A set of techniques to enhance the storage and retrieval of information.

Modeling: The acquisition of behavior as a result of observing the experiences of others.

Momentary maximization theory: The view that the behavior in a choice task is determined by which alternative is perceived as best at that moment in time.

Morpheme: The smallest meaningful amount of language.

Negative attributional (or explanatory) style: A belief system assuming that negative life events are due to stable and global factors, which makes the person vulnerable to depression.

Negative contrast (or depression) effect: The effect in which a shift from high to low reward magnitude produces a lower level of responding than if the reward magnitude had always been low.

Negative punishment: A loss or unavailability of reinforcement because of inappropriate behavior.

Negative reinforcement: The termination of an aversive event, which reinforces the behavior that preceded it.

Negative reinforcer: The termination of an aversive event, which reinforces the behavior that terminated the aversive event.

Negative rule: A concept is defined by the rule that any object or event having a certain attribute is not a member of the concept.

Nigrostriatal pathway: A neural pathway that begins in the substantia nigra and projects to the neostriatum and that serves to facilitate reinforcement-induced enhancement of memory consolidation.

Noncontinuity theory of discrimination learning: The idea that discrimination is learned rapidly once an animal discovers the relevant dimension and attends to relevant stimuli.

Nucleus accumbens (NA): A basal forebrain structure that plays a significant role in the influence of reinforcement on behavior.

Occasion setting: The ability of one stimulus to enhance the response to another stimulus.

Omission training: A schedule of reinforcement in which the absence of response leads to reinforcement.

Operant chamber: An apparatus that creates an enclosed environment, used for the study of operant behavior within it.

Operant conditioning: When a specific response produces reinforcement, and the frequency of the response determines the amount of reinforcement obtained.

Operant response: A behavior that controls the rate at which specific consequences occur.

Opponent-process theory: The theory that an event produces an initial instinctive affective response, which is followed by an opposite affective reaction.

Outcome expectation: The perceived consequences of either a behavior or an event.

Overshadowing: In a compound conditioning situation, the prevention of conditioning to one stimulus due to the presence of a more salient or intense stimulus.

Pain-induced aggression: Anger and aggressive behavior elicited by punishment.

Parallel distributed processing model: The idea that memory is composed of a series of interconnected associative networks and that knowledge is distributed throughout the entire system.

Partial reinforcement effect (PRE): The greater resistance to extinction of an instrumental or operant response following intermittent rather than continuous reinforcement during acquisition.

Partial report technique: Sperling's procedure requiring subjects to report one of three lines of a visual array shortly after the visual array ended.

Passive avoidance response: A contingency in which the absence of responding leads to the prevention of an aversive event.

Peak shift: The shift in the maximum response, which occurs to a stimulus other than S^D and in the stimulus direction opposite that of the S^Δ.

Personal helplessness: A perceived incompetence that leads to failure and feelings of helplessness.

Phobia: An unrealistic fear of a specific environmental event.

Phoneme: The simplest functional speech sound.

Phonological loop: A rehearsal system that holds and analyzes verbal information.

Phonology: The rules that dictate how phonemes can be combined into morphemes.

Phrase: A group of two or more related words that expresses a single thought.

Phrase-structure grammar: The analysis of the constituent elements of a sentence.

Positive attributional style: A belief system that negative life events are controllable, which leads to hopefulness and a resilience to depression.

Positive contrast (or elation) effect: The effect in which a shift from low to high reward magnitude produces a greater level of responding than if the reward magnitude had always been high.

Positive punishment: The use of a physically or psychologically painful event as the punisher.

Positive reinforcer: An event whose occurrence increases the frequency of the behavior that precedes it.

Postreinforcement pause: A cessation of behavior following reinforcement on a ratio schedule, which is followed by resumption of responding at the intensity characteristic of that ratio schedule.

Potentiation: The enhancement of an aversion to a nonsalient stimulus when a salient stimulus is also paired with the UCS.

Predisposition: Instances where learning occurs more rapidly or in a different form than expected.

Preparedness: An evolutionary predisposition to associate a specific conditioned stimulus and a specific unconditioned stimulus.

Primary reinforcer: An activity whose reinforcing properties are innate.

Priming: The facilitation of recall of a specific event following exposure to a closely related event.

Proactive interference (PI): The inability to recall recent experiences as a result of the memory of earlier experiences.

Probability-differential theory: The idea that an activity will have reinforcing properties when its probability of occurrence is greater than that of the reinforced activity.

Problem: An obstacle that prevents the attainment of a desired goal.

Procedural memory: A skill memory or the memory of a highly practiced behavior.

Prototype: The object that has the greatest number of attributes characteristic of the concept and that is therefore the most typical member of that concept.

Punishment: A means of eliminating undesired behavior by using an aversive event that is contingent upon the occurrence of the inappropriate behavior.

Ratio schedule of reinforcement: A contingency that specifies that a certain number of behaviors are necessary to produce reinforcement.

Reaction time: The time it takes to react to a stimulus, which provides an implicit measure of the strength of a memory.

Reactive inhibition: The temporary suppression of behavior due to the persistence of a drive state after unsuccessful behavior.

Reciprocal inhibition: Wolpe's term for the idea that only one emotional state can be experienced at a time.

Recognition measure: An explicit measure of memory requiring identification of a previous experience.

Rehearsal: The repetition of an event that keeps the memory of an event in the short-term store.

Rehearsal systems approach: The view that information is retained in several sensory registers for analysis by working memory.

Reinforcer: An event (or termination of an event) that increases the frequency of the operant behavior that preceded it.

Reinforcer devaluation effect: The association of a reinforcer with an aversive event, which reduces the behavioral control that reinforcer exerts.

Representativeness heuristic: A heuristic that solves problems based only on the obvious characteristics of the problem.

Repressed memory: The view that extremely disturbing events are submerged into the unconscious.

Rescorla-Wagner associative model: The view that a particular UCS can support only a specific level of conditioning and that when two or more stimuli are paired with a UCS, each stimulus must compete for the associative strength available for conditioning.

Resemblance: The similarity in appearance of two or more events.

Response cost: A negative punishment technique in which an undesired response results in either the withdrawal of or failure to obtain reinforcement.

Response deprivation theory: The idea that when a contingency restricts access to an activity, it causes that activity to become a reinforcer.

Response-outcome expectation: The belief that a particular response leads to a specific consequence or outcome.

Response prevention (or flooding): A behavior therapy in which a phobia is eliminated by forced exposure to the feared stimulus without an aversive consequence.

Retrieval: The ability to access a memory and recall a past experience.

Retroactive interference (RI): The inability to recall distant events because of the memory of more recent events.

Retrograde amnesia: The inability to recall events that occurred prior to a traumatic event.

Retrospective processing: The continual assessment of contingencies, which can lead to a reevaluation of prior conditioning of a CS with a UCS.

Reward: An event that increases the occurrence of the instrumental behavior that precedes the event.

Rule: The rule that defines whether the objects or events are examples of a particular concept.

Salience: The property of a specific stimulus that allows it to become readily associated with a particular UCS.

Savings score: The number of trials needed to learn a task minus the number of trials relearn the task, with a score that provides an implicit measure of the strength of a memory.

Scallop effect: A pattern of behavior characteristic of a fixed-interval schedule, where responding stops after reinforcement and then slowly increases as the time approaches when reinforcement will be available.

Schedule-induced behavior: The high levels of instinctive behavior that occur following reinforcement on an interval schedule.

Schedule-induced polydipsia: The high levels of water consumption following food reinforcement on an interval schedule.

Schedule of reinforcement: A contingency that specifies how often or when to act to receive reinforcement.

S^D: A stimulus that indicates the availability of reinforcement contingent upon the occurrence of an appropriate operant response.

S$^\Delta$: A stimulus that indicates that reinforcement is unavailable and that the operant response will be ineffective.

Secondary reinforcer: An event that has developed its reinforcing properties through its association with primary reinforcers.

Secure relationship: The establishment of a strong bond between a mother who is sensitive and responsive to her infant and that infant.

Semantic memory: The memory of knowledge concerning the use of language and the rules for the solution of problems or acquisition of concepts.

Semantics: The meaning of language.

Sensitization: An increased reactivity to all environmental events following exposure to an intense stimulus.

Sensory preconditioning: The initial pairing of two stimuli, which will enable one of the stimuli (CS$_2$) to elicit the CR without being paired with a UCS if the other stimulus (CS$_1$) is paired with UCS.

Sensory register: The initial storage of memory for a very brief time as an exact duplicate of the event.

Sentence: Two or more phrases that convey an assertion, question, command, wish, or exclamation.

Serial position effect: The faster learning and greater recall of items at the beginning and end of a list rather than at the middle of the list.

Set: The tendency to use an established method for solving problems.

Shaping (or successive approximation procedure): A technique of acquiring a desired behavior by first selecting a highly occurring operant behavior, then slowly changing the contingency until the desired behavior is learned.

Short-term store: A temporary storage facility where information is modified to create a more meaningful experience.

Sidman avoidance: A procedure in which an animal experiences periodic aversive events unless it responds to prevent them, with the occurrence of the avoidance response delaying the occurrence of the aversive event for a specific time.

Sign stimulus: A distinctive environmental event that can activate the IRM and release stored energy.

Simple idea: The mind's representation of a sensory impression.

Simultaneous conditioning: A paradigm in which the CS and UCS are presented together.

Sometimes opponent-process (SOP) theory: Wagner's idea that the CS becomes able to elicit the secondary A2 component of the UCR as the CR, and the A2 component is sometimes the opposite of and sometimes the same as the A1 component.

Spatial-temporal hierarchy: A hierarchy where phobic scenes are related to distance (either physical or temporal) to the phobic object.

Species-specific defense reaction (SSDR): An instinctive reaction, elicited by signals of danger, allowing the avoidance of an aversive event.

Specific attribution: The belief that a particular outcome is limited to a specific situation.

Spontaneous recovery: The return of a CR when an interval intervenes between extinction and testing without additional CS-UCS pairings, or when the instrumental or operant response returns without additional reinforced experience.

Spreading activation theory: The idea that once a concept or property of a concept is activated, activation spreads to associated concepts or properties.

S-R (stimulus-response) associative theories: The view that learning involves the association of a specific stimulus with a specific response.

Stable attribution: The assumption that the factors that resulted in a particular outcome will not change.

State-dependent learning: Learning based on events experienced in one state; the events will not be recalled if the subject is tested in a different state.

Stimulus-bound behavior: Behavior tied to the prevailing environmental conditions and elicited by stimulation of the brain's reinforcement center.

Stimulus generalization: Responding in the same manner to similar stimuli.

Stimulus narrowing: The restriction of a response to a limited number of situations.

Stimulus-outcome expectation: The belief that a particular consequence or outcome will follow a specific stimulus.

Stimulus-substitution theory: Pavlov's view that the pairing of the CS and UCS allows the CS to elicit the UCR as the CR.

Successive approximation procedure (or shaping): A technique for acquiring a desired behavior by first selecting a behavior with a high operant rate, then slowly changing the contingency until the desired behavior is learned.

Superstitious behavior: A "ritualistic" stereotyped pattern of behavior exhibited during the interval between reinforcements.

Suppression ratio: A measure of the fear produced by a specific conditioned stimulus obtained by dividing the number of operant responses during that CS by the number of responses during the CS and without the CS.

Surface structure (of a sentence): The arrangement of the words in a sentence.

Sustained contrast: The long-lasting change in responding due to the anticipated change in the reinforcement contingency.

Sutherland-Mackintosh attentional theory: The theory that attention to the relevant dimension is strengthened in the first stage, and association of a particular response to the relevant stimulus occurs in the second stage of discrimination learning.

Syntax: The system of rules for combining the various units of speech.

Systematic desensitization: A graduated counterconditioning treatment for phobias in which the relaxation state is associated with the phobic object.

Tegmentostriatal pathway: A neural pathway that begins in the lateral hypothalamus, goes through the medial forebrain bundle and ventral tegmental area, terminates in the nucleus accumbens, and governs the motivational properties of reinforcers.

Temporal attribute: The time that an event occurred can be a retrieval cue for that experience.

Temporal conditioning: A technique in which the presentation of the UCS at regular intervals causes the time of the UCS to become able to elicit the CR.

Terminal behavior: The behavior that just precedes reinforcement when an animal is reinforced on an interval schedule of reinforcement.

Thematic hierarchy: A hierarchy in which phobic scenes are related to a basic theme.

Time-out from reinforcement: A negative punishment technique in which an inappropriate behavior leads to a period of time during which reinforcement is unavailable.

Token economy: A contingency management program where tokens are used as secondary reinforcers for appropriate behaviors.

Tolerance: The reduced reactivity to an event with repeated experience.

Trace conditioning: When the CS is presented and terminated prior to UCS onset with this conditioning paradigm.

Transposition: Kohler's idea that animals learn relationships between stimuli and that they respond to different stimuli based on the same relationship as the original training stimuli.

Two-choice discrimination learning: A task when the S^D and S^Δ are on the same stimulus dimension.

Two-factor theory of avoidance learning: Mowrer's view that in the first stage, fear is conditioned through the classical conditioning process, and in the second stage, an instrumental or operant response is acquired that terminates the feared stimulus.

Two-factor theory of punishment: Mowrer's view that fear is classically conditioned to the environmental events present during punishment in the first stage. Any behavior that terminates the feared stimulus will be acquired through instrumental conditioning in the second stage. The reinforcement of the escape response causes the animal or person to exhibit the escape response rather than the punished response in the punishment situation.

UCS preexposure effect: The effect caused by exposure to the UCS prior to conditioning; it impairs later conditioning when a CS is paired with that UCS.

Unconditioned reflex: An instinctual response to an environmental event.

Unconditioned response (UCR): An innate reaction to an unconditioned stimulus.

Unconditioned stimulus (UCS): An environmental event that can elicit an instinctive reaction without any experience.

Universal helplessness: A belief that environmental forces produce failure and result in helplessness.

Unstable attribution: The belief that other factors may affect outcomes in the future.

Variable-interval (VI) schedule: A contingency in which there is an average interval of time between available reinforcements, but the interval varies from one reinforcement to the next contingency.

Variable-ratio schedule: A contingency in which an average number of behaviors produces reinforcement, but the actual number of responses required to produce reinforcement varies over the course of training.

Ventral tegmental area (VTA): A structure in the tegmentostriatal reinforcement system that projects to the nucleus accumbens.

Vicarious conditioning: The development of the CR to a stimulus after observation of the pairing of CS and UCS.

Vicious-circle behavior: An escape response that continues despite punishment, due to a failure to recognize that the absence of the escape behavior will not be punished.

Visual code: The transformation of a word into an image.

Visuospatial sketchpad: A rehearsal system that holds and analyzes visual and spatial information.

Well-defined problem: A problem with clear initial and goal states.

Whole report technique: Sperling's procedure requiring subjects to report all three lines of a visual array shortly after the visual array ended.

Withdrawal: An increase in the intensity of the affective opponent B state following the termination of the event.

Within-compound association: The association of two stimuli, both paired with a UCS, which leads both to elicit the CR.

Working-backward heuristic: A technique for finding the solution to a problem by starting with the end point and working back to the start point.

Working memory: Information being actively processed by rehearsal systems.

References

Aan het Rot, M., Charney, D. S., & Mathew, S. J. (2008). Intravenous ketamine for treatment-resistant major depressive disorder. *Primary Psychiatry, 15,* 39–47.

Abramowitz, A. J., & O'Leary, S. G. (1990). Effectiveness of delayed punishment in an applied setting. *Behavior Therapy, 21,* 231–239.

Abramowitz, J. S. (1997). Effectiveness of psychological and pharmacological treatments for obsessive-compulsive disorder: A quantitative review. *Journal of Consulting and Clinical Psychology, 65,* 44–52.

Abramson, L. Y. (1977). *Universal versus personal helplessness: An experimental test of the reformulated theory of learned helplessness and depression.* Unpublished doctoral dissertation, University of Pennsylvania, Philadelphia.

Abramson, L. Y., Garber, J., & Seligman, M. E. P. (1980). Learned helplessness in humans: An attributional analysis. In J. Garber & M. E. P. Seligman (Eds.), *Human helplessness: Theory and applications* (pp. 3–35). New York: Academic Press.

Abramson, L. Y., Metalsky, G. I., & Alloy, L. B. (1989). Hopelessness depression: A theory-based subtype of depression. *Psychological Review, 96,* 358–372.

Abramson, L. Y., & Sackeim, H. A. (1977). A paradox in depression: Uncontrollability and self-blame. *Psychological Bulletin, 84,* 838–851.

Abramson, L. Y., Seligman, M. E. P., & Teasdale, J. D. (1978). Learned helplessness in humans: Critique and reformulation. *Journal of Abnormal Psychology, 87,* 49–74.

Adams, C. D. (1982). Variations in the sensitivity of instrumental responding to reinforcer devaluation. *Quarterly Journal of Experimental Psychology, 34*(B), 77–98.

Adams, C. D., & Dickinson, A. (1981). Instrumental responding following reinforcer devaluation. *Quarterly Journal of Experimental Psychology, 33*(B), 109–122.

Adelman, H. M., & Maatsch, J. L. (1956). Learning and extinction based upon frustration, food reward, and exploratory tendency. *Journal of Experimental Psychology, 52,* 311–315.

Ainslie, G. (1975). Specious reward: A behavioral theory of impulsiveness and impulse control. *Psychological Bulletin, 82,* 485–489.

Ainsworth, M. D. S. (1982). Attachment: Retrospect and prospect. In C. M. Parkes & J. Sevenson-Hinde (Eds.), *The place of attachment in human behavior* (pp. 3–30). New York: Basic Books.

Airplane. (n.d.). In *Merriam-Webster Online.* Retrieved from http://www.merriam-webster.com/dictionary/airplane?show = 0&t = 1293482499

Akins, C. A., Domjan, M., & Gutierrez, G. (1994). Topography of sexually conditioned behavior in male Japanese quail (Coturnix japonica) depends on the CS-US interval. *Journal of Experimental Psychology: Animal Behavior Processes, 20,* 199–209.

Albert, U., & Brunatto, C. (2009). Obsessive-compulsive disorder in adults: Efficacy of combined and sequential treatments. *Clinical Neuropsychiatry: Journal of Treatment Evaluation, 6,* 83–93.

Alberto, P. A., & Troutman, A. C. (2006). *Applied behavior analysis for teachers* (7th ed.). Englewood Cliffs, NJ: Merrill.

Alferink, L. A., Critchfield, T. S., Hitt, J. L., & Higgins, W. J. (2009). Generality of the matching law as a descriptor of shot selection in basketball. *Journal of Applied Behavior Analysis, 42,* 595–608.

Allen, R. J., Baddeley, A. D., & Hitch, G. J. (2006). Is the binding of visual features in working memory resource-demanding? *Journal of Experimental Psychology: General, 135,* 298–313.

Allison, J. (1993). Response deprivation, reinforcement, and economics. *Journal of the Experimental Analysis of Behavior, 60,* 129–140.

Alloway, T.M. (1969). Effects of low temperature upon acquisition retention in the grain beetle (Tenebrio molitor). *Journal of Comparative and Physiological Psychology, 69,* 1–8.

Alloy, L. B., Abramson, L. Y., Safford, S. M., & Gibb, B. E. (2006). The cognitive vulnerability to depression (CVD) project: Current findings and future directions. In B. L. Alloy & J. H. Riskind (Eds.), *Cognitive vulnerability to emotional disorders* (pp. 33–61). Mahwah, NJ: Lawrence Erlbaum.

Alvarez-Royo, P., Clower, R. P., Zola-Morgan, S., & Squire, L. R. (1991). Stereotaxic lesions of the hippocampus in monkeys: Determination of surgical coordinates and analysis of lesions using magnetic resonance imaging. *Journal of Neuroscience Methods, 38,* 223–232.

Amaral, D. G., Price, J. L., Pitkanen, A., & Carmichael, S. T. (1992). Anatomical organization of the primate amygdaloid complex. In J. P. Aggleton (Ed), *The amygdala: Neurobiological aspects of emotion, memory, and mental dysfunction* (pp. 1–66). New York: Wiley.

American Psychological Association. (2002). Ethical principles of psychologists and code of conduct. *American Psychologist, 57,* 1060-1073.

Amsel, A. (1958). The role of frustrative nonreward in noncontinuous reward situations. *Psychological Bulletin, 55,* 102–119.

Amsel, A. (1967). Partial reinforcement effects on vigor and persistence. In K. W. Spence & J. T. Spence (Eds.), *The psychology of learning and motivation* (Vol. 1, pp. 1–65). New York: Academic Press.

Amsel, A. (1994). Precis of frustration theory: An analysis of dispositional learning and memory. *Psychonomic Bulletin and Review, 1,* 280–296.

Anderson, M. C., & Levy, B. J. (2006). Encouraging then ascent cognitive neuroscience of repression. *Behavioral and Brain Sciences, 29,* 511–513.

Anderson, M. C. & Levy, B. J. (2009). Suppressing unwanted memories. *Current Directions* in *Psychological Science, 18,* 189–194.

Anderson, M. C., Ochsner, K. N., Kuhl, B., Cooper, J., Robertson, E., Gabrieli, et al., (2004). Neural systems underlying the suppression of unwanted memories. *Science, 303,* 232–235.

Andersson, P. (2004). Does experience matter in lending? A process-tracing study on experienced loan officers' and novices' decision behavior. *Journal of Economic Psychology, 25,* 471–492.

Andres, P. (2003). Frontal cortex as the central executive of working memory: Time to revise our view. *Cortex: A Journal Devoted to the Study of the Nervous System and Behavior, 39,* 871–895.

Anthony, J. C., Tien, A. Y., & Petronis, K. R. (1989). Epidemiological evidence on cocaine use and panic attacks. *American Journal Epidemiology, 129,* 543–549.

Anthony, J. C., Warner, L. A., & Kessler, R. C. (1994). Comparative epidemiology of dependence on tobacco, alcohol, controlled substances, and inhalants: Basic findings from the National Comorbidity Survey. *Experimental and Clinical Psychopharmacology, 2,* 244–268.

Antonov, I. Antonova, I., Kandel, E. R., & Hawkins, R. D. (2001). The contribution of activity-dependent synaptic plasticity to classical conditioning in Aplysia. *Journal of Neuroscience, 21,* 6413–6422.

Antonuccio, D. O., Ward, C. H. & Tearnan, B. H. (1989). The behavioral treatment of unipolar depression in adult outpatients. In M. Hersen, R. Eisler, & P. M. Miller (Eds), *Progress in behavior modification* (pp. 152–191). Thousand Oaks, CA: SAGE.

Aou, S., Oomura, Y., Woody, C. D., & Nishino, H. (1988). Effects of behaviorally rewarding hypothalamic electrical stimulation on intracelluarly recorded neuronal activity in the motor cortex of awake monkeys. *Brain Research, 439,* 31–38.

Aoyama, K. & McSweeney, F. K. (2001). Habituation contributes to within-session changes in free wheel running. *Journal of the Experimental Analysis of Behavior, 76,* 289–302.

Appel, J. B. (1964). Analysis of aversively motivated behavior. *Archives of General Psychiatry, 10,* 71–83.

Arana, F. S. Parkinson, J. A., Holland, A. J., Owen, A. M. & Roberts, A. C. (2003). Dissociable contributions of the human amygdala and orbitofrontal cortex to incentive motivation and goal selection. *Journal of Neuroscience, 23,* 9632–9638.

Archer, B. U., & Margolin, R. R. (1970). Arousal effects in intentional recall and forgetting. *Journal of Experimental Psychology, 86,* 8–12.

Armus, H. L. (1959). Effect of magnitude of reinforcement on acquisition and extinction of a running response. *Journal of Experimental Psychology, 58,* 61–63.

Aronson, L., Balsam, P. D., & Gibbon, J. (1993). Temporal comparator rules and responding in multiple schedules. *Animal Learning & Behavior, 21,* 293–302.

Ashbaugh, R. & Peck, S. (1998). Treatment of sleep problems in a toddler: A replication of the faded bedtime with response cost protocol. *Journal of Applied Behavior Analysis, 31,* 127–129.

Atkinson, J. W. (1958). *Motives in fantasy, action, and society.* Princeton, NJ: Van Nostrand.

Atkinson, J. W. (1964). *An introduction to motivation.* Princeton, NJ: Van Nostrand.

Atkinson, R. C., & Shiffrin, R. M. (1971). The control of short-term memory. *Scientific American, 225,* 82–90.

Aurand, J. C., Sisson, L. A., Aach, S. R., & Van Hasselt, V. B. (1989). Use of reinforcement plus interruption to reduce self-stimulation in a child with multiple handicaps. *Journal of the Mutlihandicapped Person, 2,* 51–61.

Averbach, E., & Sperling, G. (1961). Short-term storage of information in vision. In C. Cherry (Ed.), *Fourth London symposium on information theory* (pp. 196–211). London: Butterworth.

Ayllon, T., & Azrin, N. H. (1965). The measurement and reinforcement of behavior of psychotics. *Journal of the Experimental Analysis of Behavior, 8,* 357–383.

Ayllon, T., & Azrin, N. H. (1968). *The token economy: A motivation system for therapy and rehabilitation.* New York: Appleton-Century-Crofts.

Azrin, N. H. (1956). Some effects of two intermittent schedules of immediate and non-immediate punishment. *Journal of Psychology, 42,* 3–21.

Azrin, N. H. (1964, September). *Aggression.* Paper presented at the meeting of the American Psychological Association, Los Angeles.

Azrin, N. H. (1970). Punishment of elicited aggression. *Journal of the Experimental Analysis of Behavior, 14,* 7–10.

Azrin, N. H., Hake, D. F., Holz, W. C., & Hutchinson, R. R. (1965). Motivational aspects of escape from punishment. *Journal of the Experimental Analysis of Behavior, 8,* 31–44.

Azrin, N. H., & Holz, W. C. (1966). Punishment. In W. K. Honeg (Ed.), *Operant behavior: Areas of research and application* (pp. 380–447). New York: Appleton-Century-Crofts.

Azrin, N. H., Holz, W. C., & Hake, D. F. (1963). Fixed-ratio punishment. *Journal of the Experimental Analysis of Behavior, 6,* 141–148.

Azrin, N. H., Hutchinson, R. R., & McLaughlin, R. (1965). The opportunity for aggression as an operant reinforcer during aversive stimulation. *Journal of the Experimental Analysis of Behavior, 8,* 171–180.

Azrin, N. H., Hutchinson, R. R., & Sallery, R. D. (1964). Pain aggression toward inanimate objects. *Journal of the Experimental analysis of Behavior, 7,* 223–228.

Azrin, N. H., Sneed, T. J., & Foxx, R. M. (1973). A rapid method of eliminating bedwetting (enuresis) of the retarded. *Behavior Research and Therapy, 11,* 427–434.

Azrin, N. H., Vinas, V., & Ehle, C. T. (2007). Physical activity as reinforcement for classroom calmness of ADHD children: A preliminary study. *Child and Family Behavior Therapy, 29,* 1–8.

Baddeley, A. (1990). *Human memory: Theory and practice.* Boston: Allyn & Bacon.

Baddeley, A. (2003). Working memory and language: An overview. *Journal of Communication Disorders, 36,* 189–208.

Baddeley, A. U., & Wilson, B. A. (2002). Prose recall and amnesia: Implications for the structure of working memory. *Neuropsychologia, 40,* 1737–1743.

Baer, D. M. (1962). Laboratory control of thumb sucking by withdrawal and representation of reinforcement. *Journal of the Experimental Analysis of Behavior, 5,* 525–528.

Baerends, G. P., Brouwer, R., & Waterbolk, H. T. (1955). Ethological studies of *Lebistes reticulatus* (Peters): I. An analysis of the male courtship pattern. *Behaviour, 8,* 249–334.

Bailey, C. H., Giustetto, M., Zhu, H., Chen, M., & Kandel, E. R. (2000). A novel function for serotonin-mediated short-term facilitation in *Aplysia*: Conversion of a transient, cell-wide homosynaptic Hebbian plasticity into a persistent, protein synthesis-independent synapse-specific enhancement. *Proceedings of the National Academy of Sciences of the United States of America, 97,* 11581–11586.

Bailey, C. H., Kandel, E. R., & Si, K. (2004). The persistence of long-term memory: A molecular approach to self-sustaining changes in learning-induced synaptic growth. *Neuron, 44,* 49–57.

Baker, A. G. (1976). Learned irrelevance and learned helplessness: Rats learn that stimuli, reinforcers, and responses are uncorrelated. *Journal of Experimental Psychology: Animal Behavior Processes, 2,* 131–141.

Baker, A. G., & Baker, P. A. (1985). Does inhibition differ from excitation? Proactive interference, contextual conditioning, and extinction. In R. R. Miller & N. S. Spear (Eds.), *Information processing in animals: Conditioned inhibition* (pp. 151–184). Hillsdale, NJ: Lawrence Erlbaum.

Baker, A. G., & Mackintosh, N. J. (1977). Excitatory and inhibitory conditioning following uncorrelated presentations of CS and US. *Animal Learning and Behavior, 5,* 315–319.

Baker, A. G., & Mackintosh, N. J. (1979). Preexposure to the CS alone, US alone, or CS and US uncorrelated: Latent inhibition, blocking by context, or learned irrelevance? *Learning and Motivation, 10,* 278–294.

Baker, A. G., & Mercier, P. (1989). Attention, retrospective processing, and cognitive representations. In S. B. Klein & R. R. Mowrer (Eds.), *Contemporary learning theories: Pavlovian conditioning and the status of traditional learning theory* (pp. 85–101). Hillsdale, NJ: Lawrence Erlbaum.

Baker, A. G., Mercier, P., Gabel, J., & Baker, P. A. (1981). Contextual conditioning and the US preexposure effect in conditioned fear. *Journal of Experimental Psychology: Animal Behavior Processes, 7,* 109–128.

Balleine, B. W. (2001). Incentive process in instrumental conditioning. In R. R. Mowrer & S. B. Klein (Eds.), *Handbook of contemporary learning theories* (pp. 307–366). Mahwah, NJ: Lawrence Erlbaum.

Balleine, B. W., & Dickinson, A. (1991). Instrumental performance following reinforcer devaluation depends upon incentive learning. *Quarterly Journal of Experimental Psychology, 43*(B), 279–296.

Balleine, B. W., & Dickinson, A. (1992). Signalling and incentive processes in instrumental reinforcer devaluation. *Quarterly Journal of Experimental Psychology, 45*(B), 285–301.

Balleine, B. W., Garner, C., & Dickinson, A. (1995). Instrumental outcome devaluation is attenuated by the antiemetic ondansetron. *Quarterly Journal of Experimental Psychology, 48*(B), 235–251.

Balsam, P. D., & Schwartz, A. L. (1981). Rapid contextual conditioning in autoshaping. *Journal of Experimental Psychology: Animal Behavior Processes, 7,* 382–393.

Bandura, A. (1971). *Social learning theory.* Morristown, NJ: General Learning.

Bandura, A. (1977). Self-efficacy: Toward a unifying theory of behavior change. *Psychological Review, 84,* 191–215.

Bandura, A. (1982). The self and mechanisms of agency. In J. Suls (Ed.), *Psychological perspectives on the self* (Vol. 1, pp. 3–39). Hillsdale, NJ: Lawrence Erlbaum.

Bandura, A. (1986). *Social foundations of thought and action: A social cognition theory.* Englewood Cliffs, NJ: Prentice-Hall.

Bandura, A., & Adams, N. E. (1977). Analysis of the self-efficacy theory of behavioral change. *Journal of Personality and Social Psychology, 1,* 287–310.

Bandura, A., Adams, N. E., & Beyer, J. (1977). Cognitive processes mediating behavioral change. *Journal of Personality and Social Psychology, 35,* 125–129.

Bandura, A., Blanchard, E. B., & Ritter, R. (1969). The relative efficacy of desensitization and modeling approaches for inducing behavioral, affective, and attitudinal changes. *Journal of Personality and Social Psychology, 13,* 173–199.

Bandura, A., Grusec, J. E., & Menlove, F. L. (1967). Vicarious extinction of avoidance behavior. *Journal of Personality and Social Psychology, 5,* 16–23.

Bandura, A., Jeffrey, R. W., & Gajdos, F. (1975). Generalizing change through participant modeling with self-directed mastery. *Behavior Research and Therapy, 13,* 141–152.

Bandura, A., & Locke, E. A. (2003). Negative-self efficacy and goal effects revisited. *Journal of Applied Psychology, 88,* 87–99.

Bandura, A., & Perloff, B. (1967). Relative efficacy of self-monitored and externally imposed reinforcement systems. *Journal of Personality and Social Psychology, 7,* 11–16.

Bandura, A., & Rosenthal, T. L. (1966). Vicarious classical conditioning as a function of arousal level. *Journal of Personality and Social Psychology, 3,* 54–62.

Bandura, A., Ross, D., & Ross, D. A. (1963). Imitation of film-mediated aggressive models. *Journal of Abnormal and Social Psychology, 66,* 3–11.

Banks, R. K., & Vogel-Sprott, M. (1965). Effect of delayed punishment on an immediately rewarded response in humans. *Journal of Experimental Psychology, 70,* 357–359.

Barber, N. (1994). Reducing fear of the laboratory rat: A participant modeling approach. *Teaching of Psychology, 21,* 228–230.

Barnes, G. W. (1956). Conditioned stimulus intensity and temporal factors in spaced-trial classical conditioning. *Journal of Experimental Psychology, 51,* 192–198.

Barnes, J. M., & Underwood, B. J. (1959). "Fate" of first-list associations in transfer theory. *Journal of Experimental Psychology, 58,* 97–105.

Baron, A. (1965). Delayed punishment of a runway response. *Journal of Comparative and Physiological Psychology, 60,* 131–134.

Bartlett, F. C. (1932). *Remembering: A study in experimental and social psychology.* London: Cambridge University Press.

Barton, E. S., Guess, D., Garcia, E., & Baer, D. M. (1970). Improvement of retardates' mealtime behaviors by time-out procedures using multiple baseline techniques. *Journal of Applied Behavior Analysis, 3,* 77–84.

Bass, M. J., & Hull, C. L. (1934). The irradiation of a tactile conditioned reflex in man. *Journal of Comparative Psychology, 17,* 47–65.

Bassareo, V., De Luca, M. A., & Di Chiara, G. (2007). Differential impact of Pavlovian drug conditioned stimuli on in vivo dopamine transmission in the rat accumbens shell and core and in the prefrontal cortex. *Psychopharmacology, 191,* 689–703.

Bassareo, V., & Di Chiara, G. (1999). Modulation of feeding-induced activation of mesolimbic dopamine transmission by appetitive stimuli and its relation to motivational state. *European Journal of Neuroscience, 11,* 4389–4397.

Bateson, P. P. G. (1969). Imprinting and the development of preferences. In A. Ambrose (Ed.), *Stimulation in early infancy* (pp. 109–132). New York: Academic Press.

Batsell, W. R. (2000) Augmentation: Synergistic conditioning in taste-aversion learning. *Current Directions in Psychological Science, 9,* 164–168.

Batsell, W. R., Trost, C. A., Cochran, S. R., Blankenship, A. G., & Batson, J. D. (2003). Effects of postconditioning inflation on odor + taste compound conditioning. *Learning and Behavior, 31,* 173–184.

Baum, M. (1970). Extinction of avoidance responding through response prevention (flooding). *Psychological Bulletin, 74,* 276–284.

Baumrind, D. (1996). A blanket injunction against disciplinary use of spanking is not warranted by the data. *Pediatrics, 98,* 828–831.

Baumrind, D. (1997) The discipline controversy revisted. *Family Relations, 45,* 405–414.

Baumrind, D. (2001, August). *Does causally relevant research support a blanket injunction against disciplinary spanking by parents?* Invited address at the American Psychological Association Convention, San Francisco.

Baumrind, D., Larzelere, R. E., & Cowan, P. A. (2002). Ordinary physical punishment: Is it harmful? *Psychological Bulletin, 128,* 580–589.

Bechterev, V. M. (1913). *La psychologie objective.* Paris: Alcan.

Becker, H. C., & Flaherty, C. F. (1982). Influence of ethanol on contrast in consummatory behavior. *Psychopharmacology, 77,* 253–258.

Becker, H. C., & Flaherty, C. F. (1983). Chlordiazepoxide and ethanol additively reduce gustatory negative contrast. *Psychopharmacology, 80,* 35–37.

Becker, H. C., Jarvis, M. F., Wagner, G. C. & Flaherty, C. F. (1984). *Physiology & Behavior, 33,* 707–712.

Bedard, J., & Chi, M. T. H. (1992). Expertise. *Current Directions in Psychological Science, 1,* 135–139.

Benbassat, D. & Abramson, C. I. (2002). Errorless discrimination learning in simulated landing flares. *Human Factors and Aerospace Safety, 2,* 319–338.

Bender, H. L., Allen, J. P., McElhaney, K. B., Antonishak, J., Moore, C. M., Kelly, H. O., et al. (2007). Use of harsh physical discipline and developmental outcomes in adolescence. *Development and Psychopathology, 19,* 227–242.

Bennett, C. H., Wills, S. J., Oakeshott, S. M., & Mackintosh, N. J. (2000). Is the context specificity of latent inhibition a sufficient explanation of learned irrelevance? *The Quarterly Journal of Experimental Psychology B: Comparative and Physiological Psychology, 53*(B), 239–253.

Berger, S. M. (1962). Conditioning through vicarious instigation. *Psychological Review, 69,* 450–466.

Berkowitz, L. (1971). The contagion of violence: An S-R mediational analysis of some effects of observed aggression. In M. Page (Ed.), *Nebraska symposium on motivation* (pp. 95–135). Lincoln: University of Nebraska Press.

Berkowitz, L. (1978). Do we have to believe we are angry with someone in order to display "angry" aggression toward that person? In L. Berkowitz (Ed.), *Cognitive theories in social psychology: Papers reprinted from the advances in experimental social psychology* (pp. 455–463). New York: Academic Press.

Berkowitz, L., & LePage, A. (1967). Weapons as aggression-eliciting stimuli. *Journal of Personality and Social Psychology, 7,* 202–207.

Bernard, L. L. (1924). *Instinct: A study in social psychology.* New York: Henry Holt.

Bernard, R. S. (2005). Use of a token economy to increase exercise in children with cystic fibrosis. *Dissertation Abstracts International, Section B: The Sciences and Engineering, 65,* 6641.

Bernstein, I. L. (1978). Learned taste aversions in children receiving chemotherapy. *Science, 200,* 1302–1303.

Bernstein, I. L. (1991). Aversion conditioning in response to cancer and cancer treatment. *Clinical Psychology Review, 11,* 185–191.

Bernstein, I. L., & Webster, M. M. (1980). Learned taste aversions in humans. *Physiology and Behavior, 25,* 363–366.

Bersh, P. J. (1951). The influence of two variables upon the establishment of a secondary reinforcer for operant responses. *Journal of Experimental Psychology, 41,* 62–73.

Best, J. B. (1995). Cognitive psychology (4th ed.). Minneapolis, MN: West.

Betts, S. L., Brandon, S. E., & Wagner, A. R. (1996). Differential blocking of the acquisition of conditioned eyeblink responding and conditioned fear with a shift in UCS locus. *Animal Learning and Behavior, 24,* 459–470.

Bever, T. G. (1970). The cognitive basis for linguistic structures. In J. R. Hayes (Ed.), *Cognition and development of language* (pp. 277–360). New York: Wiley.

Biederman, G. B., D'Amato, M. R., & Keller, D. M. (1964). Facilitation of discriminated avoidance learning by dissociation of CS and manipulandum. *Psychonomic Science, 1,* 229–230.

Birch, H. G., & Rabinowitz, H. S. (1951). The negative effect of previous experience on productive thinking. *Journal of Experimental Psychology, 41,* 121–125.

Birch, L.L., McPhee L., Sullivan, S., & Johnson, S. (1989). Conditional meal initiation in young children. *Appetite, 13,* 105–113.

Bitensky, S. H. (2006) *Corporal punishment of children: A human rights violation.* Ardsley, NY: Transnational Publishers.

Bjork, R. A. (1989). Retrieval inhibition as soon an adaptive mechanism in human memory. In H. L. Roediger & F. I. M. Craik (Eds.), *Variety of memory and consciousness* (pp. 309–330). Hillsdale, NJ: Lawrence Erlbaum.

Black, R. W. (1968). Shifts in magnitude of reward and contrast effects in instrumental selective learning: A reinterpretation. *Psychological Review, 75,* 114–126.

Blaisdell, A. P., Gunther, L. M., & Miller, R. R. (1999). Recovery from blocking through deflation of the block stimulus. *Animal Learning and Behavior, 27,* 63–76.

Blanchard, R. J., & Blanchard, D. C. (1969). Crouching as an index of fear. *Journal of Comparative and Physiological Psychology, 67,* 370–375.

Blass, F.M. & Hall, W.G. (1976). Drinking termination: Interactions armorg hydrational, orogastric, and behavioral controls. *Psychological Record, 83,* 356–374.

Blehar, M. C., Lieberman, A. F., & Ainsworth, M. D. S. (1977). Early face-to-face interaction and its relation to later infant-mother attachment. *Child Development, 48,* 182–194.

Blodgett, H. C., & McCutchan, K. (1947). Place versus response learning in a simple T maze. *Journal of Experimental Psychology, 37,* 412–422.

Blodgett, H. C., & McCutchan, K. (1948). The relative strength of place and response learning in the T-maze. *Journal of Comparative and Physiological Psychology, 41,* 17–24.

Bloomfield, T. M. (1972). Contrast and inhibition in discrimination learning by the pigeon: Analysis through drug effects. *Learning and Motivation, 3,* 162–178.

Boakes, R. A., Poli, M., Lockwood, M. J., & Goodall, G. (1978). A study of misbehavior: Token reinforcement in the rat. *Journal of the Experimental Analysis of Behavior, 29,* 115–134.

Bolles, R. C. (1969). Avoidance and escape learning: Simultaneous acquisition of different responses. *Journal of Comparative and Physiological Psychology, 68,* 355–358.

Bolles, R. C. (1970). Species-specific defense reactions and avoidance learning. *Psychological Review, 77,* 32–48.

Bolles, R. C. (1972). Reinforcement, expectancy and learning. *Psychological Review, 79,* 394–409.

Bolles, R. C. (1978). The role of stimulus learning in defensive behavior. In S. H. Hulse, H. Fowler, & W. K. Honig (Eds.), *Cognitive processes in animal behavior* (pp. 89–108). Hillsdale, NJ: Lawrence Erlbaum.

Bolles, R. C. (1979). *Learning theory* (2nd ed.). New York: Holt, Rinehart & Winston.

Bolles, R. C., & Collier, A. C. (1976). The effect of predictive cues on freezing in rats. *Animal Learning and Behavior, 4,* 6–8.

Bolles, R. C., & Riley, A. (1973). Freezing as an avoidance response: Another look at the operant-respondent distinction. *Learning and Motivation, 4,* 268–275.

Bolles, R. C., & Tuttle, A. V. (1967). A failure to reinforce instrumental behavior by terminating a stimulus that had been paired with shock. *Psychonomic Science, 9,* 255–256.

Bolton, D., & Perrin, S. (2008). Evaluation of exposure with response-prevention for obsessive compulsive disorder in childhood and adolescence. *Journal of Behavior Therapy and Experimental Psychiatry, 39,* 11–22.

Bonardi, C., Hall, G., & Ong, S. Y. (2005). Analysis of the learned irrelevance effect in appetitive Pavlovian conditioning. *The Quarterly Journal of Experimental Psychology* 58(B), 141–162.

Bonardi, C., & Yann Ong, S. (2003). Learned irrelevance: A contemporary overview. *The Quarterly Journal of Experimental Psychology, 56*(B), 80–89.

Bondavera, T., Wesolowska, A., Dukat , M., Lee, M., Young, R., & Glennon, R. A. (2005) S(+)-and R(-)N-Methyl-1-(3,4-methylenedioxy-phenyl)-2-aminopropane (MDMA) as discriminative stimuli: effect of cocaine. *Pharmacology, Biochemistry, and Behavior, 82,* 531–538.

Booth, M. L., Siddle, D. A., & Bond, N. W. (1989). Effects of conditioned stimulus fear-relevance and preexposure on expectancy and electrodermal measures of human Pavlovian conditioning. *Psychophysiology, 26,* 281–291.

Booth, N. P. (1980). An opponent-process theory of motivation for jogging. Cited in R. L. Solomon. The opponent-process theory of motivation. *American Psychologist, 35,* 691–712

Borkovec, T. D. (1976). Physiological and cognitive processes in the regulation of fear. In G. E. Schwartz & D. Shapiro (Eds.), *Consciousness and self-regulation: Advances in research* (pp. 261–312). New York: Plenum Press.

Boudewyns, P. A., Fry, T. J., & Nightingale, E. J. (1986). Token economy programs in VA medical centers: Where are they today? *The Behavior Therapist, 9,* 126–127.

Bouton, M. E., Jones, D. L., McPhillips, S. A., & Swartzentruber, D. (1986). Potentiation and overshadowing in odor-aversion learning: Role of method of odor presentation, the distal-proximal area distinction, and the conditionality of odor. *Learning and Motivation, 17,* 115–138.

Bower, G. H. (1981). Mood and memory. *American Psychologist, 36,* 129–148.

Bower, G. H., Fowler, H., & Trapold, M. A. (1959). Escape learning as a function of amount of shock reduction. *Journal of Experimental Psychology, 48,* 482–484.

Bower, G. H., & Hilgard, E. R. (1981). *Theories of learning* (5th ed.). Englewood Cliffs, NJ: Prentice Hall.

Bower, G. H., & Springston, F. (1970). Pauses as recording points in letter sequences. *Journal of Experimental Psychology, 83,* 421–430.

Bower, G. H., Starr, R., & Lazarovitz, L. (1965). Amount of response-produced change in the CS and avoidance learning. *Journal of Comparative and Physiological Psychology, 59,* 13–17.

Bradley, L., & Houghton, S. (1992). The reduction of inappropriate sucking behaviour in a 7-year-old girl through response-cost and social-reinforcement procedures. *Behaviour Change, 9,* 254–257.

Brady, J. V. (1961). Motivational-emotional factors and intracranial self-stimulation. In D. E. Sheer (Ed.), *Electrical stimulation of the brain* (pp. 288–310). Austin: University of Texas Press.

Brandon, S. E., Vogel, E. H., & Wagner, A. R. (2002). Stimulus representation in SOP: 1. Theoretical rationalization and some implications. *Behavioural Processes, 62,* 5–25.

Brandon, S. E., & Wagner, A. R. (1991). Modulation of a discrete Pavlovian conditioned reflex by a putative emotive Pavlovian conditioned stimulus. *Journal of Experimental Psychology: Animal Behavior Process, 17,* 299–311.

Braveman, N. S. (1974). Poison-based avoidance learning with flavored or colored water in guinea pigs. *Learning and Motivation, 5,* 182–194.

Braveman, N. S. (1975). Formation of taste aversions in rats following prior exposure to sickness. *Learning and Motivation, 6,* 512–534.

Bregman, E. O., (1934). An attempt to modify the emotional attitudes of infants by conditioned response technique. *Journal of Genetic Psychology, 45,* 169–198.

Breland, K., & Breland, M. (1961). The misbehavior of organisms. *American Psychologist, 61,* 681–684.

Breland, K., & Breland, M. (1966). *Animal behavior.* New York: Macmillan.

Brewer, W. F., & Treyens, J. C. (1981). Role of schemata in memory for places. *Cognitive Psychology, 13,* 207–230.

Briere, J., & Conte, J. R. (1993). Self-reported amnesia for abuse in adults molested as children. *Journal of Traumatic Stress, 6,* 21–31.

Brigham, F. J., & Brigham, M. M. (1998). Using mnemonic keywords in general music classes: Music history meets cognitive psychology. *Journal of Research and Development in Education, 31,* 205–213.

Bristol, M. M., & Sloane, H. N., Jr. (1974). Effects of contingency contracting on study rate and test performance. *Journal of Applied Behavior Analysis, 7,* 271–285.

Britt, M. D., & Wise, R. A. (1983). Vental tegmental site of opiate reward: Antagonism by a hydrophilic opiate receptor blocker. *Brain Research, 258,* 105–108.

Brogden, W. J. (1939). Sensory preconditioning. *Journal of Experimental Psychology, 25,* 323–332.

Brooks, C. I. (1980). Effect of prior nonreward on subsequent incentive growth during brief acquisition. *Animal Learning and Behavior, 8,* 143–151.

Brown, J. L. (1975). *The evolution of behavior.* New York: Norton.

Brown, J. S., & Jacobs, A. (1949). The role of fear in the motivation and acquisition of responses. *Journal of Experimental Psychology, 39,* 747–759.

Brown, J. S., Martin, R. C., & Morrow, M. W. (1964). Self-punitive behavior in the rat: Facilitative effects of punishment on resistance to extinction. *Journal of Comparative and Physiological Psychology, 57,* 127–133.

Brown, R., Cazden, C., & Bellugi, U. (1969). The child's grammar from I to III. In J. P. Hill (Ed.), *Minnesota symposium on child psychology* (Vol. 2, pp. 28–73). Minneapolis: University of Minnesota Press.

Brucke, E. (1874). *Lectures on physiology.* Vienna: University of Vienna.

Bruner, J. S., Goodnow, J. J., & Austin, G. A. (1956). *A study of thinking.* New York: Wiley.

Bugelski, B. R. (1968). Images as mediators in one-trial paired-associated learning: II. Self-timing in successive lists. *Journal of Experimental Psychology, 77,* 328–334.

Burke, A., Heuer, F., & Reisberg, D. (1992). Remembering emotional events. *Memory and Cognition, 20,* 277–290.

Bush, D. E. A., DeSousa, N. J., & Vaccarino, F. J. (1999). Self-administration of intravenous amphetamine: Effect of nucleus accumbens CCK-sub(B) receptor activation on fixed-ratio responding. *Psychopharmacology, 147,* 331–334.

Butter, C. M., & Thomas, D. R. (1958). Secondary reinforcement as a function of the amount of primary reinforcement. *Journal of the Experimental Analysis of Behavior, 51,* 346–348.

Cain, M. E., Smith, C. M., & Bardo, M. T. (2004). The effect of novelty on amphetamine self-administration in rats classified as high and low responders. *Psychopharmacology* (Berlin), *176,* 129–138.

Camerer, C., & Johnson, E. J. (1991). The process-performance paradox in expert judgment: How can experts know so much and predict so badly? In K. M. Ericsson & J. Smith (Eds.), *Toward a theory of expertise: Prospects and limits* (pp. 195–217). Cambridge, UK: Cambridge University Press.

Camp, D. S., Raymond, G. A., & Church, R. M. (1967). Temporal relationship between response and punishment. *Journal of Experimental Psychology, 74,* 114–123.

Campbell, B. A., & Church, R. M. (1969). *Punishment and aversive behavior.* New York: Appleton-Century-Crofts.

Campbell, B. A., & Kraeling, D. (1953). Response strength as a function of drive level and amount of drive reduction. *Journal of Experimental Psychology, 45,* 97–101.

Campfield, L. A., & Smith, F. J. (2003). Blood glucose dynamics and control of meal initiation: A pattern detection and recognition theory. *Physiological Reviews, 83,* 25–58.

Cantor, M. B., & Wilson, J. F. (1984). Feeding the face: New directions in adjunctive behavior research. In F. R. Brush & J. B. Overmier (Eds.), *Affect, conditioning, and cognition* (pp. 299–311). Hillsdale, NJ: Lawrence Erlbaum.

Capaldi, E. J. (1971). Memory and learning: A sequential viewpoint. In W. K. Honig & P. H. R. James (Eds.), *Animal memory* (pp. 115–154). New York: Academic Press.

Capaldi, E. J. (1994). The relation between memory and expectancy as revealed by percentage and sequence of reward investigations. *Psychonomic Bulletin and Review, 1,* 303–310.

Capaldi, E. J., Hart, D., & Stanley, L. R. (1963). Effect of intertrial reinforcement on the aftereffect of nonreinforcement and resistance to extinction. *Journal of Experimental Psychology, 65,* 70–74.

Capaldi, E. J., & Spivey, J. E. (1964). Stimulus consequences of reinforcement and nonreinforcement: Stimulus traces or memory. *Psychonomic Science, 1,* 403–404.

Capretta, P. J. (1961). An experimental modification of food preference in chickens. *Journal of Comparative and Physiological Psychology, 54,* 238–242.

Carboni, E., Silvagni, A., Rolando, M. T., & Di Chiara, G. (2000). Stimulation of in vivo dopamine transmission in the bed nucleus of stria terminalis by reinforcing drugs. *The Journal of Neuroscience, 15,* RC102.

Carew, T. J., Hawkins, R. D., & Kandel, E. R. (1983). Differential classical conditioning of a defensive withdrawal reflex in *Aplysia californica. Science, 219,* 397–420.

Carlson, C. L., Mann, M., & Alexander, D. K. (2000). Effects of reward and response cost on the performance and motivation of children with ADHD. *Cognitive Therapy and Research, 24,* 87–98.

Carr, G. D., & White, N. (1984). The relationship between stereotype and memory improvement produced by amphetamine. *Psychopharmacology, 82,* 203–209.

Carr, G. D., & White, N. (1986). Anatomical dissociation of amphetamine's rewarding and aversive effects: An intracranial microinjection study. *Psychopharmacology, 39,* 340–346.

Carrell, L. E., Cannon, D. S., Best, M. R., & Stone, M. J. (1986). Nausea and radiation-induced taste aversions in cancer patients. *Appetite, 7,* 203–208.

Carter, L. F. (1941). Intensity of conditioned stimulus and rate of conditioning. *Journal of Experimental Psychology, 28,* 481–490.

Castro, L., Kennedy, P. L., & Wasserman, E. A. (2010). Conditional same-different discrimination by pigeons: Acquisition and generalization to novel and few-item displays. *Journal of Experimental Psychology: Animal Behavior Processes, 36,* 23–38.

Castro, L. & Rachlin, H. (1980). Self-reward, self-monitoring, and self-punishment as feedback in weight control. *Behavior Therapy, 11,* 38–48.

Castro, L., Young, M. E., & Wasserman, E. A. (2006) Effect of number of items and visual display variability on same-different discrimination behavior. *Memory and Cognition, 34,* 1689–1703.

Catania, A. C. (1979). *Learning.* Englewood Cliffs, NJ: Prentice-Hall.

Catania, A. C., & Reynolds, G. S. (1968). A quantitative analysis of the responding maintained by interval schedules of reinforcement. *Journal of Experimental Analysis of Behavior, 11,* 327–383.

Chandler, C. C. (1991). How memory for an event is influenced by related events: Interference in modified recognition tests. *Journal of Experimental Psychology: Learning, Memory, and Cognition, 17,* 115–125.

Charness, N. (1991). Expertise in chess: The balance between knowledge and search. In K. A. Ericsson & J. Smith (Eds.), *Toward a general theory of expertise* (pp. 39–63). Cambridge, UK: Cambridge University Press.

Cherek, D. R. (1982). Schedule-induced cigarette self-administration. *Pharmacology, Biochemistry, and Behavior, 17,* 523–527.

Chester, J. A., Price, C. S. & Froehlich, J. C. (2002). Inverse genetic association between alcohol preference and severity of alcohol withdrawal in two sets of rat lines selected for the same phenotype. *Alcoholism: Clinical and Experimental Research, 26,* 19–27.

Cheyne, J. A., Goyeche, J. R., & Walters, R. H. (1969). Attention, anxiety, and rules in resistance-to-deviation in children. *Journal of Experimental Child Psychology, 8,* 127–139.

Childress, A. R., Ehrman, R., McLellan, T. A., & O'Brien, C. P. (1986). Extinguishing conditioned responses during opiate dependence treatment: Turning laboratory findings into clinical procedures. *Journal of Substance Abuse Treatment, 3,* 33–40.

Chomsky, N. (1957). *Syntactic structures.* The Hague: Mouton.

Chomsky, N. (1965). *Aspects of the theory of syntax.* Cambridge, MA: MIT Press.

Chomsky, N. (1975). *Reflections on language.* New York: Pantheon.

Chomsky, N. (1987). Language in a psychological setting. *Sophia Linguistic Working Papers in Linguistics,* No. 22 (pp. 322–323). Tokyo: Sophia University.

Church, R. M. (1969). Response suppression. In B. A. Campbell & R. M. Church (Eds.), *Punishment and aversive behavior* (pp. 111–156). New York: Appleton-Century-Crofts.

Church, R. M., & Black, A. H. (1958). Latency of the conditioned heart rate as a function of the CS-UCS interval. *Journal of Comparative and Physiological Psychology, 51,* 478–482.

Clare, L., Wilson, B. A., Carter, G., Roth, I., & Hodges, J. R. (2002). Relearning face-name associations in early Alzheimer's disease. *Neuropsychology, 16,* 538–547.

Clum, G. A., Clum, G. A., & Surls, R. (1993). A meta-analysis of treatments for panic disorder. *Journal of Consulting and Clinical Psychology, 61,* 317–326.

Cohen, P. S., & Looney, T. A. (1973). Schedule-induced mirror responding in the pigeon. *Journal of the Experimental Analysis of Behavior, 19,* 395–408.

Cohen, T. E., Kaplan, S. W., Kandel, E. R., & Hawkins, R. D. (1997). A simplified preparation for relating cellular events to behavior: Mechanisms contributing to habituation, dishabituation, and sensitization of the *Aplysia* gill-withdrawal reflex. *Journal of Neuroscience, 17,* 2886–2899.

Collias, N. E., & Collias, E. C. (1956). Some mechanisms of family integration in ducks. *Auk, 73,* 378–400.

Collier, G., Hirsch, E., & Hamlin, P. H. (1972). The ecological determinants of reinforcement in the rat. *Physiology & Behavior, 9,* 705–716.

Collins, A. M., & Loftus, E. F., (1975). A spreading activation theory of semantic processing. *Psychological Review, 82,* 407–428.

Collins, A. M., & Quillian, M. R. (1969). Retrieval time from semantic memory. *Journal of Verbal Learning and Verbal Behavior, 8,* 240–247.

Colotla, V. A. (1981). Adjunctive polydipsia as a model of alcoholism. *Behavioral Biology, 23,* 238–242.

Colwill, R. C., & Rescorla, R. A. (1985). Instrumental conditioning remains sensitive to reinforcer devaluation after extensive training. *Journal of Experimental Psychology: Animal Behavior Processes, 11,* 520–536.

Commons, M. L., Mazur, J. E., Nevin, J. A., & Rachlin, H. (1987). The effect of delay and of intervening events on reinforcement value. *Quantitative analyses of behavior* (Vol. 5). Hillsdale, NJ: Lawrence Erlbaum.

Conners, F. A. (1992). Reading instruction for students with moderate mental retardation: Review and analysis of research. *American Journal of Mental Retardation, 96,* 577–597.

Conrad, C. (1972). Cognitive economy in semantic memory. *Journal of Experimental Psychology, 92,* 149–154.

Conrad, R. (1964). Acoustic confusions in immediate memory. *British Journal of Psychology, 55,* 75–84.

Conyers, C., Miltenberger, R. G., Maki, A., Barenz, R., Jurgens, M., Sailer, A., et al. (2004). A comparison of response cost and differential reinforcement of other behavior to reduce disruptive behavior in a preschool classroom. *Journal of Applied Behavior Analysis, 37,* 411–415.

Cook, R. G. (2002). The structure of pigeon multiple-class same-different learning. *Journal of the Experimental Analysis of Behavior, 78,* 345–364.

Cook, R. G., & Blaisdell, A. P. (2006). Short-term item memory in successive same-different discriminations. *Behavioural Processes, 72,* 255–264.

Cook, R. G., & Brooks, D. I. (2009). Generalized auditory same-different discriminations by pigeons. *Journal of Experimental Psychology: Animal Behavior Processes, 35,* 108–115.

Cook, R. G., Kelly, D. M., & Katz, J. S. (2003). Successive two-item same-different discrimination and concept learning by pigeons. *Behavioural Processes, 62,* 125–144.

Coons, E. E., & Cruce, J. A. F. (1968). Lateral hypothalamus: Food and current intensity in maintaining self-stimulation of hunger. *Science, 159,* 1117–1119.

Cooper, J. O., Heron, T. E., & Heward, W. C. (2007). *Applied behavior analysis* (2nd ed.). New York: Prentice-Hall.

Corey, J. R., & Shamov, J. (1972). The effects of fading on the acquisition and retention of oral reading. *Journal of Applied Behavior Analysis, 5,* 311–315.

Corkin, S., Amaral, D. G., Gonzalez, R. G., Johnson, K. A., & Hyman, B. T. (1997). H. M.'s medial temporal lobe lesion: Findings from magnetic resonance imaging. *Journal of Neuroscience, 17,* 3964–3979.

Cornoldi, C., & De Beni, R. (1991). Memory for discourse: Loci mnemonics and the oral presentation effect. *Applied Cognitive Psychology, 5,* 511–518.

Correia, C. J., & Benson, T. A. (2006). The use of contingency management to reduce cigarette smoking among college students. *Experimental and Clinical Psychopharmacology, 14,* 171–179.

Coulombe, D., & White, N. (1982). The effect of posttraining hypothalamic self-stimulation on sensory preconditioning in rats. *Canadian Journal of Psychology, 36,* 57–66.

Coulter, X., Riccio, D. C., & Page, H. A. (1969). Effects of blocking an instrumental avoidance response: Facilitated extinction but persistence of "fear." *Journal of Comparative and Physiological Psychology, 68,* 377–381.

Cowan, N. (1994). Mechanisms of verbal short-term memory. *Current Directions in Psychological Science, 6,* 185–189.

Cowan, N., Day, L., Saults, J. S., Keller, T. A., Johnson, T., & Flores, L. (1992). The role of verbal output time in the effects of word length on immediate memory. *Journal of Memory and Language, 31,* 1–17.

Craft, R. M., Kalivas, P. W., & Stratmann, J. A. (1996) Sex differences in discriminative stimulus effects of morphine in the rat. *Behavioral Pharmacology, 7,* 764–778

Craig, K. D., & Weinstein, M. S. (1965). Conditioning vicarious affective arousal. *Psychological Reports, 17,* 955–963.

Craig, R. L., & Siegel, P. S. (1980). Does negative affect beget positive effect? A test of opponent–process theory. *Bulletin of the Psychonomic Society, 14,* 404–406.

Craik, F. I. M., & Watkins, M. J. (1973). The role of rehearsal in short-term memory. *Journal of Verbal Learning and Verbal Behavior, 12,* 599–607.

Creer, T. L., Chai, H., & Hoffman, A. (1977). A single application of an aversive stimulus to eliminate chronic cough. *Journal of Behavior Research and Experimental Psychiatry, 8,* 107–109.

Crespi, L. P. (1942). Quantitative variation of incentive and performance in the white rat. *American Journal of Psychology, 55,* 467–517.

Croce, R. V. (1990). Effects of exercise and diet on body composition and cardiovascular fitness in adults with severe mental retardation. *Education and Training in Mental Retardation, 25,* 176–187.

Cromer, R. F. (1981). Reconceptualizing language acquisition and cognitive development. In R. L. Schiefelbusch & D. D. Brinker (Eds.), *Early language: Acquisition and intervention* (pp. 51–138). Baltimore: University Park Press.

Crooks, J. L. (1967). *Observational learning of fear in monkeys.* Unpublished manuscript, University of Pennsylvania, Philadelphia.

Crovitz, H. F. (1971). The capacity of memory loci in artificial memory. *Psychonomic Science, 24,* 187–188.

Crowder, R. G., & Morton, J. (1969). Precategorical acoustic storage (PAS). *Perception and Psychophysics, 5,* 365–373.

Crowell, C. R., Hinson, R. E., & Siegel, S. (1981). The role of conditional drug responses in tolerance to the hypothermic effects of ethanol. *Psychopharmacology, 73,* 51–54.

Cruser, L., & Klein, S. B. (1984). The role of schedule-induced polydipsia on temporal discrimination learning. *Psychological Reports, 58,* 443–452.

Dallery, J., Glenn, I. M., & Raiff, B. R. (2007). An Internet-based abstinence reinforcement treatment for cigarette smoking. *Drug and Alcohol Dependence, 86,* 230–238.

Daly, H. B. (1974). Reinforcing properties of escape from frustration aroused in various learning situations. In G. H. Bower (Ed.), *The psychology of learning and motivation* (Vol. 8, pp. 87–231). New York: Academic Press.

D'Amato, M. R. (1955). Secondary reinforcement and magnitude of primary reinforcement. *Journal of Comparative and Physiological Psychology, 48,* 378–380.

D'Amato, M. R. (1970). *Experimental psychology: Methodology, psychophysics, and learning.* New York: McGraw-Hill.

D'Amato, M. R., Fazzaro, J., & Etkin, M. (1968). Anticipatory responding and avoidance discrimination as factors in avoidance conditioning. *Journal of Experimental Psychology, 77,* 41–47.

D'Amato, M. R., & Schiff, E. (1964). Further studies of overlearning and position reversal learning. *Psychological Reports, 14,* 380–382.

D'Amato, M. R., & Van Sant, P. (1988). The person concept in monkeys (*Cebus paella*). *Journal of Experimental Psychology: Animal Behavior Processes, 14,* 43–55.

Datla, K. P., Ahier, R. G., Young, A. M., Gray, J. A., & Joseph, M. H. (2002). Conditioned appetitive stimulus increases extracellular dopamine in the nucleus accumbens of the rat. *European Journal of Neuroscience, 16,* 1987–1993.

Davidson, G. C., & Neale, J. M. (1994). *Abnormal psychology* (6th ed.). New York: Wiley.

Davidson, R. S. (1972). *Aversive modification of alcoholic behavior: Punishment of an alcohol-reinforced operant.* Unpublished manuscript, U.S. Veterans Administration Hospital, Miami, Florida.

Davidson, T. L., Aparicio, J., & Rescorla, R. R. (1988). Transfer between Pavlovian facilitators and instrumental discriminative stimuli. *Animal Learning and Behavior, 16,* 285–291.

Davis, H. (1968). Conditioned suppression: A survey of the literature. *Psychonomic Monograph Supplements, 2*(14, 38), 283–291.

Davis, J. C., & Okada, R. (1971). Recognition and recall of positively forgotten words. *Journal of Experimental Psychology, 89,* 181–186.

Davis, M. (1974). Sensitization of the rat startle response by noise. *Journal of Comparative and Physiological Psychology, 87,* 571–581.

Davis, S. F., Best, M. R., & Grover, C. A. (1988). Toxicosis-mediated potentiation in a taste/taste compound: Evidence for within-compound associations. *Learning and Motivation, 19,* 183–205.

De Beni, R., & Pazzaglia, F. (1995). Memory for different kinds of mental images: Role of contextual and autobiographic variables. *Neuropsychologia, 33,* 1359–1371.

de Brugada, I., Hall, G., & Symonds, M. (2004). The US-preexposure effect in lithium-induced flavor-aversion conditioning is a consequences of blocking by injection cues. *Journal of Experimental Psychology: Animal Behavior Processes, 30,* 58–66.

De la Casa, L. G., Diaz, E., & Lubow, R. E. (2005) Delay induced attenuation of latent inhibition with a conditional emotional response depends on CS-US strength. *Learning and Motivation, 36,* 60–76.

De Martini-Scully, D., Bray, M. A., & Kehle, T. J. (2000). A packaged intervention to reduce disruptive behaviors in general education students. *Psychology in the Schools, 37,* 149–156.

de Villiers, P. A. (1977). Choice in concurrent schedules and a quantitative formulation of the law of effect. In W. K. Honig & J. E. R. Staddon (Eds.), *Handbook of operant conditioning* (pp. 233–287). Englewood Cliffs, NJ: Prentice Hall.

Dean, S. J., Denny, M. R., & Blakemore, T. (1985). Vicious-circle behavior involves new learning. *Bulletin of the Psychonomic Society, 23,* 230–232.

Denniston, J. C., Savastano, H. I., Blaisdell, A. P., & Miller, R. R. (2003). Cue competition as a retrieval deficit. *Learning and Motivation, 34,* 1–31.

Denniston, J. C., Savastano, H. I., & Miller, R. R. (2001). The extended comparator hypothesis: Learning by contiguity, responding by relative strength. In R. R. Mowrer & S. B. Klein (Eds.), *Handbook of contemporary learning theories* (pp. 65–117). Mahwah, NJ: Lawrence Erlbaum.

Denny, M. R. (1971). Relaxation theory and experiments. In F. R. Brush (Ed.), *Aversive conditioning and learning* (pp. 235–299). New York: Academic Press.

Denny, M. R., & Weisman, R. G. (1964). Avoidance behavior as a function of the length of nonshock confinement. *Journal of Comparative and Physiological Psychology, 58,* 252–257.

Derwinger, A., Stigsdotter, N, A., Person, M., Hill, R. D., & Backman, L. (2003). Remembering numbers in old age: Mnemonic training versus self-generated strategy training. *Aging, Neuropsychology, and Cognition, 10,* 202–214.

DeSousa, N. J., Bush, D. E. A., & Vaccarino, F. J. (2000). Self-administration of intravenous amphetamine is predicted by individual differences in sucrose feeding in rats. *Pharmacology, Biochemistry, and Behavior, 148,* 52–58.

DeSousa, N. J., & Vaccarino, F. J. (2001). Neurobiology of reinforcement: Interaction between dopamine and cholecystokinin systems. In R. R. Mowrer & S. B. Klein (Eds.), *Handbook of contemporary learning theories* (pp. 441–468). Mahwah, NJ: Lawrence Erlbaum.

Devine, D. P., & Wise, R. A. (1994). Self-administration of morphine, DAMGO, and DPDPE into the ventral tegmental area of rats. *The Journal of Neuroscience, 14,* 1978–1984.

Dewey, J. (1886). *Psychology.* New York: Harper & Row.

DeYoung, D. M. (2002). An evaluation of the implementation of ignition interlock in California. *Journal of Safety Research, 33,* 473–482.

Di Ciano, P., & Everitt, B. J. (2002). Reinstatement and spontaneous recovery of cocaine-seeking following extinction and different durations of withdrawal. *Behavioral Pharmacology, 13,* 397–406.

Dickinson, A. (1989). Expectancy theory in animal conditioning. In S. B. Klein & R. R. Mowrer (Eds.), *Contemporary learning theories: Pavlovian conditioning and the states of traditional learning theory* (pp. 279–308). Hillsdale, NJ: Lawrence Erlbaum.

Dickinson, A. (2001). Causal learning: An associate analysis. *The Quarterly Journal of Experimental Psychology B: Comparative and Physiological Psychology, 54*(B), 3–25.

Dickinson, A., & Balleine, B. W. (1994). Motivational control of goal-directed action. *Animal Learning and Behavior, 22,* 1–18.

Dickinson, A., & Balleine, B. W. (1995). Motivational control of instrumental action. *Current Directions in Psychological Science, 4,* 162–167.

Dickinson, A., Balleine, B., Watt, A., Gonzalez, F., & Boakes, R. A. (1995). Motivational control after extended instrumental training. *Animal Learning & Behavior, 23,* 197–206.

Dickinson, A., & Dawson, G. R. (1987). Pavlovian processes in the motivation control of instrumental performance. *Quarterly Journal of Experimental Psychology, 39*(B), 201–213.

Dickinson, A., & Nicholas, D. J. (1983). Irrelevant incentive learning during instrumental conditioning: The role of drive-reinforcer and response-reinforcer relationships. *Quarterly Journal of Experimental Psychology, 35*(B), 249–263.

Dickinson, A., Wood, N., & Smith, J. W. (2002). Alcohol seeking by rats: Action or habit? *The Quarterly Journal of Experimental Psychology B: Comparative and Physiological Psychology, 55*(B), 331–348.

Domjan, M. (1976). Determinants of the enhancement of flavor-water intake by prior exposure. *Journal of Experimental Psychology: Animal Behavior Processes, 2,* 17–27.

Domjan, M. (1977). Selective suppression of drinking during a limited period following aversive drug treatment in rats. *Journal of Experimental Psychology: Animal Behavior Processes, 3,* 66–76.

Domjan, M. (2005). Pavlovian conditioning: A functional perspective. *Annual Review of Psychology, 56,* 179–206.

Dorry, G. W., & Zeaman, D. (1975). The use of a fading technique in paired-associate teaching of a reading vocabulary with retardates. *Mental Retardation, 11,* 3–6.

Dorry, G. W., & Zeaman, D. (1976). Teaching a simple reading vocabulary to retarded children: Effectiveness of fading and on fading procedures. *American Journal of Mental Deficiency, 79,* 711–716.

Doyle, T. F., & Samson, H. H. (1988). Adjunctive alcohol drinking in humans. *Physiology & Behavior, 44,* 775–779.

Drabman, R., & Spitalnik, R. (1973). Social isolation as a punishment procedure: A controlled study. *Journal of Experimental Child Psychology, 16,* 236–249.

Ducker, G.,& Rensch, B. (1968). Verzogerung des Vergessens erlernter visuellen Aufgaben bei Fischen durch Dunkelhaltung. *Pfluengers Archiv fur die Gasamte Physiolgie des Menschen und der Tiere, 301,* 1–6.

Duker, P. C., & Seys, D. M. (1996). Long-term use of electrical aversion treatment with self-injurious behavior. *Research in Developmental Disabilities, 17,* 293–301.

Duker, P. C. & Seys, D. M. (2000). A quasi-experimental study on the effect of electrical aversion treatment on imposed mechanical restraint for severe self-injurious behavior. *Research in Developmental Disabilities, 21,* 235–242.

DuNann, D. G., & Weber, S. J. (1976). Short- and long-term effects of contingency managed instruction on low, medium, and high GPA students. *Journal of Applied Behavior Analysis, 9,* 375–376.

Dunn, K. E., Sigmon, S. C., Thomas, C. S., Heil, S. H., & Higgins, S. T. (2008). Voucher-based contingent reinforcement of smoking abstinence among methadone-maintained patients: A pilot study. *Journal of Applied Behavior Analysis, 41,* 527–538.

Durlach, P. (1989). Learning and performance in Pavlovian conditioning: Are failures of contiguity failures of learning or performance? In S. B. Klein & R. R. Mowrer (Eds.), *Contemporary learning theories: Pavlovian conditioning and the status of traditional learning theory* (pp. 19–69). Hillsdale, NJ: Lawrence Erlbaum.

Ebbinghaus, H. (1885). *Memory: A contribution to experimental psychology* (H. A. Ruger & C. E. Bussenius, Trans.). New York: Dover.

Ehrman, R. N., Robbins, S. J., Childress, A. R., & O'Brien, C. P. (1992). Conditioned responses to cocaine-related stimuli in cocaine abuse patients. *Psychopharmacology, 107,* 523–529.

Eibl-Eibesfeldt, I. (1970). *Ethology: The biology of Behavior.* New York: Holt

Eich, J. E. (1980). The cue-dependent nature of state-dependent retrieval. *Memory and Cognition, 8,* 157–173.

Eich, J. E., Weingartner, H., Stillman, R. C., & Gillin, J. C. (1975). State-dependent accessibility of retrieval cues in the retention of a categorized list. *Journal of Verbal Learning and Verbal Behavior, 14,* 408–417.

Eimas, P. D., & Corbit, J. D. (1973). Selective adaptation of linguistic feature detectors. *Cognitive Psychology, 4,* 99–109.

Eimas, P. D., Siqueland, E. R., Jusczyk, P., & Vigorito, J. (1971). Speech perception in infants. *Science, 171,* 303–306.

Eisenstein, E. M., & Eisenstein, D. (2006). A behavioral homeostatsis theory of habituation and sensitization: II. Further developments and predications. *Reviews in the Neurosciences, 17,* 533–557.

Eisenstein, E. M., Eisenstein, D., & Smith, J. C. (2001). The evolutionary significance of habituation and sensitization across phylogeny: A behavioral homeostasis model. *Integrative Physiological & Behavioral Science, 36,* 251–265.

Ekstrand, B. R. (1967). Effect of sleep on memory. *Journal of Experimental Psychology, 75,* 64–72.

Elkind, D. (1981). Recent research in cognitive and language development. In L. T. Benjamin (Ed.), *The G. Stanley Hall lecture series* (Vol. 1). Washington, DC: American Psychological Association.

Elkins, R. L. (1973). Attenuation of drug-induced bait shyness to a palatable solution as an increasing function of its availability prior to conditioning. *Behavioral Biology, 9,* 221–226.

Elmes, D. G., Adams, C., & Roediger, H. (1970). Cued forgetting in short-term memory. *Journal of Experimental Psychology, 86,* 103–107.

Emmelkamp, P. M. G., van der Helm, M., van Zanten, B. L., & Plochg, I. (1980). Treatment of obsessive-compulsive patients: The contribution of self-instructional training to the effectiveness of exposure. *Behavior Research and Therapy, 18,* 61–66.

Epstein, D. M. (1967). Toward a unified theory of anxiety. In B. A. Maher (Ed.), *Progress in experimental personality research* (pp. 1–89). New York: Academic Press.

Ernst, M. M., & Epstein, L. H. (2002). Habituation of responding for food in humans. *Appetite, 38,* 224–234.

Ervin, F. R., Mark, V. H., & Stevens, J. R. (1969). Behavioral and affective responses to brain stimulation in man. In J. Zubin & C. Shagass (Eds.), *Neurological aspects of psychopathology* (pp. 178–189). New York: Grune & Stratton.

Esber, G. R., Pearce, J. M., & Haselgrove, M. (2009). Enhancement of responding to A after A + /AX + training; challenges for a comparator theory of learning. *Journal of Experimental Psychology; Animal Behavior Processes, 35,* 405–497.

Estes, W. K. (1944). An experimental study of punishment. *Psychological Monographs, 57,* (Whole No. 263).

Estes, W. K. (1969). Outline of a theory of punishment. In B. A. Campbell & R. M. Church (Eds.), *Punishment and aversive behavior* (pp. 57–82). New York: Appleton-Century-Crofts.

Estes, W. K., & Skinner, B. F. (1941). Some quantitative properties of anxiety. *Journal of Experimental Psychology, 29,* 390–400.

Ettenberg, A. (2004). Opponent process properties of self-administered cocaine. *Neuroscience and Biobehavioral Reviews, 27,* 721–728.

Ettenberg, A., Pettit, H. O., Bloom, F. E., & Koob, G. F. (1982). Heroin and cocaine intravenous self-administration in rats: Mediation by separate neural systems. *Psychopharmacology, 78,* 204–209.

Evans, K. R., & Vaccarino, F. J. (1990). Amphetamine- and morphine-induced feeding: Evidence for involvement of reward mechanisms. *Neuroscience, Biobehavioral Reviews, 14,* 9–22.

Eysenck, M. W. (1978). Levels of processing: A critique. *British Journal of Psychology, 68,* 157–169.

Eysenck, H. J. (1960). Learning theory and behavior therapy. In H. J. Eysenck (Ed.), *Behavior Therapy and the neurosis: Readings in modern methods of treatment derived from learning theory.* Oxford, UK: Pergamon.

Fabricius, E. (1951). Zur ethologie junger anatiden. *Acta Zoologica Fennica, 68,* 1–175.

Fadda, P., Scherma, M., Fresu, A., Collu, M., & Fratta, W. (2003). Baclofen antagonizes nicotine-, cocaine-, and morphine-induced dopamine release in the nucleus accumbens of rat. *Synapse, 50,* 1–6.

Falk, J. L. (1961). Production of polydipsia in normal rats by an intermittent food schedule. *Science, 133,* 195–196.

Falk, J. L. (1966). The motivational properties of schedule-induced polydipsia. *Journal of the Experimental Analysis of Behavior, 9,* 19–25.

Falk, J. L. (1998). Drug abuse as an adjunctive behavior. *Drug and Alcohol Dependence, 52,* 91–98.

Falk, J. L., & Samson, H. H. (1976). Schedule-induced physical dependence on ethanol. *Pharmacological Reviews, 27,* 449–464.

Falk, J. L., Samson, H. H., & Tang, M. (1973). Chronic ingestion techniques for the production of physical dependence on ethanol. In M. M. Gross (Ed.), *Alcohol intoxication and withdrawal: Experimental studies* (pp. 197–211). New York: Plenum Press.

Falk, J. L., Samson, H. H., & Winger, G. (1976). Polydipsia-induced alcohol dependency in rats. *Science, 192,* 492.

Fanselow, M. S., & Baackes, M. P. (1982). Conditioned fear-induced opiate analgesia on the formalin test: Evidence for two aversive motivational systems. *Learning and Motivation, 13,* 200–221.

Fanselow, M. S., & Bolles, R. C. (1979). Naloxone and shock-elicited freezing the rat. *Journal of Comparative and Physiological Psychology, 93,* 736–744.

Fantino, E., Preston, R. A., & Dunn, R. (1993). Delay reduction: Current status. *Journal of the Experimental Analysis of Behavior, 60,* 159–169.

Faure, S., Haberland, U., Conde, F., El Massioui, N. (2005). Lesion to the nigrostriatal dopamine system disrupts stimulus-response habit formation. *The Journal of Neuroscience, 25,* 2771–2780.

Faust, J., Olson, R., & Rodriquez, H. (1991). Same-day surgery preparation: Reduction of pediatric patient arousal and distress through participant modeling. *Journal of Consulting and Clinical Psychology, 59,* 475–478.

Fazzaro, J., & D'Amato, M. R. (1969). Resistance to extinction after varying amounts of nondiscriminative or cue-correlated escape training. *Journal of Comparative and Physiological Psychology, 68,* 373–376.

Feather, B. W. (1967). Human salivary conditioning: A methodological study. In G. A. Kimble (Ed.), *Foundations of conditioning and learning* (pp. 117–141). New York: Appleton-Century-Crofts.

Feeney, D. M. (1987). Human rights and animal welfare. *American Psychologist, 42,* 593–599.

Fehr, B., & Russell, J. A. (1991). The concept of love viewed from a prototype perspective. *Journal of Personality and Social Psychology, 60,* 425–438.

Felton, J., & Lyon, D. O. (1966). The postreinforcement pause. *Journal of the Experimental Analysis of Behavior, 9,* 131–134.

Feltz, D. L. (1982). The analysis of the causal elements in Bandura's theory of self-efficacy and an anxiety-based model of avoidance behavior. *Journal of Personality and Social Psychology, 42,* 764–781.

Feltz, D. L., Chow, G. M., & Hepler, T. J. (2008) Path analysis of self-efficacy and diving performance revisited. *Journal of Sport and Exercise Psychology, 30,* 401–411.

Fenwick, S., Mikulka, P. J., & Klein, S. B. (1975). The effect of different levels of preexposure to sucrose on acquisition and extinction of conditioned aversion. *Behavioral Biology, 14,* 231–235.

Ferster, C. B., & Skinner, B. F. (1957). *Schedules of reinforcement.* New York: Appleton-Century-Crofts.

Filcheck, H. A., McNeil, C. B., Greco, L. A., & Bernard, R. S. (2004). Using a whole-class token economy and coaching of teacher skills in a preschool classroom to manage disruptive behavior. *Psychology in the Schools, 41,* 351–361.

Files, F. J., Denning, C. E., & Samson, H. H. (1998). Effects of the atypical antipsychotic remoxipride on alcohol self-administration. *Pharmacology, Biochemistry, and Behavior, 59,* 281–285.

Flaherty, C. F. (1985). *Animal learning and cognition.* New York: Knopf.

Flaherty, C. F. (1996). *Incentive relativity.* New York: Cambridge University Press.

Flaherty, C. F., & Davenport, J. W. (1972). Successive brightness discrimination in rats following regular versus random intermittent reinforcement. *Journal of Experimental Psychology, 96,* 1–9.

Flaherty, C. F., & Driscoll, C. (1980). Amobarbital sodium reduces successive gustatory contrast. *Psychopharmacology, 69,* 161–162.

Flaherty, C. F., Hamilton, L. W., Gandelman, R. J., & Spear, N. E. (1977). *Learning and memory.* Chicago: Rand McNally.

Flakus, W. J., & Steinbrecher, B. C. (1964). Avoidance conditioning in the rabbit. *Psychological Reports, 14,* 140.

Flavell, J. H., Cooper, A., & Loiselle, R. H. (1958). Effect of the number of preutilization functions on functional fixedness in problem solving. *Psychological Reports, 4,* 343–350.

Fletcher, P. J. (1998). A comparison of the effects of risperidone, raclopride, and ritanserin on intravenous self-administration of d-amphetamine. *Pharmacology, Biochemistry, and Behavior, 60,* 55–60.

Flory, R. K. (1971). The control of schedule-induced polydipsia: Frequency and magnitude of reinforcement. *Learning and Motivation, 2,* 215–227.

Foder, J. A., Bever, T. G., & Garrett, M. F. (1974). *The psychology of language: An introduction to psycholinguistics and generative grammar.* New York: McGraw-Hill.

Ford, K. A. & Riley, A. L. (1984). The effects of LiCl preexposure on amphetamine-induced taste aversions: An assessment of blocking. *Pharmacology, Biochemistry, and Behavior, 20,* 643–645.

Forster, K. I. (1979). Levels of processing and the structure of the language processor. In W. E. Cooper & T. Walker (Eds.), *Sentence processing* (pp. 27–85). Hillsdale, NJ: Lawrence Erlbaum.

Fournier, A. K., Ehrhart, I. J., Glindemann, K. E., & Geller, E. S. (2004). Intervening to decrease alcohol abuse at university parties: Differential reinforcement of intoxication level. *Behavior Modification, 28,* 167–181.

Fowler, H., & Miller, N. E. (1963). Facilitation and inhibition of runway performance by hind- and forepaw shock of various intensities. *Journal of Comparative and Physiological Psychology, 56,* 801–805.

Fowler, H., & Trapold, M. A. (1962). Escape performance as a function of delay of reinforcement. *Journal of Experimental Psychology, 63,* 464–467.

Freedman, P. E., Hennessy, J. W., & Groner, D. (1974). Effects of varying active/passive shock levels in shuttle box avoidance in rats. *Journal of Comparative and Physiological Psychology, 86,* 79–84.

Freeman, J. B., & Marrs Garcia, A (2009). *Family-based treatment for young children with OCD: Therapist guide.* New York: Oxford University Press.

Frey, P. W. (1969). Within- and between-session CS intensity performance effects in rabbit eyelid conditioning. *Psychonomic Science, 17,* 1–2.

Friesen, W. O. (1989). Neuronal coding of leech swimming movements. In J. W. Jacklet (Ed.), *Neuronal and cellular oscillators* (pp. 269–316). New York: Dekker.

Fulkerson, J. A. (2003). Blow and go: The breath-analyzed ignition interlock device as a technological response to DWI. *American Journal of Drug and Alcohol Abuse, 29,* 219–235.

Gabrieli, J. D. E. (1998). Cognitive neuroscience of human memory. *Annual Review of Psychology, 49,* 87–115.

Gabrieli, J. D. E., Cohen, N. J., & Corkin, S. (1988). The impaired learning of semantic knowledge following bilateral medial temporal-lobe resection. *Brain and Cognition, 7,* 157–177.

Galbraith, D. A., Byrick, R. J., & Rutledge, J. T. (1970). An aversive conditioning approach to the inhibition of chronic vomiting. *Canadian Psychiatric Association Journal, 15,* 311–313.

Ganz, L. (1968). An analysis of generalization behavior in the stimulus-deprived organism. In G. Newton & S. Levine (Eds.), *Early experience and behavior* (pp. 365–411). Springfield, IL: Charles C Thomas.

Ganz, L., & Riesen, A. H. (1962). Stimulus generalization to hue in the dark-reared macaque. *Journal of Comparative and Physiological Psychology, 55,* 92–99.

Garb, J. J., & Stunkard, A. J. (1974). Taste aversions in man. *American Journal of Psychiatry, 131,* 1204–1207.

Garcia, J. (1989). Food for Tolman: Cognition and cathexis in concert. In T. Archer & L. Nillson (Eds.), *Aversion, avoidance, and anxiety: Perspectives on aversively motivated behavior* (pp. 45–85). London: Lawrence Erlbaum.

Garcia, J., Brett, L. P., & Rusiniak, K. W. (1989). Limits of Darwinian conditioning. In S. B. Klein & R. R. Mowrer (Eds.), *Contemporary learning theories: Instrumental conditioning theory and the impact of biological constraints on learning* (pp. 181–203). Hillsdale, NJ: Lawrence Erlbaum.

Garcia, J., Clark, J. C., & Hankins, W. G. (1973). Natural responses to scheduled rewards. In P. P. G. Bateson & P. H. Klopfer (Eds.), *Perspectives in ethology* (Vol. 1, pp. 1–41). New York: Plenum Press.

Garcia, J., & Garcia y Robertson, R. (1985). Evolution of learning mechanisms. In B. L. Hammonds (Ed.), *Psychology and learning* (pp. 191–243). Washington, DC: American Psychological Association.

Garcia, J., Hankins, W. G., & Rusiniak, K. W. (1974). Behavioral regulation of the milieu interne in man and rat. *Science, 185,* 824–831.

Garcia, J., Kimeldorf, D. J., & Hunt, E. L. (1957). Spatial avoidance in the rat as a result of exposure to ionizing radiation. *British Journal of Radiology, 30,* 318–322.

Garcia, J., Kimeldorf, D. J., & Koelling, R. A. (1955). Conditioned aversion to saccharin resulting from exposure to gamma radiation. *Science, 122,* 157–158.

Garcia, J., & Koelling, R. A. (1966). Relation of cue to consequence in avoidance learning. *Psychonomic Science, 4,* 123–124.

Garcia, J., & Rusiniak, K. W. (1980). What the nose learns from the mouth. In D. Muller-Schwarze & R. M. Silverskin (Eds.), *Chemical senses* (pp. 141–156). New York: Plenum Press.

Garcia-Palacios, A., Hoffman, H., Carlin, A., Furness, T. A., III, & Botella, C. (2002). Virtual reality in the treatment of spider phobia: A controlled study. *Behaviour Research and Therapy, 40,* 983–993.

Gardner, B. J., & Gardner, R. A. (1971). Two-way communication with an infant chimpanzee. In A. M. Schrier & F. Stolnitz (Eds.), *Behavior of nonhuman primates: Modern research trends* (pp. 117–184). New York: Academic Press.

Gathercole, S. E., & Baddeley, A. D. (1993). *Essays in cognitive psychology. In Working memory and language.* London: Lawrence Erlbaum.

Gaudiano, B. A., & Herbert, J. D. (2007). Self-efficacy for social situations in adolescents with generalized social anxiety disorder. *Behavioural and Cognitive Psychotherapy, 35,* 209–223.

Geiselman, R. E., Bjork, R. A., & Fishman, D. (1983). Disrupted retrieval in directed forgetting: A link with posthypnotic retrieval. *Journal of Experimental Psychology: General, 112,* 58–72.

Gelder, M. (1991). Psychological treatment for anxiety disorders: Adjustment disorder with anxious mood, generalized anxiety disorders, panic disorder, agoraphobia, and avoidant personality disorder. In W. Coryell & G. Winokur (Eds.), *The clinical management of anxiety disorders* (pp. 10–27). New York: Oxford University Press.

Gelfand, D. M., Hartmann, D. P., Lamb, A. K., Smith, C. L., Mahan, M. A., & Paul, S. C. (1974). The effects of adult models and described alternatives on children's choice of behavior management techniques. *Child Development, 45,* 585–593.

Geller, E. S., & Hahn, H. A. (1984). Promoting safety belt use at industrial sites: An effective program for blue collar employees. *Professional Psychology: Research and Practice, 15,* 553–564.

Genn, R. F., Barr, A. M. & Phillips, A. G. (2002). Effects of amisulpride on consummatory negative contrast. *Behavioural Pharmacology, 13,* 659–662.

Gentry, G. D., Weiss, B., & Laties, V. G. (1983). The microanalysis of fixed-interval responding. *Journal of the Experimental Analysis of Behavior, 39,* 327–343.

Gerrits, M., & Van Ree, J. M. (1996). Effects of nucleus accumbens dopamine depletion on motivational aspects involved in initiation of cocaine and heroin self-administration in rats. *Brain Research, 713,* 114–124.

Gershoff, E. T. (2002). Corporal punishment by parents and associated child behaviors and experiences: A meta-analytic and theoretical review. *Psychological Bulletin, 128,* 539–579.

Gershoff, E. T. & Bitensky, S. H. (2007) The case against corporal punishment: Converging evidence from social science research and international human rights law and implications for U.S. public policy. *Psychology, Public Policy, and Law, 13,* 231–272.

Gianoulakis, C. (2004). Endogenous opioids and addiction to alcohol and other drugs of abuse. *Current Topics in Medicinal Chemistry, 4,* 39–50.

Gibb, B. E., Alloy, L. B., Abramson, L. Y., & Marx, B. P. (2003). Childhood maltreatment and maltreatment-specific inferences: A test of Rose and Abramson's (1992) extension of the hopelessness theory. *Cognition & Emotion, 17,* 917–931.

Gibb, B. E., Beevers, C. G., Andover, M. S., & Holleran, K. (2006). The hopelessness theory of depression: A prospective multi-wave test of the vulnerability-stress hypothesis. *Cognitive Therapy and Research, 30,* 763–772.

Gilbert, R. M. (1974). Ubiquity of schedule-induced polydipsia. *Journal of the Experimental Analysis of Behavior, 21,* 277–284.

Givon, T., & Savage-Rumbaugh, S. (2009). Can apes learn grammar? A short detour into language evolution. In J. Guo, E. Lieven, N. Budwig, S. Ervin-Tripp, K. Nakamura, & S. Ozcaliskan (Eds.), *Crosslinguistic approaches to the psychology of language: Research in the tradition of Dan Issac Slobin* (pp. 299–309). New York: Psychology Press.

Glasgow, R. E., Klesges, R. C., Mizes, J. S., & Pechacek, T. F. (1985) Quitting smoking: Strategies used and variables associated with success in a stop-smoking contest. *Journal of Consulting and Clinical Psychology, 53,* 905–912.

Glass, A. L., & Holyoak, K. J. (1975). *Cognition.* New York: Random House.

Glasscock, S. G., Friman, P. C., O'Brien, S., & Christopherson, E. F. (1986). Varied citrus treatment of ruminant gagging in a teenager with Batten's disease. *Journal of Behavior Therapy and Experimental Psychiatry, 17,* 129–133.

Gleitman, H. (1971). Forgetting of long-term memories in animals. In W. K. Honig & P. H. R. James (Eds.), *Animal memory* (pp. 2–46). New York: Academic Press.

Glenberg, M. A. (1997). What memory is for. *Behavioral and Brain Sciences, 20,* 1–19.

Glenberg, M. A., Schroeder, J. I., & Robertson, D. A. (1998). Averting the gaze disengages the environment and facilitates remembering. *Memory and Cognition, 26,* 651–658.

Glueck, S., & Glueck, E. (1950). *Unraveling juvenile delinquency.* Cambridge, MA: Harvard University Press.

Gobet, F., & Simon, H. A. (1996). Recall of random and distorted chess positions: Implications for the theory of expertise. *Memory and Cognition, 24,* 493–503.

Goeders, N. E., Lane, J. D., & Smith, J. E. (1984). Self-administration of methionine enkephalin into the nucleus accumbens. *Pharmacology, Biochemistry and Behavior, 20,* 451–455.

Gold, J. J., & Squire, L. R. (2006). The anatomy of amnesia: Neurohistological analysis of three new cases. *Learning and Memory, 13,* 699–710.

Gollin, E. S., & Savoy, P. (1968). Fading procedures and conditional discrimination in children. *Journal of the Experimental Analysis of Behavior, 48,* 371–388.

Gooden, D. R., & Baddeley, A. D. (1975). Context-dependent memory in two natural environments: On land and underwater. *British Journal of Psychology, 66,* 325–331.

Gooding, P. A., Isaac, C. L., & Mayes, A. R. (2005). Prose recall and amnesia: More implications for the episodic buffer. *Neuropsychologia, 43,* 583–587.

Goodman, I. J., & Brown, J. L. (1966). Stimulation of positively and negatively reinforcing sites in the avian brain. *Life Sciences, 5,* 693–704.

Goodwin, D. W., Powell, B., Bremer, D., Hoine, H., & Stein, J. (1969). Alcohol and recall: State-dependent effects in man. *Science, 163,* 1358–1360.

Goomas, D. T. (1981). Multiple shifts in magnitude of reward. *Psychological Reports, 49,* 335–338.

Gordon, W. C. (1983). Malleability of memory in animals. In R. L. Mellgren (Ed.), *Animal cognition and behavior* (pp. 399–426). New York: North Holland.

Gordon, W. C. & Klein, R. L. (1994). Animal memory: The effects of context change on retention performance. In N. J. Mackintosh (Ed.), *Animal learning and cognition* (pp. 255–279). San Diego, CA: Academic Press.

Gordon, W. C., McCracken, K. M., Dees-Beech, N., & Mowrer, R. R. (1981). Mechanisms for the cueing phenomenon: The addition of the cueing context to the training memory. *Learning and Motivation, 12,* 196–211.

Gormezano, I. (1969). Classical conditioning. In J. B. Sidowski (Ed.), *Experimental methods of instrumentation in psychology* (pp. 385–420). New York: McGraw-Hill.

Gormezano, I. (1972). Investigations of defense and reward conditioning in the rabbit. In A. H. Black & W. F. Prokasy (Eds.), *Classical conditioning II: Current theory and research* (pp. 151–181). New York: Academic Press.

Graham, D. (1989). *Ecological learning theory.* Florence, KY: Taylor & Francis/Routledge.

Grady, K. E., Goodenow, C., & Borkin, J. R. (1988). *Journal of Behavioral Medicine, 11,* 43–57.

Grant, D. A., & Schneider, D. E. (1948). Intensity of the conditioned stimulus and strength of conditioning: I. The conditioned eyelid response to light. *Journal of Experimental Psychology, 38,* 690–696.

Grant, D. A., & Schneider, D. E. (1949). Intensity of the conditioned stimulus and strength of conditioning: II. The conditioned galvanic skin response to an auditory stimulus. *Journal of Experimental Psychology, 39,* 35–40.

Grant, M. M., & Weiss, J. M. (2001). Effects of chronic antidepressant drug administration and electroconvulsive shock on locus coeruleus electrophysiological activity. *Biological Psychiatry, 49,* 117–129.

Grau, J. W. (1987). The central representation of an aversive event maintains opioid and nonopioid forms of analgesia. *Behavioral Neuroscience, 101,* 272–288.

Greiner, J. M., & Karoly, P. (1976). Effects of self-control training on study activity and academic performance: An analysis of self-monitoring, self-reward, and systematic planning components. *Journal of Counseling Psychology, 23,* 495–502.

Grether, W. F. (1938). Pseudo-conditioning without paired stimulation encountered in attempted backward conditioning. *Journal of Comparative Psychology, 25,* 91–96.

Grice, G. R. (1948). The relation of secondary reinforcement to delayed reward in visual discrimination learning. *Journal of Experimental Psychology, 38,* 1–16.

Grice, G. R., & Hunter, J. J. (1964). Stimulus intensity effects depend upon the type of experimental design. *Psychological Review, 71,* 247–256.

Groves, P. M., & Thompson, R. F. (1970). Habituation: A dual-process theory. *Psychological Review, 77,* 419–450.

Guthrie, E. R. (1934). Reward and punishment. *Psychological Review, 41,* 450–460.

Guthrie, E. R. (1935). *The psychology of learning.* New York: Harper.

Guthrie, E. R. (1942). Conditioning: A theory of learning in terms of stimulus, response, and association. In N. B. Henry (Ed.), *The forty-first year book of the National Society of Education: II. The psychology of learning* (pp. 17–60). Chicago: University of Chicago Press.

Guthrie, E. R. (1952). *The Psychology of Learning* (Rev. ed). New York: Harper & Brothers.

Guthrie, E. R. (1959). Association by contiguity. In S. Koch (Ed.), *Psychology: A study of a science* (Vol. 2, pp. 158–195). New York: McGraw-Hill.

Gutman, A., & Fenner, D. (1982). Signaled reinforcement, extinction, behavioral contrast, and autopecking. *Psychological Record, 32,* 215–224.

Gutman, A., Sutterer, J. R., & Brush, R. (1975). Positive and negative behavioral contrast in the rat. *Journal of the Experimental Analysis of Behavior, 23,* 377–384.

Guttman, N. (1953). Operant conditioning, extinction, and periodic reinforcement in relation to concentration of sucrose used as reinforcing agent. *Journal of Experimental Psychology, 46,* 213–224.

Guttman, N. (1954). Equal reinforcing values for sucrose and glucose solutions compared with sweetness values. *Journal of Comparative and Physiological Psychology, 47,* 358–361.

Guttman, N., & Kalish, H. I. (1956). Discriminability and stimulus generalization. *Journal of Experimental Psychology, 51,* 79–88.

Hake, D. F., Azrin, N. H., & Oxford, R. (1967). The effects of punishment intensity on squirrel monkeys. *Journal of the Experimental Analysis of Behavior, 10,* 95–107.

Hall, G. (1979). Exposure learning in young and adult laboratory rats. *Animal Behavior, 27,* 586–591.

Hall, G., & Channell, S. (1985). Differential effects of contextual change on latent inhibition and on the habituation of an orienting response. *Journal of Experimental Psychology: Animal Behavior Processes, 11,* 470–481.

Hall, G., & Honey, R. (1989). Perceptual and associative learning. In S. B. Klein & R. R. Mowrer (Eds.), *Contemporary learning theories: Pavlovian conditioning and the status of traditional learning theory* (pp. 117–147). Hillsdale, NJ: Lawrence Erlbaum.

Hall, J. F. (1976). *Classical conditioning and instrumental learning: A contemporary approach.* Philadelphia: Lippincott.

Hammen, C. L., & Krantz, S. (1976). Effect of success and failure on depressive cognitions. *Journal of Abnormal Psychology, 85,* 577–586.

Han, Y.-S. (1996). Cognitive predictors of recovery from depression in psychiatric inpatients. *Dissertation Abstracts International: Section B: The Sciences and Engineering, 56,* 6391.

Hanratty, M. A., Liebert, R. M., Morris, L. W., & Fernandez, L. E. (1969). Imitation of film-mediated aggression against live and inanimate victims. *Proceedings of the 77th Annual Convention of the American Psychological Association,* 457–458.

Hanson, H. M. (1959). Effects of discrimination training on stimulus generalization. *Journal of Experimental Psychology, 58,* 321–334.

Hanson, T., Alessi, S. M., & Petry, N. M. (2008). Contingency management reduces drug-reduced human immunodeficiency virus risk behaviors in cocaine-abusing methadone patients. *Addiction, 103,* 1187–1197.

Hantula, D. A., & Crowell, C. R. (1994). Behavioral contrast in a two-option analogue task of financial decision making. *Journal of Applied Behavior Analysis, 27,* 607–617.

Hardimann, P. T., Dufresne, R., & Mestre, J. (1989). The relation between problem categorization and problem solving among experts and novices. *Memory and Cognition, 17,* 627–638.

Harlow, H. F. (1971*). Learning to love.* San Francisco: Albion.

Harlow, H. F., & Suomi, S. J. (1970). Nature of love—simplified. *American Psychologist, 25,* 161–168.

Harris, B. (1979). What happened to Little Albert? *American Psychologist, 34,* 151–160.

Harris, V. W., & Sherman, J. A. (1973). Use and analysis of the "Good Behavior Game" to reduce disruptive classroom behavior. *Journal of Applied Behavior Analysis, 6,* 405–417.

Hashimoto, K. (2009). Emerging role of glutamate in the pathophysiology of major depressive disorder. *Brain Research Reviews, 61,* 105–123.

Hartman, T. F., & Grant, D. A. (1960). Effect of intermittent reinforcement on acquisition, extinction, and spontaneous recovery of the conditioned eyelid response. *Journal of Experimental Psychology, 60,* 89–96.

Hawkins, R. D., Cohen, T. E., & Kandel, E. R. (2006). Dishabituation in Aplysia can involve either reversal of habituation or superimposed sensitization. *Learning and Memory, 13,* 397–403.

Hawkins, R. D., Kandel, E. R., & Seigelbaum, S. A. (1993). Learning to modulate transmitter release: Themes and variations in synaptic plasticity. *Annual Review of Neuroscience, 16,* 625–665.

Hawkins, S. A., & Hastie, R. (1990). Hindsight: Biased judgments of past events after the outcomes are known. *Psychological Bulletin, 107,* 311–327.

Hayes, J. R. (1978). *Cognitive psychology.* Homewood, IL: Dorsey.

Hayes, K. J., & Hayes, C. (1951). The intellectual development of a home-raised chimpanzee. *Proceedings of the American Philosophical Society, 95,* 105–109.

Hayes, S. C., & Cone, J. D. (1977). Reducing residential energy use: Payments, information, and feedback. *Journal of Applied Behavior Analysis, 10,* 425–435.

Heil, S. H., Higgins, S. T., Bernstein, I. M., Solomon, L. J., Rogers, R. E., Thomas, C. S., et al. (2008). Effects of voucher-based incentives on abstinence from cigarette smoking and fetal growth among pregnant women. *Addiction, 103,* 1009–1018.

Helmreich, W. B. (1992). *Against all odds: Holocaust survivors and the successful lives they made in America.* New York: Simon and Schuster.

Henderson, H. S., Jenson, W. R., & Erken, N. F. (1986). Using variable interval schedules to improve on-task behavior in the classroom. *Education and Treatment of Children, 9,* 250–263.

Henke, P. G. & Maxwell, D. (1973). Lesions in the amygdala and the frustration effect. *Physiology & Behavior, 10,* 647–650.

Herrnstein, R. J. (1961). Relative and absolute strength of response as a function of frequency of reinforcement. *Journal of the Experimental Analysis of Behavior, 4,* 267–272.

Herrnstein, R. J. (1979). Acquisition, generalization, and discrimination reversal of a natural concept. *Journal of Experimental Psychology: Animal Behavior Processes, 5,* 116–129.

Herrnstein, R. J., & de Villiers, P. A. (1980). Fish as a natural category for people and pigeons. In G. H. Bower (Ed.), *Psychology of learning and motivation* (Vol. 14, pp. 60–97). New York: Academic Press.

Herrnstein, R. J., Loveland, D. H., & Cable, C. (1976). Natural concepts in pigeons. *Journal of Experimental Psychology: Animal Behavior Processes, 2,* 285–302.

Herrnstein, R. J., & Vaughn, W. (1980). Melioration and behavioral allocation. In J. E. R. Staddon (Ed.), *Limits to action: The allocation of individual behavior* (pp. 143–176). New York: Academic Press.

Hersen, M., & Rosqvist, J. (Eds.). (2005). *Encyclopedia of behavior modification and therapy. Volume I: Adult clinical applications.* Thousand Oaks, CA: SAGE.

Hess, E. H. (1973). *Imprinting.* Princeton, NJ: Van Nostrand Reinhold.

Higgins, J. W., Williams, R. L., & McLaughlin, T. F. (2001). The effects of a token economy employing instructional consequences for a third-grade student with learning disabilities: A data-based case study. *Education and Treatment of Children, 24,* 99–106.

Higgins, S. T, Budney, A. J., & Bickel, W. K. (1994). Applying behavioral concepts and principles to the treatment of cocaine dependence. *Drug and Alcohol Dependence, 34,* 87–97.

Hikita, K. (1986). The effects of token economy procedures with chronic schizophrenic patients. *Japanese Journal of Behavior Therapy, 11,* 55–76.

Hilgard, E. R., & Marquis, D. G. (1940). *Conditioning and learning.* New York: Appleton-Century-Crofts.

Hill, W. F., & Spear, N. E. (1963). Extinction in a runway as a function of acquisition level and reinforcement percentage. *Journal of Experimental Psychology, 65,* 495–500.

Hilton, H. (1986). *The executive memory guide.* New York: Simon and Schuster.

Hines, B., & Paolino, R. M. (1970). Retrograde amnesia: Production of skeletal but not cardiac response gradient by electroconvulsive shock. *Science, 169,* 1224–1226.

Hinson, R. E. (1982). Effects of UCS preexposure on excitatory and inhibitory rabbit eyelid conditioning: An associate effect of conditioned contextual stimuli. *Journal of Experimental Psychology: Animal Behavior Processes, 8,* 49–61.

Hiroto, D. S. (1974). Locus of control and learned helplessness. *Journal of Experimental Psychology, 102,* 187–193.

Hiroto, D. S., & Seligman, M. E. P. (1975). Generality of learned helplessness in man. *Journal of Personality and Social Psychology, 31,* 311–327.

Hoebel, B. G. (1969). Feeding and self-stimulation: Neural regulation of food and water intake. *Annals of the New York Academy of Sciences, 157,* 758–778.

Hoffman, H. S. (1968). The control of stress vocalization by an imprinting stimulus. *Behavior, 30,* 175–191.

Hoffman, H. S. (1969). Stimulus factors in conditioned suppression. In B. A. Campbell & R. M. Church (Eds.), *Punishment and aversive behavior* (pp. 185–234). New York: Appleton-Century-Crofts.

Hogan, J. A. (1989). Cause and function in the development of behavior systems. In E. M. Blass (Ed.), *Handbook of behavioral and neurobiology* (Vol. 8, pp. 129–174). New York: Plenum Press.

Hokanson, J. E. (1970). Psychophysiological evaluation of the catharsis hypothesis. In E. I. Megargee & J. E. Hokanson (Eds.), *The dynamics of aggression* (pp. 74–86). New York: Harper & Row.

Holder, H. D., & Garcia, J. (1987). Role of temporal order and odor intensity in taste-potentiated odor aversions. *Behavioral Neuroscience, 101,* 158–163.

Holland, P. C. (1983). Occasion setting in Pavlovian feature discriminations. In M. L. Commons, R. J. Herrnstein, & A. R. Wagner (Eds.), *Quantitative analysis of behavior: Discrimination processes* (Vol. 4, pp. 182–206). New York: Ballinger.

Holland, P. C. (1992). Occasion setting in Pavlovian conditioning. In D. L. Medin (Ed.), *The psychology of learning and motivation* (Vol. 28, pp. 69–125). San Diego, CA: Academic Press.

Holland, P. C., & Petrovich, G. D. (2005). A neural systems analysis of the potentiation of feeding by emotional stimuli. *Physiology & Behavior, 86,* 747–761.

Holland, P. C., Petrovich, G. D., & Gallagher, M. (2002). The effects of amygdala lesions on conditioned stimulus-potentiated eating in rats. *Physiology & Behavior, 76,* 117–129

Holland, P. C., & Rescorla, R. A. (1975). The effects of two ways of devaluing the unconditioned stimulus after first- and second-order appetitive conditioning. *Journal of Experimental Psychology: Animal Behavior Processes, 1,* 355–363.

Holliday, R. E., Reyna, V. F., & Hayes, B. K. (2002). Memory processes underlying misinformation effects in child witnesses. *Developmental Review, 22,* 37–77.

Holmes, D. (1990). The evidence for repression: An examination of sixty years of research. In J. Singer (Ed.), *Repression and dissociation: Implications for personality theory, psychopathology, and health* (pp. 85–102). Chicago: University of Chicago Press.

Holyoak, K. J. (1990). Problem solving. In D. N. Osherson & E. E Smith (Eds.), *Thinking: An invitation to cognitive science* (Vol. 3, pp. 117–146). Cambridge, MA: MIT Press.

Homel, R., McKay, P., & Henstridge, J. (1995). The impact on accidents of random breath testing in New South Wales; 1982–1992. In C. N. Kloeden & A. J. Mclean (Eds.), *Proceedings of the 13th International Conference on Alcohol,*

Drugs and Traffic Safety, Adelaide, 13 August–19 August 1995 (Vol. 2, pp. 849–855). Adelaide, Australia: NHMRC Road Accident Research Unit, The University of Adelaide 5005.

Homme, L. W., de Baca, P. C., Devine, J. V., Steinhorst, R., & Rickert, E. J. (1963). Use of the Premack principle in controlling the behavior of nursery-school children. *Journal of the Experimental Analysis of Behavior, 6,* 544.

Hooks, M. S., Colvin, A. C., Juncos, J. L., & Justice, J. B., Jr. (1992). Individual differences in basal and cocaine-stimulated extracellular dopamine in the nucleus accumbens using quantitative microdialysis. *Brain Research, 587,* 306–312.

Horel, J. A., & Misantone, L. G. (1976). Visual discrimination impaired by cutting temporal lobe connections. *Science, 193,* 336–338.

Horner, R. D., & Keilitz, I. (1975). Training mentally retarded adolescents to brush their teeth. *Journal of Applied Behavior Analysis, 8,* 301–310.

Houston, J. P. (1986). *Fundamentals of learning and memory* (3rd ed.). Orlando, FL: Harcourt Brace Jovanovich.

Hoveland, C. I. (1937). The generalization of conditioned responses: II. The sensory generalization of conditioned responses with varying frequencies of tones. *Journal of General Psychology, 17,* 125–148.

Howard, D. V. (1983). *Cognitive psychology: Memory, language, and thought.* New York: Macmillan.

Hudson, D., Foster, T. M., & Temple, W. (1999). Fixed-ratio schedule performance of possum (*Trichosaurus vulpecula*). *New Zealand Journal of Psychology, 28,* 79–85.

Hughes, C. W., Kent, T. A., Campbell, J., Oke, A., Croskill, H., & Preskorn, S. H. (1984). Central blood flow and cerebrovascular permeability in an inescapable shock (learned helplessness) animal model of depression. *Pharmacology, Biochemistry, and Behavior, 21,* 891–894.

Hull, C. L. (1920). Quantitative aspects of the evolution of concepts: An experimental study. *Psychological Monographs, 28* (Whole No. 123).

Hull, C. L. (1943). *Principles of behavior.* New York: Appleton.

Hull, C. L. (1952). *A behavior system.* New Haven, CT: Yale University Press.

Hulse, S. H., Jr. (1958). Amount and percentage of reinforcement and duration of goal confinement in conditioning and extinction. *Journal of Experimental Psychology, 56,* 48–57.

Hume, D. (1955). *An inquiry concerning human understanding.* Indianapolis, IN: Bobbs-Merrill. (Original work published 1748; "My own life," a brief autobiographical sketch, was originally published 1776.)

Humphreys, L. G. (1939). Acquisition and extinction of verbal expectations in a situation analogous to conditioning. *Journal of Experimental Psychology, 25,* 294–301.

Hunter, A. M., Balleine, B. W., & Minor, T. R. (2003). Helplessness and escape performance: Glutamate-adenosine interactions in the frontal cortex. *Behavioral Neuroscience, 117,* 123–135.

Hutchinson, R. R., Azrin, N. H., & Hunt, G. M. (1968). Attack produced by intermittent reinforcement of a concurrent operant response. *Journal of the Experimental Analysis of Behavior, 11,* 498–495.

Hux, K., Manasse, N., Wright, S., & Snell, J. (2000). Effect of training frequency on face-name recall by adults with traumatic brain injury. *Brain Injury, 14,* 907–920.

Hyson, R. L., Sickel, J. L., Kulkosky, P. J., & Riley, A. L. (1981). The insensitivity of schedule-induced polydipsia to conditioned taste aversions: Effect of amount consumed during conditioning. *Animal Learning and Behavior, 9,* 281–286.

Innis, N. K. (1979). Stimulus control of behavior during postreinforcement pause of FI schedules. *Animal Learning and Behavior, 7,* 203–210.

Isseroff, A., Rosvold, H. E., Galkin, T. W., & Goldman-Rakic, P. S. (1982). Spatial memory impairments following damage to the mediodorsal nucleus of the thalamus in rhesus monkeys. *Brain Research, 232,* 97–113.

Iwata, B. A., & Michael, J. L. (1994). Applied implications of theory and research on the nature of reinforcement. *Journal of Applied Behavior Analysis, 27,* 183–193.

Jackson, R. L., Alexander, J. H., & Maier, S. F. (1980). Learned helplessness, inactivity, and associative deficits: Effects of inescapable shock on response choice escape learning. *Journal of Experimental Psychology: Animal Behavior Processes, 6,* 1–20.

Jacobs, B. (1968). Predictability and number of pairings in the establishment of a secondary reinforce. *Psychonomic Science, 10,* 237–238.

Jacobson, E. (1938). *Progressive relaxation.* Chicago: University of Chicago Press.

Jacquet, Y. F. (1972). Schedule-induced licking during multiple schedules. *Journal of the Experimental Analysis of Behavior, 17,* 413–423.

Jaffe, P. G., & Carlson, P. M. (1972). Modelling therapy for text anxiety: The role of affect and consequences. *Behavior Research and Therapy, 10,* 329–339.

James, W. A. (1890). *The principles of psychology* (Vols. 1–2). New York: Holt.

Jason, L. A., Ji, P. Y., Anes, M. D., & Birkhead, S. H. (1991). Active enforcement of cigarette control laws in the prevention of cigarette sales to minors. *Journal of the American Medical Association, 266*(22), 3159–3161.

Jason, L. A., Ji, P. Y., Anes, M. D., & Xaverius, P. (1992). Assessing cigarette sales rates to minors. *Evaluation and the Health Professions, 15,* 375–384.

Jason, L. A., Pokorny, S. B., Adams, M., Hunt, Y., Gadiraju, P., & Schoeny, M., (2007). Do fines for violating possession-use-purchase laws reduce youth tobacco use? *Journal of Drug Education, 37,* 393–400.

Jasper, H. H., Proctor, L. D., Knighton, R. S., Noshav, W. C., & Costello, R. T. (Eds.). (1958) *Reticular formation of the brain.* Boston: Little, Brown.

Javidi, Z., Battersby, M. W., & Forbes, A. (2007). A case study of trichofillomania with social phobia: Treatment and 4-year follow-up using cognitive-behaviour therapy. *Behaviour Change, 24,* 231–243.

Jaynes, J. (1956). Imprinting: The interaction of learned and innate behavior: I. Development and generalization. *Journal of Comparative and Physiological Psychology, 49,* 201–206.

Jenkins, J. G., & Dallenbach, K. M. (1924). Obliviscence during sleep and waking. *American Journal of Psychology, 35,* 605–612.

Jenkins, H. M., Barnes, R. A. & Barrera, F. J. (1981). Why autoshaping depends on trial spacing. In C. M. Locurto, H. S. Terrace & J. Gibbon (Eds.), *Autoshaping and conditioning theory* (pp. 255–284). New York: Academic Press.

Jenkins, H. M., & Harrison, R. H. (1960). Effect of discrimination training on auditory generalization. *Journal of Experimental Psychology, 59,* 246–273.

Jenkins, J. R., & Gorrafa, S. (1974). Academic performance of mentally handicapped children as a function of token economies and contingency contracts. *Education and Training of the Mentally Retarded, 9,* 183–186.

Jenkins, W. O., McFann, H., & Clayton, F. L. (1950). A methodological study of extinction following aperiodic and continuous reinforcement. *Journal of Comparative and Physiological Psychology, 43,* 155–167.

Johnson, A. W. Gallagher, M., & Holland, P. C. (2009). The basolateral amygdala is critical to the expression of Pavlovian and instrumental outcome-specific reinforcer devaluation effects. *The Journal of Neuroscience, 29,* 696–704.

Johnson, J. G., Metalsky, G. I., Rabkin, J. G., Williams, J. B. W., & Remien, R. H. (2000). Attributional style, self-esteem, and human immunodeficiency virus: A test of the hopelessness and self-esteem theories of depression. *Journal of Psychopathology and Behavioral Assessment, 22,* 23–46.

Johnson, J. S., & Newport, E. L. (1989). Critical period effects in second language learning: The influence of maturational state on the acquisition of English as a second language. *Cognitive Psychology, 21,* 60–99.

Jones, M. C. (1924). The elimination of children's fears. *Journal of Experimental Psychology, 7,* 383–390.

Jones, R. S., & Eayrs, C. B. (1992). The use of errorless learning procedures in teaching people with a learning disability: A critical review. *Mental Handicap Research, 5,* 204–212.

Kahneman, D., Slovic, P., & Tversky, A. (Eds.). (1982). *Judgment under uncertainty: Heuristics and biases.* New York: Cambridge University Press.

Kahneman, D., & Tversky, A. (1972). Subjective probability: A judgment of representativeness. *Cognitive Psychology, 3,* 430–454.

Kahneman, D., & Tversky, A. (1973). On the psychology of prediction. *Psychological Review, 80,* 237–251.

Kako, E. (1999). Elements of syntax in the systems of three language-trained animals. *Animal Learning and Behavior, 27,* 1–14.

Kalat, J. W., & Rozin, P. (1971). Role of interference in taste-aversion learning. *Journal of Comparative and Physiological Psychology, 77,* 53–58.

Kalat, J. W., & Rozin, P. (1973). "Learned safety" as a mechanism in long-delay learning in rats. *Journal of Comparative and Physiological Psychology, 83,* 198–207.

Kalish, H. I. (1969). Stimulus generalization. In M. H. Mary (Ed.), *Learning: Processes.* London: Macmillan.

Kalish, H. I. (1981). *From behavioral science to behavior modification.* New York: McGraw-Hill.

Kamin, L. J. (1954). Traumatic avoidance learning: The effects of CS-UCS interval with a trace-conditioning procedure. *Journal of Comparative and Physiological Psychology, 47,* 65–72.

Kamin, L. J. (1956). The effects of termination of the CS and avoidance of the US on avoidance learning. *Journal of Comparative and Physiological Psychology, 49,* 420–424.

Kamin, L. J. (1968). "Attention-like" processes in classical conditioning. In M. R. Jones (Ed.), *Miami symposium on the prediction of behavior: Aversive stimulation* (pp. 9–31). Miami, FL: University of Miami Press.

Kamin, L. J., Brimer, C. J., & Black, A. H. (1963). Conditioned suppression as a monitor of fear of the CS in the course of avoidance training. *Journal of Comparative and Physiological Psychology, 56,* 497–501.

Kamin, L. J., & Schaub, R. E. (1963). Effects of conditioned stimulus intensity on the conditioned emotional response. *Journal of Comparative and Physiological Psychology, 56,* 502–507.

Kanarek, R. B. (1974). *The energetics of meal patterns.* Unpublished doctoral dissertation, Rutgers-The State University, New Brunswick, NJ.

Kandel, E. R. (2000). Cellular mechanisms and the biological basis of individuality. In E. R. Kandel, J. H. Schwartz, & T. M. Jessel (Eds.), *Principles of neural science* (4th ed., pp. 1247–1279). New York: McGraw-Hill.

Kaplan, M., Jackson, B., & Sparer, R. (1965). Escape behavior under continuous reinforcement as a function of aversive light intensity. *Journal of the Experimental Analysis of Behavior, 8,* 321–323.

Karolewicz, B., Klimek, V., Zhu, H., Szebeni, K., Nail, E., Stockmeier, C. A., et al. (2005). Effects of depression, cigarette smoking, and age on monoamine oxidase B in amygdaloid nuclei. *Brain Research, 1043,* 57–64.

Kasvikis, Y., Bradley, B., Powell, J., Marks, I., & Gray, J. A. (1991). Postwithdrawal exposure treatment to prevent relapse in opiate addicts: A pilot study. *International Journal of the Addictions, 26*(11), 1187–1195.

Katcher, A. H., Solomon, R. L., Turner, L. H., LoLordo, V. M., Overmeir, J. B., & Rescorla, R. A. (1969). Heart-rate and blood pressure responses to signaled and unsignaled shocks: Effects of cardiac sympathetomy. *Journal of Comparative and Physiological Psychology, 42,* 163–174.

Kaufman, M. A., & Bolles, R. C. (1981). A nonassociative aspect of overshadowing. *Bulletin of the Psychonomic Society, 18,* 318–320.

Kazdin, A. E. (1972). Response cost: The removal of conditioned reinforcers for therapeutic change. *Behavior Therapy, 3,* 533–546.

Kazdin, A. E. (1974a). Covert modeling, modeling similarity, and reduction of avoidance behavior. *Behavior Therapy, 5,* 325–340.

Kazdin, A. E. (1974b). Effects of covert modeling, multiple models, and model reinforcement on assertive behavior. *Behavior Therapy, 7,* 211–222.

Kazdin, A. E. (2000). Token economy. In A. E. Kazdin (Ed.), *Encyclopedia of psychology* (Vol. 8, pp. 90–92). Washington, DC: American Psychological Association.

Kazdin, A. & Benjet, C. (2003) Spanking children: evidence and issues. *Current Directions in Psychological Science, 12,* 99–103.

Keele, S. W., & Chase, W. G. (1967). Short-term visual storage. *Perception and Psychophysics, 2,* 383–385.

Keeney, K. M., Fisher, W. W., Adelinis, J. D., & Wilder, D. A. (2000). The effects of response cost in the treatment of aberrant behavior maintained by negative reinforcement. *Journal of Applied Behavior Analysis, 33,* 255–258.

Keith-Lucas, T., & Guttman, N. (1975). Robust-single-trial delayed backward conditioning. *Journal of Comparative and Physiological Psychology, 88,* 468–476.

Keller, F. S., & Hull, L. M. (1936). Another "insight" experiment. *Journal of Genetic Psychology, 48,* 484–489.

Kellogg, W. N., & Kellogg, L. A. (1933). *The ape and the child.* New York: McGraw-Hill.

Kenealy, P. M. (1997). Mood-state-dependent retrieval: The effects of induced mood on memory reconsidered. *The Quarterly Journal of Experimental Psychology, 50A,* 290–317.

Kendler, H. H., & Gasser, W. P. (1948). Variables in spatial learning: I. Number of reinforcements during training. *Journal of Comparative and Physiological Psychology, 41,* 178–187.

Kenny, F. T., Solyom, L., & Solyom, C. (1973). Faradic disruption of obsessive ideation in the treatment of obsessive neurosis. *Behavior Therapy, 4,* 448–457.

Kern, R. S., Green, M. F., Mintz, J., & Liberman, R. P. (2003). Does 'errorless learning' compensate for neurocognitive impairments in the rehabilitation of persons with schizophrenia? *Psychological Medicine: A Journal of Research in Psychiatry and the Allied Sciences, 33,* 433–442.

Kessels, R. P. C., & de Haan, E. H. F. (2003). Mnemonic strategies in older people: A comparison of errorless and errorful learning. *Age and Aging, 32,* 539–533.

Kihlstrom, J. F. (2004). An unbalanced balancing act: Blocked, recovered, and false memories in the laboratory and clinic. *Clinical Psychology, 11,* 34–41.

Kimble, G. A. (1961). *Hilgard and Marguis's conditioning and learning* (2nd ed.). New York: Appleton-Century-Crofts.

Kimble, G. A., Garmezy, N., & Zigler, E. (1984). *Psychology* (6th ed.). New York: Wiley.

Kimble, G. A., & Reynolds, B. (1967). Eyelid conditioning as a function of the interval between conditioned and unconditioned stimuli. In G. A. Kimble (Ed.), *Foundations of conditioning and learning* (pp. 279–287). New York: Appleton-Century-Crofts.

Kimmel, H. D. (1965). Instrumental inhibitory factors in classical conditioning. In W. F. Prokasy (Ed.), *Classical conditioning: A symposium* (pp. 148–171). New York: Appleton-Century-Crofts.

King, G. D. (1974). Wheel running in the rat induced by a fixed-time presentation of water. *Animal Learning and Behavior, 2,* 325–328.

Kintsch, W. (1980). Semantic memory: A tutorial. In T. D. Nickerson (Ed.), *Attention and performance VIII* (pp. 595–620). Hillsdale, NJ: Lawrence Erlbaum.

Kintsch, W., & Witte, R. S. (1962). Concurrent conditioning of bar-press and salivation responses. *Journal of Comparative and Physiological Psychology, 55,* 963–968.

Kirkpatrick-Steger, J., Wasserman, E. A., & Biederman, I. (1996). Effects of spatial rearrangement of object components on picture recognition in pigeons. *Journal of the Experimental Analysis of Behavior, 65,* 465–475.

Kishiyama, M. M., Yonelinas, A. P., Kroll, N. E. A., Lazzara, M. M., Nolan, E. C., Jones, E. G., & Jagust, W. J. (2005). Bilateral thalamic lesions affect recollection- and familiarity-based recognition memory judgments. *Cortex: A Journal Devoted to the Study of the Nervous System and Behavior, 41,* 775–788.

Klein, D. C., & Seligman, M. E. P. (1976). Reversal of performance deficits and perceptual deficits in learned helplessness and depression. *Journal of Abnormal Psychology, 85,* 11–26.

Klein, S. B., Domato, G. C., Hallstead, C., Stephens, I., & Mikulka, P. J. (1975). Acquisition of a conditioned aversion as a function of age and measurement technique. *Physiological Psychology, 3,* 379–384.

Klein, S. B., Freda, J. S., Mikulka, P. J. (1985). The influence of a taste cue on an environmental aversion: Potentiation or overshadowing? *Psychological Record, 35,* 101–112.

Klein, S. B., & Thorne, B. M. (2007). *Biological psychology.* New York: Worth.

Kline, S. B., & Groninger, L. D. (1991). The imagery bizarreness effect as a function of sentence complexity and presentation time. *Bulletin of the Psychonomic Society, 29,* 25–27.

Klopfer, P. H. (1971). Imprinting: Determining its perceptual basis in ducklings. *Journal of Comparative and Physiological Psychology, 75,* 378–385.

Klopfer, P. H., Adams, D. K., & Klopfer, M. S. (1964). Maternal "imprinting" in goats. *National Academy of Science Proceedings, 52,* 911–914.

Knackstedt, L. A. A, Samimi, M. M., & Ettenberg, A. (2002). Evidence for opponent-process actions of intravenous cocaine and cocaethylene. *Pharmacology, Biochemistry, and Behavior, 72,* 931–936.

Knecht v. Gillman, 488 F. 2nd 1136 (8th Cir. 1973).

Kneebone, I. I., & Dunmore, E. (2004). Attributional style and symptoms of depression in persons with multiple sclerosis. *International Journal of Behavioral Medicine, 11,* 110–115.

Kneebone, I. I., & Al-Daftar, S. (2006). Flooding treatment of phobia to have her feet touched by physiotherapists, in a young woman with Down's syndrome and a traumatic brain injury. *Neuropsychological Rehabilitation, 16,* 230–236.

Knutson, J. F., & Kleinknecht, R. A. (1970). Attack during differential reinforcement of low rate of responding. *Psychonomic Science, 19,* 289–290.

Kohlenberg, R. J. (1970). The punishment of persistent vomiting: A case study. *Journal of Applied Behavior Analysis, 3,* 241–245.

Kohler, W. (1925). *The mentality of apes.* London: Routledge & Kegan Paul.

Kohler, W. (1939). Simple structural functions in the chimpanzee and the chicken. In W. D. Ellis (Ed.), *A source book of gestalt psychology* (pp. 217–227). New York: Harcourt Brace.

Komatsu, S., Mimura, M., Kato, M., Wakamatsu, N., & Kashima, H. (2000). Errorless and effortful processes involved in the learning of face-name associations by patients with alcoholic Korsakoff's syndrome. *Neuropsychological Rehabilitation, 10,* 113–132.

Konarski, E. A., Jr. (1985). The use of response deprivation to increase the academic performance of EMR students. *Behavior Therapist, 8,* 61.

Konarski, E. A., Jr., Crowell, C. R., & Duggan, L. M. (1985). The use of response deprivation to the academic performance of EMR students. *Applied Research in Mental Retardation, 6,* 15–31.

Konarski, E. A., Jr., Johnson, M. R., Crowell, C. R., & Whitman, T. L. (1980). Response deprivation, reinforcement, and instrumental academic performance in an EMR classroom. *Behavior Therapy, 13,* 94–102.

Koob, G. F. (1992). Drugs of abuse: Anatomy, pharmacology, and function of reward pathways. *Trends in Pharmacological Science, 13,* 177–184.

Korsakoff, S. S. (1889). Etude médico-psychologique sur une forme des maladies de la mémoire [Medical-psychological study of a type of memory illness]. *Revue philosophique, 5,* 501–530.

Kovach, J. K., & Hess, E. H. (1963). Imprinting: Effects of painful stimulation upon the following response. *Journal of Comparative and Physiological Psychology, 56,* 461–464.

Krakauer, J. (1997). *Into thin air.* New York: Villard.

Krechevsky, I. (1932). "Hypotheses" in rats. *Psychological Review, 39,* 516–532.

Krishnan-Sarin, S., Duhig, A. M., McKee, S. A., McMahon, T. J., Liss, T., McFetridge, A., & Cavallo, D. A. (2006). Contingency management for smoking cessation in adolescent smokers. *Experimental and Clinical Psychopharmacology, 14,* 306–310.

Kueh, D., & Baker, L. E. (2007). Reinforcement schedule effects in rats trained to discriminate 3, 4 methyledioxymethamphetamine (MDMA) or cocaine. *Psychopharmacology, 189,* 447–457.

Laney, C., & Loftus, E. F. (2005). Traumatic memories are not necessarily accurate memories. *The Canadian Journal of Psychiatry/La Revue Canadienne de Psychiatrie, 50,* 823–828.

Laney, C. & Loftus, E. F. (2009). Eyewitness memory. In R. N. Kocsis (Ed.), *Applied criminal psychology: A guide to forensic behavioral sciences* (pp. 121–145). Springfield, IL: Chares C Thomas.

Lang, A. J., Craske, M. G., Brown, M., & Ghaneian, A. (2001). Fear-related state dependent memory. *Cognition and Emotion, 15,* 695–703.

Lang, P. J. (1978). Self-efficacy theory: Thoughts on cognition and unification. In S. Rachman (Ed.), *Advances in behaviour research and therapy* (Vol. 1, pp. 187–192). Oxford, UK: Pergamon.

Lang, P. J., & Melamed, B. G. (1969). Avoidance conditioning of an infant with chronic ruminative vomiting. *Journal of Abnormal Psychology, 74,* 1–8.

Langer, E. J. (1983). *The psychology of control.* Beverly Hills, CA: SAGE.

Larew, M. B. (1986). *Inhibitory learning in Pavlovian backward conditioning procedures involving a small number of US-CS trials.* Unpublished doctoral dissertation, Yale University, New Haven, CT.

Larson, S. J., & Siegel, S. (1998). Learning and tolerance to the ataxic effect of ethanol. *Pharmacology, Biochemistry, and Behavior, 61,* 131–142.

Larzelere, R. E. (1996). A review of the outcomes of parental use of nonabusive or customary physical punishment. *Pediatrics, 98,* 824–828.

Larzelere, R. E. (2000). Child outcomes of nonabusive and customary physical punishment by parents: An updated literature review. *Clinical Child and Family Psychology Review, 3,* 199–221.

Larzelere, R. E. (2008) Disciplinary spanking: The scientific evidence. *Journal of Developmental and Behavioral Pediatrics, 29,* 334–335.

Larzelere, R. E., Schneider, W. N., Larson, D. B., & Pike, L. (1996). The effects of discipline responses in delaying toddler misbehavior recurrences. *Child and Family Behavior Therapy, 18,* 35–57.

Lashley, K. S. (1929). *Brain mechanisms and intelligence.* Chicago: University of Chicago Press.

Lashley, K. S. (1950). In search of the engram. *Symposia of the Society for Experimental Biology, 4,* 454–482.

Lashley, K. S., & Wade, M. (1946). The Pavlovian theory of generalization. *Psychological Review, 53,* 72–87.

Lasky, R. E., Syrdal-Lasky, A., & Klein, R. E. (1975). VOT discrimination by four- to six-and-a-half-month-old infants from Spanish environments. *Journal of Experimental Child Psychology, 20,* 215–225.

Lau, C. E., Neal, S. A., & Falk, J. L. (1996). Schedule-induced polydipsic choice between cocaine and lidocaine solutions: Critical importance of associate history. *Behavioral Pharmacology, 7,* 731–741.

Lawrence, D. H., & DeRivera, J. (1954). Evidence for relational transposition. *Journal of Comparative and Physiological Psychology, 47,* 465–471.

Lazarus, A. A. (1971). *Behavior therapy and beyond.* New York: McGraw-Hill.

Le, A. D., Poulos, C. X., & Cappell, H. (1979). Conditioned tolerance to the hypothermic effect of ethyl alcohol. *Science, 206,* 1109–1110.

Leahey, T. H., & Harris, R. J. (2001*). Learning and cognition* (5th ed.). Upper Saddle River, NJ: Prentice-Hall.

Leander, J. D., McMillan, D. E., & Ellis, F. W. (1976). Ethanol and isopropanol effects on schedule-controlled responding. *Psychopharmacology, 47,* 157–164.

Leeming, F. C. & Robinson, J. E. (1973). Escape behavior as a function of delay of negative reinforcement. *Psychological Reports, 32,* 63–70.

Leff, R. (1969). Effects of punishment intensity and consistency on the internalization of behavioral suppression in children. *Developmental Psychology, 1,* 345–356.

Lehnert, H., Reinstein, D. K., Strowbridge, B. W., & Wurtman, R. J. (1984). Neurochemical and behavioral consequences of acute, uncontrollable stress: Effects of dietary tyrosine. *Brain Research, 303,* 215–223.

Lehr, R. (1970). Partial reinforcement and variable magnitude of reward effects in a T maze. *Journal of Comparative and Physiological Psychology, 70,* 286–293.

Lenneberg, E. H. (1969). On explaining language. *Science, 164,* 635–643.

Lett, B. T. (1982). Taste potentiation in poison-avoidance learning. In M. Commons, R. Herrnstein, & A. Wagner (Eds.), *Harvard symposium on quantitative analysis of behavior* (Vol. 4). Hillsdale, NJ: Lawrence Erlbaum.

Levi, A. S., & Pryor, J. B. (1987). Use of the availability heuristic in probability estimates of future events. *Organizational Behavior and Human Decision Processes, 40,* 219–234.

Levine, M. (1966). Hypothesis behavior by humans during discrimination learning. *Journal of Experimental Psychology, 71,* 331–338.

Levis, D. J. (1976). Learned helplessness: A reply and an alternative S-R interpretation. *Journal of Experimental Psychology: General, 105,* 47–65.

Levis, D. J. (1989). The case for a return to a two-factor theory of avoidance: The failure of nonfear interpretations. In S. B. Klein & R. R. Mowrer (Eds.), *Contemporary learning theories: Pavlovian conditioning and the status of traditional learning theory* (pp. 227–277). Hillsdale, NJ: Lawrence Erlbaum.

Levis, D. J. (2008). The prolonged CS exposure techniques of implosive (flooding) therapy. In W. T. O'Donohue & J. E. Fisher (Eds.), *Cognitive behavior therapy* (pp. 272–282). Hoboken, NJ: John Wiley & Sons.

Levis, D. J., & Boyd, T. L. (1979). Symptom maintenance: An intrahuman analysis and extension of the conservation of anxiety principle. *Journal of Abnormal Psychology, 88,* 107–120.

Levitsky, D., & Collier, G. (1968). Schedule-induced wheel running. *Physiology and Behavior, 3,* 571–573.

Lewis, D. J. (1952). Partial reinforcement in the gambling situation. *Journal of Experimental Psychology, 43,* 447–450.

Lewis, D. J. (1959). A control for the direct manipulation of the fractional anticipatory goal response. *Psychological Reports, 5,* 753–756.

Lewis, D. J. (1960). Partial reinforcement: A selective review of the literature since 1950. *Psychological Bulletin, 57,* 1–28.

Lewis, D. J., & Duncan, C. P. (1958). Expectation and resistance to extinction of a lever-pulling response as a function of percentage of reinforcement and amount of reward. *Journal of Experimental Psychology, 55,* 121–128.

Li, N., He, S., Parrish, C., Delich, J., & Grassing, K. (2003). Differences in morphine and cocaine reinforcement under fixed and progressive ratio schedules; effects of extinction, reacquisition and schedule design. *Behavioural Pharmacology, 14,* 619–630.

Lindsey, G., & Best, P. (1973). Overshadowing of the less salient of two novel fluids in a taste-aversion paradigm. *Physiological Psychology, 1,* 13–15.

Linscheid, T. R., Iwata, B. A., Ricketts, R. W., Williams, D. E., & Griffin, J. C. (1990). Clinical evaluation of the self-injurious behavior inhibiting system (SIBIS). *Journal of Applied Behavior Analysis, 23,* 53–78.

Linscheid, T. R., & Reichenbach, H. (2002). Multiple factors in the long-term effectiveness of contingent electric shock treatment for self-injurious behavior: A case example. *Research in Developmental Disabilities, 23,* 161–177.

Lippman, M. R. & Motta, R. W. (1993). Effects of positive and negative reinforcement on daily skills in chronic psychiatric patients in community residences. *Journal of Clinical Psychology, 49,* 654–662.

Lloyd, J. W., Kauffman, J. M., & Weygant, A. D. (1982). Effects of response cost contingencies on thumbsucking and related behaviours in the classroom. *Educational Psychology, 2,* 167–173.

Locke, J. (1964). *An essay concerning human understanding.* New York: New American Library. (Original work published 1690)

Lockwood, K., & Bourland, G. (1982). Reduction of self-injurious behaviors by reinforcement and toy use. *Mental Retardation, 20,* 169–173.

Loftus, E. F. (1975). Leading questions and the eyewitness report. *Cognitive Psychology, 7,* 560–572.

Loftus, E. F. (1992). When a lie becomes memory's truth: Memory distortion after exposure to misinformation. *Psychological Science, 3,* 121–123.

Loftus, E. F. (1997). Repressed memory accusations: Devastated families and devastated patients. *Applied Cognitive Psychology, 11,* 25–30.

Loftus, E. F. (2005). Planting misinformation in the human mind: A 30-year investigation of the malleability of memory. *Learning and Memory, 12,* 361–366.

Loftus, E. F., Coan, J. A., & Pickrell, J. E. (1996). Manufacturing false memories using bits of reality. In L. M. Reder (Ed.), *Implicit memory and metacognition* (pp. 195–220). Mahwah, NJ: Erlbaum.

Logan, F. A. (1952). The role of delay of reinforcement in determining reaction potential. *Journal of Experimental Psychology, 43,* 393–399.

Logue, A. W. (1985). Conditioned food aversion learning in humans. In N. S. Braveman & P. Bronstein (Eds.), *Experimental assessment and clinical applications of conditioned food aversions. Annals of the New York Academy of Sciences, 443,* 316–329.

Logue, A. W., Ophir, I., & Strauss, K. E. (1981). The acquisition of taste aversions in humans. *Behaviour Research and Therapy, 19,* 319–333.

Lorayne, H., & Lucas, J. (2000). *The memory book.* New York: Ballantine.

Lorenz, K. (1935). Der kumpan in der umwelt des vogels. *Journal of Ornithology, 83,* 137–213, 289–413.

Lorenz, K. (1950). The comparative method of studying innate behavior patterns. *In Society for Experimental Biology, Symposium No. 4, Physiological mechanisms in animal behaviour.* New York: Academic Press.

Lorenz, K. (1952). The past twelve years in the comparative study of behavior. In C. H. Schiller (Ed.), *Instinctive behavior* (pp. 288–317). New York: International Universities Press.

Lorenz, K. (1969). Innate bases of learning. In K. H. Pibram (Ed.), *On the biology of learning.* New York: Harcourt, Brace & World.

Lorenz, K. (1970). Companions as factors in the bird's environment. In R. Martin (Trans.), *Studies in animal and human behaviour* (Vol. 1, pp. 101–258). Cambridge, MA: Harvard University Press.

Lorenz, K., & Tinbergen, N. (1938). Taxis und instinkhandlung in der eirollbewegung der graigrans. *Zeitschrift fur Tierpsychologie, 2,* 1–29.

Lovaas, O. I., & Simmons, J. Q. (1969). Manipulation of self-destruction in three retarded children. *Journal of Applied Behavior Analysis, 2,* 143–157.

Lovitt, T. C., Guppy, T. E., & Blattner, J. E. (1969). The use of free-time contingency with fourth graders to increase spelling accuracy. *Behaviour Research and Therapy, 7,* 151–156.

Lubow, R. E., & Moore, A. U. (1959). Latent inhibition: The effect of nonreinforced preexposure to the conditioned stimulus. *Journal of Comparative and Physiological Psychology, 52,* 415–419.

Luchins, A. S. (1942). Mechanization in problem solving. *Psychological Monographs, 54* (Whole No. 248).

Ludwig, T. D., Biggs, J., Wagner, S., & Geller, E. S. (2001). Using public feedback and competitive rewards to increase the safe driving of pizza drivers. *Journal of Organizational Behavior Management, 21,* 75–104.

Luthans, F., Paul, R., & Baker, D. (1981). An experimental analysis of the impact of contingent reinforcement of salespersons' performance behavior. *Journal of Applied Psychology, 66,* 314–323.

Lynch, G. (1986). *Synapses, circuits, and the beginnings of memory.* Cambridge, MA: MIT Press.

Lynch, G., & Baudry, M. (1984). The biochemistry of memory: A new and specific hypothesis. *Science, 224,* 1057–1063.

Lynch, M. A. (2004). Long-term potentiation and memory. *Physiological Reviews, 84,* 87–136.

Lynd-Stevenson, R. M. (1996). A test of the hopelessness theory of depression in unemployed young adults. *British Journal of Clinical Psychology, 35,* 117–132.

MacCorquodale, K., & Meehl, P. E. (1954). Edward C. Tolman. In W. K. Estes et al. (Eds.), *Modern learning theory* (pp. 177–266). New York: Appleton-Century-Crofts.

Mace, F. C., Neef, N. A., Shade, D., & Mauro, B. C. (1996). Effects of problem difficulty and reinforcer quality on time allocated to concurrent arithmetic problems. *Journal of Applied Behavior Analysis, 27,* 585–596.

Mackintosh, N. J. (1975). A theory of attention: Variations in the associability of stimuli with reinforcement. *Psychological Review, 82,* 276–298.

Mackintosh, N. J. (1983). *Conditioning and associative learning.* Oxford, UK: Oxford University Press.

MacPherson, E. M., Candee, B. L., & Hohman, R. J. (1974). A comparison of three methods for eliminating disruptive lunchroom behavior. *Journal of Applied Behavior Analysis, 7,* 287–297.

Magura, S., & Rosenblum, A. (2000). Modulating effect of alcohol use on cocaine use. *Addictive Behaviors, 25,* 117–122.

Major, R., & White, N. (1978). Memory facilitation by self-stimulation reinforcement mediated by nigrostriatal bundle. *Physiology and Behavior, 20,* 723–733.

Maki, R. (1990). Memory for script: Effects for script actions: Effects of relevance and detail expectancy. *Memory and Cognition, 18,* 5–14.

Maki, W. S., & Hegvik, D. K. (1980). Directed forgetting in pigeons. *Animal Learning and Behavior, 8,* 567–574.

Makin, P. J., & Hoyle, D. J. (1993). The Premack principle: Professional engineers. *Leadership & Organization Development Journal, 14,* 16–21.

Malamut, B. L., Saunders, R. C., & Mishkin, M. (1984). Monkeys with combined amygdalo-lesions succeed in object discriminations learning despite 24-hour interval. *Behavioral Neuroscience, 98,* 759–769.

Malleson, N. (1959). Panic and phobia. *Lancet, 1,* 225–227.

Malmquist, C. P. (1986). Children who witness parental murder. Posttraumatic aspects. *Journal of the American Academy of Child Psychiatry, 25,* 320–325.

Marchant, G., Robinson, J. P., Anderson, U., & Schadewald, M. (1991). Analogical transfer and expertise in legal reasoning. *Organizational Behavior and Human Decision Processes, 48,* 272–290.

Marcus, E. A., Nolen, T. G., Rankin, C. H., & Carew, T. J. (1988). Behavioral dissociation of dishabituation, sensitization, and inhibition in Aplysia. *Science, 241,* 210–213.

Marks, J. M. (1987). *Fears, phobias, and rituals: Panic, anxiety, and their disorders.* New York: Oxford University Press.

Marques, P. R., Tippetts, A. S., & Voas, R. B. (2003). Comparative and joint prediction of DUI recidivism from alcohol recidivism from alcohol ignition interlock and driver records. *Journal of Studies on Alcohol, 64,* 83–92.

Marshall, W. L., Boutilier, J., & Minnes, P. (1974). The modification of phobic behavior by covert reinforcement. *Behavior Therapy, 5,* 469–480.

Martin, G. & Pear, J. (1999). *Behavior modification: What it is and how to do it* (6th ed). Englewood Cliffs, NJ: Prentice Hall.

Martin, R. B. (1984). Punishment-induced facilitation and suppression in the shuttlebox. *Psychological Record, 34,* 381–388.

Marx, J. L. (1980). Ape-language controversy flares up. *Science, 207,* 1330–1333.

Masters, J. C., Burish, T. G., Hollon, S. D., & Rimm, D. C. (1987). *Behavior therapy: Techniques and empirical findings* (3rd ed.). San Diego, CA: Harcourt Brace Jovanovich.

Masterson, F. A. (1969). Escape from noise. *Psychological Reports, 24,* 484–486.

Mastropieri, M. A., Scruggs, T. E., & Whedon, C. (1997). Using mnemonic strategies to teach information about U.S. Presidents: A classroom-based investigation. *Learning Disability, 20,* 13–21.

Matzel, L. D., Brown, A. M., & Miller, R. R. (1987). Associative effects of US preexposure: Modulation of conditioned responding by an excitatory training context. *Journal of Experimental Psychology: Animal Behavior Processes, 13,* 65–72.

Matzel, L. D., Schachtman, T. R., & Miller, R. R. (1985). Recovery of an overshadowed association achieved by extinction of the overshadowing stimulus. *Learning and Motivation, 16,* 398–412.

McCalden, M., & Davis, C. (1972). *Report on priority lane experiment on the San Francisco-Oakland Bay Bridge.* Sacramento, CA: Department of Public Works.

McCance-Katz, E. F., Price, L. H., McDougle, C. J., Kosten, T. R., Black, J. E., & Jatlow, P. I. (1993). Concurrent cocaine-ethanol ingestion in humans: Pharmacology, physiology, behavior, and the role of cocaethylene. *Psychopharmacology, 111,* 39–46.

McCloskey, M., Wible, C. G., & Cohen, N. J. (1988). Is there a special flashbulb-memory mechanism? *Journal of Experimental Psychology: General, 117,* 171–181.

McCord, W., McCord, J., & Zola, I. K. (1959). *Origins of crime: A new evaluation of the Cambridge-Somerville Youth Study.* New York: Columbia University Press.

McDonald, R.V. & Siegel, S. (2004). Intra-administration associations and withdrawal symptoms: Morphine-elicited morphine withdrawal. *Experimental and Clinical Psychopharmacology, 12,* 3–11.

McEvoy, M. A., & Brady, M. P. (1988). Contingent access to play materials as an academic motivator for autistic and behavior disordered children. *Education and Treatment of Children, 11,* 5–18.

McGaugh, J. L., & Landfield, P. W. (1970). Delayed development of amnesia following electroconvulsive shock. *Physiology and Behavior, 5,* 1109–1113.

McGeoch, J. A. (1932). Forgetting and the law of disuse. *Psychological Review, 39,* 352–370.

Mcilroy, D., Sadler, C., & Boojawon, N. (2007). Computer phobia and computer self-efficacy: Their association with undergraduates' use of university computer facilities. *Computers in Human Behavior, 23,* 1285–1299.

McIlvane, W. J., Kledaras, J. B., Iennaco, F. M., McDonald, S. J., & Stoddard, L. T. (1995). Some possible limits on errorless discrimination reversals in individuals with severe mental retardation. *American Journal of Mental Retardation, 99,* 430–436.

McLaughlin, T. F., Mabee, W. S., Byram, B. J., & Reiter, S. M. (1987). Effects of academic positive practice and response cost on writing legibility of behaviorally disordered and learning-disabled junior high school students. *Journal of Child and Adolescent Psychotherapy, 4,* 216–221.

McMillan, D. E., & Li, M. (2000). Drug discrimination under two concurrent fixed-interval schedules. *Journal of the Experimental Analysis of Behavior, 74,* 55–77.

McMillan, D. E., Wessinger, W. D., Paule, M. G., & Wenger, G. R. (1989). A comparison of interoceptive and exteroceptive discrimination in the pigeon. *Pharmacology, Biochemistry, and Behavior, 34,* 641–647.

McNally, R. J. (2003). *Remembering trauma.* Cambridge, MA: Belknap Press/Harvard University Press.

McNeill, D. (1966). Developmental psycholinguistics. In F. Smith & G. A. Miller (Eds.), *The genesis of language* (pp. 15–84). Cambridge, MA: MIT Press.

McSweeney, F. K. & Murphy, E. S.(2009). Sensitization and habituation regulate reinforcer effectiveness. *Neurobiology of Learning and Memory, 92,* 189–198.

Mechoulam, R., & Parker, L. (2003). Cannabis and alcohol—a close friendship. *Trends in Pharmacological Sciences, 24,* 266–268.

Medin, D. L., & Ross, B. H. (1992). *Cognitive psychology* (2nd ed.). Fort Worth, TX: Harcourt Brace Jovanovich.

Meichenbaum, D. H. (1972). Examination of model characteristics in reducing avoidance behavior. *Journal of Behavior Therapy and Experimental Psychiatry, 3,* 225–227.

Meisch, R. A., & Thompson, T. (1974). Ethanol intake as a function of concentration during food deprivation and satiation. *Pharmacology, Biochemistry and Behavior, 2,* 589–596.

Melamed, B. G., & Siegel, L. J. (1975). Reduction of anxiety in children facing hospitalization and surgery by use of filmed modeling. *Journal of Consulting and Clinical Psychology, 43,* 511–521.

Melendez, R. I., Rodd-Hendricks, A. Z., Engleman, E. A., Li, T., McBride, W. J., & Murphy, J. M. (2002). Microdialysis of dopamine in the nucleus accumbens of alcohol-preferring (P) rats during anticipation and operant self-administration of ethanol. *Alcoholism: Clinical and Experimental Research, 26,* 318–325.

Mellgren, R. L. (1972). Positive and negative contrast effects using delayed reinforcement. *Learning and Motivation, 3,* 185–193.

Mendelson, J. (1967). Lateral hypothalamic stimulation in satiated rats: The rewarding effects of self-induced drinking. *Science, 157,* 1077–1979.

Mendelson, J., & Chorover, S. L. (1965). Lateral hypothalamic stimulation in satiated rats: T-maze learning for food. *Science, 149,* 559–561.

Merikle, P. M. (1980). Selection from visual persistence by perceptual groups and category membership. *Journal of Experimental Psychology: General, 109,* 279–295.

Merzenich, M. M., Jenkins, W. M., William, M., Johnston, P., Schreiner, C., Miller, S. L., et al. (1996). Temporal processing deficits of language-learning impaired children ameliorated by training. *Science, 271,* 77–81.

Meyer, D. E., & Schvaneveldt, R. W. (1971). Facilitation in recognizing pairs of words. Evidence of a dependence between retrieval options. *Journal of Experimental Psychology, 90,* 227–234.

Mikulka, P. J., Leard, B., & Klein, S. B. (1977). The effect of illness (US) exposure as a source of interference with the acquisition and retention of a taste aversion. *Journal of Experimental Psychology: Animal Behavior Processes, 3,* 189–210.

Mikulka, P. J., Pitts, E., & Philput, C. (1982). Overshadowing not potentiation in taste aversion conditioning. *Bulletin of the Psychonomic Society, 20,* 101–104.

Miller, G. A. (1956). The magical number seven, plus or minus two: Some limits on our capacity for processing information. *Psychology Review, 63,* 81–97.

Miller, G. A. (1965). Some preliminaries to psycholinguistics. *American Psychologist, 20,* 15–20.

Miller, N. E. (1941). The frustration-aggression hypothesis. *Psychological Review, 48,* 337–342.

Miller, N. E. (1948). Studies of fear as an acquirable drive: I. Fear as motivation and fear-reduction as reinforcement in learning of new responses. *Journal of Experimental Psychology, 38,* 89–101.

Miller, N. E. (1951). Comments on multiple-process conceptions of learning. *Psychological Review, 58,* 375–381.

Miller, N. E. (1985). The value of behavioral research on animals. *American Psychologist, 40,* 423–440.

Miller, R. R., & Matzel, L. D. (1989). Contingency and relative associative strength. In S. B. Klein & R. R. Mowrer (Eds.), *Contemporary learning theories: Pavlovian conditioning and the status of traditional learning theory* (pp. 61–84). Hillsdale, NJ: Lawrence Erlbaum.

Mills, C. B. (1980). Effects of context on reaction time to phonemes. *Journal of Verbal Learning and Verbal Behavior, 19,* 75–83.

Milner, B. (1965). Memory disturbance after bilateral hippocampal lesions. In P. Milner & S. Glickman (Eds.), *Cognitive processes and the brain* (pp. 91–111). Princeton, NJ: Van Nostrand.

Milner, B. (1970). Memory and the temporal regions of the brain. In K. H. Pribram & D. E. Broadbent (Eds.), *Biology of memory* (pp. 29–50). New York: Academic Press.

Milvy, P. (Ed.). (1977). *The marathon: Physiological, medical, epidemiological, and psychological studies* (Annals, Vol. 301). New York: New York Academy of Sciences.

Mineka, S., Davidson, M., Cook, M., & Keir, R. (1984). Observational conditioning of snake fear in rhesus monkeys. *Journal of Abnormal Psychology, 93,* 355–372.

Mischel, W. (1974). Processes in delay of gratification. In L. Berkowitz (Ed.), *Advances in experimental social psychology* (Vol. 7, pp. 249–291). New York: Academic Press.

Mischel, W., & Grusec, J. E. (1966). Determinants of the rehearsal and transmission of neutral and aversive behaviors. *Journal of Personality and Social Psychology, 3,* 197–205.

Mitani, H., Shirayama, Y., Yamada, T., Maeda, K., Ashby, C. R., & Kawahara, R. (2006). Correlation between plasma levels of glutamate, alanine, and serine with severity of depression. *Progress in Neuro-Psychopharmacology, and Biological Psychiatry, 30,* 1155–1158.

Miyawaki, K., Strange, W., Verbugge, R. R., Liberman, A. M., Jenkins, J. J., & Fujimura, O. (1975). An effect of linguistic experience: The discrimination of r and l by native speakers of Japanese and English. *Perception and Psychophysics, 18,* 331–340.

Moe, A., & De Beni, R. (2004). Stressing the efficacy of the loci method: Oral presentation and the subject-generation of the loci pathway with expository passages. *Applied Cognitive Psychology, 19,* 95–106.

Mohr, H., Goebel, R., & Linden, D. E. J. (2006). Content- and task-specific dissociations of frontal activity during maintenance and manipulation in visual working memory. *The Journal of Neuroscience, 26,* 4465–4471.

Moltz, H. (1960). Imprinting: Empirical basis and theoretical significance. *Psychological Bulletin, 57,* 291–314.

Moltz, H. (1963). Imprinting: An epigenetic approach. *Psychological Review, 70,* 123–138.

Monti, P. M., & Smith, N. F. (1976). Residual fear of the conditioned stimulus as a function of response prevention after avoidance or classical defensive conditioning in the rat. *Journal of Experimental Psychology: General, 105,* 148–162.

Mooney, M., Babb, D., Jensen, J., & Hatsukami, D. (2005). Interventions to increase use of nicotine gum: A randomized, controlled, single-bind trial. *Nicotine and Tobacco Research, 7,* 565–579.

Moore, J. W. (1972). Stimulus control: Studies of auditory generalization in rabbits. In A. H. Black & W. F. Prokasy (Eds.), *Classical conditioning II* (pp. 206–230). New York: Appleton-Century-Crofts.

Moore, R., & Goldiamond, I. (1964). Errorless establishment of visual discrimination using fading procedures. *Journal of the Experimental Analysis of Behavior, 7,* 269–272.

Moray, N., Bates, A., & Barnett, R. (1965). Experiments on the four-eared man. *Journal of the Acoustical Society of America, 38,* 196–201.

Morgan, R. E., & Riccio, D. C. (1998). Memory retrieval process. In W. T. O'Donohue (Ed.), *Learning and behavior therapy* (pp. 464–482). Needham Heights, MA: Allyn & Bacon.

Morse, W. H., Mead, R. N., & Kelleher, R. T. (1967). Modulation of elicited behavior by a fixed-interval schedule of electric shock presentation. *Science, 157,* 215–217.

Mortiz, S. E., Feltz, D. L., Farbach, K. R., & Mack, D. E. (2000). The relation of self-efficacy measures to sport performance: A meta-analytic review. *Research Quarterly for Exercise and Sport, 71,* 280–294.

Moscovitch, A., & LoLordo, V. M. (1968). Role of safety in Pavlovian backward fear conditioning procedure. *Journal of Comparative and Physiological Psychology, 66,* 673–678.

Moscovitch, M. (1992). Memory and working-with-memory: A component-process model based on modules and central systems. *Journal of Cognitive Neuroscience, 4,* 257–267.

Mottram, L. M., Bray, M. A., Kehle, T. J, Broudy, M., & Jenson, W. R. (2002). A classroom-based intervention to reduce disruptive behaviors. *Journal of Applied School Psychology, 19,* 65–74.

Moulds, M. L. & Nixon, R. D. V. (2006). In vivo flooding for anxiety disorders: Proposing its utility in the treatment of posttraumatic stress disorder. *Journal of Anxiety Disorders, 20,* 498–509.

Mowrer, O. H. (1938). Preparatory set (Expectancy): A determinant in motivation and learning. *Psychological Review, 45,* 62–91.

Mowrer, O. H. (1939). A stimulus-response analysis and its role as a reinforcing agent. *Psychological Review, 46,* 553–565.

Mowrer, O. H. (1947). On the dual nature of learning—a reinterpretation of "conditioning" and "problem solving." *Harvard Educational Review, 17,* 102–148.

Mowrer, O. H. (1956). Two-factor learning theory reconsidered, with special reference to secondary reinforcement and the concept of habit. *Psychological Review, 63,* 114–128.

Moyer, K. E., & Korn, J. H. (1964). Effects of UCS intensity on the acquisition and extinction of an avoidance response. *Journal of Experimental Psychology, 67,* 352–359.

Moyer, K. E., & Korn, J. H. (1966). Effect of UCS intensity on the acquisition and extinction of a one-way avoidance response. *Psychonomic Science, 4,* 121–122.

Mueller, M. M., Palkovic, C. M., Maynard, C. S. (2007). Errorless learning: Review and practical application for teaching children with pervasive developmental disorders. *Psychology in the Schools, 44,* 691–700.

Mui, R., Haselgrove, M., McGregor, A., Futter, J., Heyes, C., & Pearce, J. M. (2007). The discrimination of natural movement by budgerigars (*Melopsittacus undulates*) and pigeons (*Columba livia*). *Journal of Experimental Psychology: Animal Behavior Processes, 33,* 371–380.

Murdock, B. B., Jr. (1961). The retention of individual items. *Journal of Experimental Psychology, 62,* 618–625.

Musser, E. H., Bray, M. A., Kehle, T. J., & Jenson, W. R. (2001). Reducing disruptive behaviors in students with serious emotional disturbance. *School Psychology Review, 30,* 294–304.

Nader, M. A., & Woolverton, W. L. (1992). Further characterization of adjunctive behavior generated by schedules of cocaine self-administration. *Behavioural Pharmacology, 3,* 65–74.

Nakamura, T., Croft, D. B., & Westbrook, R. F. (2003). Domestic pigeons (Columba livia) discriminate between photographs of individual pigeons. *Learning and Behavior, 31,* 307–317.

Nakamura, T., Ito, M., Croft, D. B., & Westbrook, R. F. (2006). Domestic pigeons (Columba livia) discriminate between photographs of male and female pigeons. *Learning and Behavior, 34,* 327–339.

Narayana, K. C., Chakrabarti, S., & Grover, S. (2004). Insecticide phobia treated with exposure and response prevention: A case report. *German Journal of Psychiatry, 7,* 12–13.

National Highway Traffic Safety Administration. (2004). *Repeat intoxicated driver laws. Traffic safety facts.* Washington, DC: Author.

National Highway Traffic Safety Administration. (2007). *2006 Traffic safety annual assessment—alcohol-related fatalities. Traffic safety facts.* DOT/HS/810/FL/. Washington, DC: Author.

National Transportation Safety Board. (2003, March 17). *Testimony of Steve before the Committee on Law Enforcement, Texas House of Representatives, regarding H.B. 226–Sobriety Checkpoints, Austin, Texas.* Washington, DC: Author.

Naus, M. J., & Halasz, F. G. (1979). Developmental perspectives on cognitive processing and semantic memory. In L. S. Cermak & F. I. M. Craik (Eds.), *Levels of processing in human memory* (pp. 259–288). Hillsdale, NJ: Lawrence Erlbaum.

Needleman, L. D., & Geller, E. S. (1992). Comparing interventions to motivate work-site collection of home-generated recyclables. *American Journal of Community Psychology, 20,* 775–785.

Neisser, U. (1982). *Memory observed.* San Francisco: W. H. Freeman.

Nelson v. Heyne 491, F. 2nd 352 (1974).

Nevin, J. A. (1973). The maintenance of behavior. In J. A. Nevin (Ed.), *The study of behavior: Learning, motivation, emotion, and instinct* (pp. 201–227). Glenview, IL: Scott, Foresman.

Newell, A., Shaw, J. C., & Simon, H. A. (1958). Elements of a theory of human problem solving. *Psychological Review, 65,* 151–166.

Newell, A., & Simon, H. A. (1972). *Human problem solving.* Englewood Cliffs, NJ: Prentice Hall.

Nichols, C. S., & Russell, S. M. (1990). Analysis of animal rights literature reveals the underlying motives of the movement: Ammunition for counter offensive by scientists. *Endocrinology, 127,* 985–989.

Nissen, H. W. (1951). Analysis of a complex conditional reaction in chimpanzees. *Journal of Comparative and Physiological Psychology, 44,* 9–16.

Noble, C. E. (1966). S-O-R and the psychology of human learning. *Psychological Reports, 18,* 923–943.

Noble, M., & Harding, G. E. (1963). Conditioning of rhesus monkeys as a function of the interval between CS and US. *Journal of Comparative and Physiological Psychology, 56,* 220–224.

Norman, A. B., Norman, M. K., Hall, J. F., & Tsibulsky, V. L. (1999). Priming threshold: A novel quantitative measures of the reinstatement of cocaine self-administration. *Brain Research, 831,* 165–174.

O'Brien, C. P., Childress, A. R., Ehrman, R., & Robbins, S. J. (1998). Conditioning factors in drug use: Can they explain compulsion? *Journal of Psychopharmacology, 12,* 15–22.

Office of Civil Rights (2007) *2004 civil rights data collection: Projected values for the nation.* Washington, DC: U.S. Department of Education.

O'Hara, K., Johnson, C. M., & Beehr, T. A. (1985). Organizational behavioral management: A review of empirical research and recommendations for further investigations. *Academy of Management Review, 10,* 848–864.

O'Hara, R., Brooks, J. O., Friedman, L., Schroder, C. M., Morgan, K. S., & Kraemer, H. C. (2007). Long-term effects of mnemonic training in community-dwelling older adults. *Journal of Psychiatric Research, 41,* 585–590.

Ohio Rev. Code Ann. § 5122.271(e) (1977).

O'Kane, G., Kensinger, E. A., & Corkin, S. (2004). Evidence for semantic learning in profound amnesia: An investigation with patient H. M. *Hippocampus, 14,* 417–425.

Olds, J. (1962). Hypothalamic substrates of reward. *Psychological Review, 42,* 554–604.

Olds, J., & Milner, P. (1954). Positive reinforcement produced by electrical stimulation of septal area and other regions of rat brain. *Journal of Comparative and Physiological Psychology, 47,* 419–427.

Olmstead, T. A. & Petry, N. M. (2009). The cost-effectiveness of prize-based and voucher-based contingency management in a population of cocaine-or opoid-dependent-outpatients. *Drug and Alcohol Dependence, 102,* 108–115.

Omdal, H. & Galloway, D. (2008). Could selective mutism be re-conceptualised as a specific phobia of expressive speech? An exploratory post-hoc study. *Child and Adolescent Mental Health, 13,* 74–81.

Osaka N., Osaka M., Kondo H., , Morishita M., Fukuyama H., & Shibasaki H. (2004). The neural basis of executive function in working memory: An fMRI study based on individual differences. *NeuroImage, 21,* 623–31.

Ost, L.-G. (1989). One-session treatment for specific phobias. *Behaviour Research and Therapy, 27,* 1–7.

Ostlund, S. B., & Balleine, B. W. (2008). Differential involvement of the basolateral amygdala and mediodorsal thalamus in instrumental action selection. *The Journal of Neuroscience, 28,* 4398–4405.

Overmier, J. B., & Seligman, M. E. P. (1967). Effects of inescapable shock upon subsequent escape and avoidance learning. *Journal of Comparative and Physiological Psychology, 63,* 28–33.

Overton, D. A. (1982). Memory retrieval failures produced by changes in drug state. In R. L. Isaacson & N. E. Spear (Eds.), *The expression of knowledge* (pp. 113–140). New York: Plenum Press.

Paivio, A. (1986). *Mental representation: A dual-coding approach.* New York: Oxford University Press.

Paletta, M. S., & Wagner, A. R. (1986). Development of context-specific tolerance to morphine: Support for a dual-process interpretation. *Behavioral Neuroscience, 100,* 611–623.

Palmatier, M. I., & Bevins, R. A. (2008). Occasion setting by drug states: Functional equivalence following similar training history. *Behavioural Brain Research, 195,* 260–270.

Palmer, S., Schreiber, G., & Fox, C. (1991, November 22–24). *Remembering the earthquake: "Flashbulb" memory of experienced versus reported events.* Paper presented at the 32nd annual meeting of the Psychonomic Society, San Francisco.

Papagno, C., Valentine, T., & Baddeley, A. (1991). Phonological short-term memory and foreign-language vocabulary learning. *Journal of Memory of Language, 30,* 331–347.

Parke, R. D., & Deur, J. L. (1972). Schedule of punishment and inhibition of aggression in children. *Developmental Psychology, 7,* 266–269.

Parke, R. D., & Walters, R. H. (1967). Some factors determining the efficacy of punishment for inducing response inhibition. *Monograph of the Society for Research in Child Development, 32* (Whole No. 19).

Pate, J. L., & Rumbaugh, D. M. (1983). The language-like behavior of Lana Chimpanzee: Is it merely discrimination learning and paired-associate learning? *Animal Learning and Behavior, 11,* 134–138.

Paul, G. L. (1969). Behavior modification research: Design and tactics. In C. M. Franks (Ed.), *Behavior therapy: Appraisal and status* (pp. 29–62). New York: McGraw-Hill.

Paul G. L., & Menditto, A. A. (1992). Effectiveness of inpatient treatment programs for mentally ill adults in public psychiatric facilities. *Applied and Preventive Psychology: Current Scientific Perspectives, 1,* 41–63.

Paulson, K., Rimm, D. C., Woodburn, L. T., & Rimm, S. A. (1977). A self-control approach to inefficient spending. *Journal of Consulting and Clinical Psychology, 45,* 433–435.

Pavlov, I. (1927). *Conditioned reflexes.* Oxford, UK: Oxford University Press.

Pavlov, I. (1928). *Lectures on conditioned reflexes: The higher nervous activity of animals* (Vol. 1, H. Gantt, Trans.). London: Lawrence and Wishart.

Pearce, J. M., Kaye, H., & Hall, G. (1982). Predictive accuracy and stimulus associability: Development of a model for Pavlovian learning. In M. L. Commons, R. J. Herrnstein, & A. R. Wagner (Eds.), *Quantitative analyses of behavior* (Vol. 3, pp. 241–255). Cambridge, MA: Ballinger.

Pelchat, M. L., Johnson, R., Chan, R., Valdez, J., & Ragland, J. D. (2004). Images of desire: Food-craving activation during FMRI. *Neuroimage, 23,* 1486–1493.

Penney, R. K. (1967). Children's escape performance as a function of schedules of delay of reinforcement. *Journal of Experimental Psychology, 73,* 109–112.

Penney, R. K., & Kirwin, P. M. (1965). Differential adaptation of anxious and nonanxious children in instrumental escape conditioning. *Journal of Experimental Psychology, 70,* 539–549.

Perez-Reyes, M., & Jeffcoat, A. R. (1992). Ethanol/cocaine interaction: Cocaine and cocaethylene plasma concentrations and their relationship to subjective and cardiovascular effects. *Life Sciences, 51,* 553–563.

Perin, C. T. (1943). A quantitative investigation of the delay-of-reinforcement gradient. *Journal of Experimental Psychology, 32,* 37–51.

Peterson, C., & Seligman, M. E. P. (1984). Causal explanations as a risk factor in depression: Theory and evidence. *Psychological Review, 91,* 347–374.

Peterson, L. R., & Peterson, M. J. (1959). Short-term retention of individual verbal items. *Journal of Experimental Psychology, 58,* 193–198.

Peterson, N. (1962). The effect of monochromatic rearing on the control of responding by wavelength. *Science, 136,* 774–775.

Peterson, R. F., & Peterson, L. R. (1968). The use of positive reinforcement in the control of self-destructive behavior in a retarded boy. *Journal of Experimental Child Psychology, 6,* 351–360.

Petitto, L. A., & Marentette, P. F. (1991). Babbling in the manual mode: Evidence for the ontogeny of language. *Science, 251,* 1493–1496.

Petrovich, G. D. & Gallagher, M. (2007). Control of food consumption by learned cues: A forebrain-hypothalamic network. *Physiology & Behavior, 91,* 397–403.

Petrovich, G. D., Ross, C. A., Gallagher, M, & Holland, P. C. (2007). Learned contextual cue potentiates eating in rats. *Physiology & Behavior, 90,* 362–367.

Petrovich, G. D., Ross, C. A., Holland, P. C., & Gallagher, M. (2007). Medial prefrontal cortex is necessary for an appetitive contextual conditioned stimulus to promote eating in sated rats. *Journal of Neuroscience.* 27: 6436–6441.

Pezdek, K. (2006). Memory of event of September 11, 2001. In L. Nilsson & N. Ohta (Eds.), *Memory and society: Psychological perspectives* (pp. 73–90). New York: Psychology Press.

Piliavin, I. M., Piliavin, J. A., & Rodin, J. (1975). Costs, diffusion, and the stigmatized victim. *Journal of Personality and Social Psychology, 32,* 429–438.

Piliavin, J. A., Dovidio, J. F., Gaertner, S. L., & Clark, R. D., III. (1981). Responsive bystanders: The process of intervention. In J. Grzelak & V. Derlega (Eds.), *Living with other people: Theory and research on cooperation and helping* (pp. 279–304). New York: Academic Press.

Pillimer, D. B. (1984). Flashbulb memories of the assassination attempt on President Reagan. *Cognition, 16,* 63–80.

Pinker, S. (1999). *Words and rules: The ingredients of language.* New York: Basic Books.

Pittenger, D. J. & Pavlik, W. B. (1988). Analysis of the partial reinforcement extinction effect in humans using absolute and relative comparisons of schedules. *American Journal of Psychology, 101,* 1–14.

Plotnick, R., Mir, D., & Delgado, J. M. R. (1971). Aggression, noxiousness, and brain stimulation in unrestrained rhesus monkeys. In B. E. Eleftheriou & J. P. Scott (Eds.), *The physiology of aggression and defeat* (pp. 143–221). New York: Plenum Press.

Plummer, S., Baer, D. M., & LeBlanc, J. M. (1977). Functional considerations in the use of procedural time out and an effective alternative. *Journal of Applied Behavior Analysis, 10,* 689–706.

Poling, A. D. & Ryan, C. (1982). Differential reinforcement of other behavior schedules: Therapeutic applications. *Behavior Modification, 6,* 3–21.

Pollack, I. (1953). The information in elementary auditory displays: II. *Journal of the Acoustical Society of America, 25,* 765–769.

Porter, D., & Neuringer, A. (1984). Music discrimination by pigeons. *Journal of Experimental Psychology: Animal Behavior Processes, 10,* 138–148.

Posner, M. I. (1982). Cumulative development of attentional theory. *American Psychologist, 37,* 168–179.

Postman, L. (1967). *Mechanisms of interference in forgetting.* Vice-presidential address given at the annual meeting of the American Association for Advancement of Science, New York.

Postman, L., Stark, K., & Fraser, J. (1968). Temporal changes in interference. *Verbal Learning and Verbal Behavior, 7,* 672–694.

Powell, J., & Azrin, N. (1968). The effects of shock as a punisher for cigarette smoking. *Journal of Applied Behavior Analysis, 1,* 63–71.

Prados, J., Sansa, J. & Artigas, A. A. (2008). Partial reinforcement effects on learning and extinction of place preference in the water maze. *Learning and Behavior, 36,* 311–318.

Premack, D. (1959). Toward empirical behavior laws: I. Positive reinforcement. *Psychological Review, 66,* 219–233.

Premack, D. (1965). Reinforcement theory. In D. Levine (Ed.), *Nebraska symposium on motivation* (pp. 123–180). Lincoln: University of Nebraska.

Prendergast, M., Podus, D., Finney, J., Greenwell, L., & Roll, J. (2006). Contingency management for treatment of substances use disorders: A meta-analysis. *Addiction, 101,* 1546–1560.

Prokasy, W. F., Jr., Grant, D. A., & Myers, N. A. (1958). Eyelid conditioning as a function of unconditional stimulus intensity and intertrial intervention. *Journal of Experimental Psychology, 55,* 242–246.

Purcell, A. T., & Gero, J. S. (1998). Drawings and the design process. *Design Studies, 19,* 389–430.

Rachlin, H., Battalio, R. C., Kagel, J. H., & Green, L. (1981). Maximization theory in behavioral psychology. *The Behavioral and Brain Sciences, 4,* 371–388.

Rachlin, H., & Green, L. (1972). Commitment, choice and self-control. *Journal of the Experimental Analysis of Behavior, 17,* 15–22.

Rachman, S. J. (1990). *Fear and courage.* New York: W. H. Freeman.

Raj, J. D., Nelson, J. A., & Rao, K. S. P. (2006). A study on the effects of some reinforcers to improve performance of employees in a retail industry. *Behavior Modification, 30,* 848–866.

Ramsden, R., Friedman, B. & Williamson, D. A. (1983). Treatment of childhood headache reports with contingency management procedures. *Journal of Clinical Child Psychology, 12,* 202–206.

Randich, A., & Ross, R. T. (1985). Contextual stimuli mediate the effects of pre- and postexposure to the unconditioned stimulus on conditioned suppression. In P. D. Balsam & A. Tomie (Eds.), *Context and learning* (pp. 105–132). Hillsdale, NJ: Lawrence Erlbaum.

Rapport, M. D., & Bostow, D. E. (1976). The effects of access to special activities on the performance in four categories of academic tasks with third-grade students. *Journal of Applied Behavior Analysis, 9,* 372.

Raynor, H. A. & Epstein, L. H. (2001). Dietary variety, energy regulation, and obesity. *Psychological Bulletin, 127,* 325–341.

Razran, G. H. S. (1949). Stimulus generalization of conditioned responses. *Psychological Bulletin, 46,* 337–365.

Reber, A. S., Kassin, S. M., Lewis, S., & Cantor, G. (1980). On the relationship between implicit and explicit modes in the learning of a complex rule structure. *Journal of Experimental Psychology: Human Learning and Memory, 6,* 492–502.

Redd, W. H., Morris, E. K., & Martin, J. A. (1975). Effects of positive and negative adult-child interactions on children's social preference. *Journal of Behavior Therapy and Experimental Psychiatry, 19,* 153–164.

Reed, D. D., Critchfield, T. S., & Martens, B. K. (2006). The generalized matching law in elite sport competition: Football play calling as operant choice. *Journal of Applied Behavior Analysis, 39,* 281–297.

Reed, P. (2003). Human causality judgments and response rates on DRL and DRH schedules of reinforcement. *Learning and Behavior, 31,* 205–211.

Reese, R. M., Sherman, J. A., & Sheldon, J. B. (1998). Reducing disruptive behavior of a group-home resident with autism and mental retardation. *Journal of Autism and Developmental Disorders, 28,* 159–165.

Regalado, M., Sareen, H., Inkelas, M., Wissow, L. S., & Halfron, N. (2004). Parents' discipline of young children: Results from the survey of early childhood health. *Pediatrics, 113,* 1952–1958.

Reitman, D., & Drabman, R. S. (1999). Multifaceted uses of a simple timeout record in the treatment of a noncompliant 8-year-old boy. *Education and Treatment of Children, 22,* 136–145.

Reitman, W. R. (1965). *Cognition and thought: An information processing approach.* New York: Wiley.

Renner, K. E., & Tinsley, J. B. (1976). Self-punitive behavior. In G. Bower (Ed.), *The psychology of learning and motivation* (Vol. 10, pp. 155–198). New York: Academic Press.

Rensch, B., & Ducker, G. (1996). Versogerung des Vergessens erlenter visuellen Aufgabenbei Tieren durch Chlorpromazin. *Pfluegers Archiv Fur die Gesante Physiologiedes Menschen und der Tiere, 289,* 200–214.

Repovs, G., & Baddeley, A. (2006). The multi-component model of working memory: Explorations in experimental cognitive psychology. *Neuroscience, 139,* 5–21.

Rescorla, R. A. (1968). Probability of shock in presence and absence of CS in fear conditioning. *Journal of Comparative and Physiological Psychology, 66,* 1–5.

Rescorla, R. A. (1971). Summation and retardation tests of latent inhibition. *Journal of Comparative and Physiological Psychology, 75,* 77–81.

Rescorla, R. A. (1973). Effects of US habituation following conditioning. *Journal of Comparative and Physiological Psychology, 82,* 137–143.

Rescorla, R. A. (1978). Some implications of a cognitive perspective on Pavlovian conditioning. In S. H. Hulse, H. Fowler, & W. K. Honig (Eds.), *Cognitive processes in animal behavior* (pp. 15–50). Hillsdale, NJ: Lawrence Erlbaum.

Rescorla, R. A. (1981). Simultaneous associations. In P. Harzum & M. D. Zeiler (Eds.), *Predictability, correlation and contiguity* (pp. 47–80). New York: Wiley.

Rescorla, R. A. (1985). Conditioned inhibition and facilitation. In R. R. Miller & N. E. Spear (Eds.), *Information processing in animals: Conditioned inhibition* (pp. 299–326). Hillsdale, NJ: Lawrence Erlbaum.

Rescorla, R. A. (1986). Facilitation and excitation. *Journal of Experimental Psychology: Animal Behavior Processes, 12,* 325–332.

Rescorla, R. A. (1990). Evidence for an association between the discriminative stimulus and the response-outcome association in instrumental learning. *Journal of Experimental Psychology: Animal Behavior Processes, 16,* 326–334.

Rescorla, R. A., & Durlach, P. J. (1981). Within-event learning in Pavlovian conditioning. In N. E. Spear & R. R. Miller (Eds.), *Information processing in animals: Memory mechanisms* (pp. 81–112). Hillsdale, NJ: Lawrence Erlbaum.

Rescorla, R. A., & LoLordo, V. M. (1965). Inhibition of avoidance behavior. *Journal of Comparative and Physiological Psychology, 59,* 406–412.

Rescorla, R. A., & Solomon, R. L. (1967). Two-process learning theory: Relations between Pavlovian conditioning and instrumental learning. *Psychological Review, 74,* 151–182.

Rescorla, R. A., & Wagner, A. R. (1972). A theory of Pavlovian conditioning: Variations in the effectiveness of reinforcement and nonreinforcement. In A. H. Black & W. F. Prokasy (Eds.), *Classical conditioning II* (pp. 64–99). New York: Appleton-Century-Crofts.

Resnik, R. B., & Resnick, E. B. (1984). Cocaine abuse and its treatment. *Psychiatric Clinics of North America, 7,* 713–728.

Revusky, S. (1971). The role of interference in association over a delay. In W. K. Honig & P. H. R. James (Eds.), *Animal memory* (pp. 155–214). New York: Academic Press.

Revusky, S. (1977). The concurrent interference approach to delay learning. In L. J. Barker, M. R. Best, & M. Domjan (Eds.), *Learning mechanisms in food selection* (pp. 319–363). Waco, TX: Baylor University Press.

Revusky, S., & Parker, L. A. (1976). Aversions to drinking out of a cup and to unflavored water produced by delayed sickness. *Journal of Experimental Psychology: Animal Behavior Processes, 2,* 342–353.

Reynolds, B., Dallery, J., Shroff, P., Patak, M., & Leraas, K. (2008). A web-based contingency management program with adolescent smokers. *Journal of Applied Analysis of Behavior, 41,* 597–601.

Reynolds, G. S. (1961). Behavioral contrast. *Journal of the Experimental Analysis of Behavior, 4,* 57–71.

Reynolds, G. S. (1968). *A primer of operant conditioning.* Glenview, IL: Scott, Foresman.

Reynolds, L. K., & Kelley, M. L. (1997). The efficacy of a response cost-based treatment package for managing aggressive behavior in preschoolers. *Behavior Modification, 21,* 216–230.

Riccio, D. C., & Haroutunian, V. (1977). Failure to learn in a taste-aversion paradigm: Associative or performance deficit? *Bulletin of the Psychonomic Society, 10,* 219–222.

Rice, J. R. (1989). Children's language acquisition. *American Psychologist, 44,* 149–156.

Riley, A. L., Lotter, E. C., & Kulkosky, P. J. (1979). The effects of conditioned taste aversions on the acquisition and maintenance of schedule-induced polydipsia. *Animal Learning and Behavior, 7,* 3–12.

Riley, A. L., & Wetherington, C. L. (1989). Schedule-induced polydipsia: Is the rat a small furry human? (An analysis of an animal model of alcoholism). In S. B. Klein & R. R. Mowrer (Eds.), *Contemporary learning theories: Instrumental conditioning theory and the impact of biological constraints on learning* (pp. 205–233). Hillsdale, NJ: Lawrence Erlbaum.

Rips, L. J., Shoben, E. J., & Smith, E. E. (1973). Semantic distance and the verification of semantic relationships. *Journal of Verbal Learning and Verbal Behavior, 12,* 1–20.

Risley, T. R. (1968). The effects and side effects of punishing the autistic behaviors of a deviant child. *Journal of Applied Behavior Analysis, 1,* 21–34.

Rizley, R. C. (1978). Depression and distortion in the attribution of causality. *Journal of Abnormal Psychology, 87,* 32–48.

Rizley, R. C., & Rescorla, R. A. (1972). Associations in higher-order conditioning and sensory preconditioning. *Journal of Comparative and Physiological Psychology, 81,* 1–11.

Roberts, W. A., Mazmaniam, D. S., & Kraemer, P. J. (1984). Directed forgetting in monkeys. *Animal Learning and Behavior, 12,* 29–40.

Robins, C. J. (1988). Attributions and depression: Why is the literature so inconsistent? *Journal of Personality and Social Psychology, 54,* 880–889.

Robinson, N. M., & Robinson, H. B. (1961). A method for the study of instrumental avoidance conditioning with children. *Journal of Comparative and Physiological Psychology, 54,* 20–23.

Robleto, K., Poulos, A. M., & Thompson, R. F. (2004). Effects of a corneal anesthetic on extinction of the classically conditioned nicitating membrane response in the rabbit (*Oryctolagus cuniculus*). *Behavioral Neuroscience, 118,* 1433–1438.

Rodebaugh, T. L. (2006). Self-efficacy and social behavior. *Behaviour Research and Therapy, 44,* 1831–1838.

Roediger, H. L. (1980). The effectiveness of four mnemonics in ordering recall. *Journal of Experimental Psychology: Human Learning and Memory, 6,* 558–567.

Roehrig, H. R. (1997). Do hopelessness/ hopefulness manipulations affect reasons for living, suicidality, and/or depression in older adolescents? *Dissertation Abstracts International: Section B: The Sciences and Engineering, 57,* 6590.

Rogers, M. E., Hansen, N. B., Levy, B. R., Tate, D. C., & Sikkema, K. J. (2005). Optimism and coping with loss in bereaved HIV-infected men and women. *Journal of Social and Clinical Psychology, 24,* 341–360.

Rohner, R. P. (1986). *The warmth dimension: Foundations of parental acceptance rejection theory.* Beverly Hills, CA: SAGE.

Roll, J. M. (2007). Contingency management: An evidence-based component of methamphetamine use disorder treatments. *Addiction, 102,* 114–120.

Roll, J. M., & Shoptaw, S. (2006). Contingency management: Schedule effects. *Psychiatry Research, 144,* 91–93.

Romanowich, P., Bouret, J., & Vollmer, T. R. (2007). Further analysis of the matching law to describe two- and three-point shot allocation by professional basketball players. *Journal of Applied Behavior Analysis, 40,* 311–315.

Roper, K. L., & Zantall, T. R. (1993). Directed forgetting in animals. *Psychological Review, 113,* 513–532.

Rosch, E. (1975). Cognitive representations of semantic categories. *Journal of Experimental Psychology: General, 104,* 192–253.

Rosch, E. (1978). Principles of categorization. In E. Rosch & B. Lloyd (Eds.), *Cognition and categorization* (pp. 28–48). Hillsdale, NJ: Lawrence Erlbaum.

Rosellini, L. (1998, April 13). When to spank. *U.S. News & World Report,* pp. 52–58.

Rosenzweig, M. R. (1984). Experience, memory, and the brain. *American Psychologist, 39,* 365–376.

Ross, H. L. (1981). *Deterring the drinking driver: Legal policy and social control* (2nd ed.). Lexington, MA: Lexington Books.

Roth, S., & Kubal, L. (1975). The effects of noncontingent reinforcement on tasks of differing importance: Facilitation and learned helplessness effects. *Journal of Personality and Social Psychology, 32,* 680–691.

Roth, E. M., & Shoben, E. E. (1983). The effect of context on the structure of categories. *Cognitive Psychology, 15,* 346–379.

Rothbaum, B. O., Hodges, L., Anderson, P. L., Price, L., & Smith, S. (2002). Twelve-month follow-up of virtual reality and standard exposure therapies for the fear of flying. *Journal of Consulting and Clinical Psychology, 70,* 428–432.

Rothbaum, B. O., Hodges, L. F., Kooper, R., & Opdyke, D. (1995). Effectiveness of computer-generated (virtual reality) graded exposure in the treatment of acrophobia. *American Journal of Psychiatry, 152,* 626–628.

Routtenberg, A., & Lindy, J. (1965). Effects of the availability of rewarding septal and hypothalamic stimulation on bar-pressing for food under conditions of deprivation. *Journal of Comparative and Physiological Psychology, 60,* 158–161.

Rowa, K., Antony, M. M., & Swinson, R. P. (2007). Exposure and response prevention. In M. M. Antony & C. Purden (Eds.), *Psychological treatment of obsessive compulsive disorders: Fundamental and beyond* (pp. 79–109). Washington, DC: American Psychological Association.

Ruder, M. & Ronnberg, J. (2008). The role of the episodic buffer in working memory for language processing. *Cognitive Processing, 9,* 19–28.

Rudy, J. W. (1994). Ontogeny of context-specific latent inhibition of conditioned fear: Implications for configural associations theory and hippocampal formation development. *Developmental Psychobiology, 27,* 367–379.

Rumbaugh, D. M. (1990). Comparative psychology and the great apes: Their competency in learning, language, and numbers. *Psychological Record, 40,* 15–39.

Rumelhart, D. E., & McClelland, J. L. & the PDP Research Group. (1986). *Parallel distributed processing: Explorations in the microstructure of cognition: Vol. 1. Foundations.* Cambridge, MA: Bradford Books/MIT Press.

Rundus, D. (1971). Analysis of rehearsal processes in free recall. *Journal of Experimental Psychology, 89,* 63–77.

Rundus, D., & Atkinson, R. C. (1970). Rehearsal processes in free recall: A procedure for direct observation. *Journal of Verbal Learning and Verbal Behavior, 9,* 99–105.

Rusiniak, K. W., Palmerino, C. C., & Garcia, J. (1982). Potentiation of odor by taste in rats: Tests of some nonassociative factors. *Journal of Comparative and Physiological Psychology, 96,* 775–780.

Russell, R. K., & Sipich, J. F. (1973). Cue-controlled relaxation in the treatment of test anxiety. *Journal of Behavior Therapy and Experimental Psychiatry, 4,* 47–49.

Saigh, P. A., Yasik, A. E., Oberfield, R. A., & Inamdar, S. C. (1999). Behavioral treatment of child-adolescent posttraumatic stress disorder. In P. A. Saigh & D. J Bremer (Eds), *Posttraumatic stress disorder: A comprehensive textbook* (pp. 354–375). Needham Heights, MA: Allyn & Bacon.

Sajwaj, T., Libet, J., & Agras, S. (1989). Lemon-juice therapy: The control of life-threatening rumination in a six-month-old infant. In D. Wedding & R. J. Corsini (Eds.), *Case studies in psychotherapy* (pp. 113–122). Itasca, IL: F. E. Peacock.

Salvy, S. J., Mulick, J. A., Butter, E., Bartlett, R. K., & Linscheid, T. R. (2004). Contingent electric shock (SIBIS) and a conditioned punisher eliminate severe head banging in a preschool child. *Behavioral Interventions, 19,* 59–72.

Samson, H. H., & Falk, J. L. (1974). Ethanol and discriminative motor control: Effects on normal and dependent animals. *Pharmacology, Biochemistry and Behavior, 2,* 791–801.

Samson, H. H., & Pfeffer, A. O. (1987). Initiation of ethanol-maintained responding using a schedule-induction procedure in free feeding rats. *Alcohol and Drug Research, 7,* 461–469.

Samuel, A. L. (1963). Some studies in machine learning using the game of checkers. In E. A. Feigenbaum & J. Feldman (Eds.), *Computers and thought* (pp. 406–456). New York: McGraw-Hill.

Sanger, D. J. (1986). Drug taking as adjunctive behavior. In S. R. Goldberg & I. P. Stolerman (Eds.), *Behavioral analysis of drug dependence* (pp. 123–160). New York: Academic Press.

Saufley, W. H., Otaka, S. R., & Bavaresco, J. L. (1985). Context effects: Classroom tests and context independence. *Memory and Cognition, 13,* 522–528.

Savage-Rumbaugh, E. S., Segerdahl, P., & Fields, W. M. (2005). Individual differences in language competencies in apes resulting from unique rearing conditions imposed by different first epistemologies. In L. L. Namy (Ed.), *Symbol use and symbolic representation: Developmental and comparative perspectives* (pp. 199–219). Mahwah, NJ: Lawrence Erlbaum.

Savage-Rumbaugh, E. S., Sevcik, R. A., Brakke, K. E., & Rumbaugh, D. M. (1992). Symbols: Their communicative use, communication, and combination by bonobos (Pan panicus). In L. P. Lipsitt & C. Rovee-Collier (Eds.), *Advances in infancy research* (Vol. 7, pp. 221–278). Norwood, NJ: Ablex.

Savage-Rumbaugh, E. S., Shanker, S., & Taylor, T. T. (1996). Apes with language. *Critical Quarterly, 38,* 45–57.

Savastano, H. I., Escobar, M. & Miller, R. R. (2001). A comparator hypothesis account of the CS-preexposure effects. Cited in Denniston, J. C., Savastano, H. I., & Miller, R. R. The extended comparator hypothesis. In R. R. Mowrer & S. B. Klein (Eds) *Handbook of Contemporary Learning Theories.* Mawrah, N. J.: Erlbaum.

Savastano, H. I., & Fantino, E. (1994). Human choice in concurrent ratio-interval schedules of reinforcement. *Journal of the Experimental Analysis of Behavior, 61,* 453–463.

Schaffer, H. R., & Emerson, P. E. (1964). The development of social attachments in infancy. *Monographs Social Research in Child Development, 29,* 1–77.

Schleidt, W. (1961). Reaktionen von truthuhnern auf fliegende rauvogel und versuche zur analyse inhrer AAM's. *Zeitschrift fur Tierpsychologie, 18,* 534–560.

Schlosberg, H., & Solomon, R. L. (1943). Latency of response in a choice discrimination. *Journal of the Experimental Psychology, 33,* 22–39.

Schneider, K., & Pinnow, M. (1994). Olfactory and gustatory stimuli in food-aversion learning of rats. *The Journal of General Psychology, 121,* 169–183.

Schooler, J. W., Gerhard, D., & Loftus, E. F. (1986). Quantities of the unreal. *Journal of Experimental Psychology: Learning, Memory and Cognition, 12,* 171–181.

Schulman, A. H., Hale, E. B., & Graves, H. B. (1970). Visual stimulus characteristics of initial approach response in chicks (Gallus domesticus). *Animal Behavior, 18,* 461–466.

Schultz, W. (2002). Getting formal with dopamine and reward. *Neuron, 36,* 241–263.

Schuster, C. R., & Woods, J. H. (1966). Schedule-induced polydipsia in the rhesus monkey. *Psychological Reports, 19,* 823–828.

Schuster, R., & Rachlin, H. (1968). Indifference between punishment and free shock: Evidence for the negative law of effect. *Journal of the Experimental Analysis of Behavior, 11,* 777–786.

Schwartz, B., & Reisberg, D. (1991). *Learning and memory.* New York: Norton.

Schwitzgebel, R. L., & Schwitzgebel, R. K. (1980). *Law and psychological practice.* New York: Wiley.

Scott, W. D., & Cervone, D. (2008). Self-efficacy interventions: Guided mastery therapy. In W. T. O'Donohue & J. E. Fisher (Eds.), *Cognitive behavior therapy: Applying empirically supported techniques in your practice* (pp. 390–395). Hoboken, NJ: John Wiley & Sons.

Scoville, W. B., & Milner, B. (1957). Loss of recent memory after bilateral hippocampal lesions. *Journal of Neurology, Neurosurgery and Psychiatry, 20,* 11–21.

Seaver, W. B., & Patterson, A. H. (1976). Decreasing fuel-oil consumption through feedback and social commendation. *Journal of Applied Behavior Analysis, 9,* 147–152.

Seligman, M. E. P. (1970). On the generality of laws of learning. *Psychological Review, 77,* 406–418.

Seligman, M. E. P. (1975). *Helplessness: On depression, development, and death.* San Francisco: W. H. Freeman.

Seligman, M. E. P., & Campbell, B. A. (1965). Effects of intensity and duration of punishment on extinction of an avoidance response. *Journal of Comparative and Physiological Psychology, 59,* 295–297.

Seligman, M. E. P., & Maier, S. F. (1967). Failure to escape traumatic shock. *Journal of Experimental Psychology, 74,* 1–9.

Seligman, M. E. P., & Schulman, P. (1986). Explanatory style as a predictor of productivity and quitting among life insurance agents. *Journal of Personality and Social Psychology, 50,* 832–838.

Seligman, M. E. P., Schulman, P., & Tryon, A. M. (2007). Group prevention of depression and anxiety symptoms. *Behaviour Research and Therapy, 45,* 1111–1126.

Sem-Jacobson, C. W. (1968). *Depth-electrographic stimulation of the human brain and behavior: From fourteen years of studies and treatment of Parkinson's disease and mental disorders with implanted electrodes.* Springfield, IL: Charles C Thomas.

Senkowski, P. C. (1978). Variables affecting the overtraining extinction effect in discrete-trial lever pressing. *Journal of Experimental Psychology: Animal Behavior Processes, 4,* 131–143.

Seyfarth, R. M., Cheney, D. L., & Marler, P. (1980). Monkey responses to three different alarm calls: Evidence of predator classification and semantic communication. *Science, 210,* 801–803.

Shallice, T. (2002). Fractionation of the supervisory system. In D. T. Stuss & R. T. Knight (Eds), *Principles of frontal lobe function* (pp. 261–277). New York: Oxford University Press.

Shanab, M. E., Molayem, O., Gordon, A. C., & Steinhauer, G. (1981). Effects of signaled shifts in liquid reinforcement. *Bulletin of the Psychonomic Society, 18,* 263–266.

Shanab, M. E., & Peterson, J. L. (1969). Polydipsia in the pigeon. *Psychonomic Science, 15,* 51–52.

Shahan, T. A., & Podlesnik, C. A. (2006). Matching and conditioned reinforcement rate. *Journal of the Experimental Analysis of Behavior, 85,* 167–180.

Shanteau, J. (1992). The psychology of experts: An alternative view. In G. Wright & F. Bolger (Eds.), *Expertise and decision support* (pp. 11–23). New York: Plenum Press.

Shaw, D. W., & Thoresen, C. E. (1974). Effects of modeling and desensitization in reducing dentist phobia. *Journal of Counseling Psychology, 21,* 415–420.

Sheffield, F. D. (1965). Relation between classical conditioning and instrumental learning. In W. F. Prokasy (Ed.), *Classical conditioning* (pp. 302–322). New York: Appleton-Century-Crofts.

Sheffield, F. D. (1966). New evidence on the drive-induction theory of reinforcement. In R. N. Haber (Ed.), *Current research in motivation* (pp. 98–111). New York: Holt.

Sheffield, F. D., & Roby, T. B. (1950). Reward value of a nonnutritive sweet taste. *Journal of Comparative and Physiological Psychology, 43,* 471–481.

Sherman, M. (1927). The differentiation of emotional responses in infants: Judgments of emotional responses from motion picture views and from actual observations. *Journal of Comparative Psychology, 7,* 265–284.

Sherrington, C. S. (1906). *Integrative action of the nervous system.* New Haven, CT: Yale University Press.

Shimoff, E., Catania, A. C., & Matthews, B. A. (1981). Uninstructed human responding: Sensitivity of low-rate performance to schedule contingencies. *Journal of the Experimental Analysis of Behavior, 36,* 207–220.

Shipley, R. H. (1974). Extinction of conditioned fear in rats as a function of several parameters of CS exposure. *Journal of Comparative and Physiological Psychology, 87,* 699–707.

Sidman, M. (1953). Avoidance conditioning with brief shock and no exteroceptive warning signal. *Science, 118,* 157–158.

Sidman, M., & Stebbins, W. C. (1954). Satiation effects under fixed-ratio schedules of reinforcement. *Journal of Comparative and Physiological Psychology, 47,* 114–116.

Siegel, S. (1975). Evidence from rats that morphine tolerance is a learned response. *Journal of Comparative and Physiological Psychology, 89,* 498–506.

Siegel, S. (1977). Morphine tolerance acquisition as an associative process. *Journal of Experimental Psychology: Animal Behavior Processes, 3,* 1–13.

Siegel, S. (1978). A Pavlovian conditioning analysis of morphine tolerance. In N. A. Krasnegor (Ed.), *Behavioral tolerance: Research and treatment implications* (NIDA Research Monograph No. 18, U.S. DHEW Publ. No. ADM 78–551). Washington, DC: Government Printing Office.

Siegel, S. (1984). Pavlovian conditioning and heroin overdose: Reports by overdose victims. *Bulletin of the Psychonomic Society, 22,* 428–430.

Siegel, S. (1991). Feedforward processes in drug tolerance and dependence. In R. G. Lister & H. J. Weingartner (Eds.), *Perspectives in cognitive neuroscience* (pp. 405–416). New York: Oxford University Press.

Siegel, S. (2001). Pavlovian conditioning and drug overdose: When tolerance fails. *Addiction Research and Theory, 9,* 503–513.

Siegel, S. (2005) Drug tolerance, drug addiction, and drug anticipation. *Current Directions in Psychological Science, 14,* 296–300.

Siegel, S., & Andrews, J. M. (1962). Magnitude of reinforcement and choice behavior in children. *Journal of Experimental Psychology, 63,* 337–341.

Siegel, S., Baptista, M. A., Kim, J. A., McDonald, R. V., & Weise-Kelly, L. (2000). Pavlovian psychopharmacology: The associative basis of tolerance. *Experimental and Clinical Psychopharmacology, 8,* 276–293.

Siegel, S., & Domjan, M. (1971). Backward conditioning as an inhibitory procedure. *Learning and Motivation, 2,* 1–11.

Siegel, S., Hinson, R. E., & Krank, M. D. (1978). The role of predrug signals in morphine analgesic tolerance: Support for a Pavlovian conditioning model of tolerance. *Journal of Experimental Psychology: Animal Behavior Processes, 4,* 188–196.

Siegel, S., Hinson, R. E., Krank, M. D., & McCully, J. (1982). Heroin "overdose" death: Contribution of drug-associated environmental cues. *Science, 216,* 436–437.

Siegel, S., Kim, J. A., & Sokolowska, M. (2003). Situational specificity of caffeine tolerance. *Circulation, 108,* 38.

Siegel, S., & Ramos, B. M. (2002). Applying laboratory research: Drug anticipation and the treatment of drug addiction. *Experimental and Clinical Psychopharmacology, 10,* 162–183.

Silberberg, A., Warren-Boulton, F. R., & Asano, T. (1988). Maximizing present value: A model to explain why moderate response rates obtain on variable-interval schedules. *Journal of the Experimental Analysis of Behavior, 49,* 331–228.

Sills, T. L., Onalaja, A. O., & Crawley, J. N. (1998). Mesolimbic dopamine mechanisms underlying individual differences in sugar consumption and amphetamine hypolocomotion in Wisrar rats. *European Journal of Neuroscience, 10,* 1895–1902.

Silverman, K., Preston, K. L., Stitzer, M. L, & Schuster, C. R. (1999). Efficacy and versatility of voucher-based reinforcement in drug abuse treatment. In S. T. Higgins & K. Silverman (Eds.), *Motivating behavior change among illicit-drug abusers: Research on contingency management interventions* (pp. 163–181). Washington, DC: American Psychological Association.

Silverstein, A. U., & Lipsitt, L. P. (1974). The role of instrumental responding and contiguity of stimuli in the development of infant secondary reinforcement. *Journal of Experimental Child Psychology, 17,* 322–331.

Simon, G. A. (1973). The structure of ill-structured problems. *Artificial Intelligence, 4,* 181–202.

Simon, S. J., Ayllon, T., & Milan, M. A. (1982). Behavioral compensation: Contrast like effects in the classroom. *Behavior Modification, 6,* 407–420.

Skinner, B. F. (1938). *The behavior of organisms: An experimental analysis.* New York: Appleton-Century-Crofts.

Skinner, B. F. (1948). Superstition in the pigeon. *Journal of Experimental Psychology, 38,* 168–172.

Skinner, B. F. (1953). *Science and human behavior.* New York: Macmillan.

Skinner, B. F. (1957). *Verbal behavior.* New York: Appleton-Century-Crofts.

Slobin, D. I. (1966). Grammatical transformations and sentence comprehension in childhood and adulthood. *Journal of Verbal Learning and Verbal Behavior, 5,* 219–227.

Smith, M. C., Coleman, S. R., & Gormezano, I. (1969). Classical conditioning of the rabbit's nictitating membrane response at backward, simultaneous, and forward CS US intervals. *Journal of Comparative and Physiological Psychology, 69,* 226–231.

Smith, S. M. (1982). Enhancement of recall using multiple environment contexts during learning. *Memory and Cognition, 19,* 405–412.

Smith, S. M., & Vela, E. (2001). Environmental context-dependent memory: A review and meta-analysis. *Psychonomic Bulletin and Review, 8,* 203–220.

Smoke, K. L. (1933). Negative instances in concept learning. *Journal of Experimental Psychology, 16,* 583–588.

Sokolowska, M., Siegel, S., & Kim, J. A. (2002). Intraadministration associations: Conditional hyperalgesia elicited by morphine onset cues. *Journal of Experimental Psychology: Animal Behavior Processes, 28,* 309–320.

Solnick, J. V., Rincover, A., & Peterson, C. R. (1977). Some determinants of the reinforcing and punishing effects of time-out. *Journal of Applied Behavior Analysis, 10,* 415–424.

Solomon, R. L. (1977). An opponent-process theory of acquired motivation: The affective dynamics of addiction. In J. D. Maser & M. E. P. Seligman (Eds.), *Psychopathology: Experimental models* (pp. 66–103). San Francisco: W. H. Freeman.

Solomon, R. L. (1980). The opponent-process therapy of acquired motivation: The costs of pleasure and the benefits of pain. *American Psychologist, 35,* 691–712.

Solomon, R. L., & Corbit, J. D. (1974). An opponent-process theory of motivation: Temporal dynamics of affect. *Psychological Review, 81,* 119–145.

Solomon, R. L., & Wynne, L. C. (1953). Traumatic avoidance learning: Acquisition in normal dogs. *Psychological Monographs, 67* (Whole No. 354).

Sorensen, J. L., Masson, C. L., & Copeland, A. L. (1999). Coupons-vouchers as a strategy for increasing treatment entry for opiate-dependent injection drug users. In S. T. Higgins & K. Silverman (Eds.), *Motivating behavior change among illicit-drug abusers: Research on contingency management interventions* (pp. 147–161). Washington, DC: American Psychological Association.

Spence, K. W. (1936). The nature of discrimination learning in animals. *Psychological Review, 43,* 427–449.

Spence, K. W. (1956). *Behavior theory and conditioning.* New Haven, CT: Yale University.

Sperling, G. (1960). The information available in brief visual presentations. *Psychological Monographs, 74* (Whole No. 498).

Sperling, G. (1963). A model for visual memory task. *Human Factors, 5,* 19–31.

Squire, L. R. (1986). Mechanisms of memory. *Science, 232,* 1612–1619.

Squire, L. R. (1987). *Memory and brain.* New York: Oxford University Press.

Squire, L. R. (1998). Memory and brain systems. In S. Rose (Ed.), *From brains to consciousness* (pp. 53–72). London: Penguin Press.

Squire, L. R. (2004). Memory systems of the brain: A brief history and current perspective. *Neurobiology of Learning and Memory, 82,* 171–177.

Squire, L. R., Amaral, D. G., & Press, G. A. (1990). Magnetic resonance measurements of hippocampal formation and mammillary nuclei distinguish medial temporal lobe and diencephalic amnesia. *Journal of Neuroscience, 10,* 3106–3117.

Squire, L. R., Stark, C. E. L., & Clark, R. E. (2004). The medial temporal lobe. *Annual Review of Neuroscience, 27,* 279–306.

Squire, L. R., Zola-Morgan, S., & Chen, K. (1988). Human amnesia and animal models of amnesia: Performance of amnesic patients on tests designed for the monkey. *Behavioral Neuroscience, 11,* 210–221.

Staats, C. K., & Staats, A. W. (1957). Meaning established by classical conditioning. *Journal of Experimental Psychology, 54,* 74–80.

Staddon, J. E. R. (1988). Quasi-dynamic choice models: Melioration and ratio invariance. *Journal of the Experimental Analysis of Behavior, 49,* 303–320.

Staddon, J. E. R., & Ayres, S. L. (1975). Sequential and temporal properties of behavior induced by a schedule of periodic food delivery. *Behavior, 54,* 26–49.

Staddon, J. E. R., & Motheral, S. (1978). On matching and maximizing in operant choice situations. *Psychological Review, 85,* 436–444.

Staddon, J. E. R., & Simmelhag, V. L. (1971). The "Superstition" experiment: A reexamination of its implications for the principles of adaptive behavior. *Psychological Review, 78,* 3–43.

Stapleton, J. V. (1975). Legal issues confronting behavior modification. *Behavioral Engineering, 2,* 35.

Starr, M. D. (1978). An opponent process theory of motivation: VI. Time and intensity variables in the development of separation-induced distress calling in ducklings. *Journal of Experimental Psychology: Animal Behavior Processes, 4,* 338–355.

Stein, B. S. (1978). Depth of processing reexamined: The effects of the precision of encoding and test appropriateness. *Journal of Verbal Learning and Verbal Behavior, 17,* 165–174.

Stein, D. B. (1999). Outpatient behavioral management of aggressiveness in adolescents: A response cost paradigm. *Aggressive Behavior, 25,* 321–330.

Stein, L., & Wise, C. D. (1973). Amphetamine and noradrendergic reward pathways. In E. Usdin & S. H. Snyder (Eds), *Frontiers in catecholamine research* (pp. 963–968). New York: Pergamon.

Steinbrecher, C. D., & Lockhart, R. A. (1966). Temporal avoidance conditioning in the cat. *Psychonomic Science, 5,* 441–442.

Stephens, C. E., Pear, J. J., Wray, L. D., & Jackson, G. C. (1975). Some effects of reinforcement schedules in teaching picture names to retarded children. *Journal of Applied Behavior Analysis, 8,* 435–447.

Steur, F. B., Applefield, J. M., & Smith, R. (1971). Televised aggression and the interpersonal aggression of preschool children. *Journal of Experimental Child Psychology, 11,* 442–447.

Stolerman, I. P. (1989) Comparison of fixed-ratio and tandem schedules of reinforcement in discrimination of nicotine in rats. *Drug Development Research, 16,* 101–109.

Stonebraker, T. B., & Rilling, M. (1981). Control of delayed matching-to-sample performance using directed forgetting techniques. *Animal Learning and Behavior, 9,* 196–220.

Storms, L. H., Boroczi, G., & Broen, W. E., Jr. (1962). Punishment inhibits an instrumental response in hooded rats. *Science, 135,* 1133–1134.

Straus, M. A. (2001). *Beating the devil out of them: Corporal punishment in American families and its effects on children.* Piscataway, NJ: Transaction Publishing.

Sutherland, N. S., & Mackintosh, N. J. (1971). *Mechanisms of animal discrimination learning.* New York: Academic Press.

Swanson, J. M., & Kinsbourne, M. (1979). State-dependent learning and retrieval: Methodological cautions against theoretical considerations. In J. F. Kihlstrom & F. J. Evans (Eds.), *Functional disorders of memory* (pp. 275–299). Hillsdale, NJ: Lawrence Erlbaum.

Sweeney, P. D., Anderson, K., & Bailey, S. (1986). Attributional style in depression: A meta-analytic review. *Journal of Personality and Social Psychology, 50,* 974–991.

Symonds, M. & Hall, G. (1999). Overshadowing not potentiation of illness-based contextual conditioning by a novel taste. *Animal Learning and Behavior, 27,* 379–390.

Tait, R. W., Marquis, H. A., Williams, R., Weinstein, L., & Suboski, M. S. (1969). Extinction of sensory preconditioning using CER training. *Journal of Comparative and Physiological Psychology, 69,* 170–172.

Tait, R. W., & Saladin, M. E. (1986). Concurrent development of excitatory and inhibitory associations during backward conditioning. *Animal Learning and Behavior, 14,* 133–137.

Talarico, J. M., & Rubin, D. C. (2003). Confidence, not consistency, characterizes flashbulb memories. *Psychological Science, 14,* 455–461.

Tang, M., Kenny, J., & Falk, J. L. (1984). Schedule-induced ethanol dependence and phenobarbital preference. *Alcohol, 1,* 55–58.

Tarpy, R. M., & Mayer, R. E. (1978). *Foundations of learning and memory.* Glenview, IL: Scott, Foresman.

Tarpy, R. M., & Sawabini, F. L. (1974). Reinforcement delay: A selective review of the last decade. *Psychological Bulletin, 81,* 984–987.

Tennen, H., & Eller, S. J. (1977). Attributional components of learned helplessness and facilitation. *Journal of Personality and Social Psychology, 35,* 265–271.

Terrace, H. S. (1963a). Discrimination learning with and without "errors." *Journal of the Experimental Analysis of Behavior, 6,* 1–27.

Terrace, H. S. (1963b). Errorless discrimination learning in the pigeon: Effects of chlorpromazine and imipramine. *Science, 140,* 318–319.

Terrace, H. S. (1963c). Errorless transfer of a discrimination across two continents. *Journal of the Experimental Analysis of Behavior, 6,* 223–232.

Terrace, H. S. (1964). Wavelength generalization after discrimination learning with and without errors. *Science, 144,* 78–80.

Terrace, H. S. (1966). Stimulus control. In W. K. Honig (Ed.), *Operant behavior: Areas of research and application* (pp. 271–344) New York: Appleton-Century-Crofts.

Terrace, H. S. (1979). *Nim.* New York: Knopf.

Terrell, G., & Ware, R. (1961). Role of delay of reward in speed of size and form discrimination learning in childhood. *Child Development, 32,* 409–415.

Tharp, R. G., & Wetzel, R. J. (1969). *Behavior modification in the natural environment.* New York: Academic Press.

Theios, J., Lynch, A. D., & Lowe, W. F., Jr. (1966). Differential effects of shock intensity on one-way and shuttle avoidance conditioning. *Journal of Experimental Psychology, 72,* 294–299.

Thomas, D. R., Mood, K., Morrison, S., & Wiertelak, E. (1991). Peak shift revisited: A test of alternative interpretations. *Journal of Experimental Psychology: Animal Behavior Processes, 17,* 130–140.

Thomas, E., & DeWald, L. (1977). Experimental neurosis: Neuropsychological analysis. In J. D. Maser & M. E. P. Seligman (Eds.), *Psychopathology: Experimental models* (pp. 214–231). San Francisco: W. H. Freeman.

Thompson, C. R., & Church, R. M. (1980). An explanation of the language of a chimpanzee. *Science, 208,* 313–314.

Thompson, R. F. (2009). Habituation: A history. *Neurobiology of Learning and Memory, 92,* 127–134.

Thompson. R. F., Clark, G. A., Donegan, N. H., Lavond, D. G., Lincoln, J. S., Madden, J., et al. (1984). Neuronal substrates of learning and memory: A "multiple-trace" view. In G. Lynch, J. L. McGaugh, & N. M. Weinberger (Eds.), *Neurobiology of learning and memory* (pp. 137–164). New York: Guilford Press.

Thompson, R. F., & Krupa D. J. (1994) Organization of memory traces in the mammalian brain. *Annual Review of Neuroscience, 17,* 519–549.

Thompson, R. F., & Spencer, W. A. (1966). Habituation: A model phenomenon for the study of neural substrates of behavior. *Psychological Review, 73,* 16–43.

Thorndike, E. L. (1898). Animal intelligence: An experimental study of the associative processes in animals. *Psychological Review Monograph Supplement, 2,* 1–109.

Thorndike, E. L. (1913). *Educational psychology, vol. II: The psychology of learning.* New York: Teachers College, Columbia University.

Thorndike, E. L. (1932). *Fundamentals of learning.* New York: Teachers College, Columbia University.

Timberlake, W. (1986). Unpredicted food produces a mode of behavior that affects rats' subsequent reactions to a conditioned stimulus: A behavior-system approach to context blocking. *Animal Learning and Behavior, 14,* 276–286.

Timberlake, W. (2001). Motivated modes in behavior systems. In R. R. Mowrer & S. B. Klein (Eds.), *Handbook of contemporary learning theories* (pp. 155–209). Mahwah, NJ: Lawrence Erlbaum.

Timberlake, W., & Allison, J. (1974). Response deprivation: An empirical approach to instrumental performance. *Psychological Review, 81,* 146–164.

Timberlake, W., & Farmer-Dougan, V. A. (1991). Reinforcement in applied settings: Figuring out ahead of time what will work. *Psychological Bulletin, 110,* 379–391.

Timberlake, W., & Lucas, G. A. (1989). Behavior systems and learning: From misbehavior to general principles. In S. B. Klein & R. R. Mowrer (Eds.), *Contemporary learning theory: Instrumental conditioning theory and the impact of biological constraints on learning* (pp. 237–275). Hillsdale, NJ: Lawrence Erlbaum.

Timberlake, W., Wahl, G., & King, D. (1982). Stimulus and response contingencies in the misbehavior of rats. *Journal of Experimental Psychology: Animal Behavior Processes, 8,* 62–85.

Tinbergen, N. (1951). *The study of instinct.* Oxford, UK: Clarendon.

Tinbergen, N., & Van Iersel, J. J. A. (1947). Displacement reactions in the three-spined stickleback. *Behavior, 1,* 56–63.

Todd, G. E., & Cogan, D. C. (1978). Selected schedules of reinforcement in the black-tailed prairie dog (*Cynomys ludovicianus*). *Animal Learning and Behavior, 6,* 429–434.

Tolman, E. C. (1932). *Purposive behavior in animals and men.* New York: Century.

Tolman, E. C. (1959). Principles of purposive behavior. In S. Koch (Ed.), *Psychology: A study of a science,* (Vol. 2, pp. 92–157). New York: McGraw-Hill.

Tolman, E. C., & Honzik, C. H. (1930a). Degrees of hunger, reward and nonreward, and maze learning in rats. *University of California Publications in Psychology, 4,* 241–256.

Tolman, E. C., & Honzik, C. H. (1930b). "Insight" in rats. *University of California Publications in Psychology, 4,* 215–232.

Tolman, E. C., Ritchie, B. F., & Kalish, D. (1946). Studies of spatial learning: II. Place learning versus response learning. *Journal of Experimental Psychology, 36,* 221–229.

Toufexis, A. (1991, October 28). When can memories be trusted? *Time,* pp. 86–88.

Trapold, M. A., & Fowler, H. (1960). Instrumental escape performance as a function of the intensity of noxious stimulation. *Journal of Experimental Psychology, 60,* 323–326.

Traupmann, K. L. (1972). Drive, reward, and training parameters and the overlearning-extinction effect (OEE). *Learning and Motivation, 3,* 359–368.

Trenholme, I. A., & Baron, A. (1975). Intermediate and delayed punishment of human behavior by loss of reinforcement. *Learning and Motivation, 6,* 62–79.

Tripp, D. A., Catano, V., & Sullivan, M. J. L. (1997). The contributions of attributional style, expectancies, depression, and self-esteem in a cognition-based depression model. *Canadian Journal of Behavioural Science Revue canadienne des Sciences du comportement, 29,* 101–111.

Trocki-Ables, P., French, R. & O'Connor, J. (2001). Use of primary and secondary reinforcers after performance of a 1-mile walk/run by boys with attention deficit hyperactivity disorder. *Perceptual and Motor Skills, 93,* 461–464.

Troland, L. T. (1928). *The fundamentals of human motivation.* New York: Van Nostrand.

Tulving, E. (1972). Episodic and semantic memory. In E. Tulving & W. Donaldson (Eds.), *Organization of memory* (pp. 381–403). New York: Academic Press.

Tulving, E. (1983). *Elements of episodic memory.* Oxford, UK: Clarendon Press/Oxford University Press.

Tulving, E. (1998). Brain/mind correlates of human memory. In M. Sabourin, F. Craik, & M. Robert (Eds.), *Advances in psychological science: Vol. 2. Biological and cognitive aspects* (pp. 441–460). East Sussex, UK: Psychology Press.

Tulving, E., & Markowitsch, H. J. (1997). Memory beyond the hippocampus. *Current Opinion in Neurobiology, 7,* 209–216.

Turek, P. W., Grubaugh, A. L., Hamner, M. B., & Foa, E. B. (2009). Diagnosis and treatment of PTSD-related compulsive checking behaviors in veterans of the Iraq War: The influence of military context on the expression of PTSD symptoms. *The American Journal of Psychiatry, 166,* 762–767.

Ullman, L. P., & Krasner, L. (1965). *Case studies in behavior modification.* New York: Holt, Rinehart & Winston.

Ulrich, R. E., Wolff, P. C., & Azrin, N. H. (1964). Shock as an elicitor of intra- and inter-species fighting behavior. *Animal Behavior, 12,* 14–15.

Underwood, B. J. (1957). Interference and forgetting. *Psychological Review, 64,* 48–60.

Underwood, B. J. (1969). Attributes of memory. *Psychological Review, 76,* 559–573.

Underwood, B. J. (1983). *Attributes of memory.* Glenview, IL: Scott, Foresman.

Underwood, B. J., & Ekstrand, B. R. (1966). An analysis of some shortcomings in the interference theory of forgetting. *Psychological Review, 73,* 540–549.

Underwood, B. J., & Freund, J. S. (1968). Effect of temporal separation of two tasks on proactive inhibition. *Journal of Experimental Psychology, 78,* 50–54.

Urcelay, G. P., & Miller, R. R. (2006). A comparator view of Pavlovian and differential inhibition. *Journal of Experimental Psychology: Animal Behavior Processes, 32,* 271–283.

Vaccarino, F. J., Schiff, B. B., & Glickman, S. E. (1989). Biological view of reinforcement. In S. B. Klein & R. R. Mowrer (Eds.), *Contemporary learning theories: Instrumental conditioning and the impact of biological constraints on learning* (pp. 111–142). Hillsdale, NJ: Lawrence Erlbaum.

Valenstein, E. S., & Beer, B. (1964). Continuous opportunities for reinforcing brain stimulation. *Journal of Experimental Analysis of Behavior, 7,* 183–184.

Valenstein, E. S., Cox, V. C., & Kakolewski, J. W. (1969). The hypothalamus and motivated behavior. In J. T. Tapp (Ed.), *Reinforcement and behavior* (pp. 242–287). New York: Academic Press.

Valentine, C. W. (1930) The innate bases of fear. *Journal of Genetic Psychology, 37,* 394–420.

Vancouver, J. B., Thompson, C. M., Tischner, E. C., & Putka, D. J. (2002). Two studies examining the negative effect of self-efficacy on performance. *The Journal of Applied Psychology, 87,* 506–516.

Vandercar, D. H., & Schneiderman, N. (1967). Interstimulus interval functions in different response systems during classical conditioning of rabbits. *Psychonomic Science, 9,* 9–10.

Van der Werf, Y. D., Jolles, J., Witter, M. P., & Uylings, H. B. M. (2003). Contributions of thalamic nuclei to declarative memory functioning. *Cortex, 39,* 1047–1062.

Van Hamme, L. J., & Wasserman, E. A. (1994). Cue competition in causality judgments: The role of nonpresentation of compound stimulus elements. *Learning and Motivation, 25,* 127–151.

Viken, R. J., & McFall, R. M. (1994). Paradox lost: Implications of contemporary reinforcement theory for behavior therapy. *Current Directions in Psychological Science, 3,* 121–125.

Voeks, V. W. (1954). Acquisition of S-R connections: A test of Hull's and Guthrie's theories. *Journal of Experimental Psychology, 47,* 137–147.

Voelz, Z. R., Haeffel, G. J., Joiner, T. E., Jr., & Wagner, K. D. (2003). Reducing hopelessness: The interation [sic] of enhancing and depressogenic attributional styles for positive and negative life events among youth psychiatric inpatients. *Behaviour Research and Therapy, 41,* 1183–1198.

Vollmer, T. R., & Bourret, J. (2000). An application of the matching law to evaluate the allocation of two- and three-point shots by college basketball players. *Journal of Applied Behavior Analysis, 33,* 137–150.

Von Holst, E., & Von St. Paul, U. (1962). Electrically controlled behavior. *Scientific American, 206,* 50–59.

Vonk, J., & MacDonald, S. E. (2002). Natural concepts in a juvenile gorilla (gorilla gorilla gorilla) at three levels of abstraction. *Journal of the Experimental Analysis of Behavior, 78,* 315–329.

Vyse, S. A., & Belke, T. W. (1992). Maximizing versus matching on concurrent variable-interval schedules. *Journal of the Experimental Analysis of Behavior, 58,* 325–334.

Wagner, A. R. (1981). SOP: A model of automatic memory processing in animal behavior. In N. E. Spear & R. R. Miller (Eds.), *Information processing in animals: Memory mechanisms* (pp. 5–47). Hillsdale, NJ: Lawrence Erlbaum.

Wagner, A. R., & Brandon, S. E. (1989). Evolution of a structured connectionist model of Pavlovian conditioning (AESOP). In S. B. Klein & R. R. Mowrer (Eds.), *Contemporary learning theories: Pavlovian conditioning and the status of traditional learning theory* (pp. 149–189). Hillsdale, NJ: Lawrence Erlbaum.

Wagner, A. R., & Brandon, S. E. (2001). A componential theory of Pavlovian conditioning. In R. R. Mowrer & S. B. Klein (Eds.), *Handbook of contemporary learning theories* (pp. 23–64). Mahwah, NJ: Lawrence Erlbaum.

Wagner, A. R., Logan, F. A., Haberlandt, K., & Price, T. (1968). Stimulus selection in animal discrimination learning. *Journal of Experimental Psychology, 76,* 171–180.

Wahler, R. G., Winkel, G. H., Peterson, R. F., & Morrison, D. C. (1965). Mothers as behavior therapists for their own children. *Behaviour Research and Therapy, 3,* 113–124.

Wald, B. A. & Cheney, C. D. (1975). Matching behavior and deprivation. *Bulletin of the Psychonomic Society, 6,* 4–6.

Walk, R. D., & Walters, C. P. (1973). Effect of visual deprivation on depth discrimination of hooded rats. *Journal of Comparative and Physiological Psychology, 85,* 559–563.

Walker, J. R., Ahmed, S. H., Gracy, K. N., & Koob, G. F. (2000). Microinjections of an opiate receptor antagonist into the bed nucleus of the stria terminalis suppress heroin self-administration in dependent rats. *Brain Research, 854,* 85–92.

Wall, A. M., Walters, G. D., & England, R. S. (1972). The lickometer: A simple device for the analysis of licking as an operant. *Behavior Research Methods and Instrumentation, 4,* 320–322.

Wallace, R. F. & Mulder, D. W. (1973). Fixed-ratio responding with human subjects. *Bulletin of the Psychonomic Society, 1,* 359–362.

Walters, G. C., & Glazer, R. D. (1971). Punishment of instinctive behavior in the Mongolian gerbil. *Journal of Comparative and Physiological Psychology, 75,* 331–340.

Walters, G. C., & Grusec, J. F. (1977). *Punishment*. San Francisco: W. H. Freeman.

Wanner, E., & Maratsos, M. (1978). An ATN approach to comprehension. In M. Halle, J. Bresnan, & G. A. Miller (Eds.), *Linguistic theory and psychological reality* (pp. 119–161). Cambridge, MA: MIT Press.

Ward-Maguire, P. R. (2008). Increasing on-task behavior and assignment completion of high school students with emotional behavioral disorders. *Dissertation Abstracts International Section A: Humanities and Social Sciences, 68*, 4256.

Warner, L. T. (1932). An experimental search for the "conditioned response." *Journal of Genetic Psychology, 41*, 91–115.

Warrington, E. K. (1985). A disconnection analysis of amnesia. *Annals of the New York Academy of Sciences, 444*, 72–77.

Warrington, E. K., & Weiskrantz, L. (1968). A study of learning and retention in amnesic patients. *Neuropsychologia, 6*, 283–291.

Warrington, E. K., & Weiskrantz, L. (1970). Amnesic syndrome: Consolidation or retrieval? *Nature, 228*, 628–630.

Wasserman, E. A. (1993). Comparative cognition: Beginning the second century of the animal intelligence. *Psychological Bulletin, 113*, 211–228.

Wasserman, E. A., & Young, M. E. (2010). Same-different discrimination: The keel and backbone of thought and reasoning. *Journal of Experimental Psychology: Animal Behavior Processes, 36*, 3–22.

Watanabe, S., Sakamoto, J., & Wakita, M. (1995). Pigeons' discrimination of paintings by Monet and Picasso. *Journal of the Experimental Analysis of Behavior, 63*, 165–174.

Watkins, M. H., & Tulving, E. (1975). Episodic memory: When recognition fails. *Journal of Experimental Psychology: General, 104*, 5–29.

Watkins, M. J. (1974). When is recall spectacularly higher than recognition? *Journal of Experimental Psychology, 102*, 161–163.

Watson, J. B. (1916). The place of the conditioned reflex in psychology. *Psychological Review, 23*, 89–116.

Watson, J. B. (1919). A schematic outline of emotions. *Psychological Review, 26*, 165–196.

Watson, J. B., & Rayner, R. (1920). Conditional emotional reactions. *Journal of Experimental Psychology, 3*, 1–14.

Waugh, N. C., & Norman, D. A. (1965). Primary memory. *Psychological Review, 72*, 89–104.

Wauquier, A. & Sadowski, B. (1978). Behavioural measurements of excitability changes in reward sites in the dog: A frequency dependent effect. *Physiology & Behavior, 21*, 165–168.

Weidman, U. (1956). Some experiments on the following and the flocking reaction of mallard ducklings. *British Journal of Animal Behavior, 4*, 78–79.

Weingarten, H. P., & Martin, G. M. (1989). Mechanisms of conditioned meal initiation. *Physiological Behavior, 45*, 735–740.

Weinstock, S. (1958). Acquisition and extinction of a partially reinforced running response at a 24-hour intertrial interval. *Journal of Experimental Psychology, 56*, 151–158.

Weiskrantz, L., & Warrington, E. K. (1975). The problem of the amnesic syndrome in man and animals. In R. L. Isaacson & K. H. Pribram (Eds.), *The hippocampus* (pp. 411–428). New York: Plenum Press.

Weisman, R. G., & Litner, J. S. (1972). The role of Pavlovian events in avoidance training. In R. A. Boakes & M. S. Halliday (Eds.), *Inhibition and learning* (pp. 253–270). London: Academic Press.

Weisman, R. G., & Palmer, J. A. (1969). Factors influencing inhibitory stimulus control: Discrimination training and prior non differential reinforcement. *Journal of the Experimental Analysis of Behavior, 12*, 229–237.

Weiss, B., Dodge, K. A., Bates, J. E., & Pettit, G. S. (1992). Some consequences of early harsh discipline: Child aggression and a maladaptive social information. *Child Development, 63*, 1321–1335.

Weiss, J. M., Goodman, P. A., Losito, P. G., Corrigan, S., Charry, J., & Bailey, W. (1981). Behavioral depression produced by an uncontrolled stressor: Relation to norepinephrine, dopamine, and serotonin levels in various regions of the rat brain. *Brain Research Review, 3*, 167–205.

Weiss, J. M., Simpson, P. G., Ambrose, M. J., Webster, A., & Hoffman, L. J. (1985). Chemical basis of behavioral depression. In E. Katkin & S. Manuck (Eds.), *Advances in behavioral medicine* (Vol. 1, pp. 233–275). Greenwich, CT: JAI Press.

Weiss, J. M., Simpson, P. G., Hoffman, L. J., Ambrose, M. J., Cooper, S., & Webster, A. (1986). Infusion of adrenergic receptor agonist and antagonists into the locus coeruleus and ventricular system of the brain: Effects on swim-motivated and spontaneous motor activity. *Neuropharmacology, 25*, 367–384.

Weiss, S. J., & Schindler, C. W. (1981). Generalization peak shift in rats under conditions of positive reinforcement and avoidance. *Journal of the Experimental Analysis of Behavior, 35*, 175–185.

Welsh, D. H., Bernstein, D. J., & Luthans, F. (1992). Application of the Premack principle of reinforcement to the quality performance of service employees. *Journal of Organizational Behavior Management, 13*, 9–32.

Wessels, M. G. (1982). *Cognitive psychology.* New York: Harper & Row.

West, R. F., & Stanovich, K. E. (2003). Is probability matching smart? Associations between probabilistic choices and cognitive ability. *Memory and Cognition, 31,* 243–251.

Wetherington, C. L. (1982). Is adjunctive behavior a third class of behavior? *Neuroscience and Biobehavioral Reviews, 6,* 329–350.

Wheeler, D. D., & Miller, R. R. (2009). Potentiation and overshadowing in Pavlovian fear conditioning. *Journal of Experimental Psychology: Animal Behavior Processes, 35,* 340–356.

Whiteside, S. P. & Brown, A. M. (2008). Five-day intensive treatment for adolescent OCD: A case series. *Journal of Anxiety Disorders, 22,* 495–504.

Whitfield, C. L. (1995). *Memory and abuse: Remembering and healing the effects of trauma.* Deerfield Beach, FL: Health Communications.

Wickelgren, W. A. (1974). *How to solve problems.* San Francisco: W. H. Freeman.

Wickens, C. D., Stokes, A., Barnett, B., & Hyman, F. (1993). The effects of stress on pilot judgment in a MIDIS stimulator. In O. Svenson & A. J. Maule (Eds.), *Time pressure and stress in human judgment and decision making* (pp. 271–292). New York: Plenum Press.

Wiggam, J., French, R., & Henderson, H. (1986). The effects of a token economy on distance walked by senior citizens in a retirement center. *American Corrective Therapy Journal, 40,* 6–12.

Wikler, A., & Pescor, F. T. (1967). Classical conditioning of a morphine abstinence phenomenon, reinforcement of opioid-drinking behavior and "relapse" in morphine-addicted rats. *Psychopharmacologia, 10,* 255–284.

Wilcott, R. C. (1953). A search for subthreshold conditioning at four different auditory frequencies. *Journal of Experimental Psychology, 46,* 271–277.

Wilcoxon, H. C., Dragoin, W. B., & Kral, P. A. (1971). Illness-induced aversions in rat and quail: Relative salience of visual and gustatory cues. *Science, 7,* 489–493.

Williams, B. A. (1983). Another look at contrast in multiple schedules. *Journal of the Experimental Analysis of Behavior, 39,* 345–384.

Williams, B. A. (1991a). Choice as a function of local versus molar contingencies of reinforcement. *Journal of the Experimental Analysis of Behavior, 56,* 455–473.

Williams, B. A. (1991b). Marking and bridging versus conditioned reinforcement. *Animal Learning and Behavior, 19,* 264–269.

Williams, B. A. (2002). Behavioral contrast redux. *Animal Learning and Behavior, 30,* 1–20.

Williams, D. E., Kirkpatrick-Sanchez, S., & Crocker, W. T. (1994). A long-term follow-up of treatment for severe self-injury. *Research in Developmental Disabilities, 15,* 487–501.

Williams, S. L. (1995). Self-efficacy, anxiety, and phobic disorders. In J. E. Madduz (Ed.), *Self-efficacy, adaptation, and adjustment: Theory, research, and application* (pp. 69–107). New York: Plenum Press.

Willows, A. O. D., & Hoyle, G. (1969). Neuronal network triggering a fixed action pattern. *Science, 166,* 1549–1551.

Wilson, F. C., & Manly, T. (2003). Sustained attention training and errorless learning facilities self-care functioning in chronic ipsilesional neglect following severe traumatic brain injury. *Neuropsychological Rehabilitation, 13,* 537–548.

Wingfield, A., & Byrnes, D. L. (1981). *The psychology of human memory.* New York: Academic Press.

Winn, P., Williams, S. F., & Herberg, L. J. (1982). Feeding stimulated by very low doses of d-amphetamine administered systemically or by microinjection into the striatum. *Psychopharmacology, 78,* 336–341.

Wise, R. A. (2004). Dopamine, learning, and motivation. *Nature Reviews Neuroscience, 5,* 483–494.

Wise, R. A., & Rompre, P. O. (1989). Brain dopamine and reward. *Annual Review of Psychology, 40,* 191–225.

Wolf, M. M., Risley, T., & Mees, H. L. (1964). Application of operant conditioning procedures to the behavior problems of an autistic child. *Behavior Research and Therapy, 1,* 305–312.

Wolpe, J. (1958). *Psychotherapy by reciprocal inhibition.* Stanford, CA: Stanford University Press.

Wolpe, J. (1976). *Theme and variations: A behavior therapy casebook.* Elmsford, NJ: Pergamon.

Wolpe, J. (1978). Self-efficacy theory and psychotherapeutic change: A square peg for a round hole. In S. Rachman (Ed.), *Advances in behavior research and therapy* (Vol. 1, pp. 231–236). Oxford, UK: Pergamon.

Wolpe, J. & Rachman, S. (1950) Psychoanalytic "evidence": A critique based on Freud's case of Little Hans. *Journal of Nervous and Mental Disease, 130,* 135–148.

Wolters, G., & Raffone, A. (2008). Coherence and recurrency: Maintainence, control, and integration in working memory. *Cognitive Processing, 9,* 1–17.

Wood, F., Taylor, B., Penny, R., & Stump, D. (1980). Regional cerebral blood flow response to recognition memory versus semantic classification tasks. *Brain and Language, 9,* 113–122.

Woods, P. J., Davidson, E. H., & Peters, R. J. (1964). Instrumental escape conditioning in a water tank: Effects of variations in drive stimulus intensity and reinforcement magnitude. *Journal of Comparative and Physiological Psychology, 57,* 466–470.

Wright v. McMann, 460 F. 2d 126 (2d Cir. 1972).

Wright, A. A. & Katz, J. S. (2007). Generalization hypothesis of abstract-concept learning: Learning strategies and related issues in Macaca mulatta, Cebus paella, and Columba livia. *Journal of Comparative Psychology, 121,* 387–397.

Wright, D. B., & Loftus, E. F. (2008). Eyewitness memory. In G. Cohen & M. A. Conway (Eds.), *Memory in the real world* (3rd ed., pp. 91–105). New York: Psychology Press.

Wynne, C. D. L. (2007). What the ape said. *Ethology, 113,* 411–413.

Young Welch, C. (2009). A mixed-method study utilizing a token economy to shape behavior and increase academic success in urban students. *Dissertation Abstracts International Section A: Humanities and Social Sciences, 69,* 3022.

Zaragoza, M. S., Belli, R. F., & Payment, K. E. (2007). Misinformation effects and the suggestibility of eyewitness memory. In G. Maryanne & H. Harlene (Eds.), *Do justice and let the sky fall: Elizabeth Loftus and her contributions to science, law, and academic freedom* (pp. 35–63). Mahwah, NJ: Lawrence Erlbaum.

Zaragoza, M. S., McCloskey, M., & Jamis, M. (1987). Misleading post-event information and recall of the original event: Further evidence against the memory impairment hypothesis. *Journal of Experimental Psychology: Learning, Memory, and Cognition, 13,* 36–44.

Zazdeh, L. A., Fu, K. S., Tanak, K., & Shimura, M. (Eds.). (1975). *Fuzzy sets and their applications to cognitive and decision processes.* New York: Academic Press.

Zeaman, D. (1949). Response latency as a function of the amount of reinforcement. *Journal of Experimental Psychology, 39,* 466–483.

Zhang, D., Zhang, X., Sun, X., Li, Z., Wang, Z., He, S., & Hu, X., (2004). Cross-modal temporal order memory for auditory digits and visual locations: An fMRI study. *Human Brain Mapping, 22,* 280–289.

Zhang, Y., Loonam, T. M., Noailles, P.-A. H., & Angulo, J. A. (2001). Comparison of cocaine and methamphetamine-evoked dopamine and glutamate overflow in somatodendritic and terminal field regions of the rat brain during acute, chronic, and early withdrawal conditions. In V. Quinones-Jenab (Ed.), *The biological basis of cocaine addiction* (pp. 93–120). New York: New York Academy of Sciences.

Zink, M., Vollmayr, B., Gebicke-Haerter, P. J., & Henn, F. A. (2010) Reduced expression of glutamate transporters vGluT1, EAAT2 and EAAT4 in learned helpless rats, an animal model of depression. *Neuropharmacology, 58,* 465–473.

Zironi, I., Burattini, C., Aicardi, G., & Janak, P. H. (2006). Context is a trigger for relapse to alcohol. *Behavioral Brain Research, 167,* 150–155.

Zoellner, L. A., Abramowitz, J. S., Moore, S. A., & Slagle, D. M. (2008). Flooding. In W. T. O'Donohue & J. E. Fisher (Eds.), *Cognitive behavior therapy: Applying empirically supported techniques in your practice* (2nd ed., pp. 202–210). Hoboken, NJ: John Wiley & Sons.

Zola-Morgan, S., & Squire, L. R. (1986). Memory impairment in monkeys following lesion limited to the hippocampus. *Behavioral Neuroscience, 100,* 155–160.

Zola-Morgan, S., & Squire, L. R. (1993). Neuroanatomy of memory. *Annual Review of Neuroscience, 16,* 547–563.

Zola-Morgan, S., Squire, L. R., & Amaral, D. G. (1986). Human amnesia and the medial temporal region: Enduring memory impairment following a bilateral lesion limited to field CA1 of the hippocampus. *Journal of Neuroscience, 6,* 2950–2967.

Zola-Morgan, S., Squire, L. R., & Ramus, S. J. (1994). Severity of memory impairment in monkeys as a function of locus and extent of damage within the medial temporal lobe memory system. *Hippocampus, 4,* 483–495.

Zoppelt, D., Koch, B., Schwarz, M., & Daum, I. (2003). Involvement of the mediodorsal thalamic nucleus in mediating recollection and familiarity. *Neuropsychologia, 41,* 1160–1170.

Zygmont, D. M., Lazar, R. M., Dube, W. V., & McIlvane, W. J. (1992). Teaching arbitrary matching via sample stimulus-control shaping to young children and mentally retarded individuals: A methodological note. *Journal of the Experimental Analysis of Behavior, 57,* 109–117.

Credits and Sources

Chapter 1

Figure 1.1a: Adapted from Swenson, L. C. (1980). *Theories of learning: Traditional perspectives/contemporary developments.* Belmont, CA: Wadsworth. Copyright © Leland Swenson.

Figure 1.1b: Robert M. Yerkes Papers, Manuscripts & Archives, Manuscripts and Archives, Yale University Library.

Figure 1.2: From Thorndike, E. L. (1898). Animal intelligence: An experimental study of the associative process in animals. *Psychological Review Monograph, 2* (Supp. 8). Copyright 1898 by the American Psychological Association. Public domain.

Figure 1.3a: Adapted from Yerkes, R. M., & Margulis, S. (1909). The method of Pavlov in animal psychology. *Psychological Bulletin, 6,* 257–273. Copyright 1909 by the American Psychological Association. Public domain.

Figure 1.3b: Time Life Pictures./Contributor/Getty Images.

Figure 1.4a: Adapted from Swenson, L. C. (1980). *Theories of learning: Traditional perspectives/contemporary developments.* Belmont, CA: Wadsworth. Copyright © Leland Swenson.

Figure 1.4b: © Center for the History of Psychology, Archives of the History of American Psychology—The University of Akron.

Photo 1.1: © Center for the History of Psychology, Archives of the History of American Psychology—The University of Akron.

Photo 1.2: © Time Life Pictures./Contributor/Getty Images.

Photo 1.3: © Center for the History of Psychology, Archives of the History of American Psychology—The University of Akron.

Photo 1.4: © Center for the History of Psychology, Archives of the History of American Psychology—The University of Akron.

Chapter 2

Figure 2.1: From Klein, S. B. (1982). *Motivation: Biosocial approaches.* New York: McGraw-Hill.

Figure 2.2: From *American Journal of Psychology.* Copyright 1942 by the Board of Trustees of the University of Illinois. Used with Permission of the author and the University of Illinois Press.

Figure 2.3: From Bolles, R. C. (1979). *Learning theory* (2nd ed.). New York: Holt, Rinehart & Winston.

Figure 2.4: Nin Leen/Time & Life Pictures/Getty Images.

Photo 2.1: © Center for the History of Psychology, Archives of the History of American Psychology—The University of Akron.

Photo 2.2: © Center for the History of Psychology, Archives of the History of American Psychology—The University of Akron.

Photo 2.3: © Center for the History of Psychology, Archives of the History of American Psychology—The University of Akron.

Photo 2.4: © Center for the History of Psychology, Archives of the History of American Psychology—The University of Akron.

Photo 2.5: © Bachrach/Contributor/Getty Images.

Chapter 3

Figure 3.1: Adapted from Lorenz, K. (1950). The comparative method of studying innate behavior patterns. In J. F. Danelli & R. Brown, *Symposia of the Society for Experimental Biology: Physiological mechanisms in animal behavior.* New York: Academic Press.

Figure 3.2: Adapted from Tinbergen, N. (1951). *The study of instinct.* Oxford: Clarendon.

Figure 3.3: From *Motivation: Theory and Research,* 3rd edition by Petri, 1991. Reprinted with permission of Wadsworth, a division of Thomson Learning: www.thomsonrights.com. Fax 800–730–2215.

Figure 3.4: From Domjan, M. (1976). Determinants of the enhancement of flavor-water intake by prior exposure. *Journal of Experimental Psychology: Animal Behavior Processes, 2,* 17–27. Copyright 1976 by the American Psychological Association. Reprinted by permission.

Figure 3.5: From Davis, M. (1974). Sensitization of the rat startle response by noise. *Journal of Comparative and Physiological Psychology, 87,* 571–581. Copyright 1974 by the American Psychological Association. Reprinted by permission.

Figure 3.6: Print Credit Line: Smock, Timothy K., *Physiological Psychology: A Neuroscience Approach,* ©1999, pp.375,376. Reprinted by permission of Pearson Education, Inc. Upper Saddle River, NJ. Electronic Credit Line: Smock, Timothy K., Physiological Psychology: A Neuroscience Approach, 1st, ©1999. Electronically reproduced by permission of Pearson Education, Inc., Upper Saddle River, New Jersey.

Figure 3.7: Print Credit Line: Smock, Timothy K., Physiological Psychology: A Neuroscience Approach, ©1999, pp. 375, 376. Reprinted by permission of Pearson Education, Inc. Upper Saddle River, NJ. Electronic Credit Line: Smock, Timothy K., *Physiological Psychology: A Neuroscience Approach,* 1st, © 1999. Electronically reproduced by permission of Pearson Education, Inc., Upper Saddle River, New Jersey.

Figure 3.8: Adapted from Solomon, R. L., & Corbit, J. D. (1974). An opponent-process theory of motivation: Temporal dynamics of affect. *Psychological Review, 81,* 119–145. Copyright 1974 by the American Psychological Association. Reprinted by permission.

Figure 3.9: Adapted from Solomon, R. L., & Corbit, J. D. (1974). An opponent-process theory of motivation: Temporal dynamics of affect. *Psychological Review, 81,* 119–145. Copyright 1974 by the American Psychological Association. Reprinted by permission.

Photo 3.1: © Max-Planck-Gesellschaft/Archive Berlin.

Chapter 4

Figure 4.2: Adapted from Swenson, L. C. (1980). *Theories of learning: Traditional perspectives/contemporary developments.* Belmont, CA: Wadsworth. Copyright © Leland Swenson.

Figure 4.3: From Gormezano, I. (1969). Classical conditioning. In J. B. Sidowski (Ed.), *Experimental methods of instrumentation in psychology* (pp. 385–420). New York: McGraw-Hill. Used with permission of the McGraw-Hill Companies.

Figure 4.5: Data from Kimble, G. A., & Reynolds, B. (1967). Eyelid conditioning as a function of the interval between conditioned and unconditioned stimuli. In G. A. Kimble (Ed.), *Foundations of conditioning and learning* (pp. 279–287). New York: Appleton-Century-Crofts.

Figure 4.6: Adapted from Prokasy, W. P., Jr., Grant, D. A., & Myers, N. A. (1958). Eyelid conditioning as a function of unconditioned stimulus intensity and intertrial interval. *Journal of Experimental Psychology, 55,* 242–246. Copyright 1958 by the American Psychological Association. Public Domain.

Figure 4.7: Adapted from Rescorla, R. A. (1968). Probability of shock in the presence and absence of CS in fear conditioning. *Journal of Comparative and Physiological Psychology, 68,* 1–5. Copyright 1968 by the American Psychological Association. Reprinted by permission.

Figure 4.9: Adapted from Humphreys, L. G. (1939). The effect of random alternation of reinforcement on the acquisition and extinction of conditioned eyelid reactions. *Journal of Experimental Psychology, 25,* 141–158. Copyright 1939 by the American Psychological Association. Public Domain.

Figure 4.10: Adapted from Shipley, R. H. (1974). Extinction of conditioned fear in rats as a function of several parameters of CS exposure. *Journal of Comparative and Physiological Psychology, 87,* 669–707. Copyright 1974 by the American Psychological Association. Reprinted with permission.

Figure 4.11: From Kimmel, H. D. (1965). Instrumental inhibitory factors in classical conditioning. In W. F. Prokasy (Ed.), *Classical conditioning: A symposium* (pp. 148–171). New York: Irvington.

Table 4.1: Masters, J. C., Burish, T. G., Hollon, S. D., and Rimm, D. C. (1987). *Behavior therapy:*

Techniques and empirical findings (3rd ed.). San Diego, CA: Harcourt Brace Jovanovich. Reprinted by permission of the publisher.

Table 4.2: Wolpe, J. (1982). *The practice of behavior therapy* (3rd ed.). Oxford: Pergamon.

Chapter 5

Figure 5.2: From Siegel, S. (1977). Morphine tolerance acquisition as an associative process. *Journal of Experimental Psychology: Animal Behavior Processes, 3,* 1–13. Copyright 1977 by the American Psychological Association. Reprinted by permission.

Figure 5.3: Adapted from Wagner, A. R., & Brandon, S. E. (1989). Evolution of a structured connectionist model of Pavlovian conditioning (AESOP). In S. B. Klein & R. R. Mowrer (Eds.). *Contemporary learning theories: Pavlovian conditioning and the status of traditional learning theory* (pp. 149–189). Hillsdale, NJ: Erlbaum.

Figure 5.4: From Paletta, M. S., & Wagner, A. R. (1986). Development of context-specific tolerance to morphine: Support for a dual-process interpretation. *Behavioral Neuroscience, 100,* 611–623. Copyright 1986 by the American Psychological Association. Reprinted by permission.

Figure 5.5: Adapted from Thompson, R. F., & Krupa D. J. (1994). Organization of memory traces in the mammalian brain. *Annual Review of Neuroscience, 17,* 519–549.

Figure 5.7: From Randich, A., & Ross, R. T. (1985). Contextual stimuli mediate the effects of pre- and postexposure to the unconditioned stimulus on conditioned suppression. In P. D. Balsam & A. Tomie (Eds.), *Context and learning* (pp. 105–132). Hillsdale, NJ: Erlbaum.

Figure 5.8: Adapted from Baker, A. G., & Mackintosh, N. J. (1977). Excitatory and inhibitory conditioning following uncorrelated presentations of CS and UCS. *Animal Learning and Behavior, 5,* 315–319. Reprinted by permission of Psychonomic Society, Inc.

Chapter 6

Figure 6.1: By Edmund Fantino and Cheryl A. Logan. *The experimental analysis of behavior: A biological perspective.* Copyright 1979 by W. H. Freeman and Company. Reprinted by permission.

Figure 6.3: Adapted from Bersh, P. J. (1951). The influence of two variables upon the establishment of a secondary reinforcer for operant responses. *Journal of Experimental Psychology, 41,* 62–73. Copyright 1951 by the American Psychological Association. Public Domain.

Figure 6.6: From *Physiology and Behavior,* 9, Collier, G., Hirsch, E., & Hamlin, P. H. The ecological determinants of reinforcement in the rat. 705–716. Copyright 1972, with permission from Elsevier Science.

Figure 6.7: Reynolds, G. S. *A Primer of Operant Conditioning,* 2nd Edition, © 1975, pp. 47, 96. Reprinted by permission of Pearson Education, Inc., Upper Saddle River, NJ.

Figure 6.8: From Grice, G. R. (1948). The relation of secondary reinforcement to delayed reward in visual discrimination learning. *Journal of Experimental Psychology, 38,* 1–16. Copyright 1948 by the American Psychological Association. Public Domain.

Figure 6.9: Adapted from Guttman, N. (1954). Equal reinforcing values for sucrose and glucose solutions compared with sweetness values. *Journal of Comparative and Physiological Psychology, 47,* 358–361. Copyright 1954 by the American Psychological Association. Public Domain.

Figure 6.12: From D'Amato, M. R. (1970). *Experimental psychology: Methodology, psychophysics, and learning.* New York: McGraw-Hill. Used with permission of the McGraw-Hill Companies.

Figure 6.13: From Jenkins, W. O., McFann, H., & Clayton, F. L. (1950). A methodological study of extinction following a periodic and continuous reinforcement. *Journal of Comparative and Physiological Psychology, 43,* 155–167. Copyright 1950 by the American Psychological Association. Public Domain.

Figure 6.14: From Hulse, S. H., Jr. (1958). Amount and percentage of reinforcement and duration of goal confinement in conditioning and extinction. *Journal of Experimental Psychology, 56,* 48–57. Copyright 1958 by the American Psychological Association. Public Domain.

Table 6.1: From Masters. Behavior Therapy, 3E. © 1987 Wadsworth, a part of Cengage Learning, Inc. Reproduced by permission. www.cengage.com/permissions.

Figure 6.15: From Ayllon, T., & Azrin, N. H. (1965). *The measurement and reinforcement of behavior of psychotics. Journal of the Experimental Analysis of Behavior, 8,* 357–383. Copyright 1965 by the Society for the Experimental Analysis of Behavior, Inc.

Figure 6.16: From Higgins, J. W., Williams, R. L., & McLaughlin, T. F. (2001). The effects of a token economy employing consequences for a third-grade student with learning disabilities: A data-based case study. *Education and Treatment of Children, 24,* 96–106.

Chapter 7

Figure 7.1: Adapted from Trapold, M. A., & Fowler, H. (1960). Instrumental escape performance as a function of the intensity of noxious stimulation. *Journal of Experimental Psychology, 60,* 323–326. Copyright 1960 by the American Psychological Association. Public Domain.

Figure 7.2: Adapted from Fowler, H., & Trapold, M. A. (1962). Escape performance as a function of delay of reinforcement. *Journal of Experimental Psychology, 63,* 464–467. Copyright 1962 by the American Psychological Association. Public Domain.

Figure 7.3: From Fazzaro, J., & D'Amato, M. R. (1969). Resistance to extinction after varying amounts of nondiscriminative or cue-correlated escape training. *Journal of Comparative and Physiological Psychology, 68,* 373–376. Copyright 1969 by the American Psychological Association. Reprinted by permission.

Figure 7.4: From Brown, J. S., Martin, R. C., & Morrow, M. W. (1964). Self-punitive behavior in the rat: Facilitative effects of punishment on resistance to extinction. *Journal of Comparative and Physiological Psychology, 57,* 127–133. Copyright 1964 by the American Psychological Association. Reprinted by permission.

Figure 7.6: From Flaherty, C. F., Hamilton, L. W., Gandelman, R. J., & Spear, N. E. (1977). *Learning and memory.* Chicago: Rand McNally.

Figure 7.7: Adapted from Skinner, B. F. (1938) *The behavior of organisms: An experimental analysis.* New York: Appleton-Century-Crofts.

Figure 7.8: Adapted from Camp, D. S., Raymond, G. A., & Church, R. M. (1967). Temporal relationship between response and punishment. *Journal of Experimental Psychology, 74,* 114–123. Copyright 1967 by the American Psychological Association. Reprinted by permission.

Figure 7.9: From Azrin, N. H., Holz, W. C., & Hake, D. F. (1963). Fixed-ratio punishment. *Journal for the Experimental Analysis of Behavior, 6,* 141–148. Copyright 1963 by the Society for the Experimental Analysis of Behavior, Inc.

Figure 7.10: Adapted from Camp, D. S., Raymond, G. A., & Church, R. M. (1967). Temporal relationship between response and punishment. *Journal of Experimental Psychology, 74,* 114–123. Copyright 1967 by the American Psychological Association. Reprinted by permission.

Figure 7.11: This article was published in *Behavior Research and Therapy,* Vol. 18, Emmelkamp, P.M.G., Van der Helm, M., van Zanten, B. L., & Plochg, I. Treatment of obsessive-compulsive patients: The contribution of self-instructional training to the effectiveness of exposure, 61–66. Copyright Elsevier, 1980.

Figure 7.12: Photographs courtesy of Peter Lang.

Figure 7.13: From Lincheid, T. R., Iwata, B. A., Ricketts, R. W., Williams, D. E., & Griffin, J. C. (1990). Clinical evaluation of the self-injurious behavior inhibiting system. *Journal of Applied Behavior Analysis, 23,* 53–78.

Photo 7.2: © Center for the History of Psychology, Archives of the History of American Psychology—The University of Akron.

Chapter 8

Figure 8.1: From McEvoy, M. A., & Brady, M. P. (1988). Contingent access to play materials as an academic motivator for autistic and behavior disordered children. *Education and Treatment of Children, 11,* 5–18.

Figure 8.2: From Allison, J. (1989). The nature of reinforcement. In S. B. Klein & R. R. Mowrer (Eds.), *Contemporary learning theories: Instrumental conditioning theory and the impact of biological constraints on learning* (pp. 13–39). Hillsdale, NJ: Erlbaum.

Figure 8.3: From Viken, R. J., & McFall, R. M. (1994). Paradox lost: Implications of contemporary reinforcement theory for behavior therapy. *Current Directions in Psychological Science, 3,* 121–124.

Figure 8.4: From Herrnstein, R. J. (1961). Relative and absolute strength of response as a function of frequency of reinforcement. *Journal of the*

Experimental Analysis of Behavior, 4, 267–272. Copyright 1961 by the Society for the Experimental Analysis of Behavior, Inc.

Figure 8.5: From Kamin, L. J. (1956). The effects of termination of the CS and the avoidance of the UCS on avoidance learning. *Journal of Comparative and Physiological Psychology, 49,* 420–424. Copyright 1956 by the American Psychological Association. Public Domain.

Figure 8.6: From D'Amato, M. R., Fazzaro, J., & Etkin, M. (1968). Anticipatory responding and avoidance discrimination as factors in avoidance conditioning. *Journal of Experimental Psychology, 77,* 41–47. Copyright 1968 by the American Psychological Association. Reprinted by permission.

Photo 8.2: © Courtesy of Harvard University, Department of Psychology.

Photo 8.3: © Center for the History of Psychology, Archives of the History of American Psychology—The University of Akron.

Chapter 9

Figure 9.1: From Timberlake, W. (2001). Motivational modes in behavior systems. In R. R. Mowrer & S. B. Klein (Eds.), *Handbook of contemporary learning theories* (pp. 155–209). Mawah, NJ: Erlbaum.

Figure 9.2: Photograph courtesy of Animal Behavior Enterprises, Inc. Hot Springs, Arkansas. Used by permission of Marian Breland.

Figure 9.3: From Riley, A. L., Lotter, E. C., & Kulkosky, P. J. (1979). The effects of conditioned taste aversions on the acquisition and maintenance of schedule-induced polydipsia. *Animal Learning and Behavior, 7,* 3–12. Reprinted by permission of Psychonomic Society, Inc.

Figure 9.4: From Hyson, R. L., Sickel, J. L., Kulkosky, P. J., & Riley, A. C. (1981). The insensitivity of schedule-induced polydipsia to conditioned taste aversions: Effect of amount consumed during conditioning. *Animal Learning and Behavior, 9,* 281–286. Reprinted by permission of Psychonomic Society, Inc.

Figure 9.5: Adapted from Garcia, J., Clark, J. C., & Hankins, W. G. (1973). Natural responses to scheduled rewards. In P. P. G. Bateson & P. H. Klopfer (Eds.), *Perspectives in ethology*

(Vol. 1, pp. 1–41). New York: Plenum. With kind permission of Springer Science and Business Media.

Figure 9.6: From Kalat, J. W., & Rozin, P. (1973). "Learned safety" as a mechanism in long-delay taste-aversion learning in rats. *Journal of Comparative and Physiological Psychology, 83,* 198–207. Copyright 1973 by the American Psychological Association. Reprinted by permission.

Figure 9.7: Nina Leen/Time & Life Pictures/Getty Images.

Figure 9.8: Photographs courtesy of Harlow Primate Laboratory, University of Wisconsin-Madison.

Figure 9.9: From Bolles, R. C. (1969). Avoidance and escape learning. *Journal of Comparative and Physiological Psychology, 68,* 355–358. Copyright 1969 by the American Psychological Association. Reprinted by permission.

Figure 9.11: From Klein, S. B., & Thorne, B. M. (2007). *Biological psychology.* New York: Worth.

Figure 9.12: From Klein, S. B. (2000). *Biological psychology.* Upper Saddle River, NJ: Prentice-Hall.

Figure 9.13: From Klein, S. B., & Thorne, B. M. (2007). *Biological psychology.* New York: Worth.

Chapter 10

Figure 10.1: Adapted from Guttman, N., & Kalish, H. I. (1956). Discriminability and stimulus generalization. *Journal of Experimental Psychology, 51,* 79–88. Copyright 1956 by the American Psychological Association. Public Domain.

Figure 10.2: *Journal of General Psychology, 17,* 125–148. Reprinted with permission of Helen Dwight Education Foundation Publications, 1319 Eighteenth St., NW, Washington, DC 20036–1802. Copyright © 1937.

Figure 10.3: From Jenkins, H. M., & Harrison, R. H. (1960). Effect of discrimination training on auditory generalization. *Journal of Experimental Psychology, 59,* 246–253. Copyright 1960 by the American Psychological Association. Public Domain.

Figure 10.4: From Weisman, R. G., & Palmer, J. A. (1969). Factors influencing inhibitory stimulus control: Discrimination training and prior non-differential reinforcement. *Journal of the*

Experimental Analysis of Behavior, 12, 229–237. Copyright 1969 by the Society for the Experimental Analysis of Behavior, Inc.

Figure 10.5: Reprinted with permission from Peterson, N. (1962). Effect of monochromatic rearing on the control of responding by wavelength. *Science, 136,* 774–775. Copyright 1962 by the American Association for the Advancement of Science.

Figure 10.6: Reynolds, G. S. *A Primer of Operant Conditioning,* 2nd Edition, © 1975, pp. 47, 96. Reprinted by permission of Pearson Education, Inc., Upper Saddle River, NJ.

Figure 10.8: From Davidson, T. L., Aparicio, J., & Rescorla, R. A. (1988). Transfer between Pavlovian facilitators and instrumental discriminative stimuli. *Animal Learning and Behavior, 16,* 285–291. Reprinted by permission of Psychonomic Society, Inc.

Figure 10.9: From Spence, K. W. (1937). The difference response in animals to stimuli varying within a single dimension. *Psychological Review, 44,* 430–444. Copyright 1937 by the American Psychological Association. Public Domain.

Figure 10.10: From Hanson, H. (1959). Effects of discrimination training on stimulus generalization. *Journal of Experimental Psychology, 58,* 321–334. Copyright 1959 by the American Psychological Association. Public Domain.

Figure 10.11: Adapted from Terrace, H. S. (1963a). Discrimination learning with and without "errors." *Journal of the Experimental Analysis of Behavior, 6,* 1–27. Copyright 1963 by the Society for the Experimental Analysis of Behavior. Reprinted by permission.

Figure 10.12: From *Learning and Memory* by Berry Schwartz and Daniel Reisberg. Copyright ©W. W. Norton & Company, Inc. Used by permission of W. W. Norton & Company, Inc.

Figure 10.13: From Domjan/ Burkhard. *Principles of Learning and Behavior,* 2E. © 1986 Wadsworth, a part of Cengage Learning, Inc. Reproduced by permission. www.cengage.com/permissions.

Photo 10.1: © Center for the History of Psychology, Archives of the History of American Psychology— The University of Akron.

Photo 10.2: © Center for the History of Psychology, Archives of the History of American Psychology— The University of Akron.

Chapter 11

Figure 11.1: From Tolman, E. C., Ritchie, B. F., & Kalish, D. (1946). Studies of spatial learning: II. Place learning versus response learning. *Journal of Experimental Psychology, 36,* 221–229. Copyright 1946 by the American Psychological Association. Public Domain.

Figure 11.2: From Tolman, E. C., & Honzik, C. H. (1930b). "Insight" in rats. *University of California Publications in Psychology, 4,* 215–232. Copyright 1930 by The Regents of the University of California.

Figure 11.3: From Tolman, E. C., & Honzik, C. H. (1930a). Degrees of hunger, reward and nonreward; and maze learning in rats. *University of California Publications in Psychology, 4,* 241–256. Copyright 1930 by The Regents of the University of California.

Figure 11.4: Adapted from Dickinson, A., & Nicholas, D. J. (1983). Irrelevant incentive learning during instructional conditioning: The role of drive-reinforcer and response-reinforcer relationships. *Quarterly Journal of Experimental Psychology, 35B,* 249–263. Reprinted by permission of The Experimental Psychology Society.

Figure 11.5: Adapted from Dickinson, A., & Dawson, G. R. (1987). Pavlovian processes in the motivation control of instrumental performance. *Quarterly Journal of Experimental Psychology, 39B,* 201–213. Reprinted by permission of The Experimental Psychology Society.

Figure 11.6: From Seligman, M. E. P., & Maier, S. F. (1967). Failure to escape traumatic shock. *Journal of Experimental Psychology, 74,* 1–9. Copyright 1967 by the American Psychological Association. Reprinted by permission.

Table 11.1: Abramson, L. Y., Seligman, M. E. P., & Teasdale, J. D. (1978). Learned helplessness in humans: Critique and reformulation. *Journal of Abnormal Psychology, 87,* 40–74. Copyright 1978 by the American Psychological Association. Reprinted by permission.

Figure 11.8: From Bandura, A., & Adams, N. E. (1977). Analysis of self-efficacy theory of behavioral change. *Cognitive Therapy and Research, 1,* 287–310. With kind permission of Springer Science and Business Media.

Chapter 12

Table 12.1: Rosch, E. (1975). Cognitive representations of semantic categories. *Journal of Experimental Psychology: General, 104,* 192–253. Copyright 1975 by the American Psychological Association. Reprinted by permission.

Figure 12.2: From Smoke, K. L. (1932). An objective study of concept formation. *Psychological Monographs, 42,* whole no. 191. Copyright 1932 by the American Psychological Association. Public Domain.

Figure 12.3: Photographs provided by Richard Herrnstein.

Figure 12.4: From Hull, C. L. (1920). Quantitative aspect of the evolution of concepts: An experimental study. *Psychological Monographs, 28,* Whole No. 123. Copyright 1920 by the American Psychological Association. Public Domain.

Figure 12.5: From Kimble, G. A., Garmezy, N., & Zigler, E. (1984). *Psychology* (6th ed.). New York: Wiley.

Figure 12.6: From Levine, M. (1966). Hypothesis behavior by humans during discrimination learning. *Journal of Experimental Psychology, 71,* 331–338. Copyright 1966 by the American Psychological Association. Reprinted by permission.

Table 12.2: Luchins, A. S. (1942). Mechanization in problem solving. *Psychological Monographs, 54,* Whole No. 24B. Copyright 1942 by the American Psychological Association. Public Domain.

Figure 12.11: Photograph courtesy of the Great Ape Trust, Des Moines, Iowa .

Photo 12.1: © Donna Coveney/MIT.

Photo 12.2: Photograph courtesy of the Great Ape Trust, Des Moines, Iowa.

Chapter 13

Figure 13.1: From "Human Memory: A Proposed System and Its Control Processes." By Atkinson, R. C., & Shiffrin, R. M. *The Psychology of Learning and*

Motivation, Advances in Research and Theory (pp. 89–195), Volume 2, edited by Spence, K. W., & Spence, J. T. Copyright © 1965 by Academic Press, reproduced by permission of the publisher.

Figure 13.3: From Sperling, G. (1960). The information available in brief visual presentations. *Psychological Monographs, 74,* Whole No. 498. Copyright 1960 by the American Psychological Association. Public Domain.

Figure 13.4: From Crowder, R. G., & Morton, J. (1969). Precategorical acoustic storage (PAS). *Perception and Psychophysics, 5,* 365–373. Reprinted with the permission of the Psychonomic Society, Inc.

Figure 13.5: From Peterson, L. R., & Petersen, M. J. (1959). Short-term retention of individual verbal items. *Journal of Experimental Psychology, 58,* 193–198. Copyright Ó 1959 by the American Psychological Association. Public Domain.

Figure 13.6: This article was published in *Journal of Verbal Learning and Verbal Behavior,* Vol. 2, Melton, A. W., Implications of short-term memory for a general theory of memory, 1–21, copyright Elsevier 1963.

Figure 13.8: From Retrieval Time from Semantic Memory by Collins, A. M. & Quillian, M. R. in *Journal of Verbal Learning and Verbal Behavior,* 8, 240–247. Copyright @ 1969 by Academic Press.

Figure 13.9: From Retrieval Time from Semantic Memory by Collins, A. M. & Quillian, M. R. in *Journal of Verbal Learning and Verbal Behavior,* 8, 240–247. Copyright @ 1969 by Academic Press.

Figure 13.10: From Retrieval Time from Semantic Memory by Collins, A. M. & Quillian, M. R. in *Journal of Verbal Learning and Verbal Behavior,* 8, 240–247. Copyright @ 1969 by Academic Press.

Figure 13.11: From Collins, A. M. & Loftus, E. F. (1975). A spreading activation theory of semantic processing. *Psychological Review, 82,* 407–428. Copyright by the American Psychological Association. Reprinted by permission.

Figure 13.12: From McClelland, E. E., Rumelhart, J. L, & Hinton, G. E. (1986) The appeal of parallel distributed processing. In Rumelhart, D. E., & McClelland, J. L. and the PDP Research Group (Eds.) *Parallel distributed processing: Explorations* in the microstructure of cognition (pp. 3–44). (vol. 1). Cambridge, MA: MIT Press.

Figure 13.13: This article was published in *Journal of Communication Disorders,* Vol. 36, Baddeley, A., Working memory and language: An overview, 189–208. Copyright Elsevier, 2003.

Table 13.1: Tulving, E. (1983). *Elements of episodic memory.* Oxford: Clarendon Press/Oxford University Press. By permission of the Oxford University Press.

Figure 13.14: From Lynch, G. (1986). *Synapses, circuits, and the beginnings of memory.* Cambridge, MA: MIT Press.

Figure 13.16: Adapted from Squire, L. R. (1986). The neuropsychology of memory. In P. Marler and H. Terrace (Eds.), *The biology of learning* (pp. 667–685). Berlin: Springer-Verlag. With kind permission of Springer Science and Business Media.

Figure 13.17: Adapted from B. Milner (1965). Memory disturbances after bilateral hippocampal lesions. In P. Milner & S. Glickman (Eds.), *Cognitive processes and the brain* (pp. 91–111). Princeton, NJ: Van Nostrand.

Figure 13.18: Reprinted with permission from Squire, L. R. (1986). Mechanisms of memory. *Science, 232,* 1612–1619. Copyright 1986 by the American Association for the Advancement of Science.

Figure 13.19: From Corkin, S., Amaral, D. G., Gonzalez, R. G., Johnson, K. A., & Hyman, B. T. (1997). H. M.'s medial temporal lobe lesion: Findings from magnetic resonance imaging. *Journal of Neuroscience, 17,* 3964–3979. Copyright 1997 by the Society of Neuroscience.

Photo 13.2: Photograph courtesy of Rotman Research Institute, Baycrest Foundation, Toronto, Canada.

Chapter 14

Figure 14.1: Adapted from Gooden, D. R., & Baddeley, A. D. (1975). Context-dependent memory in two natural environments: On land and underwater. Reproduced with permission from the *British Journal of Psychology,* @ The British Psychological Society.

Figure 14.2: From Mechanisms for the cueing context to the training memory. By Gordon, W. C., McCracken, K. M., Dees-Beech, N., & Mowrer, R. R., *Learning and Motivation,* 12, 196–211. Copyright @ by Academic Press.

Figure 14.3: From Lang A. J., Craske, M.,G., Brown, M., & Gheneian, A. (2001). Fear-related state dependent memory. *Cognition and Emotion,* 15, 695–703. Taylor & Francis.

Figure 14.5: From Jenkins, J. G. & Dallenbach, K. M. (1924) Obliviscence during sleep and waking. American Journal of Psychology, 35, 605–612. Copyright 1924 by the Board of Trustees of the University of Illinois.

Figure 14.6: From Bartlett, F. C. (1932). *Remembering: A study in experimental and social psychology.* Cambridge: Cambridge University Press. Reprinted with the permission of Cambridge University Press.

Figure 14.7: From Bartlett, F. C. (1932). *Remembering: A study in experimental and social psychology.* Cambridge: Cambridge University Press. Reprinted with the permission of Cambridge University Press.

Figure 14.8: Photographs provided by Elizabeth Loftus.

Figure 14.9: From Roper, K. L. & Zentall, T. R. (1993). Directed Forgetting in animals. *Psychological Bulletin,* 113, 513–532. Copyright 1993 by the American Psychological Association. Reprinted with permission.

Figure 14.10: Warrington, E. K. & Weiskrantz, L. (1970). Amnesic syndrome: Consolidation or retrieval? *Nature,* 228, 628–630. copyright 1970-MacMillan Magazine Limited.

Figure 14.11: Anderson, M. C. & Levy, B. J. (2009). Suppressing unwanted memories. *Current Directions in Psychological Science, 18,* 189–194. Published by Blackwell Publishers.

Photo 14.1: © Center for the History of Psychology, Archives of the History of American Psychology—The University of Akron.

Author Index

Subject Index

About the Author

Stephen B. Klein is professor of psychology at Mississippi State University. He received a BS degree in psychology in 1968 from Virginia Polytechnic Institute and a PhD degree in psychology in 1971 from Rutgers University. He taught at Old Dominion University for 12 years and at Fort Hays State University for seven years prior to coming to Mississippi State University in 1990. He has written numerous articles for psychological journals in the area of the biological basis of learning and memory and is the author of *Motivation: Biosocial Approaches,* published by McGraw-Hill in 1982; *Learning: Principles and Applications,* published by McGraw-Hill in 1987, 1991, 1996, and 2002; and *Biological Psychology,* published by Prentice-Hall in 2000. He also coauthored with B. Michael Thorne *Biological Psychology,* published by Worth in 2007 and coedited with Robert Mowrer the two-volume text *Contemporary Learning Theories* in 1989 and *Handbook of Contemporary Learning Theories* in 2001, both published by Lawrence Erlbaum. His family includes his wife, Marie, and five children, Dora, David, Jason, Katherine, and William. In his spare time, he enjoys sports, most passionately baseball, and science fiction, especially *Star Trek* and *Star Wars*.